SEVENTEENTH EDITION

LAW FOR Business AND Personal Use

John E. Adamson

SOUTH-WESTERN
CENGAGE Learning

Australia • Brazil • Japan • Korea • Mexico • Singapore • Spain • United Kingdom • United States

SOUTH-WESTERN
CENGAGE Learning™

Law for Business and Personal Use

John E. Adamson

VP/Editorial Director
Jack W. Calhoun

VP/Editor-in-Chief
Karen Schmohe

Executive Editor
Eve Lewis

Project Manager
Enid Nagel

Production Manager
Patricia Matthews Boies

Production Editor
Darrell E. Frye

VP/Director of Marketing
Carol Volz

Senior Marketing Manager
Nancy Long

Marketing Coordinator
Angela A. Russo

Manufacturing Coordinator
Kevin Kluck

Art Director
Michelle Kunkler

Editorial Assistant
Linda Keith

Developmental Consultant
Hyde Park Publishing Services

Production House
New England Typographic Service

Cover Designer
Bill Spencer

Internal Designer
Joseph Pagliaro Graphic Design

Cover Photo Source
© Getty Images, Inc.

Printer
Quebecor World
Dubuque, IA

COPYRIGHT © 2006 by South-Western, a part of Cengage Learning.

Printed in the United States of America

5 6 7 8 9 09 08

10-digit ISBN: 0-538-44051-1
13-digit ISBN: 978-0-538-44051-6

For permission to use material from this text or product, submit a request online at www.cengage.com/permissions. Any additional questions about permissions can be submitted by email to permissionrequest@cengage.com.

For more information contact, South-Western
5191 Natorp Boulevard,
Mason, Ohio, 45040
USA.
Or you can visit our Internet site at: school.cengage.com

The names of all companies or products mentioned herein are used for identification purposes only and may be trademarks or registered trademarks of their respective owners. South-Western disclaims any affiliation, association, connection with, sponsorship, or endorsement by such owners.

ASIA (including India)
Cengage Learning
www.cengageasia.com
tel: (65) 6410 1200

Represented in Canada by Nelson Education, Ltd.
www.nelson.com
tel: (416) 752 9100/(800) 668 0671

AUSTRALIA/NEW ZEALAND
Cengage Learning
www.cengage.com.au
tel: (61) 3 9685 4111

UK/EUROPE/MIDDLE EAST/AFRICA
Cengage Learning
www.cengage.co.uk
tel: (44) 207 067 2500

LATIN AMERICA
Cengage Learning
www.cengage.com.mx
tel: +52 (55) 1500 6000

SPAIN (includes Portugal)
Cengage Learning
http://www.paraninfo.es

Don't Settle for the Status Quo

Intro to Business 6E

This complete revision of our market-leading text introduces students to the role of business in our economy. The text is now organized into 20 chapters, with enhanced coverage of marketing, finance, operations, and management. *Winning Edge* gets students prepared for *BPA* and *FBLA* competition.

TEXT	0-538-44063-5
WORKBOOK	0-538-44078-3

Entrepreneurship: Ideas in Action 3E

Take students step-by-step through the entire process of owning and managing a business. Focus their attention on the real skills required of entrepreneurs – start with meeting a market need and work through planning, financing, incorporating technology, hiring, managing, and avoiding legal problems. Students learn by doing using the innovative, activity-based *Build a Business Plan* in every chapter. *Winning Edge* gets students prepared for *BPA, DECA,* and *FBLA* competition.

TEXT	0-538-44122-4
WORKBOOK	0-538-44124-0

Marketing Yourself

Knowing how to sell yourself is critical to success in any field. *Marketing Yourself* shows users how to develop a self-marketing plan and portfolio. The self-marketing plan is based on the analysis of student marketable skills and abilities. Every student text includes a Portfolio CD.

TEXT/PORTFOLIO CD PACKAGE	0-538-43640-9

School Store Operations

Finally, a book that teaches students how to operate a school store – developed in conjunction with DECA! Turn your school store into a learning laboratory. Explore the planning, development, and operation functions needed for a successful school store. *Go for the Gold – SBE Certification Program Prep* in every chapter.

TEXT	0-538-43827-4

Sports and Entertainment Management

Explore the management principles practiced by successful businesses in the sports and entertainment fields. *Sports and Entertainment Management* covers topics such as leadership, finance, product management, human resources, legal and ethical issues, managing change, and customer relations. *DECA Prep* Case Studies and Event Prep included in every chapter.

TEXT	0-538-43829-0
MODULE (EXAMVIEW CD, INSTRUCTOR'S RESOURCE CD, VIDEO, AND ANNOTATED INSTRUCTOR'S EDITION)	0-538-43831-2

Investing in Your Future 2E

Start students on the path to dollars and sense. Use NAIC's respected Stock Selection Guide process to teach smart saving, investing, and planning. Students learn how to analyze the value of stocks and mutual funds. Company Profiles introduce every chapter and the lesson-plan approach makes material easy to comprehend.

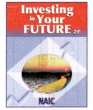

TEXT	0-538-43881-9
MODULE (EXAMVIEW CD, INSTRUCTOR'S RESOURCE CD, VIDEO, AND ANNOTATED INSTRUCTOR'S EDITION)	0-538-43885-1

INSTRUCTOR SUPPORT AND OTHER MATERIALS AVAILABLE

SOUTH-WESTERN CENGAGE Learning

Join us on the Internet at school.cengage.com

Contents

UNIT 3 The Law of Sales 212

In Practice Profile Deborah Rosado Shaw, Founder & CEO, Umbrellas Plus LLC 213
Entrepreneurs and the Law 264

Community Action Become a Consumer Activist 265
Winning Edge FBLA Public Speaking I 265

Features in Unit 3

A Question of Ethics 216, 236, 256
Cyberlaw 237, 250, 258
Economic Impact 238, 254
Hot Debate 214, 228, 244
In This Case 218, 222, 230, 234, 256
International Viewpoint 217, 230
Law Brief 218, 235, 247
Legal Research 216, 237, 246
Net Bookmark 219, 238, 247
Prevent Legal Difficulties 223, 239, 259
What's Your Verdict? 215, 218, 220, 221, 229, 231, 233, 235, 245, 246, 249, 252, 254

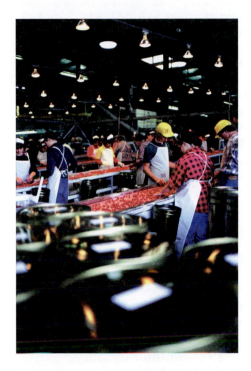

UNIT 6   Legal Forms of Business Organization   442

In Practice Profile   Bert and John Jacobs, Entrepreneurs   443
Entrepreneurs and the Law   504

Community Action   Ethical Business Conduct   505
Winning Edge   FBLA Business Plan   505

Features in Unit 6

A Question of Ethics 447, 478, 492
Cyberlaw 474, 496
Economic Impact 468, 494
Hot Debate 444, 466, 488
In This Case 447, 452, 457, 467, 476, 482, 489, 496
International Viewpoint 453, 470
Law Brief 460, 478, 498
Legal Research 451, 481, 498
Net Bookmark 446, 474, 497
Prevent Legal Difficulties 461, 483, 499
What's Your Verdict? 445, 449, 453, 456, 459, 467, 470, 473, 476, 480, 481, 489, 491, 494, 497

Reviewers

Ray L. Anderson
Marketing Instructor
Rock Bridge High School
Columbia, MO

Paula Brown
Teacher, Business Department
Benton High School
Benton, AR

Dana Dingell
Dept. Chair, Professional Technical Studies
Madison High School
Vienna, VA

Lyn Dominquez
Teacher (retired)
HS of Economics and Finance
New York, NY

Mitchell O. Hamann
Teacher, Business Department
Coal City High School
Coal City, IL

Karen M. Hanks
Chair, Technology Education
Wolfson High School
Duval County Public Schools
Jacksonville, FL

Sarah Heath
Business Education Instructor
Cedar Shoals High School
Athens, GA

Celia K. Hobbins
Teacher, Business Department
Mifflinburg High School
Mifflinburg, PA

Kristine Labbus
Business Education Instructor
Neenah High School
Neenah, WI

Stephanie J. McCall
Teacher, Business Department
Fulton County Schools
Atlanta, GA

Mary T. Pignato
Teacher, Business Department
Hilton High School
Hilton, NY

Jeanne Robinson
Teacher, Business Department
South Technical High School
Sunset Hills, MO

Delbert W. Washington
Teacher, Business Department
Corliss High School
Chicago, IL

ABOUT THE AUTHOR

John E. Adamson is Assistant Professor of Business and Law in the Department of Finance and General Business at Southwest Missouri State University. Adamson received a B.S. from the U.S. Military Academy at West Point, NY, an M.A. from Georgetown University; and an M.B.A. and J.D. from the University of Virginia at Charlottesville. A decorated, disabled veteran and past mayor and school board member of Miller, MO, Adamson is author of numerous business law publications, with a concentration on environmental law.

To the Student

You will soon find business law is one of your most valuable subjects. You will study true situations that show how business and personal law impacts not only business, but the lives of young people and adults as well. The learning package will help you achieve an understanding of legal principles you will use throughout your life. Use the following plan to help you effectively study *Law for Business and Personal Use*.

HOW TO STUDY THE TEXTBOOK

- Each chapter opens with a *Hot Debate*. Read the *Hot Debate* scenario and then discuss with your class the questions that go along with it.

- Each chapter is divided into two or three lessons. Each lesson has a list of *Goals* at the beginning. Read the *Goals* and then scan the lesson to see where each goal is addressed.

- Read each lesson slowly and carefully. Make notes of important points. In the *Student Activities and Study Guide* supplement, there is an outline of every lesson to help you take notes.

- Each main topic heading is followed by a *What's Your Verdict?* scenario. Try to answer the question. Then read the following paragraphs to learn the law that applies to *What's Your Verdict?* before you go on to the next topic.

- As you read apply what you learn to your own experiences or those of your family and friends. Think about situations within your own experience to which the law applies.

- At the end of each main topic section, ask yourself the *Checkpoint* question to review the material.

- After you have carefully studied the lesson, complete the exercises in *Think About Legal Concepts* and *Think Critically About Evidence*.

- After you complete all the lessons in a chapter, read the *Concepts in Brief* to refresh your memory. Then complete *Your Legal Vocabulary, Review Legal Concepts, Write About Legal Concepts, Make Academic Connections,* and *Analyze Real Cases.*

- The exercises in *Think Critically About Evidence* help you apply what you learned in the chapter. *Analyze Real Cases* allows you to work with the facts from real lawsuits related to the topics in each chapter.

SPECIAL FEATURES

- **A Question of Ethics** presents ethical issues that arise within the legal framework.

- **Cyberlaw** discusses emerging legal aspects of the Internet and e-commerce.

- **Economic Impact** discusses a situation in which the law is affected by a certain economic circumstance.

- **Hot Debate** promotes thoughtful discussion of important legal issues.

- **In Practice Profile** introduces you to individuals who have successful careers and highlights how the law impacts their career.

- **In This Case** demonstrates legal principles and concepts through hypothetical situations.

- **International Viewpoint** illustrates legal procedures and issues in other nations.

- **Law Brief** provides unusual or interesting facts or ideas related to the law.

- **Legal Research** helps you investigate issues relating to federal, state, and local laws using Internet and library resources.

- **Net Bookmark** encourages you to use the Internet for research. Find the URLs you need to complete the research on the Xtra! web site at lawxtra.swlearning.com.

- **Prevent Legal Difficulties** provides helpful guidelines for dealing with the legal system.

- **What's Your Verdict?** motivates you to learn new legal concepts.

REAL-WORLD CASES

- **Case for Legal Thinking** presents important real-world cases for analysis and discussion.

PROJECTS

- **Entrepreneurs and the Law** allows you to apply the law to a start-up business situation.

- **Community Action** provides ideas for getting involved and making a difference in your local, national, and global communities.

- **Winning Edge** helps you prepare for business law-related FBLA and BPA competitive events.

HOW TO ANALYZE LEGAL SITUATIONS

Following each lesson and each chapter you will find a number of legal situations in *Think Critically About Evidence*. You also will find actual cases that have been decided by courts in *Analyze Real Cases* and *Case for Legal Thinking*. You may use the same method to analyze both types of exercises. To answer the question raised in an exercise or case, first read it carefully. Be sure you understand the question and the facts involved. Then determine the rule of law involved and reach a decision. You will find it helpful to answer these questions.

- What are the facts?

- What is the disputed point?

- What rule of law is involved?

- How does this rule apply to the facts?

- What is the answer or decision?

HOW TO ANALYZE ETHICAL SITUATIONS

An ethical dilemma is posed in A Question of Ethics. You can use the ethical frameworks described in Lesson 1-3 to analyze these dilemmas.

To analyze the dilemmas using ethical reasoning based on consequences,

- Describe alternative actions that would improve the situation.

- Forecast consequences that would flow from each alternative described.

- Evaluate the consequences for each alternative by selecting a standard for judging right or wrong consequences.

To analyze the dilemmas using fundamental ethical rules,

- "Universalize" the action in question.

- Determine whether the action is irrational, illogical, or self-defeating.

HOW TO READ CASE CITATIONS

Law cases are referenced in a way that makes them easy to find. There are three parts to a citation. For example, 28 A2d 309 identifies (1) a series of law books, (2) one volume in that series, and (3) the page where the case begins. In the example, A2d identifies the series of books that report the decisions of certain courts. The A stands for Atlantic Reporter, a series that reports the cases of appellate courts in the North Atlantic Region. The 2d indicates that the case appears in the second series of the Atlantic Reporter. The 28 in this example citation refers to Volume 28 in the series. The case begins on page 309.

LEGAL ADVICE

Consult a lawyer if you have any doubts about your rights or duties when your property, life, or liberty is endangered or if significant changes occur in your circumstances.

- Familiarize yourself with local, state, and federal laws to help avoid violations. Ignorance of the law normally is no excuse.

- Remember that as a minor you generally are liable for crimes and torts and bound by contracts.

- If you are involved in a legal dispute, try to learn the other person's version and honestly seek a friendly solution out of court. In every court action at least one person loses and often both find the costs burdensome.

- If someone injures you or your property, do not rush to sign a statement releasing the person from liability in exchange for some payment of money. The damages may be greater than they appear at first. Consult your attorney immediately.

- Although oral agreements can be legally binding, you should write out all contracts that involve significant time, money, or detail and have both parties sign and receive copies.

UNIT 1

LAW, JUSTICE, AND YOU

CHAPTERS

IN PRACTICE PROFILE
Scott Hayes ■ Crime Scene Investigator

For as long as he can remember, Scott Hayes had a passion for law enforcement. At 18 he began his career with the Wichita Police Department. In his first job as a police mechanic he worked on the engines of police vehicles.

After five years, Scott became a traffic investigator. His job was to investigate traffic accidents and fatalities. While the job was rewarding, "I wanted to do more. At the end of the day I didn't feel like I was contributing enough to my community," Scott remembers. So, after ten years investigating traffic incidents, Scott changed his career again, this time to crime scene investigator. "Not once have I regretted it," he said.

Today, at age 43, Scott is crime scene supervisor with the Wichita Police Department. In addition to supervising four investigators, Scott oversees major crime scenes "to insure that everything is done correctly, and nothing is missed." He and his team investigate everything from burglaries and auto thefts to robberies, rapes, and homicides. He is a specialist in analyzing bloodstain patterns to determine if a victim was standing, sitting, kneeling, or lying down at the time of the assault.

Scott readily admits that investigating crime scenes is not as glamorous or magical as television portrays. However, he is proof that hard work and passion can have enormous payoffs.

One example was his investigation into the rape and murder of a Wichita woman. While poring over the crime scene, "I noticed the victim's bedroom closet door was open. I saw an attic access panel in the ceiling of the closet, a black mark on the wall of the closet, and what looked like a fingerprint." Because the closet shelf showed no signs of debris, indicating the access panel had

recently been removed, Scott initially dismissed his discovery. "I made a mental note of it and continued with my investigation." The next day, curiosity got the best of him and he climbed into the attic. What he discovered would become crucial evidence in the case. Scott found that the wall dividing the victim's apartment from the apartment next door had been freshly knocked through. Gift boxes in the attic were covered in dust, and recently had been disturbed. This discovery, and subsequent research, sent the victim's neighbor to death row where he remains today.

Unlike popular television programs, investigations like these can take days or even weeks just to make sure all evidence is collected. Next comes weeks of processing the evidence for fingerprints or DNA. The investigator then must write a thorough report, including detailed diagrams. "We sometimes work on a single case for a month...or longer."

The hard work is worth it, however. "We look for the truth and the evidence that supports that truth." Sometimes the evidence will put someone in prison for the crime they have committed. Other times evidence proves the suspect in the case did not commit the crime. "Let the chips fall where they may," is a favorite saying of Scott's team.

Whether a patrol officer, detective, or crime scene investigator, Scott says any job in law enforcement requires a passion for helping others. "In this line of work you see the most evil things people do to one another. Yes, we get tired of seeing dead bodies, the gore, and the stench. But having the passion to help someone who cannot help themselves is the key. It makes it all worth it."

> "We look for the truth and the evidence that supports that truth."

Laws and Their Ethical Foundation

1-1 Laws and Legal Systems

1-2 Types of Laws

1-3 Ethical Bases for Laws

HOT DEBATE

Clarisse was driving home from school in her small pickup. Her stereo system was blasting when she was pulled over by a police officer. The officer cited her for violation of the city's noise ordinance. As he did so, his voice was partially drowned out by sounds of jack hammering from a nearby construction site. Clarisse asked the officer why he had not cited the construction company as well. He replied that, even though the company was in violation, the noise ordinance had been put on the books to stop people from playing loud music in public, not to stop honest work.

© GETTY IMAGES/PHOTODISC

Where Do You Stand?

1. Is the ordinance fair?
2. Has the ordinance been fairly applied?
3. Can you suggest some changes in the ordinance that might make it a better law?

Laws and Legal Systems

▼ GOALS

- **Explain the stages in the growth of law**
- **Describe the differences between common law and positive law**
- **Identify the origin of the U.S. legal system**

WHAT IS LAW?

WHAT'S YOUR VERDICT?

Lorenzo and Bixby were discussing how much civilization had advanced since the beginning of recorded history. Bixby said he thinks that the basic nature of humankind has not changed, but the number of facts we know has been multiplied many times over. Lorenzo agreed, saying "Just compare the laws they had way back then with the ones we have now. We're still making the same mistakes and still need the same protections from the conduct of others."

Do you think they are correct?

The **laws**, or enforceable rules of conduct in a society, reflect the culture and circumstances that create them. Laws may be grouped into an organized form called a **code**. When you compare one civilization's code with the codes of other civilizations, you see many similarities. For example, the law code set down about four thousand years ago by Hammurabi, King of Babylon, had sections on criminal law, property law, business law, family law, personal injury law, labor law, and others. Such coverage is similar to that found in the U.S. law codes today.

Lorenzo and Bixby in *What's Your Verdict?* were right. The need for law has not changed much over recorded history. People still make the same mistakes and still need the same protections from the conduct of others.

STAGES IN THE GROWTH OF LAW

Most societies go through four distinct stages in forming their legal systems:

1. Individuals take revenge for wrongs done to them

2. A powerful leader or other form of central authority substitutes an award of money or goods for revenge

3. The leader or authority gives power to a system of courts

4. The leader or central authority acts to prevent and punish wrongs

In the first stage, injuries inflicted on one human being by another are matters for personal revenge. Those who are wronged feel that justice can be done only through personally punishing the wrongdoers. Gang wars in the inner cities often result from this type of attitude. Whether they occur in a big city or in a developing society, such events usually disrupt the normal routine of the people and result in harm to innocent bystanders.

© NORTH WIND PICTURE ARCHIVES

The law code set down by King Hammurabi of Babylon contained sections or categories similar to those found in modern U.S. law codes. How do you think the *specific content* of Hammurabi's codes compares to that of U.S. law codes today?

The situation often leads to one individual taking power and exerting control to bring peace to the society. To achieve this peace, the powerful leader or authority, often called the *sovereign*, forces the injured parties to accept awards of money or goods as a substitute for their taking revenge. This is the second stage in the growth of law.

The sovereign is faced with a number of such cases that need to be decided. This leads to the third stage—the sovereign sets up a system of courts and gives them appropriate powers. Elders or priests generally preside over these courts. However, the sovereign still presides over the most important matters.

In the fourth and final stage, the sovereign goes from being a passive authority working only to resolve disputes to try to prevent breaches of the peace before they can occur. The sovereign does this through enforcing a set of laws and matching punishments.

COMMON LAW VERSUS POSITIVE LAW

Laws reflect the wisdom—or lack thereof—of their creators. In any society laws should be both predictable and flexible. A system of laws that is not predictable will not produce a stable society. Chaos, unrest, and the replacement of the system by one that can exercise control and restore peace will follow.

A legal system that is too controlling and too rigid to change with the wants and needs of the people also will be overthrown. The best system of laws always evolves slowly towards a form that is most appropriate to the current standards of the people.

Law based on the current standards or customs of the people is called common law. Common law usually is formed from the rules used by judges to settle people's disputes. However, as noted earlier, some laws are set down by a sovereign or other central authority to prevent disputes and wrongs from occurring in the first place. Law dictated from above in this fashion is called positive law.

CHECKPOINT

How does common law differ from positive law?

WHAT'S YOUR VERDICT?

LaBonne, from Louisiana, was visiting his cousin in St. Louis, Missouri. While they were talking about the differences in traffic laws in the two states, LaBonne told his cousin that Louisiana's legal system was different from that used in Missouri and all the other states.

Is LaBonne correct?

The world's two great systems of law are the English common law and the Roman civil law. Countries with systems patterned after the Roman civil law have adopted written, well organized, comprehensive sets of statutes in code form. Only one state in the United States—Louisiana—has law based on a civil law system. The legal system used in the other 49 states is based on the English common law. Therefore, in *What's Your Verdict?*, LaBonne was correct.

INTERNATIONAL VIEWPOINT

Napoleonic Code

The territory that is now Louisiana was claimed for France by the explorer Lasalle in 1682. French settlers brought many French influences to the state of Louisiana—customs, food, language, and law. Louisiana's legal system was developed using the French Code Napoléon (or Napoleonic Code) as a foundation. Over the years Louisiana has modified its legal system to correspond with those of the other 49 states. The Napoleonic Code was derived from Germanic customs and Roman law. The Napoleonic Code also was the model for the civil law codes of Italy, the Netherlands, Spain, and the Canadian Province of Quebec.

Colonists from England brought the common law system to this continent. To understand how this system works, you must look back to England to see how it was developed.

ENGLISH COMMON LAW

Before the English common law system developed, feudal barons acted as judges within their territories. Disputes were settled on the basis of local customs and enforced by the barons' power. Because of this, the laws of England differed from region to region. Such differences were difficult for people to follow. They also made it hard for a central government to maintain control.

KING'S BENCH Around 1150 King Henry II decided to improve the situation. He appointed a number of judges from a group of trusted nobles. King Henry gave these judges the power to order that wrongdoers pay with money or goods the parties they injured.

In good-weather months the judges would "ride circuit" into the countryside, holding court in the villages. During bad-weather months, the judges stayed in London and sat together as a court to hear cases on appeal that might have been decided unwisely on circuit. This court so formed by the circuit riding judges came to be called King's Bench—or Queen's Bench if the regent was female.

The baron's courts, which heard local cases before the King's courts were created, kept the power to decide some of the minor cases. However, the King's courts always had the power to decide a case—or **jurisdiction**—over the most important cases.

JURY King Henry recognized that it was important to decide the court cases in harmony with the customs of the people. To do otherwise would cause unrest, if not revolution. The judges were instructed to choose citizens from each region to help interpret that region's customs for the court. This panel of citizens evolved into what we know today as the *jury*. The jury is an institution unique to the English common law system.

AN EXAMPLE The early system of English common law worked something like this. Imagine that a farmer named William is on his way to market one morning in his ox cart. He is traveling through an unfamiliar region. As he approaches an intersection, he sees another person in a similar ox cart coming into the intersection from his right.

Because he could not resolve all the disputes in the nation by himself, King Henry appointed a group of judges to decide them for him. What personal qualities do you think he looked for in these judges?

In William's home region the right of way at an intersection goes to the person on the left. So he continues on, expecting the other person to rein in. The other party, a local resident named Gwen, does not yield and a collision results. Both William and Gwen are injured. Their oxen are gored. Their carts and other property are destroyed. As a consequence, the next time the King's circuit-riding judge comes into Gwen's region, both people appear in court and request damages for their losses.

The judge needs to know who is at fault in the case in order to decide who must pay. To find out, the judge chooses a jury of 12 residents. These people must decide which person, according to their customs, acted improperly. The jury determines that, because the right of way customarily goes to the person on the right in their region, William is at fault and must pay Gwen damages. The judge accepts the decision and orders William to pay.

The decision, however, upsets William. He knows that throughout most of his travels the right of way is given to the person on the left. Therefore, he decides to take his case to the higher, or appellate, court—King's Bench in London—on appeal. That court will not be in session for several months yet, so William uses the time to collect information on the law used in other courts in England that have ruled on the issue of right of way. Finally, the time comes to appear before King's Bench. The judges listen to William's appeal and Gwen's defense of the lower court's decision.

The appellate court judges review the information presented to them by both parties, including the laws used by other courts to settle like issues. They decide that it would be wisest to reverse the holding in the lower court (that the right of way should go to the person on the right). Instead, says King's Bench, the right of way will be given to the person on the left. They send the case back down to the lower court with instructions to enter a judgment for damages in William's favor.

From that point on, anyone in the kingdom will need to give the right of way to the person on the left. If any lower court, including the one in Gwen's region, decides a case using a different rule, the result can be appealed to King's Bench and reversed.

ADVANTAGES OF ENGLISH COMMON LAW The judicial process described in the example was repeated over and over in England throughout the centuries. As a result, a uniform web of custom-based common law developed across the whole of England. The process used to achieve this end is called the English common law system. The English common law system achieves uniformity while maintaining an ability to adapt to changes in society. It has been a model for legal systems worldwide, including that in the United States.

EQUITY: AN ALTERNATIVE TO COMMON LAW

The common law courts carefully followed *precedent*. This means the courts used prior cases as a guide for deciding similar new cases as was done in *William v. Gwen* above. Following precedent helped to provide stability in the law. However, it also had the disadvantage of requiring a rigid adherence to proper form. A misplaced period or misspelled word would nullify, or void, the effect of a document.

Another disadvantage of the common law as it evolved was that the courts were limited to granting the remedy of damages. The common law courts had to wait until the harm actually occurred before they could take action.

For example, if a farmer decided to dam up the stream that watered the neighbor's crops and animals, the courts of law had to wait until the harm had occurred and then award the neighbor damages for what the farmer did. The courts of law could not order the farmer to stop building the dam. This would result in a waste of resources from the perspective of the country as a whole.

However, if the neighbor were a noble, he might be able to get around the courts and directly petition the king for help. The king would refer the matter to his chancellor, who was usually a high clergyman respected for his **equity**, or fairness.

The chancellor would conduct a hearing under rules different from those of a common

---

Cyberlaw

Ah, the joys of e-mail—instant communication of thoughts. You feel it. You say it. You send it. But, if your message is perceived as a threat, you could be prosecuted and convicted for it. In the first conviction of an online hate crime, a 21-year-old Los Angeles man was found guilty in federal court. He sent death threats by e-mail to more than 50 Asian students. The case set a precedent, as it put Internet communications on equal legal ground with telephone calls and postal mail. It also addressed civil rights violations committed online—hate crimes in this case. The defense team argued this was a "stupid prank" and that so-called flames or abusive messages are commonplace with Internet culture and discussion groups. The jury thought otherwise and took the threats seriously. At first the Net was considered to be a fantasy land where users could be anonymous. This case shows that the legal system will not treat the Net differently from other forms of communication.

THINK ABOUT IT
Do you think people should be held accountable for threats they make online? Why or why not?

law court. There would be no jury, for example, and the remedies the chancellor could impose in the king's name were different from those available to the law courts.

The chancellor might issue an order to compel that something be done. Or, he might issue an *injunction*, which stops something from being done. For example, the chancellor could issue an injunction to stop the dam from being built. If the neighbor were not a noble, he would not have been able to petition the king. The harm would be allowed to occur.

Eventually the king sensed a need for access to equitable remedies for all citizens. He created a system of equity courts and placed them under the chancellor's control. These courts were given the power to issue injunctions or to compel specific actions. In the United States today, law courts and equity courts generally are merged.

Law Brief

Four states in the United States administer law and equity separately. In Arkansas, Delaware, and Mississippi equity is administered in chancery courts. In Tennessee equity is administered in law-equity courts.

• •

Consequently, most American courts can award damages or issue orders or both.

CHECKPOINT

On which early legal system is the U.S. legal system based?

Xtra! Study Tools
lawxtra.swlearning.com

1-1 Assessment

THINK ABOUT LEGAL CONCEPTS

1. Substitution of damages for revenge is the first stage in the evolution of law. **True or False?**

2. The two systems of law in use today are the English common law and the (a) American Constitution (b) French legal code (c) Roman common law (d) none of the above.

3. A remedy of the English Courts of Equity was the (a) injunction (b) court order (c) disputation (d) none of the above.

4. Louisiana is the only one of the 50 states whose legal system was not originally based on the English common law system. **True or False?**

5. Most American law courts can use either damages or an injunction or both as remedies in civil cases. **True or False?**

THINK CRITICALLY ABOUT EVIDENCE

Study the situation, answer the questions, and then prepare arguments to support your answers.

6. You are on your daily jog when a car negligently pulls out in front of you. Unable to stop, you run into it and injure yourself. Should you be able to recover damages for the harm done to you?

7. The driver of the car in exercise 6 becomes abusive towards you after your recovery. The driver follows you on your jogs and yells threats at you. He has recently taken to driving very close to you as you jog. What can you do legally to make him stay away from you?

8. Cracked Mirror, a local rock group, contracts to play for your high school prom. A week before the dance, the group cancels its appearance. A teacher finds out that the band booked a concert that will pay them $800 more. The class president's mother is an attorney and offers her services to the school. If you sue the band for damages, what would be an appropriate amount and why?

9. For the situation in exercise 8, fashion an equitable remedy that might encourage Cracked Mirror to decide to keep its commitment to play at your prom.

Types of Laws

▼ **GOALS**

- **Identify the four sources of law**
- **Discuss how to resolve conflicts between different sources of laws**
- **Compare and contrast criminal and civil law, and substantive and procedural law**

WHAT ARE THE SOURCES OF LAW?

WHAT'S YOUR VERDICT?

The federal constitution guarantees the citizens of the United States many rights. These include freedom of speech, of press, of assembly, to petition, to bear arms, against unreasonable searches and seizures, and more.

What part of the U.S. Constitution contains these guarantees?

Laws in this country are created at all three levels of government—federal, state, and local. The forms that these laws can take include constitutions, statutes, case law, and administrative regulations.

CONSTITUTIONS

A **constitution** is a document that sets forth the framework of a government and its relationship to the people it governs. When constitutions are adopted or amended, or when courts interpret constitutions, *constitutional law* is made. You are governed by both the Constitution of the United States and the constitution of your state. The Supreme Court of the United States is the final interpreter of the federal Constitution.

Constitutions are the highest sources of law, and the federal Constitution is "the supreme law of the land" (U.S. Constitution, Article VI). This means that any federal, state, or local law is not valid if it conflicts with the federal Constitution. Similarly, within each state the state constitution is supreme to all other state laws.

Federal and state constitutions are concerned primarily with defining and allocating certain powers in our society. Constitutions allocate powers (1) between the people and their governments, (2) between state governments and the federal government, and (3) among the branches of the government.

ALLOCATION OF POWER BETWEEN PEOPLE AND THEIR GOVERNMENTS The federal Constitution is the main instrument for allocating powers between people and their governments. It does this primarily with its first ten amendments, called the *Bill of Rights.* The Bill of Rights protects people from actions of their governments. This is the section of the federal Constitution referred to in *What's Your Verdict?* The Bill of Rights will be discussed in detail in Chapter 2.

ALLOCATION OF POWER BETWEEN FEDERAL AND STATE GOVERNMENTS The federal Constitution also allocates powers between the federal and state governments. For example, many governmental powers over business are divided between state governments and the federal government on the basis of commerce. In general, the Constitution gives the federal government the power to regulate both foreign and interstate commerce. *Interstate* commerce occurs between two or more states. The power to regulate *intrastate* commerce, which occurs within one state, is left with that state.

LEGAL RESEARCH

The Fraudulent Online Identity Sanctions Act (H.R.3754) of 2004 would increase prison sentences to up to seven years for someone who provided "material and misleading false contact information to a domain name registrar, domain name registry, or other domain name registration authority." It would also make it much easier for the recording studios and movie producers to track down copyright violators and obtain the $150,000 per violation damages. Obtain a copy of this proposed act. What do you see as potential problems with the bill? What rights does the bill put in jeopardy, if any?

Railroads often are used to transport goods over long distances. What type of commerce, interstate or intrastate, does this represent, and which level of government most likely regulates it?

© GETTY IMAGES/PHOTODISC

ALLOCATION OF POWER AMONG THE BRANCHES OF GOVERNMENT State and federal constitutions also allocate governmental powers among the three branches of government: executive, legislative, and judicial. Traditionally these powers are distributed so as to create a system of checks and balances between the branches of each government. This ensures that no branch of government becomes too powerful. For example, the federal Constitution gives the courts, not Congress, the authority to conduct trials. It gives Congress the power to ordain and establish the courts in the first place.

STATUTES

The federal Constitution created the Congress of the United States. State constitutions created the state legislatures. These state and federal legislatures are composed of elected representatives of the people. Acting for their citizens, these legislatures enact laws called **statutes**.

In addition, all states delegate some legislative authority to local governments. Thus, towns, cities, and counties can legislate on matters over which the state has given them authority. These pieces of legislation created by a town or city

council or by a county board or commission are typically referred to as **ordinances**. They are only effective within the boundary of the local governments that enacted them.

CASE LAW

The judicial branch of governments creates **case law**. Case law usually is made after a trial has ended and one of the parties has appealed the result to a higher court. This appeal will be based on legal rulings made by the lower court in deciding the case.

When the appellate court publishes its opinion on a case, that opinion may state new rules to be used in deciding the case and others like it. These rules are referred to as case law at either the federal or state level.

The effectiveness of case law arises out of the doctrine of **stare decisis**. This is Latin for "let the decision stand." This doctrine requires that lower courts must follow established case law in deciding similar cases. Generally, case law doctrines are carefully established and seldom revoked. However, the doctrine of *stare decisis* generally does not bind supreme courts.

IN THIS CASE

Carol borrowed her stepfather's car without his express permission. The police stopped her and discovered the car was not registered in her name. They then phoned her stepfather. When he said he did not know where his car was, Carol was arrested. At her trial, Carol and her stepfather testified that she had his permission to use the car without asking each time. The trial judge nevertheless found Carol guilty of auto theft, which, the judge stated, occurs when one person takes the car of another without expressly asking permission. Carol appealed to the state supreme court. That appellate court issued an opinion stating implied permission is enough, and, therefore, Carol was innocent. This rule then became state case law to be applied in similar cases.

ADMINISTRATIVE REGULATIONS

Federal, state, and local legislatures all create administrative agencies. **Administrative agencies** are governmental bodies formed to carry out particular laws. The federal Social Security Administration, your state's division of motor vehicles, and your county's zoning commission are examples of administrative agencies.

Although created by legislatures, administrative agencies usually are controlled by the executive branch of government. Thus, the president, governor, or mayor will supervise the agency's activities. Legislatures sometimes give administrative agencies legislative powers and limited judicial powers. Legislative power means the agency is authorized to create administrative laws, also called *rules* and *regulations*. For example, the federal Social Security Administration might establish rules for determining when a student is depending on support from a widow or widower and thereby qualified to receive social security payments.

If an agency has judicial power, it can hold hearings, make determinations of fact, and apply the law to particular cases. In the above example, the Social Security Administration might hold a hearing to judge whether a *particular* student is in fact a dependent. Once this determination is made, the Social Security Administration would use its executive powers to carry out the rules on payments to dependents of widows or widowers.

CHECKPOINT

What are the four sources of law?

WHAT HAPPENS WHEN LAWS CONFLICT?

WHAT'S YOUR VERDICT?

When adopted, the U.S. Constitution provided that there could be no income tax. So when Congress levied a 2 percent income tax in 1894, the U.S. Supreme Court declared it unconstitutional. Many people wanted the federal government to raise money by taxing incomes because the burden imposed would be based on one's current ability to pay.

Could the people do anything to change the effect of the Supreme Court decision?

Sometimes laws created by different levels of government conflict. For example, a city ordinance setting a speed limit of 35 mph on a state highway near an elementary school may conflict with a state statute setting 45 as a minimum speed limit on state roads. Different types of laws created by the same level of government also may conflict. A federal administrative regulation requiring the phase-out of coal-fired electric-generating plants may conflict with a federal court decision holding that such regulations are unconstitutional.

In these situations, legal rules are used that determine which statement of the law is superior to the other and should therefore be enforced. Generally, these *supremacy* rules hold that federal law prevails over state law and state law prevails over local (city and county) law. Within the state and federal systems, constitutional law prevails over statutory law and statutory law over administrative law. Finally, within the state and federal court systems, a higher court's decision prevails over a lower court's.

CONSTITUTIONS AND VALIDITY Constitutions are the highest sources of law, and the federal Constitution is "the supreme law of the land" (U.S. Constitution, Article VI). This means that any federal, state, or local statute, case law or administrative decision is not valid if it conflicts with the federal Constitution. Within each state's legal framework, the state constitution is supreme to all other state laws.

When any type of law is declared invalid by a state or federal court because it conflicts with a constitution, it is said to be *unconstitutional*. Such a determination may be appealed to the highest court within the state and federal systems. Within the federal system, the U.S. Supreme Court has the final say. The highest state court wins out on state issues. Of course, even when interpreting constitutions, courts are not the ultimate authority. The people have the power to amend constitutions if they disagree with the courts' interpretations.

In answer to *What's Your Verdict?* the Sixteenth Amendment to the U.S. Constitution, adopted in 1913, gave Congress the power to lay and collect an income tax. This in effect nullified the U.S. Supreme Court decision.

STATUTES AND VALIDITY As discussed, statutes or ordinances must be constitutional to be valid. In addition, when needed in a particular case, courts also examine the statutes and ordinances involved to see whether or not the law's enactment exceeded the scope of the powers of the body that authored it.

ADMINISTRATIVE REGULATIONS AND VALIDITY

Administrative regulations also can be reviewed by courts to determine whether they are constitutional. The courts may also invalidate a rule or regulation if it is outside the scope of powers delegated to the agency by the legislature that created it.

CASE LAW AND VALIDITY A case law decision by a court holding a statute invalid is not always the end of the issue. A legislative body has the power to nullify a court's interpretation of a statute or ordinance by rewriting the statute. Administrative agencies also can revise their regulations when challenged.

CHECKPOINT

Which source of law in the United States is the highest authority?

WHAT ARE THE MAIN TYPES OF LAWS?

WHAT'S YOUR VERDICT?

Worthington was driving down the road well within the speed limit. At a stop sign he slowed to about 15 miles per hour, but he did not stop. As a result, he smashed into the side of Bates' Mercedes, causing $12,000 in damage.

Did Worthington violate civil law or criminal law or both?

Laws may be classified in various ways. Common classifications include civil laws, criminal laws, procedural laws, substantive laws, and business law.

CIVIL AND CRIMINAL LAWS

When the private legal rights of an individual are violated, the matter is governed by civil law. The use of the term **civil law** within the common law system refers to the group of laws that make up for wrongs against individual persons. (Civil law in this sense does not refer to the comprehensive system of law mentioned in Lesson 1-1.)

For example when a tenant fails to pay the rent as promised, the landlord has the right to sue the tenant. The police do not take action in civil conflicts. If a defendant loses a civil case, that defendant is liable. This means that she or he must pay money to the plaintiff. This is the primary help that courts grant in civil matters. In addition to enforcing legal promises, civil law also applies whenever one person is injured by another. Such private wrongs (civil offenses) against people or organizations are referred to as *torts*.

A *crime* is an offense against society rather than individuals. It disrupts the stable environment that we all depend upon to make civilization work. So, when the citizens' right to live in peace is violated by such activity, the offense is governed by **criminal law**. Acting in the name of all the people, the government investigates an alleged wrongdoing. If a crime has been committed and the person responsible can be found, the government will prosecute. Conviction of a crime can result in a fine, imprisonment, and in some states, execution.

Usually when a crime occurs, private injuries may be inflicted as well. A result may be both a crime and a civil offense. Thus, the civil law may also apply, and the victim of the crime may sue the wrongdoer.

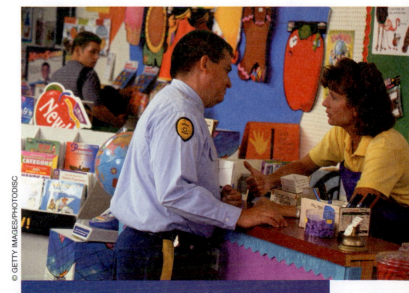

© GETTY IMAGES/PHOTODISC

Is shoplifting a crime or a tort? Explain your answer.

In *What's Your Verdict?* Worthington committed both a crime and a civil offense. Driving through the stop sign was a crime for which Worthington could be arrested, convicted in a criminal trial, and fined. In addition, Worthington committed a civil offense when he carelessly smashed into the side of Bates' Mercedes. Bates could probably win a civil trial to recover the $12,000.

PROCEDURAL AND SUBSTANTIVE LAWS

Procedural law deals with methods of enforcing legal rights and duties. Laws that specify how and when police can make arrests and what methods can be used in a trial are procedural laws. Procedural laws determine whether equitable remedies, such as an injunction, are available. The doctrine of *stare decisis* is a procedural law. Rules for determining the supremacy of conflicting laws are procedural laws.

In contrast, **substantive law** defines rights and duties. It is concerned with all rules of conduct except those involved in enforcement. Substantive laws define offenses, such as murder, theft, breach of contract, and negligence.

There are two types of procedural law: civil procedure and criminal procedure. *Criminal procedure* defines the process for enforcing the law when someone is charged with a crime. *Civil procedure* is used when a civil law has been violated. Civil law is concerned only with private offenses. When a civil law is violated the injured party is entitled to protect his or her rights. Police and public prosecutors generally do not involve themselves in the dispute.

BUSINESS LAW

Business law covers rules that apply to business situations and transactions. This book's table of contents shows that the scope of business law is broad. Business law is important for all students—not just those planning careers in business or law. Most business transactions involve a merchant and a consumer. As you study business law, you will gain legal knowledge that will make you a better consumer.

Business law mainly is concerned with civil law, especially contracts. The area of the law pertaining to commercial torts is another category of business law. Such torts are distinct from breaches of contracts. For example, torts may occur when manufacturers make defective products that injure users. Business activities are at times also governed by criminal law. For example,

Assume that the woman in this photo is a public prosecutor giving her closing argument in a case to a jury. Is this most likely a civil trial or a criminal trial? Justify your answer.

criminal law would punish a firm that conspires with competitors to fix prices or an employee who steals company tools.

UNIFORM BUSINESS LAWS Laws of our various states do not have to be alike as long as they are constitutionally valid. However, with the growth of interstate commerce and large business firms, more uniformity among state laws governing business and commercial transactions is important.

Committees of legal experts have written model laws covering such areas as sales, certain credit transactions, and business forms. Sets of these model laws were then offered to the states for adoption in place of their current statutes covering the areas. The result has been more uniformity in state commercial laws. The *Uniform Commercial Code (UCC)* is a widely adopted uniform business law. It governs such areas as sales of goods, certain aspects of banking, and leases of goods. You will learn more about the UCC throughout this book.

CHECKPOINT

Compare and contrast criminal and civil law and substantive and procedural law.

TYPES OF LAW

Constitutional law	Based on constitutions
Statutes	Enacted by legislative bodies
Administrative law	Rulings by administrative agencies
Civil law	Addresses wrongs done to individuals
Criminal law	Addresses wrongs done to society
Procedural law	Deals with methods of enforcing legal rights and duties
Substantive law	Defines legal rights and duties
Business law	Rules that apply to business transactions

1-2

Assessment

Xtra!
Study Tools
lawxtra.swlearning.com

THINK ABOUT LEGAL CONCEPTS

1. The first ten amendments to the U.S. Constitution are known as the _ ? _.

2. Contract law would be considered civil law. **True or False?**

3. Legislative enactments at the local level are called _ ? _.

4. *Stare decisis* is the doctrine that requires lower courts to adhere to existing case law in their decisions. **True or False?**

5. Torts are private wrongs committed against individuals or organizations. **True or False?**

6. Business activities are at times governed by the criminal law. **True or False?**

7. Businesses cannot commit torts. **True or False?**

8. The doctrine of *stare decisis* is a (a) substantive law (b) procedural law (c) prohibitive law (d) none of the above.

THINK CRITICALLY ABOUT EVIDENCE

Study the situation, answer the questions, and then prepare arguments to support your answers.

9. Suppose the principal of your public school required all students to recite a prayer at the start of each school day. What level of government (federal, state, or local) would most likely determine whether or not the principal's action was constitutional?

10. In exercise 9, what governmental body would make the determination?

11. Sonoma County passed a law making it legal to drive 65 mph on freeways inside the county. A state law limited all vehicles anywhere in the state to 55 mph. What is the valid speed limit on freeways inside this county?

12. In 1896, the U.S. Supreme Court held in *Plessy v. Ferguson*, 163 U.S. 537, that equal treatment of different races is provided when public and semipublic facilities, even though separate, are substantially equal in quality. For years, railroad cars, buses, schools, and other facilities had separate and supposedly equal facilities for blacks. In 1954 black plaintiffs in Delaware, Kansas, South Carolina, and Virginia sought admission for their children to public schools on an integrated basis. Does the doctrine of *stare decisis* bar the U.S. Supreme Court from changing the law declared in *Plessy v. Ferguson*? (*Brown v. Board of Education*, 347 U.S. 483)

13. On a two-week vacation in a neighboring state, you buy several large firecrackers and take them home. A police officer notices them in your car on a routine traffic stop. She cites you for possession of an illegal explosive device, which is a felony in your state. Possession of fireworks in the neighboring state is not a crime. Can this be a defense for you?

Ethical Bases for Laws

ETHICS AND THE LAW

WHAT'S YOUR VERDICT?

In the early 1960s, Dr. Martin Luther King, Jr., wanted to lead a march into Birmingham, Alabama, to protest racial segregation in that city. When he applied for a parade permit, his request was denied. Dr. King, knowing that his conduct was illegal, led the nonviolent march anyway. He was at the front of the line and allowed himself to be arrested, although he could have escaped easily. He went to jail. Community leaders were highly critical of Dr. King because he had violated the law.

Was there an ethical justification for Dr. King's violation of the law?

Ethics is a practice of deciding what is right or wrong in a reasoned, impartial manner. To involve ethics, a decision must affect you or others in a significant way. An ethical decision is one that is reasoned out typically by referring to a written authority that provides consistency. The law is such an authority. So are religious texts such as the Torah, the Bible, and the Koran. For example, a person might reason, "I believe that God is the source of the Bible and the Bible tells me not to lie. Therefore, it would be wrong, or unethical, for me to lie." To make ethical decisions, we usually must base our decisions on reason, not on emotion.

In addition to being reasonable, ethical decisions should be impartial. *Impartiality* is the idea that the same ethical standards are applied to everyone. The reason you are learning about ethics in general is to prepare you to apply ethical concepts to business decision making. *Business ethics* are the ethical principles used in making business decisions.

All too often, however, ethics are not considered when business decisions are made. The reason can be summarized in two words: profit maximization. The idea of profit maximization is supported by those who need a justification for actions that would hurt the general welfare. These actions might include moving factories offshore, having skilled jobs done overseas instead of by American workers, and buying solid, conservatively run companies only to sell the company's assets. To move toward a more ethically motivated economy, the profit maximization justification for such actions will need to be replaced by the more humane ethical standards presented in this lesson.

BASIC FORMS OF ETHICAL REASONING

Ethical reasoning about right and wrong takes two basic forms. One form is based on consequences. In this style of ethical reasoning, rightness or wrongness is based only on the results of the action. Particular acts have no ethical, or moral, character. An act that produces good consequences is good. An act that produces bad consequences is bad.

IN THIS CASE

It was a nice day so Gabe decided to walk to school instead of riding the bus. On the way, he found a wallet containing $300 in cash and a driver's license. When he saw how much money there was, he could almost feel the fun he could have with it. Gabe also asked himself how much injury the loss of $300 might cause the person who lost the wallet. At first he thought he would get much more pleasure from the money than anyone else could. In the end, he decided that he would want his wallet and money returned if he lost them, so he called the owner.

The other form of moral reasoning is based on ethical rules. In this style of reasoning, acts are either right or wrong. For example, telling the truth is always right, and lying is always wrong. In rule-based ethics, good consequences do not justify wrong or bad acts. For example, in rule-based ethics, you cannot justify lying by showing that it produces good consequences.

For almost all ethical decisions, these two forms of reasoning reach the same conclusion. In the decision of whether to lie or to tell the truth, for example, both forms usually conclude that one should not lie.

CONSEQUENCES-BASED ETHICAL REASONING

Consequences-based reasoning first looks for alternative ways to alter the current situation. Then it attempts to forecast the consequences that will arise from each alternative. Finally, it evaluates those possible consequences to select the alternative that will generate the greatest good. This last criterion often is very subjective as to how one defines the good—financial reward, pleasure, love, justice. Who will be receiving "the good" often is a major consideration in this reasoning process.

RULE-BASED ETHICAL REASONING
With fundamental ethical rules, the acts themselves are judged as right or wrong. The standard for judging usually comes from one of two sources— a recognized authority or human reasoning.

The authority, often a religious source, often clearly prescribes what is correct by time-tested rules such as those found in the Ten Commandments. Human reasoning also can show what is basically wrong or right. A test, called *universalizing,* has been developed to help in this effort. In universalizing, you picture everyone doing the action and then ask yourself, "Would the result be irrational, illogical, or demeaning?" If so, the action is considered ethically wrong.

ETHICS REFLECTED IN LAWS

Under the U.S. system of democracy, representatives must vote for laws that are acceptable to the majority of people if the representatives expect to be reelected. Because this system is grounded on majority rule, it uses many of the features of consequences-based ethics. In this system, laws are judged to be right or good when they affect the majority of the people positively. Laws are judged to be wrong when they affect the majority negatively. Thus the government, empowered by the U.S. Constitution, seeks to ensure that

A QUESTION OF ETHICS

The term *culture* refers to a society's shared values, beliefs, and behaviors. *Values* reflect the goals a society considers important. Values also express the culture's ideas of how people should act, as well as ideas about what is good, right, and desirable. Culture expresses a society's ethics. Different cultures may have very different ethical systems. What is considered ethical behavior in one culture may not be acceptable behavior in another. For example, in Islamic societies, women's activities outside the home are greatly restricted. Compare this to the role of women in U.S. society today. Every society has a unique culture, which evolves and changes over time. Each culture develops a set of laws based on the ethical values expressed at the time. Laws evolve as the culture's sense of ethics evolves.

the federal lawmaking system provides the greatest good for the greatest number.

On the other hand, the Constitution also seeks to protect the well-being of minorities that might be taken advantage of by the wrong actions of the majority. This is done primarily through the rights preserved in the first ten amendments to the Constitution. Such protection of basic human dignity afforded by the Bill of Rights and other civil rights laws reflect ethics based on rules.

Both ethics based on consequences and ethics based on rules conclude that we are obligated to obey the law. According to consequences-based reasoning, when the law is violated, many more people are injured than are benefited. With rule-based reasoning, if we say that we have agreed to obey the law but violate it, we are breaking our promise. If we universalize promise breaking by imagining that everyone always breaks promises, there would be no point to promising. In this universalized state, promise breaking is illogical or pointless and thus wrong.

Even if unethical, the ease with which laws can be broken, especially by those with superior abilities or knowledge, such as a computer programmer, makes such behavior tempting. Aware of this, employers often purchase fidelity bonds for persons who handle large sums of money, such as cashiers, managers of movie theaters, or supervisors of restaurants. A *fidelity bond* is an insurance policy that pays the employer money in the case of theft by employees.

Unethical, lawbreaking behavior does not always occur on a large scale, however. Often, individuals do not obey even minor laws. These individuals are termed *scofflaws*. These are persons who do not respect the law. They simply assess the risk of being caught and punished against the benefits they obtain by breaking the law. They lack personal *integrity,* or the capacity to do what is right in the face of temptation or pressure to do otherwise. They think they are smart because they frequently violate valid laws without being caught. A scofflaw is never ethically justified in violating the law.

In contrast to the self-serving behavior of scofflaws, some persons care passionately about ethical behavior, human rights, and justice. Their concern for justice sometimes compels them to violate what they consider to be an unjust law—a law they believe to be in conflict with ethical reasoning. They violate the law by engaging in acts of civil disobedience.

Civil disobedience is an open, peaceful, violation of a law to protest its alleged, or supposed, injustice. The goal of those who engage in civil disobedience is not to advance their self-interest but rather to make the legal system more just. The participants may be willing, or even eager, to be arrested in order to test the validity of the law in court.

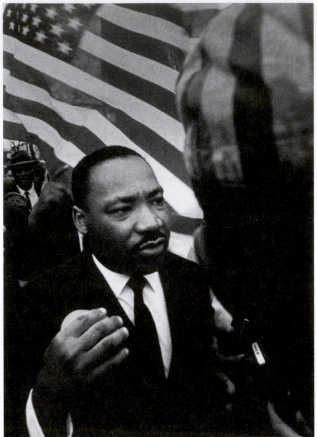

© FLIP SCHULKE/COBBS

In *What's Your Verdict?* Dr. Martin Luther King, Jr., engaged in civil disobedience. Dr. King believed that civil disobedience is justified only in very limited circumstances. He and others conclude that civil disobedience is ethical when

- a written law is in conflict with ethical reasoning
- no effective political methods are available to change the law
- the civil disobedience is nonviolent
- the civil disobedience does not advance a person's immediate self-interest
- the civil disobedience is public and one willingly accepts the punishment for violating the law

As a result of Dr. King's efforts, many human rights were extended for the first time to several minority groups in this country.

Access lawxtra.swlearning.com and click on the link for Chapter 1. Once in the ACLU web site type "civil disobedience" into the Search box. Choose one of the articles. Read it and note the context in which the term is used. Prepare a one-minute presentation explaining the article. Break into small groups and present your article. As a group, make a list of the issues which civil disobedience was used to protest. Then, present your group findings to the class.

lawxtra.swlearning.com

CHECKPOINT

In the U.S. system of democracy, how are ethics reflected in laws?

THINK ABOUT LEGAL CONCEPTS

1. Ethics is a practice of deciding what is right or wrong in a reasoned, _?_ manner.

2. The two forms of ethical reasoning almost never reach the same conclusions. **True or False?**

3. Civil disobedience involves which of the following? (a) violating the law (b) violating the law openly (c) violating the law openly and peacefully (d) violating the law openly, peacefully, and accepting punishment for the violation (e) all of the above

4. Majority rule usually advances this type of ethical reasoning. (a) reasoning based on consequences (b) rule-based reasoning

THINK CRITICALLY ABOUT EVIDENCE

Study the situation, answer the questions, and then prepare arguments to support your answers.

5. Conner walked past the candy section in the grocery store and quickly stuffed a handful of candy bars into her purse. A store security guard saw her do it, and she was arrested. Her parents came to the police station after her arrest to take her home. Did Conner's shoplifting significantly affect anyone? If so, who? Was Conner basing her conduct on emotion or reason? Was she treating herself and the other customers and stockholders of the store equally?

6. Sharon knows about tax laws and how the Internal Revenue Service (IRS) audits tax returns. She knows a way to cheat on her tax return that would save her almost $2,000. She thinks her chance of being caught is about one in 100. Can this cheating be justified by reasoning based on ethical rules? Can it be justified by ethics based on consequences?

7. An ordinance of Walker County provided that all automobiles must pass a smog emissions test once a year. Ross was ticketed because his car had not been inspected and approved at a testing center. Ross claimed to be a skilled mechanic who kept his car well tuned and cleaner than the law required. According to Ross, the law violated his natural rights. Explain why you agree or disagree with Ross.

8. If a legislature enacted a law that made it illegal to shout "fire" in a movie theater, would the dominant ethical character of the law reflect consequences-based or rule-based reasoning?

9. Assume a state legislature enacted legislation which budgeted more money to educating rich children than to educating poor children. Also assume that the majority of children are rich. Would the dominant ethical character of this law be consequences-based or rule-based?

PREVENT LEGAL DIFFICULTIES

As a citizen . . .

1. When moving to a new location, find out how the laws in that county or city may affect you.

2. Before beginning a new business, consult an attorney to learn about city, county, state, and federal laws and how they may affect you.

3. Study business law so you can become an informed citizen who is knowledgeable about legal matters.

4. Recognize that fulfilling your duties is the greatest guarantee of your maintaining your rights as an American citizen. These include:
   a. The duty to obey the law.
   b. The duty to respect the rights of others.
   c. The duty to inform yourself on political issues.
   d. The duty to vote in elections.
   e. The duty to serve on juries if called.
   f. The duty to serve and defend your country.
   g. The duty to assist agencies of law enforcement.

Chapter 1 Assessment

CONCEPTS IN BRIEF

1-1 Laws and Legal Systems

1. Laws are the enforceable rules of conduct in a society.

2. The two great systems of law in the world are the English common law and the Roman civil law. The legal systems of all the states except Louisiana are based on the common law.

3. Sources of law include constitutions, statutes, cases decided by appellate courts, and regulations and rulings of administrative agencies.

1-2 Types of Laws

4. Civil law is concerned with the private legal rights of individuals and governs relations between individuals. Criminal law deals with crimes (offenses against society) and governs violations of duties owed to society as a whole.

5. Procedural law deals with methods of enforcing legal rights and duties. Substantive law defines those rights and duties.

1-3 Ethical Bases for Laws

6. Business law is concerned with the rules that apply to business situations and transactions.

7. Ethical reasoning should be applied to reach reasonable and impartial decisions that affect people.

8. Ethics are either based on consequences or on fundamental rules.

9. Civil disobedience is the open, peaceful violation of a law to protest its alleged injustice or unfairness. It is only justified in rare and extraordinary circumstances.

YOUR LEGAL VOCABULARY

Match each statement with the term that it best defines. Some terms may not be used.

1. Doctrine requiring lower courts to adhere to existing case law in making decisions

2. Group of laws defining the methods for enforcing legal rights and duties

3. Enforceable rules of conduct in a society

4. Law based on the customs of a group of people

5. Legislative enactment by a city

6. Group of laws defining and setting punishments for offenses against society

7. An open, peaceful, violation of a law to protest its alleged injustice

8. Power of a court to decide a case

9. Law enacted by state legislatures or federal legislatures

10. Law made when an appellate court endorses a rule to be used in deciding court cases

11. The practice of deciding what is right or wrong in a reasoned, impartial manner

12. Document that sets forth the framework of a government and its relationship to the people it governs

13. Group of laws that make up for wrongs against individual persons

14. Laws grouped into an organized form

15. Fairness

16. Law dictated from above

a. **administrative agency**
b. **case law**
c. **civil disobedience**
d. **civil law**
e. **code**
f. **common law**
g. **constitution**
h. **criminal law**
i. **equity**
j. **ethics**
k. **jurisdiction**
l. **laws**
m. **ordinance**
n. **positive law**
o. **procedural law**
p. *stare decisis*
q. **statute**
r. **substantive law**

REVIEW LEGAL CONCEPTS

17. Louisiana is the only one of our 50 states whose law was not originally based on the English common law system. What system was its law based on? How did this system come to be used?

18. Why should a constitution be considered the highest law of a nation or a state?

19. What does the phrase "interstate commerce" mean to you? Would you consider growing vegetables in your garden for your own consumption interstate commerce? Why or why not?

20. Why does the doctrine of *stare decisis* not bind supreme courts?

21. Why are most fines the courts assess for criminal behavior paid to the government and not to the victim of the crime?

22. Explain how both ethics based on reasoning and consequences-based ethics conclude that people are obligated to obey the law.

23. Identify a situation in your life where someone used rule-based ethical reasoning.

24. Describe the three steps involved in making a decision using consequences-based ethics.

WRITE ABOUT LEGAL CONCEPTS

25. Would you rather be under the control of a system of common law or positive law? Write a paragraph to explain your answer.

26. Why is it important to have uniform state laws governing business? Write a paragraph to list and discuss at least four reasons.

27. Use one to three words to identify a current event that others will quickly recognize. Next, write a paragraph evaluating someone's conduct in the current event using the ethics of reasoning based on consequences.

28. Use one to three words to identify a current event that others will quickly recognize. Next, write a paragraph evaluating someone's conduct in the current event using the ethics of rule-based reasoning.

29. Create and write a scenario which raises an ethical issue. Try to create a scenario where something is wrong in rule-based reasoning but right in reasoning based on consequences.

30. **HOT DEBATE** Clarisse is convicted of a violation of the noise ordinance. Her appeal is dismissed. As a consequence, she organizes a group of friends with cars to drive through the neighborhoods of the city with their stereos going at full volume as an act of civil disobedience. Is she ethically justified in so doing? Why or why not?

THINK CRITICALLY ABOUT EVIDENCE

Study the situation, answer the questions, and then prepare arguments to support your answers.

31. You are in France and are accused of a crime. You ask for a trial by jury. Why is one not available?

32. Your friend Bill has shared with you his dream of getting rid of the income tax. He says that if the people wanted to, they could pass a constitutional amendment that would eliminate the tax. Is he correct?

33. Juana was trying to decide whom to vote for in an upcoming election. After reviewing the candidates, she said, "I've decided to vote for Gary because I just feel better about him." Is Juana's decision based on ethics? If not, why?

34. Staub, Conly, and Winfield were employees of the Prime Time Restaurant. They were aware that the owner never checked the totals on the sales checks against the cash in the register. Therefore, it would be very easy to steal from the cash register. However, they did not steal. When asked why, they gave the following reasons. Staub said he did not take the money because he was afraid of being caught. Conly said she did not take the money because she felt obligated to obey the law. Winfield said he did not take the money because of his religious beliefs. To which person do you best relate? Why?

MAKE ACADEMIC CONNECTIONS

35. **MEDICINE** As medical science moves forward, major ethical issues are developing that are likely to be encountered in the courts and legislative bodies. Identify such issues in medical fields such as cloning, cryogenic preservation, organ marketing and farms, etc. Choose one of these issues, and apply both consequences-based and rule-based ethical reasoning to determine whether it is ethical or not. Write a paragraph summarizing your findings.

ANALYZE REAL CASES

36. Alaska enacted a statute known as "Alaska Hire." It required employers in the state to hire qualified Alaskan residents in preference to non-residents. Hicklin, a nonresident, sued Orbeck, the state official charged with enforcing the statute. After the Supreme Court of Alaska found the statute constitutional, Hicklin appealed to the U.S. Supreme Court, which found the statute to be in conflict with the U.S. Constitution. Which supreme court is the final authority in this case? (*Hicklin v. Orbeck*, 437 U.S. 518)

37. The city of Chicago sued to stop the operation of the Commonwealth Edison Company's coal-burning, electricity-generating plant in nearby Hammond, Indiana. Chicago claimed that the plant emitted too much smoke, sulfur dioxide, and other harmful substances. The city also claimed that the plant was a common-law public nuisance because it caused "an unreasonable interference with a right common to the general public" to clean air. Edison argued that it had spent much money to reduce harmful emissions and that the emissions were now well below the levels prescribed by federal clean air regulations and by the city of Hammond. Edison also pointed out that "unpleasant odors, smoke, and film" already characterized the area in which the plant was located. The trial court refused to issue an injunction. Therefore, the city of Chicago appealed to a higher court, which affirmed (upheld) the trial court. How can this legal action be ethically justified? (*City of Chicago v. Commonwealth Edison Company*, 321 N.E.2d 412, Ill.)

38. On March 30, 1981, as then President Ronald Reagan left the Washington Hilton Hotel after giving a speech, he was wounded by one of a series of bullets allegedly fired by John Hinckley. Three other men also were wounded, including James Brady, the President's press secretary, who received a severe wound to the head. President Reagan underwent surgery shortly thereafter at the hospital. Hinckley was arrested at the scene literally with the smoking gun. Soon after the criminal process was begun against him, he underwent two psychiatric examinations by order of the magistrate and then the chief judge involved in the case. Both examinations found him to be competent. On August 28, after being indicted by a federal grand jury, Hinckley pled not guilty to a battery of charges, including the attempted assassination of the President of the United States. Hinckley's lawyers then began their work. In two very important rulings they were able to suppress the use of evidence that would have been very damning to the defendant. They first had thrown out all answers he had given to questions prior to having his attorney present. This was done even though he had been read his Miranda rights three times before agreeing to answer those questions. Then Hinckley's attorneys were able to suppress allegedly incriminating material in the form of a diary gathered by the jailers when they checked Hinckley's cell for contraband and instruments useful in a potential suicide attempt. These rulings by the court were based on the constitutional rights to counsel and to protection against improper searches and seizures. Do you consider their use in this case a proper application of such rights? Is the exclusion of the evidence the only possible remedy or could you come up with another one? If so, what is it and why would it be an improvement over the current policy? (*United States v. John W. Hinckley, Jr.*, 525 F. Supp. 1342)

CASE FOR LEGAL THINKING

GRIMSHAW v. FORD MOTOR COMPANY
174 CAL. RPTR. 348

EVIDENCE Mrs. Gray, accompanied by 13-year-old Richard Grimshaw, set out in the family's new Pinto from Anaheim for Barstow to meet Mr. Gray in Barstow. As Mrs. Gray approached the Route 30 off-ramp where traffic was congested, she moved from the outer fast lane to the middle lane of the freeway. Shortly after this lane change, the Pinto suddenly stalled and coasted to a halt in the middle lane. A Ford Galaxie traveling immediately behind the Pinto was unable to avoid colliding with it. The Galaxie had been traveling from 50 to 55 miles per hour but before the impact had slowed to a speed of from 20 to 37 miles per hour. At the moment of impact, the Pinto caught fire and its interior was engulfed in flames. According to plaintiff's expert, the impact of the Galaxie had driven the Pinto gas tank forward and caused it to be punctured by the flange or one of the bolts on the differential housing so that fuel sprayed from the punctured tank and entered the passenger compartment. . . . When the occupants emerged from the vehicle, their clothing was almost completely burned off. Mrs. Gray died a few days later of congestive heart failure as a result of the burns. Richard Grimshaw managed to survive but only through heroic medical measures. He underwent numerous and extensive surgeries and skin grafts and faced additional surgeries over the next ten years. He lost portions of several fingers on his left hand, portions of his left ear, and his face required many skin grafts from various portions of his body.

OPINION Ford's objective was to build a car at or below 2,000 pounds to sell for no more than $2,000. Ordinarily marketing surveys and preliminary engineering studies precede the styling of a new automobile line. The Pinto, however, was a rush project, so that styling preceded engineering and dictated engineering design to a greater degree than usual. Among the engineering decisions dictated by styling was the placement of the fuel tank. The Pinto's styling. . . . required the tank to be placed behind the rear axle, leaving only nine or ten inches of "crush space," far less than in any other American automobile or Ford overseas subcompact. Also, the Pinto was designed so that its bumper was little more than a chrome strip, less substantial than the bumper of any other American car produced then or later.

Prototypes as well as two production Pintos were crash-tested by Ford to determine, among other things, the integrity of the fuel system in rear end accidents. Prototypes struck from the rear with a moving barrier at 21 miles per hour caused the fuel tank to be driven forward and punctured, causing fuel leakage. Where rubber bladders had been installed in the tank, crash tests into fixed barriers at 21 miles per hour withstood leakage from punctures in the gas tank. The cost of the flak suit or bladder would be $4 to $8 per car. A reasonable inference may be drawn from the evidence that despite management's knowledge that the Pinto's fuel system could be made safe at a cost of but $4 to $8 per car, it decided to defer corrective measures to save money and enhance profits. Ford's institutional mentality was shown to be one of callous indifference to public safety. . .

DECISION The judgment against the Ford Motor Company is affirmed.

PRACTICE JUDGING

1. Have both criminal and civil wrongs been committed by Ford Motor Co.? Explain.

2. Which ethical system, consequences-based or reasoning based on ethical rules, most reflects the thinking used by the defendant, Ford Motor Company, in this case?

3. Which ethical system, or systems, most reflect the thinking used by the court in this case?

© BETTMANN/CORBIS

Constitutional Rights

HOT DEBATE

We the People

The original draft of the Declaration of Independence condemned the slave trade and criticized the English people. Both passages were edited out by the delegates of the Continental Congress before the Declaration was approved.

© GETTY IMAGES/PHOTODISC

Where Do You Stand?

1. Why do you think the passages were omitted?

2. Was omitting them a good or bad idea? Why?

Foundations of the U.S. Constitution

▼ GOALS
- Identify the documents written in the course of the nation's founding
- Explain how the U.S. Constitution addresses and protects citizens' civil rights.

THE DOCUMENTS THAT FORMED A NATION

WHAT'S YOUR VERDICT?

When the Constitutional Convention sent the proposed Constitution to the states for ratification, it met with strong opposition. Patrick Henry, James Monroe, and John Hancock, for example, all opposed it. Even so, the Constitution was put into effect in 1789. The vote did not become unanimous until 1790.

What caused the opposition to the Constitution? What action resolved the dispute?

DECLARATION OF INDEPENDENCE

On July 4, 1776, delegates from the 13 original American colonies to the second Continental Congress, meeting in Philadelphia, formally adopted the **Declaration of Independence**. Thomas Jefferson of Virginia drafted the Declaration in less than a month. The document asserted the rights the colonists desired. It charged King George III of England with "a history of repeated injuries and usurpation" for the purpose of establishing an "absolute tyranny. . . ." It declared that "all men are created equal, that they are endowed by their Creator with certain unalienable rights, that among these are life, liberty, and the pursuit of happiness." (See the full text of the Declaration of Independence in Appendix B on page 606.)

The authors of the Declaration of Independence believed that to secure these rights, they would need to have their own government.

This image is a reproduction of a famous painting by John Trumbull entitled "Declaration of Independence." The painting has been criticized for showing a scene that never took place. That is, according to historians, all 48 men shown in this picture were never gathered in the same place at the same time. Despite this criticism, do you think the picture is historically valuable? Why or why not?

© NORTH WIND/NORTH WIND PICTURE ARCHIVES

This new government would draw its power from the people.

At the time the Declaration was adopted, fighting between British troops and colonists had already begun. The American War of Independence that followed lasted more than eight years, with the colonies claiming ultimate victory.

ARTICLES OF CONFEDERATION

The 13 sovereign former colonies united loosely in 1781 under a charter called the **Articles of Confederation**. The Articles of Confederation contained the following provisions:

- a one-house legislature (the Continental Congress) with two to seven representatives from each state; each state had one vote

- strict term limits placed on members of Congress, who were subject to recall by their states

- power to declare war, make peace, enter into treaties and alliances, manage relations with Indian nations, coin money, settle differences between states, establish a postal system, and appoint a Commander in Chief

- a national defense that would be paid for by the national government

- states would be asked, rather than required, to make payments to the national treasury

- major legislation, including bills relating to finance, would require a two-thirds vote for passage

- amendments to the Articles would require a unanimous vote of the states

Many people felt a need for a stronger central government than the one the Articles provided. Disagreement among the states regarding the Articles led to the calling of a special convention of delegates from the original 13 states.

U.S. CONSTITUTION

The special convention, held in Philadelphia in the summer of 1787, drafted the initial U.S. Constitution. The seven articles of the **U.S. Constitution** provided a workable framework for a federal government. By June 1788, the Constitution had been ratified by delegates to special conventions held in nine of the original 13 colonies.

ORDER OF RATIFICATION OF THE U.S. CONSTITUTION

1. Delaware	December 7, 1787
2. Pennsylvania	December 12, 1787
3. New Jersey	December 18, 1787
4. Georgia	January 2, 1788
5. Connecticut	January 9, 1788
6. Massachusetts	February 6, 1788
7. Maryland	April 28, 1788
8. South Carolina	May 23, 1788
9. New Hampshire	June 21, 1788
10. Virginia	June 26, 1788
11. New York	July 26, 1788
12. North Carolina	November 21, 1789
13. Rhode Island	May 29, 1790

THE ORIGINAL 13 COLONIES

DE
PA
NJ
GA
CT
MA
MD
SC
NH
VA
NY
NC
RI

Our existence as a truly united country began on March 4, 1789. On this date, Congress declared the Constitution effective and binding because nine states had already ratified it. Critics in the other four states claimed the wording of the Constitution failed to provide adequate protection of the human rights proclaimed in the Declaration of Independence. In *What's Your Verdict?* Virginia, New York, North Carolina, and Rhode Island took longer to ratify because they felt this fundamental problem with the Constitution—the failure to protect human rights—had to be corrected. The situation was resolved by the adoption of the Bill of Rights.

THE BILL OF RIGHTS

The first ten amendments to the Constitution, known as the **Bill of Rights**, were adopted to ensure that U.S. citizens would enjoy the human rights proclaimed in the Declaration of Independence. The U.S. Bill of Rights is based on three English Documents: The Magna Carta, the Petition of Right, and the Bill of Rights. The Magna Carta is considered the basis for English constitutional liberties.

The amendments in the U.S Bill of Rights shown below are in the words of the founding fathers.

AMENDMENT I Congress shall make no law respecting an establishment of religion, or prohibiting the free exercise thereof; or abridging the freedom of speech, or of the press, or the right of the people peaceably to assemble, and to petition the Government for a redress of grievances.

AMENDMENT II A well regulated Militia, being necessary to the security of a free State, the right of the people to keep and bear Arms, shall not be infringed.

AMENDMENT III No Soldier shall, in time of peace be quartered in any house, without the consent of the Owner, nor in time of war, but in a manner to be prescribed by law.

AMENDMENT IV The right of the people to be secure in their persons, houses, papers, and effects, against unreasonable searches and seizures, shall not be violated, and no warrants shall issue, but upon probable cause, supported by oath or affirmation, and particularly describing the place to be searched, and the persons or things to be seized.

AMENDMENT V No person shall be held to answer for a capital, or otherwise infamous crime, unless on a presentment or indictment of a Grand Jury, except in cases arising in the land or naval forces, or in the Militia, when in actual service in time of War or public danger; nor shall any person be subject for the same offense to be twice put in jeopardy of life or limb, nor shall be compelled in any criminal case to be a witness against himself, nor be deprived of life, liberty, or property, without due process of law; nor shall private property be taken for public use without just compensation.

AMENDMENT VI In all criminal prosecutions, the accused shall enjoy the right to a speedy and public trial, by an impartial jury of the State and district wherein the crime shall have been committed, which district shall have been previously ascertained by law, and to be informed of the nature and cause of the accusation; to be confronted with the witnesses against him; to have compulsory process for obtaining witnesses in his favor, and to have the assistance of counsel for his defense.

AMENDMENT VII In Suits at common law, where the value in controversy shall exceed twenty dollars, the right of trial by jury shall be preserved, and no fact tried by a jury shall be otherwise re-examined in any Court of the United States, than according to the rules of the common law.

AMENDMENT VIII Excessive bail shall not be required, nor excessive fines imposed, nor cruel and unusual punishments inflicted.

AMENDMENT IX The enumeration in the Constitution of certain rights shall not be construed to deny or disparage others retained by the people.

AMENDMENT X The powers not delegated to the United States by the Constitution, nor prohibited by it to the States, are reserved to the States respectively, or to the people.

CHECKPOINT

What document's statement of human rights formed the basis for the first ten amendments to the U.S. Constitution?

CIVIL RIGHTS

The First Amendment protects your right to practice the religion of your choice. If the founding fathers believed that freedom of religion was important, why do you think they opted for separation between church and state?

© GETTY IMAGES/PHOTODISC

Through the Bill of Rights and other amendments that were to follow, the Constitution became a shield for the personal, natural rights of the individual. These rights are referred to as **civil rights**. The most vital of these rights are those protected by the First Amendment: freedom of speech, freedom of the press, and freedom to assemble.

The First Amendment also protects the people's rights to practice the religion of their choice. Religion has inspired men, women, and children to noble and caring conduct. However, misguided religious zeal also has caused great violence and destruction. The founders of the republic recognized this deep-seated religious impulse but wisely imposed a role of neutrality for the government. They created a wall of separation between church and state. The government tolerates all religions but supports none in any strictly religious efforts.

DUE PROCESS OF LAW

Another significant amendment in the Bill of Rights is the Fifth Amendment. It states, "No person shall be . . . deprived of life, liberty, or property, without due process of law. . ."

Unlike the Declaration of Independence, the Constitution does not mention "the pursuit of happiness." However, respect by others for one's life, liberty, and property surely helps one to be secure and content, if not consciously happy.

The Constitution does not spell out what is meant by due process. The term has, however, come to be defined through various U.S. Supreme Court decisions. At the present time **due process of law** is taken to mean that, at a minimum, a defendant over whom jurisdiction has been established must be provided adequate notice and a proper hearing. Due process of law requires fundamental fairness in compliance with reasonable and just laws. If convicted, the criminal may be deprived of property by fine, of liberty by imprisonment, and even of life by lawful execution.

Due process of law is a concept embodied throughout the Constitution. It is assured by guaranteeing

- the right to be secure against unreasonable searches and seizures (Fourth Amendment)
- the right not to be a witness against yourself in

any criminal case (Fifth Amendment)

- in criminal prosecutions, the right for the accused to a speedy and public trial by an impartial jury of the state and district where the crime was committed, and to be informed of the nature and cause of the accusation; the right to be confronted with the witnesses against him; to have a set process for obtaining witnesses in his favor, and to have the benefit of a defense counsel (Sixth Amendment)
- trial by jury in civil suits where the value in controversy exceeds $20 (Seventh Amendment)
- that excessive bail will not be required nor excessive fines imposed, nor cruel and unusual punishment inflicted (Eighth Amendment)

THE ABOLITION OF SLAVERY

Originally the practice of slavery was enabled under the Constitution. In particular, the Constitution provided that Congress could not prohibit, prior to 1808, the "migration or importation of such persons. . . ." Slaves were further dehumanized by a provision in Article I that counted them as only three-fifths of a person for the purpose of apportioning representatives to Congress. Under Article IV, a slave who escaped to another state had to be returned to "the party to whom such service or labor may be due."

Finally, as a consequence of the Civil War, these provisions were negated by the Thirteenth Amendment, which states in part, "Neither slavery nor involuntary servitude, except as a punishment for a crime whereof the party shall have been duly convicted, shall exist within the United States, or any place subject to their jurisdiction."

THE RIGHT TO VOTE

The Fifteenth Amendment provided the newly freed slaves the legal right to vote. It decreed, "The right of citizens of the United States to vote shall not be denied or abridged by the United States or by any State on account of race, color or previous condition of servitude." Although the Thirteenth Amendment abolished slavery, and the Fifteenth guaranteed the former slaves the right to vote, racial discrimination continued in both the North and the South. Some southern states enacted a *poll tax*. This was a fixed payment per person required before the person could vote. Many former slaves could not afford to pay a tax in order to vote.

In 1964, more than 100 years after the Civil War began, the Twenty-Fourth Amendment guar-

● ●

anteed that the right to vote in federal elections "shall not be denied or abridged . . . by reason of failure to pay any poll tax or other tax." The Supreme Court subsequently applied the same rule to all state elections, declaring such taxes unconstitutional under the Fourteenth Amendment.

DENIAL BY GENDER The exclusion of "gender" in the Fifteenth Amendment was a deliberate denial of voting rights to women of all races. This injustice was removed in 1920 with the passage of the Nineteenth Amendment. It provided "The right of citizens of the United States to vote shall not be denied or abridged by the United States or by any State on account of sex."

DENIAL BY AGE Students protested during the Vietnam War, in part, because they objected to being eligible to fight in a war at the age of 18—

During the Vietnam conflict, young men and women in this country came close to open revolt. They embraced many forms of civil disobedience to make the point that they were being asked to bleed and die for their country, but had no input into making the decisions that caused the war or that might end it. Judged from the standpoint of the political "establishment" of the 1960s, their actions were illegal and improper. How do you think the American Revolutionaries would have viewed them? Which viewpoint is the more ethical?

but not vote until age 21. One result of these student protests was the hasty enactment of an amendment that gave all citizens age 18 or older the right to vote. The Twenty-Sixth Amendment was approved overwhelmingly by the Senate and House in March 1971. It was ratified by 38 states within three months. In *What's Your Verdict?* Tom was correct.

PERIPHERAL RIGHTS

Some rights are not explicitly mentioned in the U.S. Constitution or Bill of Rights, but courts have recognized them as necessary to protecting the rights that are mentioned. The *right of privacy* is such a peripheral right—it is not specifically mentioned in the Constitution or Bill of Rights. In the 1960s the U.S. Supreme Court acknowledged the right of privacy as a separate right. The right of privacy has since been reinforced by several federal acts.

CHECKPOINT
How does the Constitution address and protect citizens' civil rights?

Xtra!
Study Tools
lawxtra.swlearning.com

2-1 Assessment

THINK ABOUT LEGAL CONCEPTS

1. The Declaration of Independence was adopted on (a) July 4, 1776 (b) July 4, 1789 (c) July 4, 1861

2. The "inalienable rights" mentioned in the Declaration of Independence are "life, liberty, and the pursuit of _ ?_."

3. The American War of Independence lasted about (a) two years (b) four years (c) eight years (d) ten years

4. The 13 colonies originally created a common government under the "Articles of Incorporation." **True or False?**

5. Critics of the original Constitution claimed the wording failed to protect human _?_.

6. _ ?_ was the thirteenth state to ratify the U.S. Constitution.

7. Which of the first 10 amendments guarantees freedom of the press? (a) First (b) Second (c) Third (d) freedom of the press is not guaranteed in the Bill of Rights

8. The original Bill of Rights contains the right of peaceful assembly. **True or False?**

9. Term limits on representatives were imposed by the Articles of Confederation. **True or False?**

10. The right of privacy was not acknowledged as a separate right until the 1960s. **True or False?**

THINK CRITICALLY ABOUT EVIDENCE

Study the situation, answer the questions, and then prepare arguments to support your answers.

11. It is 1793 and you are a citizen and editor of a newspaper in one of the original states. Your newspaper regularly carries stories about corruption in state government. Finally, the state prosecuting attorney brings charges against you for criticism of government officials, a violation of state law, and closes your newspaper. You maintain that your freedom of the press under the U.S. Constitution has been violated. The prosecutor replies that the Bill of Rights does not protect you from state actions. Is the prosecutor correct?

12. You are a citizen of one of the 13 colonies. The time is mid-July 1776. You have just heard of the issuance of the Declaration of Independence. What reasons might cause you to withhold your support of the Declaration?

13. As a protest against overseas military action by the government, about 600 sign-carrying students from a local school gathered peacefully at a major road intersection. As curious drivers slowed to observe, traffic came to a standstill. Within minutes, the police moved in and forced the crowd to break up. Several individuals who dropped their signs and "went limp" on the pavement were arrested. Did the police action violate the protesters' First Amendment constitutional right "peaceably to assemble"?

Division and Balance of Governmental Powers

▼ GOALS

- Describe the system of checks and balances in the U.S. government
- Explain how the power to govern is divided between the federal and state governments

A SYSTEM OF CHECKS AND BALANCES

WHAT'S YOUR VERDICT?

Thomas was critical of the U.S. Constitution because he said it had not been ratified by a democratic vote of the people. Shakira said in response that of course it had been.

Who is correct?

Warren E. Burger, former Chief Justice of the U.S. Supreme Court, has pointed out that at the time the Constitution was drafted and adopted, "There was not a country in the world that governed with separated and divided powers providing checks and balances on the exercise of authority by those who governed." The 55 delegates who drafted the U.S. Constitution displayed great foresight in devising a unique system of checks and balances. This system gives specific authority to each of the three basic branches of government.

BRANCHES OF GOVERNMENT

The three branches of government include the legislative, the executive, and the judicial.

LEGISLATIVE BRANCH The legislative branch at the federal level is the Congress. When the Constitution was drafted, the convention delegates were concerned with equal representation in Congress. States with small populations worried they might lose some of the sovereignty and independence they enjoyed under the Articles of Confederation. States with large populations feared they would be dominated by the less populous states (of which there were many more), if each state had an equal number of votes.

The solution? The national legislature would consist of two bodies:

1. a Senate, with two members from every state—regardless of population, and
2. a House of Representatives, with seats allocated to the states in proportion to their population.

The Senate could block any action of the House, and the House could block any action of the Senate. The existence of two bodies allows for various checks and balances. For instance, all bills for taxing or appropriating funds must originate in the House. A majority vote of both bodies is required for passage of any bill.

A further check is available to the House of Representatives. The House has the power to impeach any civil officer of the United States—including the President and Vice President—for treason, bribery, or other high crimes and misdemeanors. However, the Senate has the sole power to try all impeachment cases. **Impeachment cases** involve trying a government official for misconduct in office. Conviction in such cases requires a two-thirds vote of the members present.

Finally, the people may vote for their representatives in elections to the House (for a two-year term), the Senate (for a six-year term), and the executive office (for a four-year term).

EXECUTIVE BRANCH The executive branch is headed by the President and Vice President. These officers are elected by a vote of the people. In the electoral process, citizens vote for the electors who are pledged to support candidates selected by political parties. Because the President and Vice President are not elected directly by the people, the candidate who receives the greatest popular vote for president may not be elected. This has occurred four times, in 1824, 1876, 1888, and 2000.

A **political party** is a private organization of citizens who select and promote candidates for election to public office. Party members agree with these candidates on important governmental policies and legislation. Political parties are not mentioned in the Constitution.

JUDICIAL BRANCH The third branch of government is the judiciary. It is headed by the Supreme Court of the United States. Ultimately, the Supreme Court decides on the constitutionality of a statute passed by the legislative branch and signed by the President as head of the executive branch. The Supreme Court also may decide if a particular action or decision exceeds the powers granted to the executive branch under the Constitution. If so, the action or decision is void.

CHANGING THE CONSTITUTION

A major check is provided by the power of constitutional **amendment** meaning change or alteration. The Constitution may be amended in two ways. The first way has been used for all amendments adopted to date. The amendment is proposed by a two-thirds majority vote in both the Senate and the House. The second way requires the legislatures of two-thirds of all the states to call a convention of all the states. The convention may propose one or more amendments. Under either method of proposal, the amendment becomes a valid part of the U.S. Constitution only if it is ratified by the legislatures of three-fourths of the states, or if it is ratified by conventions in three-fourths of the states.

THE U.S. FORM OF GOVERNMENT

In a pure **democracy**, every adult citizen may vote on all issues. This is almost impossible to make happen in a nation of almost 300 million people. Instead, the United States is a **republic**

or a representative democracy. Voters select their representatives to the legislative, executive, and judicial branches of government.

Although representatives make the day-to-day decisions, the sovereign power ultimately resides in the people. This means that the highest final authority to decide what the law shall be rests with the citizens who exercise their right and duty to vote. In many elections only a minority of the total number of voters who are eligible actually exercise this right.

In *What's Your Verdict?* Thomas is correct. The Constitution was proposed, ratified, and has since been amended only by representatives of the people in Congress, in conventions, and in the state legislatures. There has never been a purely democratic vote on the Constitution.

CHECKPOINT

How did the Constitution create a system of checks and balances?

THE POWER TO GOVERN

WHAT'S YOUR VERDICT?

Several thousand people had assembled in the park for the annual Fourth of July celebration. The state's senior U.S. senator opened the ceremonies. He said, "I am proud and pleased to be a citizen of the United States of America and of this great state. But, before I am a citizen of either state or country, I, like all of you, am a human being. Our humanity precedes our citizenship. Government exists only by the will and consent of the people. The people control the government. Any control by the government of the people occurs because the people have granted permission of that control."

Does the senator's analysis conform to the governmental structure created by the framers of the Constitution?

The Constitution and the Bill of Rights were written by representatives of the people elected by voters in the 13 original states. These documents place a priority on the basic rights of human beings. This priority exists whether people act as individuals or together. The Ninth Amendment recognizes this priority by stating, "The enumeration in the Constitution of certain rights, shall not be construed to deny or disparage others retained by the people."

SOVEREIGNTY OF THE STATES

The Tenth Amendment acknowledges the continued sovereignty of all of the states to govern their own citizens within their own borders. **Sovereignty** in this sense means freedom from external control. The Tenth Amendment declares, "The powers not delegated to the United States by the Constitution, nor prohibited by it to the States, are reserved to the States respectively, or to the people." Here it is evident

INTERNATIONAL VIEWPOINT

Democratic Representation in Hungary

The history of democratic representation in Hungary is long and complicated. For nearly a thousand years, the only form of representation was a collection of nobles who met infrequently at different places around the country. The parliament was relatively weak, and Hungary was dominated by outside powers for much of the period. In 1867, the parliament gained considerable powers when the Austrian emperor Franz Joseph agreed that Hungary should be administered as a separate nation within the empire.

The parliament continued throughout the rest of the nineteenth century and into the twentieth century as a semi-representative body. For most of this time, either an elite group or a dictator dominated the parliament. After the collapse of Communism in 1989, Hungary gained its first parliament that truly represented all Hungarians.

that the Constitution is a shield against unlimited power of the federal government.

Article VI recognizes the Constitution to be "the supreme law of the land." It prevails over any possible contrary state constitution or law. At the same time, every state constitution and the respective statutes are supreme on matters that have not been given to the federal government. Powers kept by the states include control over most business law and contract law, most criminal and tort law, real property and probate law, and domestic relations law.

LIMITING STATES' POWERS

The Fourteenth Amendment opens with these sweeping provisions: "All persons born or naturalized in the United States and subject to the jurisdiction thereof, are citizens of the United States and of the state wherein they reside. No state shall make or enforce any law which shall abridge the privileges or immunities of citizens of the United States; nor shall any State deprive any person of life, liberty, or property, without due process of law; nor deny to any person within its jurisdiction the equal protection of the laws."

Recall that the Fifth Amendment had previously applied such limitations only to the powers of the federal government. The Fourteenth Amendment subjects the states to the same restraint. Due process, as outlined in the Fifth Amendment, is not the only constitutional protection that state governments are required to respect.

Other relevant amendments in the Bill of Rights also have been applied to the states. As a result, today the shield of the Constitution is effective against abuse of power by both the federal and state governments. At both levels, statutes have been enacted to provide comparable protection against abuse of power by private individuals and corporations.

POWERS OF THE FEDERAL GOVERNMENT

The federal government has the duty to protect every state against invasion. It may raise and support armies, a navy, and an air force for national defense. The federal government alone may establish post offices, coin money, and tax imports and exports. Both federal and state legislatures may impose other taxes—on sales and on incomes. The federal government has exclusive power to regulate **interstate commerce**, or commerce that affects trade between states, and foreign commerce. Each state retains authority to regulate **intrastate commerce**, or trade within its own borders.

As a result of the nationwide, or interstate, impact of the Great Depression in the 1930s, the federal government assumed more and more power in the regulation of business. Today this power is exercised through its many agencies. The figure below lists and describes some of the major federal agencies. When a federal agency properly makes regulations to control its commercial area of responsibility, those regulations

SELECTED FEDERAL REGULATORY AGENCIES AND THEIR POWERS

Federal Reserve System's Board of Governors Determines economic policies involving the money supply, credit availability, and interest rates.

Federal Trade Commission (FTC) Assists the antitrust division of the Justice Department. Enforces laws against anti-competitive business activities. It also is involved in protecting consumer rights, preventing monopolistic behavior, and eliminating unfair and deceptive trade practices.

Securities and Exchange Commission (SEC) Enforces laws regulating the disclosure of information related to the buying and selling of stocks and bonds. It also regulates the stock exchanges themselves.

National Labor Relations Board (NLRB) Charged with preserving employees' rights to join labor unions and to participate in collective bargaining. It also is charged with eliminating employer, employee, and union unfair labor practices.

Federal Communications Commission (FCC) Controls all interstate channels of communication and channels of communication between the United States and foreign nations. This includes satellite, telegraph, telephone, radio, and television forms of communication.

Equal Employment Opportunity Commission (EEOC) Charged with the elimination of workplace discrimination based on race, religion, sex, color, national origin, age, or disability.

Occupational Safety and Health Administration (OSHA) Governs health and safety in the workplace.

Consumer Product Safety Commission (CPSC) Researches the safety of various consumer products, including toys. It also collects data on mishaps with products and has banned various products including toys, baby cribs, and fireworks.

Food and Drug Administration (FDA) Enforces a number of pure food and drug acts. Tests and reviews any new drug before it can be marketed to the American public. The FDA also conducts food product inspections and regulates the availability and use of medical devices such as prosthetics and pacemakers.

Environmental Protection Agency (EPA) Enforces antipollution acts (the Clean Air and Clean Water Acts, for example) and regulates the creation, marketing, and use of various hazardous chemicals. Also handles cleanups of toxic dumpsites around the country.

Nuclear Regulatory Commission (NRC) Charged with insuring the safety of nuclear power plants in the United States.

have the force of federal law. The states often have similar agencies with jurisdiction only within their boundaries.

Congress has the power to make detailed laws it considers appropriate for executing the powers given to it in the Constitution. The people, through their votes, ultimately control the entire governmental structure. Each adult retains power over choice of a place to live and to work, a career, friends, travel, holiday activities, and many other personal lifestyle factors.

In *What's Your Verdict?* the senator's comments do accurately reflect the reality of the relationship between citizens and the government today. However, even after the Bill of Rights was added to the Constitution, certain deficiencies existed in the Constitution and in the resulting life of the nation. Additional amendments have been ratified through the years to correct these problems.

CHECKPOINT

How is the power to govern divided between the federal and state governments?

2-2 Assessment

lawxtra.swlearning.com

THINK ABOUT LEGAL CONCEPTS

1. Under the U.S. Constitution, all spending bills must originate in the _ ?_.

2. Which of the following powers was not retained by the states? (a) power to define and apply tort (personal injury) law (b) power to define and apply criminal laws (c) power to define and apply probate laws (d) the states retained all of the above powers

3. Individual states in the United States can coin money. **True or False?**

4. The legislative branch of the federal government is called the _ ?_.

5. The U.S. Senate is made up of _ ?_ members from every state.

6. The U.S. House of Representatives is made up of the same number of members from each state. **True or False?**

7. The U.S. Senate has the power to initiate impeachment proceedings against a U.S. President. **True or False?**

8. The _ ?_ branch of government is headed by the President.

THINK CRITICALLY ABOUT EVIDENCE

Study the situation, answer the questions, and then prepare arguments to support your answers.

9. You are a member of the legislature of a large Midwestern state. Your state is running short of money to carry out some much needed programs. As a possible solution you suggest that the state government issue its own currency to people who work for it. The currency can be exchanged for dollar bills at a rate that is to be fixed by the state the first of every month. Is your idea constitutional?

10. Later in the legislative session mentioned in exercise 9, you become disenchanted with your fellow citizens when you learn that only 28 percent of those eligible to vote actually did so in the last election. Consequently, you pass a law requiring that everyone vote in every election. What arguments can you make in support of such a measure? Against?

11. The Equal Rights Amendment (ERA) was formally proposed in 1972. It provided: "Equality of rights under the law shall not be denied or abridged by the United States or by any state on account of sex." For more than ten years, supporters and opponents conducted campaigns in all states. When the time limit for approval elapsed in 1982, only 35 of the required state legislatures had voted in favor. Women in a sorority at a nearby college now wonder if another campaign should be launched to pass the ERA. How would you advise them?

2-3

The Internet and
Constitutional Rights

▼ GOALS

■ Understand the issues of jurisdiction that
arise with Internet usage

■ Identify the various constitutional
issues involved in the use of electronic
communication

WHO CONTROLS THE INTERNET?

WHAT'S YOUR VERDICT?

Gutterballers Inc. is a New Jersey manufacturing company that sells a wrist stiffener for bowlers. This reinforced, glove-like device fits over a bowler's wrist and allows the bowler to throw a better, more accurate ball. The device was very popular for several years and was sold exclusively on the Internet via nogogutter.com to customers throughout the United States as well as in Japan, Canada, Mexico, Europe, and South America. Recent research into the use of this device has found that even moderate use may cause a pinched-nerve syndrome somewhat like carpel tunnel. You are the founder and president of Gutterballers. You are extremely concerned about the lawsuits that may be filed against your company.

Where may these suits be filed? What jurisdiction's law will be used to decide these cases once filed?

FOUNDATIONS OF CYBERLAW

Literally right in front of your noses an entire new area of law is being formed. **Cyberlaw**—law that is intended to govern the use of computers in e-commerce and, more generally, the Internet—is developing at a previously unheard of pace. Legal issues born in this advancing wave of technology are testing the courts and established law to the maximum. The cases in which these issues are developed involve the computer and subject areas such as jurisdiction, trademarks, copyrights, contracts, privacy, obscenity, defamation, security of data, and crime.

Often the opinions in these cases do not fully decide the issues, but clarify them. The judges in the cases leave it to Congress, the state legislatures, and federal and state administrative agencies to actually create the lasting cyberlaw.

An example can be found in the complex area of jurisdiction, where states have competing laws to determine where a case is to be tried. The courts often are faced with duplicating the work of other courts in other jurisdictions and do not have the ability to resolve the issues involved. Instead they must wait for the federal government to act.

THE BIRTH OF THE INTERNET

The U.S. Department of Defense laid the groundwork for the Internet in the late 1960s during the so-called Cold War. It did so by having its Advanced Research Projects Agency (ARPA) tie together computers on various academic campuses and research centers around the country in a network called ARPANET. The idea was to increase the pace of development of defense projects by

One of the most difficult issues in cyberlaw is determining jurisdiction, or where a case will be tried. Based on what you know about the Internet, why do you think this is so difficult?

© GETTY IMAGES/PHOTODISC

empowering the sharing of defense-related information between researchers through the use of electronic mail, file transfers, and online chats. The success of the idea was immediate and, as a result, this defense network was expanded and even connected to overseas networks.

Soon academics outside of the defense establishment began to take notice of the usefulness of the medium. As a consequence, in the late 1980s the National Science Foundation (NSF) built its own network. This more advanced NSF network—or Internet—took over the functions of the defense network and continued to grow and gain in popularity among the academics and students who had the expertise to use it.

Eventually, commercial interests began to inquire about the Internet. Their requests to use it for business purposes, however, were turned down. This was primarily because the NSF Internet, like the defense network before it, was never intended to serve a commercial purpose. In fact, until 1991, all the users of the NSF network had to agree to a contract that explicitly disallowed the use of the Internet for business purposes.

THE WORLD WIDE WEB

In 1990, 20 years of scientific and academic use of *hypertext*—a nonlinear format for the publishing of information used to send e-mails, transfer mountains of data, and converse in chat rooms—helped to open the Internet up to other users. These new users were seeking specialized information in subject areas in which they did not have a great deal of background.

The access these new users desired was developed chiefly through the work of one person, Tim Berners-Lee. Working at the European Laboratory for Particle Physics, Berners-Lee developed the World Wide Web (WWW) Program mainly in his spare time. This program's effect was to simplify the Internet to allow almost universal access to anyone with the use of a computer. Berners-Lee, who has not earned a profit from his development, is currently director of the World Wide Web Consortium, the coordinating body for Web development. His vision is that of open access to as wide a body of information as possible for every user. This access is accomplished through the use of a scanning program called a **browser.** These browsers utilize the attributes of hypertext to allow immediate access to any and all subjects and the background information necessary to comprehend them.

To quote Berners-Lee, "there is power in arranging information in an unconstrained, web-like way." To that end, he created hypertext markup language (HTML) and hypertext transfer protocol (HTTP). HTML dictates the format of standard Web documents, while HTTP provides the standard for exchanging files in the HTML format. Note that in this web-like arrangement of information, there are a multitude of connecting points and, therefore, a multitude of paths and storehouses for information. Shut down one path or storehouse and many more spring up in its place. The very decentralization of the Internet makes it nearly impossible to exercise legal control over it and what goes on within it.

EVOLVING LEGAL ISSUES IN CYBERSPACE

Cyberlaw is developing in many separate areas at once. Contracts, privacy, obscenity, defamation, security of data, trademarks, copyrights, and crime all have been the focus of many decisions intended to resolve the legal issues raised by

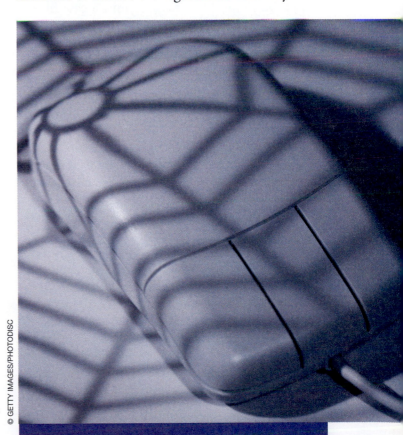

© GETTY IMAGES/PHOTODISC

Information on the Internet is arranged in a web-like fashion. How does this affect government's ability to exercise legal control over it?

computer usage and the Internet. These issues will be explored in the remainder of this lesson and in the Cyberlaw features in the chapters that follow.

THE ONGOING ISSUE OF JURISDICTION Final answers to the legal questions in all of the areas mentioned above can only be arrived at after the court responsible for giving them is determined. Traditionally, the state courts have been given jurisdiction over cases between their citizens. Cases with relatively large amounts of money at stake and between citizens of different states, along with cases that involve questions of federal law, have been left to the federal courts to decide. (See Lessons 3-2 and 3-3 in the text for more information on this topic.)

Regardless of whether or not a case is filed in state or federal court, however, the vital issue soon becomes whether or not the case is to be decided within the state where it was filed or in the state where the e-business is physically located. For example, would a corporation physically located in New Jersey and incorporated there have to fund a defense against a case filed against it in California?

The answer to this question of jurisdiction is based on two vital legal considerations. First of all, the laws of the state in which the case is filed must allow suits against non-resident defendants. Most states do have statutes—referred to as "long-arm statutes" for the long arm of the law—that, for the good of their citizens, permit such cases to be heard. However, the standards the state's long-arm statute sets for the involvement of the non-resident defendant in the state must be met or the suit will be dismissed. These standards vary from state to state.

Some standards require a concrete presence in the state in the form of an office, a traveling salesperson, a mailing address, etc. Others simply require a reasonable presumption that the defendant is doing business in the state by its level of involvement there.

The second legal consideration relating to jurisdiction is whether or not allowing the state or federal court (the latter using the state rules) to decide the case would be a violation of the due process requirements of the U.S. Constitution. As discussed earlier in this chapter, these requirements are embedded in the Fifth and Fourteenth Amendments to the Constitution. The Fifth Amendment, which applies to the actions of the federal government, prohibits the taking of life, liberty, or property without the due process of law. The Fourteenth Amendment extends this same prohibition to the states.

According to the latest decisions regarding cyberlaw issues, the establishment of jurisdiction by a state over a nonresident defendant is only proper if the defendant has either a "substantial, continuous, and systemic presence" in the state or has "minimum contacts" with the state. Most e-businesses lack the former and, therefore, are judged by the minimum contacts rule.

Soliciting business from a web site available in the state generally has been held to be a minimum contact. Accordingly, it is reasonable to presume that a lawsuit (over contracts, product liability, warranty, etc.) might be generated as a result of such activity. Simply providing an informative web site has been held not to be a minimum contact, however. In other words a car company merely providing pictures and characteristics of its cars on its web site but not providing a means by which one can be purchased through the web site itself would be free of the threat of suit based strictly on it as a "minimum contact." There must be something more to indicate that the defendant intended to serve the market in the state.

In *What's Your Verdict?* Gutterballers Inc. most likely would have to defend against the product liability suits wherever they were filed in the United States. Should they not defend and suffer a default judgment or defend and lose,

LEGAL RESEARCH

Imagine that you are a member of the governing body of the Internet. Help to set up a system of rules and a procedure for enforcement to prevent the appearance of web sites that you consider unethical. These may include sites that contain instructions on how to make bombs or how to assist or commit crimes. Research and appraise the rules that are currently in place for this purpose.

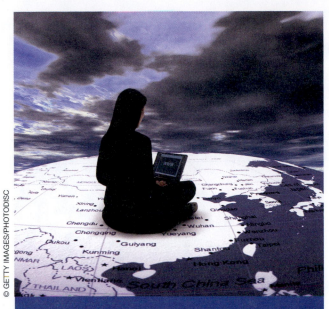

© GETTY IMAGES/PHOTODISC

What action can an e-business take to remove the uncertainty involved in both international and domestic jurisdiction issues?

CHECKPOINT
What characteristic of the Internet makes exercising legal control over it nearly impossible?

INTERNET-RELATED CONSTITUTIONAL ISSUES

WHAT'S YOUR VERDICT?

A respected Internet news service carried on its web site a picture of the U.S. Secretary of State provided by the Secretary's publicity staff. The picture depicted the Secretary of State shaking hands in front of a foreign embassy next to a statue of a nude woman. The web site does not have the controls required to ensure that minors do not have access to it. In fact, it promotes itself as a source of information for school-age children.

Would the news service be in violation of federal statutes against online pornography accessible by minors? Would the Secretary of State or the Secretary's office be in violation of the statute?

the judgment may be entered and enforced against them in a New Jersey Court without substantial review by the New Jersey Court.

INTERNATIONAL JURISDICTION International cases are governed by international law, which is currently under serious revision due primarily to e-commerce. An established, pre-e-commerce principle is that a country may exercise jurisdiction only over activities with a substantial effect on or in that country. However, new standards under consideration would impose a country-of-origination selection principle on business-to-business transactions and a country-of-residence-of-the-consumer principle on consumer transactions. The reviewability of decisions made overseas and then entered in the domestic courts of the United States for enforcement currently is covered mainly by treaties between individual countries.

Most of the uncertainty involved in the jurisdiction issue can be removed if the e-business puts a notice on its web site and clarifying section in its contracts. This notice or clause should state, in effect, that all legal issues shall be resolved in a particular jurisdiction (hopefully its home state) with favorable laws. If the laws of a particular jurisdiction do not allow such limits on suits, then the e-business should not do business in that jurisdiction.

FREEDOM OF SPEECH

The legal cornerstone of any defense against charges of limitations on freedom of speech are the rights so eloquently protected by the First Amendment to the U.S. Constitution. This protection against governmental action is extended to the states by the Fourteenth Amendment.

Note that these basic means of expression—speech, press, religion, assembly, and petition—are jealously protected not only in their fundamental forms but also in the extension of those forms. Such extensions may include flag burnings, anti-government publications, or what the vast majority would label obscene. The theme of this extended protection is that censoring these questionable forms of expression would ultimately have a chilling effect on them.

However, even these fundamental rights are not absolute. Certainly the freedom of speech does not condone your shouting "fire" in a crowded theater or a newspaper maliciously publishing lies about a celebrity. In the case of obscenity, for example, the basic law was formulated by the U.S. Supreme Court in the mid-1950s.

ROTH V. UNITED STATES The Court determined that obscenity did not have the protection of the First Amendment. To reach this conclusion the court noted that the protections given speech and the press were to ensure the open exchange of ideas that would allow necessary political and social change. Therefore, to quote the Court in *Roth v. United States,*

> All ideas having even the slightest redeeming social importance—unorthodox ideas, controversial ideas, even ideas hateful to the prevailing climate of opinion—have the full protection of the guaranties, unless excludable because they encroach upon [interfere with] the limited area of more important interests. But implicit in the history of the First Amendment is the rejection of obscenity as utterly without redeeming social importance.

Obviously, it is vital to be able to determine what is or is not obscene in order to apply the court's decision. The standards used to determine that issue have varied through the years. The Roth decision, quoted above, indicated that the key question was whether or not the questionable material had any redeeming social importance. If it did not, then it could be regulated or banned totally by the federal or state government.

MILLER V. CALIFORNIA In the 1960s the standard became whether or not the questionable material was "utterly without redeeming social value." This standard was much more difficult to prove and resulted in much greater latitude for those publishing material arguably obscene. Finally, in a 1973 case, *Miller v. California,* the Supreme Court toughened the standards by deciding that the questionable materials were to be judged by the standards of the community affected.

Unfortunately, the Miller standards proved inadequate when applied to the Internet environment. Slowly, however, case law has begun to fill in the necessary gaps. For example, the issue of

Freedom of speech is an important right protected by the First Amendment. Besides communicating orally, what other means of expression are protected under the umbrella of freedom of speech?

"community standards" raises the question, "Which community?" The answer to the question often determines whether or not someone will spend years in jail. Currently, the case law holds the sender to the standards of the recipient's community. This tends to put the responsibility on the party profiting from such an exchange to know those standards and refuse to send the material to areas in which the community standards would make such an act illegal.

Local community standards also are applicable in determining whether or not the material has any literary, artistic, political, or socially redeeming value when taken as a whole. Certainly, what is of such value will vary greatly from an urban to a suburban setting. Because of the unpredictability of the interpretation of the laws it has been suggested that the "community" be considered to be the Internet community rather than any particular geographical region. Thus far, the courts have declined to adopt this perspective.

Supreme Court decisions of the last 50 years have held that once material is determined to be obscene, it can be regulated by the local, state, and federal governments. The types of regulation and their extent, however, have been open to challenge. See "Landmark Decisions in Cyberlaw," above.

COMMUNICATIONS DECENCY ACT In 1996, Congress passed the Communications Decency Act (CDA). One purpose for CDA is to control the knowing transmittal of obscene material through the Internet. The statute provides heavy fines and imprisonment for up to five years for first-time violators with even stronger penalties for subsequent offenses. Upon passage, the CDA came under immediate legal attack from the American Civil Liberties Union, the Electronic Frontier Foundation, America Online, Apple Computer, Microsoft, and other plaintiffs. The result, due mainly to the legally ambiguous term "indecent" used in the statute, was the declaration that the statute was overbroad and chilling of protected speech. Consequently, the statutory portions relying on that term were declared unconstitutional.

CHILD ONLINE PROTECTION ACT The Child Online Protection Act of 1998 required commercial sites to use up-to-date methodology to restrict access to their sites containing material harmful to children. This act was amended due to the alleged inability of site operators to afford the necessary equipment and the overbroad definition of "harmful material" so that it would have arguably included legitimate art works and scientific information about sex. See the figure on the next page for a summary of the statutes

relating to free speech issues and citations to these statutes.

In *What's Your Verdict?* the Child Online Protection Act of 1998 might have made criminal both the actions of the news site in posting it and the actions of the Secretary of State's staff in circulating the picture.

THE RIGHT OF PRIVACY

The right of privacy was legitimized as a right by the U.S. Supreme Court in the late 1960s. Ever since then, it has been based on a person's reasonable expectations as to whether his or her actions, communications, beliefs, and other personal attributes deserve protection from those who would improperly use them. For example, a recent case involved an employee's privacy

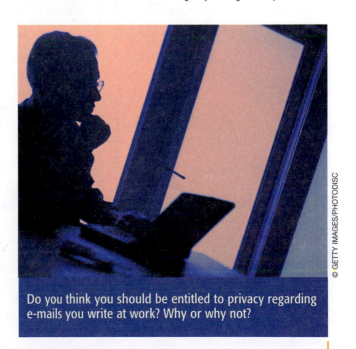

Do you think you should be entitled to privacy regarding e-mails you write at work? Why or why not?

© GETTY IMAGES/PHOTODISC

regarding personal e-mail sent at work. The court held that the employee had no true expectation of privacy on a company's e-mail system. Therefore, the employee's personal e-mails were not protected by the right of privacy.

Other issues of privacy remain unresolved. For example, *spamming*—the practice of sending unrequested bulk e-mailings to hundreds of thousands of potential customers via the Internet—is supported by the ability to generate address lists. This generation typically is performed by popular web sites compiling the "cookies" that are left behind every time such a site is visited by a web user. A cookie is a packet of information containing the Internet address and other personal information about a web site visitor, such as buying patterns. This information is then sold without the user's knowledge or permission.

Existing federal law rightfully protects against such information being gathered on the videos and cable programs you rent or purchase. But, no such law exists in the United States that covers gathering information about users while they are online. The European Union (EU) has passed a directive that requires its member nations to pass legislation protecting consumers—not companies—against such practices.

The European Union Directive forbids member nations from permitting the transfer of per-

sonal data to a nation, like the United States, that does not provide an adequate level of personal privacy protection. Should U.S. firms doing business in the European Union, especially in the areas of credit and insurance, transfer data back to the United States they could be in violation of the directive and subject to penalties

STATUTES OF IMPORTANCE TO CYBERLAW

Lanham Act of 1976 (Title 15 U.S.C. Section 1051 et. seq.)
Provides for the registration and protection of trademarks and copyrights

Trademark Dilution Act of 1996 (Title 15 U.S.C. Section 1125)
Attempts to protect the holders of famous trademarks from the effects of domain-page registrations that tend to confuse and dilute the trademark's goodwill

Computer Fraud and Abuse Act (Title 18 U.S.C. Section 1030)
An often-amended act that pioneered the treatment of computer-related crimes as unique offenses in the United States Code

Telecommunications Act of 1996, also known as **The Communications Decency Act of 1996 (CDA)** (Title 47 U.S.C. Section 223, Title V)
Makes it criminal to knowingly transport obscene material through interactive computers or interstate or foreign commerce for sale or distribution. In addition Section 230 of the CDA gives protection from defamation suits to Internet service providers.

Child Online Protection Act of 1998 (Title 47 U.S.C. Section 231)
Makes it a crime for site operators to fail to use proper technology and methodology to prevent minors from accessing "harmful" material.

and civil suits. To address this problem, the Department of Commerce negotiated with the European Union to produce a list of precautions that a U.S. firm should take in order to comply with the EU directive.

CHECKPOINT
What are the constitutional issues related to use of the Internet?

2-3 Assessment

lawxtra.swlearning.com

THINK ABOUT LEGAL CONCEPTS

1. Typically, when citizens of the same state sue one another, their case will be handled by (a) the state courts (b) the federal courts.

2. What is obscene is now determined by one uniform national standard. **True or False?**

3. An employee's personal e-mail, composed and sent at work, is protected by the right of privacy. **True or False?**

4. If you negotiate and sell your computer over the Internet to a person in another state, would the buyer have jurisdiction over you in a suit filed in her or his home state? **Yes or No?**

5. Statutes that allow a citizen of one state to file suit against a non-resident of the state are called (a) Jurisdictional Reach Acts (b) long-arm statutes (c) Interstate Commerce Acts.

THINK CRITICALLY ABOUT EVIDENCE

Study the situation, answer the questions, and then prepare arguments to support your answers.

6. Sy Bore has been receiving spam mail advertisements from adult-oriented web sites that contain pictures. Some of the pictures are very similar to ones that have been termed obscene in his state, and the senders were punished at criminal law there. However, the senders of the pictures he is receiving in the spam mail are located in states other than Bore's. Bore persuades the local prosecutor to bring charges against the senders based on the obscene nature of the pictures. At trial, the senders defend themselves by showing the material is not obscene in their home states. Can they still be convicted?

7. Consider the effects of making the European Union's privacy standards federal law here in the United States. What groups would support a movement to do so? What groups would oppose the move? What would be the effects on business?

PREVENT LEGAL DIFFICULTIES

As a citizen . . .

1. Carefully read and reread the U.S. Constitution as it has been amended. (See Appendix A on page 594.) This will enable you to become a properly informed citizen of the United States.

2. Pay special attention to the Bill of Rights and the Fourteenth Amendment to better appreciate their value in assuring your liberty and to be alert to possible threats that could erode vital freedoms for you and others.

3. When eligible, participate in government as a well-informed voter. If you are able and willing, participate in the work of the political party of your choice. If you are one of the dedicated few, become a candidate for public office.

4. When you use the Internet be aware of your rights and potential liabilities for what you say and the transactions you conduct.

Chapter 2 Assessment

CONCEPTS IN BRIEF

2-1 Foundations of the U.S. Constitution

1. The documents that formed the U.S. government include the Declaration of Independence, the Articles of Confederation, and the U.S. Constitution, including the Bill of Rights.

2. The First Amendment protects free speech, free press, free exercise of any private religion, freedom to assemble peaceably, and the right to petition the government for redress if one is wronged.

3. Civil rights are personal, natural rights of individuals guaranteed by the Constitution.

4. Although the Constitution does not spell out what is meant by "due process," U.S. Supreme Court decisions have come to define it as a defendant being provided, at a minimum, adequate notice and a proper hearing. Due process of law assured by the First, Fourth, Fifth, Sixth, Seventh, and Eighth Amendments.

5. Voting rights were extended to freed slaves by the Fifteenth Amendment and to women through the Nineteenth Amendment. The voting age for all citizens was lowered to eighteen by the Twenty-Sixth Amendment.

2-2 Division and Balance of Governmental Powers

6. A vigorous and useful balance of power exists among the three basic branches of government: legislative, executive, and judicial.

7. The Tenth Amendment allows states the freedom to govern their citizens. However, the Constitution limits states' powers through the Fourteenth Amendment.

2-3 The Internet and Constitutional Rights

8. Cyberlaw is developing at a previously unheard of pace and is nowhere near its final form.

9. Freedom of speech and the right of privacy are the two main constitutional issues related to Internet use.

YOUR LEGAL VOCABULARY

Match each statement with the term that it best defines. Some terms may not be used.

1. Personal, natural rights guaranteed by the Constitution
2. Internet scanning program
3. Governmental system wherein each citizen may vote directly to decide issues
4. Division and allocation of the powers of government between its various branches
5. Governmental systems wherein citizens elect representatives to decide issues
6. Freedom from external control
7. Loose form of charter for common government for the 13 colonies prior to the adoption of the Constitution
8. Document that provides a framework for the federal government, consisting of 7 articles and 27 amendments
9. Concept of fundamental fairness in compliance with reasonable and just laws
10. The first ten amendments to the U.S. Constitution
11. Law that is intended to govern the use of computers in e-commerce
12. Change or alteration

a. amendment
b. Articles of Confederation
c. Bill of Rights
d. browser
e. civil rights
f. cyberlaw
g. Declaration of Independence
h. democracy
i. due process of law
j. impeachment cases
k. interstate commerce
l. intrastate commerce
m. political party
n. republic
o. sovereignty
p. system of checks and balances
q. U.S. Constitution

REVIEW LEGAL CONCEPTS

13. The Constitutional Convention of 1787 was meant to make changes in the Articles of Confederation instead of create a new document. Why do you think the Articles were discarded?

14. Can you foresee a time when the U.S. might become a true democracy? If so, how could this occur?

15. While the system of checks and balances works to prevent the accumulation of too much power by any one branch of the government, it also causes problems in the functioning of government. What do you think some of these problems might be?

16. Could you get your friends and neighbors to sign the Declaration of Independence today? During the Vietnam era, young people around the country tried to do just that. Most citizens who read the document but were not told that it was the Declaration, refused to sign and, in some cases, reacted violently to its content. Why is that?

17. Susan, a manager in a local company, became romantically involved with one of her subordinates at work. They sent love messages back and forth by using the company's Internet connection. The company regularly monitored its employee's on-the-job e-mails and had a policy against such personal involvements. As a consequence, Susan was fired. She brought suit for invasion of privacy. Will she win?

WRITE ABOUT LEGAL CONCEPTS

18. Write an essay on how the framers of the Constitution and the Bill of Rights could justify the maintenance of slavery and the denial of voting rights to women.

19. Write a paragraph stating your opinion about which is the most important right preserved by the Bill of Rights.

20. The Bill of Rights is presented in this book in the language the founding fathers used. Rewrite the Bill of Rights in your own words.

21. **HOT DEBATE** While the passages denouncing the people of England and the slave trade were cut from Jefferson's draft of the Declaration, numerous direct accusations against the King of England were left in the document. Why was the King singled out for criticism and not the people? Was this a wise move on the part of the Continental Congress?

MAKE ACADEMIC CONNECTIONS

22. **HISTORY** Rhode Island was the last of the 13 colonies to ratify the Constitution. Using the Internet and the library, determine what caused them to pause for so long. Write a one-page paper summarizing your findings.

23. **SOCIAL SURVEY** Apply the standards of the Child Online Protection Act to works of art, advertisements, and other such displays easily visible to the young in your community. What conclusions can you draw about the Act and its enforcement as a consequence?

THINK CRITICALLY ABOUT EVIDENCE

Study the situation, answer the questions, and then prepare arguments to support your answers.

24. Jennifer let her cousin use her computer during a recent visit. Without Jennifer's permission the cousin visited several web sites that sold pornography. Now Jennifer is receiving spam from similar sites all around the world. No matter how often she reports the objectionable nature of the material, it keeps appearing. Evidently, the site her cousin visited sold her web address to others in the same line of business. It makes her very upset, but she cannot change her web address for some time. What practical and legal means can Jennifer use to solve this problem?

25. In 1919 the Eighteenth Amendment outlawed "the manufacture, sale, or transportation of intoxicating liquors...." This law led to widespread illegal traffic in liquor by criminals. The controversial law also led to unspoken approval of the illegal trade by many citizens who continued to buy and consume liquor. The Eighteenth Amendment was repealed by the Twenty-First Amendment, but individual states were permitted to continue to enforce Prohibition within their borders. By 1966, all individual states had abandoned

Prohibition. According to experts, abuse of alcoholic beverages is the most serious drug problem in overall harmful effect on society. Should Prohibition be reinstated? If not, what, if anything, should be done?

ANALYZE REAL CASES

26. A Champaign County, Illinois, board of education granted permission to religious teachers to give religious instruction in public school buildings in grades four to nine. Subject to approval of and supervision by the superintendent of schools, the teachers were employed by a private religious group and included representatives of the Catholic, Jewish, and Protestant faiths. Only pupils whose parents requested religious instruction were required to attend the religious classes. McCollum, a resident with a pupil who was enrolled in one of the public schools, sued for a writ, or court order, to end the religious instruction as a violation of the First Amendment to the Constitution. The writ was denied, and the Illinois Supreme Court upheld the denial. The parent appealed to the U.S. Supreme Court. Should the writ have been granted to end the practice as a violation of the First Amendment? (*McCollum v. Board of Education*, 333 U.S. 203)

27. In 1964, a motel owner in Atlanta restricted its clientele to white persons, three-fourths of whom were interstate travelers. U.S. government attorneys charged that this policy violated the Civil Rights Act of 1964, which forbids such discrimination against blacks. The trial court ordered the motel to stop refusing blacks as guests. The motel owner appealed to the U.S. Supreme Court, claiming the Civil Rights Act was unconstitutional. Was it? Why or why not? Does the federal government have the power to regulate matters that might in any way affect interstate commerce? (*Heart of Atlanta Motel, Inc. v. United States*, 379 U.S. 241)

28. Cleveland police had received information that a person wanted for questioning about a recent bombing was hiding in a particular two-family dwelling. There was said to be a large quantity of illegal lottery materials hidden in the home. Upon arrival, three officers knocked on the door and demanded entrance. Mapp, who lived on the top floor with her daughter, telephoned her attorney and then refused to admit the officers without a search warrant. Three hours later, reinforced by additional officers, the police returned. When Mapp did not answer immediately, they tried to kick in the door, then broke its glass pane, reached in, unlocked it, and entered. Meanwhile Mapp's attorney had arrived, but the officers would not let him see his client or enter the house. Mapp demanded to see a search warrant. When an officer held up a paper claiming it to be a warrant, Mapp grabbed the paper and placed it in her bosom. A struggle ensued during which the officer recovered the paper. Mapp was handcuffed for resisting the officer. The entire house was searched, but all that was found were certain allegedly "lewd and lascivious books and pictures." Mapp was convicted of knowingly having them in her possession. At the trial, no search warrant was produced nor was the failure to produce one explained. Mapp appealed to the U.S. Supreme Court for a reversal of her conviction because it was based on a search that was illegal under the U.S. Constitution. Was the evidence for conviction obtained in violation of the U.S. Constitution? If so, was it admissible in the trial against the defendant Mapp? (*Mapp v. Ohio*, 367 U.S. 643)

29. Weber was injured while staying in a hotel in Italy. When he returned to the United States, he filed suit against the hotel in a New Jersey court. Weber based his claim that the New Jersey court had jurisdiction on the fact that the hotel's web site advertising for rooms for rent was available in that state. Was Weber correct in maintaining that the New Jersey court had jurisdiction? (*Weber v. Jolly*, 977 F. Supp. 327)

30. When a company began sending literally millions of unsolicited e-mails per day to its subscribers, America Online (AOL) blocked the transmissions. The sender then sued claiming an abridgement of its First Amendment rights by the action and requested an injunction preventing AOL's actions against its spamming. How should the court decide? (*Cyber Promotions, Inc., v. America Online, Inc.*, 948 F. Supp. 436)

Court Systems

HOT DEBATE

© GETTY IMAGES/PHOTODISC

Anthony Destin works as a junior designer at a large fashion house called Berentinos. After two years on the job, Anthony learns that his co-worker Sarah Blake earns 35 percent more than he does. Anthony and Sarah were hired at the same time and have exactly the same job. Anthony has five more years experience in the field than Sarah does. Anthony discussed his concern with Tom Sortee, one of his colleagues. Tom commented that such discrimination against males has long been the rule at Berentinos. Anthony loves his work but can't help feeling he is being treated unfairly.

Where Do You Stand?

1. What alternative courses of action, other than filing suit in court, might Anthony utilize to bring about a resolution of the issue?

2. Does Anthony have a duty to anyone, legally or morally, to bring a lawsuit instead?

GIDEON v. WAINWRIGHT
372 U. S. 335

BACKGROUND Gideon was charged in a Florida court with breaking and entering with the intent to commit a misdemeanor, which is a serious crime but not punishable by death.

Gideon appeared in court without legal counsel and requested the court to appoint a lawyer to defend him. The following exchange then occurred:

> The Court: Mr. Gideon, I am sorry, but I cannot appoint Counsel to represent you in this case. Under the laws of the State of Florida, the only time the Court can appoint Counsel to represent a Defendant is when that person is charged with a capital offense. I am sorry, but I will have to deny your request to appoint Counsel to defend you in this case.
> Defendant: The United States Supreme Court says I am entitled to be represented by Counsel.

© CORBIS/BETTMANN

FACTS After his request was disallowed, Gideon conducted his own defense as well as he could. He made an opening statement, cross-examined witnesses, presented his own defense witnesses, and made a short argument maintaining his innocence.

The jury then returned a guilty verdict. Gideon was sentenced to five years in state prison from which he filed the habeas corpus petition on which this case is based.

APPEAL The state supreme court of Florida considered the habeas corpus petition and denied all relief to Gideon. After Gideon wrote a letter to the U.S. Supreme Court from his jail cell, the U.S. Supreme Court decided to review the case.

ISSUE Should a defendant in a state court have the right to counsel as mandated by the federal Constitution?

DECISION The United States Supreme Court, in an opinion written by Justice Black, held that the Sixth Amendment required that in all criminal prosecutions the accused shall enjoy right to assistance of counsel. The decision of the Florida Supreme Court was reversed and the cause remanded so that counsel can be enjoyed by Gideon and other like defendants.

PRACTICE JUDGING

1. How should the Florida Supreme Court respond and why?

2. How are the appointed counsels to be paid? Who is to determine if they do an adequate job?

3. What should be the sanction(s) imposed upon governments that fail to provide such legal services for their accused?

3-1

Forms of Dispute Resolution

▼ GOALS

- Explain how disputes can be settled without going to court
- Name the different levels of courts and describe their powers

DISPUTE RESOLUTION

WHAT'S YOUR VERDICT?

The Court Company repaired tennis courts throughout Missouri and Arkansas. Part of its standard contract with tennis court owners was a clause requiring that disputes concerning the repairs be settled by arbitration rather than by a trial in court.

Is this clause enforceable?

HOW CAN DISPUTES BE RESOLVED WITHOUT GOING TO COURT?

Many people decide too quickly to **litigate**—or take their disputes to court. When one person injures another or fails to keep a binding agreement, often the best solution is for the parties to negotiate a settlement themselves. Together, they often can reach a mutually acceptable solution.

As an alternative to face-to-face negotiations, the parties may invite an independent third party to act as a mediator. The **mediator** tries to develop a solution acceptable to both sides of the dispute. The actions of a mediator are advisory (not legally binding on the parties). In other cases, the parties may retain an arbitrator. An **arbitrator** usually holds an informal hearing to determine what happened. The arbitrator's decision, unlike that of a mediator, is binding on both parties. The decision can be enforced by court order if necessary. Sometimes a provision for arbitration is included in the original agreement between the parties. In *What's Your Verdict?*, either party to the contract can require the dispute to be resolved by arbitration.

HOW DO COURTS SETTLE DISPUTES?

A **court** can be defined as a governmental forum that administers justice under the law. Courts decide disputes between private individuals and in criminal cases. A court may award damages or order other appropriate relief in the former cases and impose punishment (fine and/or imprisonment) in the criminal cases.

Courts follow impartial and thorough procedures to make decisions. Witnesses are in some cases compelled to give testimony. The accused party is allowed equal opportunity to argue her or his side of the case. Typically, two levels of courts are involved in deciding a dispute. These two levels are trial courts and appellate courts.

TRIAL COURTS The court in which a dispute is first heard is called a **trial court**. The trial court hears the witnesses testify and reviews the other pertinent evidence firsthand so as to determine the facts of a case. The trial court will then apply what it selects as the appropriate law to the facts to reach a **verdict**, or decision, in the case. Because of this initial contact with the dispute, a trial court has **original jurisdiction** over, or original power to decide, the case.

A trial court consists not only of a judge but also of lawyers, who are officers of the court.

© GETTY IMAGES/PHOTODISC

Disputing parties may retain a mediator or an arbitrator to develop a solution. What is the difference between a solution offered by a mediator and a solution offered by an arbitrator?

Other court personnel necessary for its operation include clerks, sheriffs or marshals, bailiffs, and jury members.

Clerks enter cases on the court calendar, keep records of proceedings, and often compute court costs. Sheriffs or their deputies serve as bailiffs. Bailiffs summon witnesses, keep order in court, and take steps to carry out judgments in the state court systems. Marshals have these duties in the federal court system. Juries are citizens sworn by a court to decide issues of fact in court cases.

APPELLATE COURTS An **appellate court** reviews decisions of lower courts when a party claims an error was made during the lower court's proceeding. Because appellate court judges were not present to evaluate firsthand the truthfulness of the witnesses, their testimony, and other evidence, they do not make determinations of fact. Instead appellate jurisdiction is concerned solely with errors of law.

Appellate courts examine the **transcript**, which is a verbatim record of what went on at trial. They also read **appellate briefs**, or written arguments on the issues of law, submitted by the opposing attorneys. Appellate courts also often

LEGAL RESEARCH

Contact the clerks of your local courts—city, county, and state—to find out the types of cases over which the court has original jurisdiction (the power to give a ruling).

listen to attorneys' oral arguments in support of these briefs. During such oral argument the appellate judges question attorneys about the case. Finally, appellate courts decide whether the decision of the lower court should be affirmed (upheld), reversed (overturned), amended (changed), or remanded (sent back to the trial court for corrective action or possibly a new trial).

CHECKPOINT

What are the two levels of courts, and what is the function of each?

Which type of court, trial or appellate, is pictured here? Justify your answer.

© GETTY IMAGES/PHOTODISC

THINK ABOUT LEGAL CONCEPTS

1. Which of the following means of dispute resolution may be enforced by a court order? (a) The parties invite a mediator to develop a solution. (b) The parties retain an arbitrator to prescribe a solution. (c) The parties call the police in to resolve the dispute.

2. There is no difference between mediation and arbitration. **True or False?**

3. A trial court has _?_ jurisdiction over a case.

4. Courts (a) award damages in criminal cases (b) hear witnesses at the appellate level (c) decide questions of fact at the trial level (d) enforce mediators' decisions (e) all of the above.

5. Appellate courts review decisions of lower courts when a party claims an error was made during the lower court's proceeding. **True or False?**

6. Appellate court review of trial court decisions is normally confined to errors of _?_.

7. Which of the following are involved in appellate court proceedings? (a) bailiffs (b) juries (c) judges (d) witnesses

8. To _?_ means to resolve a dispute in court.

9. When an appellate court sends a case back down to a trial court for a new trial or other corrective action it is said to have _?_ the case. (a) affirmed (b) reversed (c) remanded (d) none of the above.

10. A decision of the lower court that has been overturned by the lower court is said to be (a) affirmed (b) reversed (c) amended (d) remanded

11. A decision of the lower court that has been upheld by the lower court is said to be affirmed. **True or False?**

12. A decision of the lower court that has been changed by the lower court is said to be (a) affirmed (b) reversed (c) amended (d) remanded

THINK CRITICALLY ABOUT EVIDENCE

Study the situation, answer the questions, and then prepare arguments to support your answers.

13. Your boss at Swift Electronics is getting ready to enter into a series of contracts with a new group of suppliers. She is concerned with avoiding the delays and high costs of any litigation that might result from the new agreements. She asks you for your recommendations. You suggest putting a binding arbitration clause in the contracts. Why?

14. Your boss at Swift Electronics decides against the recommendations you made (see exercise 13). Six months later, a supplier sends the wrong projection device in response to your order. The supplier then refuses to correct the mistake. Your boss hires an attorney at $250 per hour and takes you to lunch to admit she made a mistake in not following your ideas. Ultimately, the case is set for trial. What type of jurisdiction will this court have? What will be done during the trial?

15. In exercise 14, who may be present during the trial? If there is an appeal, which of these parties will not have to appear again?

16. Don Long is convicted of second-degree murder for killing a woman he had been seeing over the last few months. The court sentenced him to 30 years in jail. One year after his trial, Don admits that he withheld evidence that would have cleared him. He states he did so to protect his twin brother, who actually committed the crime, but who was dying of cancer at the time. He further states that he did not want his brother to spend the last years of his life behind bars. His brother has since died. The evidence is conclusive as to Don's innocence. Should the court set aside his conviction due to the new evidence? What policies would support the court in not doing so?

The Federal Court System

▼ **GOALS**

- Identify the source of power of the federal courts
- Name the various levels of federal courts and describe their jurisdictions

ORIGIN OF THE FEDERAL COURT SYSTEM

WHAT'S YOUR VERDICT?

Tom and Martina were discussing how the various federal courts were empowered to decide cases. Tom said that federal courts received their power from the U.S. Constitution. Martina maintained that Congress had created and empowered them.

Who is correct?

Through Article III of the Constitution, the people conferred the power to judge certain criminal and civil matters on a system of federal courts:

Section 1. The judicial Power of the United States shall be vested in one Supreme Court, and in such inferior Courts as the Congress may from time to time ordain and establish.

The Articles of Confederation did not allow for a Supreme Court, and some citizens did not think a Supreme Court would be needed under the Constitution. As a result, after George Washington's inauguration as the nation's first president, it took nearly six months for Congress to utilize the power it was granted under Article III and pass the Federal Judiciary Act. This act "ordained and established" the U.S. Supreme Court (USSC) and thirteen district courts. In 1891, approximately a century after passing the initial Federal Judiciary Act, Congress passed a Judiciary Act that established the federal Courts of Appeal. Certain specialized courts, such as those concerned primarily with tax or bankruptcy matters, also were created as the need for them arose.

In *What's Your Verdict?* both Tom and Martina are correct. Ultimately, the federal courts receive their power to adjudicate cases from the Constitution. However, the Constitution left to Congress the power to ordain and establish these courts if and when it deemed them necessary.

CHECKPOINT

What is the source of power of the federal courts?

JURISDICTION OF THE FEDERAL COURTS

WHAT'S YOUR VERDICT?

Susan Bean, a citizen of Illinois, sued Wallis Turk, a citizen of the state of Colorado, for the breach of a construction contract on Bean's new Chicago residence. More than $600,000 was at stake. Bean filed the suit in Illinois state court. Turk fought to remove the case to the federal courts.

Will the case be heard in federal or state court?

Currently there are three levels of federal courts with general jurisdiction. These are federal district courts, federal courts of appeals, and the U.S. Supreme Court. A court with **general jurisdiction** can hear almost any kind of case. A court with **special jurisdiction** hears only one specific type of case. The chart on page 53 illustrates the three levels of the federal court system.

FEDERAL DISTRICT COURTS

The federal (or U.S.) district court is the lowest level of federal court with general jurisdiction. This is the trial court (the first court to hear the dispute) of the federal system. It has the power to determine the facts and to make initial determinations of the law to use in deciding the case.

In general, district courts have original jurisdiction over (a) federal questions, or cases that arise under the Constitution, U.S. law, and U.S. treaties; and (b) lawsuits between citizens of different states, between a U.S. citizen and a foreign nation, or between a U.S. citizen and a citizen of a foreign nation. These parties are said to have *diversity of citizenship*. More than $75,000 must be in dispute in federal diversity of citizenship lawsuits.

Bean v. Turk in *What's Your Verdict?* will be tried in the federal courts. As the case has more than $75,000 in question and is between citizens of different states, it falls within the jurisdictional limits of the federal courts. These courts, only when at least one of the parties requests their exercising it, have priority jurisdiction over state courts in such diversity cases.

FEDERAL COURTS OF APPEALS

The federal courts of appeals have appellate jurisdiction over the district courts, certain specialized federal courts, and many federal administrative agencies. Such power is exercised when the result of a case in a lower court is appealed by one or more of the parties to the case.

Appellate courts do not accept any new evidence or call witnesses. Instead, they review the trial transcripts, appellate briefs and oral arguments of the attorneys to reach a decision. No appellate court, not even the USSC, can change the factual determinations of a jury.

There are 13 federal courts of appeal. Twelve of these are circuit courts, each of which is responsible for an assigned geographic area. The thirteenth is dedicated to the "federal circuit." As such, it handles patent cases appealed out of the district courts and appeals from federal courts with special jurisdictions.

FEDERAL COURT SYSTEM

UNITED STATES SUPREME COURT

(Cases Involving Federal Law)

13 UNITED STATES COURTS OF APPEALS
(12 Circuit Courts)
(1 Court of Appeals for the Federal Circuit)

STATE SUPREME COURTS

UNITED STATES DISTRICT COURTS

SPECIALIZED FEDERAL COURTS*

MANY FEDERAL AGENCIES

*Among the federal courts with specialized jurisdiction are the Tax Court, Court of International Trade, and the Claims Court. The Bankruptcy Court acts as an adjunct of the District Courts.

UNITED STATES SUPREME COURT

The U.S. Supreme Court (USSC) has both original and appellate jurisdiction. Its original jurisdiction, according to the Constitution, is over "cases affecting ambassadors, other public ministers and consuls and those in which a state shall be party." The most important function of the USSC, however, is the exercise of its appellate jurisdiction. This jurisdiction is exercised over cases on appeal from the U.S. Courts of Appeals or from the highest courts of the various states. If the Supreme Court believes that a case contains a constitutional issue sufficiently important to be decided by it, the Supreme Court will issue a **writ of certiorari** to the last court that heard the case. This "writ" or order compels the state court to turn over the record of the case to the Supreme Court for review.

NETBookmark

Access lawxtra.swlearning.com and click on the link for Chapter 3. Click on one of the topics on the home page of the official web site of the U.S. Supreme Court. Write a one-paragraph summary of your findings.

lawxtra.swlearning.com

Jurisdiction over state supreme court cases is limited to those in which a federal question of law has arisen. Such a question must be based on a federal law or on the U.S. Constitution. The decisions of the USSC that interpret or apply the Constitution are final and can only be overturned by the USSC itself or by a constitutional amendment.

CHECKPOINT

Name the three levels of federal courts and describe the jurisdiction of each.

IN THIS CASE

The jury in Martin's case convicted him of grand larceny partially based on evidence found in the trunk of the car he was driving. The state appellate courts upheld his conviction. The USSC, however, took jurisdiction over the case by issuing a writ of certiorari to the state supreme court. The USSC on appeal then held that the search of his trunk that discovered the items was improper. The USSC overturned his conviction, as the jury could have been improperly influenced by such evidence.

3-2 Assessment

lawxtra.swlearning.com

THINK ABOUT LEGAL CONCEPTS

1. A Supreme Court did not exist under the Articles of Confederation. **True or False?**

2. There are _ ?_ levels of courts with general jurisdiction in the federal system.

3. The federal trial courts are known as (a) district courts (b) federal county courts (c) common law courts (d) criminal courts

4. Cases involving citizens of different states in which less than $75,000 is at stake must be tried in the state courts. **True or False?**

5. An appeal to the federal court system of a ruling of a federal agency would be taken to (a) a federal district court (b) a federal court of appeals (c) the USSC.

THINK CRITICALLY ABOUT EVIDENCE

Study the situation, answer the questions, and then prepare arguments to support your answers.

6. Ms. Tant of New York City recently sued Mr. Bloom, also of New York City. She claimed that he had run into and injured her while he was jogging. She asked for $50,000 in damages. When she filed her suit in federal district court, Mr. Bloom's attorney immediately objected on two grounds. What were they?

7. Ms. Tant's case (see exercise 6) was thrown out of federal court. She later filed it in the New York state court solely as a case involving Mr. Bloom's negligent jogging. When she lost, she appealed all the way to the highest New York state court but still lost. She then sought to appeal to the U.S. Supreme Court. Will the Supreme Court hear her case?

8. Paul Stone sued his employer for assault and battery due to the actions of several of his female co-workers. While gathered around the coffee machine each morning, they would whistle at him, make lewd comments, and touch and pinch him. When the case was dismissed from the state circuit court, Stone appealed. The intermediate court of appeals sustained the result in the lower court and Stone appealed to the state supreme court. When the state supreme court also sustained, Stone sought to appeal to the U.S. Supreme Court. Are there any federal issues in this case that would allow the U.S. Supreme Court to take jurisdiction? What might prevent the nation's highest court from so doing?

A TYPICAL STATE COURT SYSTEM

WHAT'S YOUR VERDICT?

Sheila had a beautiful apartment with a view of the harbor. After she had lived there several years, her landlord gave her and the other tenants of the apartment building 30 days notice to vacate. She sued to prevent the mass evictions. After losing in the state trial court, she vowed to appeal the issue directly to the U.S. Supreme Court.

Can she do so?

The typical state legal system resembles the federal system. The state legislature makes the laws. The state executive branch enforces those laws in the courts of the state judicial branch.

The courts of general jurisdiction of this judicial branch are organized into three tiers. In the bottom tier is a geographically based trial-court system. An appellate layer of courts is next. Trial and appellate courts are controlled and supervised by a state supreme court as the ultimate level of appeal. In *What's Your Verdict?* Sheila could not take her appeal directly to the U.S. Supreme Court. Generally, there is no guaranteed right to be heard on appeal by even the state supreme court, with the exception of capital murder convictions.

STATE TRIAL COURTS

In most states trial courts—those courts with general original jurisdiction over both criminal and civil matters—are known as circuit courts. Other states refer to them as superior courts, district courts, or courts of common pleas. Regardless of their name, these trial courts are the courts of record in the state system.

A **court of record** keeps an exact account of what goes on at trial. The accuracy of this account is vital, as any appeal filed depends on it. The "record" may include a transcript of what was said, the evidence that was submitted, statements, the determinations of the court officials, and the judgment of the court.

State trial courts also review the decisions of courts of more specialized jurisdiction, such as the small claims courts. Where necessary, state trial courts retry such cases to make a proper record for the purpose of potential appeals.

Because a state trial court has original jurisdiction over cases before it, it typically makes determinations of the facts in the case by using a jury. If a jury is not requested by the parties in the case, the judge will determine the facts. Once

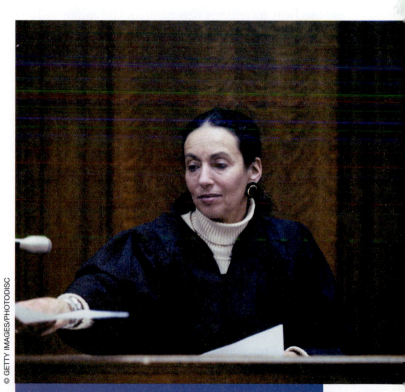

© GETTY IMAGES/PHOTODISC

If the parties to a case do not request a jury, a judge will preside over the case. Do you think it is always in the best interest of the parties to request a jury? Why or why not?

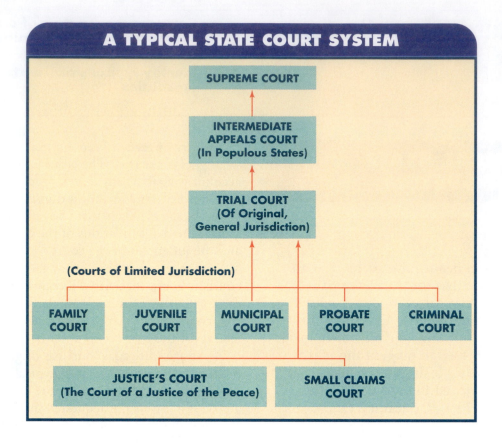

A TYPICAL STATE COURT SYSTEM

SUPREME COURT

INTERMEDIATE
APPEALS COURT
(In Populous States)

TRIAL COURT
(Of Original,
General Jurisdiction)

(Courts of Limited Jurisdiction)

FAMILY COURT

JUVENILE COURT

MUNICIPAL COURT

PROBATE COURT

CRIMINAL COURT

JUSTICE'S COURT
(The Court of a Justice of the Peace)

SMALL CLAIMS COURT

the facts have been determined, the judge will select and apply the law to the facts to reach a verdict.

STATE COURTS OF APPEALS

An appeal from a court of record is typically reviewed by a panel of judges in a state court of appeals. The panel of judges from the state court of appeals usually consists of no more than three judges. The state court appellate procedure is very similar to that of the federal courts of appeals. In particular, the state appellate panel evaluates the record of the case and the appellate briefs submitted by the attorneys for the parties. It also may hear oral arguments by those attorneys in the case. No new evidence can be introduced at this level. The judges at the appellate level check to be sure that the lower court used the correct law to conduct and resolve the case. If the correct law was used, the result in the case will be upheld.

If court of appeals judges conclude that the trial court used the incorrect law they may apply the correct law themselves to reach a new result. If, however, they conclude that the use of the incorrect law interfered with the proper determination of the facts of the case, they may send the case back down for a new trial.

STATE SUPREME COURTS

Generally, in whatever legal issue you confront, you are entitled to a trial and to one appeal, if filed in a timely manner and in the proper form. In states with the intermediate level of courts of appeals, only cases that involve the most complex legal issues are taken to the justices of the state supreme court. (*Justice* is the title given to judges who sit on state supreme courts and the federal Supreme Court.) Typically, at the state supreme court level, a panel of three or more justices reviews the cases on appeal in the same manner as the lower appellate courts.

State supreme courts issue the final decision on matters of law appealed to them. If a U.S. Constitutional or other federal question of law is involved, however, a further appeal can go to the U.S. Supreme Court. In several states, in addition to its appellate jurisdiction, the state supreme court has original jurisdiction over most state impeachment cases.

CHECKPOINT

What does a typical state court system have in common with the federal court system?

STATE COURTS WITH SPECIALIZED JURISDICTIONS

WHAT'S YOUR VERDICT?

Alton, age 15, stole a car from a mall parking lot. She was caught and referred to a juvenile court.

Will she be treated differently under the juvenile court's jurisdiction than under a regular trial court's jurisdiction?

Below the circuit court level in most states are the courts that take care of specialized or relatively minor jurisdiction. These courts include the associate circuit, municipal, small claims, juvenile, and probate courts.

ASSOCIATE CIRCUIT COURTS

Many states have a layer of courts below their main courts of general original jurisdiction. These lower courts are referred to as **associate circuit courts** or **county courts**. Such courts hear minor criminal cases, state traffic offenses, and lawsuits in which relatively small amounts are involved (usually no more than $25,000). Generally, these courts are not courts of record. However, they take a significant burden off the higher courts, even though appeals from their decisions can be taken to a state trial court for a trial on the record.

CITY OR MUNICIPAL COURTS

Cities typically have courts that administer their ordinances. These **municipal courts** are usually divided into traffic and criminal divisions. As city ordinances often overlap with or duplicate state laws, less serious violations occurring within city limits are brought before such municipal courts for their first trial. The result can then be appealed to the state trial court level if necessary. Although the penalties for violating ordinances can be as severe, ordinances are not considered criminal laws. Only state and federal governments can make an act criminal.

SMALL CLAIMS COURTS

Minor individual suits would not often be heard if not for the **small claims courts**. These courts handle disputes in which small amounts, generally $2,500 or less, are involved. Attorneys generally are not required in small claims courts. The judge hears the case without a jury or formal rules of evidence. Decisions of small claims court can also be appealed to a state trial court.

JUVENILE COURTS

Younger members of society—those over 13 and under 18 years of age in most states—are referred to as juveniles. The map in the Law Brief on page 58 shows the minimum age at which each state tries an individual as an adult. Society typically believes that juveniles should not be held as responsible as adults for their criminal acts. To carry out this policy, special **juvenile courts** have been set up. In these courts the juvenile is entitled to his or her full constitutional rights, including the right to be represented by an attorney. If the juvenile is found guilty of the charges brought, the court has wide powers in determining what should be done.

However, the emphasis for juveniles generally is on rehabilitation, not punishment. Possibilities open to the court include release into the supervision of parents, guardians, or governmental officials; placement in foster homes; and detention in correctional facilities. These courts ensure that most of the criminal cases involving juveniles do not become public knowledge. The courtroom is closed while an informal hearing into the charges is conducted. Any records made on juvenile cases are not open to the public.

Why do you think the emphasis in juvenile courts is on rehabilitation rather than punishment? Do you agree with this? Why or why not?

© GETTY IMAGES/PHOTODISC

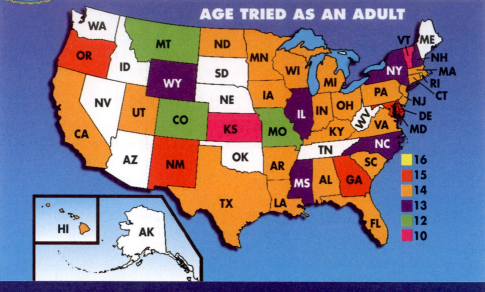

AGE TRIED AS AN ADULT

16
15
14
13
12
10

Washington, D.C., and 11 states do not have a set minimum age for a child to be tried as an adult. Thirty-nine of the states do have a set minimum age—the range is 10 to 16 years of age.

If rehabilitation fails or is shown to be impossible, the young offender can be tried and punished as an adult. This occurs only in cases involving a very serious offense. For example, murder and certain other crimes may bring about trial and punishment through the criminal law system. Appeals from actions of the juvenile courts are directed to the circuit courts.

In *What's Your Verdict?* Alton would be treated far differently under the juvenile court's jurisdiction. She would be entitled to a juvenile court hearing where her age, level of maturity, and potential would be considered in determining how she is to be treated.

PROBATE COURTS

When individuals die, their property and other interests must be divided according to their wishes and the appropriate laws. The courts that administer wills and estates to accomplish this task are called **probate courts**.

CHECKPOINT

Name the typical state courts that have specialized jurisdiction.

A QUESTION OF ETHICS

At age 17, Horace Samuels was brought before the juvenile court charged with child molestation. He was convicted and, as a juvenile, was sentenced to probation in a foster home. While in the home, he was again caught and tried for the same offense. Again, he was tried as a juvenile. Now he is 18 and about to live on his own in an area in which many children of the same age that he has been charged with molesting also live. Horace's probation officer realizes that Horace has not been rehabilitated and is a potential danger to the neighborhood's young. The law requires that the juvenile's record remain closed so that the individual may begin a new life free and clear of past mistakes. What should the probation officer do?

Assessment

THINK ABOUT LEGAL CONCEPTS

1. Which of the following is generally not included in the "record" of a case? (a) verbatim transcript (b) physical and documentary evidence (c) media coverage (d) all of the above are generally included

2. Attorneys generally are not required in a small claims court. **True or False?**

3. A state trial court has the power to hear some appeals. **True or False?**

4. A dispute between neighbors involving property damage of $8,500 would probably be heard in (a) federal district court (b) probate court (c) small claims court (d) associate circuit court

5. A state supreme court has the power to issue the final decision on all matters of law appealed to it. **True or False?**

THINK CRITICALLY ABOUT EVIDENCE

Study the situations, answer the questions, and then prepare arguments to support your answers.

6. Gwendolyn Hunt was driving while intoxicated when she hit and killed Felicia Meyers, a seven-year-old, in a school crosswalk. Gwendolyn was 16 years old at the time. However, she was on probation from a reduced sentence for driving 62 in a 35 mph residential speed zone. Should Gwendolyn be tried as an adult for vehicular manslaughter?

7. You are driving along a residential city street when you are stopped by a city police cruiser for speeding. You are given a citation and a summons to appear before a particular court. What court would that most likely be and why?

8. You are driving along the interstate highway headed for a ballgame in a nearby city. A state highway patrol car suddenly appears in your rearview mirror, lights flashing. You pull over and are cited for doing 80 in a 65 mph zone. Your receive a summons to a particular court. What court would that most likely be and why?

9. After a long illness, your uncle dies. He leaves a sizeable estate but no will is found for several weeks. Finally, one of his ex-wives appears with a document she claims to be a valid will. It shows her and her children by him receiving most of his property. Your parents and the deceased's other children contest the will. Should the federal or state courts handle this case? Why? Which court in which system is most likely to hear it?

10. George Matthews lives in the South. He ordered a $2,950 garden cultivator from a company in the Midwest. George paid for the cultivator C.O.D. (cash on delivery). After trying to use the cultivator, George found that the tines were made of a cheap, thin metal that was not adequate for use even on fairly loose soil. The company refused to refund George's money. Should George sue? What court would be available to him? Does the way jurisdictions are allocated make it unlikely certain cases will be litigated? What does this say about society's desire to afford justice to all?

PREVENT LEGAL DIFFICULTIES

Be prepared...

1. To avoid expensive litigation should a dispute develop, when you enter a contract include a provision requiring the use of a mediator or an arbitrator.

2. To be sure of the rules and costs of any litigation that might develop under a legal document you sign, specify the jurisdiction in which such disputes must be resolved.

3. Know the facts about your state's juvenile court system with respect to ages, rights, sentencing options.

4. Have your parents see an attorney to make out a will and utilize other methods to avoid the expenses of probate.

Chapter 3 Assessment

CONCEPTS IN BRIEF

3-1 Forms of Dispute Resolution

1. The levels of courts are trial courts, which have original jurisdiction, and appellate courts, which review decisions of lower courts.

2. Mediation and arbitration offer dispute resolution alternatives to litigation. Using these alternative methods of dispute resolution helps to avoid the costs, delays, and difficulties of a court trial.

3-2 The Federal Court System

3. The federal government and each state have separate court systems.

4. The federal courts receive their power from the Constitution. Federal courts can have either general or specialized jurisdiction.

3-3 State Court Systems

5. The typical state court system is similar to the federal court system. Both the federal and most state court systems have trial courts, appellate courts, and a supreme court.

6. Associate circuit courts, or county courts, hear minor criminal cases, state traffic offenses, and lawsuits involving small amounts of money.

7. Municipal or city courts usually feature two divisions, one to handle traffic and another to handle violations of all other ordinances. Penalties for ordinance violations (which are not considered crimes) are less severe than federal and state criminal law penalties.

8. Small claims courts feature relaxed rules of evidence and do not require representation by an attorney. The dollar amount that can be adjudicated usually is limited to around $2,500.

9. In every state, there are juvenile courts with specialized jurisdiction over persons under a certain age. These courts emphasize rehabilitation over punishment. In certain instances, juveniles can be bound over for trial as adults.

10. Probate courts settle the estates of decedents who die with or without a will.

YOUR LEGAL VOCABULARY

Match each statement with the term that it best defines. Some terms may not be used.

1. Verbatim record of what went on at trial
2. Court that reviews trial court decisions to determine if a significant error of law was made during trial
3. Court in which an accurate, detailed report of what went on at trial is formed
4. Independent third party who develops a binding, court-enforceable dispute resolution
5. Order to a lower court to produce the record of a case for the Supreme Court to review
6. Power to hear a case in full for the first time
7. Courts that hear cases involving individuals generally between the ages of 13 and 18
8. To take a dispute to court
9. Court that hears cases involving violations of ordinances
10. Power to hear only cases of a specific type

a. **appellate brief**
b. **appellate court**
c. **arbitrator**
d. **associate circuit court (or county court)**
e. **court**
f. **court of record**
h. **general jurisdiction**
i. **juvenile court**
j. **litigate**
k. **mediator**
l. **municipal court**
m. **original jurisdiction**
n. **probate court**
o. **small claims court**
p. **special jurisdiction**
q. **transcript**
r. **trial court**
s. **verdict**
t. **writ of certiorari**

REVIEW LEGAL CONCEPTS

11. What is the fundamental difference between arbitration and mediation?

12. Why are appeals heard by higher courts?

13. Why should the federal courts handle cases involving private matters between citizens of different states (for example, cases involving diversity of citizenship with more than $75,000 at stake)?

14. Why shouldn't the USSC be able to substitute its own factual determinations for those of a jury in a lower court?

WRITE ABOUT LEGAL CONCEPTS

15. Wherever you go you are charged with knowing all the laws, ordinances, rules, and regulations that apply to you. "Ignorance of the law is no excuse." Because of the confusion this causes, there has been a movement in the last 50 years to make state laws more uniform. From sales law to various parts of the criminal code, the effect has been positive. Should state court systems be made more uniform? What are the advantages and disadvantages of such an idea?

16. Judges cost an extraordinary amount of money. To attract competent personnel to the judiciary, salaries must be comparable to what an exceptional lawyer would earn in private practice. A way to provide the necessary salary levels is to save money elsewhere in the system. Many states use extensively trained non-lawyers to preside over municipal courts and hold other minor judiciary positions. Do you think this is a good idea? Why or why not?

17. **HOT DEBATE** Write a paragraph discussing the following question: If Anthony decides to file suit in state court against his employer, what federal court might ultimately claim jurisdiction? Under what circumstances?

MAKE ACADEMIC CONNECTIONS

18. **BIOLOGY** The jurisdictional shield of the juvenile courts ends at age 18. Research the maturation process of homo sapiens and determine whether or not, according to the scientific evidence, 18 is a good cutoff age. What implications does the result of your research have for driving age, voting age, age to enter the military, and age to drink.

THINK CRITICALLY ABOUT EVIDENCE

Study the situation, answer the questions, and then prepare arguments to support your answers.

19. Gomez wanted to sue Shapiro for failure to complete work under their contract but could not afford the expenses and time delays associated with litigation. What alternatives are available to resolve this matter?

20. If you were called to testify as a witness in a friend's criminal trial, would you have the moral strength to tell the complete truth even if your friend might be convicted as a result?

21. June lost her case in trial court. She thought that the plaintiff, Sid, had lied during the trial. On appeal, she requested that she be allowed to appear and explain why she thought Sid had lied. Will her request be granted?

22. Suppose someone has injured you. Do you have a duty to sue them for the injury even when the costs of bringing suit may be more than you can recover?

23. On May 7, Bart Masters turned 18. The evening of that day, he was caught stealing a woman's purse. "Don't worry," he told his friend Julia, "I just turned 18 today, they won't try me as an adult. I'm too close to being a juvenile." Is he correct?

24. Priscilla is being sued in small claims court by her landlord for past due rent. "Just wait," she exclaims. "Once I get in front of that jury, they won't award him the money. After all, he shut off the water several times and didn't even have heat in the building for over a month last winter." What is wrong with Priscilla's estimate of the situation?

25. In April of 2004, the U.S. Supreme Court refused to hear the appeal of a case involving Virginia Military Institute (VMI). The case centered on the issue of whether or not, at a public supported college such as VMI, a prayer traditionally offered before the evening meal should be prohibited as a violation of the constitutional mandate requiring the separation of church and state. In an unusual step, two of the Justices of the Court criticized the other Justices for avoiding the responsibility of rendering a clear decision with attendant guidelines on the matter. Failing to take the case left in place a lower court's decision against having the prayer. The two Justices pointed out that, although there were previous decisions against such prayer in the public schools where attendance was enforced, colleges were voluntary institutions. Should the court have taken the case? How do you feel the court should rule on the mandatory recital of the pledge of allegiance, with the phrase "Under God" therein, in public schools or colleges? (*Bunting v. Mellen*, USSC 03-863, 181 F. Supp. 2d 619)

26. Taylor and Fitz Coal Company had a dispute over the amount of money due under a mineral lease.They submitted the dispute to arbitration according to the provisions of the lease. The arbitrators awarded the lessor, Taylor, $37,214.67. Taylor did not like the amount awarded and filed suit in court. Will the court conduct a trial to determine whether the amount is fair? (*Taylor v. Fitz Coal Company*, 618 S.W.2d 432, Ky.)

27. A 17-year-old boy first appeared in juvenile court to answer charges of vehicular homicide. The incident had occurred when he was 16. By the time the case actually went to trial the boy was 18. Should he be tried as an adult? Why or why not? (*Commission v. A Juvenile*, 545 N.E.2d 1164)

28. When a tip was received that marijuana was being grown in his greenhouse, Michael Riley's property was observed from a helicopter by an investigating officer. The helicopter flyover was deemed necessary because the items within the greenhouse could not be observed from a nearby road. Riley was subsequently arrested and tried for offenses stemming from his cultivation efforts. The defense challenged the use of the information acquired by the helicopter flyover saying that it was an illegal search under the Fourth Amendment to the U.S. Constitution. The Florida Supreme Court agreed with the defense. Could the State of Florida appeal the decision to the U.S. Supreme Court? Why or why not? (*Florida v. Riley*, 102 L.Ed. 2d 835)

29. Colleen Donnelly filed charges with the Equal Employment Opportunity Commission (EEOC) against her employer, Yellow Freight, for sex discrimination. After she filed the charges, Colleen received notice from the EEOC that she had 90 days to bring suit. This 90-day period was a procedure for claims under the federal Civil Rights Act of 1964. Within that period Donnelly did indeed file suit but in an Illinois state court under an Illinois statute that also prohibits such discrimination. After the 90-day period had expired, however, she tried to transfer the suit to a federal court. Yellow Freight defended claiming that she could not make such a transfer as the 90-day period had expired for federal actions. Should she be allowed to go forward with her suit? Why or why not? (*Donnelly v. Yellow Freight System, Inc.*, 874 F.2d 402)

30. A government-owned P-51 fighter plane landed at a Los Angeles airport and waited on a runway for a tow truck, on instructions from the tower. Shortly thereafter, a plane owned by Douglas Aircraft Company began approaching the airfield to land. The Douglas aircraft struck the P-51, which was parked on the runway. The United States brought suit against Douglas, claiming that the Douglas pilot was negligent. During the trial, evidence was introduced indicating that the Douglas pilot was careless in not seeing the parked P-51, but that the airport was covered with a haze and the P-51 was painted in camouflage colors. Also, the Douglas pilot had "zigzagged" his plane while taxiing in order to improve his forward vision. The trial was conducted before a jury. The government claimed that the issue of whether the Douglas pilot was negligent was an issue of law for the judge to decide. Douglas claimed that is was an issue of fact for the jury to decide. Which one is correct? (*United States v. Douglas Aircraft Company*, 169 F.2d 755, 9th Cir.)

CASE FOR LEGAL THINKING

Texas v. Johnson
USSC, 109 Supreme Court
Reporter 2533

BACKGROUND In 1984, during the Republican National Convention in Dallas, Texas, a political demonstration was held. The point of the demonstration was to protest the policies of the President of the United States, Ronald Reagan. Mr. Reagan was to be re-nominated by the convention for a second term. The demonstration also targeted several Dallas-based corporations for their government-related activities.

FACTS As the demonstration was being conducted, a protestor took an American flag from a pole outside one of the buildings. The protestor passed the flag to another protestor, Johnson, who subsequently doused it with kerosene and set it afire. As the flag of the United States of America burned, the protestors chanted, "America, the red, white, and blue, we spit on you." The protestor who set the flag afire was ultimately charged with a crime and tried in a Texas trial court.

LOWER COURT The trial court found Johnson guilty of violating a state statute which prohibited the desecration of state or national flags. The statute defined desecration as the physical mistreatment of such objects so as to seriously offend individuals likely to observe or discover the act.

APPEAL Johnson appealed his conviction on the basis of the First Amendment's guarantee of freedom of speech. A Texas Court of Appeals affirmed the conviction after stating that such a statute, which might have a potentially chilling effect on speech, deserved close scrutiny in its application. However, said the court, the conviction could be upheld in this instance as being necessary to guarantee the peaceful nature of the assembly due to the highly inflammatory nature of a flag burning. The case was then appealed to the Texas Court of Criminal Appeals. The Court of Criminal Appeals reversed the decisions of the inferior courts and sent the case back to the trial court with instructions to dismiss the charges. The Court, in so doing, indicated that the statute was too broad in its reference to protecting against a breach of the peace. The

U.S. Supreme Court then took jurisdiction by a writ of certiorari.

ISSUE Was the conviction of Johnson justifiable by the state of Texas as an attempt to protect against breaches of the peace or did the flag burning have overriding elements of communication that the state statute failed to protect?

DECISION The United States Supreme Court, in an opinion written by Justice Brennan, held that the First Amendment freedom of speech protection had indeed been violated by the application of the statute.

PRACTICE JUDGING

1. Should the court affirm or reverse as a consequence?

2. The record did not contain any evidence indicating that a breach of the peace had indeed occurred. How do you think this affected the decision?

3. There is an exception for "fighting words" provided for governments who want to enforce statutes that might chill public speech. Could this exception have been applied to this situation in order to uphold the conviction?

© GETTY IMAGES/PHOTODISC

CHAPTER 4

Criminal Law and Procedure

4-1 Criminal Law

4-2 Criminal Procedure

HOT DEBATE

Sixteen-year-old Brittany's parents were hit and killed by Ann, a 21-year-old intoxicated driver trying to speed away from police. Ann's attorneys were able to have the blood test evidence that showed intoxication thrown out at trial. She was convicted only of two counts of second-degree manslaughter and leaving the scene of an accident. After serving a week of "shock" jail time, she was set free on probation. Outraged at what she termed the failure of the legal system, Brittany took her foster parent's car and ran Ann over in the street as she left the jail. Ann was crippled for life as a result.

Where Do You Stand?

1. Was Brittany morally justified in her actions?

2. What action should the law take against Brittany?

▼ GOALS

- Understand the three elements that make up a criminal act
- Classify crimes according to the severity of their potential sentences
- Identify the types of crimes that affect business

CRIMES AND CRIMINAL BEHAVIOR

WHAT'S YOUR VERDICT?

O'Brien, a vice president at the Del Norte Credit Union, cleverly juggled the company books over a period of years. During that time, he took at least $135,000 belonging to the credit union. When the theft was discovered by outside auditors, O'Brien repaid the money with interest.

Has he committed a crime despite the repayment?

The most fundamental characteristic of a **crime** is that it is a punishable offense against society. When a crime occurs, society—acting through police and prosecutors—attempts to identify, arrest, prosecute, and punish the criminal. These efforts are designed to protect society, not the victim of the crime. As a consequence, it is up to society's chosen representatives to determine what action to take against the person who committed the crime. The victim can sue identified criminals for civil damages. However, victims seldom do so because few criminals have the ability to pay judgments.

A QUESTION OF ETHICS

Not more than two centuries ago society routinely imposed a single punishment for a felony. That punishment was death. What do you think was happening at that time in history that required such a level of punishment?

Crimes should be carefully defined by statutes, or laws enacted by state or federal legislatures. A well-worded criminal statute clearly and specifically defines the behavior it prohibits. It does not interfere with protected individual rights in so doing.

ELEMENTS OF CRIMINAL ACTS

Before you can be convicted of a crime, the prosecutors must prove these three elements regarding your behavior at the trial. These elements are

1. whether you were aware of your duty to do or not to do a certain thing
2. whether you performed an act or omission in violation of that duty
3. whether or not you had criminal intent

DUTY It is everyone's *duty* to know the law and to conform his or her conduct to the law's requirements. To establish duty in a trial, the prosecutor cites to the judge a statute that prescribes the duty owed in the case at hand.

VIOLATION OF THE DUTY The *breach of duty*—the specific conduct of the defendant that violates the statute—is the *criminal act*. For example, all states have statutes that make battery a crime. These statutes often define criminal battery as "the intentional causing of bodily harm to another person." A breach of this duty could be proved in a trial by the testimony of a witness who saw the defendant punch the victim.

CRIMINAL INTENT The third element, criminal intent, also must be proven in most cases. Criminal intent generally means that the defendant (1) intended to commit the act and (2) intended to do evil. If in a basketball game you deliberately punch an opposing player, you display criminal intent. You have committed a crime. On the other hand, if you lose your balance, and while flailing your arms hit the nose of a bystander, there would be no crime. You did not intend the act nor did you intend to do evil.

In *What's Your Verdict?* O'Brien owed a duty, defined by state statute, to not take the credit union's money. Violation of this duty, the criminal conduct of taking another's property or money by a person to whom it has been entrusted, is *embezzlement*. This act could be proved with the testimony of the auditors. O'Brien's criminal intent can be inferred from his conduct. The acts were intentional and he intended to do the evil. So O'Brien did commit a crime. His return of the money does not alter this fact.

Criminal intent creates two issues for corporations. First, can a corporation, which is an organization, form criminal intent the way humans can? The answer is yes. If the corporation's employees have criminal intent, their employer may be judged to have criminal intent. If the employees were doing their assigned duties and the criminal act benefits the organization, most courts will find criminal intent in the organization.

The second issue relates to corporate presidents, treasurers, and other officers. When a corporate employee commits a crime, can officers be held criminally responsible? Again, the answer often is yes. In some situations, the officer will be held criminally liable under the doctrine of **vicarious criminal liability**. Vicarious means substituted. The criminal intent of the employee is used as a substitute for the requirement of criminal intent for an officer.

Criminal intent also is related to age. Under early common law, children under age 7 were considered incapable of forming the criminal intent necessary for crimes. Those over age 14 were presumed capable of recognizing the difference between right and wrong and so were as accountable as adults for their acts. For children ages 7 through 14, such ability had to be proved.

Today, statutes in most states fix the age of criminal liability at 18, but the figure ranges from 16 to 19. State statutes provide that minors as young as 7 may be tried and punished as adults if they are accused of serious crimes such as murder. Generally, however, what is a crime for an adult is *juvenile delinquency* for a minor.

To have criminal intent, one must have sufficient mental capacity to know the difference between right and wrong. Accordingly, insane persons are not held responsible for their criminal acts. However, people who voluntarily become intoxicated or drugged are held responsible.

Some minor crimes do not require the element of criminal intent. Traffic offenses are an example. A speeding driver who did not intend to speed or intend evil still has committed a traffic offense. In addition, in certain circumstances extreme carelessness may be considered the same as criminal intent. Suppose you drive 80 miles per hour through a residential neighborhood while drunk and kill a pedestrian. You may not have intended to speed or intended to do evil. However, your conduct was so careless that in many jurisdictions courts will treat it the same as criminal intent. You could be convicted of the crime of vehicular homicide.

ECONOMIC IMPACT

ADA ACCESSIBILITY GUIDELINES

The Americans with Disabilities Act (ADA) is a comprehensive federal civil rights statute that outlaws discrimination on the basis of disability. Recently, after years of planning and evaluation, the Architectural and Transportation Barriers Compliance Board (Access Board) proposed an amendment to the Americans with Disabilities Act Accessibility Guidelines (ADAAG) to cover newly constructed and altered recreation facilities. These rules were intended to provide access for the disabled to facilities such as amusement park rides, marinas, golf courses, physical fitness facilities, recreational camps, etc.

THINK CRITICALLY

Evaluate these new rules based on their stated cost to the owners of such facilities. (Access lawxtra.swlearning.com for a link to a detailed listing of estimated costs per type of facility.) If you were the president of a company in the recreational field, what impact might these rules have on your decision to update or build new facilities? Would you support or object to these new rules? On what grounds?

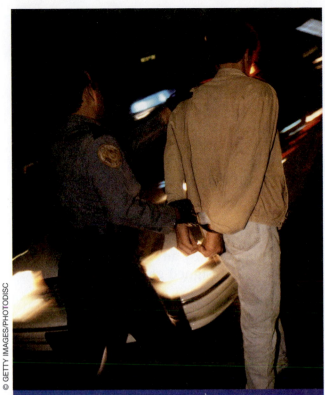

Imagine that the person in this photo killed a pedestrian while driving under the influence of alcohol. Do you think the law should treat the intent of this person as criminal? Why or why not?

CHECKPOINT

What three elements must be proven at trial before someone can be convicted of a crime?

CLASSIFICATIONS OF CRIMES

WHAT'S YOUR VERDICT?

Murdock was a witness at a civil trial for damages. Before testifying, he took an oath "to tell the truth, the whole truth, and nothing but the truth." Nevertheless, while being questioned by one of the attorneys, Murdock deliberately lied, hoping to help the defendant.

What crime has Murdock committed?

Crimes can be classified in many different ways. One method of classification is to identify against whom or what they are committed. The Law Brief lists and gives examples of these types of crimes. Crimes also can be classified as either felonies or misdemeanors according to the severity of their potential sentences.

FELONY

A **felony** is a crime punishable by confinement for more than a year in a state prison or by a fine of more than $1,000, or both—or even death.

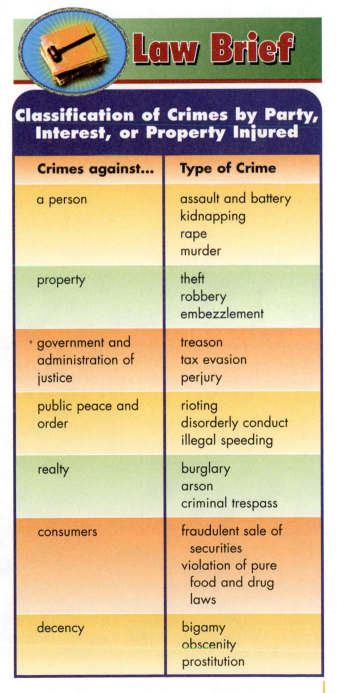

Law Brief

Classification of Crimes by Party, Interest, or Property Injured

Crimes against...	Type of Crime
a person	assault and battery kidnapping rape murder
property	theft robbery embezzlement
government and administration of justice	treason tax evasion perjury
public peace and order	rioting disorderly conduct illegal speeding
realty	burglary arson criminal trespass
consumers	fraudulent sale of securities violation of pure food and drug laws
decency	bigamy obscenity prostitution

Murder, kidnapping, arson, rape, robbery, burglary, embezzlement, forgery, theft of large sums, and perjury are examples of felonies. People who lie under oath (as Murdock did in *What's Your Verdict?*) commit the felony of *perjury*.

MISDEMEANOR

A **misdemeanor** is a less serious crime. It usually is punishable by confinement in a county or city jail for less than one year, by fine, or both. Crimes such as disorderly conduct and speeding usually are misdemeanors.

Some states classify lesser misdemeanors as *infractions*. Persons convicted of infractions can only be fined. Because there is no risk of being jailed, the defendant charged with an infraction is not entitled to a jury trial. Parking violations and littering are examples of infractions.

CHECKPOINT

Name the two categories of crimes classified by the severity of their potential sentences.

Littering in this beach town carries a fine of $1,000. Research to find out the fine for littering in your area.

BUSINESS-RELATED CRIMES

WHAT'S YOUR VERDICT?

Officers of six competing cosmetics manufacturers met at a trade convention. All of the officers agreed to use the same wholesale prices. They also agreed to follow the lead of the biggest company in making future price changes. Each officer agreed to promote sales by advertising only within an assigned geographical region.

Have the officers and their companies committed any crime?

Like people, businesses are subject to general criminal law. Offenses committed in the business world typically are referred to as **white-collar crimes.** These crimes do not involve force or violence and do not cause physical injury to people or physical damage to property.

Common examples of white-collar crimes are not paying income taxes, stock fraud, using false weighing machines, conspiring to fix prices, making false fire insurance and auto insurance claims, engaging in false advertising, committing bribery, engaging in political corruption, and embezzling. Because physical violence is not involved, courts tend to be more lenient with white-collar criminals. Punishments usually include fines or short prison sentences.

In *What's Your Verdict?* the six officers were guilty of violating criminal portions of the antitrust laws. *Antitrust laws* state that competing companies may not cooperate in fixing prices or in dividing sales regions. Antitrust laws require that business firms compete with one another. Some of the more common business-related crimes follow.

© GETTY IMAGES/PHOTODISC

LARCENY *Larceny*, commonly known as *theft*, is the wrongful taking of money or personal property belonging to someone else, with intent to deprive the owner of possession. *Robbery* is a variation of larceny. It is the taking of property from another's person or immediate presence, against the victim's will, by force or by causing fear. *Burglary* is another variation of larceny. It is entering a building without permission when intending to commit a crime. Other types of larceny include shoplifting, pick pocketing, and purse snatching.

Larceny may be either a felony or a misdemeanor. The classification is determined by the value of the property stolen and other circumstances. Robbery and burglary are always felonies. A thief who sells the stolen goods is guilty of the separate crime of *selling stolen property*.

RECEIVING STOLEN PROPERTY Knowingly receiving stolen property consists of either receiving or buying property known to be stolen, with intent to deprive the rightful owner of the property. One who receives stolen property is known as a *fence*.

FALSE PRETENSES One who obtains money or other property by lying about a past or existing fact is guilty of *false pretenses*. This crime differs from larceny because the victim parts with the property voluntarily. False pretenses is a type of fraud.

FORGERY *Forgery* is falsely making or materially altering a writing to defraud another. The most common forgeries are found on checks when one signs another's name without permission to do so. Forgery also includes altering a check, such as changing "$7" to "$70" and "Seven" to "Seventy." Forgery usually is a felony. Of course, if others authorize you to sign their names, there is no forgery.

BRIBERY *Bribery* is unlawfully offering or giving anything of value to influence performance of an official. Soliciting or accepting the bribe is also criminal. In many states, bribing nongovernmental parties is also a form of bribery called commercial bribery. Thus, paying a private company's purchasing agent to obtain a sale may be bribery. It is usually bribery when a professional gambler pays an athlete to lose a game intentionally. The federal Foreign Corrupt Practices Act of 1977 prohibits bribery in foreign countries by U.S. companies. Unlike the United States, many other nations do not make criminal or prosecute such actions by their companies.

What is the evidence that this man is committing a burglary? Is there any evidence that a robbery is in process? If so, what is it?

© GETTY IMAGES/PHOTODISC

COMPUTER CRIME The computer revolution has created a range of problems for criminal law. For example, larceny is "the wrongful taking of the personal property of others." This traditional definition of the crime made it difficult to prosecute those who steal computer data. Many courts concluded that there was not a "taking" if an

LEGAL RESEARCH

Search the Internet for state and federal laws that prohibit computer-related crimes. An example would be to research electronic identity theft in all its forms from credit card fraud to invasion of accounts.

intruder merely copied the information in the computer. Even if an intruder copied and erased computer information, some courts concluded that there was no taking of "personal property" but only the loss of electrical impulses, which no one really owns. In response, the federal and state governments have created new criminal laws, such as the federal Computer Fraud and Abuse Act (Title 18 U.S.C. Section 1030) specifically targeting computer-related crimes.

IN THIS CASE

Intercomp is a U.S. company that routinely buys surplus computers in this country and markets them overseas. Intercomp agreed to reimburse its agent for gifts given to a foreign government official. The official decided which companies were to be placed on a list of those authorized to do business in the country. Intercomp's competitors all gave similar gifts to the official. However, for doing so, Intercomp was prosecuted under the U.S. Foreign Corrupt Practices Act, convicted, and fined $500,000.

EXTORTION *Extortion* (commonly known as *blackmail*) is obtaining money or other property from a person by wrongful use of force, fear, or the power of office. For example, the extortionist (blackmailer) may threaten to inflict bodily injury. At other times, the threat may be to expose a secret crime or embarrassing fact if payment is not made.

CONSPIRACY An agreement between two or more persons to commit a crime is called *conspiracy*. Usually the agreement is secret. The conspiracy is a crime separate from the crime the parties planned to commit. Depending on the circumstances, the crime may be either a felony or a misdemeanor. Business executives of competing corporations sometimes conspire to fix prices or to divide markets.

ARSON *Arson* is the willful and illegal burning of a building. Arson occurs when someone intentionally starts a fire and burns a structure without the owner's consent. In some states, arson also occurs if you burn your own building to defraud an insurer.

CHECKPOINT

Name the types of business-related crimes.

4-1 Assessment

Xtra! Study Tools
lawxtra.swlearning.com

THINK ABOUT LEGAL CONCEPTS

1. Legally, a crime is considered an offense against (a) the victim (b) society (c) the court (d) none of the above.

2. Ben is convicted and sentenced to two to five years in jail. The crime he has committed is a (a) misdemeanor (b) felony.

3. In some situations, an officer of a corporation will be held criminally liable for the acts of an employee under the doctrine of _?_.

4. The willful and illegal burning of a building is known as inflammation. **True or False?**

THINK CRITICALLY ABOUT EVIDENCE

Study the situation, answer the questions, and then prepare arguments to support your answers.

5. Phillips developed a scheme to generate funds by sending bogus bills for small amounts for District Sanitation Services to residents of affluent areas. Enough people paid these bills to make the practice quite profitable. What crime has Phillips committed?

6. A corporation was cited and charged with illegal pollution for dumping chemical wastes into a river. The dumping happened when an employee mistakenly opened the wrong valve. The company pleaded not guilty because the dumping was not intentional. Neither the company nor the employee knew of the ban on dumping this particular chemical. Is either argument a good defense? Why or why not?

Criminal Procedure

- Know the rights a person has when arrested
- Recognize a person's potential criminal liability for the actions of others
- Name and describe the two types of defenses to criminal charges

RIGHTS AND RESPONSIBILITIES

WHAT'S YOUR VERDICT?

During a routine traffic stop of a small truck for speeding, an officer became suspicious of the cargo the truck contained due to a smell coming from inside. When his request to search the truck was refused, the officer radioed for the assistance of a drug dog. Unfortunately, the dog was unavailable. Finally, he ordered the driver to open the cargo area. When the driver did so, the officer found more than a ton of marijuana. At trial, the defense attorney maintained that it was an illegal search and seizure and that the marijuana should not be allowed to be used as evidence.

Do you agree? Why or why not?

One of the major objectives of the framers of the Constitution of the United States was to protect individuals from the powers of the federal government created under it. The constitutional limitations created as a consequence have been extended over the years so as to also apply to the state and local governments. The authors of the Constitution believed it was better for society to give individuals too much liberty than to allow the government too much power. Thus, in this country, people suspected or accused of criminal conduct have rights that are not available in many other countries. For an example of this, see the International Viewpoint feature on this page.

RIGHTS OF THE ACCUSED

The constitutional right to due process requires fundamental fairness in governmental actions. It requires fair procedures during an investigation and in court. As discussed in Chapter 2, criminal defendants may not be compelled to testify against themselves. Evidence presented against them cannot be developed by unreasonable searches and seizures by the authorities. For example, in *What's Your Verdict?* the police officer's sense of smell was not as keen as the police dog's. Therefore, the search was deemed unreasonable as it lacked **probable cause** (a reasonable ground for belief) and the marijuana could not be used as evidence.

Perhaps the most important right is the right of the accused criminal to be represented by a

INTERNATIONAL VIEWPOINT

Criminal Procedure in France

Criminal procedure in France—and most other European countries—is significantly different from criminal procedure in the United States and Great Britain. A few examples from the French system are

- persons accused of crimes are not presumed innocent until proven guilty
- victims and their families can become parties to investigations
- judges take an active role in trials, including examining and cross-examining witnesses
- persons accused of crimes have no protection from self-incrimination and can be compelled to testify
- testimony based on hearsay and opinion is allowed.

lawyer. The state will provide a lawyer for a person who cannot afford to hire one.

To convict a person of a crime, the evidence must establish guilt with proof "beyond a reasonable doubt." This means that there must be no sufficient basis placed in evidence at the trial that would logically indicate that the defendant did not commit the crime. Defendants have a constitutional right to a trial by jury. There will be a jury if either the state prosecutor or the defendant requests one. In criminal jury trials, the defendant usually is found guilty only if all the jurors vote to convict.

RESPONSIBILITY FOR THE CRIMINAL CONDUCT OF OTHERS

A person who knowingly aids another in the commission of a crime also is guilty of criminal wrongdoing. For example, one who acts as a lookout to warn a burglar of the approach of the police is an accomplice in the burglary. Similarly, one who plans the crime, or otherwise intentionally helps, is guilty of the same crime. In most jurisdictions, if someone is killed during the commission of a felony, all the people who participated are guilty of the homicide.

As discussed previously in this chapter, corporations can be held vicariously liable for the conduct of their employees. Also, officers of corporations may be criminally liable for their actions as managers.

CHECKPOINT

What constitutional rights would you have if you were accused of a crime?

DEFENSES TO CRIMINAL CHARGES

WHAT'S YOUR VERDICT?

Will and Zack were arrested for stealing a car. Both signed confessions at the police station. At their trial, they claimed that their right to due process had been violated. They said they had not been advised of their right to remain silent and to have a lawyer present when questioned.

If true, are those good defenses?

To insure the fair application of laws, a criminal defendant may often be able to avoid conviction in court by the use of one or more defenses. In criminal law, a **defense** is a legal position taken by an accused to defeat the charges against him or her. In court the state must prove that the defendant is guilty beyond a reasonable doubt.

© GETTY IMAGES/PHOTODISC

Why would it be important to be represented by an attorney if you were accused of a crime?

Even when the prosecution has conclusive evidence to show such guilt, all too often that evidence cannot be introduced due to procedural defenses. In addition, even if there is sufficient admissible evidence to show guilt, defendants also may use substantive defenses to excuse their conduct.

PROCEDURAL DEFENSES

Procedural defenses are based on problems with the way evidence is obtained or the way an accused person is arrested, questioned, tried, or punished. For example, a defendant who had confessed to a crime might say that she signed the confession only because she was threatened by the police. This would be a procedural defense.

Ignorance of the law is not a defense. The legal system assumes that everyone knows the law. Thus, if you park in a no-parking area because you did not see the sign, you have no defense. In *What's Your Verdict?* Will and Zack should have been advised of their rights at the time of the arrest. If they could prove they were not so advised, such a violation of their procedural rights under the Constitution would be a valid defense.

Why must police officers be very careful in the way that they arrest and question accused individuals?

© GETTY IMAGES/PHOTODISC

SUBSTANTIVE DEFENSES

Substantive defenses disprove, justify, or excuse the alleged crime. Most substantive defenses discredit the facts that the state sought to establish. In other words they discredit the very substance of the prosecution's case against the defendant. For example, an eyewitness may have placed the defendant at the scene of the crime. The defendant may establish a substantive defense by showing that he was in the hospital at the time of the alleged crime. Self-defense, criminal insanity, and immunity are other examples of substantive defenses.

Self-defense is the use of the force that appears to be reasonably necessary to the victim to prevent death, serious bodily harm, rape, or kidnapping. This defense also extends to members of one's family and household and to others whom one has a legal duty to protect. You may not use deadly force if non-deadly force appears reasonably sufficient. Only non-deadly force may be used to protect or recover property. You may not set deadly traps to protect unoccupied buildings. In addition, a civilian may not shoot a thief who is escaping with stolen property.

Criminal insanity generally exists when the accused does not know the difference between right and wrong. If the accused is criminally insane, there is no criminal intent and therefore no crime. At a trial, the defendant must prove the criminal insanity.

Immunity is freedom from prosecution even when one has committed the crime charged.

IN THIS CASE

A state law makes "hit-and-run" driving a crime. The law requires drivers of motor vehicles involved in an accident to stay at the scene, give their names and addresses, and show their driver's licenses. Barlow, who was arrested for violating this law, claimed that the law was unconstitutional. He said that the law violated his Fifth Amendment right against self-incrimination. In concluding the law was constitutional, the court said that the right against self-incrimination applies only to statements that would implicate a person in a crime. Merely identifying oneself as a party to an accident does not indicate guilt.

Sometimes one criminal may be granted immunity in exchange for an agreement to testify about the criminal conduct of several other criminals. In other instances, there is no agreement. Instead, the government grants immunity to a reluctant witness to remove the privilege against self-incrimination. A witness who refuses to testify after the grant of immunity is in contempt of court. **Contempt of court** is action that hinders the administration of justice. It is a crime punishable by imprisonment.

CHECKPOINT

Name the two defense categories and give an example of each.

PUNISHMENTS FOR CRIMES

WHAT'S YOUR VERDICT?

To conserve water, a city ordinance prohibited the practice of allowing water to run into the streets and sewers. Gill turned the water sprinklers on in her garden and forgot to turn them off. The water ran into the street all night. Gill was cited for violating the ordinance.

What is an appropriate penalty for this type of offense?

"Let the punishment fit the crime" is more easily said than done. Any penalty provided by law and imposed by a court is called a **punishment**. The purpose is not to remedy the wrong but rather to discipline the wrongdoer. If reasonably swift and certain, punishment should also deter others from similar behavior. Punishments for crimes range from fines, imprisonment, and in some cases, execution or death.

In *What's Your Verdict?* Gill was guilty of an infraction, which did not require criminal

© GETTY IMAGES/PHOTODISC

Why do you think society regards contempt of court a crime punishable by imprisonment?

intent. Nevertheless, her conduct was illegal so she would probably be fined. Criminal statutes ordinarily set maximum limits for punishment, but allow a judge discretion within those limits.

An accused person may agree to plead guilty to a less serious crime in exchange for having a more serious charge dropped. This is called **plea bargaining**. The accused voluntarily gives up the right to a public trial to avoid the risk of a greater penalty if convicted. Plea bargains must be approved by the judge of the court with the criminal jurisdiction over the case.

CHECKPOINT

What is the purpose of punishment for a crime?

Assessment

lawxtra.swlearning.com

THINK ABOUT LEGAL CONCEPTS

1. The authors of the Constitution believed it was better for society to give individuals too much liberty than to allow the government too much power. **True or False?**

2. An individual who helped in a car jacking in which someone was killed by another car jacker can be charged with murder. **True or False?**

3. Self-defense is a (a) procedural defense (b) substantive defense.

4. Which of the following is not a good defense to criminal accusations? (a) immunity (b) insanity (c) indebtedness (d) all are good defenses

5. Immunity is never granted to someone who has committed the crime. **True or False?**

6. A prosecutor offering an accused an opportunity to plead guilty to a lesser charge in return for the accused testifying against other involved parties is called _?_.

THINK CRITICALLY ABOUT EVIDENCE

Study the situation, answer the questions, and then prepare arguments to support your answers.

7. Sharon spent the weekend with her friend Amelia. Amelia proposed a plan for shoplifting CDs from a local music store. Sharon was to go to the store clerk, say she felt ill, and then pretend to faint. This distraction would allow Amelia, at the other end of the store, to place CDs in her shopping bag without risk of being seen. At first Sharon said she could not do something like that because it is against the law. Amelia argued that Sharon would not be breaking the law, only Amelia would. Is Amelia right? If a person can think of a way to profit by violating the law without risk, what reasons are there for not breaking the law?

8. Art is charged with kidnapping. After listening to all the evidence, 11 of the 12 jurors found him guilty. The twelfth juror voted he was not guilty. Has Art been convicted of the crime?

9. Rosa shot a burglar in her home when he was about to enter her bedroom with a knife in his hand. What would be a good defense for her?

10. John left his home state of Missouri early one afternoon to drive to New Mexico. Eventually the sun set, but John continued on. Hours later, while driving 70 mph on an interstate highway east of Amarillo, he was pulled over by the Texas highway patrol. The last speed limit sign John had seen had been in Oklahoma and had read 70 mph. As she issued the ticket, the officer noted that the speed limit in Texas on interstates is 70 during the day but drops to 65 at night. John protested he was unaware of the change. Was he still guilty of speeding?

PREVENT LEGAL DIFFICULTIES

As a citizen . . .

1. Work to know the law and to live within its requirements.

2. Never intentionally do something illegal.

3. Never misrepresent a fact to obtain the goods or services of others.

4. Never threaten others with an illegal act to cause them to do something.

5. If arrested, immediately contact a lawyer.

6. Know your rights and make use of them.

CONCEPTS IN BRIEF

4-1 Criminal Law

1. A crime is a punishable offense against society. In order to convict, the prosecution must establish a duty, an act or omission in violation of the duty, and, in most cases, criminal intent.

2. Crimes are generally categorized as felonies or misdemeanors. Some states also recognize infractions.

3. Some crimes in which a business may be the victim are robbery, burglary, shoplifting, employee theft, passing bad checks, vandalism, receiving stolen property, and embezzlement.

4. Some crimes in which a business person or firm may be the perpetrator are income tax evasion, price fixing, false advertising, and bribery.

5. Generally, any adult capable of knowing the difference between right and wrong is considered sane under the law.

4-2 Criminal Procedure

6. Anyone accused of committing a crime has certain constitutional rights. These due process rights involve freedom from arrest without probable cause; the right to be represented by a lawyer; the right to cross-examine witnesses; the right to not testify against oneself; and the right to a speedy, public, fair trial.

7. Procedural defenses relate to the way evidence is obtained or the way the accused person is arrested, questioned, tried, or punished. Substantive defenses disprove, justify, or excuse the alleged crime. Common substantive defenses are self-defense, criminal insanity, and immunity.

8. Crimes are punishable by fine, imprisonment, or both. Some states execute certain criminals.

YOUR LEGAL VOCABULARY

Match each statement with the term that it best defines. Some terms may not be used.

1. Legal position that disproves, justifies, or otherwise excuses an alleged crime

2. Accused person admitting guilt to a less serious crime in exchange for having a more serious charge dropped

3. The use of the force that appears to be reasonably necessary to the victim to prevent death, serious bodily harm, rape, or kidnapping

4. Punishable offense against society

5. Action that hinders the administration of justice

6. Crime punishable by either a fine of more than $1,000 or by confinement for more than one year in a state prison or by death

7. Substituted criminal liability

8. Freedom from prosecution even when one has committed the crime charged

9. Any penalty provided by law and imposed by a court

a. contempt of court
b. crime
c. defense
d. felony
e. immunity
f. misdemeanor
g. plea bargaining
h. probable cause
i. procedural defense
j. punishment
k. self-defense
l. substantive defense
m. vicarious criminal liability
n. white-collar crime

10. Crime punishable by confinement in a county or city jail for less than one year, by fine, or both

11. A criminal defense based on how the evidence was obtained or how the accused was arrested, questioned, or tried

REVIEW LEGAL CONCEPTS

12. Why must criminal statutes carefully and clearly define the prohibited behavior?

13. Why are certain acts crimes in one state and not another? Why are there varying levels of punishment for the same crime in different states?

14. Explain the significance of the main steps in a criminal prosecution. Is the cause of justice served when a defense attorney gets his client off because of a "loophole" in the law? Consider both the short-term and the long-term consequences.

WRITE ABOUT LEGAL CONCEPTS

15. An old adage of the law states, "As society becomes less secure, criminal punishments become more severe." Write a paragraph relating this to the United States' experience with the death penalty and other punishments in the last few decades.

16. **HOT DEBATE** Write a paragraph debating whether or not the protections afforded those accused of criminal activity by the Constitution are mainly used by individuals who are truly guilty to avoid their deserved punishment.

MAKE ACADEMIC CONNECTIONS

17. **SOCIAL STUDIES** As a result of a U.S. Supreme Court decision in the early 1960s, improperly or illegally obtained evidence cannot be used to convict an accused in the court system. This is referred to as the "exclusionary rule," as the evidence is excluded from consideration by the court. It was put into place to stop police from using the wrong tactics to obtain incriminating evidence. Other developed countries handle such actions by their police force in a different manner. Research how England and two other European countries discipline improper or illegal attempts to gather evidence by their police and whether or not the evidence developed thereby can be used against the accused at trial.

THINK CRITICALLY ABOUT EVIDENCE

Study the situation, answer the questions, and then prepare arguments to support your answers.

18. Buttler, a contractor, ordered $24,600 worth of plywood from K.C. Lumber Company without intending to pay for it. Buttler told the company it was to be used in building houses in a subdivision. When Buttler failed to pay for the plywood, the lumber company investigated. Its investigation revealed that after the plywood was delivered to the building site, Buttler had it transported across the state line, hidden, and resold for cash. A criminal complaint was then filed against Buttler. With what crimes could she be charged?

19. Bif was in Gail's office waiting to go to lunch with her. Gail owned a business in competition with Bif's business. When Gail excused herself to go to the restroom, Bif looked at her computer screen and saw part of a customer list. Bif had a blank diskette which he inserted into the computer. He quickly copied the file onto his diskette. Then he put his diskette in his pocket. The entire action took only 20 seconds. Bif finished long before Gail returned. Has Bif committed a crime? If so, what crime?

20. Paula's boyfriend moved to her home town, Oklahoma City, from Houston, Texas. Two weeks after he arrived, he asked her to phone his bank in Houston and inquire about his balance. She did so as a favor to him and found out the balance was over $40,000. As soon as she told him, he left and drove to Houston to remove it from his account. In Houston, he was arrested by the FBI for fraud and several related crimes. Paula was then charged with the federal crime of making a phone call across state lines for the furtherance of a fraudulent scheme. Her boyfriend only knew the scheme had been successful by Paula's report of the large balance in his old account. What would be a possible defense for Paula?

21. The Royal Scotsman Inn built a motel that did not comply with the building code. Therefore, Scotsman was refused an occupancy permit. The chair of the county council approached a representative of the motel and offered to have "everything taken care of" in exchange for the payment of $12,000. Scotsman was faced with the possibility of a large loss of revenue. Therefore, Scotsman agreed to pay the money. The Federal Bureau of Investigation arrested the council chairperson after tape recording the discussion and seeing the exchange of the money. What crime did the council chairperson commit? (*United States v. Price*, 507 F.2d 1349)

22. Basic Construction Company was engaged in the road-paving business. Two of its lower-level managers rigged bids by giving competitors the prices that Basic would bid for work. That is a criminal violation of the Sherman Antitrust Act. Will Basic be criminally liable for the conduct of its manager? (*United States v. Basic Construction Company*, 711 F.2d 570)

23. Pack was the president of Acme Markets, Inc., a large national retail food chain. Both Pack and Acme were charged with violating criminal provisions of the federal Food, Drug, and Cosmetics Act. They were charged with allowing interstate shipments of food contaminated by rodents in an Acme warehouse. Pack defended himself by stating that although he was aware of the problem, he had delegated responsibility for the sanitary conditions of food storage to responsible subordinates. Can Pack be criminally liable in these circumstances? (*United States v. Pack*, 95 S. Ct. 1903)

24. Feinberg owned a cigar store in a poor neighborhood of Philadelphia. He sold cans of Sterno, which contains about 4 percent alcohol, to people in the neighborhood who mixed it with water and drank it to become intoxicated. After conducting this business for some time, Feinberg purchased a quantity of Institutional Sterno. It contained 54 percent alcohol. The cans were marked "Danger—Poison," and had a picture of a skull and crossbones; Feinberg did not warn customers of the difference. As a result, 33 people died from alcohol poisoning. Did Feinberg commit a crime? (*Commonwealth v. Feinberg*, 234 A.2d 913, Pa.)

25. To help attract convention business to the city, a group of hotels, restaurants, and various other businesses in Portland, Oregon, formed an association. The association was funded by contributions. To provide incentives for contributions to the association, its members agreed to stop doing or curtail doing business with those who did not contribute. As a part of this effort, the Portland Hilton Hotel's purchasing agent threatened a Hilton supplier with the loss of the hotel's business unless such a contribution was forthcoming. Such activities and the agreement behind them are criminal violations of the federal antitrust laws. As a result, the federal government charged Hilton accordingly and a guilty verdict was returned at the trial. Hilton appealed, as it had been shown in court that the manager and assistant manager of the hotel had, on at least two occasions, told the purchasing agent not to participate in the boycott. He was instead to follow corporate policy and purchase supplies only on the basis of price, quality, and service. Should the decision be reversed on appeal given the employee's actions were clearly against corporate policy and directions by corporate executives? (*United States v. Hilton Hotels Corporation*, 467 F.2d 1000)

CASE FOR LEGAL THINKING

MIRANDA V. ARIZONA
USSC 86 S. CT. 1602

BACKGROUND In 1963 a man named Ernesto Miranda, who had previously been described in court records as "seriously disturbed and having pronounced sexual fantasies," was arrested at his home on suspicion of rape and kidnapping. He was then taken to a Phoenix police station.

FACTS At the police station, the suspect was identified by the complaining witness, an eighteen-year-old woman. Thereafter, he was questioned by two officers. He was not advised of his right to have an attorney present at such a questioning. After a lengthy interrogation of approximately two hours, during which time his defense counsel was allegedly demanding to see him but not allowed to do so, the officers convinced Miranda to sign a confession. The form of the confession as signed by Miranda included a statement that he was making the statement voluntarily and without being coerced by threats or promises of immunity. It also indicated, in a clear, typed paragraph at the top of the statement, that the statement was attested to with "full knowledge of my legal rights and the understanding that anything in the statement may be used against me."

LOWER COURT At the jury trial for his crimes, the written confession was placed into evidence over the defense counsel's objection. Both interrogating officers testified also to the nature of the oral confession Miranda made during the interrogation. Ultimately, Miranda was convicted of the crimes and sentenced to 20 to 30 years imprisonment on each count.

APPEALS Miranda appealed his conviction to the Supreme Court of Arizona. That court upheld the lower court's conviction of Miranda on both counts. The Arizona Supreme Court, in reaching its decision, emphasized that Miranda did not ever request counsel. Miranda then took his appeal to the U.S. Supreme Court, alleging that he had not been informed of all his constitutional rights.

ISSUE The U.S. Supreme Court reviewed the matter in order to decide if Miranda could or should be convicted of any crime on the basis of his confession "obtained from defendant during incommunicado interrogation in police-dominated atmosphere, without full warning as to his or her constitutional rights."

DECISION In an opinion written for the U.S. Supreme Court by then Chief Justice, Earl Warren, the Court decided that the confession was inadmissible as evidence in the trial and reversed the conviction. It also, thereafter, placed the burden on the government to demonstrate that, if the defendant waived his rights, such a waiver was made knowingly and intelligently.

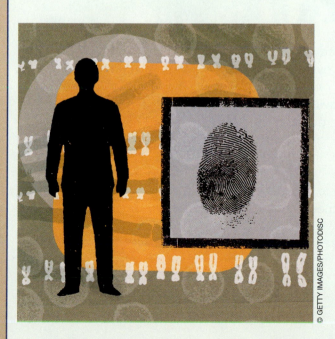

© GETTY IMAGES/PHOTODISC

PRACTICE JUDGING

1. If we are all charged with knowing the law, how could the court find that Miranda needed to be informed of his rights by the state?

2. Could Miranda be tried again for the same crime?

3. What justification would the Court have in imposing such a burden on the police? Would they not be practicing law by giving such legal advice?

4. Was excluding the evidence (the confession) the only sanction available to the U.S. Supreme Court? Can you think of some other sanctions that would still allow such evidence to be used but protect the innocent person who might be subjected to such treatment.

Civil Law and Procedure

HOT DEBATE

© GETTY IMAGES/PHOTODISC

Every time Chanelle's science teacher asked her a question during class, the teacher walked over to her desk, squatted down, and placed a hand on Chanelle's thigh. Chanelle found this behavior extremely offensive. Finally, in private, she politely asked the teacher to stop. Although the teacher seemingly agreed, the next time Chanelle raised her hand the teacher behaved the same way. However, this time when the teacher extended her hand to place it on Chanelle's leg, Chanelle twisted violently away and slammed her knee into the other side of her desk.

Where Do You Stand?

1. What corrective action could Chanelle take within the school structure?
2. Regardless of whether or not she tries to resolve the problem within the school's structure, has Chanelle received a personal injury for which she could bring suit in court?

Private Injuries vs. Public Offenses

▼ GOALS

- **Distinguish a crime from a tort**
- **Identify the elements of torts**
- **Explain why one person may be responsible for another's tort**

HOW DO CRIMES AND TORTS DIFFER?

WHAT'S YOUR VERDICT?

To support his family and still pursue a college education, JJ worked for a delivery service from 3:30 A.M. until his college classes began at 9 every weekday morning. He then student taught as a basketball coach after classes. Returning home each evening he would care for his children until his wife finished her workday at 10 P.M. Early one morning, JJ fell asleep at the wheel of the delivery truck and crashed it into an oncoming car. JJ and the other driver, Shirley, were seriously injured and the vehicles were "totaled."

Does JJ's conduct represent a criminal or civil wrong or both?

mitted an offense against society—the crime of reckless driving. Police will investigate the crime, and then give him a ticket or possibly arrest him. A county or district attorney will prosecute him in a criminal trial. If convicted, he may be fined or jailed.

JJ also committed a tort by injuring Shirley and her property (the car). She may bring a civil suit against him. If she wins, Shirley can obtain a judgment against JJ as compensation for her injuries. Thus, JJ's reckless driving caused him to be liable both criminally and civilly. He is criminally liable because his offense was committed against society. For this he may incur a fine and/or a jail term. He is civilly liable for money damages to Shirley for the injury he caused her and her property.

CHECKPOINT

What is the difference between a crime and a tort?

A crime is an offense against society. It is a public wrong. A **tort**, in contrast, is a private or civil wrong. It is an offense against an individual. If someone commits a tort, the person injured as a result can sue and obtain a judgment for **damages**. This is a monetary award intended to compensate the injured party for the harm done to her or him. From society's standpoint, the money is meant to restrain the injured individual's desire to exact revenge by taking the law into her or his own hands. Doing so would cause chaos.

One act can be both a tort and a crime. In *What's Your Verdict?* JJ com-

What is the purpose of an injured party's receiving money damages for a tort committed against him or her?

© GETTY IMAGES/PHOTODISC

ELEMENTS OF A TORT

WHAT'S YOUR VERDICT?

On a windy autumn day, Mason was burning dry leaves in his backyard. When he went inside to answer a telephone call, flames from the fire leaped to the next-door neighbor's fence and then to a tool shed where a small can of gasoline exploded. Soon the neighbor's house was ablaze, and it burned to the ground.

Did Mason commit a tort?

Like criminal law, tort law is a broad legal category. Just as there are many specific crimes, there also are many specific torts. Certain elements are common to most torts. In a trial, these elements must be proved to establish liability (legal responsibility).

The elements of a tort are

1. duty (a legal obligation to do or not to do something)
2. breach (a violation of the duty)
3. injury (a harm that is recognized by the law)
4. causation (proof that the breach caused the injury)

DUTY By law, you have certain rights. You also have certain duties related to respecting the rights of others. The following are the duties created by tort law:

1. the duty not to injure another (including bodily injury, injury to someone's reputation, or invasion of someone's privacy)
2. the duty not to interfere with the property rights of others, for example, by trespassing on their land
3. the duty not to interfere with the economic rights of others, such as the right to contract

Whether or not a duty exists in a certain situation is a question of law for the judge to decide. A judge will make this decision by consulting state case and statutory law and, on occasion, federal law.

VIOLATION OF THE DUTY A violation (or breach) of the duty must be proved before the injured party can collect damages. Whether a breach of a tort duty has occurred is almost always a question of fact for a jury to decide.

Many torts acknowledge a breach only when the defendant possesses a certain mental state at the time of the breach. Some torts require that the breach be intentional. These are classified as *intentional torts*. In other torts, intent is not required. It is enough if the breach occurred because someone was careless or negligent. These torts, based on carelessness, are classified as **negligence**.

In still other torts, even carelessness is not required. Liability is imposed simply because a duty was violated and this caused injury. The last classification, where neither intent nor carelessness is required, is classified as strict liability.

INJURY Generally, injury resulting from the breach of duty must be proved. Thus, if you act recklessly, but no one is injured, there usually is no tort.

Apply the elements of a tort to determine whether Mason in *What's Your Verdict?* committed a tort in allowing the fire to occur. Check your answer against the explanation on the next page.

© GETTY IMAGES/PHOTODISC

CAUSATION Causation means that breach of the duty caused the injury. There are degrees of causation. For example, one can argue that the first people on earth are the ultimate cause of every injury that occurs in the world today. However, when the amount of causation is great enough for it to be recognized by the law, it is called *proximate cause*. Generally, proximate cause exists when it is reasonably foreseeable that a breach of duty will result in an injury.

Applying these elements to *What's Your Verdict?* Mason committed a tort because (1) he owed a duty to the neighbors not to injure their property; (2) he breached the duty when he left the fire unattended so it spread to the neighbor's property; (3) the injury occurred when the neighbor's house was burned; and (4) leaving the fire unattended was a proximate cause of the loss of the fence, the tool shed, and the house. Therefore, the neighbor can obtain a judgment against Mason for the value of the loss.

CHECKPOINT
Name the four elements of a tort.

RESPONSIBILITY FOR ANOTHER'S TORTS

WHAT'S YOUR VERDICT?

Hunt was taking riding lessons from Saddleback Stables. Patterson, the Saddleback instructor, was a skilled rider although only 15 years old. Nevertheless, during a lesson while leading the horse Hunt was riding, Patterson negligently dropped the bridle. As a result, the horse bolted and Hunt was thrown to the ground and injured.

Who was liable for Hunt's injuries?

With few exceptions, all persons, including minors, are personally responsible for their conduct and are therefore liable for their torts. Even children or insane persons may be held liable for injuring others. Certainly, in *What's Your Verdict?* Patterson's negligence would result in his being liable to Hunt for Hunt's injuries. In addition, Saddleback Stables can be held liable for the negligence of its employee Patterson. In such cases, the injured party may sue both employer and employee.

When one person is liable for the torts of another, the liability is called *vicarious liability*. For example, parents may be liable if they give their children "dangerous instrumentalities," such as guns, without proper instruction. Similarly, parents may be liable for their children's continuing dangerous habits. For example, if a child continues to throw rocks at trains and vehicles, the parents may be liable if they fail to stop the child's behavior.

In some states parents are liable, by statute, up to a specified amount of money for property damage by their minor children. This is usually designed to cover vandalism and malicious destruction of school property. Most states also provide that parents are liable, up to the limits of financial responsibility laws, for damages negligently caused by their children while operating motor vehicles.

CHECKPOINT
What parties might be held responsible for another person's tort?

IN THIS CASE

Bottomless Barges, Inc. (BBI), contracted with a coastal city to barge the city's untreated sewerage some 300 miles into the ocean and dump it. This activity was permitted by the federal government due to the city's lack of funds needed to build an adequate treatment facility. Ollee Facktory, an employee of BBI, dumped an afternoon run only 35 miles offshore in order to get back to land in time for a date. Various diseases, including minor cases of cholera, broke out in several coastal towns. As a result, BBI was sued by individual plaintiffs and the government and recovered against due to its vicarious liability for Facktory's actions.

Assessment

lawxtra.swlearning.com

THINK ABOUT LEGAL CONCEPTS

1. A single act can be both a tort and a crime. **True or False?**

2. The degree of causation of a tort great enough to be recognized by law is called (a) proximate cause (b) intimate cause (c) incidental cause (d) none of the above

3. A tort is considered to be an offense against society. **True or False?**

4. In order to establish liability for a tort, all of the following must be proved except (a) duty (b) breach of duty (c) harm recognized by law (d) vicarious liability.

5. An insane person cannot be held liable for a tort. **True or False?**

6. When one party is held responsible for the tort of another, the liability is called _ ?_ liability.

7. Torts based on carelessness are classified as negligence. **True or False?**

THINK CRITICALLY ABOUT EVIDENCE

Study the situation, answer the questions, and then prepare arguments to support your answers.

8. Philip drove a tractor-trailer rig onto a ferry boat. He left the rig in gear because of a problem with its brakes. Posted regulations prohibited the starting of engines before docking, but when the ferry was about 50 feet from the dock, Philip started his engine. That caused the tractor-trailer to jump forward and strike Herrick's car, which in turn hit Patton's car. Patton's car, at the head of the line, crashed through the ferry's barricades and plunged into the water. The car could not be recovered. What was the tort duty in this case? Where was the breach of the duty? What were the injuries? What was the proximate cause of the injury to Patton's car?

9. Felicia carelessly left a campfire before it was completely extinguished. The fire spread through the woods and caused the destruction of a nearby lodge. Is Felicia liable to the owners of the lodge for the building? Is she liable to the lodge owners for the loss of income until the lodge can be restored? Is she liable to the persons who had reservations for the lodge but whose trips are now ruined?

10. Todd let his 10-year-old daughter, Julie, drive the family car. While she was driving, she turned her head to say something to her friend in the back seat, and swerved off the road. The car hit and destroyed a mailbox and damaged a fence. Who is liable for the damages to the property?

11. As a police officer, Maureen was authorized to carry her handgun with her. While darting into a store to pick up her dry cleaning, she left the gun in her car hidden under the seat. Her 9-year-old son found the pistol and accidently shot his friend in the leg. Is Maureen liable for the injury?

12. Patrick borrowed his friend John's car to impress a young lady he was dating. It was a new luxury car that John had saved four years to purchase. The paint on the car turned colors under various climatic and light conditions. While on the date, Patrick drove the car down a public road that had just been repaved with hot oil and gravel. The result was several nicks in the paint from flying rocks. Patrick then parked in front of his favorite restaurant, a sports pub on the far side of town. While in the restaurant, Patrick heard a special weather report that a thunderstorm with large hail was sweeping across the area and would arrive over the restaurant in ten minutes. Unfortunately, for John's car, the date was going too well to break off and move the car under cover. Consequently, the hail left a multitude of pock marks on the top of the car. Is Patrick legally responsible for the damage done by the gravel, oil, and hail? Why or why not?

Intentional Torts, Negligence, and Strict Liability

▼ **GOALS**
- **Identify common intentional torts**
- **Recognize the elements of negligence**
- **Explain the basis for strict liability**

WHAT ARE THE MOST COMMON INTENTIONAL TORTS?

WHAT'S YOUR VERDICT?

During deer-hunting season, Hart drove miles into the country in search of game. He parked his pickup truck along a dirt road, climbed a fence, and hiked into the woods. Hart thought the land was part of a national forest. However, it actually belonged to Quincy, who had posted "No Trespassing" signs. Confronted by Quincy, Hart apologized for his mistake and left.

Had Hart committed an intentional tort?

Intentional torts are torts in which the defendant possessed the intent or purpose to inflict the resultant injury. These torts contrast with negligence and strict liability, where intent to produce the injury is not required. There are numerous intentional torts. The number continues to grow as society and its environment changes. There are nine common intentional torts.

ASSAULT

The tort of assault occurs when one person intentionally puts another in reasonable fear of an offensive or harmful bodily contact. The threat can be made with words or gestures. But to be considered "reasonable" from the viewpoint of the potential victim, the threat must be believable. In other words, there has to be an ability to carry it out. The threatened injury can be physical: a person may raise a fist threatening to punch you. Or the threatened injury can be offensive: a person might threaten unwanted sexual touching by attempting to kiss you.

IN THIS CASE

Spencer, elderly and totally blind, thought Wills had swindled him. Spencer told Wills that he was going to "beat your face to a pulp." Because it was obvious that Spencer could not carry out his threat, there was no assault.

BATTERY

A person has a duty to refrain from harmful or offensive touching of another. An intentional breach of the duty is a battery. Shooting, pushing in anger, spitting on, or throwing a pie in another's face are all batteries. An assault frequently precedes a battery.

Angrily raising a clenched fist and then striking someone in the face involves first an assault (the raised fist) and then a battery (the blow to the face). When the victim is hit without warning from behind, there is a battery without an assault.

© GETTY IMAGES/PHOTODISC

Is the action in this photo an example of assault or battery? Justify your answer.

Even though there is harmful or offensive touching, there may be no battery if the contact is not intentional. Also, the contact may be justified. For example, when you act in self-defense, you have not committed a battery. Further, there may be consent to the contact. Thus, in a boxing match, there is no battery because the boxers consent to the offensive touching.

FALSE IMPRISONMENT

False imprisonment is the intentional confinement of a person against the person's will and without lawful privilege. People may be deprived of freedom of movement in many ways. For example, they may be handcuffed; locked in a room, car, or jail; told in a threatening way to stay in one place; or otherwise denied their liberty. Consent occurs when they agree to being confined. For example, when a burglary suspect sits voluntarily in a police car to describe his actions over the last hour, the suspect consents to being detained.

When the police have probable cause to arrest people, they are privileged to imprison them. Privilege justifies the imprisonment. But if the police mistake the identity of one person for another, they may commit false imprisonment in the course of the arrest. Merchants in many states have a privilege to detain a person if they have a reasonable basis for believing the person was shoplifting. If they detain persons against their will without a reasonable basis, they falsely imprison them.

DEFAMATION

Statements about people can injure them. If a false statement injures a person's reputation or good name, it may constitute the tort of **defamation**. If the defamation is spoken, it is *slander*. If the defamation is written or printed, it is *libel*. To be legally defamatory, the statement must

1. be false (truth is a complete defense)
2. be communicated to a third person (your reputation is not harmed if no other person hears or reads the lie)
3. bring the victim into disrepute, contempt, or ridicule by others.

In slander suits, you must show that you have suffered an actual physical loss, or damages, as a result of the slanderous remark. Exceptions to this occur in cases where the oral statements are to the effect that the plaintiff committed a serious crime, has a loathsome disease, or injures someone in his or her profession or business. In libel cases, you are presumed to have suffered a loss, and so these damages do not have to be shown to the court.

Exceptions are made to the law of defamation in order to encourage open discussion of issues of public concern. For example, legislators' statements, even those made with malice, are immune

Cyberlaw

Defamatory statements published on Internet bulletin boards, e-mails, and the like, are considered libel due to the somewhat permanent nature of the medium. This often is vital to a successful suit for defamation as damages are presumed to exist in the case of libel and do not have to be proven to the court. The remaining question becomes who to sue. This, however, is the hard part. Sections of the Communications Decency Act of 1996 and several court decisions provide protections to Internet service providers and bulletin board operators. Such parties generally are considered to be immune from suits brought to make up for the harm done by such statements. However, they may be held liable if it can be shown that they exercised editorial or full control of the material posted or transmitted or, at least, had knowledge of the specific defamatory contents. This has proven very difficult to do.

THINK ABOUT IT
Why do you think it has been so difficult for people to win libel suits against Internet bulletin board operators or Internet service providers?

Angstrom went into a jewelry store and asked to see an expensive ring. The clerk handed it to him. While holding it, he asked the price of a matching necklace. As the clerk looked down to check the tag on the necklace, Angstrom inadvertently laid the ring out of the clerk's sight behind a display on the counter. He then turned and started to walk out of the store. The clerk, thinking he was stealing the ring, yelled, "stop thief," and with other store personnel, grabbed him and threw him to the floor. When Angstrom was finally able to make the personnel listen, they found the ring and let him go with apologies. Now he is considering bringing suit because of their hasty action. Would it be ethical for him to do so, as it appeared to be an honest mistake on the part of the store personnel?

from liability if made during legislative meetings. Judges, lawyers, jurors, witnesses, and other parties in judicial proceedings are also immune from liability for statements made during the actual trial or hearing. Similarly, liability for defamatory statements about public officials or prominent personalities does not exist unless the statements were made with malice. That means the statement when issued was known to be false and was made with an evil intent.

INVASION OF PRIVACY

People are entitled to keep personal matters private. This is the right to privacy. Congress has stated that "the right of privacy is a personal and fundamental right protected by the Constitution of the United States." Uninvited intrusion into (or interruption of) an individual's personal relationships and activities is the tort of **invasion of privacy**. Such unwelcome and unlawful intrusion into one's private life may cause outrage, mental suffering, or humiliation.

This right includes freedom from unnecessary publicity regarding personal matters. So, unlike the law regarding the tort of defamation, publi-

cation of even a true statement about someone may be an invasion of privacy. This is because, as the U.S. Supreme Court put it, you should be protected when you have a reasonable "expectation of privacy." Thus, two-way mirrors in the women's restroom of a gas station would constitute an invasion of privacy.

The right to privacy also includes freedom from commercial exploitation of one's name, picture, or endorsement without permission. The right to privacy bans illegal eavesdropping by any listening device, interference with telephone calls, and unauthorized opening of letters and telegrams. However, the right of privacy is not unlimited. For example, the police are permitted to tap telephone lines secretly if they have a warrant to do so. Also, public figures, such as politicians, actors, and people in the news, give up much of their right to privacy when they step into the public domain.

What are some situations related to the right to privacy that affect your life?

TRESPASS TO LAND

The tort of **trespass to land** is entry onto the property of another without the owner's consent. However, trespass may consist of other forms of interference with the possession of property. Dumping rubbish on the land of another or breaking the windows of a neighbor's house also are trespasses. Intent is required to commit the tort of trespass. However, the only requirement is that the intruder intended to be on the particular property. If a person were thrown onto another's land, there would be no intent and no trespass. If a person thought she was walking on her own property, but was mistaken, there would be a trespass because she intended to be there. Thus, in *What's Your Verdict?* Hart was guilty of trespass, even though he thought he was in a national forest.

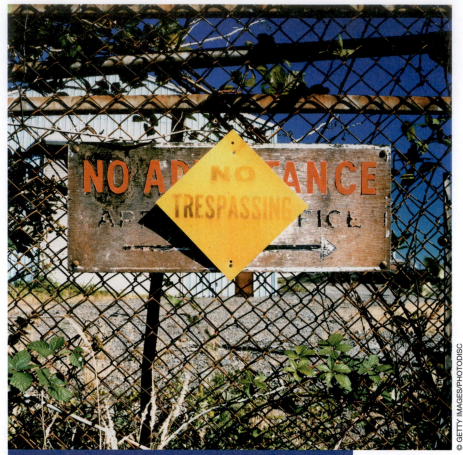

In order for the tort of trespass to occur, what would be required of the person who enters this property without the owner's permission?

© GETTY IMAGES/PHOTODISC

CONVERSION

People who own personal property, such as diamond rings, have the right to control their possession and their use. This right is violated if the property is stolen, destroyed, or used in a manner inconsistent with the owner's rights. If that happens, a **conversion** occurs. A thief is always a converter.

Conversion occurs even when the converter does not know that there is a conversion. So, the innocent buyer of stolen goods is a converter. The party injured by the conversion can receive damages. Or the converter can, in effect, be compelled to purchase the converted goods from their owner.

INTERFERENCE WITH CONTRACTUAL RELATIONS

Parties to a contract may be able to breach the contract if they pay for the injury suffered by the other party; that is, if they pay damages.

However if a third party encourages the breach party in any way, that third party may be liable in tort to the non-breaching party. This is called the tort of *interference with contractual relations.*

FRAUD

Fraud occurs when there is an intentional misrepresentation of an existing important fact (that is, a lie). The misrepresentation must be relied on and cause the victim to part with a legal right or something valuable.

Ordinarily a statement of opinion is not considered fraudulent. This is because the hearer should recognize that the statement is the speaker's personal view.

CHECKPOINT

Name at least six of the nine most common intentional torts.

WHAT CONSTITUTES NEGLIGENCE?

WHAT'S YOUR VERDICT?

Britt was driving home late one rainy night after drinking alcohol all evening. With only one working headlight, she raced down residential streets at speeds up to 50 miles per hour. Meanwhile, Yee was slowly backing her station wagon out of her driveway, but she failed to look both ways when she should have. Britt rammed into the right rear end of Yee's car. Yee's station wagon was badly damaged, and she was injured.

Can Yee collect from Britt?

Negligence is the most common tort. Intent to injure is not required for this tort. Only carelessness is required for negligence. It is determined through the recognition of a duty, breach of that duty, causation, and injury.

DUTY IMPOSED BY NEGLIGENCE

The general duty imposed by negligence law is the reasonable-person standard. This duty requires that you act with the care, prudence, and good judgment of a reasonable person so as not to cause injury to others. In court, the trier of fact (typically a jury) is asked how the reasonable person would have behaved under the circumstances. The answer to this question sets the standard of duty against which the defendant's actions will be compared.

For certain individuals, a different degree of care is applied. For example, children under age seven are held to be incapable of negligent conduct. Older children are only required to act with the care that a reasonable child of like age, intelligence, and experience would act. If, however, a child undertakes an adult activity, such as driving a boat or a car, the child is held to the adult standard.

Professionals and skilled tradespersons are held to a higher degree of care in their work. These persons are required to work with the degree of care and skill that is normally possessed by members of the profession or trade. Thus, an attorney must act with the care

If the driver of this aquacycle is twelve years old, would she be negligent if she ran into a swimmer? Why or why not?

and skill normally possessed by other attorneys in his or her community. Similarly, a plumber must perform work with the care and skill normally exercised by other plumbers in the community.

BREACH OF DUTY

The "reasonable-person" standard defines the duty. A defendant's actual conduct, such as Britt's in *What's Your Verdict?* is then compared with the reasonable-person standard to determine whether a violation of the duty has occurred. You could conclude that a reasonable person would drive a car only at a safe speed, only when sober, and at night only when the car's lights work. Because Britt engaged in speeding, driving while intoxicated, and driving at night without proper lights, she clearly breached the reasonable-person standard.

CAUSATION AND INJURY

As with other torts, the violation of the duty must be the proximate cause of the injury. In *What's Your Verdict?* Britt's speeding was a breach of the duty and it is reasonably foreseeable that speeding will cause injury. In fact, speeding was the cause of the property damage to the station wagon and the personal injury to Yee.

DEFENSES TO NEGLIGENCE

In several states a plaintiff cannot recover for loss caused by another's negligence if the plaintiff also was negligent. This is the old common law defense of *contributory negligence.* For example, in *What's Your Verdict?* Yee backed up without looking left or right. That and Britt's speeding were causes of the accident. So Yee was contributorily negligent. If she lived in a state that recognizes contributory negligence, she could not recover anything from Britt. Under this legal rule, it does not matter that one party, like Britt, was very negligent and primarily responsible for causing the collision while the other, like Yee, was only slightly negligent.

Most states have substituted comparative negligence for contributory negligence. *Comparative negligence* applies when a plaintiff in a negligence action is partially at fault. In such a case the plaintiff is awarded damages, but they are reduced in proportion to the plaintiff's negligence. Some states do not allow a plaintiff whose negligence was greater than the defendant's to recover.

Assumption of the risk is another defense to negligence. If plaintiffs are aware of a danger, but decide to subject themselves to the risk, that is a defense. Suppose you walk into a fast-food restaurant and see a sign stating "Danger! This

© GETTY IMAGES/PHOTODISC

Bart broke his leg while playing tennis at night on a dark city tennis court. Do you think he would win a judgment against the city for his injury? Why or why not?

LEGAL RESEARCH

A World Trade Organization (WTO) panel in March of 2004 held that U.S. laws prohibiting gambling on the Internet are an unfair trade barrier and should be overturned. Nonetheless, due to worries about minors gambling, Congress may not heed the warning. Research the current state of such laws as the Internet Gambling Prohibition Act. Download a copy and review it for loopholes. Can you suggest improvements? Should it be repealed to satisfy the WTO? Why or why not?

floor is slippery due to mopping." Then, as you walk through the wet area, you slip, fall, and break your arm. The danger was created by the restaurant, but you assumed the risk after being informed of the danger. You could not recover in negligence because of the defense of assumption of the risk.

CHECKPOINT

Name the four elements that must be proven for an act to be negligent.

WHY IS STRICT LIABILITY NECESSARY?

WHAT'S YOUR VERDICT?

Mrs. Lamm went to a grocery store and placed a carton of a soft drink into her shopping cart. One of the bottles exploded and the broken glass cut her leg.

Can she collect in tort from the grocery store or the bottler?

Sometimes the law holds one liable in tort on the basis of absolute or **strict liability**. This is liability that exists even though the defendant was not negligent. In essence, strict liability makes the defendant liable if he or she engaged in a particular activity that resulted in injury. In strict liability, proof of both the activity and the injury substitutes for proof of a violation of a duty.

Engaging in abnormally dangerous activities, such as target practice, blasting, crop dusting with dangerous chemicals, or storing flammable liquids in large quantities, gives rise to strict liability. If you engage in activities of this type and someone is injured as a result, you will be liable.

Ownership of dangerous animals also subjects you to strict liability. Domesticated animals (dogs, cats, cows, and horses) are not considered dangerous unless the owner knows that the particular animal has behaved in such a way. Bears, tigers, snakes, elephants, and monkeys are examples of wild or dangerous animals. If the dangerous animal causes injury, the owner is strictly liable.

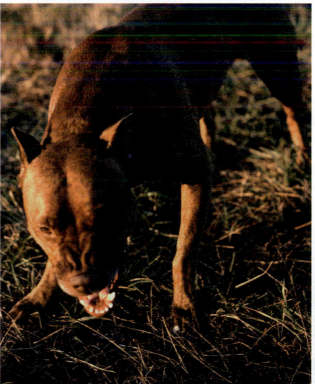

© GETTY IMAGES/PHOTODISC

Imagine you are the owner of this dog, and the dog just bit your young neighbor. Could you be held liable on the basis of strict liability? Why or why not?

A third strict liability activity is the sale of goods that are unreasonably dangerous. If the goods are defective, the defect makes them dangerous. If the defect causes an injury, any merchant who sells those goods is strictly liable, as is the manufacturer.

Under strict liability, the manufacturer and any sellers in the chain of distribution are liable to any buyer of the defective product who is injured by it. The effect of strict liability is that the manufacturer held liable will increase the price and thus spread the cost to all consumers of the product.

Without strict liability, the victim might not receive any compensation because negligence may be difficult to prove. In *What's Your Verdict?* Mrs. Lamm could collect from either the store or the bottler under strict liability. The bottle was defective, and this defect made the product unreasonably dangerous.

CHECKPOINT

What is strict liability and why is it necessary?

5-2 Assessment

lawxtra.swlearning.com

THINK ABOUT LEGAL CONCEPTS

1. An actual harmful or offensive touching must be shown to prove the tort of assault. **True or False?**

2. A person who has consented to be detained by another cannot recover for the tort of false imprisonment. **True or False?**

3. Spoken defamation is (a) libel (b) liable (c) slander (d) none of the above

4. An unwelcome and unlawful intrusion into one's personal life so as to cause outrage, mental suffering, or humiliation is the basis of the tort of _?_.

5. An innocent buyer of stolen goods cannot be liable for conversion because the buyer had no intent to keep the goods from their rightful owner. **True or False?**

6. Which of the following is not a defense to negligence? (a) contributory negligence (b) comparative negligence (c) violation of reasonable person standard (d) assumption of risk

7. Strict liability may exist even when a defendant is not negligent. **True or False?**

THINK CRITICALLY ABOUT EVIDENCE

Study the situation, answer the questions, and then prepare arguments to support your answers.

8. Betty was at a baseball game seated one row behind a famous movie star. When Betty stood up to cheer, she was bumped by the person beside her. She lost her balance and fell into the lap of the movie star. He sued her for the tort of assault. Who prevails?

9. Every morning on the way to work, Sharon rides an elevator up 14 floors. Sometimes, when it is crowded, the elevator operator intentionally bumps into her in an offensive way. What can Sharon do legally? What would be a likely defense for the operator?

10. Ham asked to borrow Lane's car to go to a movie with his girlfriend. Lane gave him permission. After the movie, Lane decided to drive to a city some 50 miles away to see a friend. Has he committed the tort of conversion?

11. Ashleigh has a pet boa constrictor named Pauline. She keeps it in the most expensive, escape-proof cage she can find. Regardless, the boa escapes and kills the neighbor's famed show cat which was valued at more than $5,000. Will Ashleigh be liable?

Civil Procedure

REMEDIES AVAILABLE IN A CIVIL SUIT

WHAT'S YOUR VERDICT?

Horsley, the owner of a dry cleaning store, lived next door to Eardly, who was the editor of a small newspaper in their town. The two quarreled frequently and became enemies. As a consequence, when Eardly published a story on the drug problem in the town, he identified Horsley as "a drug dealer." This statement was untrue and defamatory.

What kind of damages could Horsley collect from Eardly in a lawsuit?

Two types of remedies are generally available if the situation warrants in a civil lawsuit for a tort, breach of contract, or other private injury. These two types are injunctions and damages. An **injunction** is a court order for a person to do or not do a particular act. An injunction may be issued to prevent a private injury or to stop it from continuing.

Damages are a monetary award to the injured party to compensate for loss. The purpose of the award is to place the injured party in the same financial position as if the injury had not occurred. These damages often are referred to as *actual* or *compensatory damages.* However, in many cases, the loss may be difficult to measure. An example from tort law is where negligence causes bodily injury with ongoing pain and suffering or even death. Even so, a dollar value of the injury or loss must be set. This value usually is decided by a jury.

A jury decides the amount of compensatory or actual damages by deciding on a figure that would equal the plaintiff's lost wages and medical bills plus a more arbitrary amount for the plaintiff's pain and suffering. Lawyers at times

handle a civil lawsuit for a percentage of the recovery. This is referred to as taking the case on a *contingency fee* basis. Common percentages are 25 percent if the case is settled before a trial, 33 percent if the case is won at trial, and 40 percent or more if the case is won on appeal.

In *What's Your Verdict?* if Horsley could prove that Eardly's defamation injured her business, she could probably receive damages as compensation. If Horsley could prove that Eardly acted with malice, the jury might award her additional damages referred to as punitive damages. These damages would be awarded as punishment for Eardly's malicious defamation and as an example to deter others.

Although unavailable in contract law or generally for other torts, punitive damages are usually available where an intentional tort has been committed. The damage amount is meant to be set at a figure that would punish the defendant, not compensate the plaintiff.

IN THIS CASE

Grimshaw sued the manufacturer of his auto after being burned severely in a collision. He was able to show that the manufacturer willfully kept a defective gas tank in his car even after it knew of the problem. The jury awarded him nearly $7 million in actual damages and another $100 million in punitive damages. The punitive damage award was set so high because a smaller amount would not be enough to punish an auto maker making billions each year.

CHECKPOINT

Name the two remedies available in a civil suit.

WHAT PROCEDURE IS USED TO TRY A CIVIL CASE?

WHAT'S YOUR VERDICT?

When their cars collided at an intersection, Claxson and DaLucia sued each other. Claxson claimed that DaLucia caused the accident by failing to stop for his stop sign. DaLucia claimed he had stopped and then moved through the intersection. He said he had not yet reached five miles per hour when Claxson ran his stop sign and slammed into him. Two witnesses saw the accident and could testify, but they have conflicting stories.

How can the court determine what really happened?

The procedure used to try a civil court case follows a set sequence.

JUDGE OR JURY

First of all, if a jury is to be used, it is selected. Remember that judges and juries play different roles in trials. Judges always decide any issues of law. The issues of fact are left to the jury to decide, if a jury is sitting. In civil cases, you do not always have a right to a trial by jury. Even when there is a right to a civil trial by jury, both the *plaintiff* (the party that initiates the lawsuit by filing a complaint) and the *defendant* (the party complained against in a criminal or civil proceeding) may decide to forgo this right. When there is no jury, the judge decides the issues of both law and fact. In *What's Your Verdict?* the trier of fact, be it judge or jury, would listen to the witnesses, Claxson and DaLucia, and evaluate their testimony for truth and accuracy. The trier of fact also would weigh any other evidence such as sobriety tests, skid marks, and location of debris to determine what happened.

Civil juries are made up of 6 to 12 citizens who listen to witnesses, review physical evidence, and reach their decisions. In most states, jury decisions in civil trials do not have to be unanimous.

OPENING STATEMENTS AND TESTIMONY

After the jury for a specific case has been selected, the attorneys make opening statements. These statements briefly outline what the plaintiff and the defendant will try to prove. The evidence is then presented to the jury, first by the plaintiff and then by the defendant. **Evidence** includes anything that the judge allows to be presented to the jury that helps to prove or disprove the alleged facts. Evidence may consist of written documents, records, charts, sobriety test results, photographs of skid marks and debris location, and other objects.

Testimony is the most common form of evidence. **Testimony** consists of statements made by witnesses under oath. A **witness** is someone who has personal knowledge of the facts. Sometimes an *expert witness* will give an opinion. An expert witness possesses superior knowledge about important facts. For example, an engineer may be utilized as an expert witness to testify that skid marks indicate a car was going 70 miles per hour before a collision.

Witnesses often are summoned into court by subpoena. A **subpoena** is a written order by the judge commanding a witness to appear and give testimony. Willful, unexpected failure to appear

Law Brief

Expert witnesses are generally hired first as "consultants." Only after the lawyer feels comfortable with the potential of their testimony is the "consultant" designated to the court and opposition in a case as an expert witness. All information and material provided to a potential expert witness while merely a consultant is confidential. However, after he or she is designated an expert witness, the other side in the case can find out everything the expert witness knows including everything disclosed to him or her while a consultant.

after receipt of such an order is contempt of court. The judge can punish persons guilty of contempt of court by fine or jailing them without a trial.

CLOSING ARGUMENTS AND INSTRUCTIONS TO THE JURY

Following the presentation of the evidence, the attorney for each side gives a closing argument. During closing arguments, each attorney summarizes the case, trying to persuade the judge (and the jury if there is one) to favor his or her side. After consultation with the attorneys, the judge then gives instructions to the jury. These instructions tell the jury what rules of law apply to the case. They also tell the jury what issues of fact they must decide.

JURY DELIBERATION AND THE VERDICT

For example, in a civil case involving an auto accident, the judge might instruct the jury that exceeding the speed limit in bad weather is negligence (a rule of law). The judge also may tell the jury to decide if the weather was bad at the time of the accident (a question of fact) and whether the defendant was exceeding the speed limit at the time of the accident (a question of fact). The jury then retires to the jury room for deliberation in secret to decide the case. In decid-

ing, each juror must determine whether a preponderance (superior weight) of the evidence supports the plaintiff's case. In a civil action, a unanimous vote of the jurors is not required. Usually, 10 out of 12 or, in a few states having smaller jury panels, 5 out of 6 voting for the plaintiff will be enough to find for the plaintiff. The jury's decision is called the **verdict**.

After the verdict has been returned, the judge renders a judgment. The **judgment** is the final result of the trial. It will normally be for a sum of money if the plaintiff wins. If the defendant wins, the judgment will merely be "judgment for the defendant." If either party believes the judge made a mistake, an appeal may be made to a higher court.

Examples of judicial error include incorrect instructions to the jury, admission of evidence that should have been rejected, or exclusion of evidence that should have been admitted. When there has been an error, the appellate court may modify or reverse the judgment of the lower court. Or it may order a new trial. If there is no error in the record, the reviewing court will affirm the judgment of the lower court.

CHECKPOINT

List the steps in the procedure used to try a civil case.

What is this defense attorney trying to do with his closing argument to the jury?

© GETTY IMAGES/PHOTODISC

HOW ARE CIVIL DAMAGES COLLECTED?

WHAT'S YOUR VERDICT?

Stevens won a judgment for $35,000 in a civil suit against Alvarez. Alvarez objected, but did not appeal because her lawyer told her that there was no basis for appeal. Alvarez stubbornly refused to pay.

What steps could Stevens take to collect the judgment?

Ordinarily, when a civil judgment for the plaintiff becomes final, the defendant will pay the judgment. If the defendant does not pay, the plaintiff may obtain a *writ of execution*. Execution here means the process by which a judgment for money is enforced. The court directs that the defendant's property (for example, a savings account or car) be seized or sold. The proceeds, after deducting the costs of seizure and sale, are used to pay the judgment. In *What's Your Verdict?* Stevens could get a writ of execution, because Alvarez refused to pay voluntarily.

© GETTY IMAGES/PHOTODISC

Would the possibility of losing a prize possession influence you to pay a judgment against you in a civil suit?

CHECKPOINT

How does a plaintiff collect damages if the defendant refuses to pay?

lawxtra.swlearning.com

5-3 Assessment

THINK ABOUT LEGAL CONCEPTS

1. Damages meant to punish the person who has committed a tort are called compensatory damages. **True or False?**

2. Compensatory damages are also referred to as __?__ damages?

3. A jury never determines a matter of law. **True or False?**

4. In deciding the amount of compensatory or actual damages to pay a plaintiff, the jury decides on a figure that would equal lost wages and medical bills plus a more arbitrary amount for the plaintiff's __?__.

5. A witness who was at the scene of the crime and who is very sure about what happened is referred to as an expert witness. **True or False?**

6. An order that a judge writes commanding a witness to appear and give testimony is called a(n) __?__.

7. In a civil case, the judge renders a judgment after hearing the jury's (a) determination (b) resolution (c) verdict (d) none of the above

8. Seizing a defendant's car to sell it to pay a damage award against him or her is known as (a) recovery (b) liquidation (c) execution (d) all of the above

THINK CRITICALLY ABOUT EVIDENCE

Study the situation, answer the questions, and then prepare arguments to support your answers.

9. Stone had secretly criticized the large chemical company she worked for over a span of several years. Her inside information had led to many accurate stories in the local papers about toxic releases into the environment. Finally, the company discovered what she was doing and hired two thugs to rough her up. They did a very thorough job, and she had to be hospitalized for several weeks. Because she immediately reported her beating to the police, the thugs were captured. In a plea bargain with the prosecutor, they confessed who had hired them. Stone brought suit against the chemical company. For what types of damages could she sue? Why?

10. Stone lost $7,000 in wages and owed $22,000 in medical bills as a result of the beating in exercise 9. She had sustained a concussion and had a broken leg with numerous lacerations and abrasions. Thereafter, she consistently walked with a limp. The chemical company averaged $72 million in annual profits over the last five years. What damage award for each type of damages you selected in exercise 9 would be appropriate. Why?

11. Presume that the damage awards that you deemed appropriate in exercise 10 were awarded by the jury. If the company refused to pay, even after the appeals went against them, how could Stone go about collecting?

12. In preparing for the suit, Stone's attorney subpoenaed several witnesses. After they were served with the subpoenas, the company immediately assigned them to distant locations in the country. If they willfully fail to appear at the trial, what sanctions can the court utilize to punish them?

13. Because the evidence against it was overwhelming, the chemical company decides to settle the case out of court for $16 million. Typically, what would be an attorney's contingency fee percentage share of this amount? If the case had to be won at trial and $20 million was awarded by the jury, how much would Stone's attorneys receive under a typical fee arrangement? If the chemical company appealed but lost, what would be Stone's typical attorney's share of the $20 million?

PREVENT LEGAL DIFFICULTIES

As a citizen . . .

1. Avoid legal liability for torts by consistently respecting other persons and their property.

2. If you commit a tort or are the victim of a tort that may lead to a lawsuit, consult a lawyer promptly. Critical evidence may be lost if you delay.

3. Choose your attorney carefully for a tort case. Be sure that the legal issues are in their area(s) of specialty. Check their list of clients and past legal victories. If employed on a contingency fee basis, make sure they have the resources to handle the case.

4. In some states, your own negligence, however slight, may bar any recovery under the doctrine of contributory negligence. In other states, those that use the doctrine of comparative negligence, even though you are somewhat negligent you may recover. Investigate the negligence laws in your state.

5. If you injure a third party while on the job, both you and your employer may be liable.

6. The automobile is the principal source of tort liability for most persons, young and old. Drive carefully.

7. If you are injured as the result of a tort, do not be rushed by insurance adjusters or others into signing a statement releasing the other party from liability. Let your lawyer decide if the settlement offer is fair.

8. Realize that just obtaining a judgment against a defendant in a tort may not end the legal ordeal. The judgment may not be voluntarily paid and execution will have to be carried out.

9. A judgment, once obtained, may be executed in other states and over a considerable period of time. The fact that a defendant is without resources today does not mean he or she will remain so forever.

Chapter 5 Assessment

CONCEPTS IN BRIEF

5-1 Private Injuries vs. Public Defenses

1. A tort is an act that causes private injury to the person or property of another.

2. Torts may be broadly classified as intentional torts, negligence, or strict liability. The most common tort is negligence.

3. Generally every individual is personally responsible for damage resulting from any torts committed by him or her.

4. Employers are liable for the torts of their employees if the torts are committed within the scope of the employees' employment.

5-2 Intentional Torts, Negligence and Strict liability

5. A person injured by a tort is entitled to damages—monetary compensation for the loss or injury suffered. The amount of damages is typically determined by the jury.

6. With intentional torts, the defendent possess the intent or purpose to inflict the injury. There are nine common intentional torts.

7. In some states, if the injured person was also negligent and the negligence contributed to the injury, the injured person may be barred from recovering damages. In many states today, however, some recovery may be obtained under the doctrine of comparative negligence.

5-3 Civil Procedure

8. If a jury is present, it will determine the issues of fact in a civil trial. The issues of law will be determined by the judge.

9. For a civil case, lawyers can either be hired on an hourly basis or, if the case promises an adequate award to the client, for a percentage of that award. If the client's case is lost, the attorney working on a contingency fee basis receives nothing.

YOUR LEGAL VOCABULARY

Match each statement with the term that it best defines. Some terms may not be used.

1. Person who has personal knowledge of the facts in a case
2. Deprivation of freedom of movement without consent or privilege
3. Final result of a trial
4. Using property in a manner that is inconsistent with its owner's rights
5. Tort based on carelessness
6. False statement that injures a person's reputation
7. Intentionally made threat to physically or offensively injure another
8. Harmful or offensive touching
9. Written court order compelling a person to appear in court and to testify
10. Materials or statements presented in a trial to prove or disprove alleged facts
11. A monetary award to compensate for the loss caused by a tort

a. assault
b. battery
c. conversion
d. damages
e. defamation
f. evidence
g. false imprisonment
h. fraud
i. intentional tort
j. invasion of privacy
k. judgment
l. negligence
m. strict liability
n. subpoena
o. testimony
p. tort
r. trespass to land
s. verdict
t. witness

REVIEW LEGAL CONCEPTS

12. If certain acts are both crimes and torts, why couldn't you let the prosecutor both bring criminal charges against the defendant and bring suit for damages for the victim at the same time?

13. In most cases, in order to recover damages for emotional harm, a person must also show a physical harm. Why would society want to establish an additional barrier to someone who has been harmed by the commission of a tort?

14. Other countries with common law systems do not require a showing of malice in order for a public figure to recover against someone for defamation. Why do we have such a requirement in our laws?

15. Under the doctrine of strict liability, the manufacturer and any sellers in the chain of distribution are held liable for the injuries of a buyer of a defective product. Given the complexity of many modern products, is it fair to hold the sellers liable especially when the manufacturers have gone out of business and cannot pay?

WRITE ABOUT LEGAL CONCEPTS

16. Make an outline of what takes place in each of the main steps of a civil lawsuit from the filing of the complaint to the execution of the judgment. Is justice done when the process is halted by a settlement between the parties?

17. **HOT DEBATE** What parties would Chanelle likely sue over the assault? What type of relief would she likely seek?

MAKE ACADEMIC CONNECTIONS

18. **PSYCHOLOGY** Jury selection was once an art form directed by past lore taught in law schools. For example, clergy, school teachers, lawyers (and their spouses) were considered bad risks in the jury box because they were opinionated and could not be swayed by the lawyer's arguments. Good jury selections included retired businesspeople and reasonably well-educated laborers. Today, however, jury selection in important cases is done on a scientific basis utilizing psychological insights. Research and comment on the new methods and criteria for picking jurors.

THINK CRITICALLY ABOUT EVIDENCE

Study the situation, answer the questions, and then prepare arguments to support your answers.

19. Martin asked Gabrielle on a date. They went to a movie and then drove around for a while. As he drove, Martin grabbed Gabrielle, pulled her to him and tried to kiss her. After a moment she was able to break his grip and demanded he let her out of the car. Instead, Martin sped up and kept driving at a high rate of speed, saying he would only let her out if she would kiss him. What torts has Martin committed?

20. McDonald and Beck were sitting in a bar watching a professional football game. When she discovered McDonald was not rooting for her team, Beck hit McDonald in the face, breaking McDonald's glasses and nose. McDonald called the police, who arrested Beck. What legal causes of action does McDonald have against Beck? What type of damages can he recover?

21. Jackson was a lawyer, respected by his peers. He successfully represented several persons who were charged with income tax evasion. All three defendants were reputed to be leaders of an organized crime syndicate. The local newspaper then printed an editorial calling for the tightening of tax laws "to protect society against mobsters and shyster lawyers like Jackson who would sell their souls to the devil for 30 pieces of silver." Was this statement a tort?

22. Yardly and Whiple, ages 12 and 13, intentionally threw stones which smashed 57 windows in an old warehouse. The warehouse had been standing vacant for nine months. Yardly and Whiple were caught and disciplined by the juvenile court. Then the owner of the warehouse sued them and their parents for damages. The girls said they were "just having fun and not hurting anyone because the place was empty." Who, if anyone, is liable and why?

23. Town Finance Corporation (TFC) foreclosed on a mortgage following a dispute with Hughes as to whether a loan had been repaid. TFC had a locksmith remove the locks of Hughes' dwelling. When no one was home, TFC personnel then entered the house, seized household goods, and left the inside of the house in disarray. Hughes filed suit over the debt. The court held that the finance company had been paid and thus had no further right of action against Hughes. Hughes thereupon filed this action, which claimed malicious and willful trespass and asked both actual (compensatory) and punitive damages. Was Hughes entitled to judgment? (*Town Finance Corporation v. Hughes*, 214 S.E.2d 387)

24. Lewis, an undercover police officer carrying a concealed pistol, went shopping in a Dayton Hudson department store. There, a security officer became suspicious that he was a shoplifter. Lewis took some clothing into a fitting room, where there were signs stating, "This area is under surveillance by Hudson's personnel." In fact, the security guard observed Lewis from a grille in the ceiling. After he saw Lewis place the gun on a chair, he called the police. Eventually, Lewis was identified as an undercover officer. But he sued Dayton Hudson claiming that the spying in the fitting room was an invasion of his privacy. Will he recover? (*Lewis v. Dayton Hudson Corporation*, 128 Mich. App. 165)

25. A train stopped at the defendant's railroad platform. As it started up again, a man carrying a small package jumped aboard. He appeared unsteady and about to fall. Therefore a guard on the train, holding the door open, reached out to help him. Another guard, standing on the platform, pushed the man from behind. The man made it onto the train, but he dropped the package, which was about fifteen inches long. The package was wrapped in newspaper and contained fireworks that exploded when the package hit the rails. The shock of the explosion caused several scales at the other end of the platform, many feet away, to fall down. As they fell, they struck the plaintiff, injuring her. She sued the railroad, claiming the guards were negligent. Is the railroad liable? (*Palsgraf v. Long Island Railroad Company*, 162 N.E. 99, N.Y.)

26. David Allen, age two, was attacked and severely bitten in the face and ear by a dog owned by Whitehead. Whitehead admitted that the dog barked a lot, was large, looked mean, and chased cars. On the other hand, no one had ever complained about the dog, it had never bitten anyone before, and it frequently played with other children. Is Whitehead liable for the injuries to David? (*Allen v. Whitehead*, 423 So. 2d 835, Ala.)

27. When a statement appeared on its financial bulletin board claiming that individuals from a securities investment firm committed criminal and fraudulent acts during an initial public offering of a stock, Prodigy and the anonymous poster of the statement were sued for defamation. Prodigy had previously maintained that the content of its bulletin board was monitored and edited by Prodigy. Can Prodigy be held liable for the comments of the anonymous poster on its bulletin board? (*Stratton Oakmont, Inc. v. Prodigy Services Co.*, 5 Alb L J Sci & Tech 229, 237 [1996])

CASE FOR LEGAL THINKING

NADER v. GENERAL MOTORS
NEW YORK STATE COURT OF APPEALS
255 N.E.2D 765

FACTS In the mid 1960s, Ralph Nader became famous as a crusader for consumer rights. His fame was initially based on the writing of his book, *Unsafe at Any Speed.* The book alleged serious problems with the Chevrolet Corvair, a car designed and manufactured by General Motors.

SUIT After the book's publication, much to the shock of the nation, Nader brought suit against General Motors for invasion of his privacy. The case was filed in New York State Court but, before the trial could be held, an appeal was taken to the highest court of that state, the Court of Appeals.

The Court of Appeals was called upon to determine which of the claims in Nader's complaint to the trial court might be actionable as invasions of privacy. In other words, the Court had to decide which, if any, of the claims Nader made, even if proven in the lower court, were legally invasions of privacy for which he could recover. If the court decided that none of the claims were actionable, no trial would be held.

CLAIMS The claims that Nader made were as follows:

1. That General Motors had tried to entrap him into an illicit relationship with several women in their hire.
2. That people hired by GM had conducted numerous interviews with Nader's friends about his viewpoints and had indicated that his views, sexual orientation, and personal habits were improper.
3. That GM's sleuths had watched him closely in public places for extended and unreasonable periods of time.
4. That people hired by GM had made harassing phone calls to him.

5. That GM had tapped his phone and eavesdropped on his private conversations.
6. That GM had conducted an extended investigation of him.

PRACTICE JUDGING

1. Consider each of these claims. Which ones do you think the New York Court of Appeals found actionable? Explain your answer.

2. Consider the ways in which the protection of the right of privacy might have to expand given the various additional communication patterns in today's world. What guideline(s) would you use to select among the types of communications (fax, e-mail, cellular phone, cordless home phone, etc.) that should be protected?

Entrepreneurs and the Law

PROJECT 1 LAW, JUSTICE, AND YOU

THE IDEA

JJ Adamski, 25 and a recent college graduate, taught business and computer classes at Walnut Grove High School for $22,000 per year. To make ends meet, pay off student loans, and save some money for the future, he also coached men's basketball and baseball, and drove a school bus. Often he found himself getting up at 5 A.M. to get to the bus barn after coming in from a late ball game and getting to bed around midnight. However, JJ loved the coaching as he'd played basketball for his college alma mater and had lettered in both basketball and baseball in high school. He cared for his students and the feeling that he was doing something significant with his life. During the summers, to earn extra cash, JJ worked for his uncle, Stinson Adamski, at a dry cleaner in the nearby city of Springfield.

The idea came from the experience JJ had at the dry cleaner. After garments were taken in at one of the two Adamski shops or on a route run by JJ in the shop's van, they were inventoried. Then each garment had to be individually tagged and categorized with the customer ID, the type of process to be performed, and the date due back to the customer. This was extremely labor-intensive as safety pins were used to attach the proper color-coded and numbered tags to the garment. When a customer's order was to be returned, the proper garments were found by the tags, a process that occasionally required quite a bit of searching. JJ's idea would alleviate these problems. It was to use microchips embedded in the head of removable brads to mark the clothing. The chips would be reusable and could be encoded by the computer when the garments were taken in. They could carry lots of information and could be energized to report their data and location by a reader at the counter or a portable microwave emitter/reader. Instead of taking an hour to mark 60 garments by hand, with a brad gun it would take five minutes.

THE PROTOTYPE

Using his home computer and, at his own expense, buying the brad gun to be modified, the chips, counter and handheld scanners, and encoder, JJ created a prototype of his invention in his apartment. JJ now is considering discussing his invention with Amber Stacy, a college friend. Amber works as a computer programmer for a law firm that specializes in invention development and production. JJ thought she would be the ideal person to do the software programming for the device. She also might be able to get answers to some legal questions that had occurred to JJ in considering what to do with his invention.

ACTIVITIES

Divide into teams and perform one or more of the following activities, as directed by your teacher.

Role-Play

Think about how JJ is to go about bringing Amber into the project. Consider long-term issues such as secrecy, use of the idea or software by Amber in other unassociated projects, liability potential, claims on the idea by outside parties such as the dry cleaner where JJ works, and the like. Role-play negotiations between Amber and JJ. Reduce any agreement to writing and sign it.

Research

Prepare the list of questions that JJ has for Amber on the legal issues he will need to deal with and the actions he will need to take to market his invention. Use this textbook and its table of contents as your information resource. Each team member should choose a different unit of the book and prepare questions that relate to that unit. Present these questions to the group and discuss their significance.

© COMSTOCK IMAGES

COMMUNITY *ACTION*

Get Out the Vote

Did you know that in the 2004 election only 51 percent of potential voters under age 30 actually cast their ballots? Overall the voter turnout in the United States mocks the description of participatory democracy often applied to this country. In 2004, only about 60 percent of the eligible voters exercised their right to determine who makes the decisions in this land. Shocking? Actually, that was up more than 8 percent from the 2000 election. You can help change that with a campaign to get out the vote.

Do Your Part

1. Research the appropriate laws on registration and alternative means of voting. Contact your courthouse or city hall for information.
2. Devise a plan to inform potential voters how to exercise their right to vote. Often people want to vote but do not know the basics. Language barriers, employment hours, and handicaps all can be overcome with proper planning. You can provide information to assist potential voters in overcoming barriers.
3. Determine resources for assistance for those with problems getting to the polls, locations of the appropriate polling station, and so on.
4. Develop a plan to make personal contact with potential voters. It is far and away the most effective means of getting out the vote. Experience shows that it also is beneficial to recontact the potential voters before the election.
5. Create a handout, in appropriate languages, with a map of polling stations, answers to frequently asked questions, and resources.

Emerging Business Issues

This event for two- or three-member teams challenges FBLA members to develop and demonstrate research and presentation skills for an emerging business issue. Your research should find both affirmative and negative arguments for each topic.

- Setting Award Limits for Malpractice Lawsuits
- The Death Penalty
- Lemon Laws for Automobile Purchases
- Making Home Builders Accountable for Their Work

Performance Indicators Evaluated

- Understand the given emerging business issue.
- Present a relevant affirmative or negative argument for the topic.
- Conduct research to support your argument.
- Demonstrate persuasive speaking and oral presentation skills.
- Involve all team members in the research and presentation.

Fifteen minutes before your presentation time, you will draw to determine whether you will present an affirmative or negative argument for your emerging business issue. Each presentation may last no more than five minutes. Following each oral presentation, the judges have five minutes to ask questions.

For more detailed information about performance indicators, go to the FBLA web site.

Think Critically

1. Why must consumers conduct major research before receiving medical treatment or making major purchases?
2. List two strategies during the presentation that will hold the attention of the judges?
3. Does *caveat emptor* mean that the consumer is accountable for purchases even when defective?
4. List a pro and con for setting award limits on malpractice lawsuits.

http://www.fbla-pbl.org/

UNIT 2

CONTRACT LAW

CHAPTERS

IN PRACTICE PROFILE
Jenny Bent ■ Literary Agent

Jenny Bent shows up for work every day on the 36th floor of a Madison Avenue high rise in New York City. It's there that she found her dream job. Since attending college at Cambridge University in the United Kingdom, Jenny knew she wanted to be a literary agent. That's exactly what she became after earning a bachelor's and master's degree in English Literature.

"I always wanted to be in publishing, and after doing some research, determined that agenting allowed me the most freedom, the chance to make the most money, and the chance to be the most entrepreneurial," she says. Prior to becoming a literary agent, Jenny worked at *Rolling Stone* and *Ladies Home Journal* magazines.

As a literary agent, Jenny, age 35, represents writers much in the way sports agents represent athletes. "I help writers get their work ready for the marketplace." Once the preparation is complete, Jenny submits a writer's work to the publishing houses and editors she thinks are best suited for the particular piece. Once a work is accepted for publication, Jenny negotiates terms of the contract on behalf of the author, and she troubleshoots throughout the process.

Even before beginning her career, Jenny knew she'd be dealing with legal issues, specifically during the negotiating process.

"I think of every possible thing that might go wrong, and then try to make the language of the contract fit these possibilities in order to protect my client."

"I need to know my way around a contract very thoroughly to make sure my client is protected and not taken advantage of by a publisher. I also work hard to get the best possible contractual terms for my client." Jenny must be knowledgeable about warranties and indemnity language, "and I need to know the best possible terms I can get for my client in the event he or she is sued." Although none of Jenny's authors has been sued, an author potentially could be sued for plagiarism, libel, or other wrongdoing.

Because she researched her career prior to entering the field, Jenny was sure she'd enjoy the work. "But what I didn't realize was how much I'd enjoy negotiating my clients' contracts." Doing so requires extensive preparation. "I think of every possible thing that might go wrong, and then try to make the language of the contract fit these possibilities in order to protect my client." It's an intellectual challenge that keeps Jenny stimulated. "I didn't realize it would be so interesting!"

It's no surprise that Jenny finds her job rewarding. "I work with authors to help them publish their work, and for most of them, getting published is a lifelong dream. So helping them do that is an amazing thing. Plus I get to read and talk on the phone all day with interesting people. What could be better than that?"

Offer and Acceptance

6-1 Creation of Offers

6-2 Termination of Offers

6-3 Acceptances

HOT DEBATE

Trenton and Elisa were students in a class on movie production. Knowing that the final movie in the *Alien Cheerleader* trilogy was about to come out, Trenton camped out overnight at the theater. He bought two tickets, and then asked Elisa to go with him. Elisa agreed. To be able to go, however, she had to call in sick to her evening job as a waitress. Not working that evening would cost her more than $100 in wages and tips. Nonetheless, she made the call. When Trenton did not show up to get her, she confronted him. He admitted he had sold the tickets to someone else for $50 each.

Where Do You Stand?

1. Should Elisa be allowed to sue Trenton for not taking her to the movie?

2. Would your answer change depending upon whether or not Trenton knew Elisa would lose income by going?

WHAT MUST BE IN A CONTRACT?

WHAT'S YOUR VERDICT?

Juan and Susan were talking one day after school. Juan would turn 16 on the upcoming July 13 and wanted to buy Susan's car. Susan, 17, had been working and saving her money to buy a new car. Selling her old car for $2,800 would give her enough to do so. She offered it to Juan for that amount, and he accepted.

Did the two friends create a legally enforceable contract?

Because of its limited resources, the court system is very selective in what it will enforce. Criminal laws and laws allowing recovery for certain private injuries (torts) are highest on the list as they are necessary for keeping peace in society. When it comes to **contracts**, generally defined as agreements between two or more parties that create obligations, the courts are far more selective.

In particular, there are six major requirements that must be satisfied before courts will treat a transaction as a legally enforceable contract. These are offer and acceptance, genuine assent, legality, consideration, capacity, and writing.

1. **OFFER AND ACCEPTANCE** There must be an apparently serious offer to contract. The person who makes the offer is termed the **offeror**. The person to whom it is made is the **offeree**. The terms of the offer must be definite and accepted without change by the party to whom it was intended to be offered.

2. **GENUINE ASSENT** The agreement (offer and acceptance) must not be based on one party's deceiving another, on an important mistake, or on the use of unfair pressure exerted to obtain the offer or acceptance.

3. **LEGALITY** What the parties agree to must be legal. An agreement to pay someone to commit a crime or tort cannot be a contract.

4. **CONSIDERATION** The agreement must involve both sides receiving something of legal value as a result of the transaction.

5. **CAPACITY** To have a completely enforceable agreement, the parties must be able to contract for themselves rather than being forced to use parents or legal representatives. In *What's Your Verdict?* if the minimum age to contract is 18 as it is in almost every state, the courts would not enforce Juan and Susan's contract if either one later did not want to be bound by it.

6. **WRITING** Some agreements must be placed in writing to be fully enforceable in court.

CHECKPOINT

What elements are required to form a legally enforceable contract?

IN THIS CASE

When you told Sheila how nice the paint job was on her car, she responded that she painted cars in her garage for a second income. She took a close look at your vehicle. Then she said that, if you agreed, she would do a similar job on it with the color of your choice in the next week for $1,800. In this transaction, Sheila is the offeror and you are the offeree.

REQUIREMENTS OF AN OFFER

An **offer** is a proposal by an offeror to do something, provided the offeree does something in return. The offer is the basis of the bargain. If it is not valid, there can be no contract for the courts to enforce. As a consequence, the law examines would-be offers carefully. There are three tests that a valid offer must pass:

1. Contractual intent must be present in the offer.
2. The offer must be communicated to the offeree.
3. The essential terms of the offer must be complete and definite.

LEGAL RESEARCH

Take a legal resource inventory of your community. Call the municipal libraries, the bar associations, libraries of colleges or universities, and the county courthouses near you. Determine what reference materials they have available to the public, such as case reporters, digests, codes, legal encyclopedias, online legal subscription services, and so on. Keep your list for future reference.

CONTRACTUAL INTENT MUST BE PRESENT

Often, although the words themselves may indicate an offer, a reasonable person would disregard them because of the facts and circumstances under which they were spoken. When a teacher says to a business law class, "I offer to sell you my new car for $3,000," this probably isn't an offer but an example. Words that take the form of offers but which are spoken in jest (as a joke), in extreme terror or anger, or as a preliminary negotiation or social agreement would not be enforced.

JESTS The law is not concerned with what is actually in the mind of a person making a purported offer. Rather, it is concerned with the appearance of this action. If you think you are joking, but a reasonable person would interpret your conduct as indicating that you intend to contract, you have made an offer. On the other hand if you are serious, but a reasonable person would interpret your conduct as a joke, then no legally enforceable offer is made.

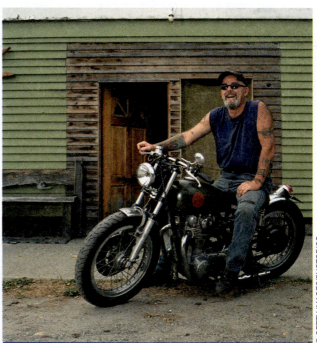

© GETTY IMAGES/PHOTODISC

Imagine that this man just told his two friends that he would gladly sell his motorcycle to the first one of them who could scrape together $1,000 in cash to pay for it. Judging from the expression on his face, has he made a legally enforceable offer? Why or why not?

STATEMENTS MADE IN ANGER OR TERROR Yelling after someone who has just stolen your watch, "Stop thief—I'll pay anyone who stops her $100," is not looked upon as being a valid offer by the law. It does not have the reasoned basis necessary for enforceable offers. So if someone ran after the person, captured her, and returned your watch, you would not, in a legal sense at least, owe the $100.

PRELIMINARY NEGOTIATIONS Information often is communicated merely to induce someone to initiate bargaining. Such statements are not seen by the law as indicating an intent to contract. You might casually say, "Would you pay $800 for my laptop computer?" without intending to be bound if he says yes. This contrasts with an offer which might take the form, "Look Jeff, I'll sell you my laptop computer today for $800." Statements of this nature, including putting signs on merchandise with a certain price or ads in newspapers to the same effect, are *invitations to negotiate*. They are not offers. The offer in such circumstances would typically come from the party responding to the ad.

In *What's Your Verdict?* Anchors Aweigh advertised boats. When would-be buyers tendered (presented for acceptance) the purchase price of the cabin cruiser, the would-be buyers were the ones making an offer. Thus, Anchors Aweigh was not bound by contract to the seven would-be buyers who came to purchase the boats after they were out of stock. To promote good customer relations, businesses try to deliver advertised merchandise to all who want to buy. Statutes prohibit false or misleading advertising. However, prosecuting an advertiser—who might be fined or imprisoned as a consequence under such a statute—does not get someone the bargain in the ad.

Advertisements may occasionally be offers. This can occur in one of two ways. First, the ad must be clearly worded in ways that address the problem of numerous people receiving the ad for a limited amount of product. Someone selling a car could create an offer by writing a complete and clear ad, and in addition, writing that the car will be sold only to the first person to accept the terms contained in the offer. Or an ad may state "subject to stock on hand."

The salesperson in this photo is about to mark the sale prices on these tags. Are these invitations to negotiate or offers?

Second, an ad may become an offer if it asks the offeree to perform an act as a way of accepting. An ad which states that a clearly described new power lawnmower will be sold for $20 "to the first person to appear at the main door of a shopping mall on Saturday morning after 6:00 A.M." will be a valid offer.

SOCIAL AGREEMENTS If two friends agree to go to the movies, no contract is intended. The friends don't think of this agreement as creating legal obligations. If either breaks the date, the other may be offended but cannot file suit for breach of contract. Social arrangements do not create legal obligations.

OFFER MUST BE COMMUNICATED TO THE OFFEREE

A person who is not the intended offeree cannot accept the offer. Nor can a person accept an offer without knowing it has been made. That is because any action taken would not have been a response to the offer. Thus, an offer of a reward that is made to certain persons or even to the general public cannot be accepted by someone who has never seen or heard of the offer. In such cases, the offeror may get what was sought. However, most courts require that anyone who claims the reward must have known of the offer and acted in response to it when performing the requested act.

ESSENTIAL TERMS MUST BE COMPLETE AND DEFINITE

The terms of an offer must be sufficiently complete and definite to allow a court to determine what the parties intended and identify the parties' legal rights and duties.

COMPLETE Nearly all offers must, at a minimum, identify the price, subject matter, and quantity, either directly or indirectly, to be legally effective.

Some offers require even more information to be valid. For example, in most states the essential terms for the sale of real estate lots would include

1. identity of the specific lot
2. price
3. full terms for payment
4. date for delivery of possession, and
5. date for delivery of the deed.

A QUESTION OF ETHICS

Sarah was talking with four friends at the entrance to their community college. When a bell called them to class, she absentmindedly left her backpack behind. It contained a pocket calculator, her driver's license, and other items of value only to her. After class, she posted an ad on a student bulletin board, offering $25 to whoever returned her pack. Major, another student, had not seen the advertisement but he found the bag and returned it to Sarah. Is Major legally entitled to the reward? Is Sarah ethically obliged to give him the reward?

If one of those terms were missing there would not be a valid offer. In contrast, an offer for the sale of a candy bar by a friend who identifies price, subject matter, and quantity (as many as are on the shelf). This is a valid offer.

What do you think would be the essential terms in a contract for a used car?

© GETTY IMAGES/PHOTODISC

DEFINITE Each essential term must be identified clearly. If a seller owned several cars but only stated that she would sell "my car" the courts would not enforce the offer. In some contracts, however, a term might be implied by law or common business practice. For example, some contracts are between individuals who regularly deal in the goods, or tangible personal property such as televisions and cars, being bought or sold. In these contracts, when the price is not specified, current market price is used as the basis for the contract.

CHECKPOINT

What are the requirements of an offer?

6-1 Assessment

THINK ABOUT LEGAL CONCEPTS

1. If the offer that was accepted to form a contract is invalid, the courts will not enforce the contract. **True or False?**

2. Which of the following is not an essential element of a contract? (a) offer and acceptance (b) genuine dissent (c) legality (d) all of the above are essential elements.

3. In some cases a person may be held to an offer that she only intended as a joke. **True or False?**

4. All agreements must be in writing to be enforceable in court. **True or False?**

5. If an offer is made, it can be accepted by anyone who learns of it. **True or False?**

THINK CRITICALLY ABOUT EVIDENCE

Study the situation, answer the questions, and then prepare arguments to support your answers.

6. The owner of a small color television set offers to sell it to a neighbor for $75. As the neighbor stands there thinking about the offer, a bystander says, "That's a bargain. I'll take it!" Is there a contract between the bystander and the owner?

7. Bill spent most of his month's allowance for expensive tickets to a rock concert after Lorene said she would go with him. On the morning of the event, Lorene phoned and said she was terribly sorry, but Tony, the high school's star fullback, had also asked her to go and she "just couldn't say no." Did she breach a contract? Could Tony be held legally liable if he knew Lorene had already promised to go with Bill? Was Lorene's conduct ethical? If Tony knew Lorene had already promised Bill she'd go with him, was Tony's conduct ethical?

8. The Nationwide Credit Union agreed to allow Heidi to borrow up to $10,000. Nothing was specified as to the length of the agreement, the rate of interest the credit union would charge, or the terms of repaying any loan. The credit union did not make a loan of $8,000 to Heidi when she requested it four months later. Is the credit union liable for breach of contract?

9. G. Whiz Sports Shop published this advertisement in the local newspaper: "Congratulations to the winners of the Tour de France! Now YOU TOO can be a champ! Get an 18-speed Blue Lightning bicycle for only $2,295—marked down from $2,795, the manufacturer's suggested retail price. What a bargain! Come and get it!" Baxter visited the discount store the following day and said, "I'll take one of the Blue Lightning bikes." The clerk replied, "Sorry, we had only ten bikes in stock and they've all been sold." Was the advertisement an offer?

Termination of Offers

HOW CAN OFFERS BE ENDED?

WHAT'S YOUR VERDICT?

On May 15th, Melissa offered to sell her collection of baseball cards for $3,000 at anytime before the first of the next month to her friend and fellow collector, Raoul. While Raoul was trying to raise the money, Melissa had second thoughts. So she called Raoul and said, "I've changed my mind, I'm not interested in selling the cards." Raoul responded, "It's too late, you said the offer would be open for this whole month. This is just the 20th, and I've got the money so I accept."

Was Melissa's offer terminated before Raoul's attempted acceptance?

Once made, an offer does not last forever. It may be terminated in a variety of ways.

REVOCATION BY THE OFFEROR

After an offer has been made, the offeror can generally revoke it anytime before it is accepted by the offeree. This is true even if the offeror promised that the offer would remain open for a particular period. In *What's Your Verdict?* because Melissa revoked first, there was no offer for Raoul to accept. The fact that she had promised to keep it open until the end of the month was not legally binding on her. Therefore there was no contract. The right to withdraw an offer before it is accepted is known as the right of **revocation**. A revocation is not effective until communicated to the offeree.

TIME STATED IN THE OFFER

In making an offer, the offeror may state how and when the offer must be accepted. For example, on October 10, the Mercantile Bank sent a letter to Boggs, who had applied for a loan. In the letter,

Mercantile offered to lend $50,000 on specified terms and stated that the acceptance had to be in writing and received no later than October 18. Boggs mailed an acceptance on October 17, but the letter did not arrive until October 20. As Mercantile did not receive Boggs's reply by the time specified, the offer expired. There was no contract.

REASONABLE LENGTH OF TIME

When nothing is said in the offer about how long it will remain open, it will end after a reasonable length of time. What is a reasonable length of time depends on all the surrounding circumstances. For example, a produce broker in New Jersey telephones a customer in Florida offering to sell a truckload of tomatoes. If the offer to sell the tomatoes is not accepted within an hour, it probably will terminate automatically. That is because tomatoes are perishable produce which rot and therefore must be marketed and shipped quickly. The seller may be in touch with many prospective buyers and they understand they must accept quickly.

In contrast, an offer to sell expensive durable equipment, such as a bulldozer, would not terminate until a longer time had elapsed. At least

Why does the length of time an offer will remain open vary with the type of goods to be sold?

© GETTY IMAGES/PHOTODISC

ECONOMIC IMPACT

several days would be reasonable. If the parties had bargained about the sale over a period of months, a week or longer might be appropriate. To avoid misunderstandings, the time available for acceptance should be specified at the outset.

REJECTION BY THE OFFEREE

When an offeree clearly rejects the offer, the offer is terminated. Unless renewed by the original offeror, the offeror can no longer accept the original offer. For example, in *What's Your Verdict?*, if Raoul had immediately declined the offer after Melissa made it, he could not have shown up with the $3000 later in May and bought the cards. His rejection ended the offer. An offer is terminated by an offeree's rejection even if a time limit set by the offeror has not expired.

COUNTEROFFER

Generally an offeree accepting an offer must accept it exactly as made. If the offeree changes the offeror's terms in important ways and sends it back to the offeror, a **counteroffer** results. In making a counteroffer, the offeree says in legal effect, "I refuse your offer; here is my proposal." The counteroffer terminates the original offer. The counteroffer then becomes a new offer.

DEATH OR INSANITY OF EITHER THE OFFEROR OR OFFEREE

Contracts are agreements voluntarily entered into by the parties and subject to their control. Death or insanity eliminates such control. Therefore the law acts for these parties when they can no longer act and terminates their offers.

DESTRUCTION OF THE SPECIFIC SUBJECT MATTER

If the offer refers to unique subject matter, such as Melissa's card collection, and it is subsequently destroyed, for example in a fire, the offer is automatically terminated.

IN THIS CASE

If, in *What's Your Verdict?* Raoul had said, "I will pay you $2,000 for them and not a penny more." His counteroffer would have terminated Melissa's original offer at that moment, even though she had promised to keep it open for the month. If, seeing that Melissa was not going to take the $2,000, Raoul immediately said he'd pay the $3,000, he would be making another offer not accepting Melissa's original.

CHECKPOINT

Explain two ways in which offers can be terminated.

HOW CAN AN OFFER BE KEPT OPEN?

WHAT'S YOUR VERDICT?

The Downings had placed their idle factory building on the market for $950,000. Robinson, a developer, was interested in buying it, but she needed time to persuade a group of investors to join her in a syndicate to purchase the building. Robinson offered $10,000 to the Downings to keep the offer open to her alone for 60 days. The Downings accepted the money.

Are they now legally bound to keep the offer open to Robinson?

As mentioned, an offeror is not legally obligated to keep an offer open for a specified time even if the offeror has promised to do so. This may cause the offeree not to pursue the offer or to act without proper consideration to close the deal. Such uncertainty may be eliminated in the following ways.

OPTIONS

If the offeree gives the offeror something of value in return for a promise to keep the offer open, this agreement is itself a binding contract. It is called an **option**. The offer may not be withdrawn during the period of the option. In *What's Your Verdict?* with the $10,000 Robinson bought an option to buy the factory building. Thus, the Downings could not legally withdraw the offer or sell to another party during the 60 days.

FIRM OFFERS

A special rule that works the same result as an option applies to merchants (individuals who regularly deal in the goods being bought or sold) who make offers in writing. If such a written offer contains a term stating how long it is to stay open, it is called a **firm offer**. The Uniform Commercial Code (UCC) makes firm offers binding for the time stated, but not more than three months. This is true even when nothing is paid by the offeree.

CHECKPOINT

How could an offeree insure that an offer will stay open for a set period of time?

INTERNATIONAL VIEWPOINT

Contract Law in China

There are two systems of contract law in the People's Republic of China—one for domestic transactions and the other for foreign contracts. The Economic Contract Law code was enacted in 1981 and is applicable to domestic transactions. The Foreign Economic Contract Law code was enacted in 1985 in order to attract foreign buyers for Chinese goods. The Chinese legal environment is not based on case law. Therefore, the role of the judges in Chinese courts is to apply the codes as written. The judges' opinions are not publicly recorded.

Do you think China's foreign trade has increased since the passage of the two law codes mentioned in the International Viewpoint? Why or why not?

THINK ABOUT LEGAL CONCEPTS

1. If a time for the offer to expire is not stated, it will expire in a reasonable time under the circumstances. **True or False?**

2. If an offeree clearly rejects the offer, the offer is termed (a) counteroffered (b) revoked (c) expired (d) terminated.

3. When an offeree changes the offeror's terms in important ways, the offeree makes a(n) _?_.

4. Which of the following does not describe an event that will terminate an offer? (a) revocation by the offeror (b) offeror is admitted to the hospital for tests (c) counteroffer (d) death of the offeree

5. An offeree who rejects an offer can later accept it if the acceptance occurs within a reasonable time after the original offer. **True or False?**

6. If an offeree gives the offeror something of value to keep an offer open, the contract thereby created is called a(n) _?_.

7. If either the offeror or offeree is deemed insane, the law will (a) uphold any offers made (b) terminate any offers made.

8. If a hardware store salesclerk said, "This price on the lawnmowers is good for 30 days," would this be a firm offer? **Yes or No?**

9. Offers between merchants that contain a term stating how long it is to stay open is called a _?_ offer.

10. If a beauty salon hair designer said to a customer, "This price on the cut and dry is good for 30 days," and then wrote it down on a piece of paper and signed it, would this be a firm offer? **Yes or No?**

THINK CRITICALLY ABOUT EVIDENCE

Study the situation, answer the questions, and then prepare arguments to support your answers.

11. While her car was in Prescott's garage for repairs, Wood noticed a large, seemingly unused, metal tool chest in the corner, complete with about 400 standard and metric tools. Wood offered to buy it for $3,000 and said, "You can take a week to think about it before you decide whether to accept." Four days later, before Prescott had responded, Wood told Prescott that she was withdrawing her offer as she had found a better set for less money. Can Prescott still accept Wood's original offer? If Wood had put the offer in writing, could she have withdrawn it before the week was over?

12. Frank saw a wheelchair advertised in the paper for sale for $900. When he called the seller, who had bought it to use while he was recovering from a skiing accident, the seller said it had not yet been sold. Frank drove out to see it but found it needed work. So Frank offered $700. The seller seemed insulted, and said he wasn't interested at that price. Frank left. About an hour later, he went back and found the wheelchair had not been sold. He then offered the $900 specified in the ad.

However, the seller refused to sell it to him. Frank became upset and sued to get the court to force the owner to sell it to him for $900. Will the seller have to do so? Why or why not?

13. Gus walked into his local hardware store to buy exterior paint for his house. It was on sale for $35 a gallon. Gus wanted to check around but didn't want to lose the chance to buy at the sale price. In response to Gus's request, the manager of the paint department wrote Gus a note stating, "Gus Almondson may buy up to 15 gallons of Old Dutch Exterior Grade paint for $35 per gallon anytime within the next two weeks." The manager signed and dated the note. Is this offer binding?

14. Phil was talking with Sharon about Opie, his Springer Spaniel dog. Phil explained that Opie has a strong personality, loves to snuggle up to people, likes to eat "people food," and is a good watchdog. Sharon liked Opie a lot and needed a dog. She asked Phil how much he paid for Opie. Phil said, "I paid $75, but I wouldn't sell Opie for ten times that amount. Sara said, "Well okay, it's a deal then. I'll give you $800, more than ten times the $75." Has Opie been sold?

WHAT IS REQUIRED OF AN ACCEPTANCE?

WHAT'S YOUR VERDICT?

When Blithely found Entitee on Blithely's used car lot looking at an SUV, she introduced herself and then showed him the features of the vehicle. After a period of time they discussed the price, and then she opened the driver's door for him. As he slid behind the wheel, she said, "Tell you what, I believe that once a customer gets behind the wheel of one of these beauties, he's sold. So, if you don't say no within the next ten seconds, we've got a deal at $15,750." Entitee said nothing within the ten seconds.

Did Entitee legally agree to Blithely's offer by his silence?

Acceptance occurs when a party to whom an offer has been made agrees to the proposal. To create an enforceable contract, the acceptance must

1. come from the person or persons to whom the offer was made
2. match the terms in the offer
3. be communicated to the offeror

ONLY OFFEREES MAY ACCEPT

An offer made to one person cannot be accepted by another. Sometimes, however, an offer is made to a particular group or to the public and not to an individual. For example, a reward offer may be made to the general pub-

lic. Any member of the general public who knows of the offer may accept it.

THE ACCEPTANCE MUST MATCH THE OFFER

The **mirror image rule** requires that the acceptance must exactly match the terms contained in the offer. This is true even as to when and how the acceptance must be made and even if the change is advantageous to the original offeror. If the attempted acceptance is not identical to the offer, it is a counteroffer.

Currently, courts in most states apply the mirror image rule only when the term altered in the attempted acceptance is material (important) and related to the providing of services or the sale of real property. Even in these states, however, if the offeror requires that acceptance must exactly match the terms contained in the offer, then any variation is legally a counteroffer.

Under the UCC, absent such a requirement for identity in the offer, an attempted acceptance of an offer for a contract for a sale of goods can be valid even if it does include new or conflicting terms. In these cases, there is a contract on the terms where the offer and acceptance agree.

What three characteristics of acceptances must be present in order for the contract to be enforceable?

© GETTY IMAGES/PHOTODISC

Then the new or modified terms are treated as follows:

1. If a party is a consumer, not a merchant, then the new or changed terms are mere proposals and not a part of the contract unless agreed to by the original offeror.
2. If both parties are merchants, the new or changed terms are not a part of the contract if the original offeror objects, or in the absence of an objection, if the terms are material.
3. If the parties are merchants, the new or changed terms are part of the contract if the original offeror is silent and the terms are minor (not material).

ACCEPTANCE MUST BE COMMUNICATED TO THE OFFEROR

An acceptance must be more than a mental decision. It must be communicated to the offeror.

SILENCE AS ACCEPTANCE One is not obligated to reply to offers made by others. An offeror's attempt to word the offer so that silence would appear to be an acceptance will not work. In *What's Your Verdict?* no contract would result from Entitee's silence.

BILATERAL ACCEPTANCE Most offers are bilateral. This means the offer implies that it can be accepted by giving a promise instead of performing the contracted-for act. For example, a seller promises to deliver a load of topsoil in exchange for a homeowner's promise to pay $65. Offers for **bilateral contracts** require that the offeree accept by communicating the requested promise to the offeror. Until this is done, there is no contract. The promise can be implied from the offeree's conduct as well as from words.

UNILATERAL ACCEPTANCE In some offers, the offeror requires that the offeree indicate acceptance by performing his or her obligations under the contract. Contracts offered under these conditions are **unilateral contracts**. The offeror in a unilateral contract promises something in return for the offeree's performance and indicates that this performance is the way acceptance is to be made. For example, the offeror may publicly promise to pay a $100 reward to anyone who returns a lost camera. Many people learn of the offer. All may join the search. A promise to look for the camera does not create a contract. Only one person may find and return the camera, thus performing the act required to accept the offer and earn the reward.

Note that if the person performing the act does not know of the reward, that person is not legally entitled to it. Also, if the words used are not clear as to whether an offer is unilateral or bilateral, courts will presume that the offer is for a bilateral contract.

IN THIS CASE

Stirrup found Buster, Fenton's lost dog and returned the animal to Fenton. After doing so, Stirrup noticed several reward posters by which Fenton offered $500 for the return of the dog. As he did not know of the reward prior to returning Buster, Stirrup was not entitled to it.

MODES OF CONTRACTUAL COMMUNICATION

Contractual communications such as offers, acceptances, rejections, revocations, and counteroffers may generally be communicated in person or by other effective means. These means include by telephone, mail, delivery service, e-mail, facsimile (fax) machine or other methods.

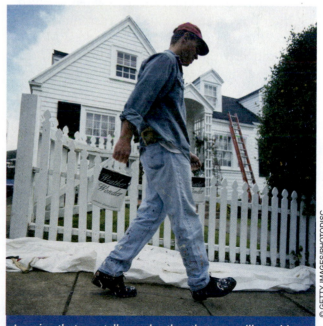

© GETTY IMAGES/PHOTODISC

Imagine that you tell your brother that you will pay him $100 if and when he paints your fence. If he agrees, have you formed a bilateral contract or a unilateral contract with him? Explain your answer.

The UCC provides that an acceptance of an offer to buy or sell goods may be made "in any manner and by any medium reasonable in the circumstances" unless otherwise clearly "indicated by the language or circumstances."

WHEN ACCEPTANCES ARE EFFECTIVE

When the communication takes time, for example when sent through the surface mail, the question of when the communication is effective can become very important. All forms of contractual communications but one take effect only when received. The exception to this is the acceptance, which often is effective when sent.

The offeror may require the offeree to use a certain communication method. If a different method is used, then it is treated as a modification of the offer. Business custom often implies a method to be used in an acceptance. On some stock and commodity exchanges, hand signals are used to communicate offers and acceptances. In many industries, next-day delivery service is the custom. When the required or the customary method is used, the acceptance is effective when sent unless the offeror specified the acceptance would be effective when received.

Often there is no specified or customary method for communicating acceptances. Most courts then say the acceptance is effective when sent by the same means used for the offer, or by faster means.

Under the UCC, if the acceptance of an offer for the sale or purchase of goods is by a reasonable means, it is effective when sent. A "reasonable" method incorporates all of the above rules but opens the door for a slower means to be reasonable in some situations.

It often becomes important to determine even more precisely when acceptance is effective. Oral acceptances are effective at the moment the words are spoken directly to the offeror. Acceptances sent by mail generally take effect when properly posted. That is, they are placed, with correct address and sufficient postage, under the control of the U.S. Postal Service. A telegram takes effect as an acceptance when it is handed to the clerk at the telegraph office or telephoned to the telegraph office. A fax transmission is instan-

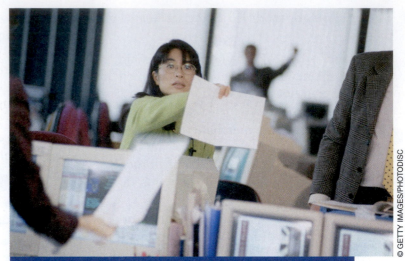

How are these stock exchange floor traders communicating offers and acceptances? Do you think this is an efficient communication method in this market? Why or why not?

© GETTY IMAGES/PHOTODISC

taneous when the transmission lines are open and both sending and receiving equipment work properly. Therefore the effect is similar to instantaneous oral communication, but in a more durable form that is easier to prove in court.

The offeror may specify that an acceptance will not be binding until it is actually received. This avoids the confusion that arises when an acceptance is mailed yet never reaches the offeror because it is lost in the mail. It also avoids the requirement for using the rules above.

CHECKPOINT

What are the requirements of an effective acceptance?

Law Brief

To facilitate proof of your acceptance of a contract by mail, use certified mail with return receipt requested. Also, keep a copy of your acceptance letter and other documents, including the offer. These items will be useful as evidence in court to establish a particular contractual communication.

Assessment

THINK ABOUT LEGAL CONCEPTS

1. A(n) _?_ is an offeree's agreement to an offeror's proposal.

2. If an offeror specifies in the offer that the acceptance must be made by fax, an e-mailed acceptance will not be effective. **True or False?**

3. All forms of contractual communication take effect only when received. **True or False?**

4. An offer that can be accepted only by an offeree's performance creates a(n) _?_ contract.

5. When there is no specified or customary means for communicating acceptances, a faster means than that employed by the offeror to make the offer would be considered effective by the courts. **True or False?**

THINK CRITICALLY ABOUT EVIDENCE

Study the situation, answer the questions, and then prepare arguments to support your answers.

6. To help pay for housing renovations, Jeanne placed an ad on the bulletin board at the public golf course showing a picture of her prized set of golf clubs, her phone number, and the figure $2,000. Eve, after seeing the ad, called Jeanne and then drove to her house with $2,000 in hand. When she presented the $2,000 to Jeanne, the latter refused it, stating that she had received several calls wanting the clubs for that price, so she was raising it to $2,500. Can Eve sue and force Jeanne to accept her $2,000 for the clubs. Why or why not?

7. Jonas wrote to Smith offering to sell 42 acres of farmland at $5,000 per acre with the purchase price to be paid at the closing. Smith replied, "I accept for the 42 acres, for the $5,000 per acre, but will pay the purchase price two days after closing." Is this an acceptance?

8. Office Suppliers, Inc., ordered 2,000 reams of 20-lb. paper from Dimension Paper for $1.75 per ream to be delivered at the Office Suppliers warehouse on April 24. Dimension responded that 2,000 reams would be delivered on April 25 at the price of $1.75 per ream. Office Suppliers made no further response. Has a valid contract been formed? If so, what are the terms? If not, why not?

PREVENT LEGAL DIFFICULTIES

When you seek to enter into a contract . . .

1. When negotiating, assume the worst and include terms in the contract addressing potential problems.

2. For important contracts, put offers and acceptances in writing. If either an offer or an acceptance is made orally, promptly confirm it in writing.

3. Obtain and keep a copy of every important document you sign.

4. Express your intentions in offers and acceptances with clear, complete, and understandable language.

5. Remember that the offeror may specify how and when the offer must be accepted. Otherwise the offeree may use the same means used by the offeror, a faster means, or other reasonable means.

6. When appropriate, buy an option, if one is available, to keep the offer open for as long as you need.

7. Remember that for an offeror to withdraw or revoke an offer, the offeree must receive notice. For speed, use the telephone, e-mail, or fax machine to withdraw or revoke an offer.

Chapter 6 Assessment

CONCEPTS IN BRIEF

6-1 Creation of Offers

1. Contracts are agreements between two or more parties that create obligations.

2. To be legally enforceable contracts require a valid offer and acceptance, genuine agreement, legality, consideration, and capacity. Some contracts must be placed in writing.

3. The party making the offer is the offeror. The party accepting the offer is the offeree.

4. An offer must (a) be made with the offeror's apparent intention to be bound by it, (b) be complete and definite, and (c) be communicated to the offeree.

6-2 Termination of Offers

5. If not accepted, an offer is ended (a) by revocation of the offeror, (b) at the time stated in the offer, (c) at the end of a reasonable time if no time is stated, (d) by rejection of the offeree, (e) by counteroffer, (f) by death or insanity of either of the parties, or (g) by destruction of the specific subject matter.

6. In general, an offeror is not obliged to keep an offer open for a specified time even if the offeror has promised to do so.

7. The offeree may give the offeror something of value in return for a promise to keep the offer open. This is called an option.

8. A firm offer, made between two merchants, is an offer that contains a term stating how long the offer is to stay open.

6-3 Acceptances

9. In contracts for the sale of services or realty, the offeree must accept the offer unconditionally and in the exact form and manner indicated by the offeror. In contracts for the sale of goods, acceptances can vary the terms of offer.

10. Contractual communication is effected by a constantly increasing variety of means to include phone, fax, e-mail, face-to-face negotiations, ground mail, and hand signals.

11. Although most contractual communications are effective when received, acceptances are generally effective when sent.

YOUR LEGAL VOCABULARY

Match each statement with the term that it best defines.

1. Binding agreement created by an offer that is accepted by a promise of performance

2. Offeror's withdrawal of an offer before it is accepted

3. Party to whom an offer is made

4. Signed writing by a merchant stating how long it is to stay open

5. Response by offeree, with new terms, which ends the original offer

6. Requirement that the terms in an acceptance exactly match the terms in the offer

7. Affirmative response necessary to transform an offer into a contract

8. Contract to leave an offer open for a period of time in exchange for other consideration

9. Agreement that is legally effective and enforceable in court

10. The person who makes the offer

a. **acceptance**
b. **bilateral contract**
c. **contract**
d. **counteroffer**
e. **firm offer**
f. **mirror image rule**
g. **offer**
h. **offeree**
i. **offeror**
j. **option**
k. **revocation**
l. **unilateral contract**

REVIEW LEGAL CONCEPTS

11. It is vital for a businessperson to be able to review a contract quickly to see if it is likely to be legally enforceable. This means being certain that the six essential elements of a valid contract are present. Without consulting the material in the book, list these elements, and give a short description of each.

12. Imagine you have made an offer to buy your friend's mountain bike. Make a list of the different ways your offer could be terminated.

WRITE ABOUT LEGAL CONCEPTS

13. Imagine that you are a portrait painter. Create an ad for your services to be placed in a local paper.

14. Write a reward offer for the return of your missing pet skunk. It has not been deodorized.

15. **HOT DEBATE** Assume that Elisa were allowed to bring a lawsuit against Trenton and was successful. Write a paragraph examining possible remedies that might be appropriate, such as damages or court orders.

MAKE ACADEMIC CONNECTIONS

16. **HISTORY** The feudal period in Europe did not have the level of trade and commerce that is such a part of our lives. Read about the quality of life during this period. Make a list of businesses and transactions that were not allowed or severely limited during that time.

17. **ENVIRONMENTAL SCIENCE** Could you pass a law requiring that every contract have a term in it requiring all parties to it to not hurt the environment in any way? What would be the economic consequences of such a requirement? Write a paragraph explaining your answer.

THINK CRITICALLY ABOUT EVIDENCE

Study the situation, answer the questions, and then prepare arguments to support your answers.

18. Caryn offered to tutor Dottie in business law for six hours on the day before the final exam in return for $100. Dottie responded, "Let me think about it for a day, okay?" Two hours later Jim offered Caryn $150 to tutor him on the day before the final and she accepted. Dottie called Caryn an hour later and said, "I accept." Caryn said, "I'm sorry but I've already agreed to tutor Jim that day so I can't tutor you." Was there a contract between Caryn and Dottie?

19. Sam advertised his ski boat for sale, priced at $4,500, complete with outboard engine and trailer. Barbara paid Sam $100 for a ten-day option, the money to be applied to the purchase price if she exercised her right to buy. Two days later, Sam was killed. Is Barbara's option still valid?

20. On Monday, Abner offers to sell his trained golden retriever, Track, to Bob for $300 cash. "My offer is open until we go hunting next Saturday." On Tuesday, Carl offers Abner $400 for Track, in eight equal monthly payments of $50. Abner says "Sorry, my price is $300 cash." On Wednesday, Dan learns that Abner has offered to sell Track. Dan tells Abner, "I'll pay $300 cash when you deliver the dog at the end of this year's duck hunting season. But you can keep Track until then." Abner says, "Sounds like a good deal. Okay, you now own Track." He phones Bob and tells him of the sale. On Thursday, Carl phones Abner and says, "I accept your offer. I'll pay $300 cash. When can I pick up Track?" Abner replies, "Sorry, but Track's been sold." Has Abner breached a contract with Bob or Carl? Has he been ethical in his conduct?

21. Lee Calan Imports, Inc., advertised a 1964 Volvo station wagon for sale in a Chicago newspaper. Because of an error by the newspaper, the price was listed at $1,095 instead of $1,795. Plaintiff O'Brien came in and said he wished to buy the station wagon. One of the defendant's sales representatives at first agreed but, upon discovering the erroneous price, refused to sell. Was there a binding contract? (*O'Keefe-Administrator of Estate of O'Brien v. Lee Calan Imports, Inc.,* 128 Ill. App. 2d 410, 262 N.E.2d 758)

22. Scheck wanted to sell a parcel of his real property. He made an offer to pay a commission to Marchiondo, a real estate broker, if Marchiondo caused the sale of the property to a particular buyer within six days. However, Scheck revoked his offer to Marchiondo on the morning of the sixth day. Later that day, Marchiondo obtained the prospect's acceptance of Scheck's offer, but Scheck refused to pay the commission. Marchionado sued, claiming the offer could not be revoked because he had begun performance. The trial court dismissed the complaint, stating that Scheck could revoke his offer at any time before completion of the requested act. Marchiondo appealed. Who should win the case? (*Marchiondo v. Scheck,* 78 N.M. 440, 432 P.2d 405)

23. On December 23, the First National Bank had its sales agent, Wyman, mail a written offer to Zeller to sell a parcel of real property for $240,000. On January 10, Zeller had his purchasing agent mail a written offer to buy the property for $230,000. The same counteroffer was made in a telephone conversation on that day to Wyman, but Wyman told Zeller's agent that the offer to sell the land was no longer in effect. When Zeller's agent reported this news to Zeller, he promptly told his agent to wire an acceptance of the original offer at $240,000. Zeller's agent did as ordered and the telegram of acceptance arrived before the letter containing Zeller's counteroffer. The bank refused to sell, reminding Zeller that the offer to sell had been revoked and that its agent Wyman had so informed Zeller's agent in the telephone conversation on January 10. Nevertheless, Zeller sued the bank for specific performance and for damages. Who should win? (*Zeller v. First National Bank,* 79 Ill. App. 3d 170, 398 N.E.2d 148)

24. Epton orally bargained for an option to buy a 54 percent share of the ownership of the Chicago White Sox baseball club for $4.8 million from the defendant, CBC Corporation. The option, which was to have been reduced to writing, was to last one week in exchange for the payment of $1,000 by Epton. To exercise the option within the week, Epton was supposed to give CBC a certified or cashier's check for $99,000 as a down payment. Epton was also to notify the corporation in writing that he was exercising his option. Twice during the week, Epton orally assured CBC of his intent to exercise the option and he also offered to pay the $99,000 as soon as the option was signed by CBC. After the week had passed, CBC refused to sell, and Epton sued. He claimed that his oral notice of intent to exercise the option was sufficient. He said that failure of CBC to sign a written option agreement excused both the requirement of a written exercise of the option by him and the necessity of the $99,000 deposit. Who should win? (*Epson v. CBC Corporation,* 48 Ill. App. 2d 274, 197 N.E.2d 727)

25. A brokerage sued its customers to recover for the purchase price of certain uranium stock. The brokerage contends it was directed to buy the stock "as close to two cents as possible," while the customers contend the price was to be two cents per share. Pursuant to the order, the brokerage purchased the stock and several days thereafter sent a confirmation listing purchase of the stock at two and one-eighth cents per share. The trial court found the order to buy was given at two cents per share which plaintiff executed by purchasing the stock at two and one-eighth cents per share. Is there an enforceable contract? (*Baldwin v. Peters, Writer & Christensen,* 41 Colo. 529)

LEFKOWITZ v. GREAT MINNEAPOLIS SURPLUS STORE
251 MINN. 188, 86 N.W.2D 689

FACTS On April 6, the defendant published the following advertisement in a Minneapolis newspaper:

Saturday 9 A.M. — 3 Brand New Fur Coats Worth $100.00 — First Come, First Served — $1 Each

On April 13, the defendant again published an advertisement in the same newspaper as follows:

Saturday 9 A.M. — 2 Brand New Pastel Mink 3-Skin Scarves Selling for $89.50. Out they go Saturday, $1 Each — 1 Black Lapin Stole Beautiful, worth $139.50, $1 Each — First Come, First Served

The record supports the findings of the trial court that on each of the Saturdays following the publication of the above-described ads, the plaintiff [Lefkowitz] was the first to present himself at the appropriate counter in the defendant's store.

On each occasion he demanded the coat and the scarf so advertised and indicated his readiness to pay the sale price of $1. Both times the defendant refused to sell the merchandise to the plaintiff, stating on the first occasion that by a "house rule" the offer was intended for women only and sales would not be made to men, and on the second visit that plaintiff knew defendant's house rules.

REASONING The defendant contends that a newspaper advertisement offering items of merchandise for sale at a named price is a "unilateral offer" which may be withdrawn without notice. He relies upon authorities which hold that, where an advertiser publishes in a newspaper that he has a certain quantity or quality of goods which he wants to dispose of at certain prices and on certain terms, such advertisements are not offers which become contracts as soon as any person to whose notice they may come signifies his acceptance by notifying the other that he will take a certain quantity of them. Such advertisements have been construed as an invitation for an offer of sale on the terms stated, which offer, when received, may be accepted or rejected and which therefore does not become a contract of sale until accepted by the seller; and until a contract has been so made, the seller may modify or revoke such prices or terms.

The test of whether a binding obligation may originate in advertisements addressed to the general public is "whether the facts show that some performance was promised in positive terms in return for something requested." The authorities cited emphasize that, where the offer is clear, definite, and explicit, and leaves nothing open for negotiation, it constitutes an offer, acceptance of which will complete the contract.

Whether in any individual instance a newspaper advertisement is an offer rather than an invitation to make an offer depends on the legal intention of the parties and the surrounding circumstances. We are of the view on the facts before us that the offer by the defendant of the sale of the Lapin fur was clear, definite, and explicit, and left nothing open for negotiation. The plaintiff, having successfully managed to be the first one to appear at the seller's place of business to be served, as requested by the advertisement, and having offered the stated purchase price of the article, was entitled to performance on the part of the defendant. We think the trial court was correct in holding that there was in the conduct of the parties a sufficient mutuality of obligation to constitute a contract of sale.

CONCLUSION Judgment affirmed.

PRACTICE JUDGING

1. If the store had not identified the quantity as "3...fur coats," or "1...stole," would this have affected the outcome of the decision?

2. If the store had advertised in the same way, but left out the statement, "First come, first served" would there have been a contract?

© GETTY IMAGES/PHOTODISC

Genuineness of Assent

7-1 Duress and Undue Influence

7-2 Mistake, Misrepresentation, and Fraud

HOT DEBATE

Responding to an ad from the local electronics store, your friend buys a personal data assistant (PDA) for $250, including a foldout keyboard and a portable printer. The keyboard and printer were shown with the PDA in the ad but noted as optional equipment.

In her excitement, your friend signs the credit card sales receipt, which is not itemized. She fails to note that the two items add an extra $198 to the price. When the credit card statement listing the total purchase price of $448 plus sales tax arrives, your friend objects.

Where Do You Stand?

1. State two reasons why it would be fair to allow your friend to withdraw from the contract.

2. State two reasons why it would be fair for your friend to be bound to the contract.
3. Which reasons are more persuasive?

Duress and Undue Influence

▼ GOALS
- Recognize when genuine assent is not present
- Identify the two key elements in undue influence

GENUINE ASSENT AND DURESS

WHAT'S YOUR VERDICT?

Cameron owned a promising race-horse that Link had offered to buy for undisclosed parties. When Cameron refused to sell, Link lowered his voice and slowly said, "Listen, the people I represent don't take 'no' for an answer. If you don't sell, they'll hurt you. They'll hurt your family. Like a good friend, I'm telling you to sell. You're getting a fair price, just sign the contract." Cameron, who had secretly recorded the conversation, sold. Then he called the police.

Can he now rescind and get his horse back?

Whether oral or written, an agreement will be treated as valid (legally binding and enforceable) as long as it meets all the proper legal requirements. One of the most important of these requirements is genuineness of assent. **Genuine assent** (true and complete agreement) is at times shown to be lacking in court. This is due to a variety of causes such as duress, undue influence, mistake, misrepresentation, and fraud. Without genuine assent a contract typically is **voidable**. This means that, if the injured party desires, that party can cancel their obligation under the contract and get back what they have already put into it. Such an action is referred to as a **rescission**.

To be effective, a rescission must be prompt. It must occur shortly after you discover that there is no genuine agreement. In addition, it must occur before you ratify the contract. **Ratification** is conduct suggesting you intend to be bound by the contract.

IN THIS CASE

Steven inspected a 5-year-old car with the intention of buying it. He asked the owner, Allan, how many miles were on the engine. Allan said, "As you can see from the odometer, it only has 30,000 miles on it, and I'm the only one who has ever owned it." A written contract was executed and Steven took the car to the local automobile dealer to be inspected. The dealer informed Steven that the car had often been serviced there, and that the odometer had been replaced at about 100,000 miles. This was fraud on Allan's part, making the contract voidable by Steven. However, if Steven continued to make his monthly payments to Allan after discovering the fraud, this would ratify the contract and Steven would lose his ability to rescind.

DURESS

Certainly, most parties are subject to duress in the form of apprehension and pressure when negotiating a contract. However, the law only allows a contract to be undone because of it in a few instances. Legal **duress** only occurs when one party uses an improper threat or act to obtain an expression of agreement. The resulting contract is voidable. Much of the law of duress focuses on the nature of the threat.

THREATS OF ILLEGAL CONDUCT The threat to engage in illegal conduct, such as a crime or tort, to win agreement is always duress. Committing an act of violence (for example, stabbing), threatening a crime (threatening to stab), committing a tort (for example, unlawful detention), or threatening a tort to obtain a signature on a written contract is duress. The actual crime or tort, or the threat, may be to the physical life, liberty, or property of the victim, the victim's immediate family, or the victim's near relatives. In *What's Your Verdict?* Cameron acted under duress in making the contract and therefore could rescind it.

THREATS TO REPORT CRIMES If you observe a crime, you have a duty to report it to the proper authorities. If you use a threat of reporting to force the criminal to contract with you, this is duress. It may also be the crime of extortion.

THREATS TO SUE The law encourages parties to settle conflicts without a suit. An important part of this process involves communicating a threat that you will sue if the other side doesn't settle. This happens frequently. When the threat to sue is really made for a purpose unrelated to the suit, this may be duress.

For example, during divorce negotiations, a husband threatens to sue for custody of the children if the wife doesn't sign over valuable shares of stock. Because he doesn't really want custody of the children, this threat to sue makes the contract for the stock voidable. If the threatened suit is completely groundless, a resulting contract may be voidable for duress.

ECONOMIC THREATS Often when parties are bound by a valid contract, they will seek to modify it. Parties then are tempted to use the economic power they have over one another to negotiate a favorable modification or settlement. If a manufacturer has a contract to pay a supplier $15 for a special computer part needed to maintain production, the supplier might threaten to withhold the parts unless the manufacturer agrees to a price of $20 each. If a disruption in the flow of parts would cause substantial injury to the manufacturer, then the courts would find the agreement on the new price an economic threat voidable for duress.

© GETTY IMAGES/PHOTODISC

Explain under what circumstances a court might find a price increase in factory parts voidable due to duress.

In economic duress cases, the courts look at both the threat and the alternatives available to the threatened party. If the threatened party had no choice but to enter into or modify a contract, then duress exists.

CHECKPOINT
List the various forms of legal duress.

UNDUE INFLUENCE AND ASSENT

WHAT'S YOUR VERDICT?

Albert had cancer and was being treated by Dr. Bennington. He had carefully followed the doctor's advice, and the treatment had been successful. One day, during a periodic checkup, Dr. Bennington said to Albert, "To prevent the cancer from recurring, you need to reduce the stress in your life. Long drives in the country are great for that. Come to think of it, I'm selling my convertible right now. You should buy it." Without investigating, Albert followed the doctor's directions and contracted to buy the car. Later he found the price he'd agreed to pay was nearly double the market value.

Could Albert avoid the contract due to undue influence?

Undue influence occurs when one party to the contract is in a position of trust and wrongfully dominates the other party. The dominated person then does not exercise free will in accepting the contractual terms. The two key elements in undue influence are the relationship and the wrongful or unfair persuasion. When a contract arises because of undue influence, the contract is voidable by the victim.

THE RELATIONSHIP

A relationship of trust, confidence, or authority must exist between the parties to the contract. This relationship is presumed to exist between an attorney and client, wife and husband, parent and child, guardian and ward, physician and patient, or minister and congregation member. In *What's Your Verdict?* the contract would be voidable by Albert. Although more difficult to prove when it is not present, a formal relationship is not necessary. The type of relationship necessary to prove undue influence could arise between a housekeeper and her elderly employer. It also could arise between a disabled person and his neighbor.

UNFAIR PERSUASION

Often the best evidence of unfair persuasion is found in the terms of the contract. For example, an elderly person, who is dependent on one child for daily care, may sell her home to that child for half its value. This is strong evidence of lack of free will.

To prevent a claim of undue influence, the stronger party should act with total honesty, fully disclose all important facts, and insist that the weaker party obtain independent counsel before contracting. Persuasion or nagging do not necessarily mean undue influence exists. Whether action rises to the level of undue influence is a difficult question of fact for a jury.

CHECKPOINT
What are the key elements in undue influence?

7-1 Assessment

Xtra! Study Tools

lawxtra.swlearning.com

THINK ABOUT LEGAL CONCEPTS

1. Rescission for duress must be timely and occur before ratification. **True or False?**

2. Contracts created or modified by duress are voidable. **True or False?**

3. Which of the following is a threat that can create duress? (a) threat to shoot the contracting party if she doesn't sign the contract (b) threat to sue (without grounds) the contracting party if she doesn't modify the contract (c) threat to report the contracting party to the IRS for tax evasion if she doesn't sign an agreement (d) all of the above

4. In economic duress cases the courts look at the _?_ and the victim's alternatives.

5. A formal relationship between parties to the contract must always be shown to prove undue influence. **True or False?**

6. Which of the following need not be done by the dominating party to prevent a claim of undue influence? (a) act with total honesty (b) fully disclose all important facts (c) insist the weaker party seek independent legal advice before contracting (d) submit the contract to a judge for review

7. If there is an offer and acceptance with no duress, undue influence, mistake, fraud, or misrepresentation, then there is _?_ assent.

THINK CRITICALLY ABOUT EVIDENCE

Study the situation, answer the questions, and then prepare arguments to support your answers.

8. Manuela rented an apartment and later discovered that the roof leaked. She asked the landlord to make repairs, but he refused. Manuela said that she would move out unless the landlord either made the repairs or lowered the rent. The landlord lowered the rent. Does Manuela's conduct make the modification to the contract voidable due to duress?

9. Evelyn was 86 years old and of sound mind. However, she relied upon her nephew Jamal, an accountant, to advise her in business matters. During one of Jamal's visits, he persuaded her to sell him a valuable painting for about 80 percent of its true value. Evelyn agreed and signed a contract. Then she had the painting appraised and learned its true value. She continued with the transaction by accepting payment for the painting. About a year later she died. Her estate sued for rescission of the contract. Jamal defended by claiming that Evelyn had ratified by accepting payment after learning of the value of the painting. Who prevails, Evelyn's estate or Jamal?

Mistake, Misrepresentation, and Fraud

WHAT ARE THE TYPES OF CONTRACTUAL MISTAKES?

WHAT'S YOUR VERDICT?

Bugliosi saved more than $25,000 to buy the new car of his dreams. At the dealership, the sales staff convinced him to purchase option after option until his $25,000 was totally exhausted. When he went to register the vehicle, he found that the state expected him to pay an 8% sales tax on the purchase price. Bugliosi thought the $2,000 in sales tax had been included in the $25,000 paid at the dealership, just as it is with purchases at other retail stores.

Is the contract voidable by Bugliosi because of his mistake?

Generally, mistakes are categorized as either unilateral or mutual. A **unilateral mistake** occurs when only one party holds an incorrect belief about the facts related to a contract. Generally, this does not affect the validity of the contract. In *What's Your Verdict?* Bugliosi alone was mistaken, so the contract is valid.

A mistake from failure to read a contract before signing is a unilateral mistake. So is a misunderstanding from a hurried or careless reading. Similarly, signing a contract written in language you don't understand will bind you even if you are mistaken about some of the contract's content.

When there is a **mutual mistake** (also called a *bilateral mistake*) both parties have an incorrect belief about an important fact. Important facts that influence the parties' decisions about a contract are called **material facts**. If a mutual mis-take of fact occurs, the contract is **void** (without legal effect). For example, suppose both a buyer and seller think that a property is 41 acres in size and they contract for the sale based on this belief. Later they learn that it is only 28 acres. This is a mutual mistake of fact. Their agreement is not binding.

When the mutual mistake is about the applicable law, the contract is still valid. For example, if both parties to a sale of raw land mistakenly believe that local zoning laws permit construction of duplexes on the lot, the contract would be valid though there was a mutual mistake and the duplexes could not be constructed. This is because all persons are presumed to know the law. Similarly, unilateral mistakes of law (such as Bugliosi's in *What's Your Verdict?*) generally have no effect upon the contract rights of the parties.

IN THIS CASE

Falkhausen, who lived in Indianapolis, owned a Formula One racing car that he kept in Miami. On March 18, he sold the car to Firenzi. When they concluded their contract that day, neither party knew that the car had been destroyed on March 17 when the parking garage in which the car was stored burned to the ground. Because of the mutual mistake as to the existence of the car, there was no contract.

CHECKPOINT

Name the types of mistakes that can make a contract voidable or void.

WHAT IS MISREPRESENTATION?

WHAT'S YOUR VERDICT?

Nutri-Life offered a dietary supplement for sale. The package contained a statement that clinical studies at Harvard University had shown the drug reduced the risk of cancer by more than 30 percent if taken regularly. This statement was untrue.

Can customers get their money back if they learn of the deception?

In many contract negotiations, the parties make statements that turn out to be untrue. For example, in the sale of a car, a seller, unaware that a previous owner replaced the odometer, might say that it has 70,000 miles on it when in fact it has 150,000 miles on it. This is an **innocent misrepresentation**. If the seller had known the statement was untrue, the seller would have engaged in **fraudulent misrepresentation**. In both of these situations the contract that results is voidable by the party to whom the misrepresentation is made. Statements are treated as misrepresentations by the law only if

1. the untrue statement is one of fact or there is active concealment, and
2. the statement is material to the transaction or is fraudulent, and
3. the victim reasonably relied on the statement.

UNTRUE STATEMENT OF FACT

In misrepresentation, the statement must be one of fact rather than opinion. Therefore the statement must be about a past or existing fact. If someone says, "This car will suit your needs well for at least the next year," this is a statement about the future and therefore must be an opinion. It cannot be the basis for misrepresentation. A seller's statement that, "I'm sure land values will increase at least 15 percent a year for the next three years," is a statement of opinion. Opinions also can be distinguished from facts based on how concrete they are. Saying, "it really runs well," is a statement of opinion about the condition of the car. Statements like "This is the best tasting cola on the market" are mere sales talk. In contrast, if the seller said, "the engine was rebuilt 7,000 miles ago," this is the expression of a concrete fact. It is a misrepresentation if untrue.

When experts express an opinion, the law will treat the statement as a statement of fact which can be the basis for misrepresentation. If an expert auto mechanic says, "The engine is in A-1 shape," and this is not true, it is a misrepresentation and the buyer could rescind. The packaging of the Nutri-Life dietary supplement in *What's Your Verdict?* involved an expert's opinion that constituted misrepresentation.

ACTIVE CONCEALMENT Active concealment is a substitute for a false statement of fact. If the seller of a house paints the ceiling to cover stains which indicate the roof leaks, this is active concealment. Similarly, if a seller places the price sticker on the TV screen to cover a wide scratch, this is active concealment.

SILENCE While in many situations the seller may remain silent about defects, there are three important situations where disclosure is required. The first is where a statement about a material fact omits important information. If a seller says, "I only drove this car once a week," then the seller also must disclose that this occurred while

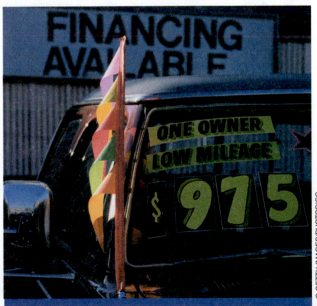

With what you just read about active concealment, what would you do if you were interested in buying the vehicle in this picture?

racing the car at the local drag strip. Half-truths cannot be used to conceal or mislead.

The second duty to break silence arises when a true statement is made false by subsequent events. A seller says, "No, the roof doesn't leak." Later that night, it begins leaking and the seller ends up sleeping under an umbrella. This seller must break silence and disclose the defect to correct the buyer's misimpression.

The third situation arises when one party knows the other party has made a basic mistaken assumption. For example a buyer may assume that a foundation is solid, but the seller knows of a defect allowing water to flood the basement each spring. The seller knows repairs will cost 25 percent of the sale price. This mistaken assumption must be corrected.

MATERIALITY

There are three ways an untrue statement can be determined to be material. First, a statement is material if the statement would cause a reasonable person to contract. Statements about total miles on a car and the number of miles since an engine was rebuilt probably would cause a reasonable person to complete the contract. A statement that a star's signature on a baseball card is his authentic autograph, when in fact it is a forgery, is a statement that would be material to a reasonable person.

Second, a statement can be material if the defendant knew this plaintiff would rely on the statement. Suppose a seller says the oil in the car was changed every 3,000 miles when it was only changed every 4,000 miles. This slight discrepancy would probably not be material to a reasonable person. If, however, a buyer says that the frequency of oil changes is very important to her, then statements about the frequency of oil changes would be material.

Third, if the defendant knew the statement was false, this makes the statement material. Therefore, if a seller lies about an otherwise non-material fact, this is material. If a seller says, "I always had the car serviced at the local Chevrolet dealership," when in fact he had it serviced at the local gas station, this statement would be material.

REASONABLE RELIANCE

Even though the statement is material, there is no misrepresentation unless the victim reasonably relied on it. A buyer may be told by an art gallery owner that an oil painting was created by "one of the great masters of the Renaissance era." She then learns from an art appraiser that it is a mere imitation. If the buyer still completes the sale, the buyer isn't relying upon the statement. If a car dealer says the tires are new, but the buyer responds, "Two are as bald as you," there is no reliance.

© CORBIS/ADAM WOOLFITT

You are told by a jewelry store salesperson that the diamond you are looking at is a perfect stone. Then you learn from an appraiser that it is not. If you purchase the diamond, did you rely on the salesperson's statement? Did a misrepresentation occur?

Law Brief

American contract law is built on the principle that individuals can take care of themselves when contracting, but still advises "let the buyer beware." The American approach generally allows silence as to material facts the seller knows that might adversely affect his or her bargaining position. It is up to the buyer to ask the seller about specific product attributes. Then, out of the seller's answer, if factually inaccurate, the basis for active concealment, fraud, and the potential avoidance of the contract is laid. If the buyer does not ask, the bargain generally will stand even when problems present themselves later.

CHECKPOINT

What are the three criteria for a statement to be treated as a misrepresentation?

FRAUD AND REMEDIES FOR FRAUD

WHAT'S YOUR VERDICT?

Graffter sold a used car to Camacho for $16,000. Graffter told her that the car had been driven only 50,000 miles, had never been in an accident, and had the original paint. In fact, Graffter had stolen the car, set back the odometer from 90,000 miles, and repainted the exterior in the original color. Graffter stood between Camacho and the right rear end of the car to prevent her from seeing a crudely repaired fender that had been damaged in the accident. Later Camacho learned the truth.

What remedies are available to Camacho?

Fraud is based on misrepresentation. All the elements of misrepresentation must be proven to show fraud plus two additional elements: intent and injury. If a victim can show fraud, courts will grant the victim assistance beyond the rescission available for misrepresentation.

THE MISREPRESENTATION MUST BE INTENTIONAL OR RECKLESS

Fraud clearly exists when a person deliberately lies or conceals a material fact. Fraud also exists if a person recklessly makes a false statement of fact, without knowing whether it is true or false. To constitute fraud, in addition to intending to deceive, the misrepresentation also must be intended to induce the victim to contract.

THE MISREPRESENTATION OR CONCEALMENT MUST INJURE

To establish fraud, there must be proof of injury. If there is an intentional misrepresentation, but no injury, there is no liability for fraud. Suppose

NETBookmark

Access lawxtra.swlearning.com and click on the link for Chapter 7. Read the article entitled "Material Misrepresentation to the Federal Government." What does the author of the article suggest that you do if and when you are questioned by the federal government?

lawxtra.swlearning.com

you are looking at an antique motorcycle. The seller says, "It is a 1938 Indian." The seller knows it is a 1937 Indian but intentionally lies, thinking the newer bike is more valuable. If you buy it for $9,000 and it turns out to be worth $14,000, you haven't suffered an injury. While you could rescind based on misrepresentation, you could not establish fraud.

REMEDIES FOR FRAUD

If a seller innocently misrepresents a material fact, the buyer may rescind. This remedy also is available for fraud. If a victim can establish fraud, courts also will allow recovery of actual damages and punitive damages.

In *What's Your Verdict?* Graffter was a criminal who intentionally lied about the car and actively concealed the damaged rear fender. The deception

A QUESTION OF ETHICS

Paul, a tax protestor, refused to pay income taxes. Although he only had a daughter, he listed so many children as dependents that his employer did not withhold any federal taxes from Paul's paycheck. Each April 15, Paul would appear on local TV holding up a blank 1040 Internal Revenue Service form and state his belief that the income tax was only intended for corporate income. He would then cite Congressional debate at the time of the passage of the Constitutional amendment allowing the income tax in support of his position. Is Paul's behavior illegal, unethical or both?

injured Camacho because the car was not worth $16,000. Accordingly, as Camacho could establish fraud, she could have her contract rescinded and be awarded compensatory and punitive damages.

RESCISSION As mentioned, contracts entered into as a result of misrepresentation or fraud are voidable by the injured party and can be rescinded. Normally when you rescind, anything you received must be returned. A deceived party who has performed part of the contract may recover what has been paid or given. A deceived party who has done nothing may cancel the contract with no further obligation. If sued on the contract, the deceived party can plead fraud or misrepresentation as a defense.

DAMAGES Damages are available if fraud is proven. The party defrauded may choose to ratify the agreement rather than rescind. Then either party may enforce the contract. However the defrauded party who ratified may seek damages for loss created by the fraud. In *What's Your Verdict?* Camacho could recover the difference in value for a car with 50,000 miles on it (the fraudulent misrepresentation) and one with 90,000 miles on it (the truth). Note that, under the UCC, damages are available when there is only an innocent misrepresentation in a sale of goods (tangible personal property).

LEGAL RESEARCH

Elect a class representative to contact your local police department and inquire as to whether any fraudulent schemes have occurred in your area. Possibilities include "con games" such as the pigeon-drop scenario as well as the techniques of short-change artists, pickpockets, and others. Discuss the findings in class.

PUNITIVE DAMAGES If fraud is proven, then punitive damages also become available. Punitive damages are a form of punishment. For instance, a judge might award a victim $5,000 in addition to actual damages as a way to punish the party who committed fraud.

CHECKPOINT
What are the remedies available for fraud?

Cyberlaw

Fraud is one of the fastest-growing threats facing consumers today. Because many consumer transactions now take place over the Internet, consumers also face the prospect of online fraud. In 1996, the National Consumers League started the Internet Fraud Watch project and the National Fraud Information Center web site. Consumers can access the web site to get tips on how to avoid scams and fraud 7 days a week, 24 hours a day. Many of the scams involve travel fraud. Travel fraud is growing quickly and involves bargain vacation packages, travel vouchers, and prize trips "for a small fee." In Operation Trip-Up, the Federal Trade Commission and 12 other law enforcement agencies brought 36 separate actions against travel-related scams. Attorneys general in many states have established special task forces to handle Internet fraud. To curb Internet fraud, education is the key to protection. Before you purchase, check it out!

THINK ABOUT IT
Type "National Fraud Information Center" into an Internet search engine to check out this web site. Click on "Internet Fraud" and then "Internet Fraud Tips." Choose one tip that you think is especially helpful to share with your class.

Assessment

THINK ABOUT LEGAL CONCEPTS

1. Which type of mistake gives both parties the right to rescind? (a) unilateral mistake (b) bilateral mistake

2. Unilateral mistakes of law generally have no effect on the rights of the parties under the resultant contract. **True or False?**

3. A statement of opinion by an expert _?_ be treated as fact. (a) will (b) will not

4. Misrepresentation is an element in both innocent misrepresentation and fraud. **True or False?**

5. For misrepresentation, which of the following elements need not be proven? (a) a false statement of fact (b) the fact must be material (c) the statement must be relied upon (d) all of the above must be shown

6. Which of the following remedies is not available for an innocent misrepresentation? (a) rescission (b) damages if the transaction is governed by the UCC (c) punitive damages

THINK CRITICALLY ABOUT EVIDENCE

Study the situation, answer the questions, and then prepare arguments to support your answers.

7. Anne was shopping for a used washing machine. She found one she thought was in good condition. She asked the seller what shape it was in and the seller replied, "It is in great shape." In fact it needed major repairs. Is the seller's statement a misrepresentation?

8. Chip was shopping for a used computer. He found one and asked the seller if the processor's speed was greater than 2 megahertz. The seller said, "Yes, it runs at 2.5 megahertz." In fact it was a much slower chip. Is the seller's statement a misrepresentation?

9. Glenna found a computer she wanted. While describing all the components, the seller said it had a fast modem. Glenna said modem speed was very important to her and asked

how fast it was. The seller said, "It's 56K," but she didn't really know how fast it was. In fact, it was a much slower modem. Has this seller committed misrepresentation? Has this seller committed fraud?

10. For years, Salazar, the lead mechanic at the Pull On In gas station, saved his money and eventually bought the business. Two weeks after the purchase, he found out that, a month previous, the Environmental Protection Agency had passed a regulation that would make the dispensing of petroleum-based fuels within a mile of a drinking water reservoir illegal. The station was only a few blocks from such a reservoir. Salazar also discovered that the previous owners knew of the regulation when they sold but did not inform him. Can he get the transaction rescinded?

PREVENT LEGAL DIFFICULTIES

In making contracts...

1. Research important transactions before entering into them. Verify claims of the seller by outside means or through firsthand personal experience.

2. Do not rush into a decision. Take time to review and understand the advantages and disadvantages of the proposed contract. Legitimate proposals will usually survive a delay.

3. Do not hesitate to ask questions about vague or uncovered issues. Forcing the other party to

make statements about them may lay the groundwork for proving fraud or misrepresentation later.

4. If the other party does not properly answer your questions, proceed with great caution or abandon the negotiations.

5. If you believe you have been defrauded, act promptly to rescind the contract.

Chapter 7 Assessment

CONCEPTS IN BRIEF

7-1 Duress and Undue Influence

1. One of the most important legal requirements for a valid contract is genuineness of assent.

2. Genuine assent is at times shown to be lacking in court due to a variety of causes such as duress, undue influence, mistake, misrepresentation, and fraud.

3. Duress consists of either an improper act or threat that induces the victim to make an unwanted contract. Such contracts are voidable by the victim.

4. Undue influence exists when one person, with trust, confidence, or authority, uses that power over the victim to obtain an unfavorable contract. The contract is voidable by the victim who acted without free will.

7-2 Mistake, Misrepresentation and Fraud

5. Generally a unilateral mistake of fact does not affect the validity of a contract.

6. Generally a mutual or bilateral mistake of material fact makes the agreement void.

7. Generally a unilateral or mutual mistake concerning applicable law leaves the contract valid.

8. Misrepresentation occurs if a victim reasonably relied on a material or fraudulent misstatement of fact or a material fact was actively concealed. Misrepresentation leaves the contract voidable by the victim.

9. Fraud exists when there is a deliberate false representation or a deliberate concealment of a material fact which influences the decision of the other party, causing injury. Contracts induced by fraud are voidable by the victim.

10. If a contract is voidable, the injured party must rescind shortly after the discovery that there is no genuine agreement. The injured party also must not engage in any activity that might ratify the contract.

YOUR LEGAL VOCABULARY

Match each statement with the term that it best defines. Some terms may not be used.

1. Of no legal effect

2. Consent or agreement not clouded by fraud, duress, undue influence, or mistake

3. Contract in which the injured party can withdraw from the transaction

4. One party holds an incorrect belief about the facts related to a contract

5. Deliberate false representation or concealment of a material fact, which is meant to and which does induce another to make an unfavorable contract

6. Approval of a voidable contract

7. Overpowering of another's free will by taking unfair advantage to induce the person to make an unfavorable contract

8. Use of an improper act or threat to obtain an expression of agreement

9. To offer to give back what you received via a contract while demanding return of what you gave

a. duress
b. fraud
c. fraudulent misrepresentation
d. genuine assent
e. innocent misrepresentation
f. material fact
g. mutual mistake
h. ratification
i. rescission
j. undue influence
k. unilateral mistake
l. void
m. voidable

REVIEW LEGAL CONCEPTS

10. Describe the concept of mutual mistake.

11. Distinguish the effect of the passage of time on the potential for rescission versus the potential for ratification.

12. What does reliance mean?

13. Explain all the elements that must be proven to establish fraud.

14. How is innocent misrepresentation different from fraud?

WRITE ABOUT LEGAL CONCEPTS

15. Write a short paragraph explaining why undue influence would be presumed in certain cases, such as the attorney and client relationship, but not in others.

16. Describe in writing a scenario where a mutual mistake of a material fact might cause a contract to be void.

17. Write a paragraph describing a television ad that could be the basis for misrepresentation if the statement made were untrue.

18. **HOT DEBATE** Write a letter for your friend to the credit card company. In the letter argue that the amount billed for the PDA was incorrect and should be changed.

MAKE ACADEMIC CONNECTIONS

19. **ENGLISH** Read Frank Abagnale's book, *Catch Me If You Can.* Prepare a report on the nature and level of complexity of his fraudulent schemes. What, in your opinion, made them so successful?

THINK CRITICALLY ABOUT EVIDENCE

Study the situation, answer the questions, and then prepare arguments to support your answers.

20. In negotiations for the purchase of a ranch, Adler (the seller) discussed water rights with Folt, the buyer. Adler never mentioned an ongoing dispute she had over such rights with a neighboring rancher. After the purchase, Folt realized that he had "bought a lawsuit" when his neighbor sued him over the water rights. In turn, he therefore sued Adler for rescission of their contract. Who will prevail, and why?

21. During negotiations for the sale of a well to be used to water animals, Hutton said the well was free of gypsum and brine (salty water). In fact, the well did contain gypsum, although there was no brine. The gypsum made the well unusable for watering animals. Curry, the purchaser, refused to pay, claiming the contract was voidable because of misrepresentation. Was it?

22. Ashbery, a salesperson, told Gelman that a new computer and its accounting software should do the work of at least five employees. Relying on this statement, Gelman bought the products. When Gelman found that he could eliminate only three employees but needed a new specialist, he claimed fraud. Was fraud committed?

23. Moser had no automobile liability insurance, although it was required by state law. She negligently collided with Chang's car. Chang threatened to sue if Moser failed to pay $1,000 for pain and suffering and $2,000 for car repairs. Moser gave Chang a check for $3,000. Then she stopped payment on it, claiming duress. Was it duress?

24. Olga Mestrovic, the widow of the successful artist Ivan Mestrovic, died. 1st Source Bank was the representative of her estate. It entered into a contract for the sale of Olga's home to the Wilkins. There was a lot of personal property in the home including a stove, dishwasher, and other items. The contract of sale provided that these items of personal property also were being sold to the Wilkins. When the Wilkins took possession of the realty, they found it in a cluttered condition which would require substantial cleaning. When they complained to the bank, it sent a bank officer to the scene. That person offered the Wilkins two options: Either the bank would pay to have the rubbish removed or the Wilkins could remove it and, "keep any items of personal property they wanted." No one thought there were any works of art on the property. The Wilkins accepted the latter option and later found eight very valuable drawings by Ivan Mestrovic. Was there a mutual mistake? Was there a mistake about the subject matter of the transaction? (*Wilkin v. 1st Source Bank*, 548 N.E. 2d 170, Ind. Ct. App.)

25. Using a smuggled-in .38 caliber pistol, Gorham and Jones took control of their cell block in a District of Columbia (Washington, D.C.) jail. They and other prisoners released by them ultimately took several hostages and demanded to be freed. One hostage was Kenneth Hardy, the Director of Corrections for the District of Columbia. The hostages were threatened with violence and used as human shields. Ultimately the authorities reestablished control of the cell block. Gorham and Jones were then transferred to the maximum security part of the prison from which, with the use of smuggled-in hacksaw blades, they later escaped. After their recapture, they appealed their subsequent criminal convictions (on 22 counts) of charges relating to their efforts. They said that the transfer to maximum security was in violation of the agreement they had extracted from Hardy while he was a hostage. They said he promised they would not be punished for their first attempt at jailbreak. Should the court recognize the agreement as binding and overturn the convictions? (*United States v. Gorham and Wilkerson (a/k/a Jones)*, 532 F. 2d 1088)

26. Treasure Salvors, Inc. located a Spanish ship on the ocean bottom in 55 feet of water about 46 miles off the Florida coast. The ship, the Nuestra Señora de Atocha, sank in a hurricane while heading from Havana to Spain in 1622. It was carrying "a treasure worthy of Midas: 160 gold bullion pieces, 900 silver ingots, more than 250,000 silver coins, 600 copper planks, 350 chests of indigo and 25 tons of tobacco." On the mistaken assumption that the seabed where the Atocha lay was state land, Treasure Salvors made a series of contracts with Florida whereby the state was to receive 25 percent of all items recovered. After the U.S. Supreme Court, in another case, had decided that the continental shelf where the ship rested was federal land, Treasure Salvors sued to rescind its contract with Florida and to recover all items as the exclusive owner of the Atocha. Should Treasure Salvors be able to rescind? Why or why not? (*Florida v. Treasure Salvors, Inc.*, 621 F.2d 1340)

27. Snap-On manufactures and sells hand tools such as wrenches to professional mechanics. It sold a distributorship to Eulich, but he was not successful and encountered significant financial difficulties. In Eulich's view his sales territory was too small. As a result Eulich terminated the dealership agreement. That agreement included a clause stating that on termination of the agreement, Snap-On might buy back any new tools owned by the distributor. Eulich attempted to turn in his tools but Snap-On delayed. Eulich's financial situation deteriorated to the point where he was unable to pay his personal bills and his wife needed to be hospitalized, though he had no medical insurance. Snap-On knew this. Finally, Snap-On accepted the tools. Before paying for the tools, Snap-On asked Eulich to sign an agreement promising not to sue Snap-On for claims arising out of the distributorship. He signed but later sued. What factors do you think the court considered in deciding whether the agreement not to sue was based on duress? (*Eulich v. Snap-On Tool Corp.*, 853 P.2d 1350)

NOBLE v. SMITH
164 CAL. APP. 3D 1001 (1985)

FACTS Noble contracted with the U.S. Navy to remodel the engine maintenance shop at El Toro Marine Corps Air Station. The contract price was some $647,500. The work included installation of heating, ventilating and air conditioning systems (HVAC) with a chilled water system.

In preparing his bid for the work, Noble totaled the informal bids he had received from subcontractors plus a percentage for his profit. In particular, he used $90,000 to cover the HVAC based on a bid for a subcontract by John Berry, president of American. Later the bid from Berry was reduced to $86,500.

Noble sent Berry a contract for the HVAC work to be performed by American at its bid price of $86,500. Learning this, Coast (another bidder) warned Noble the $86,500 was not a reasonable bid as Coast's $94,000 bid had excluded the chilled water system from the HVAC.

Four weeks later, Berry told Noble he would not sign the contract. He testified he had a number of questions and "I knew going in it was a low bid." [Then Berry recommended Smith as a contractor who might do the work.]

Berry told Smith his $86,500 bid had a 20 percent profit margin. Smith signed that same day a contract identical to that turned down by Berry. Smith told Noble he had not done "much examination" of the plans or specifications and Ruff was going to look the job over. After checking the job site and the plans, Ruff told Smith the cost of the job "far exceeded" the contract price. The plans included the chilled water system in the HVAC which cost an additional $16,000 not contemplated by the [bid]. Smith promptly told Noble the $86,500 price would not cover the HVAC with the chilled water system. Noble responded with the comment he would get another contractor and "sue [Smith] for the difference." Noble then awarded Coast two subcontracts, one for $94,000 and one for $16,000 for the chilled water system and sued Smith for the difference between his bid and the Coast bids.

REASONING Unilateral mistake is grounds for relief where the mistake is due to the fault of the other party or the other party knows or has reason to know of the mistake. Substantial evidence supports the conclusion Noble knew Smith's contract for the HVAC did not include the chilled water system.

To rely on a unilateral mistake of fact, Smith must demonstrate his mistake was not caused by his "neglect of a legal duty." This was Smith's first venture into contract waters deeper than $10,000. He told Noble the plans and specifications had not been reviewed by him; Ruff was to undertake that task after the contract was signed. Importantly, Smith related to Noble the profit assurance given him by Berry. In these circumstances, neither the trial court nor we could find Smith's conduct neglect of a legal duty.

While the [lower] court relied on mistake to void the contract, we find an alternative ground in fraud. Smith's consent was obtained by Noble's fraud in the suppression by Noble of the fact Berry's contract price for the HVAC did not include the cost of the chilled water system.

CONCLUSION Judgment affirmed that the contract should be voided.

© GETTY IMAGES/PHOTODISC

PRACTICE JUDGING

1. Is the mistake material?

2. Is the mistake unilateral or bilateral?

3. What evidence supports the conclusion that fraud occurred?

Consideration

HOT DEBATE

For a college graduation present, a wealthy aunt promised to give Maureen two round-trip tickets for a cruise for her and a friend. The promised trip was to be along the "Mexican Riviera" from Long Beach, California, to Acapulco, Mexico. At the graduation exercises, however, her aunt gave her a kiss instead and said, "The stock market is down. Sorry, darling!"

© GETTY IMAGES/PHOTODISC

Where Do You Stand?

1. State two reasons why you think the aunt is legally obligated to provide the tickets.

2. State two reasons why you think the aunt should not have to pay.

8-1

▼ GOALS
- Identify the three requirements of consideration
- Recognize the various forms of consideration

Types of Consideration

CONSIDERATION

WHAT'S YOUR VERDICT?

John, a writer, gets a call from his editor and, consequently, has to leave immediately on a research trip to Hudson Bay and Newfoundland in Canada. As the trip should take a couple of weeks, he leaves a note offering to pay his neighbor, Jordan, $100 to watch his house and feed and walk his dog during the absence. John then leaves without ever speaking to Jordan. Jordan gets the note and complies.

Is there an enforceable contract? What is the consideration for each party?

Consideration is what a person demands and generally must receive in order to make her or his promise legally binding. There are three requirements of consideration.

1. Each party must give an act, forbearance, or promise to the other party.

2. Each party must trade what they contribute to the transaction (act, forbearance, or promise) for the other party's contribution.

3. What each party trades must have legal value, that is, it must be worth something in the eyes of the law.

Consideration distinguishes a contractual promise from a promise to make a gift. A **gift** is a transfer of ownership without receiving anything in return. A promise to make a gift is generally not legally enforceable. Only after a **donor** (the person giving the gift) intentionally transfers the gift to the **donee** (the person receiving the gift) and the donee accepts it does the transaction become legally binding.

ACT, FORBEARANCE, OR PROMISE

In *What's Your Verdict?* what Jordan contributed was watching John's house and feeding and walking the dog each day. These acts were consideration for John's consideration, that is, John's promise to pay the $100. Both the acts and promise have value in the eyes of the law. Therefore, there was consideration and a valid contract.

When looking for consideration, look for legal value in the underlying act that is promised. If someone promises **forbearance**—or, to not do something—look beneath the promise and ask if the forbearance has legal value.

TRADING

In a typical contract, one party in effect says to another, "If you do this for me (pick up my mail and watch the house), I shall do that for you

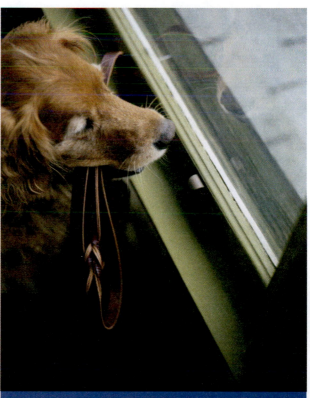

In *What's Your Verdict?* was Jordan's consideration an act or a forbearance in the contract that was created? Explain.

© GETTY IMAGES/PHOTODISC

(pay you $100)." A person promising an action or forbearance is the **promisor**. The person to whom the promise is made is the **promisee**. In most contracts, trading arises as one party exchanges a promise for the promise of the party on the other side. There has been a bargaining, or trading, of one promise for the other.

Consideration must be mutual. This means that each party must give consideration, and each must receive consideration. Consideration can be given by conferring, or promising to confer, a benefit. Consideration also can be given by incurring, or promising to incur, a *detriment*, or harm. If either of the parties does not give consideration, the other has no duty to perform as promised.

IN THIS CASE

Tyrone, a ten-year-old boy, attended a mineral show in Dallas, Texas. He bought several different crystal-like stones there. One such stone was purchased from Edwards for the marked price of $5. Later the stone was identified as a diamond and valued at more than $50,000. Edwards sued to recover the stone alleging he had not received proper consideration for the purchase. The courts held in Tyrone's favor as Edwards had received what he had demanded for the stone. (This is based on an actual case. Later, Tyrone did share part of the $50,000 with Edwards.)

© GETTY IMAGES/PHOTODISC

Your dad tells you that he will let you stay out until midnight tonight if you clean your room this afternoon. Who is the promisor and who is the promisee in this situation?

LEGAL VALUE

Legal value means there has been a change in a party's legal position as a result of the contract. In *What's Your Verdict?* Jordan performed acts which involved a benefit to his neighbor (feeding and walking the dog and watching the house). There is legal value because this changed (benefited) the neighbor's legal position. John, as promisor, benefited Jordan's legal position by promising the $100. Because both the act and the promise (to pay $100) have legal value and were traded, consideration is present and there is a contract. Legal value (a change in legal

position) is most commonly found in this form—in the exchange of two benefits.

Legal value also can be found in the exchange of benefit for a detriment. With regard to legal value, the detriment is the giving up of a legal right. A detriment always arises when you promise forbearance—that is, promise to refrain from doing what you have a right to do. If your uncle said on your eighteenth birthday, "Look, if you refrain from driving until your twenty-first birthday, I'll give you $25,000." You respond, "Yes, I accept." What you have promised is not a benefit to your uncle, but rather a detriment to yourself—you have given up a legal right. This is a change in your legal position and is thus valid consideration.

Legal value also can arise from the exchange of two detriments. If you say to your neighbor that you will forbear buying a dog if she will forbear building a fence, both parties have changed their legal positions. Therefore, there is consideration.

ADEQUACY OF CONSIDERATION

Generally, what the parties give and get as consideration need not be of equal economic value. This idea is sometimes expressed as, "The courts do not inquire into the adequacy of consideration."

The values that different people place on the same property may vary widely. For example, one person might gladly pay $60,000 for an original and exclusive high-fashion gown by a famous designer. Others would not be interested in owning such a gown for $60. A person also might place a higher value on a product at one time than at another. For example, when you have been baking for hours on the sunny side of a baseball stadium, you might willingly pay three times the grocery-store price for a cold soft drink.

Economic value is unimportant as long as there is genuine agreement. However, a big difference in economic value of what one gives and receives may be evidence of mutual mistake, duress, undue influence, or fraud. If the consideration received by one of the parties is so grossly inadequate so as to shock the conscience of the court, the contract will be declared *unconscionable* (grossly unfair or oppressive). In such a case, the contract or the unconscionable clause may not be enforceable.

NOMINAL CONSIDERATION

In certain written contracts, such as publicly recorded deeds, consideration from one party may be identified as "one dollar ($1) and other good and valuable consideration." In such situations, the actual consideration may be substantially more. However, the parties either cannot state the amount precisely or do not want to publicize it. This token amount is known as **nominal consideration**.

CHECKPOINT

List the three requirements of consideration.

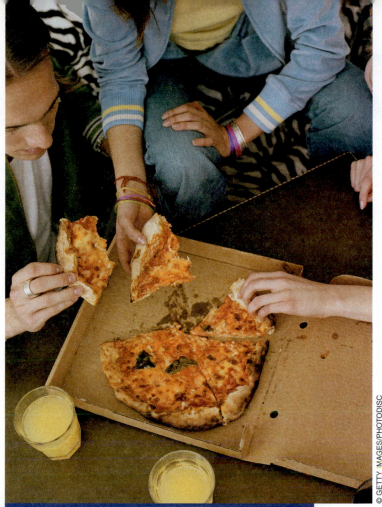

Would you be willing to pay more for a slice of pizza if you were really hungry? If so, why might this be?

© GETTY IMAGES/PHOTODISC

INTERNATIONAL VIEWPOINT

Contracts in Medieval England

Contracts have not always been as important as they are in today's society. The rigid hierarchy of the feudal society in medieval England required very few contracts. Nobles, knights, serfs and peasants all knew their place in society and understood their rights.

Formal contracts, known as "solemn promises," were more common in England by the fourteenth century. The royal courts required that these promises be written down and sealed. In order to seal the contract, a noble would use the imprint of his signet ring in a wax seal. Today, you can seal a document by writing the word "seal" in parentheses after your name.

THINK ABOUT LEGAL CONCEPTS

1. Forebearance cannot be consideration. **True or False?**

2. The presence or absence of consideration distinguishes a legally enforceable promise from a promise to make a _?_.

3. The person who makes a gift is called the donee. **True or False?**

4. Consideration can be found in the exchange of benefits, or in the trading of a benefit for a detriment, but not in the exchange of two detriments. **True or False?**

5. Courts do not consider the _?_ of consideration.

6. Token amounts given as consideration are referred to as _?_ consideration. (a) nominal consideration (b) normal consideration (c) insufficient consideration.

THINK CRITICALLY ABOUT EVIDENCE

Study the situation, answer the questions, and then prepare arguments to support your answers.

7. After graduation from high school in June, you and three classmates plan to travel around the United States. The plan is to visit the capital cities of all 48 contiguous states, taking numerous pictures along the way. The Sunnyside Camera Shop offers to give you a dozen rolls of 36-exposure color film for the trip free if you agree to let it develop and print all the rolls you use, for a stated price per roll. You agree. Are both you and the Sunnyside Camera Shop legally bound? What is the consideration for each party?

8. A three-piece high school rock band practiced for at least one hour most days of the week. Its studio was the garage of the drummer's home. The music was so loud that it violated a noise ordinance. Several neighbors offered to pay the rent at a local mini-warehouse as a practice room for a year if the group agreed to stop practicing at the drummer's home. The players agreed. Did the neighbors receive consideration? Did the rock band receive consideration? Did the rock band receive a benefit, endure a detriment, both, or neither? Was the contract enforceable? Would it make a difference if the band's music didn't violate the noise ordinance?

9. Gil found a nearly new engine in his neighbor's garage. He was experienced enough to see that it was in good shape. When he asked the neighbor how much she wanted for it, she said "you can have it if you'll get it out of here by the weekend and clean up the oil and grease around where it was." Gil said, "Okay," even though he knew the engine was worth nearly $1200. Is this a valid contract?

Questionable Consideration

▼ GOALS

- Describe situations in which consideration is present only under limited circumstances
- Recognize when what appears to be binding consideration is not

CIRCUMSTANTIAL CONSIDERATION

WHAT'S YOUR VERDICT?

Bovine Construction was a company that built custom homes for the very wealthy. Bovine contracted to buy from Greener Grass Inc. all the sod necessary for the yards of every home it constructed in May, June, and July of a particular year. During late May of that year, Bovine discovered it could get a comparable sod at half the price that it was paying Greener Grass. As a consequence, Bovine put off laying the sod on homes it had completed in June and July until August when it could buy the sod more cheaply.

Was Bovine able to do this without breaching its contract with Greener? Why or why not?

Certain forms of consideration are only legally binding in the proper circumstances. If these circumstances, in the form of properly worded contract provisions or patterns of behavior are not present, what would appear to be valid consideration is not.

ILLUSORY PROMISES

To be consideration, a promise must be binding. In other words, the promise must create a duty or impose an obligation. If a contract contains a clause that allows you to escape the legal obligation, the promise is said to be *illusory*. For example, you might have a clause stating that you will "paint the house—if you have time." This does not increase your legal obligation because you may never have time to paint the house.

TERMINATION CLAUSES Businesses often want the power to withdraw from a contract if business circumstances change. Therefore they include termination clauses in their contracts. If the clause gives one party the power to terminate the contract for any reason, the promise to perform would be illusory.

The promise is not illusory if termination is allowed only after a change in defined circumstances, after the passage of a certain length of time, or after a set period after a notice of termination is given. There is clearly a change in the party's legal obligations.

OUTPUT AND REQUIREMENTS CONTRACTS Buyers sometimes agree to purchase all of a particular producer's production. For instance, a steel company may buy all of the output of a nearby coal mining company. This is an **output contract**. On the other hand, a seller may agree to supply all of the needs of a particular buyer. For instance, a carburetor manufacturer may agree to supply all the carburetors needed for the production of a certain make of vehicle. This is a **requirements contract**.

It may seem that one party could elect to stop production and thereby eliminate the obligation. However, courts recognize these contracts as supported by consideration because they imply a duty of fair dealing.

NETBookmark

Access lawxtra.swlearning.com and click on the link for Chapter 8. Using the online dictionary at Law.com, look up the terms *illusory promise, output contract,* and *requirements contract.* Think of an example for each of these concepts, and write your examples down on a sheet of paper. Share your examples in class.

lawxtra.swlearning.com

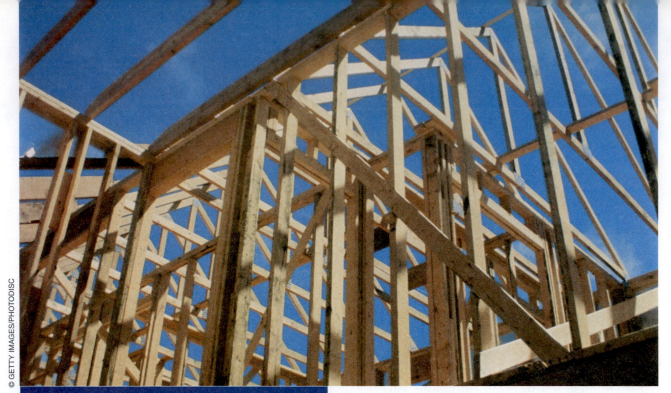

If a lumber company agrees to supply all of the lumber needs of a builder, what kind of contract would the two parties enter into?

This means that production cannot be stopped arbitrarily. Instead any action terminating the obligation of an output or requirement contract must be taken in a way that constitutes *fair dealings.* By finding an implied duty of fair dealings, the courts have maintained the basis for the presence of consideration. In *What's Your Verdict?* the courts would imply the fair dealings standard against Bovine and find them in breach of their contract with Greener.

EXISTING DUTY

A person sometimes promises to do something that he or she already is obligated to do by law or by prior contract. Such a promise, or act, cannot serve as consideration to bind the other party to the contract.

EXISTING PUBLIC DUTY If on your sixteenth birthday, your aunt promised to pay you $10,000 if you promised to not purchase alcohol for two years and you said, "Okay," this would not be a contract. There is no consideration because it is illegal for you to purchase alcohol when you are 16 and 17 years old. While the agreement creates a benefit for you ($10,000), you don't incur a detriment because you are not giving up a legal right.

EXISTING PRIVATE DUTY If a contract creates a duty, this duty cannot be the basis of consideration in a different contract. The same rule holds true when a person demands further compensation for carrying out a contract already made.

SETTLEMENT OF LIQUIDATED DEBTS A **liquidated debt** is one where the parties agree that the debt exists and on the amount of the debt. When a *creditor* (a person to whom a debt is owed) agrees to accept less than the total amount due in full settlement from a *debtor* (a person who owes money to a creditor) there is no consideration if the debt is liquidated.

Assume that Shawver borrows $1,000 from Reno. The loan is to be paid in one year with interest at 10 percent per year, or a total amount of $1,100. On the due date, Shawver sends Reno a check for only $1,000, saying "Sorry, I'm strapped for cash. You will have to accept this in full payment." Reno endorses (signs) and cashes the check. Reno may later sue and recover the unpaid balance of $100. She has received no consideration for the suggested agreement to reduce the amount due.

A debtor can settle a claim by paying less than the full amount if additional consideration is given. For example payment of less than the full amount before the due date could be consideration. However, there must be mutual agreement between the creditor and debtor to do so.

Valid consideration exists because the creditor receives the benefit of early payment. If something extra is given by the debtor, the new consideration supports a voluntary release by the creditor.

SETTLEMENT OF UNLIQUIDATED DEBTS When there is a genuine dispute between the parties about how much is owed, the debt is referred to as unliquidated. In such case, a payment offered in full settlement by the debtor and accepted by a creditor settles the claim. This process is called an **accord and satisfaction**. For example, a debtor may in good faith claim that a certain debt is $500. The creditor in good faith contends that it is $1,000. If the parties compromise on $750, their new agreement on that sum is referred to as the *accord*. Consideration for the accord is found in their mutual forbearance from litigating over the amount owed. When the subsequent agreement is performed, in this case the amount of $750 is paid, the act is referred to as the *satisfaction*.

RELEASE At the time most torts occur, the liability is unliquidated because the extent of damages is uncertain. If a party settles a claim at this point, this is called a **release**. The payment of money is sufficient consideration for the promise not to sue. Many people are hurt financially by signing releases too soon.

IN THIS CASE

Fillmore loaned Grant his riding lawnmower. While mowing a sloping piece of ground, the right rear wheel came off and the lawnmower rolled over Grant causing severe injuries. Fillmore knew that the wheel had been wobbling but hadn't warned Grant. When Grant threatened to sue Fillmore and the lawnmower company, Fillmore offered Grant $5,000 for a release from the unliquidated claim. Grant, owing for his hospital stay, accepted and gave the release knowing she could still pursue suit against the lawnmower company. The question only remains as to whether or not it would be successful.

COMPOSITION OF CREDITORS Occasionally a group of creditors will cooperatively agree to accept less than what they are entitled to, in full satisfaction of their claims against a debtor. In return, the debtor agrees not to file for bankruptcy. This is called a **composition of creditors**. Consideration for the promise of each creditor to release the debtor from full payment is found in the reciprocal promises of the other creditors to refrain from suing for the entire amounts due them. If the creditors did not agree to this arrangement, the debtor could file for bankruptcy, and the creditors might receive much less.

CHECKPOINT
Why is consideration not binding in illusory contracts?

FALSE CONSIDERATION

WHAT'S YOUR VERDICT?

Francis, a pedestrian, saw a car pulled over by the side of the road with a flat tire. He came to the driver's aid, replacing the flat with the spare tire. Then he accompanied the driver to the nearest gas station where her flat was repaired. She thanked Francis and said she would give him $20 on her next payday. Later she changed her mind, and Francis sued.

Can Francis win the $20?

Unlike forms of consideration that are only legally binding in certain circumstances, certain acts or promises are falsely identified as consideration but can never be.

MUTUAL GIFTS

When something of value is given by one party to another without demanding anything in return, the something of value is not consideration for anything later promised or provided. For example, in *What's Your Verdict?* Francis' service of changing the tire was not consideration for the promise of a payment of $20 made afterward by the driver. Neither party sought to exchange one thing for the other. Francis' service was a completed gift. The promised transfer of $20 was merely a stated intent to make a gift. It was unsupported by consideration and therefore unenforceable in court.

PAST PERFORMANCE

Contractual bargaining takes place in the present, for immediate or future performance by both parties. Therefore, an act that has already been performed cannot serve as consideration. Such act is called **past consideration**.

CHECKPOINT

What distinguishes a gift from a valid contract?

A QUESTION OF ETHICS

A motorist and her two young children are stranded in the parking lot of a shopping mall with a dead car battery. Having just completed your driver's education course, you know how to jump-start a dead battery. You connect the batteries of the two vehicles with your jumper cables. With your engine running, she turns her ignition key and her engine starts smoothly. Grateful, she asks for your address and promises to send you $25. Is she legally bound to keep her promise? Is she ethically bound to do so?

8-2 Assessment

lawxtra.swlearning.com

THINK ABOUT LEGAL CONCEPTS

1. If a contractual obligation can be negated by a particular action, the contractual promise is said to be _?_.

2. Termination clauses always make a contract invalid for lack of consideration. **True or False?**

3. Output clauses make contracts invalid. **True or False?**

4. If you already owe a duty, that duty cannot be used as consideration. **True or False?**

5. Legal value means a change in one's legal position as a result of the contract. **True or False?**

6. When there is a dispute over the amount owed, a subsequent agreement stipulating that amount and promising its payment is referred to as a(n) (a) accord (b) satisfaction (c) output contract

THINK CRITICALLY ABOUT EVIDENCE

Study the situation, answer the questions, and then prepare arguments to support your answers.

7. If a contract contains a clause stating that all the buyer's obligations could be extinguished by giving 30-days' notice, would this make the buyer's obligations under the contract illusory?

8. Georgia's neighbors approached her right after she received her driver's license and said they felt that she drove too fast on the roads where their kids often played. They struck a deal with her that if she stayed within the speed limit for the next three months they would pay her $200. Georgia agreed. Is there a benefit to the neighbors? Is there a benefit to Georgia? Is there an enforceable contract?

9. Kamiar owed Rubio $5,000, which was due in one year. There was no dispute as to the amount. However, Rubio needed money immediately, so Kamiar offered to pay $4,000 early in full settlement of the debt. If Kamiar pays the $4,000 early, will Rubio be able to successfully sue and collect the $1,000 later.

8-3 When Consideration Is Not Required

EXCEPTIONS TO THE REQUIREMENT OF CONSIDERATION

WHAT'S YOUR VERDICT?

The Constantine children, in memory of their father who had died of cancer, promised to pay for the local hospital's purchase of new cancer-fighting equipment. As a consequence, the board of directors of the facility entered into a contract for more than $450,000 worth of advanced devices. When presented with the bill, the Constantine children, reacting to a downturn in the stock market, refused to pay saying they weren't contractually obligated.

Can they be held to their pledge?

There are important exceptions to the general rule that, under contract law, consideration is necessary to bind someone to their promise. These exceptions include promises made to a charitable organization, promises covered by the UCC, promises to renew a debt barred from collection by certain statutes, and promises enforceable under the doctrine of promissory estoppel.

PROMISES TO CHARITABLE ORGANIZATIONS

Individuals and business firms often contribute to charitable organizations, such as churches, schools, and hospitals not operated for profit. The contributions may be completed gifts or promises (pledges) to pay in the future. Because the party who makes the pledge receives nothing in return, one might assume that the pledge is unenforceable.

Courts generally enforce such promises provided the charity states a specific use for the money and actually acts in reliance on the pledge. For example, a hospital may have contracted for new facilities, as in *What's Your Verdict?* As it would be unjust to deprive the hospital of the promised support it reasonably relied on, the Constantine children are legally obligated to make good on their pledge.

PROMISES COVERED BY THE UCC

FIRM OFFERS Under the UCC, a merchant who makes an offer in a signed writing to buy or sell goods and promises to leave the offer open is bound for up to three months even when no payment or other consideration has been given for the promise. This is called a *firm offer.*

MODIFICATIONS At common law modification of a contract needs consideration. Under the UCC, however, a good-faith agreement that modifies an

© GETTY IMAGES/PHOTODISC

A store owner promises to fund the building of an addition to her church. Then the economy takes a downturn, and the store's business decreases. Is she legally obligated to fulfill her promise to the church?

existing contract for the sale of goods needs no new consideration. For example, after a sale has been made, a seller could agree to give the buyers a valid warranty without further charge. This modification is enforceable though not supported by consideration.

PROMISES BARRED FROM COLLECTION BY STATUTE

STATUTE OF LIMITATIONS A state's **statute of limitations** specifies a time limit for bringing a lawsuit. Once you become aware of a legal claim, you must sue before the statute of limitations passes or you lose the right to sue. In many states, the statute of limitations for breach of contract or torts is three years. If there is a breach of contract or a tort, you must bring suit within three years after the claim arises.

Some states will enforce a promise to pay a claim after the passage of the statute of limitations even though there is no consideration for the promise. These states do require that the promise be in writing.

DEBTS DISCHARGED IN BANKRUPTCY Sometimes, even after a debt has been discharged as a result of the debtor declaring bankruptcy, the obligation may be reaffirmed or (reinstated) by a promise of the debtor. This is often done when someone close to the debtor cosigned or guaranteed payment on the debt. Such a promise does not have to be supported by additional consideration to be legally binding. To avoid taking advantage of other creditors, however, the debts to be reaffirmed have to be listed with the bankruptcy court during the proceeding.

If you cosign a loan for a friend or family member, you may have to pay that debt. This is true even if the person you cosigned for takes bankruptcy. In such a situation, you can ask the bankrupt [person] to reaffirm the debt and thereby prevent your having to pay it instead.

PROMISSORY ESTOPPEL

At times a rigid adherence to the letter of the law can produce injustice. As a consequence, the law allows courts to counteract this effect by taking certain actions in the name of equity, or basic fairness. One such action that the courts can take is the use of the doctrine of **promissory estoppel**. When brought into use—or "invoked"—by the courts, promissory estoppel prevents promisors from stating in court that they did not receive consideration for their promises. Under the doctrine of consideration, if a person cannot claim they did not get what they demanded in return for being bound to their promises, then those promises can be enforced against them.

For the courts to invoke promissory estoppel, the following conditions must be met:

- The promisor should reasonably foresee that the promisee will rely on the promise.
- The promisee does, in fact, act in reliance on the promise.
- The promisee would suffer a substantial economic loss if the promise is not enforced.
- Injustice can be avoided only by enforcement of the promise.

CHECKPOINT

Name four exceptions to the requirement of consideration.

Assessment

lawxtra.swlearning.com

THINK ABOUT LEGAL CONCEPTS

1. Promissory estoppel can only be invoked if the only way to avoid injustice is by enforcing the promise. **True or False?**

2. At common law, changes to a contract must be supported by consideration. **True or False?**

3. There is no time limit under a typical statute of limitations for lawsuits based on breaches of contract. **True or False?**

4. Promises to charities are generally enforceable in court. **True or False?**

5. Under the UCC a merchant's signed, written offer to buy or sell goods is binding for a limited time without consideration. **True or False?**

6. Debts discharged in bankruptcy can still be reaffirmed by the debtor. **True or False?**

THINK CRITICALLY ABOUT EVIDENCE

Study the situation, answer the questions, and then prepare arguments to support your answers.

7. Laura wanted to go to graduate school after college and she knew it would be very expensive. Her dad told her that if she would major in math instead of history, he would pay tuition in graduate school for a master's degree. Laura majored in math but her dad refused to pay for her graduate school tuition. Can Laura compel her father to pay?

8. Welt entered into a contract with Carbonaro, Inc. for the purchase of two dozen ultralight bike frames that he planned to resell from his retail bike shop. The price was $600 each. The parties wrote out all the terms of their contract and each signed. Later Welt learned that he could acquire similar frames for $525 each. Welt told Carbonaro that if it wanted to maintain Welt's goodwill it would reduce the price to $525. Carbonaro agreed. What is the consideration in the original contract? Is the price of $525 enforceable? Explain.

9. When they were both freshmen in college, Steiner borrowed $200 from Faber so he could attend a big game in Chicago. Steiner never repaid the debt, and after five years it was barred by the statute of limitations. Then Steiner sent Faber a Christmas card on which he added this note: "I haven't forgotten those four 50's I borrowed from you for the big game. Now that I am working, I'll pay you. In addition, I'll take you to this year's big game at my expense." Is Steiner legally obligated to repay the $200?

10. Lemke's son bought a videocassette recorder from Dyer on an installment plan. When her son was unable to keep up the payments, Dyer came to repossess the recorder. Lemke promised in writing to make the payments if Dyer would allow her son to keep the recorder. If Dyer agreed, could Lemke hold him to his promise?

PREVENT LEGAL DIFFICULTIES

Remember that under contract law...

1. Generally both parties must give and receive consideration if their agreement is to be enforceable as a contract.

2. Adequacy of consideration generally is immaterial to whether or not a contractual promise is enforceable.

3. Accepting money in exchange for giving up a legal right constitutes consideration and is binding. Consult a lawyer before making such an agreement in any major dispute.

4. A pledge to a charitable institution is generally binding without consideration and should not be made unless you intend to fulfill it.

5. Generally, however, promises to make gifts cannot be enforced by the intended donee.

6. You should use care and good judgment in making contracts. Courts generally will not rescue you from "bad bargains" or unfavorable deals voluntarily made.

Chapter 8 Assessment

CONCEPTS IN BRIEF

8-1 Definition and Types of Consideration

1. Consideration is what a person demands and generally must receive in order to make her or his contractual promise legally binding.

2. Consideration may consist of a promise, an act, or a forbearance.

3. The adequacy, equality, or fairness of the consideration given and received is immaterial as long as the consideration has some value and is voluntarily agreed to by both parties.

8-2 Questionable Consideration

4. Performing or promising to perform an existing obligation is not consideration.

5. Past performance is not consideration for a promise given now or in the future.

8-3 When Consideration Is Not Required

6. Pledges to pay money to charitable organizations are usually enforceable even though no consideration was given in return.

7. Agreements between merchants modifying contracts for the sale of goods need no consideration to be binding.

8. Promises barred by statute may be enforceable if reaffirmed.

9. If basic fairness demands it, the courts may invoke the doctrine of promissory estoppel to prevent promisors from stating that they did not receive consideration for their promises.

YOUR LEGAL VOCABULARY

Match each statement with the term that it best defines. Some terms may not be used.

1. Agreement by all creditors to accept something less than the total amount of their claims in full satisfaction of a debtor's obligations

2. Token consideration, which bears no relation to the real value of the contract

3. What a person demands and generally must receive in order to make her or his promise legally binding

4. Refraining from doing what one has a right to do

5. Voluntary transfer of ownership of property without consideration

6. Change in the legal position of a party as a result of the contract

7. Act that has already been performed and thus cannot be consideration for a promise in the present

8. Enforcement of a promise to avoid injustice, even though no consideration is given for it

9. Person who makes a promise

10. Person to whom a promise is made

11. Contractual situation in which a seller agrees to supply all the needs of a particular buyer

a. accord and satisfaction
b. composition of creditors
c. consideration
d. donee
e. donor
f. forbearance
g. gift
h. legal value
i. liquidated debt
j. nominal consideration
k. output contract
l. past consideration
m. promisee
n. promisor
o. promissory estoppel
p. requirements contract
q. release
r. statute of limitations

REVIEW LEGAL CONCEPTS

12. Give an example of an output contract associated with school.

13. Give an example of a requirements contract associated with school.

14. Think of three promises you've made to your family or friends today. Might they be enforceable in court? Why or why not?

WRITE ABOUT LEGAL CONCEPTS

15. Write an analysis of why a deputy sheriff should not be able to collect a standing reward for capturing a criminal.

16. **HOT DEBATE** Write a paragraph about whether or not the doctrine of promissory estoppel should be applied to the situation involving Maureen's promised graduation trip. Who would win if the doctrine was applied?

MAKE ACADEMIC CONNECTIONS

17. **PSYCHOLOGY** Contact a charity and ask about how people are about fulfilling their pledges. Ask if the charity relies on the pledges or waits to get the money before budgeting expenditures and what steps, including lawsuits, the charity takes to enhance the receipt of the promised money.

THINK CRITICALLY ABOUT EVIDENCE

Study the situation, answer the questions, and then prepare arguments to support your answers.

18. Glenn contracted to provide the labor for an addition to Reid's home for $10,000. When Glenn was partially through, he realized that the job was more time-consuming than anticipated. Therefore he refused to continue until Reid promised to pay an additional $2,000. Reid did so. Is Glenn legally entitled to the extra $2,000?

19. Kari promised to deed ten acres of land to the Ezlers. In reliance on the promise, they took possession of the land, cleared it, installed an irrigation system over a one-acre section, and planted 50 young fruit trees. Then Kari, seeing the improved property, changed her mind. Will a court compel the transfer to the Ezlers even though they gave Kari no consideration?

20. Mary received a diamond lapel pin from the estate of her maternal grandmother. It was appraised at $7,500. Because it did not fit in with her sports-oriented lifestyle, Mary sold the pin to a jeweler who told her, "The setting is old-fashioned, but the diamond is forever the same. I'll give you $3,500 cash." Later Mary wondered whether she received legally sufficient consideration. Did she? Can she rescind the transaction if she can prove that she received much less than the pin was worth?

21. When Bob began college at age 21, his godmother promised to give him $1,000 at the end of each of the following four years if he remained in school and refrained from smoking and/or chewing tobacco. She also promised a bonus of $1,000 if and when he received his bachelor of science degree. Are the godmother's promises legally enforceable? What are the ethical implications of her promises?

22. Marine Contractors Company, Inc., did various kinds of marine repair work within a 100-mile radius of Boston, Massachusetts. The company maintained a trust fund for the benefit of retired employees. The trust agreement provided that employees who resigned could withdraw their share of the fund after waiting five years. Hurley, general manager of the company, had accumulated $12,000 in the trust fund. When Hurley resigned, the president of Marine offered to pay his $12,000 immediately if he would agree not to compete with Marine directly or indirectly within 100 miles of Boston for five years. The parties made a written contract which set forth a "consideration of One Dollar and other good and valuable consideration." The contract also stated that the parties have "set their hands and seals" to the contract. Within four months after leaving Marine's employ, Hurley began doing repair work similar to that of Marine. Soon after, he organized his own company, hiring two supervisors of Marine. Marine sued to stop Hurley from breaking his contract. Hurley defended with a plea of no consideration. Was there consideration, and was Hurley therefore bound to the agreement not to compete? Why or why not? (*Marine Contractors Company, Inc. v. Hurley*, 310 N.E.2d 915)

23. Under a written contract with the Robert Chuckrow Construction Company, Gough agreed to do the carpentry work on a commercial building. Gough was to supply all necessary labor, materials, and other requirements to complete the work "in accordance with the drawings and specifications." After Gough's employees had erected 38 trusses, 32 of them fell off the building. Gough did not claim that the plans or specifications were defective or that Chuckrow was to blame for the collapse. Gough was told by a Chuckrow representative to remove the fallen trusses and to rebuild and erect them. Gough also was told to submit an additional bill for this work. He completed the job and submitted the additional bill. However, Chuckrow paid only the amount promised under the original written contract. Therefore Gough sued Chuckrow for the extra costs of reconstruction. Is he entitled to the added money? (*Robert Chuckrow Construction Company v. Gough*, 159 S.E.2d 469, Ga.)

24. Hoffman and his wife owned a bakery in Wautoma, Wisconsin. Lukowitz, an agent for Red Owl Stores, Inc., represented to and agreed with Hoffman that Red Owl would erect a grocery store building for them in Chilton and stock it with merchandise. In return, the Hoffmans were to invest $18,000 and Hoffman was to operate the store as a Red Owl franchise. In reliance on Red Owl's assurances and advice, the Hoffmans sold their bakery, paid $1,000 down on a lot in Chilton, and rented a residence there. In negotiations over some seventeen months, Red Owl boosted the required investment to $24,100; then to $26,000; and finally to $34,000, which was to include $13,000 from Hoffman's father-in-law. Red Owl insisted the $13,000 must either be a gift or a loan that would be inferior in claim to all general creditors. Hoffman balked and sued for damages. Should the Hoffmans win? If so, on what grounds? (*Hoffman v. Red Owl Stores*, 133 N.W.2d 267, 26 Wis. 2d 683)

25. Petty, a general contractor, made a series of purchases from Field Lumber Company. Field's records showed a total price of $1,752.21. Petty admitted he owed $1,091.96, but denied liability for the difference of $660.25. He claimed the difference was a result of an unauthorized $292.60 purchase by an employee, plus related finance charges. Petty sent a check for $500 along with a letter stating that the check must be accepted in full settlement of the total claim or returned. Field phoned to say the lumber company required full payment, but nevertheless Field cashed the check and sued for the full balance it claimed was due. Can Field Lumber Company now recover the full amount? (*Field Lumber Company v. Petty*, 512 P.2d 764, Wash.)

26. Burt made two pledges of $50,000 each to the Mt. Sinai Hospital of Greater Miami. He made the pledges "in consideration of and to induce the subscriptions of others." Nothing was said as to how the funds were to be used. Mt. Sinai Hospital did not use his pledge to induce others to subscribe. Nor did the hospital undertake any work in reliance on Burt's pledge. Burt died in the following year. Up to the time of his death, he had paid $20,000 on his pledge. The executors of his estate now refuse to pay the balance. Must they do so? (*Mount Sinai Hospital of Greater Miami, Inc., v. Jordan*, 290 So. 2d 484, Fla.)

THIRD STORY MUSIC, INC., v. TOM WAITS
48 CAL. RPTR. 2D 747

BACKGROUND Tom Waits agreed to be a recording artist and songwriter for Third Story Music (TSM). TSM transferred its rights in Waits' music to Elektra/Asylum Records (a division of Warner Communications). Under this agreement, Warner obtained from TSM the worldwide right to "manufacture, sell, distribute and advertise records or other reproductions and to permit others to do any or all of the foregoing. . ." This clause also specifically stated that Warner "may at our election refrain from any or all of the foregoing." TSM was to receive as a royalty a percentage of the amount earned by Warner.

Bizarre/Straight Records sought to compile and market an album of previously released Waits' compositions. Bizarre presented a licensing proposal to Warner. However, Warner would not enter the deal unless Waits agreed. Waits refused.

TSM brought suit against Warner for contract damages. Warner defended by asserting that the clause in the agreement permitting it to "at (its) election refrain" from doing anything to profitably exploit the music is controlling.

REASONING Both sides rely on different language in the California Supreme Court decision in *Carma v. Marathon*. In Carma, the court recognized that "in situations where one party is invested with a discretionary power affecting the rights of another," that "[s]uch power must be exercised in good faith."

The Carma court also stated: "The general rule [regarding the covenant of good faith] is plainly subject to the exception that the parties may, by express provisions of the contract, grant the right to engage in the very acts and conduct which would otherwise have been forbidden by an implied covenant of good faith . . . there can be no implied covenant where the subject is completely covered by the contract."

[An implied covenant of good faith can be the basis for consideration when there otherwise would be none because the promise is illusory.] "If what appears to be a promise is an illusion, there is no promise. . . ."

"The tendency of the law is to avoid the finding that no contract arose due to an illusory promise when it appears that the parties intended a contract. . . .The TSM/Warner agreement states that Warner may market the Waits recordings, or "at [its] election" refrain from all marketing efforts.

Read literally, this is a textbook example of an illusory promise. At the same time, there can be no question that the parties intended to enter into an enforceable contract with binding promises on both sides. Were this the only consideration given by Warner, a promise to use good faith would necessarily be implied under the authorities discussed.

The illusory promise was not, however, the only consideration given by the licensee. Warner promised to pay TSM a guaranteed minimum amount no matter what efforts were undertaken. It follows that consideration is present.

Warner bargained for and obtained all rights to Waits' musical output, and paid legally adequate consideration. That it chose not to grant a license in a particular instance cannot be the basis for complaint on the part of TSM as long as Warner made the agreed minimum payments and paid royalties when it did exploit the work.

CONCLUSION The judgment is for Warner.

© GETTY IMAGES/PHOTODISC

PRACTICE JUDGING

1. What is the consideration for each side?

2. If Warner had not promised the royalty payments, would the court have found consideration present here?

3. If the promise of royalty payments had not been made, would the court have still found for Warner?

Legal Capacity to Contract

9-1 Contractual Capacity of Individuals and Organizations

9-2 Limits on the Rights of Those Without Capacity

HOT DEBATE

© GETTY IMAGES/PHOTODISC

When John Eric turned 16 he received a new car for a birthday present. The same month, he responded to a magazine ad from a "club" offering his choice of 10 music CDs for only one penny. His response included his address and correct age. The ad noted that in return for this bargain, anyone who subscribed to it would have to buy one CD at full price for the next 6 months. The 10 CDs arrived and John Eric ignored any further letters from the club. The next month, however, he received a CD entitled "Bach's Bombs" and a bill for $23.99 from the club. John Eric ignored the bill and filed the CD in the back of his CD stack. Over the next several months, John Eric continued to receive a CD a month and notice of an ever-increasing amount owed to the club. Finally, when the bill reached over $200, John Eric talked to his dad about the situation. His dad, a lawyer, wrote a letter for John Eric telling the club that the sender was canceling the contract and would send back any CDs previously received if the club would pay for postage. John Eric signed the letter and sent it. The club didn't respond but the CDs and bills stopped coming.

Where Do You Stand?

1. Which party or parties has acted improperly in a legal sense? Explain.

2. Which party or parties has acted improperly in a moral sense? Discuss.

Contractual Capacity of Individuals and Organizations

WHAT IS CAPACITY?

WHAT'S YOUR VERDICT?

Alexis, 16, was getting ready for a tour of Europe with her family when she walked into a luggage shop in a specialty mall. A salesperson convinced her that she should spend $750 of the $1,000 she had saved for the trip on a matching set of cases, carry on, and an overnight bag. When she had time to consider her purchase that evening at home, she realized she had made a mistake by spending so much. Now she hardly had any money to buy clothes.

Can Alexis get her money back?

Certain parties to contracts are assumed by the law to lack the maturity and experience to protect their self-interests in contractual negotiations. The law grants these parties special contractual protections designed to keep them from being cheated due to their lack of such contractual capacity. Contractual capacity is defined by the law to mean the ability to understand the consequences of a contract. Note that this definition does not require that a person understand the actual terms of the contract which may be written in technical legal terminology. Nor does the definition require that the person have merely the understanding of the terms. Contractual capacity means only that she or he possess the ability to understand them.

Parties who have such special contractual rights due to a legally recognized lack of such capacity include minors, the intoxicated, and the mentally incapacitated. All of these parties are said to be *incapacitated.* For contract law purposes, minors are defined as individuals under the age of majority. This is the age at which a person is entitled to the management of his or her own affairs. The age of majority is 18 in most states. In a few states, it is 19 or 21. A person who has not yet reached the age of majority is called a minor. Minority, or the state of being below the age of majority, ends the *day before* the birthday of the age set as the age of majority.

PROTECTIONS FOR THOSE WHO LACK CAPACITY

The contracts of most parties who lack capacity are considered voidable. As a consequence, the primary protection granted to those who lack contractual capacity is disaffirmance. Disaffirmance in contract law means a refusal to be bound by a previous legal commitment. Generally, when a protected party disaffirms a contract, by law the protected party is to receive back whatever they have put into the contract. The other party may or may not get back their consideration. For example, assume a protected party bought a four-wheel ATV from a dealership and then wrecked it. He or she could disaffirm the contract and recover any payments made. The dealership would only be able to recover the damaged ATV. In *What's Your Verdict*

INTERNATIONAL VIEWPOINT

Current Age Limits

Around the world there are many differences in the ages youthful individuals are permitted to leave school, work, and be married. For example a child may leave school as early as 10 years of age in Bangladesh but no earlier than 16 in the United States and the Netherlands. There is no minimum age of employment in New Zealand, but it is set at 16 in Armenia. A 16-year-old Japanese woman may marry, but a male in India must wait until he turns 21.

Alexis could disaffirm her contract, return the luggage, and receive back the money she paid for the luggage.

The problem with giving certain parties, especially minors, the legal ability to disaffirm a contract and get back whatever they had given to the other party is that no one will want to contract with them. As a consequence, another protection was afforded those who lack capacity. It applies when protected parties purchase things classified as **necessaries**—things needed to maintain life—typically food, clothing, and shelter.

When the protected, or special, parties contract for such items they must at least pay a reasonable value for the necessaries even if they disaffirm the actual purchase contract. For example, if a minor purchased a fur coat for $5,000, she could disaffirm the contract. However she would still be required to pay the cost of a good cloth coat (say $200, a reasonable price), for the fur if she chose to keep it. This price may be seemingly unfair to the seller. However, in the eyes of the law, receiving only $200 for the fur serves as punishment for taking advantage of minors in contractual dealings.

MINORS

Minors' contracts are considered voidable, and they may disaffirm contracts during their minority. They also may disaffirm for a reasonable length of time after achieving their majority.

After the age of majority, the power to disaffirm is immediately cut off if the person ratifies the contract. **Ratification** is acting toward the contract as though one intends to be bound by it. Note that ratification can never occur before the age of majority.

Minors also may find themselves bound to their contracts if they are emancipated. **Emancipation** is the severing of the child-parent relationship. It

If this minor decides to purchase this bottle of expensive perfume, could she later disaffirm the contract and get back the money she paid for it? Or, upon disaffirmance, would she still have to pay a reasonable price for it? Explain your answer.

ends the duty of the parent to support a child and the duty of the child to obey the parent. A minor naturally becomes emancipated upon reaching the age of majority. However, a minor also may be emancipated before that time.

Early emancipation can occur formally or informally. Formal emancipation occurs when a court decrees the minor emancipated. Informal

Law Brief

To the normal list of food, clothing, and shelter as necessaries found in most states, the state of California adds cars and televisions. Cell phones are not considered necessaries anywhere as yet.

NETBookmark

Click on the link for Chapter 9 on lawxtra.swlearning.com to access the web site of the National Conference of State Legislatures. Locate your state in the chart entitled "Termination of Child Support and Support Beyond Majority." Write down the age in your state at which parents can legally terminate support. Then write the description of parents' duty to provide post-majority support in your state. Compare your state's treatment with that in surrounding states. Write a paragraph describing any major differences you notice among the states, citing specific examples.

lawxtra.swlearning.com

emancipation arises from the conduct of the minor and the parent. The following are evidence of informal emancipation:

1. The parent and minor agree that the parent will cease support.
2. The minor marries.
3. The minor moves out of the family home.
4. The minor becomes a member of the armed forces.
5. The minor gives birth.
6. The minor undertakes full-time employment.

States differ greatly in their treatment of emancipated minors. Some give them full contractual capacity and others don't. If you become emancipated, you may lose your capacity protection.

THOSE MENTALLY INCAPACITATED

Mental incapacity is much less precisely defined than minority. Under contract law mental incapacity means that a person lacks the ability to understand the consequences of his or her contractual acts. Thus people with severe mental illness, severe mental retardation, or severe senility lack capacity.

If a judge rules that a person is permanently insane, then this person has a complete lack of capacity. All contracts executed by this person are void. However, the rules surrounding necessaries are applied to an insane person's purchases of food, clothing, and shelter. If the judge rules that a person was insane when the contract was made but the condition was only temporary, the contract is considered voidable.

IN THIS CASE

Emily was 88 years old when she contracted to sell her family home to her daughter Gail for about 15 percent of its value. At the time, she was suffering from advanced Alzheimer's disease and didn't understand the consequences of the transaction. Two months later Emily died. Her will provided for all her property to be split equally among her four children. The other children sued to have the deed set aside because Emily lacked the mental capacity to contract. As Emily did not understand the consequences when she deeded the home to Gail, the contract was voided.

THE INTOXICATED

Intoxication can arise from using alcohol such as beer or vodka, from using drugs such as marijuana or crack cocaine, or inhaling products such as glue or aerosols. The courts often refer to the same definition of incapacity as for the mentally impaired—that is, can the person understand the consequences of their contractual acts. However, most courts are reluctant to consider an intoxicated party's contracts voidable. This would allow disaffirmance for intoxication even though it may injure an innocent party. Therefore courts typically allow disaffirmance only for those who are so intoxicated they do not know they are contracting. This stricter standard is used because intoxication is a voluntary act. If a judge holds that a person is in a permanent state of alcoholism, that person's contracts are considered void.

CHECKPOINT
What three classifications of individuals lack contractual capacity?

A QUESTION OF ETHICS

Perkins is a regional sales manager for an automobile manufacturer. She is responsible for visiting 15 car dealerships in one state. Perkins' job is to "push" certain models at different times to compensate for oversupply from the manufacturer. As part of her job, she often takes the owner and salespeople of a dealership to lunch. Over lunch, Perkins' guests often order several drinks. After these lunches, Perkins then gets down to business. She often does not know if her guests are drunk or not when she begins her pitch. Does Perkins have an ethical obligation to determine whether the dealers have had too much to drink? Do the owners have an ethical obligation to refrain from drinking at lunch, knowing that they will be asked to commit to deals after lunch?

WHO HAS CONTRACTUAL CAPACITY IN ORGANIZATIONS?

WHAT'S YOUR VERDICT?

Alicia was a wholesaler of flowers. Her friend, Caryn, worked for a grocery store as a checker. One day Alicia stopped by during Caryn's break and asked if she could sell her flowers through that store. Caryn said yes and signed a contract to purchase 10 dozen roses for the store. When Alicia tried to deliver the roses, they were refused by the store and Alicia sued.

Is the store bound by Caryn's contract?

Some people who work for businesses or other types of organizations have the capacity to bind the organizations to contracts. If someone has this capacity, it is said to be within his or her **scope of authority**, or within the range of acts the organization has authorized him or her to do. Capacity to contract can be created when the employer tells an employee that they are authorized to bind the organization.

Capacity also can be created when the organization leads others to believe that a person has certain authority. For example a person who holds the title of purchasing agent in an organization is assumed to have the authority to make purchases in its behalf. As another example, a person selling shoes probably could not bind the shoe store to a contract for the lease of a new store in a shopping center. The salesperson has capacity to sell the shoes, but doesn't have the capacity to contract for the store in any other way. It would be within the shoe store owner's scope of authority to contract for the lease.

When doing business with organizations, it is important to ensure that the person signing the contract has the scope of authority to bind the organization. People acting outside the scope of their authority generally are personally liable when the organization isn't. In *What's Your Verdict?* the store is not bound by the contract but Caryn may be liable to Alicia for the lost profit on the sale of the roses.

CHECKPOINT

In what two ways is capacity to contract on behalf of an organization created?

This photo shows the manager (middle), a bagger (left), and a sales clerk (right) who work for a supermarket. Which of these employees do you think has the broadest scope of authority, and why?

© DIGITAL VISION

In mid-2004, the U.S. Supreme Court again put on hold the enforcement of the Child Online Protection Act of 1988. The Court in its majority opinion stood behind First Amendment free-speech advocates who had maintained that there were less-restrictive means of preventing children's access to pornography on the web. The opinion by Justice Kennedy stated: "[c]ontent-based prohibitions, enforced by severe criminal penalties, have the constant potential to be a repressive force in the lives and thoughts of a free people. To guard against that threat, the Constitution demands that content-based restrictions on speech be presumed invalid and that the government bear the burden of showing their constitutionality." By content-based prohibitions, Justice Kennedy was pointing to the part of the Act that made it a criminal act to knowingly and for commercial purposes make any material that is "harmful to minors" accessible to minors. Justice Kennedy also noted that such a pervasive and ambiguous law would chill legitimate speech. A lawyer for the American Civil Liberties Union who agreed with the Court in putting enforcement of the Act on hold stated: "The Court has made it safe for artists, sex educators and Web publishers to communicate with adults about sexuality without risking jail time."

THINK ABOUT IT

Do you think the court struck the right balance between free speech and the danger of children accessing porn on the Internet? Why or why not? Can you propose any other solutions to the problem?

9-1 Assessment

Xtra!
Study Tools
lawxtra.swlearning.com

THINK ABOUT LEGAL CONCEPTS

1. The contracts of all those who lack capacity are void. **True or False?**

2. The law treats all the contracts of those lacking capacity in the same way. **True or False?**

3. Which of the following contracts are for necessaries? (a) a purchase of a high definition television (b) the purchase of groceries at a market (c) the rental of a truck for moving (d) all of the above are necessaries

4. What is the most common age of majority? (a) 21 (b) 18 (c) 16 (d) 9

5. The three most common necessaries are food, education, and shelter. **True or False?**

6. If a person acts within his or her scope of authority in entering into a contract for an organization, he or she is not personally liable for any losses that might occur. **True or False?**

THINK CRITICALLY ABOUT EVIDENCE

Study the situation, answer the questions, and then prepare arguments to support your answers.

7. Clare was age 17, a minor in her state, when she bought a week's worth of groceries at a local supermarket. Later she discovered she spent too much money and was going to be over her weekly budget. So she took the groceries back and asked for her money back. If she sues, will she get her money back?

8. Tanya, a minor, was the daughter of a construction worker. When she was 17, she bought an evening gown for $400 to wear to a school dance. After the dance, Tanya decided she didn't like the dress and returned it asking for the money back. Is she legally entitled to the money?

9. Janice had been drinking all afternoon before she went into a used car lot. There she signed a contract to purchase a two-year-old car for as much as it would cost for the same model new. She sought to disaffirm the contract based on intoxication. At the trial, she testified that, at the time of purchase, she knew she was buying a car but could not understand any of the terms of the contract. Will the court hold her to the terms of the contract?

Limits on the Rights of Those Without Capacity

▼ **GOALS**

- Recognize the time frame during which a contract can be disaffirmed
- Identify contracts that cannot be disaffirmed
- Discuss the effects of misrepresentation of age on contractual responsibilities

WHEN CAN DISAFFIRMANCE OCCUR AND WHAT MUST BE DONE AT THAT TIME?

WHAT'S YOUR VERDICT?

While still a minor, Beach bought a stereo system on credit from McReam's Electronic Cloud for $500. Beach paid $100 down and promised to pay $50 a month on the unpaid balance until the debt was paid. After making four payments, two of which were made after he reached the age of majority, Beach decided to disaffirm the contract and return the equipment.

Can Beach do so?

Generally, a person lacking contractual capacity can disaffirm a contract for necessaries or goods or services that are not necessaries

1. any time while still under the incapacity, or
2. within a reasonable time after attaining capacity.

After attaining capacity, a person may ratify the contract made while under an incapacity. Ratification is action by the party indicating intent to be bound by the contract. For a minor, ratification must occur after achieving majority. Ratification may consist of either of the following:

1. giving a new promise to perform as agreed, or
2. any act (such as making payments to the seller)

that clearly indicates the party's intention to be bound.

In *What's Your Verdict?* Beach ratified the contract by making payments after reaching majority. These actions cut off his power to disaffirm. Once ratification occurs, it may not be withdrawn.

WHAT MUST BE DONE UPON DISAFFIRMANCE

In all states, when a minor disaffirms, anything of value the minor received and still has must be returned. The minor is then entitled to get back everything that was given to the other party.

LOSS OF VALUE In most states, if minors are unable to return exactly what was received under the contract, they can still get back everything they gave. This is true even if a minor returns used or damaged goods. It is also true even if a minor returns nothing because the goods have been lost, consumed, or destroyed.

In some states, however, a minor must return everything received in a condition as good as it was when it was received. If this cannot be done, the minor must pay the difference in value, or deduct the difference from the amount to be refunded.

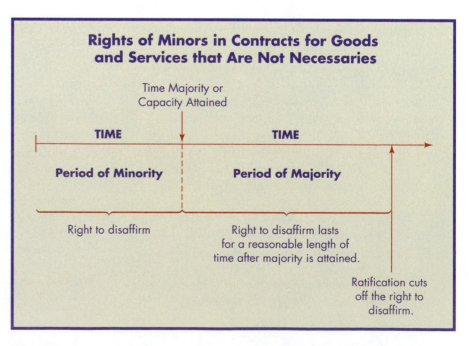

Rights of Minors in Contracts for Goods and Services that Are Not Necessaries

Time Majority or Capacity Attained

TIME | TIME

Period of Minority | **Period of Majority**

Right to disaffirm | Right to disaffirm lasts for a reasonable length of time after majority is attained.

Ratification cuts off the right to disaffirm.

OBLIGATIONS OF PARTY WITH CAPACITY Not only can the party lacking capacity generally disaffirm contracts for goods and services that are not necessaries, but, should he or she choose to, the party lacking capacity can enforce them against the party with capacity. On the other hand, generally the party with capacity can neither enforce nor avoid all or any part of a contract for goods or services that are not necessaries against a party lacking capacity.

CHECKPOINT

When can a person who lacks contractual capacity disaffirm a contract?

IN THIS CASE

Lamon, a minor, bought a diamond engagement ring and a necklace for his fiancée, Morgan. He paid for the items in weekly installments of $10. One day while still a minor, he and Morgan quarreled. Morgan returned the ring to Lamon but refused to part with the necklace.

Morgan was legally entitled to keep the necklace because it was an ordinary gift not connected with the proposed marriage. Lamon could return the ring to the jeweler and demand a refund of the money he had paid for both pieces of jewelry. Lamon is entitled to the money he had paid on the ring. In most states, he is even entitled to what he had paid on the necklace. That is because he returned everything that was still in his possession. In some states, however, a minor must return everything received in a condition as good as it was when it was received. If this cannot be done, the minor must pay the difference in value, or deduct the difference from the amount to be refunded. In these states, Lamon could be unable to recover the price of the necklace.

CONTRACTS THAT CANNOT BE DISAFFIRMED

WHAT'S YOUR VERDICT?

Upon graduation from high school, Robinson, age 17, began a business doing electrical work. He bought $375 in tools from Muller. The venture was a disappointing failure. Discouraged after a month, Robinson asked Muller to take back the tools and to return his $375 payment.

Must Muller do so?

Some contracts of minors for goods or services that are not necessaries cannot be disaffirmed. These exceptional situations vary considerably from state to state. The statutes and cases of your state are the only definitive source on this topic. The most common examples follow.

COURT-APPROVED CONTRACTS In all states, minors cannot void any contracts approved for them by a court. For example, minors who are employed as actors or actresses or as professionals in sports usually have their contracts approved by a court. Once approved, these contracts may not be disaffirmed.

MAJOR COMMITMENTS In all states, contracts to enlist in the armed services and contracts for educational loans cannot be disaffirmed. Similarly, marriage contracts of minors cannot be disaffirmed.

BANKING CONTRACTS In most states, minors are permitted to make deposits in banks and in savings and loan associations. Most states also permit minors to make withdrawals as if they were adults, without any right to disaffirm these transactions.

INSURANCE CONTRACTS More than one-half of the states provide that minors who are over a certain age may not disaffirm certain contracts of life insurance.

WORK-RELATED CONTRACTS In most states, minors who engage in a business or trade cannot disaffirm agreements involving their businesses. In *What's Your Verdict?* Robinson would not be able to avoid his contract if he lived in a state with such a law.

SALE OF REALTY In some states, a minor who owns real property and sells it or borrows money against it cannot disaffirm until after achieving majority.

APARTMENT RENTAL In a few states, the lease of an apartment cannot be disaffirmed even if the apartment is not a necessary.

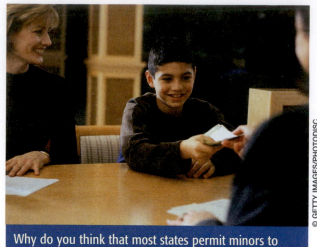

© GETTY IMAGES/PHOTODISC

CHECKPOINT

Which contracts that cannot be disaffirmed apply in all 50 states?

Why do you think that most states permit minors to make deposits and withdrawals to their bank accounts without the right to disaffirm these transactions?

CONTRACTUAL EFFECT OF MISREPRESENTING AGE

WHAT'S YOUR VERDICT?

Ron, a mature-looking minor, lied about his age when he bought an extensive wardrobe of clothing from the Casuals Shop. Ron showed his older brother's driver's license as identification. He also used his brother's name on the installment contract. By October, Ron had paid $325 on the $785 contract. He then became bored with the wardrobe and returned it to the store and demanded the return of all payments.

Must the store return his money?

In *What's Your Verdict?* Ron is within his rights as a minor in disaffirming the contract. However, he also committed the tort of fraud. Therefore in most states, the Casuals Shop probably could hold back from the refund an amount of money sufficient to cover the decrease in value of the wardrobe as returned. Or the store could hold back the full amount if nothing was returned. Ron could be held liable in damages for deceiving the seller. These damages could exceed the price of the goods he lied to get.

CHECKPOINT

If minors lie about their age, what happens in most states with regard to their ability to disaffirm contracts for goods and services that are not necessaries?

Minors have been known to misrepresent their ages. In most states, minors who lie about their age may nevertheless disaffirm their contracts. However, in these states, a minor who gives a false age may be held liable for the tort of false representation.

Minors are liable for their torts and delinquent or criminal conduct growing out of a contractual transaction, although typically they still have the right to disaffirm their contracts. Thus, the other party to the contract may collect from a minor any damages suffered because of the minor's fraud even though the minor may be able to disaffirm the contract.

LEGAL RESEARCH

Investigate the effect in your state of using fake identification in contracts to purchase alcohol or tobacco, or for entering age-restricted areas. Summarize your findings in a paragraph. Note especially the effect on the ability to rescind the contract.

Assessment

THINK ABOUT LEGAL CONCEPTS

1. A disaffirmed contract for a necessary may still be enforced against a minor for a reasonable value. **True or False?**

2. A contract for goods or services that are not necessaries entered into while a minor can be disaffirmed (a) anytime (b) anytime after achieving majority (c) anytime during minority (d) within a reasonable time after achieving majority (e) both c and d.

3. Generally, a minor who lies to appear in his or her majority loses the right to disaffirm a contract that might result. **True or False?**

4. Which of the following is not an example of a contract that a minor cannot disaffirm in some or all states. (a) bank depository contracts, (b) enlistment contracts in the armed services, (c) gambling contracts, (d) none of the above can be disaffirmed by a minor.

THINK CRITICALLY ABOUT EVIDENCE

Study the situation, answer the questions, and then prepare arguments to support your answers.

5. Richard bought car insurance while he was 16. He had a perfect driving record until he reached the age of majority, 21 in his state. The day after his birthday, Richard disaffirmed the insurance contract and asked for the return of his payments. In most states would he be legally entitled to the money?

6. Linda subscribed to a "Book of the Month" program on her sixteenth birthday. She received monthly books from the publisher until her twenty-first birthday. She continued receiving books for another six months, and then attempted to disaffirm. Will she succeed?

7. In Juan's state, the age of majority is 21. Three weeks after his eighteenth birthday, Juan joined the Marine Corp. After two weeks of boot camp, he decided he didn't like the lifestyle. He told the Marines he was disaffirming his contract to join. Will he succeed?

8. Beverly was 14 when she bought a used motorcycle that wouldn't run. Beverly made repairs and got it going. She rode it illegally for more than six months. Then a leak developed in a gas line and the bike caught fire. It was a total loss. Beverly returned the burned-out motorcycle to the seller and asked for all her money back. Will she succeed?

PREVENT LEGAL DIFFICULTIES

In making contracts . . .

1. When contracting, always observe and remember factors about the other person indicating whether or not they have full contractual capacity. If you are dealing with a representative of a business, ask questions about the person's ability to bind the organization in contract.

2. When judging age, be skeptical. Ask for identification for anyone who looks like they are within a decade of the age of majority.

3. If the people you want to contract with have alcohol on their breath, watch for signs of drunkenness: whether or not they slur their words, weave as they walk, and exaggerate behavior. If they display these symptoms and you still want to contract with them, be sure you have a witness or other proof of the fact that they know they are making a contract.

4. Remember the other party in a transaction is seldom primarily concerned with your best interest and generally is not obligated to volunteer information about their capacity.

5. When contracting with the elderly, be certain that they can understand the consequences of any contract you enter into with them.

6. If you are a minor, do not misrepresent your age. The consequences may hurt you more than not being allowed to contract.

Chapter 9 Assessment

CONCEPTS IN BRIEF

9-1 Contractual Capacity of Individuals and Organizations

1. Generally, the contracts of individuals lacking contractual capacity are voidable and can be disaffirmed by the incapacitated party. Upon so doing they are to receive back what they put into the bargain and must return what they received from it, if possible.

2. Necessaries are those things needed to sustain life. In most states, necessaries are limited to food, clothing, and shelter. Even after disaffirming a contract for these items, a party without capacity is liable for their reasonable value.

3. Minors are those under the age of majority.

4. If a court has held that an individual is permanently insane or is permanently addicted to alcohol, that person's contracts are void. However, the doctrine of necessaries will apply where appropriate.

5. The contractual party having capacity has no right to disaffirm the contract just because the party lacking capacity has the right to do so.

6. Employees bind their employers to contracts they execute on their behalf if they are acting within their actual or apparent scope of authority.

9-2 Limits on the Rights of Those Without Capacity

7. Generally, those lacking contractual capacity can only disaffirm contracts during the time of their incapacity and for a reasonable time thereafter.

8. Ratification of a contract cannot occur before an incapacity is removed.

9. Ratification may consist of either giving a new promise to perform as agreed, or any act (such as making payments to the seller) that clearly indicates the previously incapacitated party's intention to be bound.

10. In many states certain types of contracts, such as insurance and banking contracts, cannot be disaffirmed.

11. Generally, misrepresentation of age does not affect the right to disaffirm but may expose a minor to a subsequent lawsuit.

YOUR LEGAL VOCABULARY

Match each statement with the term that it best defines. Some terms may not be used.

1. Severing of the parent-child relationship
2. Within the range of authorized acts
3. Goods and services needed to sustain life
4. State of being unable to understand the consequences of a contract because of alcohol or drugs
5. Act after regaining capacity indicating an intent to be bound by the contract
6. Ability to understand that a contract is being made and the consequences thereof
7. Giving back what you have received under a contract and requesting the return of what you gave
8. Period of time when a young person lacks full contractual capacity
9. A severe mental illness, retardation, or senility
10. Either 18, 19, or 21 in most states
11. One who has not yet reached the age of majority

a. age of majority
b. contractual capacity
c. disaffirmance
d. emancipation
e. intoxication
f. mental incapacity
g. minor
h. minority
i. necessaries
j. ratification
k. scope of authority

REVIEW LEGAL CONCEPTS

12. Assume you were going to buy a two-year-old car at a bargain price from a woman who was 86 years old. Explain the steps you would take to create evidence that she has mental capacity.

13. Assume you were going to buy a two-year-old car at a bargain price from a man with alcohol on his breath. Explain the steps you would take to create evidence that he has capacity.

14. Identify three things you've bought recently that are necessaries and three things that are not.

15. If any of the three purchases in exercise 14 can be ratified, describe the exact conduct you might engage in after achieving majority to constitute ratification.

WRITE ABOUT LEGAL CONCEPTS

16. Write a one-paragraph summary of the law of capacity as it applies to minors.

17. Write a one-paragraph summary of the law of capacity as it applies to the intoxicated.

18. Write a one-paragraph description of what you would do to protect your legal interests if dealing with a 90-year-old man who wanted to rent an apartment to you.

19. **HOT DEBATE** John Eric kept a copy of the letter his father wrote. Thereafter, he subscribed to similar offers from several other clubs, and then cancelled the contracts with the letter. All of the other clubs responded in the same manner as the first. He amassed a large CD collection at almost no cost to himself. Should John Eric still be under the protection of the law in these later contractual circumstances?

THINK CRITICALLY ABOUT EVIDENCE

Study the situation, answer the questions, and then prepare arguments to support your answers.

20. A month after he turned 16, Chris, a resident of Missouri, answered a classified newpaper ad and, after prolonged negotiations, bought a used car from Dowdy. Chris spent $8,500 of the $10,000 in cash given to him by his father on his birthday on the purchase. Six months after buying the car, the crankshaft in the engine broke. The cost of a new engine would have been about $3,200 so Chris decided to disaffirm the contract to purchase the car. Legally, can he do so?

21. On her sixteenth birthday, Laurisa bought a used computer from Stuart for $100 cash. Laurisa is from a wealthy family and receives an allowance of $200 a week. Six months after buying the computer, the hard drive crashed so Laurisa decided to disaffirm. Legally, can she?

22. June stopped by a bar on the way home from work and drank three gin and tonics. Then she bought a six-pack of beer at the local grocery store and drank three cans before her husband came home. June and her husband then began drinking whiskey and water and each finished two drinks. A salesperson from Metropolitan Life Insurance came over and sold June a life insurance policy that cost $900 per year. Is there evidence indicating that June may be able to disaffirm?

23. Larson was 69 years old and trying to sell his home. He had it appraised, and the estimated value was $300,000. He listed the home with a local real estate broker for $330,000. When Perry offered him $305,000 he counteroffered at $320,000. When Perry balked at the price, he lowered his offer to $315,000 and she accepted. Is there evidence that Larson possesses the mental capacity to contract?

MAKE ACADEMIC CONNECTIONS

24. **MARKETING** Interview people who work in telemarketing, Internet sales, banking, insurance, and like industries to see how they determine if the parties they are dealing with have capacity to contract. Evaluate the methods and report to the class on those you consider effective and those that you consider ineffective. State why.

25. Sixteen-year-old Johnny Hays went to Quality Motors, Inc., in Tennessee, to buy a car. When a salesperson asked about his age, Johnny side-stepped the question. The salesperson refused to sell except to an adult. Hays left and returned shortly with a companion of 23, whom he had just met. The salesperson then sold Hays the car. The bill of sale was made out to the companion who, with the help of the salesperson, later transferred the title to Hays. When Hays' father, Dr. D. J. Hays, discovered the sale, he called Quality Motors and asked them to take the car back. The company refused. Dr. Hays tried to return the car on three more occasions. Finally, the car was put into storage. Johnny Hays found the keys to the car and took it on a trip, damaging it in two accidents. As a result, the car was not in running condition at the time of the trial. Can Johnny disaffirm? Who will bear the loss due to the damage? (*Masterson v. Sine*, 216 Ark. 264)

26. W. O. Lucy and J. C. Lucy, the plaintiffs, sued A. H. Zehmer and Ida Zehmer, the defendants, to force the Zehmers to transfer the title to the Ferguson Farm to the Lucys for $50,000. The Lucys alleged that the Zehmers had agreed to do so one night when Mr. Lucy had stopped in to visit the Zehmers in the combination restaurant, filling station, and motor court they operated. While there, Lucy tried to buy the Ferguson Farm just as he had tried many times before. This time he tried a new approach. Lucy said to Zehmer, "I bet you wouldn't take $50,000 for that place." Zehmer replied, "Yes, I would too; you wouldn't give fifty." Throughout the evening, the conversation returned to the sale of the Ferguson Farm for $50,000. At the same time, the parties continued to drink whiskey and engage in light conversation. Eventually Lucy got Zehmer to write up an agreement to the effect that Zehmer would sell to Lucy the Ferguson Farm for $50,000 complete. Later, Lucy sued Zehmer to go through with the sale. Zehmer argued that he had been drunk and that the offer had been made in jest and hence was unenforceable. What evidence supports the conclusion that Zehmer was intoxicated? What evidence supports the conclusion that Zehmer was not intoxicated? Is Zehmer bound? (*Lucy v. Zehmer*, 196 Va. 493)

27. Webster Street Partnership owned real estate in Omaha, Nebraska. It leased an apartment to Matthew Sheridan and Pat Wilwerding for one year at a rental of $250 per month. Although Webster Street did not know this, both Sheridan and Wilwerding were younger than the age of majority when the lease was signed. Both minors had moved out of their homes voluntarily and were free to return there at any time. Sheridan and Wilwerding paid $150 as a security deposit. They paid for two months, for a total of $500, then failed to pay for the next month on time. Webster Street notified them that they would be required to move out unless they paid immediately. Unable to pay rent, Sheridan and Wilwerding moved out of the apartment. Webster Street later demanded that they pay the expenses it incurred in attempting to re-rent the property and assorted damages and fees, amounting to $630.94. Sheridan and Wilwerding refused on the ground of minority to pay any of the amount demanded. Further, they demanded the return of their security deposit. Webster Street then sued. Is the apartment a necessary? Can Sheridan and Wilwerding disaffirm? (*Webster Street Partnership v. Sheridan*, 368 N.W. 2d 439, Neb.)

28. Kevin Green was 16 years old when he purchased a 1979 Camaro for $4,642.50 from Star Chevrolet. Shortly after the purchase, the car blew a head gasket and couldn't be driven. Thereafter Kevin informed Star that he was disaffirming the contract. He offered to return the car, but Star would not accept it unless it was repaired. In January 1982 Kevin brought suit for the purchase price. The car was not used for four or five months until Kevin repaired the blown head gasket himself. In June 1982 the car was in an accident which substantially reduced its value. In an insurance settlement arising out of the accident, Kevin received $1,500 as a salvage payment for the Camaro. He used the salvage money to buy another car. Star then sued Green. What resulted? (*Star Chevrolet v. Green*, 473 So. 2d 157, Miss.)

CASE FOR LEGAL THINKING

HAUER V. UNION STATE BANK OF WAUTOMA
192 WIS. 2D 576

EVIDENCE Kathy Hauer suffered a brain injury in a motorcycle accident. She was subsequently judged to be incompetent, and the court appointed a guardian for her. Hauer's guardianship was later terminated based upon a letter from her treating physician. Ben Eilbes met Hauer and convinced her to take out a $7,600 loan to help him in his business, using her mutual fund as collateral. Eilbes then contacted Shroeder, assistant vice president of the bank, to arrange for the loan. Shroeder called Hauer's stockbroker and financial consultant to verify Hauer's mutual fund. He was told that Hauer needed the interest from the mutual fund to live on. Upon default, the bank brought suit to collect the amount due from the collateral.

TRIAL The jury found that Hauer lacked the mental capacity to enter into the loan and that the Bank failed to act in good faith toward Hauer in the loan transaction. The Bank appeals.

REASONING A review of the record reveals that there is credible evidence the jury could have relied on in reaching its verdict. First, Hauer was under court-appointed guardianship approximately one year before the loan transaction. Second, Hauer's testimony indicates a complete lack of understanding of the nature and consequences of the transaction. Third, Hauer's psychological expert testified that Hauer was "very deficient in her cognitive abilities, her abilities to remember and to read, write and spell . . . Barnes further testified she was "incompe-

tent and . . . unable to make reasoned decisions" on the date she made the loan.

The trial court offered two explanations for voiding the contract and not holding Hauer liable for repayment of the loan: (1) the law and policy of the "infancy doctrine," and (2) the jury's finding that the Bank failed to act in good faith.

The Supreme Court held that a minor who disaffirms a contract might recover the purchase price without liability for use, depreciation, or other lessening in value. Generally, a minor who disaffirms a contract is expected to return as much of the consideration as remains in the minor's possession. However, the minor's right to disaffirm is permitted even where the minor cannot return the property.

However, a "contract made by a person who is mentally incompetent requires the reconciliation of two conflicting policies: the protection of justifiable expectations and of the security of transactions, and the protection of persons unable to protect themselves against imposition." Absent fraud or knowledge of the incapacity by the other contracting party, the contractual act of an incompetent is voidable by the incompetent only if avoidance accords with equitable principles.

The Bank argues that it does not have an affirmative duty to inquire into the mental capacity of a loan applicant to evaluate his or her capacity to understand a proposed transaction. We agree.

However, a contracting party exposes itself to a voidable contract where it is put on notice or given a reason to suspect the other party's incompetence such as would indicate to a reasonably prudent person that inquiry should be made of the party's mental condition.

Judgment affirmed.

© GETTY IMAGES/PHOTODISC

PRACTICE JUDGING

1. What evidence indicates that Hauer had mental capacity?

2. What evidence indicates Hauer did not have mental capacity?

3. Which evidence do you think is weightier, that indicating capacity or that indicating lack of capacity?

Legal Purpose and Proper Form

10-1 Illegal Agreements

10-2 The Statute of Frauds

© GETTY IMAGES/PHOTODISC

HOT DEBATE

"The winner is number 3913. Who's won this incredible classic? Who's got the winning ticket?" The voice echoed throughout the gym. Sanford Davis looked around. A man was running toward the stage from the other side of the floor. It was Brandon Johnson, the son of Michael Johnson. Michael Johnson was the owner of Johnson's Exotic Car Shop and the donor of the '67 Mustang that was the prize in the lottery. Odd, thought Sanford, that out of more than 2,000 purchasers of the $25 tickets, the son of the man who had donated the car had won it. Of course, buying new uniforms for the high school's Marching Terrapins band was a great cause. Still, it was too much of a coincidence. Sanford pushed his way through the crowd. Near the stage he found the band director carrying a box with the receipts in it. "I want my money back," said Sanford, "or I'll swear out a criminal complaint against everybody involved in this for holding an illegal lottery." Sanford knew that the state statute on gambling only allowed bingo games run by licensed charitable organizations and the state lotteries. The band director replied that it had been an honest lottery for a good cause and that she would not refund Sanford's money. Sanford immediately knew what he had to do. The next afternoon, after a lengthy session with Sanford, the local prosecutor called the school and said she would bring felony gambling charges against the band director and other school officials if the receipts were not refunded to the ticket purchasers.

Where Do You Stand?

1. Were Sanford's actions ethical?
2. Would a statute that allowed "honest lotteries for a good cause" be acceptable? Why or why not?

Illegal Agreements

WHICH AGREEMENTS ARE ILLEGAL?

WHAT'S YOUR VERDICT?

Razer agreed with several published articles that criticized laws prohibiting the production, possession, and use of marijuana. The authors of the articles claimed such legislation was unrealistic and often violated civil rights. Razer agreed so heartily that he bought several dozen marijuana plants from a friend, Sara. Then he rented a patch of isolated land and persuaded the owner, Tom, to accept a share of the proceeds from the sale of the anticipated crop as rent. After harvesting the first crop, Razer sold most of the product to a local drug dealer for $7,500.

Were any of Razer's agreements illegal?

Agreements that involve contracting for an illegal act generally are void and unenforceable. For example, almost any agreement to commit a felony (a serious crime) will be an illegal agreement. In *What's Your Verdict?* all of Razer's agreements were criminal and therefore void. Examples of the most frequently prosecuted types of illegal contracts are discussed in the following sections.

ILLEGAL LOTTERIES

Most states either forbid or regulate gambling. Usually they have statutes which make gambling agreements, typically termed illegal lotteries, void. A **lottery** has three elements: a *prize* (something of value for one or more winners), *chance* (the winner determined solely by luck) and *consideration* (a payment to participate). A **wager**, one of the most common forms of gambling, is a bet on the uncertain outcome of an event, such as a football game.

Most states have legalized various forms of gambling under regulated conditions:

- *Casinos*—where most forms of traditional gaming are permitted such as keno, blackjack, roulette and the like

ECONOMIC IMPACT

NATIVE AMERICANS AND TRIBAL GAMING

In many states that permit gambling or "gaming," casinos are being operated by Native American tribes. The tribes, recognized as "sovereign nations," depend on the revenue from the casinos as an important part of their tribal economy. Tribal gaming has stimulated community growth and economic development within many once-impoverished Native American nations. The large-scale tribal gaming operations began in the early 1980s, about the same time as the emergence of lotteries in many states. Since then, several court cases have shaped the relationship between the sovereign nations' gaming operations and

the states. In 1987 in *California v. Cabazon* the Supreme Court upheld the tribes' rights as sovereign nations to conduct gaming on Native American lands. They may conduct the gaming free of state control if similar gaming is permitted outside the reservation. The Indian Gaming Regulatory Act, passed by Congress in 1988, affirms the tribes' right to conduct gaming on their lands.

THINK CRITICALLY

What is your opinion of Native American tribes raising revenue through casino gambling?

- *Pari-mutuel betting*—a form of betting in which those who bet on the winner of a horse race share the total prize pool
- *State-run lotteries*—often with millions in the jackpot to be split between the winner(s) and state educational institutions
- *Bingo games and pull-tab betting*—permitted in many states when conducted by licensed institutions for financing charitable, religious, or educational projects.

AGREEMENTS TO PAY USURIOUS INTEREST

Almost all states provide that, with certain exceptions, lenders of money may not charge more than a specified maximum rate of interest. Generally, the penalties specified by these statutes vary. In some states, the lender cannot collect some or all of the interest. However, the borrower usually must repay the principal. The maximum interest rate varies among the states, and 18 percent is a common maximum. Lending money at a rate higher than the state's maximum allowable rate is *usury*.

Sometimes a person borrows money for which interest will be charged but no exact rate is stated. In such a case, the rate to be paid is the *legal rate of interest,* which is specified by state statute. In about one-half of the states, this rate is 7 percent or less per year. In most of the other states, the legal rate ranges between 8 and 12 percent.

Many states permit licensed loan companies and pawnbrokers to charge a *small loan rate of interest.* This rate typically is 36 percent a year, usually on loans of up to $2,000. Because the dollar amount loaned is relatively small, the overhead cost per dollar loaned is high. Presumably the risk of loss from defaults also is high on such loans. Therefore the states allow a higher interest rate to loan companies and pawnbrokers to protect people against criminal loan sharks, who illegally charge extremely high rates, often 50 percent monthly.

AGREEMENTS INVOLVING ILLEGAL DISCRIMINATION

Some agreements are unenforceable because they violate anti-discrimination statutes. For example, an agreement between a motel chain and a local manager to not accept guests of a particular race or national origin would be unenforceable because it violates the federal Civil Rights Act of 1964.

Agreements also may be illegal as violations of the Constitution. For example, a contract between a residential subdivision developer and a home buyer providing that the buyer would not sell to a member of a particular race would be unenforceable because it violates the Fourteenth Amendment to the Constitution.

AGREEMENTS THAT OBSTRUCT LEGAL PROCEDURES

Agreements that delay or prevent justice are void. Examples include promises to

- pay non-expert witnesses in a trial to testify, or pay for false testimony
- bribe jurors
- refrain from informing on or prosecuting an alleged crime in exchange for money or other valuable consideration. This is called **compounding a crime**.

A court or prosecutor may make a penalty dependent upon a criminal's making restitution (for example, returning a stolen car). However, the victim may not make reporting a crime dependent upon restitution.

AGREEMENTS MADE WITHOUT A REQUIRED COMPETENCY LICENSE

All states require that persons in certain occupations and businesses pass exams and receive a **competency license** to ensure that they can perform adequately. Persons engaged in trades, such as barbers, plumbers, and electrical wiring installers typically require a competency license. Professionals such as physicians, teachers,

Who benefits from mandatory competency licensing of tradespeople and professionals?

lawyers, and pharmacists also must have competency licenses. Real estate brokers, insurance agents, and building contractors are subject to such regulation as well. Persons who lack the required competency license may not enforce the contracts they make in doing the regulated work.

In contrast, if the license is a **revenue license**, whose purpose is only to raise revenue rather than to protect the public, contracts made by the unlicensed person are valid. Generally the only penalty for failure to get such a license is a higher fee when the license is obtained later.

AGREEMENTS THAT AFFECT MARRIAGE NEGATIVELY

The law encourages marriage and family life by making agreements that harm or interfere with marriage unenforceable. For example, Mimi is an illegal immigrant and Bill is a U.S. citizen. It would be an illegal contract if Mimi agreed to pay Bill $5,000 in exchange for his promise to marry her so she could obtain citizenship. Similarly, a father's promise to pay his daughter for not marrying would be unenforceable. Also it would be illegal for a boss to agree to pay her assistant money in exchange for his promise to divorce his spouse.

AGREEMENTS THAT RESTRAIN TRADE UNREASONABLY

The U.S. economic system is based on the concept of free and open competition. This creates profits for producers who benefit consumers the most. Hence, both state and federal laws seek to prevent monopolies and combinations that restrict competition unreasonably.

PRICE FIXING When competing firms agree on the same price to be charged for a product or service, this injures consumers. It deprives them of the lower prices which competition would produce. **Price fixing** is a crime under federal law. Agreements to fix prices are therefore unenforceable.

One form of price fixing is **bid rigging**. This occurs when competitors who bid on jobs agree that one bidder will have the lowest bid for a particular job. It is illegal because typically the bid riggers take turns being the lowest bidder and set the bid price higher than if there were real competition.

IN THIS CASE

All ten pharmacy owners in the city of Weston meet to discuss common problems. During the discussion, they agree that all the stores would match the prices charged for certain items by a discount outlet that had recently opened in the town. They also agree that they will charge no less than specified minimum prices for some 50 other high-volume items. Because these agreements restrained free trade and controlled prices, they were illegal and void.

RESALE PRICE MAINTENANCE Manufacturers engage in *resale price maintenance* when they want retailers to sell their product at particular prices. They may identify a "suggested retail price." This is legal. However, manufacturers may not agree or contract with retailers to sell the product at a particular price because that would involve two parties fixing the price. On the other hand, manufacturers can identify a suggested price and refuse to sell to retailers who will not charge that amount.

ALLOCATION OF MARKETS The same injury to competition produced by price fixing can be achieved if competitors divide markets between themselves. This practice is known as *allocation of markets*. If the Ford dealers in a state agree that they will not sell to residents outside the county where their dealership is located, this eliminates price competition for Fords and injures consumers. Therefore agreements to allocate markets are illegal and unenforceable.

AGREEMENTS NOT TO COMPETE

Price fixing and market allocations are agreements not to compete. One type of agreement not to compete is sometimes enforceable. When persons are hired they may agree that they will not compete with their employer after the employment terminates. However, these agreements become illegal if they are unreasonable in

- time period for the limitation
- geographic area to which the limitation applies
- employer's interest protected by the limitation

An agreement not to compete for 20 years would likely be illegal. Often an agreement not to compete anywhere in the United States is ruled to be illegal. In contrast, an agreement not to engage in the printing business for two years in the city or county where the former employer is located probably would be enforceable. The employer's interests protected by the agreement not to compete must be significant. Trade secrets are the most commonly recognized employer interests.

CHECKPOINT

Name four of the eight illegal agreements discussed in this section.

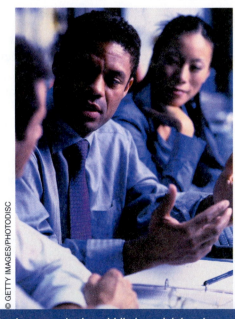

The businessman in the middle is explaining the company's "non-compete" contract to two new salespeople. The contract states that upon termination of their employment, they are not to work in the same industry anywhere in the world for five years. Is this a legal agreement?

© GETTY IMAGES/PHOTODISC

WHEN WILL THE COURTS ENFORCE ILLEGAL AGREEMENTS?

WHAT'S YOUR VERDICT?

A young couple, the Guptas, wanted to provide for the college education of their infant daughter. They received this offer in the mail from the True Bonanza Mining Corporation, which seemed perfect for their need: "Join us now for only 10 cents a share of stock. Become part owner of a gold and silver mine with already proven mineral deposits. In ten years, you will be rich enough to retire!" The Guptas used all their savings to buy 250,000 shares of Bonanza stock. Months later they learned that Bonanza had violated the law. Its "proven mineral deposits" were commercially worthless aluminum oxides. The sales agreement was illegal.

Can the Guptas recover their $25,000?

Most illegal contracts are void and unenforceable. However, when the connection between the illegality and the agreement is slight or a party is relatively innocent of wrongdoing or both, the law will allow restitution (the recovery of your consideration) or the agreement to be enforced in court. Examples of the circumstances under which such treatment may be afforded include cases involving protected victims, the excusably ignorant, those who rescind before the prohibited act, and cases in which the contract is divisible.

PROTECTED VICTIMS

In some cases the law that was violated was designed to protect a party to the agreement. For example, *blue-sky laws* prohibit sales of worthless stocks and bonds. Such securities have no more value than a section of the blue sky. The victim may obtain restitution to recover money paid. Thus, in *What's Your Verdict?* restitution would be available to the Guptas.

Parties to an illegal agreement often are not equally to blame. For example, one party might lie to persuade another person to enter an illegal agreement. Where the illegal agreement was created by fraud, duress, misrepresentation, or undue influence, the victim may obtain restitution.

THE EXCUSABLY IGNORANT

The excusably ignorant can either enforce the legal part of the contract or obtain restitution. A person is *excusably ignorant* who

- does not know the contract is illegal, but
- the other party knows the transaction is illegal, and
- the illegality is minor

RESCISSION PRIOR TO ILLEGAL ACT

If a party rescinds before the illegal act occurs, then restitution will be available. For example, suppose you paid $50 to another student to steal an advance copy of a final exam. Then you changed your mind and called off the deal before the theft. You could recover the $50 payment. In this way, the law creates an incentive to stop illegal acts.

DIVISIBLE CONTRACTS

Illegal contracts often contain a combination of legal and illegal provisions. Courts may enforce the legal part of a contract if it is divisible. *Divisible* generally means that separate consideration is given for the legal and illegal parts of the contract. Suppose a retailer contracts to sell camping and hunting supplies, including a pistol. If the seller fails to comply with a state law that requires a 30-day waiting period and a police clearance of sale of a handgun, this part of the contract is illegal. However, a court would

probably enforce the legal provisions of the contract because the amount paid for the pistol (the illegal part) can be distinguished from the amount paid for everything else (the legal part).

On the other hand, suppose a single bid for all electrical contracting work on an office building specifies wiring and terminals in conflict with the building code. This contract probably would not be divisible because labor, wiring, terminals, and other costs were not broken out as separate items. This contract is *indivisible*.

A major provision in the UCC governing the sale of goods makes agreements or contract clauses that are unconscionable unenforceable. The UCC establishes an additional remedy for courts when dealing with such agreements. **Unconscionability** occurs when there is a grossly unfair contract that parties under ordinary circumstances would not accept. The UCC makes unconscionable contracts for the sale of goods subject to the rules for illegality. Such a contract has two elements: procedural and substantive unconscionability.

Procedural unconscionability is shown by how the contract is created. It arises when contracts contain very fine print, light typesetting, or elements of fraud, duress, undue influence, or misrepresentation. It also can be established by showing that a party had no real alternatives, was time pressured, or possessed unequal bargaining power.

Substantive unconscionability arises from unfair terms in the agreement. It can take the form of a price so high that it shocks the conscience of the court or very one-sided terms such as the elimination of important remedies (for example, restitution) for one party.

Most, but not all, courts require both procedural and substantive unconscionability before the contract is deemed unconscionable and illegal. When the court finds a contract illegal for unconscionability, it can refuse to enforce the contract, or it can enforce the legal part and refuse to enforce the illegal part. In addition, courts also can modify the terms of an agreement to make it fair.

CHECKPOINT

Under what circumstances will the courts enforce illegal agreements?

Assessment

THINK ABOUT LEGAL CONCEPTS

1. Contracts in which one person pays another to commit a felony are unenforceable. **True or False?**

2. Charging interest at a rate higher than allowed by law is called (a) compounding a crime (b) wagering (c) excessive interest (d) usury.

3. Typically, illegal contracts are held by the courts to be _?_ and unenforceable. (a) valid (b) voidable (c) void

4. A lottery has three elements: prize, chance, and consideration. **True or False?**

5. Restitution is (a) the enforcement of an agreement (b) getting back your consideration in a contract.

6. If you agreed to pay a non-expert witness to make sure that she testified for you at a trial, this agreement would be unenforceable. **True or False?**

7. A party to an illegal contract may be able to either enforce the agreement or obtain restitution if he or she (a) is excusably ignorant (b) is a protected victim (c) rescinds before the illegal act occurs (d) all of the above.

THINK CRITICALLY ABOUT EVIDENCE

Study the situation, answer the questions, and then prepare arguments to support your answers.

8. Crump was coming up for trial on felony charges. He paid the judge in the case $10,000 to make errors in conducting the trial so that Crump's conviction could be overturned on appeal. When the appeal failed, Crump sought to sue for restitution of the $10,000. Should he be allowed to recover the bribe? Why or why not?

9. Dixon, a wholesaler, was on the brink of bankruptcy. He bought fire insurance policies for more than twice the value of the building and contents from two companies. Then he arranged to pay a character known only as "Sparky" $5,000 to "torch" his business building. If Sparky did so but Dixon did not pay him, could Sparky enforce the contract for the $5,000? Could Dixon legally collect on his insurance policies if Sparky torched the building?

10. A new boss was scheduled to take over Patty's department in three weeks. Patty agreed to pay Nancy $600 to remove unflattering information from her personnel file so she would look good to the new boss. The day before Nancy was going to do it, Patty called and told her not to. She also asked for her money back. Nancy never took the information. Could Patty sue and recover her money?

11. Cliff worked as a site manager for an oil-drilling company. When a drill bit broke, he called Texas Bit Company, a bit manufacturer. Cliff asked for a bit able to cut quickly through granite. The salesperson recommended their model 2123 which was described as a high carbon steel bit with diamonds embedded on the cutting edges. The salesperson quoted a fair price but she said there were no warranties and that the product was being sold, "as is." This is an unusual practice in this industry. Cliff didn't think he could get that type of bit from anyone else without a big delay, so he ordered it. It turned out that the bit was made only of low-carbon steel and it cut very slowly. Is there procedural unconscionability here? Is there substantive unconscionability here? Did the bit company create an unconscionable contract?

12. A remote community and the surrounding countryside had no doctor. The city council advertised for help, offering free office space, a six-bed infirmary, and a three-year contract. Glamorgan applied and was accepted. Three months later, the council learned that although Glamorgan had a medical degree, she had failed to pass the state examination required to practice medicine. No patients complained, but the council summarily discharged her. Glamorgan sued for breach of contract. Will she win the lawsuit?

13. Randy entered into a contract to provide a computer program to a New Jersey school district. He used without permission parts of a computer program copyrighted by another programmer. The portion of the program that violated the copyright law cost $12,000 and the part that didn't violate the copyright law cost $44,000. He delivered both parts to the school district. Can he recover anything for his work?

The Statute of Frauds

- Explain why the Statute of Frauds is necessary and what it requires
- Identify the main instances when the Statute of Frauds requires a writing
- Understand the rules of contract interpretation

WHY HAVE A STATUTE OF FRAUDS?

WHAT'S YOUR VERDICT?

While they were playing golf, Haka orally agreed to buy an apartment building from Simon. In a later telephone conversation, Haka promised Simon $100,000 as a down payment on the purchase price with the balance to be paid within five years. Simon promised to deliver the deed to the property at the time the down payment was made. Both parties were satisfied that all the terms had been completely negotiated. Later Haka found a better deal and told Simon he was backing out.

Is Haka's contract with Simon enforceable?

Although oral contracts are generally valid and binding, because they are subject to fraudulent claims, the law requires that several of the most important types of contracts be placed in writing to be enforceable in court. These types are determined in most states by a law entitled the **Statute of Frauds**. For example, under such a statute in every state, contracts to transfer an interest in real property (land, buildings, and things permanently attached to them) must be evidenced by a writing and signed by the party against whom enforcement is sought. In *What's Your Verdict?* the oral agreement between Haka and Simon would not be enforceable in court.

Note that most agreements, oral or written, are carried out without resort to the courts for enforcement. Nonetheless, it is always a good idea to put an important contract in writing whether it is required by the Statute of Frauds or not.

IN THIS CASE

Sue orally agreed to provide interior decorating services for a law firm for two years at a rate she found attractive. She wrote and signed a letter to the law firm expressing her appreciation for the business, which she described as "interior decorating services, not to exceed 10 hours per week." The law firm replied with its own signed letter which described the transaction as, "services for 24 months at $3,500 per month." The two letters would be considered together by a court as evidence of a contract under the Statute of Frauds.

CONTRACTS WITHIN THE STATUTE OF FRAUDS

A contract is said to be *within the Statute of Frauds* if it is required to be in writing. It is *without the Statute of Frauds* if it is not required to be in writing. Contracts within the Statute of Frauds include

- contracts to buy and sell goods for a price of $500 or more
- contracts to buy and sell real property or any interest in real property
- contracts that require more than one year to complete
- promises to pay the debt or answer for a legal obligation of another person
- promises to give something of value in return for a promise of marriage

If a contract is within the Statute of Frauds, but there is either no writing or no signature, how courts will treat the parties depends on the extent of contractual performance.

EXECUTED CONTRACTS An **executed contract** is one that has been fully performed. Both parties have done all they promised to do. If an executed contract is within the Statute of Frauds, but there is either no writing or no signature, the courts leave the parties where they are. Neither party can reverse the contract.

EXECUTORY CONTRACTS An **executory contract** is one that has not been fully performed. Something agreed upon remains to be done by one or both of the parties.

An executory contract within the Statute of Frauds, but not signed or not in writing, is unenforceable. This means neither party can compel performance from the other.

The executory contract in violation of the Statute of Frauds is different from an illegal contract. One difference is that restitution is available. Further, if a benefit was conferred in reliance on the oral agreement, its value can be recovered. It is recovered by suing based on quasi-contract. A **quasi-contract** exists when some element of an enforceable contract is missing (such as a signed writing), yet courts award money to prevent the unjust enrichment of one party.

REQUIREMENTS OF THE WRITING

Generally a writing need not utilize any special form to satisfy the Statute of Frauds as long as it contains certain key elements. Even within a state there usually are two sets of such requirements for a writing. One is specified in a state's Statute of Frauds, the other in the state's version of the Uniform Commercial Code covering sales of goods.

STATUTE OF FRAUDS REQUIREMENTS Such statutes vary widely from state to state in their requirements. The least demanding Statutes of Frauds merely require that the writing indicate the existence of a contract. The most demanding standard used by states is that the writing must contain all the essential terms that would be required to create a valid offer. In general, this includes

1. names of the parties
2. subject matter description
3. price
4. quantity
5. signature
6. other essential terms

"Other essential terms" can include time or method of delivery, terms of payment, methods of financing, date for transfer of possession and so on, depending on the nature of the transaction. Most states require contracts for the sale of real estate to provide a legal description (as opposed to a street address) of the realty.

© GETTY IMAGES/PHOTODISC

On a recent trip to Singapore, you fell in love with these statues of Tang Dynasty warriors, each worth at least $1,000. You then learn that an import-export business in the United States has several of these statues for sale. Write up a contract that contains all the essential terms required to create a valid offer for one of the statues. Assume that the sale is taking place in a state that uses the most demanding Statute of Frauds standard.

LEGAL RESEARCH

Assume you are about to get engaged. Research the issue of who gets to keep the ring if the engagement is called off. What rules are utilized to make the determination? Find out if the rules have stayed the same for many years, or if they change frequently.

UCC REQUIREMENTS Because the UCC is essentially the same in each state, it establishes a uniform content standard. Under the UCC, the writing must indicate only

- the quantity of goods
- that a contract has been created between the parties

SPECIAL RULES FOR SIGNATURES Note that, under the Statute of Frauds requirements, only the parties whose signatures actually appear on the contract may be sued for enforcement. The signature may be written, stamped, engraved, or printed. It may consist of any mark that is intended as a signature or authentication of the writing. Under the UCC, however, this rule is changed for those who regularly deal in the type of goods being sold in the contract. For such parties a writing signed by one party and sent to the other is enforceable against the other party unless the other party objects to the terms within 10 days of receipt of the contract.

CHECKPOINT
Name the six essential elements in a writing required by the most demanding Statutes of Frauds standards.

How do the Statute of Frauds requirements for signatures differ from the UCC requirements?

TYPES OF CONTRACTS WITHIN THE STATUTE OF FRAUDS

WHAT'S YOUR VERDICT?

Cervante and Joan were good friends. When they graduated from high school, both were 18. They planned to marry, but first they wanted to become financially secure. So they shook hands and agreed to become partners in operating a small restaurant serving Indian cuisine. "This is just the beginning," Joan said. "'Til death do us part!" both said.

Are they legally bound to remain partners in business until one of them dies?

To be enforceable under the Statute of Frauds, five types of executory contracts must be evidenced by a writing and signed by the party against whom the contract is to be enforced. As an alternative, the contract may be provable by some other writing, such as a letter signed by the party who is being sued. A plaintiff seeking to enforce the contract can readily sign if his or her signature is missing. Because either party might later want to sue for breach, both parties should sign when the contract is made.

The following sections discuss the five types of executory contracts within the Statute of Frauds, that is, those contracts that must be evidenced by a writing and signed by the party against whom the contract is to be enforced.

CONTRACT FOR THE SALE OF GOODS FOR $500 OR MORE

Goods (such as a book, car, or TV) are tangible personal property. If parties agree to buy and sell goods for a price of $500 or more, their contract must be evidenced by a writing. If a contract for the sale of goods is for less than $500, then it need not be in writing. However, a modification of that contract which brings the total price above $500 must be in writing and signed.

The Uniform Commercial Code provides exceptions to the Statute of Frauds. In these cases, a writing and signature is not required

- when goods are ordered to be specially manufactured and they are not suitable to be sold to others in the ordinary course of the seller's business
- when goods have been ordered and paid for and the seller has accepted payment
- when goods have been received and accepted by the buyer
- when the party against whom enforcement is sought admits during legal proceedings that the oral contract was made

CONTRACT TO SELL AN INTEREST IN REAL PROPERTY

Real property includes land and buildings permanently attached to land. Transfers of real property or of lesser interests—such as a lease, the right to pump oil or to cut timber—must be in a properly signed writing to be enforceable. In most states, oral leases for one year or less are enforceable. Some states require that contracts employing real estate brokers satisfy the Statute of Frauds.

As an exception to the general rule, courts will enforce the oral contract if the seller has delivered the deed or if the buyer also has done all of the following: (1) made partial or full payment, (2) occupied the land, and (3) made substantial improvements to the land.

CONTRACTS THAT REQUIRE MORE THAN ONE YEAR TO COMPLETE

Courts will not enforce a contract that cannot be performed within one year unless there is a signed writing to prove the agreement. The year begins at the time the contract is made, not at the time contractual performance is to begin.

This time provision does not apply to agreements that might be executed within one year. This is true even if such agreements are not actually carried out within that time. The test is not whether the agreement is actually performed within one year, but whether there is a possibility of performance within one year. To illustrate, two persons, such as Cervante and Joan in *What's Your Verdict?* shake hands and orally agree to be business partners. But they do not specify a definite time period. Because either partner may quit or die within one year, their agreement does not require more than one year to complete, and it need not be in writing. Either party could withdraw at anytime.

CONTRACT TO PAY A DEBT OR ANSWER FOR ANOTHER'S DEBT

Another provision of the Statute of Frauds requires a writing for a promise to answer for the debt or default of another. For example, if a father tells his daughter's landlord that he will pay the rent if she defaults on a three-month lease, this promise is called a *collateral promise*. It must be in writing to be enforceable. This contrasts with a primary promise to pay. A *primary promise* exists if Dad says, "I'll rent the apartment and you bill me. Then I'll let my daughter stay there." This agreement is enforceable without a writing.

Often a person dies without enough assets to pay all the debts. In these cases, the person in charge of settling the deceased person's unpaid debts, often a relative, may agree to pay the debt personally instead of trying to pay it from the deceased person's assets. This is a promise to answer for the debts of another. Such a promise is not enforceable unless placed in writing.

INTERNATIONAL VIEWPOINT

Writing Requirement

The laws regarding a writing requirement for contracts differ among nations. Stemming from the 1677 English Parliament law, some common law countries may still have writing requirements in effect. (England, however, repealed this law in 1954.) Countries with civil law codes have not required that contracts be in writing. The United Nations Convention on Contracts for the International Sale of Goods (CISG) is in effect in approximately 60 countries. Under the CISG, contracts for the sale of goods need not be in writing.

Puccini predicted a revival of "one-man bands" featuring accordion music. Mike's Music Box shop had the accordion Puccini needed, but it cost $1,495. Puccini had neither the necessary cash nor credit. His friend, Muniz, told the music shop owner, "Sell Puccini the accordion on a 15-month installment contract. If he fails to make any payment, I will pay the balance due." After three months, Puccini defaulted. However, the oral promise Muniz made is not enforceable as a promise to stand good for the debts of another must be in writing.

EXCEPTION—MAIN PURPOSE RULE A third party is liable for an oral promise to pay another's debt if the main purpose of the promise serves the promisor's own interest. This is called the *main purpose rule.* Suppose an owner of a house under construction is anxious to see it completed. After the building contractor fails to pay on time, the driver of the delivery truck refuses to unload a shipment of lumber. If the homeowner orally promises to pay the lumberyard if the contractor does not pay for needed supplies, the homeowner cannot defend using the Statute of Frauds. The main purpose rule applies.

CONTRACT FOR WHICH THE CONSIDERATION IS MARRIAGE

A signed writing is required for agreements in which one party promises to marry in return for something other than the other's promise to marry. If Sue and Bill agree to marry each other, this is outside the Statute of Frauds. If Alice agrees to marry Buck because he promised to deed his house to her, this is within the Statute of Frauds. In some U.S. subcultures, a parent of the woman may promise to pay a dowry to the man in return for his promise to marry. This agreement must be placed in writing to be enforceable.

In some states, if one party breaches either an oral or written contract to marry, the victim of the breach may successfully sue for damages. The trend, however, is to ban such "heart balm" suits.

HOW ARE CONTRACTS INTERPRETED?

WHAT'S YOUR VERDICT?

Highman bought a new personal computer from Advanced Electronics. She signed the store's usual contract, which contained a clause stating that it was the complete agreement between the parties. Later, Highman alleged that as part of the bargain, the salesperson orally promised that if the list price were reduced within two months, Highman would be refunded the amount of the reduction. The list price was reduced, but Advanced Electronics refused to pay the refund to Highman.

Can Highman recover the refund?

At times parties to a written agreement claim that it does not include everything that was agreed upon or is not clear about such terms. In court these claims are settled either by an examination of the agreement itself or by a set of rules specifically devoted to the interpretation of contracts.

INTEGRATION CLAUSE

Often, in anticipation of issues involving preceding oral agreements not reflected in the ultimate contract, writings will include an **integration clause**. This is a contract clause stating that both parties agree that the terms in the written contract constitute the entire and final agreement. An example of an integration clause is: "It is agreed that the terms written here constitute the entire and final contract between the parties."

SPECIFIC RULES OF INTERPRETATION

ANALYSIS The first thing a court will do is interpret the contract in terms of the parties' principal objective. By looking at the main objective, courts can see which clauses should prevail over others. Further, if an agreement can be interpreted in two ways, the courts will choose the way that renders the agreement a contract. Interpreting each clause in the light of all other provisions of the contract is another way to follow the parties' principal objective.

CONFLICTING TERMS If there is a conflict between a printed form contract and something typewritten or handwritten thereon, the later writings—not the conflicting typeset print—determine the contract's meaning. This is because the writing is likely to have occurred after the typesetting. Similarly a typewritten agreement which includes a conflicting handwritten statement or clause will be interpreted based on the handwritten portion.

When contracts refer to amounts of money, they often describe the amount with numerals, such as "10," and also with words such as "ten." If there is a conflict between the numeral and the word, and one of them is ambiguous, then the unambiguous expression will prevail. For example, "Two twenty-five dollars ($2.25)" will be

Find the conflicting terms in this contract. Which numbers prevail?

REAL ESTATE MORTGAGE

THIS MORTGAGE made this _____**20th**_____ day of **October**_____, 20--, between **Bernard and Mariah Easton (husband and wife), 6720 Observatory Lane, Cuyahoga Falls, Ohio**_____, Mortgagors, and the LAST NATIONAL BANK of Akron, Summit County, Ohio, a corporation doing business under the laws of the United States with its principal office in Akron, Ohio, Mortgagee.

WITNESSETH: That whereas, Mortgagors are jointly indebted to Mortgagee for money borrowed in the sum of $____**one hundred thirty-four thousand, five hundred**____ Dollars ($ **134,900**____) to secure the payment of which Mortgagors have executed their promissory note of even date herewith in the said amount together with interest as stated in said note, payable within ten (1) years.

interpreted by reliance on the numerals. When both the writing and the numerals are unambiguous, then the writing prevails. For example, "Two hundred twenty-five and 00/100 ($235.00)" will be interpreted in reliance on the words. The reason is that more mistakes are made when writing numerals.

A QUESTION OF ETHICS

Andy watched an elderly customer fill out a check to purchase one of his original watercolor paintings. They had orally agreed to $340, but the customer wrote "$540" and "five hundred forty and no/100" dollars on the check. If you were Andy, would you correct the customer if you thought you would never do business with her again?

WORDS The plain and normal meaning of ordinary words will be used to determine the meaning of the contract. Prior relationships of the parties may indicate how the words should be interpreted. Legal and other technical terms are given their technical meaning unless the contract as a whole shows that a different meaning is intended. Where both parties are members of a trade or profession, both parties are presumed to know the trade custom or practice, and the contract is interpreted in light of that trade custom or practice.

AUTHORS OF AMBIGUITY Courts will interpret ambiguities (things that can be understood in two or more possible ways) against the party who drafted the contract. Often consumers are asked to accept and sign **contracts of adhesion**. These are contracts such as credit purchases or life insurance policies. They are prepared by the stronger parties (usually the sellers), with the help of skilled lawyers, who naturally favor the interests of their clients. Generally, the terms of such contracts are not negotiable. The weaker parties (usually the consumers) must "take it or leave it." In such contracts, courts interpret ambiguity against the author. Statutes in some states now require that the language of consumer contracts be clear, simple, and understandable to the average person.

IMPLIED REASONABLENESS Contracts often include implied terms as a matter of reasonableness. Thus, a clause requiring "payment in cash" usually may be satisfied by check. Promised services must be performed with reasonable care and skill even when this is not stated. When no time for performance is mentioned, a reasonable time is allowed.

Consumers who purchase appliances on credit often are required to sign contracts of adhesion. What can you do to protect yourself against contract terms that strongly favor the interests of the offering parties?

© GETTY IMAGES/PHOTODISC

PAROL EVIDENCE RULE

Generally, when a contract is placed in final written form, the courts feel that it is a reasonable expectation that the parties will consider the terms carefully. If a party to a contract does not understand it, he or she may exercise one of several options such as not entering the contract or getting the help of an attorney to interpret it. Certainly, given the volume of contracts that are made each day, we can never have enough judges to review and save parties from their contractual errors.

This wise conclusion is supported by the *parol evidence rule.* This rule makes the final writing the source of evidence about the terms of the contract. **Parol evidence** consists of words spoken prior to the execution of the final writing or at the time of signing. Parol evidence generally is inadmissible in court proceedings. For example, if a complete final written agreement for the sale of a house is signed, then a court will not admit oral testimony that, prior to the parties' signing the written agreement, the seller had said he would paint the exterior before vacating. The rule keeps out preliminary inquiries, initial proposals, negotiations, and other discussions that are not the final agreement.

In *What's Your Verdict?* Highman could not recover the refund. Evidence of the salesperson's oral promise would be parol evidence. In complete and final writings, both parties should carefully include all terms that they deem essential.

EXCEPTION TO THE PAROL EVIDENCE RULE Parol evidence may be admissible in the following exceptional instances:

1. to clarify ambiguities in the written agreement
2. if the written contract was not intended to be a complete agreement
3. if a condition necessary to the existence of the contract never occurred
4. if fraud, forgery, illegality, mistake, or misrepresentation occurred
5. to show the parties reached another agreement or terminated the contract under consideration after executing the written contract
6. to show that the contract is voidable because a party lacked contractual capacity

CHECKPOINT

Explain the parol evidence rule.

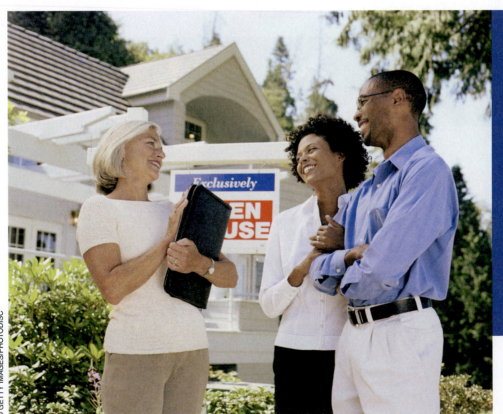

© GETTY IMAGES/PHOTODISC

Stan and Lauretta attend an open house for a home they are interested in buying. They tell the agent that they would be serious about buying this house if the owner would remove some of the bushes in front of the house. The salesperson says that would not be a problem. Later, they sign a contract to buy the house, but it doesn't mention removing the bushes. If the couple later decided to sue to make the home owners remove the bushes, would they win the case? Why or why not?

THINK ABOUT LEGAL CONCEPTS

1. Enforceable contracts can often be created without a writing. **True or False?**

2. Ambiguity in the terms of a written contract will be interpreted against the author. **True or False?**

3. Where there are contractual obligations unperformed, the contract is called _ ? _.

4. Parol statements can be admitted to prove which of the following? (a) fraud (b) illegality (c) a conflicting agreement existed before the signing (d) a and b

THINK CRITICALLY ABOUT EVIDENCE

Study the situation, answer the questions, and then prepare arguments to support your answers.

5. Jason's father, Phil, died. He left credit card bills totaling $17,000 and some additional small bills. His only asset at the time of death was a savings account with $6,000 in it. One of the credit card companies called Jason. In his grief, Jason orally promised to pay them the balance on his dad's account, $2,000. Is this promise enforceable in court?

6. A salesperson tries to persuade you to buy an electronic musical instrument. The price is $499, plus carrying charges of $72. The salesperson says, "You'll soon be the life of the party. If not, just return it and get your money back." You sign an installment payment contract, which includes an integration clause but which says nothing about a return

privilege. Can you hold the seller to the promise to accept a return?

7. Under a written contract, Cabrera bought a used sedan from Sharpe's Previously Owned Cars Inc. The salesperson had knowingly falsely assured her that the car was in "tip-top condition...with just 45,000 miles driven by only one previous owner." Later, in checking official registration records, Cabrera discovered that the sedan had three previous owners and that the odometer had been set back from 70,000 miles. In court, Sharpe's attorney claims that under the parol evidence rule, introduction of the salesperson's oral statements is barred because there was an integration clause in the written contract. Is this parol evidence admissible?

PREVENT LEGAL DIFFICULTIES

In making contracts...

1. Deal only with persons who are reputable and properly licensed when contracting for professional or skilled services.

2. Do not rush into a decision. Take time to review and understand the advantages and disadvantages of the contract. Legitimate proposals usually will survive a delay.

3. If the contract is complex or involves much time or money, put it in writing even when the Statute of Frauds does not require this. Try to anticipate and provide for all possible problems. If needed, obtain the assistance of a qualified lawyer.

4. If a prepared contract is presented to you for your signature read it carefully, especially if it is a contract of adhesion. If the contract involves a

large sum of money, or if it is complex, have your lawyer review it before you sign.

5. Insist that all terms of the contract that you do not understand be defined and explained. Make necessary changes, or reject the entire contract.

6. Make sure that all changes are written into a contract on all copies as well as on the original, and that all changes are initialed by both parties. Retain a copy with the other party's signature on it.

7. Be sure all desired terms are expressed in writing or included by specific reference to any other relevant document(s).

8. When any payments have been made in cash, be sure to get a receipt if payment is not acknowledged in the contract.

Chapter 10 Assessment

CONCEPTS IN BRIEF

10-1   Illegal Agreements

1. To be valid, a contract must not violate the law (constitutional, statutory, or case), nor be contrary to public policy in its formation, purpose, or performance.

2. Among agreements that violate law or public policy and are therefore void and unenforceable are those that require committing a crime or tort, obstruct legal procedures, injure public service, are made by persons without a required competency license, involve usury, involve illegal lotteries, threaten marriage, involve price fixing or market allocation, include an unreasonable promise not to compete, and are unconscionable.

3. Illegal agreements usually are unenforceable and restitution is not available. Exceptions are made to this rule when the violated law was meant to protect one of the parties, one party is excusably ignorant, a party rescinds before the illegal act occurs, the contract is divisible into legal and illegal parts.

10-2   The Statute of Frauds

4. Unless so required by the Statute of Frauds, contracts need not be in writing to be enforceable.

5. An express contract is stated in words—written or spoken. An implied contract is shown by conduct of the parties and by surrounding circumstances.

6. An executory contract has not been fully performed. An executed contract has been completed by both parties.

7. A quasi-contract exists when some element of a valid contract is missing, yet it is enforced as if it were a contract. This is done to prevent unjust enrichment of one party.

8. To be enforceable, the following contracts must be in writing (or evidenced by some other written proof) and signed by the party against whom enforcement is sought: (1) contracts to buy and sell goods for a price of $500 or more, (2) contracts to buy and sell real property or any interest in real property, (3) contracts that cannot be performed within one year after being made, (4) contracts to pay a debt or answer for a legal obligation of another person, (5) contracts having marriage as the consideration.

9. A memorandum of an agreement need not be in any special form. The requirements for the content of a writing under the common law vary greatly from state to state.

10. The terms of a written contract may not be changed by parol evidence unless the original writing is clearly ambiguous. Parol evidence also may be used to show that a written agreement is not binding because of mistake, fraud, illegality, or because a party was a minor.

YOUR LEGAL VOCABULARY

Match each statement with the term that it best defines. Some terms may not be used.

1. To refrain from informing on or prosecuting an alleged crime in exchange for money or other valuable consideration

2. Contract that has been fully performed

3. Composed of prize, chance, and consideration

4. When competing firms agree on the same price to be charged for a product or service

5. A bet on the outcome of an event

6. License required of professionals certifying they can perform adequately

7. Created by court action to prevent unjust enrichment

8. "Take it or leave it" contracts

9. License granted only to earn revenue for the licensing body

a. **bid rigging**
b. **competency license**
c. **compounding a crime**
d. **contracts of adhesion**
e. **executed contract**
f. **executory contract**
g. **integration clause**
h. **lottery**
i. **parol evidence**
j. **price fixing**
k. **quasi-contract**
l. **revenue license**
m. **Statute of Frauds**
n. **unconscionability**
o. **wager**

REVIEW LEGAL CONCEPTS

10. Describe the ways courts handle contracts for which a required license is missing.

11. Assume the usury limit is 20 percent in your state. What is the annual dollar amount of interest charged on a loan of $1,000 where the interest rate is a legal 20 percent? Compare that with the dollar amount of interest on a $1,000 loan carrying a usurious 25 percent? Does the difference in the interest amounts indicate to society criminal behavior on one lender's part and not another? Does it indicate criminal behavior to you? What about a business that buys goods at $1,000 each and sells them with a 100 per-cent markup the same day for $2,000? Is that much markup criminal? Why or why not?

12. Describe the elements of unconscionability.

13. Name the categories of contracts that are within the Statute of Frauds.

14. Describe how the parol evidence rule effects the court's evaluation of the facts underlying a contractual dispute by identifying the times when parol evidence can be introduced to clarify a contract. What other rules help a court in such evaluations?

WRITE ABOUT LEGAL CONCEPTS

15. Select a type of local business. Next write three sentences that describe three different illegal agreements that might be entered into by such a business.

16. List four licenses that are held by people you know. For each license, indicate whether it is a revenue or competency license.

17. Invent a situation involving the sale of a used car. Write a related contract which includes the minimum content required to satisfy the UCC.

18. Write a dialogue between two people that creates some oral statements which would be admissible and some which would not be admissible for a contract of employment for three years.

19. **HOT DEBATE** Did the prosecutor act impartially by giving the organizers of the illegal lottery a way out without being indicted? What would you have done if you were the prosecutor?

THINK CRITICALLY ABOUT EVIDENCE

Study the situation, answer the questions, and then prepare arguments to support your answers.

20. Trent, a minor, bought a copyrighted CD of a current hit from Shawn. After making a copy of the disc, Trent found a defect in the CD. He tried to return it to Shawn for a full refund. Shawn suspected the illegal copying and refused the refund. Can Shawn assert illegality as a defense here? Why or why not?

21. Moser had no automobile liability insurance, although state law required it. She negligently collided with Chang's car. Chang threatened to call the police if Moser failed to pay $1,000 for pain and suffering and $2,000 for car repairs. Moser gave Chang a check for $3,000. Then she stopped payment on it. If Chang sues, will she recover?

22. During the final week of March in Al's junior year at East High, a recruiter from Granite Inc. offered him a job. "After you get that diploma," the officer said, "show up ready for work." Al replied, "I'll be there." Was this a contract enforceable in court?

23. Kelley was admitted to University Hospital as an emergency heart transplant patient. The next day, the hospital's business manager discussed the cost of the surgery with Kelley's two sons. Both sons told the manager, "Do whatever is necessary to save his life, and we will pay you." When the hospital presented the staggering bill to the junior Kelleys, they said the contract was oral and, therefore, they were not liable. Is that true?

24. Cornelius, an elderly bachelor, was at the town cafe. In front of several witnesses who will vouch for the story, Cornelius made the following statement to Barbara, a young waitress: "I can't give you a castle in Spain. But if you marry me, I will deed to you a half interest in Meadowland Acres, the best farm in the county. And I'll give you 75 cows, 200 hogs, and 5,000 chickens." Barbara said, "I will," and they were married. Is Cornelius legally bound to keep his promise?

MAKE ACADEMIC CONNECTIONS

25. **LAW** Research the procedure by which a lawyer may lose her or his license in your state. Call the State Bar Association and obtain statistics about how many lawyers there are in your state and how many have been complained against, reviewed, brought up on charges and disbarred in the last five years.

ANALYZE REAL CASES

26. Blubaugh, a farmer, leased a combine from John Deere Leasing (JDL). The lease document was printed on two sides of the paper but one side was printed in very small, light type. Blubaugh read and signed the front side but did not notice or read the other side of the document. It contained unusual provisions making Blubaugh liable in the event of breach for much more money than the unpaid lease payments. When Blubaugh breached, JDL sued. The trial judge required a magnifying glass to read the fine print. Is there evidence of procedural unconscionability here? Is there evidence of substantive unconscionability? Was the contract illegal? Must Blubaugh pay more than the balance of the lease payments? (*John Deere Leasing Company v. Blubaugh*, 636 F. Supp. 1569, Kan.)

27. Dixon, a motor vehicle purchaser, sued the Wisconsin Finance Company with which he had entered into an installment contract. He also sued its Illinois sister corporation, alleging that the contract was void under the Sales Finance Agency Act because the finance company was not licensed to do business in the state of Illinois. The license was not a competency license. Will Dixon prevail? (*Dixon v. Mercury Finance Company of Wisconsin*, 694 N.E.2d 693, Ill.)

28. For a nine-year period, Kiyosi served as a teaching associate and lecturer at Indiana University, Bloomington. Meanwhile, he continued to study and write to qualify for a Ph.D. degree. He relied on an oral promise by the defendant university that upon obtaining the degree, he would be appointed to a permanent position with perpetual renewals, starting at the rank of assistant professor. It was customary for the university to make such appointments for terms of three years. When Kiyosi received his Ph.D., he was appointed assistant professor. However, he was told that he would not be reappointed for the following year. He then sued for damages for breach of contract. The university officials claimed that the Statute of Frauds barred his action because a lifetime contract cannot be performed within one year. Who should win this case? (*Kiyosi v. Trustees of Indiana University*, 166 Ind. App. 34, 333 N.E.2d 886)

29. Franklin Life Insurance Co. issued a policy that named Burne as a beneficiary. The policy provided for double indemnity accidental death benefits because of the death of the insured. The insured had been struck by an automobile and was kept alive in a vegetative state for four and a half years before he died. The policy provided that the accidental death benefits would be paid only if death occurred within 90 days of the accident, and that such benefits would not be paid if death occurred during a time when premiums were being waived due to the insured's disability. Will the beneficiary be allowed to recover on the policy? (*Burne v. Franklin Life Ins. Co.*, 301 A.2d 799, Pa.)

30. For safekeeping, Kula deposited $18,300 with the cashier of a Nevada hotel casino and was given a receipt for the money. Kula and a friend, Goldfinger, gambled in the hotel's casino. (Casino gambling is legal in Nevada.) Kula made withdrawals and deposits from time to time with the casino cashier and at the time had a balance of $18,000. One evening Goldfinger lost $500 in gambling and was unable to pay it. He asked the shift boss, Ponto, to telephone Kula for a guarantee of the loss. Ponto did so and received Kula's authorization to give Goldfinger credit up to $1,000 but no more. Ponto confirmed this but stated that Kula had also said Goldfinger could gamble the entire deposit of $18,000. Goldfinger was permitted to gamble until he lost $18,000. The casino tried to collect the amount from Kula on his alleged oral promise to cover Goldfinger's debt to $18,000. The casino did this by refusing to return to Kula the amount he had on deposit. Kula was willing to honor his oral guarantee of Goldfinger's debt up to $1,000 but no more. Kula sued the hotel for return of his deposit. Should he get it? (*Kula v. Karat, Inc.*, 531 P.2d 1353)

CASE FOR LEGAL THINKING

RANSBURG V. HAASE
586 N. E. 2D 1295 (ILL. CT. APP.)

EVIDENCE The Ransburgs resided in Peoria, Illinois. They orally hired David William Haase Associates, a local business, to act as the architect, construction manager, designer, and decorator of a house that the Ransburgs wanted to have built in Vail, Colorado. The parties discussed this project both in Peoria and in Colorado. The parties agreed that Haase would provide budgetary control. They also agreed to a construction budget of $949,500 and a completion date. Haase was to receive $80,000 as compensation for services. The cost of the project exceeded $1.2 million. The Ransburgs alleged that Haase had failed to meet contract terms and that he held himself out as an architect but is not a registered architect in Illinois or any other state. They sought recovery of the fees paid to Haase. The trial court dismissed this count. The Ransburgs appealed

OPINION The initial question is whether Haase acted in violation of the Illinois Architecture Act when he represented to the Ransburgs that he is an architect and undertook to provide architectural services in connection with the construction of a residence in Colorado.

The allegations in the complaint plainly charge Haase with offering professional services as an architect in Peoria where he operated a design and decorating business. Regardless of where the services were furnished, holding himself out to the Ransburgs as an architect in Illinois was a violation of the Illinois Architecture Act.

As a general rule, courts will not enforce a contract involving a party who does not have a license called for by legislation that expressly prohibits the carrying on of the particular activity without a license where the legislation was enacted for the protection of the public, not as a revenue measure. The purposes of the Illinois statute prohibiting the practice of architecture without the required registration have long been held to be for the protection of the public.

Applying the general rule to the case before us, it does not appear that the contract would be enforceable. Do Illinois courts recognize a cause of action to recover money previously paid to a defendant for architectural services which have been rendered but for which defendant was not licensed? Although it is a general rule that parties to a void contract will be left where they have

placed themselves with no recovery of money paid for illegal services, exceptions to the rule have been recognized under two different rationales:

- that the person who paid for the Service is not in pari delicto [equally at fault] with the unlicensed person, and

- that the law in question was passed for the protection of the person who paid and it appears that the purposes of the law would be better effectuated by granting relief than by denying it.

To allow the unlicensed architect to retain the fee paid is to allow him to practice architecture in the state of Illinois without a license and to reap the rewards thereof. The purpose of the Illinois licensing act can best be effectuated by recognizing the Ransburgs' right to recovery.

DECISION Case remanded for further proceedings.

PRACTICE JUDGING

1. Would the outcome be different if the Ransburgs' had known Haase was not an architect?

2. Are Haase's failures to meet the terms of the contract relevant to this case?

© GETTY IMAGES/PHOTODISC

Contractual Obligations and their Enforcement

11-1 Transfer and Discharge of Obligations

11-2 Remedies for Breach of Contract

11-3 The Marriage Contract and Divorce

© GETTY IMAGES/PHOTODISC

HOT DEBATE

Ben, 16, had been dating Betsy for several months when he told his parents about the relationship. Ben's father had been in business with Betsy's dad and the partnership ended poorly. When his father heard the news, he told Ben to stop seeing Betsy. Ben refused, and his father took away the car Ben bought with his own money, stopped paying Ben's tuition, and spent the funds saved for Ben's college. With his mother's backing, Ben brought suit against his father for "improper parenting." Ben's father's attorney filed a motion to dismiss the suit. The motion stated that "improper parenting" was not a legitimate cause of action and that the father had acted within his powers as a parent under the law. The lower court dismissed the suit, and Ben appealed to the state court of appeals.

Where Do You Stand?

1. Make a persuasive argument that emphasizes the legal reasons supporting Ben's suit.

2. Make a persuasive argument that emphasizes the legal reasons supporting his father's actions.

Transfer and Discharge of Obligations

▼ **GOALS**

■ Identify what rights can be assigned and what duties delegated
■ Describe the various ways in which contractual obligations may be discharged

THE TRANSFER OF CONTRACT RIGHTS AND DUTIES

WHAT'S YOUR VERDICT?

Whipple bought a high-powered sports coupe from Oriental Motors for $32,000. After a down payment of $2,000, the balance, plus a finance charge, was to be paid by mail in installments over the following 48 months. Oriental Motors needed cash to restore its inventory of new cars. It immediately sold Whipple's contract to a finance company, Palmout Inc., and told Whipple to mail all installment payments to Palmout.

Is such a transfer of contract rights legal?

A transfer of a right a party may have under a contract to another is called an **assignment**. For example, one party may transfer to another the right to collect a payment. The party who transfers the contractual right is the *assignor.* The party who receives this contractual right is the *assignee.* An assignment does not need to be supported by consideration to be legally effective, although it often is. In *What's Your Verdict?* it was perfectly legal for Oriental Motors to assign to the finance company its right to receive Whipple's payments in return for needed cash. When Whipple was notified of the assignment, he became obligated to pay the finance company instead of Oriental Motors.

From the perspective of the courts the assignee "stands in the shoes of the assignor." This means that the assignee receives exactly the same contractual rights and duties as the assignor had—no more and no less. If a contractual right is transferred, this does not change the legal rights of the other party to the contract. For example, if Whipple's newly purchased automobile is defective and it takes $2,000 to fix it, he may withhold that

amount from Palmout, the assignee, if he would have had the right to withhold it from Oriental.

In all assignments, the assignor guarantees to the assignee that the assignor has a right to assign and that the assigned right is legally enforceable. However, the assignor typically does not promise that the **obligor** (the one who owes a duty under a contract) will perform as promised in the original contract. If the obligor breaches, the assignee, not the assignor, must sue for the breach. This means that, in *What's Your Verdict?,* if Whipple (the obligor) stops making payments, Palmout (the assignee) must bring suit instead of Oriental (the assignor) to enforce against Whipple his duty to pay. Often, the assignment will include specific language making the assignor liable for breach by the obligor.

ASSIGNABLE RIGHTS

Generally, a party may assign contractual rights to another, provided performance will not be materially changed, that is, changed in an

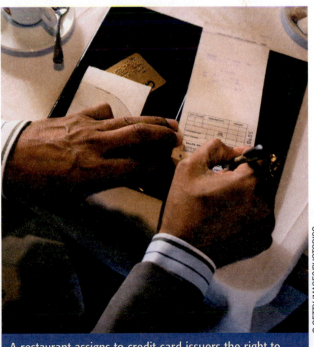

A restaurant assigns to credit card issuers the right to collect amounts due from customers who use the card. Which party is the assignor and which is the assignee?

© GETTY IMAGES/PHOTODISC

important way. **Performance** is the fulfillment of contractual promises as agreed. In *What's Your Verdict?* Whipple's payment was to be sent by mail regardless of to whom, so the assignment was proper. In a similar way, retailers and restaurants assign to issuers of credit cards the right to collect the amounts due from customers who have used the cards. In exchange, the credit card companies immediately pay the retailers and restaurants the face amount of the credit slips, less an agreed percentage.

NON-ASSIGNABLE RIGHTS

Contractual rights may not be assigned if performance requirements would be materially changed as a consequence. Other situations in which rights may not be transferred include

1. a right created under a contract that prohibits transfer of the contractual rights
2. claims for damages for personal injuries
3. claims against the United States
4. rights to personal services, especially those of a skilled nature, or when personal trust and confidence are involved
5. assignments of future wages, as limited by state statutes

FORM OF ASSIGNMENTS

Assignment of contractual rights usually is made voluntarily by the assignor. While an assignment usually is valid whether oral or written, a written assignment is always wiser. State statutes sometimes require that certain assignments be in writing. No consideration is necessary to make a valid assignment.

NOTICE OF ASSIGNMENTS

Until notified that an assignment has occurred, the obligor may continue to pay the assignor. After notification, however, the obligor is liable to the assignee for performance. To protect newly acquired rights, the assignee should promptly notify the obligor of the assignment.

DELEGATION OF CONTRACTUAL DUTIES

The routine obligations of a party that must be performed to fulfill a contract often can be transferred to another to perform. This is known as *delegation of duties*. However a person who delegates contractual duties remains legally obligated and responsible for proper performance even

though someone else may do the required work. A person cannot delegate to another any duty where performance requires unique personal skill or special qualifications. Also, a contract creating a duty can prohibit delegation.

CHECKPOINT
Under what conditions may you assign contractual rights to another person?

DISCHARGE OF CONTRACTUAL OBLIGATIONS

WHAT'S YOUR VERDICT?

When Sheila told him that she could not pay the full $1,000 she owed him by August 1 as required by their contract, Effriham suggested a new agreement. After some negotiations, he agreed to take $500 as payment in full if Sheila could provide it by July 15. When Sheila failed to make the payment by July 15, Effriham demanded the $1,000 be paid according to the terms of the original contract.

Does Sheila owe $500 or $1,000?

BY PERFORMANCE

Discharge of a contract is a termination of duties that ordinarily occurs when the parties perform as promised. Most contracts are discharged by complete performance of the terms of the contract. Failure to provide complete performance is a **breach of contract**. The significance of the breach determines what the non-breaching party can do in response.

When one party fails to perform a crucial duty under a contract, the other party may treat such a failure as a major breach and regard her or his own obligation as discharged. In sales contracts under the Uniform Commercial Code (UCC) this is termed a *cancellation*.

When just about all the duties are performed, but a minor duty under the contract remains, **substantial performance** has occurred. In this case there has been only a minor breach. A minor breach does not discharge the duties of the non-breaching party the way a major breach does. The party who has substantially performed can sue and recover what is due, less the cost of completing the remaining work. If the failure to perform is deliberate, however, the non-breaching party may treat it as a major breach.

Sometimes a party who **defaults**, or fails to perform, notifies the other party to a contract before the time of performance has arrived that he or she will not perform. This is called an **anticipatory breach**. In this situation, the non-breaching party may wait until the promised time of performance, or may treat the notice as evidence of a breach of contract and immediately sue for damages.

IN THIS CASE

Jerome's Gang Construction Co. Inc. remodeled Jeanne's kitchen. The new cabinets were made of top-grade plywood instead of solid wood as specified in the contract. (The mistake was caused by a purchasing department error.) The plywood was as strong and functional as the wood. The contract was substantially performed because the breach was unintentional and minor. Therefore, by law, Jeanne was responsible for the full price less a deduction for the lower cost of the plywood. Is the law's resolution of the issue ethical?

TIMING OF PERFORMANCE Contracts often identify a duty but don't say when it must be performed. In these cases, the duty must be performed within a reasonable time. If it is not performed within a reasonable time, this is a breach. A judge or jury determines a reasonable time after examining the circumstances in each case. Thus a contract to ship tomatoes—which rot quickly—might have a reasonable time for performance of several hours. Alternatively, a contract to ship furniture—which doesn't change in value as quickly—might have a reasonable time of several weeks.

In other instances, the contract identifies a date for performance. Most courts will rule that performance shortly after the date is only a minor breach. Again, the circumstance in each

A QUESTION OF ETHICS

On January 5, Graham Roofers contracted to remove the old shingles and to install a new fireproof roof on the home of the Sterlings. The job was to be completed "by March 30, at the latest," to be ready for anticipated heavy spring rains. Late in February, Graham notified the Sterlings that because of a rush of orders, his crews were "swamped" and he could not get to the job until late April or early May. This was an anticipatory breach. The Sterlings have the choice of waiting for performance or immediately proceeding as though Graham had breached the contract.

case will influence how much time after the specified date will be allowed before the delay is treated as a major breach.

When a contract states that performance is to occur by a specified date, and that "time is of the essence," failure to perform by that date may be regarded as a major breach. If so, the duties of the non-breaching party are discharged. Time will be "of the essence" when a contract deals with property that rapidly fluctuates in value or property that is perishable. Courts look to the subject matter of the contract and the individual circumstances of the case to determine whether time is "of the essence." Just having the words placed in a contract is not the deciding factor.

BY THE INITIAL TERMS

When the parties prepare their contract, they may agree that it will terminate

- on a specified date or upon the expiration of a specified period of time (for example, a fresh food supply contract with a school district to terminate on the last day of school)

- upon the occurrence of a specified event (for example, a contract to have someone mow your yard until you return from vacation and resume doing it yourself)

- upon the failure of a certain event to happen (for example, a construction loan contract upon failure to get a required building permit)

- at the free will of either party upon giving notice (for example, when one partner decides to retire from business and gives the required notice as specified in the business agreement with her associates)

BY SUBSEQUENT AGREEMENT

The parties who have made a contract may later mutually agree to change either the terms of the contract or the nature of their relationship. They may do so without any liability for breach in any of the following ways.

RESCISSION By rescission the parties may agree to unmake or to undo their entire contract from its very beginning. Each party returns any consideration already received. Both parties are placed in their original positions to the extent possible.

ACCORD AND SATISFACTION Parties may decide that the present contract is not what they want, and so replace it with a new contract. This discharges their original contract by *substitution*. An agreement to make such a change is an *accord*. Performance of the new obligation is called a *satisfaction*.

A compromise of a disputed claim is an accord. Carrying out the new agreement is the satisfaction. Thus, an accord and satisfaction discharges the previous obligation. However, if the performance in the accord is not rendered, the old contract remains in effect. That is the situation in *What's Your Verdict?* Sheila failed to perform under the accord (to pay $500 by the 15), and so the original contract was not discharged. She still owes $1,000.

NOVATION A party entitled to receive performance under a contract may release the other party from the duty of performance and accept a substitute party. This is a *novation*. In effect, a new contract is formed by agreement of the three parties who are involved.

BY IMPOSSIBILITY OF PERFORMANCE

Generally, impossibility of performance refers to extreme external conditions rather than an obligor's personal inability to perform. A surprise war or an unexpected embargo (the legal stoppage of commerce) may lead to impossibility of performance. On the other hand, increased prices of needed supplies, a strike of workers, difficulty in obtaining materials or equipment, or natural disasters (such as a flood or earthquake) that only delay performance do not discharge the contractual obligations.

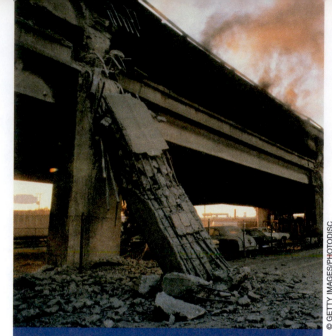
Inspectors determined that this bridge, damaged in an earthquake, would not be usable until it is repaired. The bridge provides your company's only connection for transporting goods. Would your company's contracts be discharged due to this situation? Why or why not?

Impossibility of performance also may be used to discharge contractual obligations when events on a smaller scale than wars or earthquakes interfere. For example,

- unique subject matter identified in the contract is destroyed before it can be delivered to the buyer (for example, a Picasso is burned to a crisp in a fire at an auction house)
- a performance becomes illegal before it can be rendered (for example, installing asbestos shingles on a new building)
- the death or disability of someone who was to provide a personal service that only that person could render

Parties commonly do include "escape hatch" language in their contracts. Such language permits modification, or even termination, of performance without liability for damages in the event of an inability to perform on schedule because of specified conditions.

BY OPERATION OF LAW

A contract may be discharged or the right to enforce it may be barred by operation of law. This happens when the person's debts are discharged in bankruptcy. It also happens when the time allowed for enforcement of the contract has elapsed because of the statute of limitations.

Alteration of a written agreement also usually discharges the agreement by operation of law. **Alteration** is a material change in the terms of a written contract without the consent of the other party. To discharge the contract, the alteration must be

- material, thus changing the obligation in an important way
- made intentionally, and not by accident or mistake
- made by a party to the agreement, or by an authorized agent
- made without consent of the other party.

BY TENDER OF PERFORMANCE

A ready, willing, and able offer to perform an obligation is a **tender**. If the duty requires the doing of an act, a tender that is made in good faith but is rejected will discharge the obligation of the one offering to perform. If the obligation requires the payment of money, rejection of an offer to pay the money does not discharge the debt nor does it prevent the creditor from collecting later. It merely relieves the debtor of court costs or future interest charges that might otherwise become due. To be valid, the tender of money must consist of the exact amount due in currency or coins, or *legal tender*.

A tender of only part of the debt is not a valid tender. If the debtor offers less than the amount due, the creditor may refuse it without losing the right to later collect the entire amount due.

CHECKPOINT
Identify the six ways in which contractual obligations can be discharged.

lawxtra.swlearning.com

11-1 Assessment

THINK ABOUT LEGAL CONCEPTS

1. The party transferring a right in an assignment is called the (a) assignee (b) assignor (c) obligor.

2. An assignment has to be supported by consideration. **True or False?**

3. Which of the following is the most frequent cause of a discharge of all contractual duties? (a) complete performance (b) major breach (c) promissory estoppel

4. If the contract creating the rights prohibits assignment, the parties may still assign. **True or False?**

5. Where the parties agree to substitute one party for another, this is called a(n) (a) novation (b) substitution (c) accord

6. A tender of money will not discharge a contractual obligation. **True or False?**

THINK CRITICALLY ABOUT EVIDENCE

Study the situation, answer the questions, and then prepare arguments to support your answers.

7. Tori operated a business that provided graphic design and printing services. Gerov contracted to have Tori design and print 25,000 brochures in full color promoting a variety of international tours. Under their contract, Tori also agreed to address and mail envelopes containing the brochures to a select list of prospects. Tori delegated the addressing, stuffing, and mailing of the envelopes. Is this a valid delegation? Does Tori remain liable to Gerov for proper completion of the entire job?

8. Your school orders 50 new uniforms for its marching band. The contract is with Quality Uniforms Inc., a firm with whom the school has done business for 12 years. A week before the first public performance by the band, Quality states that it has overbooked its business and has delegated the sewing to New Era Uniforms. Is the delegation legally proper?

9. Your school orders 50 new uniforms for its marching band. The contract states that "time is of the essence," and if the goods are not received in time for the first performance by the band on September 1, the old uniforms will be used for another year. The performance is the major part of a contest to see which area band will go to New York City to take part in its Thanksgiving Parade. The manufacturer does not deliver the uniforms until September 3. Can the school cancel the contract?

Remedies for Breach of Contract

▼ GOALS

- Name and describe various remedies possible for minor or major breach of contract
- Discuss the factors that affect the choice of remedies

REMEDIES POSSIBLE FOR BREACH

WHAT'S YOUR VERDICT?

Liu contracted to buy 160 acres of land from McCall. She planned to build an amusement park on the land that was near the junction of two interstates and had adequate utilities and population density. When McCall learned of her plan, he refused to transfer the title.

What is the optimal remedy for Liu?

A **remedy** means the action or procedure followed to enforce a right or to get damages for an injury to a right. Different remedies are available depending on whether a breach is a major or minor one. Whether a breach is major or minor is an issue of fact in a trial. The primary guideline in making the classification is the significance of the breach in relation to the entire contract.

REMEDY FOR A MINOR BREACH

The only remedy generally available for a minor breach is money damages. The party injured by a minor breach generally must continue to perform the duties defined by the contract. The amount of damages would be whatever it took to complete the minor duty. They could be recovered by suit if the victim had already paid. They could be deducted from the money due the breaching party under the contract if the victim had not yet paid.

REMEDIES FOR A MAJOR BREACH

If the breach is classified as a major breach, then the injured party need not continue performing the duties defined by the contract. In addition, the victim can choose among the following remedies:

1. *Rescission and restitution* Canceling the contract and returning whatever has been received under it
2. *Money damages* The payment of money to compensate for injury
3. *Specific performance* A court order commanding the breaching party to perform what was promised in the contract

Do you think the contract breach in the *What's Your Verdict?* situation on this page would be a major breach or a minor breach? Explain your answer.

© GETTY IMAGES/PHOTODISC

RESCISSION AND RESTITUTION These remedies are intended to place the parties in the same legal position they were in before contracting. Rescission allows the parties to treat the contract as canceled. *Restitution* permits the injured party to recover money or property (or the value thereof) given to the defaulting party. Thus, if a seller of realty committed a major breach by failing to deliver the deed, the buyer could sue for restitution and recover any money paid for the property. When rescission is granted, all the contractual obligations of the parties are canceled. Restitution also is usually available when the parties have attempted to contract, but failed, and in the process one party has delivered something of value to the other.

MONEY DAMAGES Money damages may be compensatory, consequential, liquidated, punitive, or nominal.

COMPENSATORY An award of *compensatory money damages* seeks to place injured parties in the same financial position they would have been in if there had been no breach. Specifically, the remedy grants the "benefit of the bargain." For example, if a homeowner contracted to sell at $65,000, when the fair market value of the property was $75,000, the buyer would be receiving a $10,000 "bargain." If the seller then committed a material breach, the buyer could recover the amount of her "bargain," $10,000, as compensatory money damages.

CONSEQUENTIAL In awarding *consequential money damages,* the court again tries to place injured parties in the same financial position they would have been in if the contract had been performed. This remedy grants money for the foreseeable injuries caused by the breach. Consequential damages generally are foreseeable when a reasonable person would know that a breach would cause the injury.

Consequential damages specifically are foreseeable if the defaulting party has been told that breach will cause the injury. For example, suppose a buyer tells the seller that she needs to take possession of her commercial property on or before January 1. She says that eight boxcars of ski boots will be arriving then and must be stored on the property. The buyer also may say she'll need to rent other property to store the boots if delivery of possession is delayed. This makes the injury specifically foreseeable. The seller will be liable if her breach causes the buyer to be forced to rent storage space. Consequential damages may be granted for both major and minor breaches.

PUNITIVE Under certain circumstances, such as fraud or when an intentional tort is involved in a breach of contract, the courts will award *punitive damages.* Such damages are added to other money damages. Their purpose is to punish and to make an example of the defendant. This could happen, for example, when a dishonest seller cheats a buyer by falsely saying a necklace is made of solid, 18-carat gold when in fact it is gold-plated copper or highly polished brass.

LIQUIDATED Parties to a contract sometimes agree that a certain amount of money will be paid if a certain breach occurs. This is called *liquidated money damages.* A liquidated damages clause might state

> "In the event the purchaser fails to pay the balance of the purchase price for said computer, the seller shall retain the amounts already paid hereon as liquidated damages."

Not all liquidated damages clauses are enforceable. When the amount of the liquidated damages is excessive in relation to the injury, the clause will not be enforced. A liquidated damages clause will be enforced only when it stipulates an amount reflecting a reasonable attempt to forecast the damages that would result from the breach. If it does reflect a reasonable forecast, it will be enforced even when no damages actually are suffered. When the liquidated damages clause is not enforceable, the injured party can collect damages only by proving other money damages.

NOMINAL Failure to perform a duty under a contract is a legal wrong. Therefore courts, even when no substantial harm has been done, will still award a token amount called *nominal damages* to acknowledge that a wrong has been committed. This could happen when, after a breach, the plaintiff finds a replacement product at a lower price. Nominal damages are granted in recognition of the rights that have been violated.

SPECIFIC PERFORMANCE Sometimes the only appropriate remedy for breach of contract is to decree (order) that the breaching party do exactly what was required under the contract. This is termed the remedy of **specific performance**.

Specific performance generally is available when the subject of the contract is unique such as in the purchase of an antique custom made 1932 Rolls Royce or a specific parcel of land. In

What's Your Verdict? Liu could likely win a suit for specific performance. The court would order McCall to transfer title to the property with a properly signed deed delivered to Liu.

Courts are reluctant to grant specific performance in situations where they would have great difficulty in supervising the result. For example, watching over the construction of a home or other structure to be sure it was up to contract specifications would absorb too much of the court's time. Similarly, it is very difficult for courts to supervise personal service or employment contracts. Therefore these contracts usually are not specifically enforceable. However, a court may grant an injunction prohibiting the defaulting party, such as an athletic coach or a key laboratory scientist, from working for anyone else during the period of employment agreed to under the contract. The person who breached the contract still would be liable for any money damages suffered by the employer. In addition to personal service and employment contracts, courts will not specifically enforce contracts in which terms are vague or ambiguous.

Finally, note that specific performance is an equitable remedy. A court will not award the remedy unless the party seeking it is blameless and has acted reasonably and fairly throughout the transaction. This is often called "clean hands."

CHECKPOINT

Explain the remedies available for a major breach of contract.

FACTORS AFFECTING CHOICE OF REMEDY

WHAT'S YOUR VERDICT?

Jim "high and tight" Brushback, an unknown baseball pitcher, signed a two-year contract to play for a major league team for $120,000 a year. After two months, Brushback had won all four games he'd started with 37 strikeouts and an earned-run average (ERA) of 1.75. He then contracted with a competing team for $12 million a year, thereby breaching his contract

What remedies are available to the original team?

IN THIS CASE

Rod McFink, a well-known rock and roll star, contracted with TickXX, Inc., a promotion company, to play in Springfield, Missouri's new convention center on December 15. TickXX had rented the venue, printed 15,000 tickets, and sold more than 1,000 in advance, when Rod announced that he would not be able to appear. TickXX personnel quickly found out that Rod had cancelled in order to play on the same date in Minneapolis for almost double the money. TickXX sued for its expenditures, lost profits on the 1,000 tickets (the potential sale of the other 14,000 was too speculative to get a lost profits award for them), and for a court order prohibiting Rod from playing anywhere other than Springfield on that weekend. Upon hearing of the suit, Rod called TickXX and agreed to perform in Springfield as scheduled. TickXX then dropped the suit.

CONFLICT OF REMEDIES

A party injured by a breach of contract must elect, or choose, a remedy when suing. Often, the electing to pursue one remedy will rule out pursuing another. For example, specific performance and damages cannot be recovered for the same breach because specific performance is not available when damages are an adequate remedy. Similarly, as rescission and restitution place the victim in the pre-contract position and damages places the victim in the same post-contract financial position, the combining of these remedies is not permitted for most contracts. Under the UCC, however, these remedies can be combined for a breach of contract for the sale of goods.

Restitution and specific performance are essentially opposites, so you could not combine these remedies. In *What's Your Verdict?* Brushback's original team could recover the two months' wages ($20,000) as restitution. However, if the team elects this remedy, they would lose the ability to sue for damages and the ability to obtain an injunction to stop Brushback from playing for the competition.

DUTY TO MITIGATE

A party injured by a breach of contract is required by law to take reasonable steps to minimize the harm done or, in legal terminology, to mitigate the damages. Suppose you contracted for a daily supply of 10-cent bolts used to assemble a car. If the supplier breached, you could not recover the consequential damages associated with the production line's being halted unless you made a reasonable attempt to find substitute bolts. Similarly, in most states, a landlord must take reasonable steps to re-rent an apartment vacated in breach of a lease. If an injured party fails to take reasonable steps to mitigate the damages, the amount of potential recovery is lessened by the amount that could have been mitigated.

WAIVERS

Sometimes a party intentionally and explicitly gives up a contractual right. This is called a waiver. If a creditor says, "I will accept your late payment without a late charge," this is a waiver. Waivers also arise by implication from conduct. For instance, if one party consistently sends late payments and is not charged the late fee specified in the contract, the rights to collect a late fee on future payments may be waived.

STATUTE OF LIMITATIONS

Statutes in all states deny any remedy if suit is not brought within a certain time after a legal claim, such as breach of contract, arises. Such laws are called statutes of limitations. While the time period varies among the states, four years is a common time for contracts and three years is a common time for torts. About half of the states allow more time to sue on written contracts than on oral ones. The UCC provides that an action for breach of a contract for the sale of goods must be begun within four years after the cause of action arises. In their original agreement, the parties may shorten the period to not less than one year, but they may not lengthen it. The statute of limitations begins to run from the moment there is a right to sue for a breach or default.

In the case of minors and others who lack capacity to contract, allowance is made for their period of incapacity. Thus, a minor is given a reasonable time after reaching majority to file suit.

BANKRUPTCY

Under the U.S. Constitution, Congress has established uniform laws on bankruptcies that permit the discharge (or excusing) of debts. Under these laws, debtors can get a fresh start, and creditors share fairly in whatever assets are available. *Bankruptcy* is a legal proceeding whereby a debtor's assets are distributed among his or her creditors to discharge the debts.

CHECKPOINT
What does it mean to "mitigate the damages"?

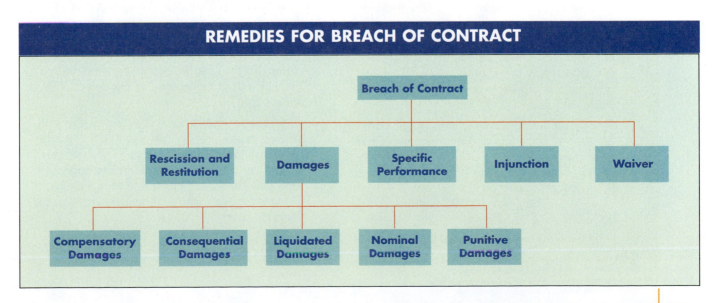

REMEDIES FOR BREACH OF CONTRACT

Breach of Contract

- Rescission and Restitution
- Damages
  - Compensatory Damages
  - Consequential Damages
  - Liquidated Damages
  - Nominal Damages
  - Punitive Damages
- Specific Performance
- Injunction
- Waiver

THINK ABOUT LEGAL CONCEPTS

1. Which remedy seeks to place the parties in exactly the same position they would have been in if the contract had been performed? (a) liquidated damages (b) restitution (c) specific performance.

2. If a liquidated damages clause is excessive, the clause will not be enforced and the injured party only can collect by proving other money damages. **True or False?**

3. Specific performance will be granted if (a) money damages are an adequate remedy (b) the subject matter of the contract is unique (c) the duty to be performed is difficult for the court to supervise (d) any of the above.

4. Which of the following remedies can be pursued at the same time? (a) damages and restitution for services (b) specific performance and damages (c) specific performance and restitution (d) none of the above can be pursued at the same time.

5. In contracts for the sale of goods, rescission can be combined with damages. **True or False?**

6. The party injured by a breach has a duty to _ ?_ the damages.

7. Specific performance and damages cannot be recovered for the same breach. **True or False?**

THINK CRITICALLY ABOUT EVIDENCE

Study the situation, answer the questions, and then prepare arguments to support your answers.

8. A college football coach has directed his team to division championships five times. With two years remaining in his current three-year employment contract, he notifies the college president that he is resigning in order to coach a professional team at a higher salary. Is the coach legally free to change employers? Is the professional team legally free to hire him? What can the college legally do?

9. The Bethlehem Steel Company contracted with the city of Chicago to supply and erect the steelwork for a certain section of an interstate highway. The price agreed upon was $1,734,200. The contract also provided that the steel company would pay as liquidated damages $1,000 for each day the work was extended and uncompleted beyond a specified date. The work was completed 52 days after the date agreed upon. Is the company liable for $52,000?

10. Rivera had the concession rights to sell food, drinks, and souvenirs at a post-season football bowl game. Some 60,000 reserved seat tickets had been sold for the event. As part of her preparations, Rivera contracted with Ace High Novelty Company for 10,000 pennants, noisemakers, and other items imprinted with the emblems and in the colors of the two competing teams. Although Rivera had emphasized the absolute necessity of delivery at least eight hours before game time, the goods arrived two days after the game had been played. Can Rivera recover lost profits from Ace? Why?

11. Taipei Yang ordered 900 solid brass bowls for indoor plants from the East-Meets-West Company, which imports such goods from Singapore. Yang had included the bowls as a special in his holiday gift catalog and expected to generate a net profit of at least $9,000 from their sale. When the shipment arrived and was opened, Yang scratched the bottom of one bowl and determined that it was steel with a surface plating of brass. Yang complained to the supplier, who pleaded ignorance and apologized. Nothing further was said and Yang paid the full price. Three months later he thought he should get a reduction in price because of the defect. Will he succeed?

12. While under contract with the county, Pyramid Paving improperly applied asphalt to the public gravel road in front of your family's home. Soon after application, large cracks appeared and your family complained. It took the city six years to file suit. What defense can Pyramid assert?

11-3 The Marriage Contract and Divorce

MARRIAGE AND CONTRACTS

WHAT'S YOUR VERDICT?

Jim and Mary are both 16 years old. While dating they have intimate relations, and Mary becomes pregnant.

Will the law compel them to marry?

Marriage is a legal union of a man and woman as husband and wife. No law specifies a minimum age for dating, although there are still state laws setting a minimum age for marriage without parental permission. Typically, this minimum age is 18. No law restricts the choice of marital partners, with one exception—close relatives may not marry.

If parents tell their minor child not to date or not to see a specific person, they can enforce that order only with the "reasonable force" that they may use to see that their other directions are carried out. If that fails, parents have no legal means to achieve their ends short of having their child labeled "incorrigible" in a juvenile delinquency proceeding. Parental use of excessive force may result in charges of child abuse.

Criminal laws against consensual premarital sexual intercourse between adults generally have been eliminated over the past couple of decades. However, if pregnancy results and the male responsible is identified, he will be required to pay his share of the female's medical bills and to contribute to the child's support until the child reaches adulthood. This is true even if the father is a minor. Beyond that requirement, no law exists to force the parents of an illegitimate child to marry. In *What's Your Verdict?* Mary and Jim may remain single.

A man and woman who live together outside of marriage are said to *cohabitate*. Such living arrangements were considered illegal in most states until the late 1970s. Cohabitation is still illegal in some states, although such laws are seldom enforced.

CONTRACTUAL ELEMENTS OF PREMARITAL RELATIONSHIPS

If one party in a heterosexual relationship proposes marriage and the other accepts, a binding contract results. If both later mutually agree to end their engagement, the law considers their agreement void and never to have existed. If only one party wants out of the contract and refuses to perform, a breach-of-promise suit may be brought by the other party.

Such suits at one time were notorious because juries set abnormally high figures to compensate the jilted party (usually the woman) for the actual damages, humiliation, and hurt feelings that accompanied the breakup. Today, some states allow such suits only where the woman is

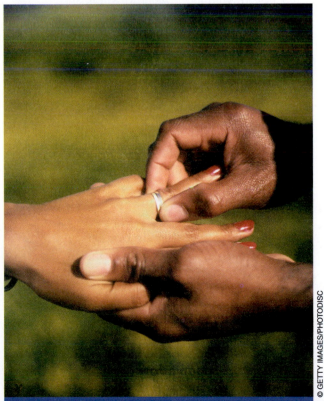

What happens, legally, if a couple mutually decides to end their engagement to be married?

© GETTY IMAGES/PHOTODISC

pregnant and her ex-fiancé is the father. Other states have placed a cap on the amount of damages that can be awarded. Many states have banned breach-of-promise suits altogether.

If third parties interfere with the engagement, a few states allow damage suits against the intruders. Such suits, however, cannot be brought against the parents who try to prevent their son or daughter from marrying.

When a relationship breaks down, gifts given by one party to the other may create legal problems. If the gift, such as a ring, is given in expectation of marriage, the courts generally order it to be returned. However, some states allow the woman to keep the ring if the man breaks off the engagement. The recipient can keep gifts other than those given in expectation of marriage.

IN THIS CASE

When Amanda said yes to his proposal, Antonio gave her several gifts including a five-carat engagement ring, a new sports car, and some plastic surgery. Two months later, Amanda fell in love with the jeweler to whom she had gone for an appraisal of the ring. Consequently, she broke off the engagement to Antonio. In most states, she must return the ring but can keep the car (and the plastic surgery).

STATUTORY REQUIREMENTS Each state has its own requirements for marriage. Most couples begin the process by appearing before the city or town clerk. The couple must apply for a marriage license and pay a fee to obtain it. In the vast majority of states, if the parties are over 18 years of age, they do not need their parents' consent. With parental consent, most states allow minors as young as 16 years old to marry.

Some states require a blood test before the license is issued to show that the applicants are free from various communicable diseases. A mandatory waiting period of three days from application to issuance is common. Once the license has been issued, any authorized religious or civil officials—court clerks, mayors, judges, rabbis, ministers, priests, and even ship captains at sea—can perform the ceremony.

NETBookmark

Access lawxtra.swlearning.com and click on the link for Chapter 11. Examine the table entitled "Marriage Laws of the Fifty States, the District of Columbia, and Puerto Rico." Locate the marriage laws for your state, and write a paragraph explaining them.

lawxtra.swlearning.com

An attempt has been made to standardize state laws for marriage and divorce. The Uniform Marriage and Divorce Act has been adopted by eight states. These states include Illinois, Kentucky, Missouri, Minnesota, Colorado, Montana, Arizona, and Washington. Marriage laws in the other states vary.

CONTRACTUAL ELEMENTS OF MARITAL RELATIONSHIPS

Traditionally, the law sees husband and wife as parties to a marriage contract for life and for the benefit of each other. The practical and legally recognized purposes for marriage are procreation, raising children, and filling sexual, economic, and companionship needs.

MARITAL CONSORTIUM The law recognizes these purposes as mutual duties of the wife and husband and calls them the **marital consortium**. In most states, if either spouse suffers an injury that prevents fulfillment of these marital duties, the other can sue the party who caused the harm for damages for "loss of consortium."

The most important duty of both spouses is to provide for the support, nurture, welfare, and education of their children. Other obligations jointly entered into, such as contracts, notes, and income tax returns, also are the mutual responsibility of the marital partners.

RIGHTS AND DUTIES OF PARENTHOOD Parents are obligated by state laws to support their children until they reach adulthood. An exception applies if a minor child takes legal measures to become emancipated.

Financial support of a couple's children is a joint obligation. This duty may be divided according to each spouse's financial position. Both parents in a married couple have custody rights to their children. Likewise, both have an equal voice in decisions that arise while raising them.

Some couples may choose to adopt children. The legal process of *adoption* creates a parent-child relationship. Adoptive parents have the same rights and duties to the adoptive child as they would to a child born of their union. Adoptions are governed by state law and must be approved by the courts.

Today adoption laws are the focus of attention in many states. Much of the attention is centered on access to adoption records. Laws vary from state to state, but most states allow some access. As new adoption laws are enacted, they also are being challenged. In 1997 the U.S. Supreme Court let stand a decision by the U.S. court of Appeals for the Sixth Circuit that Tennessee's open records statute does not violate the federal Constitution.

PROPERTY RIGHTS AND DUTIES Property acquired during the marriage may be kept in the name of the husband, the wife, or both. Either marital partner can buy and sell property of all types in her or his own name and have sole control of the respective earnings and credit. Such was not always the case, especially for the woman in the relationship.

At times, spouses bring property into marriage that they want to keep in their own names. They don't want the other spouse to have claim over it, especially in the event of death or divorce. Keeping a spouse from getting property rights can be accomplished with a **prenuptial agreement**.

A prenuptial agreement is an agreement in which the marital partners-to-be typically give up any future claim they might have to part or all of the other's property. Such a contract is especially useful when one or both are entering into their second or subsequent marriage and want to reserve the property from a previous marriage for the children of that bond.

The actions of one spouse may incur liability for the other. For example, the wife or husband may take care of the household while the other works outside the home. This often happens when there are young children in the family. In such a circumstance, the wage-earning spouse is legally responsible for the debts incurred by the other spouse in purchasing food, clothing, medical care, furniture, and any other items necessary to run the household.

Law Brief

States that Recognize Common-Law Marriages

Alabama
Colorado
Georgia (if created before 1/1/97)
Idaho (if created before 1/1/96)
Iowa
Kansas
Montana
New Hampshire (for inheritance purposes only)
Ohio (if created before 10/10/91)
Oklahoma
Pennsylvania
Rhode Island
South Carolina
Texas
Utah
Washington, D.C.

COMMON-LAW MARRIAGE

Common-law marriages have their roots in the American frontier. Because of the absence of suitable authorities, many pioneers could not follow the legal methods for becoming husband and wife. As a consequence, the law recognized common-law marriages that occurred when a single woman and a single man lived together, shared common property, and held themselves out as husband and wife over a prolonged period of time (usually 10 years or longer).

Today, about one-fourth of our states fully allow common-law marriages. All states must recognize such a union if it is legal in the state in which it occurred.

CHECKPOINT

What rights and duties are associated with the marriage contract?

ENDING THE MARRIAGE CONTRACT

WHAT'S YOUR VERDICT?

After they were married for two months, Ashley admitted to Scarlett that he was 15 years older than what he had previously stated.

What is the legal status of their marriage as a consequence?

A marriage may end in several ways. The death of either spouse, annulment, divorce, or a variety of illegalities may bring about the end of a marriage. Legal consequences of a spouse's death are discussed in Chapter 19.

BY ANNULMENT

Annulment ends many marriages. An **annulment** is a court order that cancels a marriage because of a problem that existed from the beginning of the marriage. Annulments serve to end marriages considered to be either voidable or void.

Problems such as refusal to have children or fraudulent grounds for the marriage contract may produce a *voidable marriage.* Fraudulent grounds for marriage include either spouse lying to the other as to wealth, condition of pregnancy, freedom from disease, willingness to have a child, past marriage, or age. Such a marriage may be terminated within a reasonable time by an annulment proceeding. The marriage stays valid until the annulment. In *What's Your Verdict?* Scarlett and Ashley's marriage is voidable and may be ended by annulment.

A *void marriage,* on the other hand, creates no rights or duties for either party and is considered invalid from the beginning. Such a marriage typically occurs whenever laws are violated by the matrimonial union. For example, if one partner is already married when the second marriage occurs, the second is a void marriage. A person who knowingly marries a second spouse while still married to the first is a *bigamist.* Bigamy is a crime. Another example of a void marriage is one between close relatives.

BY DIVORCE

The method usually used to end a marriage is *divorce.* In many states this is referred to as the dissolution of marriage. It is a court action that terminates the marriage and divides the property and responsibilities between the parties.

SEPARATION In many states, the first step toward divorce is *separation.* In such an event the spouses maintain separate living quarters, but their marital rights and obligations remain intact. To alter these rights and obligations, the parties or their lawyers must negotiate a legal separation agreement. This separation agreement contains terms covering such items as child custody, child support, alimony, and property division. If the parties fail to reconcile their differences during the period of separation and instead go through a divorce proceeding, the separation agreement often becomes the basis for the final divorce decree.

NO-FAULT DIVORCE Divorce has been made more available with no-fault divorce laws. In a no-fault divorce proceeding there is no assignment of fault

What do spouses cite as the legal reason for dissolution of marriage in states that have no-fault divorce laws?

© GETTY IMAGES/PHOTODISC

for the dissolution. The requesting spouse does not have to list a grievance, such as adultery, desertion, or cruelty against the other. Instead the court recognizes the right of either the wife or the husband to terminate a marriage unilaterally or of both spouses to end the marriage by mutual agreement.

A no-fault marriage dissolution may be initiated by either spouse. The dissolution is granted after testimony that there is no chance of repairing the marriage relationship. In most no-fault states *irreconcilable differences* are stated as the legal reason for dissolution. After the dissolution request is filed, the couple must usually wait about six months before it is final. In some states couples must meet with a marriage counselor to try to save their marriage.

TYPICAL ISSUES IN A DIVORCE

Many issues need to be resolved when a couple divorces. These include the issues of division of marital property, child custody and support, and alimony payments.

DIVISION OF PROPERTY In most states marital property laws are based on the English common law. The property brought into a marriage by a spouse will remain that spouse's property should the marriage end. During the marriage, whatever is earned, inherited, or received as a gift also remains the property of the spouse who earned or received it. States that do not follow this common-law rule are called *community property* states. In such states, half of all property acquired by the marital partners during the marriage is presumed to belong to each. Property owned by either spouse at the time of the marriage or

received by gift or inheritance during the marriage remains each spouse's own. You will learn more about community property laws in Chapter 15.

Regardless of the law followed, most state laws provide some type of equitable distribution of marital property upon the dissolution of a marriage. Judges distribute property fairly between the spouses. They consider issues such as the age and earning power of each spouse, length of the marriage, and contributions of each spouse to the marriage. If one of the spouses has stayed home to raise children and or take care of the household, the value of those services is considered as well.

CHILD CUSTODY AND SUPPORT The issue of *child custody* is concerned with the division of the physical and other care and control responsibilities for a child. The welfare of the child is the most important consideration in determining who will have custody of the child. Under the Marriage and Divorce Act, the factors a court must consider in awarding custody include

- parents' wishes as to custody
- child's wishes as to custody
- child's relationship with parents, siblings, and others who may affect the child's best interest
- child's adjustment to home, school, and community
- physical and mental health of all persons concerned.

Many divorcing couples are awarded *joint custody* of their children. In these situations the responsibility of raising the children is shared. With joint custody, both parents usually remain more interested and involved with their children.

Even if joint custody is not awarded, both parents have a duty to support minor children. The court typically orders the non-custodial parent to pay child support to the custodial parent. *Child support* is the monetary payment by a parent to provide a dependent child with appropriate economic maintenance. These payments help pay for the needs and wants of the child, including housing, food, clothing, schooling, and other expenses.

ALIMONY *Alimony* is the support paid by the wage earner of the family to the other spouse. Alimony usually is paid at regular intervals. It may, in some cases, be a lump-sum payment. Alimony is not intended to penalize the person ordered to pay it. The amount to be paid is set

What are some examples of community property?

LEGAL RESEARCH

Compare the differences in procedures and formulas used to determine the amount of child support due the custodial parent in a Pacific state, a Midwestern state, a Southern state, and an Eastern seaboard state. Why do you think these differences exist?

by the court. Factors considered by the court are the paying spouse's income, financial resources, earnings outlook, current debts, number of dependents, and number of spouses (former and subsequent).

CHECKPOINT

Name three ways in which a marriage contract is ended.

© GETTY IMAGES/PHOTODISC

What do you see as the pros and cons of divorced parents having joint custody of their children rather than one or the other having full custody?

11-3

Assessment

lawxtra.swlearning.com

THINK ABOUT LEGAL CONCEPTS

1. The voiding of a marital contract is referred to as an (a) alleviation (b) alteration c) annulment (d) none of the above.

2. If one party to a marital agreement wants out before the wedding but the other party does not, a _ ?_ suit may result.

3. A parent-child relationship is artificially created by the legal process of (a) adhesion (b) alignment (c) assignment (d) none of the above.

4. By entering into a(n) _ ?_ agreement, the marital partners-to-be typically give up any future claim they might have to any or all of the other's property.

5. Is common-law marriage still possible in some of the states of the United States? **Yes or No?**

6. Child support is a part of alimony. **True or False?**

7. Before no-fault divorces, which of the following was not a typical ground for divorce? (a) desertion (b) cruelty (c) adoption (d) all of the above were such grounds

8. Which of the following usually is given as the legal reason in a no-fault marriage dissolution? (a) bigamy (b) irreconcilable differences (c) cruelty (d) desertion

THINK CRITICALLY ABOUT EVIDENCE

Study the situation, answer the questions, and then prepare arguments to support your answers.

9. Maria is an only child. Her mother died when she was eight years old. Now, seven years

later, her father is engaged to remarry, and Maria objects. She is afraid that her father's new wife will come between her and her father and that the new wife will end up with

---

the family home after her father dies. Ethically, should Maria try to persuade her father not to marry? What legal device would help resolve part of her worries if she could get both her father and his intended to enter into it?

10. Marcel is 22 years old and Heather is 16. They are very much in love and planned to get married right away. After Heather's parents refused to consent to her marriage, Heather and Marcel eloped. Can Heather's parents have the marriage annulled even though Marcel is an adult?

11. Michael was driving home late one night when a tractor trailer truck ran a red light and struck his vehicle. Even though Michael was wearing a seat belt and his air bag properly deployed, he was critically injured. Several months later it became obvious that he was permanently paralyzed from the waist down. Michael has grounds for a lawsuit against the trucking company and the driver of the tractor semi-trailer. What cause of action does his wife have? How do you think a judge will decide?

12. Orlando and Mary lived together for 14 years in Oklahoma City. During the latter part of their cohabitation, they both claimed to be married to one another. In addition, they added Mr. and Mrs. to their address and held a joint bank account in those names. Now they are living apart from one another. Orlando currently lives in California. He has fallen in love with another woman and plans to marry her. As a consequence, he hires an attorney to determine whether he and Mary were legally married. What will the attorney check first? What other elements of common-law marriage might be significant in the determination? Is Orlando free to marry another?

13. The night after Zeke and Shanda were married, Shanda admitted that she was pregnant by another man. Can Zeke end their marriage? How?

14. Bernice and Bernie are married. He is a Certified Public Accountant making $75,000 per year. She is an architect making almost exactly the same amount. In the event of divorce, who will pay whom alimony?

PREVENT LEGAL DIFFICULTIES

In the execution of contracts . . .

1. As a prospective assignee, determine whether the assignor is subject to any defense that may affect your claim. Do this by promptly checking with the obligor (debtor). Remember that you, as the assignee, acquire only the rights as the assignor possessed.

2. If you are an assignee, be sure to notify the obligor (debtor) of the assignment as soon as practicable.

3. Be aware that "time is of the essence" in many contracts. If a contract calls for performance by a certain time, failure to perform may be a breach of contract. When appropriate, include this requirement in your contract, and clearly state that failure to perform at the time agreed upon may be treated as a breach.

4. Remember that hardship and higher costs do not make performance impossible. Bad weather, fires, strikes, inability to obtain materials, or similar difficulties could cause hardship. To be pro-

tected against damages for failure to fulfill a contract because of such events, include in the contract a clause to that effect.

5. Negotiate, and if possible, mediate or voluntarily arbitrate, before you litigate. A lawsuit should be the final resort because it is costly in time, money, and goodwill.

6. Always keep accurate records and be prepared to show that you actually suffered a monetary loss from a breach of contract. Make and keep evidence of a reasonable effort to mitigate the damages.

7. Use prenuptial agreements to avoid subsequent conflicts over property ownership and division.

8. If your marriage ends in divorce, make all decisions relative to your children with their best interest in mind. Joint custody with cooperating and involved parents helps the children grow up in a balanced and healthy environment.

Chapter 11 Assessment

CONCEPTS IN BRIEF

11-1 Transfer and Discharge of Obligations

1. A party may generally assign rights under a contract as long as the performance will not be materially changed. One is not released from contractual duties by making an assignment of them.

2. Duties may not be delegated when they involve personal judgment or skill, as with artists and professional experts.

3. An assignee acquires only such rights as the assignor has under the contract.

4. A material breach of contract generally permits the other party to regard his or her obligation to perform as discharged.

5. An obligation calling for an act, except that of paying money, is discharged by a tender of performance.

11-2 Remedies for Breach of Contract

6. In case of a breach of contract, the injured party has various remedies. An injured party may rescind or cancel the contract, recover the amount of loss through damages, and in certain cases, require specific performance or obtain an injunction.

7. The courts will not punish even an intentional breach of contract by awarding punitive damages unless an intentional tort or crime is involved. Rather, the court will award compensatory damages, possibly including special consequential damages. Sometimes the court will award either liquidated or nominal damages.

8. When the legal remedy of damages is not adequate, the court may grant the equitable remedy of specific performance, or of rescission, or it may grant an injunction prohibiting specified acts.

9. A remedy for breach of contract may be barred by the lapse of the time prescribed by a statute of limitations or by the debtor's discharge in bankruptcy.

11-3 The Marriage Contract and Divorce

10. Parental consent to marry generally is required for individuals in their minority.

11. Annulments are available based upon a variety of causes. Fraud is the most common, where either spouse lied about such things as freedom from diseases, past marriages, age, preference towards having children, and wealth.

12. In a prenuptial contract, marital partners-to-be may renounce any claim to their future spouse's property that they might otherwise acquire through marriage.

YOUR LEGAL VOCABULARY

Match each statement with the term that it best defines. Some terms may not be used.

1. The fulfillment of contractual promises as agreed
2. A court order that cancels a marriage because of a problem that existed from the beginning of the marriage
3. An agreement in which the marital partners-to-be typically give up any future claim they might have to part or all of the other's property
4. A ready, willing, and able offer to perform contractual obligations
5. One who owes a duty under a contract
6. The result of a court decree that the breaching party do exactly what was required under the contract
7. A termination of duties that ordinarily occurs when the parties perform as promised
8. The action or procedure followed to enforce a right or to get damages for an injury to a right
9. The injured party takes reasonable steps to minimize the harm done

a. **alteration**
b. **annulment**
c. **anticipatory breach**
d. **assignment**
e. **breach of contract**
f. **default**
g. **discharge**
h. **marital consortium**
i. **mitigate the damages**
j. **obligor**
k. **performance**
l. **prenuptial agreement**
m. **remedy**
n. **specific performance**
o. **statute of limitations**
p. **substantial performance**
q. **tender**
r. **waiver**

REVIEW LEGAL CONCEPTS

10. Tell how to determine whether a right can be assigned.

11. Describe those situations where specific performance will not be granted.

12. Explain how a statute of limitations works.

13. Why should the government require parental consent for marriages of persons in their minority?

14. What conditions produce a voidable marriage?

WRITE ABOUT LEGAL CONCEPTS

15. Write a short contract for the fictitious sale of a car between two of your classmates. Stipulate that the money is to be paid in two weeks and the title is to be delivered in one week. Now for each of the two classmates, write a sentence describing the rights and duties created by this contract.

16. Imagine that you are engaged to be married. Write a letter to your fiancée stating reasons for or against having a prenuptial agreement.

17. Make a list of five things that might be the subject of a contract but where specific performance would not be available. After each item write one sentence which states why this remedy is not available.

18. **HOT DEBATE** Write a persuasive opening argument that emphasizes the legal and ethical points in Ben's favor. Or, write a persuasive opening argument that emphasizes the legal and ethical points in his father's favor.

THINK CRITICALLY ABOUT EVIDENCE

Study the situation, answer the questions, and then prepare arguments to support your answers.

19. The Conch Oil Company, located at Marathon in the Florida Keys, contracted to sell and to deliver 500 barrels of fuel oil on the first of each month for one year to the Monsoon Mushroom Factory, an indoor farm. Conch delivered the oil for the first two months, but only two barrels at the beginning of the third month. Conch said there was unprecedented demand due to hurricane Sunny heading their way and it was allocating available supplies to customers on a pro-rata basis. There was nothing in the contract covering such a circumstance. The hurricane missed Marathon, and the mushroom crop died for want of fuel to help the climate control system keep it at an even temperature and humidity. Monsoon sued Conch. How should Conch defend against the suit? Who would likely win?

20. Hoglund reneged on his promise to sell his car to Elsen. Elsen went to nearby Los Angeles and found the same model with lower mileage, in better condition, and priced $600 below Hoglund's. Nevertheless, Elsen was incensed by Hoglund's conduct and wanted to sue him. To what damages, if any, is Elsen entitled?

21. Good contracted to build a house for Stern according to Stern's plans. After the house was completed, there were several defects that Good refused to fix. Stern then contracted with Madden to do the necessary corrective work for $8,000 and then sued Good for $8,000 in compensatory damages. Stern also demanded $10,000 in punitive damages "to punish Good and set an example for others." Is Stern entitled to compensatory damages? Is Stern legally or ethically entitled to punitive damages?

22. Stephanie and Alfred moved to Missouri after 15 years of living in Oklahoma. While they were together in Oklahoma, they held themselves out as husband and wife, lived together, and shared common property. Now Alfred wants to leave Stephanie. He has been the sole wage earner the whole time they have been together. Therefore, he wants to take all the property except a bed and an old car. Stephanie believes that Alfred owes her far more than that. She feels they have been married at common law and, therefore, she has the same rights as any other divorcing spouse. Alfred points out that Missouri does not have common-law marriage, so she has no such rights. Who is correct?

MAKE ACADEMIC CONNECTIONS

23. **SCIENCE** Development of products to be used in the frontiers of space can be expensive. The process is often saddled with delays, cost overruns, and failures. Research how NASA writes its contracts for the projects it funds. Be especially observant for liquidated damage clauses, waivers, assignment restrictions, testing, security precautions and any unusual clauses that are specific to such undertakings. Keep in mind the legendary aside of an astronaut to another as the countdown neared an end. "Did you ever think we're about to blast off in a rocket built by a host of lowest bidders?"

24. Eugene Plante was a general contractor who built a house for Frank and Carol Jacobs for a contract price of $26,765. The buyers paid $20,000 but refused to pay the balance, claiming that the contract had not been substantially performed. Plante sued, and the court ruled in his favor but first deducted the cost of repairing plaster cracks in the ceilings and a number of other defects. The buyers were dissatisfied with the judgment and appealed, notably because the trial court had allowed nothing for the misplacement of a wall between the kitchen and the living room. This enlarged the kitchen and narrowed the living room by one foot. Real estate experts testified during the trial that this did not affect the market price of the house, yet to move the wall would cost about $4,000. How should the appellate court decide? (*Plante v. Jacobs*, 103 N.W.2d 296, Wis.)

25. The Washington Trader was a giant oil tanker owned by the plaintiff, American Trading and Production Corporation. In March 1967, the defendant, Shell International Marine, Ltd., contracted for the ship to carry a load of oil from Texas to India. The total fee agreed upon was $417,327.36. No reference was made in the contract for the route to be taken; this was to be a decision of the shipping company. The route around Africa's Cape of Good Hope was an acceptable route. However, the price was based on passage through the Suez Canal (the invoice contained a Suez Canal toll charge). The Washington Trader headed for the Mediterranean Sea and the Suez. When the ship reached Gibraltar, it was warned of possible violence in the Middle East. Nevertheless, it continued. Upon reaching the Suez Canal, the ship found the canal closed by the Arab-Israeli War. The ship turned back and took the long route around Africa, at an added cost of $131,978.44. It arrived in Bombay some 30 days later than originally expected. American Trading then billed Shell for the full amount. When Shell refused to pay, American Trading sued. American claimed that the war made it impossible to perform as originally agreed. Shell, it said, should pay the extra cost because otherwise Shell would be unjustly enriched. You decide. (*American Trading and Production Corporation v. Shell International Marine, Ltd.*, 453 F.2d 939, 2d Cir.)

26. Under a written contract, plaintiff Shirley MacLaine Parker agreed to play the female singing-dancing lead in defendant 20th Century-Fox Film Corporation's planned production of a musical entitled "Bloomer Girl," to be filmed in Los Angeles. Fox Films was to pay MacLaine a minimum of $53,571.42 a week for 14 weeks, starting May 23. Before then, Fox decided not to produce the picture. In a letter dated April 4, Fox offered to employ MacLaine in a dramatic, western-type movie to be produced in Australia instead. She was given one week in which to accept. She did not, and the offer lapsed. She then sued for the agreed-upon $750,000 guaranteed compensation. Fox defended by saying MacLaine had unreasonably refused to mitigate damages by rejecting the substitute role. Is MacLaine entitled to receive the damages? (*Parker v. 20th Century-Fox Film Corporation*, 474 P.2d 689, Cal.)

27. More than four years after they were married, George Woy sought an annulment of his marriage to Linda Woy on the basis of fraud. In his petition he alleged that at the time of the marriage ceremony he was unaware that she had a dependence on illegal drugs, and that, had she not concealed the fact from him, he would have refused to marry her. Should the court grant an annulment on this basis? (*Woy v. Woy*, 737 S.W.2d 769)

28. When they remarried each other, Robert Root owed Nila Root several thousand dollars of unpaid child support from their first marriage. A month and a half after their second marriage ceremony, Nila filed to dissolve their second marriage and demanded payment of the back child support. Should the court allow her to collect the money, as she is still married to Robert? (*In re Marriage of Root*, 774 S.W.2d 521)

29. James and Anna Nesbit were contemplating divorce. They entered into a property settlement agreement, but James died before the divorce became final. His will provided a greater amount of property for Anna than did the settlement agreement. Which document should be enforced? (*Crist v. Nesbit*, 352 S.W.2d 53)

CASE FOR LEGAL THINKING

IVANA TRUMP v. DONALD J. TRUMP
SUPREME COURT OF NEW YORK, APPELLATE DIVISION,
582 N.Y.S.2D 1008

EVIDENCE The Trumps were married in 1977. On December 24, 1987, they entered into a postnuptial agreement. Both spouses did so under the advice of separate counsel. The agreement of December 1987 superceded three previous agreements of 1977, 1979, and 1984, respectively.

Two paragraphs of the 1987 agreement are under primary scrutiny in this case. The first is Paragraph 9(b) which set out the parties' rights and obligations in the event of divorce. These rights and obligations included the husband's obligation to pay $350,000 per year to the wife as maintenance and $10,000,000 in a lump sum within 90 days after the entry of the final divorce decree.

The second paragraph (Paragraph 10) provides that without obtaining Mr. Trump's advance written consent, Mrs. Trump can not publish, or cause to be published, any diary, memoir, letter, story, photograph, interview, article, essay, account, or description or depiction of any kind, whether fictionalized or not, concerning their marriage or any other aspect of Mr. Trump's personal, business, or financial affairs. She also could not assist or provide information to others in connection with the publication or dissemination of any such material or excerpts.

The agreement goes on to terminate any of Mr. Trump's obligations under paragraph 9(b) if a breach of the agreement occurs. It also provides that, in the event of divorce, the terms and conditions of this agreement shall supercede any divorce decree.

In 1990, Mrs. Trump initiated a divorce action against Donald J. on the grounds of cruel and inhuman treatment. Concurrently, she brought suit to have the agreement voided as she maintained it violated her rights to a property division available under state law.

TRIAL COURT DECISION The court granted Mrs. Trump her divorce. Later, after extensive negotiations between the parties, the court issued a judgment that reflected the result of these negotiations, i.e., that Mrs. Trump would accept the lump sum payment of the $10 million in return for allowing the agreement to be enforceable. Regrettably, the court, although including all the other terms of the agreement by reference, did not include paragraph 10 of the agreement in its judgment. Mr. Trump appealed the court's unilateral action which was taken without explanation or notice to the parties.

APPELLATE COURT DECISION "Since it is clear that the trial court exceeded its limited authority to disturb the terms of a separation agreement and paragraph 10 does not, on its face, offend public policy as a prior restraint on protected speech, we modify to incorporate the terms of said agreement into the . . . judgment as agreed to by the parties."

PRACTICE JUDGING

1. What is the significance of the omitted term? Could you infer that Mrs. Trump gave up anything of value in the negotiations in return for its being omitted?

2. Do you think the courts should have the discretion to pick and choose what sections of a contract they are going to enforce, even though all sections are valid under the law?

3. Mrs. Trump argued against the reinclusion of the term by saying that it involved a "prior restraint" on what she might publish. This, she maintained, would be a violation of her Constitutional rights. Do you agree? Why or why not?

© MICHAEL JACOBS/SAGA/LANDOV

PROJECT 2 CONTRACT LAW

PROTECTING THE IDEA

JJ's idea seemed to be working out. He'd come up with a name: DataDart. The prototype of the system had functioned well. Amber agreed to work with him in its development and marketing and had focused his attention on the legal issues he needed to take care of before he could start marketing the devices. Foremost among these issues was the necessity that JJ's idea be legally protected so that it could not be claimed or exploited by anyone else. As a consequence he met with a lawyer from Amber's law firm to discuss how to go about securing such protection. The lawyer listened to JJ's description of the DataDart and his assessment of the market for it. Then he made several recommendations.

First, JJ should not explain the interior workings of the DataDart to anyone else without having them sign a non-disclosure agreement beforehand. Next, JJ should meet with his uncle to see if he would give up all claims to JJ's invention. Stinson Adamski might argue that because JJ is employed there, the idea is his company's property to use and develop. The lawyer suggested that JJ be prepared to offer consideration to Stinson Adamski for giving up these claims. JJ also should have a preliminary patent search run to see if a similar device has been patented. If the preliminary patent search finds no conflicts, JJ should contract for a professional engineer to draft blueprints of the DataDart for a patent application. Then, he should contract with a lawyer specializing in patent law to draft the claims and file the actual application.

ADDITIONAL ISSUES

The lawyer also advised JJ that making the devices in

© GETTY IMAGES/PHOTODISC

his apartment is against the zoning laws of the city. Therefore, as soon as possible, JJ should see about leasing a small manufacturing facility for any production line he might set up. The lawyer closed the meeting by telling JJ that as the business progresses, many other steps will need to be taken to insure the optimal running of the concern.

After the meeting, JJ told Amber he was worried about how he would finance the project. He had used all of his savings to pay for building the prototype and did not know how he would find the money for the legal and engineering work that needed to be done. After listening carefully, Amber considered JJ's dilemma. She then said, "JJ, I've known you a long time and I believe in you. I have some savings set aside. Let me lend you the money and you can pay me back when you are able." JJ declined. "I can't ask you to do that Amber. This is a risk. It might not work." Amber said, "It will work. Go for it." Then seeing that Amber was serious, he said, "All right but we'll get the lawyers to make it a real business deal. Thank you so much."

ACTIVITIES

Divide into teams and perform one or more of the following activities, as directed by your teacher.

Prepare Legal Documents

As a team, prepare the following legal documents that JJ's lawyer has recommended
1. Non-disclosure agreement (how should this be worded to protect JJ?)
2. Lease agreement for an assembly plant
3. Promissory note to Amber to ensure that JJ will pay back the money he borrows

Negotiate

JJ needs to settle the issue of Stinson Adamski's possible claims on his invention. The lawyer suggests that JJ be prepared to offer consideration to Stinson Adamski for agreeing to give up these claims. Divide the class into two teams. One side should represent JJ's interests and the other side, Stinson Adamski's. Prepare different contract alternatives, dependent upon Stinson Adamski's attitude towards giving up his claims on the DataDart.

Use Technology

Have one or more group members conduct an Internet search to find out how to apply for a patent. The member(s) who conduct(s) the search should then present the findings of the group.

COMMUNITY ACTION

Positive Peer Pressure

Motor vehicle crashes are the number one cause of death among youth ages 15 to 20 according to the National Highway Traffic Safety Administration. In 2000 there were 6,131 youth motor vehicle deaths. Of these, 2,339 were alcohol-related.

You can help combat these frightening statistics through an organization called SADD—Students Against Destructive Decisions. With thousands of chapters in middle schools, high schools, and colleges, SADD student volunteers help peers with destructive behaviors and attitudes including underage drinking, substance abuse, impaired driving, violence, and suicide. SADD volunteers work through a variety of peer-led educational projects including classes, forums, workshops, conferences, rallies, and legislative work. SADD has 10,000 chapters with 350,000 active student members and more than seven million students in schools with a SADD chapter.

Do Your Part

1. Use the Internet to research a SADD chapter in or near your community. Contact them to learn how you can use your talents and abilities to help. Then make an appointment to volunteer your help.
2. If SADD is not already in your school or community, gather a group of your peers and go to work. Use the Internet for information on setting up a chapter.
3. Set a date and agenda for your first meeting. Arrange to hold the meeting in a large room at your school
4. Advertise the meeting. Post flyers around the school and campus. Send a press release to the school newspaper and radio station.
5. Create a handout with information about SADD, frequently asked questions, and the time and place of the next meeting.
6. At the meeting, provide information about SADD and your chapter, and invite students to become volunteers.

Multimedia Presentation

This event may be completed by one to three individuals. Using technology to support a presentation enhances a business leader's effectiveness. This event recognizes FBLA members who demonstrate the effective use of presentation technologies and software to prepare and deliver their message.

You have been asked to prepare a presentation that covers common types of contracts that young people sign (college loan, car loan, rental agreement, etc.) Your presentation must cover all elements of a contract (offer and acceptance, genuine agreement, mutual consideration, capacity, legality). The presentation should relate all of the contract elements to one type of contract entered by a young person.

The individual or team has five minutes to set up equipment and five minutes to present. The presentation is an explanation of the Multimedia Presentation, not a viewing of the presentation.

Performance Indicators Evaluated
• Understand the elements of a contract.

• Describe common contracts that young people sign.
• Use multimedia effectively for thorough coverage of all elements of contracts.
• Design an effective multimedia presentation.
• Explain all aspects of the multimedia presentation.
• Involve all members in the multimedia project.

For more detailed information about performance indicators, go to the FBLA web site.

Think Critically
1. Why is multimedia an effective means to cover the elements of a contract?
2. What effect does the use of pictures have in a multimedia presentation?
3. List three characteristics for an effective multimedia presentation.

http://www.fbla-pbl.org/

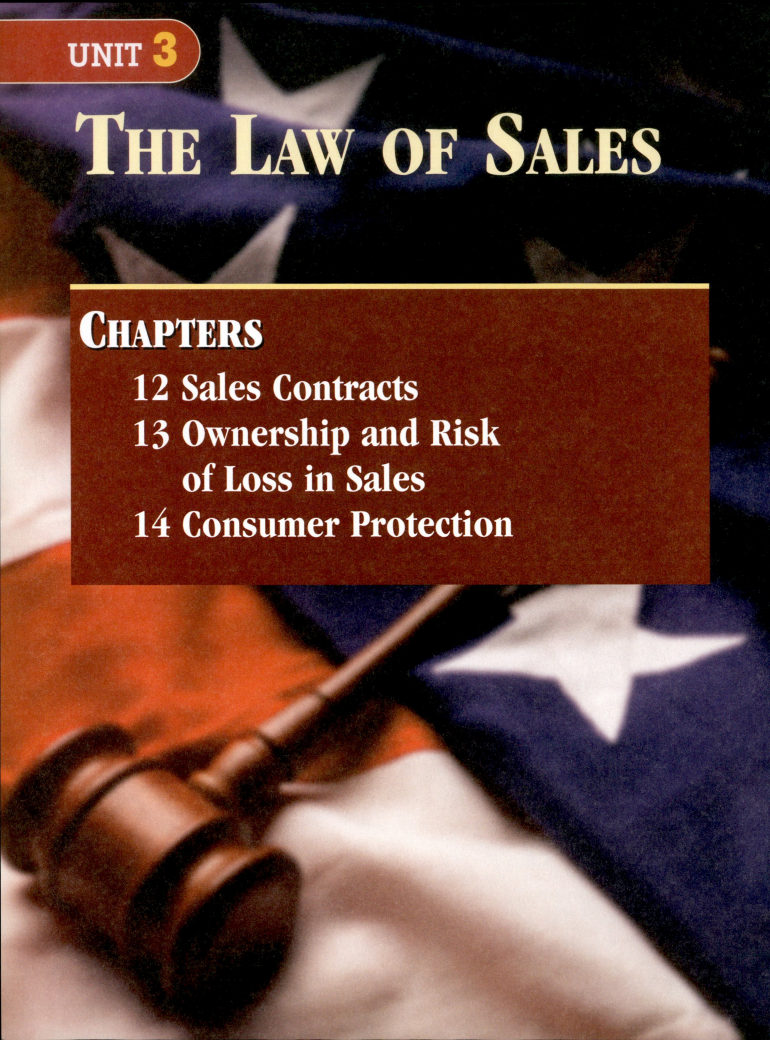

UNIT 3

THE LAW OF SALES

CHAPTERS

IN PRACTICE PROFILE

Deborah Rosado Shaw ■ Founder and CEO Umbrellas Plus LLC

Deborah Rosado Shaw didn't choose a career in sales. "A sales career chose me," she explains. While attending Barnard College at Columbia University in New York City, Deborah took a job as a customer service representative for a company that made umbrellas and tote bags. The job helped pay her tuition. She planned to attend law school after earning a Bachelor of Arts in Political Science. Then her customer service job opened her eyes to new possibilities.

"As I was working, I watched and listened and started to really enjoy what the sales team got to do. They were creative and got to travel to meet with interesting people. And they made very good money." Although she never had considered a career in sales, "I was really drawn to the hustle and bustle of it all." In an effort to be promoted to a salesperson, Deborah secretly arranged a meeting with the executives of the Museum of Natural History in New York. She left the meeting with a $140,000 order which she placed in front of her company president. Her sales career had begun.

Today Deborah is the founder and chief executive officer of Umbrellas Plus, LLC, a multi-million dollar wholesaler and importer of fashion and sun accessories. Although she runs the company, she considers her primary job to be sales. "I sell the credibility of the business: who we are, what our company is about, our values." Because big deals require big attention,

PHOTO BY SIGRID ESTRADA

"I sell the credibility of the business: who we are, what our company is about, our values. . . . I also sell to our banker when I ask them to continue to lend us money to finance and grow our business."

Deborah makes sales calls to key executives and visits the company's most important accounts. "I also sell to our banker when I ask them to continue to lend us money to finance and grow our business."

Although she never earned her law degree, Deborah finds the law is a part of everything she does. "We need to meet all hiring and employment laws, and get correct contracts for the buying and delivery agreements we make with our vendors in China and in the United States." She knows that incorrectly written contracts can mean missed delivery dates and cancelled orders.

Facing challenges is nothing new to Deborah. As a child she was challenged with safely getting to and from school each day. "I grew up in a place were shots were fired from rooftops, drug dealers in the streets." Wanting to share her strategies for success with others, Deborah wrote *Dream BIG!—A Roadmap for Facing Life's Challenges and Creating the Life You Deserve.* In doing so she became the first Hispanic person to have a self-help book published by a major publisher.

Her success in business and in life has placed her on numerous national television shows. Top business magazines tout her achievements, as do numerous organizations that have given her such titles as "Hispanic Businesswoman of the Year" and included her as one of the "100 Most Successful Latinos in the U.S."

Sales Contracts

12-1 Sales

12-2 Special Rules for Sales Contracts

HOT DEBATE

Amanda and Bob, a successful young married couple, began the redecoration of the kitchen in the antebellum house they had just purchased outside of New Orleans. They contracted with several artisans in the effort. Anton, the owner of a custom cabinet shop, worked closely with Amanda to develop a pattern in the period of the house. After taking measurements, Anton set about making the cabinets to fit the unique dimensions and style of the house's cooking area. As the work was nearing completion, Amanda and Bob decided to divorce. They notified Anton to stop work and told him he would not be paid as he had not completed the job. Anton sued.

Where Do You Stand?

1. Should Anton be able to recover? Why or why not?

2. Discuss the ethical reasons in Anton's favor.

▼ GOALS
- Define sale and explain how the UCC governs the sale of goods
- Explain how the UCC treats unconscionable contracts and contracts of adhesion

WHAT IS A SALE?

WHAT'S YOUR VERDICT?

At the Dan-Dee Discount Department Store, Jack and Jean Medina signed a contract to buy a clothes washer and dryer set. The Dan-Dee salesperson explained that although the set on display was not in stock, "We will deliver and install it within two weeks." While shopping at the store, the Medinas left their car in the store's automobile service department to have the engine's idling speed adjusted and to have squeaks in the door eliminated. The charge for labor was $45. There was no charge for parts or supplies. The service attendant recommended replacing the car's tires, and the Medinas agreed. The cost of the tires was $300, plus $25 for balancing and installation. The Medinas also bought a new battery for $59. It was installed free of charge.

Were all of these agreements sales?

A **sale** is a contract in which ownership of goods transfers immediately from the seller to the buyer for a price. **Ownership** entails a collection of rights that allow the use and enjoyment of property. If the transfer of ownership is to take place in the future, the transaction is a **contract to sell** rather than a sale. **Price** is the consideration for a sale or contract to sell goods. It may be expressed in money, in services, or in other goods. When parties exchange goods for goods, the sale is a **barter**.

The Uniform Commercial Code (UCC) governs sales of goods. It also governs contracts to sell goods in the future. **Goods** are tangible (touchable), movable personal property, such as airplanes, books, clothing, and dogs. By

UCC definition, goods do not include the following:

1. Money (except rare currency or rare coins, which are collectible items with value that may exceed their face amounts)

2. Intangible (not touchable) personal property, such as legal rights to performance under a contract, transferred by assignment rather than by sale

3. Patents and copyrights, which are exclusive rights given by the federal government to inventors and writers

4. Land and other forms of real property, which are transferred by conveyance and are subject to special rules (as discussed in Unit 4 on Property)

© DIGITAL VISION

This girl is listening to a song on a music CD. When she decides to buy the CD, will the transaction be considered a sale or a contract to sell? Explain your answer.

Under the UCC a sales contract may be made in any manner sufficient to show agreement. The resulting contract suffices if the parties, by their actions, recognize the existence of a contract. This is true even though a court might not be able to determine precisely when the contract was made, and even though one or more terms are left open in accordance with customs of the trade.

In general, as applied to the sale of goods, the law of contracts (as discussed in Unit 2) has been simplified and made less strict. For example, the price for goods usually is fixed in the contract. However, the parties may indicate that the price is to be set in a certain way at a later date. This method is used in long-term contracts due to the fluctuation of prices over time. Ordinarily, when nothing is said about the price, a contract results if all other essentials are present, and provided the parties do not express a contrary intent. In such a case, the buyer is required to pay the price that is reasonable when the goods are received.

CONTRACTS THAT ARE NOT SALES

In some contractual situations, goods may be included but the primary purpose of the contract is to provide a service. Such contracts are not sales because any goods supplied are merely incidental. In *What's Your Verdict?* the work on the car engine and the doors was a contract for services. Any goods supplied, such as lubricants, were incidental. Even if a specific charge was made for them, the contract would remain one for the services that were the dominant part of that agreement. Such a contract would not fall under the UCC rules and requirements as a consequence.

On the other hand, the transfer to the Medinas of title to the tires was a sale of goods, even though a small charge was made for related

LEGAL RESEARCH

Determine how the tax laws treat sales for money versus barter contracts. What is the justification for the difference(s)?

labor. The battery also was acquired in a sale of goods, with no charge for labor. The Medinas' agreement to buy the washer and dryer at a later date was not a sale. Instead, it was a contract to sell—a contract in which ownership of goods is to transfer in a sale in the future. In both sales of goods and contracts to sell, the seller is known as a **vendor**. The buyer is known as the **vendee** or the *purchaser*.

PAYMENT AND DELIVERY

Payment occurs when the buyer transfers the agreed-upon consideration and the seller accepts it. **Delivery** is the act by which the subject matter of the contract is placed within the possession or control of the buyer. **Receipt of goods** means that the buyer takes physical possession or control of the goods. Receipt usually involves actual delivery. However, delivery may be constructive. This means that there is no actual transfer of possession of the goods, but the recipient has the power to control them, as intended by the parties involved. Examples would be when the buyer gets the

CISG

The Convention on Contracts for the International Sale of Goods (CISG) is a United Nations agreement that regulates international sales contracts. The CISG has been adopted in nearly 40 countries. Once a country adopts the CISG, it becomes part of that country's domestic law.

The CISG applies to international transactions under the following conditions: (1) the contract involves the commercial sale of goods (2) the contract is between parties whose "places of business" are located in different countries (3) the places of business are located in countries that have adopted the convention.

keys to a car or receives a warehouse receipt for stored goods.

In the basic sales transaction, payment, delivery, and transfer of title take place simultaneously at the seller's place of business. Even if payment or delivery, or both, take place later, title still passes when the buyer selects and agrees to buy existing goods in the seller's store.

At the appropriate time fixed in the sales contract, the buyer has a duty to pay, and the seller has a duty to transfer possession. Generally neither is obligated to perform until the other does. Thus, unless it is otherwise agreed (as when the sale is on credit), or if it is the custom of the trade, the seller may retain the goods until the buyer makes payment in full. Similarly, the buyer may refuse to pay the price until the seller delivers all the goods.

The buyer is entitled to a receipt when payment is made.

BILL OF SALE A **bill of sale** is a receipt that serves as written evidence of the transfer of ownership of goods. Such a document is sometimes required by statute, as in the case of automobile sales. If a bill of sale is signed by the seller, buyer, or both, it can satisfy the requirements of the Statute of Frauds for a signed writing. However, neither a sales contract nor a bill of sale necessarily identifies the parties nor explains the terms of the transaction.

A bill of sale makes resale of the property easier because it provides the owner with written evidence of ownership. When goods are lost, stolen, or destroyed, as in a fire, the document can be used to help prove value. The bill of sale is not absolute proof of ownership because other persons may have acquired claims against the goods since the bill of sale was issued. Also, dishonest persons may forge such documents to help dispose of stolen property.

USE OF CREDIT To encourage business, most sellers extend credit to qualified buyers, including other business firms. Some retailers do most of their business selling to customers who use credit cards or charge accounts, or who pay in installments. Thus, the buyer may get both title and possession before payment.

This candy retailer just received this bill of sale from Becksmith Candies, one of her vendors. What does the bill of sale indicate about the ownership of the candy she purchased?

© GETTY IMAGES/PHOTODISC

ACCEPTANCE OF GOODS Acceptance of goods means that the buyer has agreed, by words or by conduct, that the goods received are satisfactory. Acceptance is shown when the goods are used, resold, or otherwise treated as if they were owned by the buyer. Acceptance also may be indicated when a buyer fails to reject the goods within a reasonable time, if the buyer has had adequate opportunity to inspect them.

IN THIS CASE

The Baumgartens bought Hannukah gifts for their three young children during the Sunrise Center's October lay-away sale. Delivery was scheduled for early December, and payment was due before January 15 of the following year. Assuming the goods were set aside for the Baumgartens at the time of the sale, they received title in October, possession in December, and paid for the goods in January.

Law Brief

Several important changes recently were proposed by the National Conference of Commissioners on Uniform State Laws to UCC Article 2: Sales. The changes represent the impact of e-commerce, inflation, and an increasing international focus. These changes, especially those relating to e-commerce, have met with great resistance. As of mid-2004, not a single state had adopted the proposed changes. The states are reluctant to accept the change that proposes to redefine "sign" to include electronic signatures and to create other definitions pertaining to electronic commerce such as "electronic agent," "electronic record," and others. The states also object to considering an electronic record of a transaction as the "writing" required by the Statute of Frauds.

OTHER WAYS TO CONTRACT

Sales contracts may be made through a traditional exchange of offer and acceptance. However, the UCC also recognizes alternative methods. Instead of telephoning, sending a facsimile (fax), or mailing an acceptance, the seller may simply ship the goods and thereafter notify the buyer of this action.

CHECKPOINT

What is the definition of a sale?

UNCONSCIONABLE SALES CONTRACTS

WHAT'S YOUR VERDICT?

Piotr, a recent immigrant, bought a refrigerator from a rent-to-own store that advertised its willingness to deal with people with unestablished credit. Piotr spoke, read, and wrote Russian and German, but only spoke a few words of English. The negotiations and sale of the refrigerator were conducted in German. However, although the seller knew that Piotr could not understand it, the written contract was entirely in English. The store had paid the manufacturer $348 for the refrigerator but the total cost to Piotr under the three-year installment contract was $2,567. When Piotr defaulted on his payments after more than a year, the store sued for the $1,805 left to be paid.

Why shouldn't the store recover the remainder due under the contract?

The UCC provides that a court may find that a contract or a clause of a contract is *unconscionable,* that is, grossly unfair. An unconscionable contract or clause offends an honest person's conscience and sense of justice, as does the contract in *What's Your Verdict?* The terms need not be criminal nor violate a statute, but they are unethical.

Contracts of adhesion are more likely to be unconscionable. This is so because in such contracts one of the parties dictates all the important terms. The weaker party must generally accept the terms as offered or not contract at all. A court that decides whether a clause of a contract is unconscionable may do any of the following:

- refuse to enforce the contract
- enforce the contract without the unconscionable clause
- limit the clause's application so that the contract is no longer unfair.

In *What's Your Verdict?* Piotr would probably receive title to the appliance without further payment as it is the unconscionable result of a contract of adhesion and Piotr has paid double the cost to the store already. The law is not designed to relieve a person of a bad bargain. A person may be legally bound by the purchase of over-priced, poor quality, or unneeded goods.

NETBookmark

Access lawxtra.swlearning.com and click on the link for Chapter 12. Read the Insurance Foundation glossary entry for "adhesion." Why do courts generally interpret ambiguous provisions in insurance contracts in favor of the insured?

lawxtra.swlearning.com

CHECKPOINT

Why are contracts of adhesion likely to be unconscionable?

Xtra! Study Tools

lawxtra.swlearning.com

12-1 Assessment

THINK ABOUT LEGAL CONCEPTS

1. Rare coins, even though currency, can be considered goods under the UCC. **True or False?**

2. Intellectual property, such as a patent or a copyright, is not considered a good under the UCC. **True or False?**

3. A(n) _?_ delivery occurs when there is no actual transfer of possession of the goods, but the recipient has the power to control them, as intended by the parties involved.

4. Contracts to sell are not governed by the UCC's law of sales. **True or False?**

5. Which of the following would not be considered goods under the UCC's law of sales? (a) passenger plane (b) computer (c) six acres of land (d) All of the above are goods under the UCC.

6. Can a court refuse to enforce an entire contract that if finds to be unconscionable? **Yes or No?**

THINK CRITICALLY ABOUT EVIDENCE

Study the situation, answer the questions, and then prepare arguments to support your answers.

7. The Caribbean Mill sold a quantity of standard electrolytic copper bars to Pollard. The contract was complete in all respects except that it failed to state the price. Was the contract enforceable in court?

8. As Brackston was examining a china plate in the Nook and Cranny Shoppe, it slipped from her hands. The plate smashed into countless pieces when it hit the floor. After the store owner swept up the mess, she pointed to a sign on the wall that said, "Handle with Care! If You Break It, You Buy It." She then rang up a sales charge of $300 plus $18 sales tax. Was Brackston the vendee in a sales contract?

9. After their business law class, Alexa and Ronald were discussing contracts of adhesion. Ronald insisted that when a "big-ticket item," such as a television, is sold on credit terms, the seller prepares the contract. "You agree to it as written or you're out of luck. No sale." Alexa argued, "That's the truth, but not the whole truth." Can you explain what Alexa meant by her comment? Is it ethical for a seller to use contracts of adhesion?

Special Rules for Sales Contracts

SPECIAL RULES FOR MERCHANTS

WHAT'S YOUR VERDICT?

During the week, Adonis would buy property at auctions and then sell it to others on weekends at one of his garage sales. After 33 consecutive weekends of garage sales, the city in which he lived claimed that he was a merchant as a result and so had to pay sales tax.

Is the city correct?

In most cases, the UCC treats all buyers and sellers alike. However, specialized rules may be applied to individuals who are merchants. A **merchant** is someone who deals regularly in the type of goods being exchanged or claims special knowledge or skill in the type of sales transaction being conducted. Individuals who do not qualify as merchants in a transaction are known as **casual sellers**.

You would be a casual seller if you sold your private automobile. A used-car dealer selling an identical car would be a merchant. In general, the UCC holds merchants to a higher standard of conduct than it does casual sellers. Merchants may be required to have licenses to sell. They also usually are subjected to special taxation and closer regulation by the government. In *What's Your Verdict?* Adonis was indeed a merchant and would have to pay sales tax.

MERCHANT STATUS IN SALES CONTRACTS

Under the UCC, an offeror may state that the offer to buy or to sell goods must be accepted exactly as made or not at all. Otherwise the offeree may accept and still change some terms of the contract or add new ones. Recall that in contract negotiations governed by the common law such changes would end the original offer and

would be considered a counteroffer. Under the law of sales of goods, however, the new term is treated as a *proposal for addition* to the contract. What happens then depends on whether both parties are merchants.

When both parties are merchants, a new term inserted by the offeree automatically becomes part of the contract if the offeror fails to object within a reasonable time. However, the new term must not materially alter the offer. In addition, the original offer must not expressly bar such changes. If the new term is a *material* (important) alteration, it is included in the contract only if the original offeror expressly shows an intention to be bound by it.

Other special rules applying to merchants will be pointed out as the appropriate topic area is covered.

© GETTY IMAGES/PHOTODISC

Your cousin's hobby is making surfboards for friends. He makes three or four a year. Occasionally someone offers to buy one of the boards from him before he gives it away. Is your cousin a merchant or a casual seller of surfboards?

CHECKPOINT

How do merchants differ from casual buyers in a sales situation?

HOW DOES THE STATUTE OF FRAUDS APPLY TO SALES?

WHAT'S YOUR VERDICT?

Chilton orally agreed to buy an imported camera from the Open Shutter Shop for $748.98. The camera she wanted was not in stock, but a shipment was expected any day. Therefore the salesclerk prepared a memorandum of the sale, signed it, and gave Chilton a copy. A week later the clerk phoned and said, "Your camera is ready." Chilton replied that she did not want it because she had learned that the identical model could be purchased for much less by mail from a New York City discount store.

Is Chilton liable to Open Shutter for breach of contract?

Sales contracts, like other contracts, are generally valid and enforceable in court whether they are oral, written, or implied from the conduct of the parties. However, as you may recall, under the Statute of Frauds, sales contracts for goods valued at $500 or more must be evidenced by a writing to be enforceable in court.

In good business practice, both parties sign a written sales contract and each party gets a copy. This provides both parties with a useful legal record, and it reinforces mutual good faith. Normally both parties expect to perform, but either party could breach the contract. If that happens, the injured party can sue. In court, the written contract goes a long way towards proving the existence and terms of the agreement.

In *What's Your Verdict?* the price of the goods was more than $500. Therefore the sale was governed by the Statute of Frauds. Open Shutter is bound because its clerk signed the contract.

Chilton is not bound because she did not sign, but she could enforce the agreement against Open Shutter if she so desired.

Not all the terms of a sales contract have to be in writing to satisfy the Statute of Frauds. Essentially, all that is required is a writing, signed by the party being sued, which satisfies the court that a contract to sell, or a sale, has been made. The number or quantity of goods involved in the transaction must be contained in the writing. The contract is not enforceable beyond the stated quantity.

However, the time and manner of performance; credit and warranty terms; packaging, labeling, and shipping instructions; and even the price need not be included for the writing to satisfy the statute. If necessary, this information can be provided later in oral testimony in court.

A variation of the Statute of Frauds applies only to contracts between merchants. The law generally requires a signature of the person being sued. Between merchants, however, the signature of the party who is suing may be enough to prove an otherwise unenforceable sales contract. If a merchant sends a written confirmation of an oral contract to another merchant within a reasonable time after this oral agreement was made, the confirmation binds both parties. If the second merchant sends a written objection to the confirmation within ten days, the confirmation is not binding.

EXCEPTIONS TO THE STATUTE OF FRAUDS FOR SALES CONTRACTS

Under certain circumstances, oral contracts for the sale of goods priced at $500 or more may be valid and enforceable. These exceptions to the requirements of the Statute of Frauds include the following:

GOODS RECEIVED AND ACCEPTED BY THE BUYER

Receiving the goods does not in itself make an oral contract binding under the Statute of Frauds. Both receipt and acceptance are necessary. A buyer may receive goods without accepting them. Under the UCC a buyer can accept goods in three ways.

1. After a reasonable opportunity to inspect the goods, the buyer signifies to the seller that the goods conform to the contract or will be retained in spite of their nonconformity.

2. The buyer acts inconsistently with the seller's ownership (for example, uses, consumes, or resells the goods).

3. The buyer fails to make an effective rejection after having a reasonable opportunity to inspect the goods.

Note that if the buyer has received and accepted only some of the goods, the oral contract is enforceable only for those goods received and accepted.

BUYER PAYS FOR GOODS AND SELLER ACCEPTS PAYMENT When payment in full has been accepted by the seller, the oral contract is enforceable in full. When partial payment has been accepted by the seller, the oral contract is enforceable only for the goods paid for if the goods can be divided and the price can be apportioned fairly. If the goods are indivisible and there can be no dispute as to quantity, the contract is enforceable in full.

GOODS SPECIALLY MADE NOT SUITABLE FOR SALE TO OTHERS A seller can enforce an oral contract for non-salable goods if

1. the seller has substantially begun to manufacture them, or

2. the seller has made contracts to obtain the goods from third parties.

PARTY AGAINST WHOM ENFORCEMENT SOUGHT ADMITS ORAL CONTRACT MADE A party against whom enforcement of an oral contract is sought may admit in legal pleadings or testimony that he or she agreed to part or all of a contract. In

such a case, a signed writing is not necessary for the enforcement of the part of the contract that was admitted.

CHECKPOINT

Name the four situations in which the Statute of Frauds does not apply to sales contracts.

12-2 Assessment

Xtra! Study Tools

lawxtra.swlearning.com

THINK ABOUT LEGAL CONCEPTS

1. Generally, orally made sales or contracts to sell are valid and enforceable in court. **True or False?**

2. Under the Statute of Frauds, sales of goods valued at _?_ or more need to be evidenced by a writing to be enforceable in court.

3. If a buyer resells the goods, the UCC treats the buyer's action as an acceptance. **True or False?**

4. Do both parties have to sign the writing to satisfy the Statute of Frauds? **Yes or No?**

5. If a party admits in court the existence of a contract, it becomes enforceable against that party even if the admission is only oral. **True or False?**

6. An individual who does not qualify as a merchant in a sales situation must be a(n) _?_.

THINK CRITICALLY ABOUT EVIDENCE

Study the situation, answer the questions, and then prepare arguments to support your answers.

7. A pottery manufacturer offered to sell red clay flowerpots in three different sizes to a garden supply store. The store accepted the offer but specified that the pots had to be packaged in sets of three (with one of each size) rather than in bulk as described in the offer. This was a material change in the terms. The pottery maker did not object or revoke the original offer. Instead the maker packaged and shipped in threes the goods as requested. Later, the pottery maker did a cost evaluation of shipping the pots in threes and stopped doing so. Could the maker be sued under the sales contract and be forced to ship in threes?

8. When Soule bought a sweater for his wife, the clerk deliberately lied to him. She said that the garment was a pure silk and mohair, hand-knitted import from Italy. In fact, it was a machine-made, domestic, polyester-and-wool mix. Did the clerk violate the Statute of Frauds by her conduct? Did the clerk act ethically?

9. Grant had long admired Kahn's collection of records featuring the big bands of the 1930s. One day Kahn orally agreed to sell the collection to Grant for $275. When Grant appeared with the money, however, Kahn said she had changed her mind and refused to deliver. Moreover, she insisted she was acting within her legal rights. Kahn said she had learned that her collection was worth at least $1,000. Therefore, she said, a signed writing was required to make the contract enforceable. Did Kahn state the law correctly?

10. Harrison orally agreed to buy two electric guitars and a matched set of drums from Rudolph. The price was $1,250, payable with $800 in cash and a bass saxophone. Harrison paid the price in full. However, Rudolph refused to deliver the guitars and drums, and he sent the saxophone back and mailed a certified check for $800 to Harrison. He explained that he had decided to start another rock group. Rudolph claimed that their oral agreement was not enforceable. Is he right?

PREVENT LEGAL DIFFICULTIES

In sales, be aware that . . .

1. During your lifetime, you will probably enter into more sales contracts than any other type of contract—as both buyer and seller. Knowledge of the law of sales will help you to make successful transactions.

2. Your best protection against poor quality merchandise is knowledge of goods and their value, followed by careful comparison shopping.

3. Your best protection against sales fraud is the integrity of the seller (as reflected in the seller's established reputation) coupled with your caution.

4. When you make a major purchase, make sure your insurance is adequate. It should provide for coverage against possible loss of valuable purchased property. If appropriate (as in automobile purchases), it also should provide protection against possible liability for injury to others.

5. It is a good idea to put a sales agreement in writing even if it is for goods worth less than $500. Although this is not required by the Statute of Frauds, doing so can avoid misunderstandings and prevent costly litigation. If the goods are worth $500 or more, insist on compliance with the Statute of Frauds.

6. To have an enforceable writing be sure the other party signs the contract or memorandum and gives you a copy. The other party may properly require that you do likewise.

7. You are bound by oral contracts for goods priced at $500 or more if you have received them and accepted delivery. You may be bound in full or in part if you have made some payment. You usually are bound when you order custom-made goods.

8. For expensive items, you should get a bill of sale marked "paid" when you pay the full price.

Chapter 12 Assessment

CONCEPTS IN BRIEF

12-1 Sales

1. Both sales of goods and contracts to sell goods are governed by a combination of basic contract law and special UCC provisions on sales.

2. Neither payment nor delivery is essential for transfer of title.

3. Price may consist of anything such as money, services, or goods—whatever was agreed upon by the parties as consideration.

4. Payment occurs when the buyer delivers the price and the seller accepts it.

5. Receipt of goods occurs when the buyer takes physical possession or control of the goods.

6. Acceptance of the goods occurs when the buyer indicates that the goods received are satisfactory.

7. A bill of sale may provide useful evidence of the transfer of title to goods.

12-2 Special Rules for Sales Contracts

8. Merchants generally are held to a higher standard of conduct by the UCC than are casual sellers.

9. Unless otherwise required by statute, sales or contracts to sell may be oral, written, or implied from the conduct of the parties.

10. To be enforceable, a sale or contract to sell goods for $500 or more must be evidenced by a writing. The writing must specify at least a quantity of goods involved and must be signed by the party who is sued or by that party's agent. The writing is not essential when the

    - buyer has received and accepted the goods
    - buyer has paid for the goods in full and the seller has accepted payment
    - goods custom-made for the buyer are not suitable for sale to others in the ordinary course of business, and the seller has begun manufacturing or has contracted to obtain the goods
    - party seeking to avoid the contract admits during legal proceedings that the oral agreement was made.

YOUR LEGAL VOCABULARY

Match each statement with the term that it best defines. Some terms may not be used.

1. Immediate transfer of ownership of goods from a seller to a buyer for a price

2. Consideration for a sale or a contract to sell

3. An exchange of goods for goods

4. Tangible, movable, personal property

5. Label for a seller who claims special knowledge in a certain type of sales transaction

6. Receipt showing evidence of a transfer of ownership of goods

7. Seller who does not meet the definition of a merchant

8. Occurs when the buyer transfers the agreed-upon consideration and the seller accepts it

9. Collection of rights that allow the use and enjoyment of property

10. Purchaser

11. The act by which the subject matter of the contract is placed within the possession or control of the buyer

a. barter
b. bill of sale
c. casual seller
d. contract to sell
e. delivery
f. goods
g. merchant
h. ownership
i. payment
j. price
k. receipt of goods
l. sale
m. vendee
n. vendor

REVIEW LEGAL CONCEPTS

12. Why should the law of sales be different from the law of contracts?

13. Give specific examples of a barter transaction, a sale for money transaction, and a transaction that combines the two. Identify the advantages and disadvantages of each kind of transaction.

14. Arguably, the law of sales helps facilitate the smooth transfer of goods in commerce. It also provides clear standards that are in general uniform from state to state. Why should the governments of the states devote their time and resources to accomplish such ends?

15. Compare the sale of 10,000 feet of irrigation pipe in a retail sale from a Farmer's Supply to a farmer versus the commercial sale of that same amount of pipe from a wholesaler to the Farmer's Supply. Label the parties to each transaction. List the specialized knowledge of the law of sales that might be required by the various parties.

16. What is the justification for requiring a higher standard from merchants than casual sellers? Would the merchants likely support such a situation?

WRITE ABOUT LEGAL CONCEPTS

17. Consider the concept of ownership. What rights and duties do you think come with it?

18. Why is a bill of sale not considered a contract?

19. **HOT DEBATE** Would it make a difference if Anton had refused Bob's requests to put the contract in writing and the amount demanded by Anton is twice what Bob and Anton had shaken hands on?

MAKE ACADEMIC CONNECTIONS

20. **ART** Research how artists, sculptors, architects, composers, and other creative individuals handle contracting when they are to produce unique goods (portraits, statues, fountains, etc.) as a result of personal commissions.

THINK CRITICALLY ABOUT EVIDENCE

Study the situation, answer the questions, and then prepare arguments to support your answers.

21. Paul, a graduate student at the university, repeatedly sold his blood to a blood bank to pay for his tuition and books. Does the law of sales apply to these transactions?

22. One day, on his way back from selling his blood, Paul became light headed and crashed his car into a light pole. The car was repairable but the charges for parts and labor totalled more than $2,000. Should he have to pay sales tax on this whole amount? Why or why not?

23. When the economy turned sour and a large number of people sought to sell their blood, the blood bank wrote a term in its contracts that, in order to sell blood to the blood bank, each "donor" had to sell at least three pints a month to it or would have to refund any payments made to them in a month where the quota was not met. This meant that the donors would be very low on their own blood supply. What might a court do when confronted by such a term in a contract? What would be the result?

24. On one visit Paul could only bleed out three quarters of a pint of blood. The blood bank refused to pay anything for what had been donated until Paul could complete the donation of a full pint of blood that the sales contract called for. Paul maintained that he should be paid pro rata for the amount he had given. Who is correct under the law of sales?

25. When Paul returned to complete the delivery of blood, the blood bank refused to pay, yet kept the full pint and resold it to a hospital. Paul then maintained that the blood bank had accepted the goods he had for sale and should pay. Is he correct?

26. Paul had type B-negative blood. It was extremely rare. As a consequence, when the blood bank received a request for that type, it called Paul and orally promised to pay him $645 per pint. Paul gave two pints in less than three weeks, but the blood bank only paid him the standard $35 per pint. Was the oral contract enforceable? Why or why not?

27. Gillispie, a minor, was injured when two bottles of a soft drink exploded. The accident occurred as Gillispie was carrying the bottles to the checkout counter in the defendant's self-service store. If a sale had taken place even though Gillispie had not yet paid for the goods, the store could be partially liable for the injury. Has a sale taken place? (*Gillispie v. Great Atlantic and Pacific Tea Company,* 187 S.E.2d 441, N.C.)

28. In July of 1977 Dr. Sedmak read in Vett Vues, a Corvette fancier's magazine, that the Pace Car, a special edition of the Corvette, would soon be manufactured. He was a collector of Corvettes and wanted one of the 6,000 that were to be placed on sale. In January of 1978 Mrs. Sedmak gave Charlie's Chevrolet a $500 check as a deposit on a Pace Car and specified the options the Sedmaks desired. She was then informed that the purchase price of the car would be around $15,000. In April of 1978 the Sedmaks were notified that the Pace Car, equipped as specified, had arrived. However, because of the unanticipated high demand for the car, it would be put up for sale to the highest bidder. The Sedmaks did not submit a bid; instead they filed a suit for specific performance. The trial court found that the parties had entered into an oral contract. If that contract could be excepted from the application of the Statute of Frauds, the court would order specific performance as petitioned by the Sedmaks. Charlie's Chevrolet would then have to sell them the car at a reasonable price which, given the options added, would be around $15,000. What exception to the application of the Statute of Frauds would this transaction fall under? (*Sedmak v. Charlie's Chevrolet, Inc.* 622 S.W. 2d 694.)

29. Cargill, Inc., the plaintiff, is a large grain company. Warren, an agent of Cargill, managed its grain elevator in Hingham, Montana. On August 24, Warren orally contracted to buy from Wilson, the defendant farmer, 28,000 bushels of wheat at $1.48 per bushel and 6,000 bushels of higher protein wheat at $1.63 per bushel. Warren prepared two standard grain purchase written contracts. He signed them for Cargill, as its agent, and he also signed Wilson's name. A few days later, he delivered copies to Wilson, who made no objection. On August 30, Wilson received a $10,000 loan from Cargill. The check was attached to a detachable part of the standard grain contract, and it incorporated the two con-

tracts by specific references to their numbers. Wilson endorsed and cashed the check. The loan was interest-free because it was an advance payment for the wheat. During September and October, Wilson delivered 11,000 bushels of ordinary wheat at the agreed-upon price of $1.48, and 6,000 bushels at the then-current, higher market price. Then Wilson refused to deliver any more wheat. Cargill sued for damages. Wilson claimed he was not bound because of the Statute of Frauds. Who should win? (*Cargill, Inc. v. Wilson,* 532 P.2d 988, Mont.)

30. Jordan Paper Products, Inc., sued to recover $22,089.48 owed to it under an oral contract by Burger Man, Inc., an Indiana fast-food chain. The contract was for various paper products that Jordan had prepared at Burger Man's order, to specially identify the fast-food chain to its customers. Burger Man maintained that the oral contract was unenforceable because of the Statute of Frauds. Was the contract unenforceable? (*Burger Man, Inc. v. Jordan Paper Products, Inc.,* 352 N.E.2d 821, Ind.)

31. Albert Reifschneider knew farming. Born and raised on a farm, he had been selling his crops for more than 20 years. He also had a lot of experience in farm futures (contracts made between farmers and buyers for the purchase of crops to be harvested at some future time). One year he orally contracted to sell more than 12,000 bushels of corn from the fall harvest to the Colorado-Kansas Grain Company. Treating Reifschneider as a merchant, the company sent him a written confirmation of the deal to which he did not respond. When Reifschneider refused to deliver the corn, the Grain Company sued him for breach of contract. Who won, and why? (*Colorado-Kansas Grain Co. v. Reifschneider,* 817 P. 2d 637)

32. The Palermos needed carpeting for their home. Colorado Carpet Installation, Inc., agreed to do the job for a price that, including carpet and labor, totalled more than $500. Mrs. Palermo did not like how the job was being done and so sought the services of another contractor. Colorado Carpet then sued for enforcement of the oral contract. The Palermos replied that, as the contract was for more than $500, it was unenforceable under the Statute of Frauds. The issue at trial became whether or not the contract was for the sale of goods or services. How do you think the court ruled? (*Colorado Carpet Installation, Inc. v. Palermo,* 668 P.2d 1384)

ADVENT SYSTEMS, LTD., v. UNISYS CORPORATION
U.S. COURT OF APPEALS, THIRD CIRCUIT, 925 F. 2D 670

FACTS In the pre-1990 developing world of computers, Unisys Corporation and IBM were major competitors. When Unisys was approached in the mid-1980s by Advent Systems, Ltd., a software developer, Unisys saw a chance to make a major improvement in its market position. Advent had developed a computer-based data management system that allowed engineering drawings and specialized documents to be transformed into a database. The database could then be improved, tailored, and reused again and again for different projects. In June of 1987, Unisys agreed with Advent to sell the system throughout the United States for an initial two-year period. Advent was required to provide the technical personnel that might be necessary to produce a successful installation of each individual system.

In the summer of 1987, however, Unisys failed in an attempt to sell the Advent-developed system to Arco, a large oil company. This cast a negative light on the properties and marketability of the Advent system. Regardless, progress continued on the product's joint sales and training programs in the United States.

Finally, however, the relationship split apart. Unisys, in a period of downsizing, determined that it would be better off if it developed its own system. Therefore, in December, 1987, Unisys informed Advent that their relationship was at an end. Similarly, negotiations between Unisys' United Kingdom subsidiary and Advent came to an end. Advent promptly filed a complaint against Unisys alleging a breach of contract. Unisys defended by contending the sale of the software was, in essence, a sale of goods and, therefore, there was no breach of contract suit. Advent countered that software was not a good and that Advent was basically contracting to sell Unisys the services of its technical personnel.

LOWER COURT DECISION The trial court found in favor of Advent. A jury awarded Advent $4,550,000 as a result of Unisys' "breach of contract." The case was appealed to the U.S. Court of Appeals.

APPELLATE ARGUMENTS On appeal before the federal 3rd Circuit Court of Appeals, Advent continued to base its arguments on a breach of contract claim for the providing of services. Unisys also followed its previous line of reasoning in the lower court. Before the appellate court, it basically said that the transaction was a sale of goods and, therefore, subject to the Statute of Frauds in the Uniform Commercial Code. As the agreement lacked an explicit term on quantity, the Statute of Frauds would, therefore, preclude any suit and recovery.

DECISIVE ISSUE Was the transaction a sale of goods or a providing of services?

PRACTICE JUDGING

1. Should the trial court's decision be reversed because the transaction was a sales contract, or should the decision be affirmed as the transaction was for services?

2. What is the legal reasoning that led you to this conclusion?

3. Can you envision any time when computer software would not be as you decided it should be? What are the circumstances of the transaction, if so?

CHAPTER 13

Ownership and Risk of Loss in Sales

13-1 Transfer of Ownership

13-2 Risk of Loss and Insurable Interest in Sales

HOT DEBATE

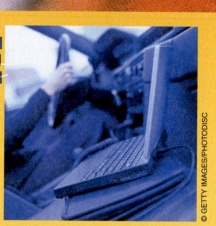

While you are having dinner one evening, your laptop computer is stolen from the front seat of your car. You do not report the theft for a week and a half. The police discover that the computer was sold to an innocent purchaser by a pawn shop that has since gone out of business. The new "owner" of the laptop is a pastor of a church that ministers to the homeless. She bought the laptop from the pawn shop before you reported the theft to the police. When you approach the pastor to get the computer back, she refuses. She says that the church needs it desperately to keep track of its "flock." It is especially important during the current winter season, when knowing where the homeless can seek shelter means life or death. You file suit for the return of the computer.

Where Do You Stand?

1. What are the legal reasons for your suit?

2. What legal arguments could you anticipate the attorney for the church making?

Transfer of Ownership

WHO MAY TRANSFER OWNERSHIP?

WHAT'S YOUR VERDICT?

Brad was walking through a part of town near the docks for ocean going cargo vessels when he came upon an electronic goods store. Attracted by the goods and prices in the window, Brad went inside and eventually haggled Standon, the owner and only sales clerk, into selling a surround-sound system to him. Brad bought the system, available even in discount stores for more than $600, for $110. Standon turned out to be a dock worker who stocked his store with stolen goods. When police showed up to take back the surround-sound system, which had been stolen by Standon, Brad protested that he had paid for it in good faith and didn't know it was stolen property.

Who has title to the sound system?

Generally, only the true owner of goods may legally transfer ownership of those goods. Further, the buyer of goods receives only the property rights that the seller has in the goods and nothing more.

As with most general rules, there are exceptions to these rules about transfer of ownership. Such exceptions include the following.

1. Persons authorized to do so may transfer another's title.

2. Buyers in a sale induced by fraud may transfer better title than they have.

3. Holders of negotiable documents of title may transfer better title than they have.

4. Merchants who keep possession of goods they have sold may transfer better title than they have.

AUTHORIZED PERSONS

Persons may sell what they do not own if the owner has authorized them to do so. Salespeople in retail stores are so authorized. Auctioneers and sheriffs also are authorized when they sell, under court order, stolen or repossessed goods or foreclosed property.

BUYERS IN A SALE INDUCED BY FRAUD

If an owner of goods is induced by fraud to sell the goods, the transfer of title is voidable by the seller. Upon discovering the fraud, the victimized seller may cancel the contract and recover the goods unless an innocent third party already has given value and acquired rights in them. Such a third party is known as a **good faith purchaser**. Thus, a fraudulent buyer with voidable title may transfer valid title to a good faith purchaser. To act in good faith, the purchaser

What gives salespeople the ability to sell goods they don't own?

© DIGITAL VISION

must not have reason to suspect the person who has the voidable title. The defrauded seller must seek damages from the original fraudulent buyer.

In contrast, the person who buys stolen goods from a thief receives possession, but not title, because the thief did not have good title to give. This is true whether the buyer is innocent or knows that the goods were stolen. In *What's Your Verdict?* Brad did not receive title to the surround-sound system. Because Standon knew it was stolen, he is guilty of the crime of receiving stolen property.

Unfortunately, stolen goods are seldom recovered. If they are recovered, they often have been damaged or stripped of parts. Even when recovered in good condition by the police, stolen goods often cannot be identified clearly as property of the victim and therefore are not returned. The police are compelled to sell such goods at public auction.

HOLDERS OF NEGOTIABLE DOCUMENTS OF TITLE

In business, certain documents often are used as a substitute for possession of goods. One example is a warehouse receipt issued by public warehouses when goods are stored there. Other examples are bills of lading and air bills issued by common carriers when goods are shipped by them. These documents may be negotiable or nonnegotiable. If the documents are negotiable, the goods are to be delivered to the bearer, who is the person in possession of the document, or to the order of a named party. Such persons, also known as *holders*, are deemed to have title to the goods. They may transfer ownership of the goods by transferring the documents alone. A holder who is named in the negotiable document must sign as well as deliver the document to transfer it to a third party.

MERCHANTS WITH POSSESSION OF SOLD GOODS

Occasionally a buyer will allow the merchant seller to temporarily retain possession of the goods after the sale. If, during this period, the merchant resells and delivers these goods to a good faith purchaser, the latter receives good title. However, the merchant must replace the resold goods or be liable in damages to the original buyer for the tort of *conversion*.

CHECKPOINT

Besides the owner, who may transfer ownership of goods?

IN THIS CASE

As the construction of their new home neared completion, the Howlands bought a set of new living room furniture from Eaton's Fine Furniture Shop. Though they paid the full price, Eaton was to retain possession of the furniture until the house was finished. Assuming that she would have no trouble replacing the furniture before the completion date, Eaton sold the Howlands' furniture to Hopkins, a good faith purchaser who took immediate delivery. Hopkins thus obtained a valid title. If Eaton is unable to replace the set when the Howlands demand delivery, she will be liable to them for damages for the tort of conversion.

INTERNATIONAL VIEWPOINT

Negotiable Bills of Lading

Negotiable bills of lading have been a part of commerce for centuries. Many European countries used them as early as the sixteenth century. In today's international transactions, ownership still is often transferred using negotiable bills of lading. These documents are bought and sold while cargo is literally floating on the open seas. When the document is sold, so is the cargo. It is not uncommon for oil to change hands 20 times between the time it leaves the Persian Gulf and arrives in the United States.

REQUIREMENTS FOR OWNERSHIP TRANSFER

WHAT'S YOUR VERDICT?

Chien Huang ordered electronic equipment worth more than $3 million from Inter-Continental Traders, a Seattle exporter. The equipment was to be shipped to a company in the People's Republic of China. The sales agreement, signed by both parties, stated that title and risk of loss would pass "when all necessary governmental permits are obtained." The Chinese government granted an import permit and necessary clearance to allow the exchange of Chinese currency into dollars to pay for the order. However, the U.S. State Department refused to grant an export permit because of the classified nature of some of the equipment

Did a sale take place?

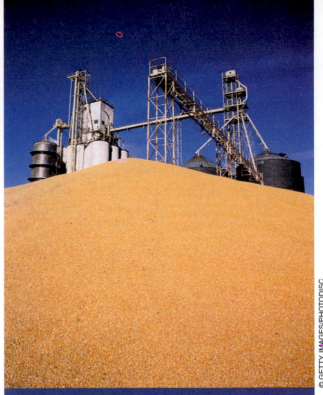

Do you think this grain would be considered a fungible good? Why or why not?

© GETTY IMAGES/PHOTODISC

For ownership of goods to be transferred in a sale, the goods must be both existing and identified. **Existing goods** are physically in existence even though they may not be in a fully assembled and immediately deliverable condition. Existing goods also are owned by the seller. **Identified goods** have been designated specifically as the subject matter of a particular sales contract. The identification of such goods may be done by the buyer, the seller, both, or by a mutually agreed-upon third party. Typically, when identified, the goods are marked, separated, or in some way made distinct from similar goods that the seller might have on hand.

Unless goods are both existing and identified, they are **future goods**. Any contract for the sale of future goods is a contract to sell rather than a sale. Neither ownership nor risk of loss passes at the time of the agreement.

An important exception to the process of identification is made for *fungible goods*. These are goods of a homogeneous or essentially identical nature. With fungible goods, by nature or trade usage, each unit is regarded as equal to every other unit. Examples are a quantity of corn or oil of a given variety and grade, or thousands of cases of identical canned fruit in a warehouse. In many states, ownership and risk of loss in fungible goods pass without selection or identification of specific goods. The buyer therefore becomes the owner at the time of the agreement.

WHEN DOES OWNERSHIP TRANSFER?

Once goods are existing and identified, disputes still may arise over who has title and risk of loss to the goods at particular times. Sometimes creditors of the seller, or creditors of the buyer, may claim possession in order to collect money due. Other disputes may concern who bears the risk of loss if the goods are damaged, stolen, or destroyed before the transaction is completed. A risk-bearer may want or need the protection of casualty insurance. Generally, the person who has title to the goods will bear the loss, but this is not always the case.

In deciding when title transfers from seller to buyer, courts first examine the sales agreement to see if the parties have specified clearly when they intended for title to pass. If they have expressed such intent, courts generally will uphold their agreement. In *What's Your Verdict?* no sale took place. The agreement said that title and risk of loss would pass "when all necessary governmental permits" were obtained. Therefore Inter-Continental Traders would retain title to the goods because this condition had not been met.

If the parties do not specify when title is to pass, courts first determine if there is any applicable custom or usage in the particular trade that can settle the question. If there is no agreement on the matter and no available trade custom or usage, courts look to the UCC for a solution.

COMMON SITUATIONS

Common situations involving transfer of title are discussed below. Note that neither the method nor the time of payment governs the outcome.

SELLER DELIVERS GOODS TO THEIR DESTINATION If the contract requires the seller to deliver the goods to their destination, title passes when the goods are tendered at that specified destination. **Tender of delivery** means that the seller places (or authorizes a carrier to place) the proper goods at the buyer's disposal and notifies the buyer so that delivery can be received. The manner, time, and place for tender are determined by the agreement and the UCC. When the seller is required to do additional work, title does not pass until such work is completed.

SELLER SHIPS, BUT DOES NOT DELIVER, GOODS TO THEIR DESTINATION If the contract requires or authorizes the seller to ship the goods but does not obligate the seller to deliver them to the destination, title passes to the buyer at the time and place of shipment, when possession is transferred to the carrier.

SELLER DELIVERS DOCUMENT OF TITLE When customary, or when the parties have agreed that the seller is to deliver a document of title (for example, an airbill), title passes when and where the document is delivered. For example, Degory bought 600 tons of oats from Delta. The oats were stored in a public grain elevator. Title passed when an authorized agent of Delta delivered a negotiable warehouse receipt for the oats to Degory.

BUYER TAKES POSSESSION AT PLACE OF SALE If the seller is to tender the goods at the place of sale, title passes at the time and the place where the sales contract is made.

CHECKPOINT

What two characteristics must goods have in order to have ownership of them transferred?

13-1

Assessment

Xtra! Study Tools
lawxtra.swlearning.com

THINK ABOUT LEGAL CONCEPTS

1. The buyer of stolen goods receives good title if he or she did not know the goods were stolen. **True or False?**

2. If an owner of goods is induced by fraud to sell the goods, the transfer of title is _?_ by the seller. (a) valid (b) voidable (c) void

3. If the seller is to tender the goods at the place of sale, title passes at the time and place where the sales contract is made. **True or False?**

4. Goods that are not both existing and identified are referred to as false goods. **True or False?**

THINK CRITICALLY ABOUT EVIDENCE

Study the situation, answer the questions, and then prepare arguments to support your answers.

5. Conch lied about his income and assets when he bought a dinette from Furniture World on credit. After making the first of 12 payments, Conch defaulted. Furniture World then checked Conch's credit record and discovered the fraud. Conch had already sold the dinette to Tilly, who honestly thought that Conch was the owner. Furniture World sued to recover the furniture from Tilly. Who wins? Why?

6. After Carr refurbished her home, she held a yard sale for things she did not need. Included was a large crosscut saw, which she sold to Sutro. She did not know that her husband had borrowed the saw from a neighbor. Did Sutro become the owner?

13-2 Risk of Loss and Insurable Interest in Sales

13-2

▼ GOALS

- **Explain the general rules for identifying when risk of loss transfers**
- **Identify the point at which insurable interest of goods transfers**
- **Identify when risk of loss and insurable interest transfer in specific situations**

WHEN DOES RISK OF LOSS TRANSFER?

WHAT'S YOUR VERDICT?

Knowing that high definition DVD's would soon hit the market, Correlone ordered two copies of each of the major movie titles he sold in his high-end video store. He ordered them from DVDistribution in Osaka, Japan, to be shipped directly to his location by a carrier that the seller would select. Two weeks later the goods arrived and the carrier notified Correlone that they could be picked up at its warehouse. When Correlone arrived at the warehouse's address the next day, he found the building a smoldering ruin. It had been hit by lightning and caught fire the previous evening destroying all of its contents.

Who has the risk of loss for the goods, Correlone or DVDistribution?

A wise buyer and seller of goods in a sales transaction will be sure to pay special attention to identifying the point at which the risk of loss transfers. At that point, insurance coverage can be terminated by the buyer to minimize costs. By this time as well insurance coverage should also be in place for the seller to minimize exposure to the consequences of damage to or destruction of the goods. The following discussions provide the general rules for identifying this important point.

IF SELLER SHIPS GOODS BY CARRIER

If the seller is required to deliver the goods to a particular destination but is allowed to use a carrier, such as a railroad, to make the delivery, the risk of loss passes to the buyer at the destination, upon tender of delivery. This is true even if goods that are shipped by carrier are still in the possession of the carrier. In *What's Your Verdict?* Correlone had the risk of loss as soon as the shipper gave its tender of the goods by notifying him they were available for pickup. Hopefully, Correlone had insurance that covered property loss under these circumstances.

Suppose the seller is not required to deliver the goods to the buyer at a particular destination. If the seller then uses a carrier to transport the

The seller of the goods being shipped on this vessel is required to deliver the goods to a particular destination. When and where would the risk of loss pass to the buyer?

© GETTY IMAGES/PHOTODISC

goods, the risk of loss passes to the buyer when the goods are delivered to the carrier.

Commercial buyers often use the shipment term **FOB**, which means "free on board." Assume that the seller is in Atlanta and the buyer is in New York City. In this case, "FOB Atlanta" means the seller agrees to deliver the goods no further than the carrier's freight station in Atlanta. Title and risk of loss transfer to the buyer at that point. On the other hand, if the terms are "FOB, buyer's warehouse, New York City," the seller must deliver the goods to the buyer's warehouse in New York City. The title and the risk of loss remain with the seller until delivery takes place. In the absence of contrary arrangements, the buyer pays the transportation charges in the first situation described and the seller pays the charges in the second.

In shipments from foreign countries, it is not uncommon for the seller to quote a **CIF** (cost, insurance, freight) price. This means that the seller contracts for adequate insurance and for proper shipment to the named destination and then adds these items to the price or cost of the goods. The risk of loss passes to the buyer when the seller delivers the goods to the carrier, such as a seagoing ship. However, the insurance provides protection against loss from any identified risks.

IF THE GOODS ARE HELD BY A BAILEE

Sometimes goods are held for a seller by a bailee. A *bailee* has temporary possession of another person's goods, holding them in trust for a specified purpose. A public warehouse is an example of a bailee. (Bailments are discussed more fully in Chapter 16.)

The goods may be sold by the owner, yet the contract may call for delivery to the buyer without the warehoused goods being moved. The risk of loss transfers to the buyer under such circumstances upon any of the following events:

- when the buyer receives a negotiable document of title covering the goods (for example, a negotiable warehouse receipt)
- when the bailee acknowledges the buyer's right to possession of the goods
- after the buyer receives a non-negotiable document of title (for example, a non-negotiable warehouse receipt) or other written direction

to a bailee to deliver the goods. (The buyer must have had a reasonable time to present the document to the bailee, who must have honored it.)

IF EITHER PARTY BREACHES AFTER THE GOODS ARE IDENTIFIED

The seller sometimes breaches by providing goods so faulty that the buyer rightly rejects them. The risk of loss then remains with the seller until the defects are corrected.

IN THIS CASE

Galaxy Furniture Company shipped a truckload of chairs and sofas to Brenda's Bargain Basement. Without unloading the tractor-trailer, inspection disclosed that Galaxy had mistakenly shipped sofas and chairs upholstered in costly Italian leather. Brenda had ordered the durable but much cheaper vinyl upholstery models. Brenda promptly notified Galaxy of the error and asked for instructions on what to do with them. After a week, the unloaded trailer was still parked in back of Brenda's warehouse. Then a fire of undisclosed origin destroyed the trailer (along with some other vehicles). Galaxy suffers the loss as the goods were faulty and risk of loss therefore remained with it.

IN OTHER CASES

In any case not covered previously, the risk of loss falls on the buyer upon receipt of the goods if the seller is a merchant. If the seller is not a merchant, the risk of loss transfers to the buyer as soon as the seller makes a tender of delivery

CHECKPOINT

Explain when the risk of loss transfers from seller to buyer when the seller ships the goods by carrier.

WHEN DOES INSURABLE INTEREST TRANSFER?

WHAT'S YOUR VERDICT?

Frosty-Frolic Company was a fresh-food packer and processor. In a sales contract with Goodman, Frosty-Frolic agreed to pack a quantity of head lettuce grown near Salinas, California, and to place the "Soaring Eagle" brand label on the cartons. The lettuce was routinely dehydrated, cooled, packaged, placed in the special cartons, and stacked on pallets in Frosty-Frolic sheds for daily shipment as ordered by Goodman.

At what point did Goodman obtain the right to insure the goods against possible loss?

The buyer obtains certain rights in goods at the time of their identification to a sales contract. One such right, called an *insurable interest,* gives the buyer the right to buy insurance on the goods. This often is necessary as, even though the risk of loss may still reside with the seller, the buyer may lose money should the goods be destroyed and the buyer cannot satisfactorily find them elsewhere. The physical act of identifying goods usually takes the form of setting aside, marking, tagging, labeling, boxing, branding, shipping, or in some other way indicating that specific goods are to be delivered or sent to the buyer in fulfillment of the contract. In *What's Your Verdict?* Goodman obtained an insurable interest when the lettuce was identified as hers (when placed in "Soaring Eagle" cartons).

If the goods already exist and have been identified to the contract when the contract is made, an insurable interest arises in the buyer at that time.

In addition to the insurable interest, the buyer has the following rights:

1. to inspect the identified goods at a reasonable hour
2. to compel delivery if the seller wrongfully withholds delivery
3. to collect damages from third persons who take or injure the goods.

CHECKPOINT

When does a buyer obtain an insurable interest in the goods?

TRANSFER OF RIGHTS AND RISKS IN SPECIFIC SALES

WHAT'S YOUR VERDICT?

With a high bid of $145, Angelina and Tom bought a king-sized mattress at an auction held outside the house of a neighbor who had died the previous month. Before they could pay for and receive their goods, a sudden storm dumped an inch of rain on the mattress ruining it.

Who had the risk of loss at the time the mattress was ruined?

The following sales transactions merit special attention because of the frequency with which they occur or because of the uniqueness of the rules that apply to them.

CASH-AND-CARRY SALES

When the buyer in a sales contract is a consumer who pays cash and takes immediate delivery, title passes to the buyer at the time of the transaction.

The euro is now the only legal tender in the following countries: Austria, Belgium, Finland, France, Germany, Greece, Republic of Ireland, Italy, Luxembourg, the Netherlands, Portugal, and Spain. These countries' old national currencies, such as the German mark and the French franc, have been withdrawn from circulation.

This is the most common type of transaction for groceries and other low-priced items. Risk of loss passes upon the buyer's receipt of the goods from a merchant and on tender of goods by a casual seller.

The seller may insist on payment in legal tender. Checks are commonly used but are not legal tender. Acceptance of a check by the seller is not considered payment until the check is paid at the bank. However, use of a check by the consumer in a cash-and-carry sale does not affect the timing of the transfer of title or risk of loss.

The clothes that these shop assistants are unloading were sold to the shop on a sale or return transaction. What would be the benefit of this type of sale to the store? What would be the benefit to the seller?

SALES ON CREDIT

The fact that a sale is made on credit does not affect the passing of title or risk of loss. A **credit sale** is simply a sale that, by agreement of the parties, calls for payment for the goods at a later date. Ownership and risk of loss may pass even though the time of payment or delivery is delayed.

COD SALES

Goods often are shipped **COD**, which means collect on delivery. The carrier collects the price and transportation charges upon delivery and transmits this amount to the seller. If the buyer does not pay, the goods are not delivered. Thus, in effect, the seller retains control over the possession of the goods until the price is paid. In a COD arrangement, the buyer loses the right otherwise available to inspect the goods before payment. Nevertheless, ownership and risk of loss transfer just as though there were no such provisions.

SALE OR RETURN

A **sale or return** is a completed sale in which the buyer has an option of returning the goods. When goods are delivered to a merchant buyer in a sale or return, the ownership and risk of loss pass to the buyer upon delivery. Such a transaction is a true sale. In a sale or return transaction, if the buyer returns the goods within the fixed or a reasonable amount of time, ownership and risk of loss pass back to the seller. This is true

A QUESTION OF ETHICS

Dorothy owned her own plumbing business. She bought her tools from a nationwide retailer that offered an unconditional guarantee that tools sold under its trademark could be returned and exchanged for new ones any time the customer was dissatisfied for any reason. Dorothy made it a policy to use the retailer's tools until they were worn out and then return them, demanding and receiving a new replacement. She did this even though the retailer's tools outlasted comparable tools by a wide margin. Are her actions legal? Ethical?

whether the sale is made for cash or on credit. The returned goods must essentially be in their original condition. Normally goods held on sale or return are subject to the claims of the buyer's creditors, who can seize the goods under court order.

The sale or return provision should not be confused with the return privilege granted to customers of some retail stores. These stores allow customers to return most purchases that have not been used, even if they are not defective. This return privilege is not required by law, but stores offer it to promote goodwill and increase sales in the long run.

SALE ON APPROVAL

Sometimes goods are delivered to the buyer in a **sale on approval**, "on trial," or "on satisfaction." In such a case, ownership and risk of loss do not pass until the prospective buyer approves the goods. This may be done by words, payment, any conduct indicating approval, or retention of the goods beyond a specified or reasonable time. While in possession of the goods, the prospective buyer is liable for any damage to them caused by his or her negligence. Normally, the prospective buyer may reject the goods for any cause, whether or not it is reasonable.

SALE OF AN UNDIVIDED INTEREST

A person who sells a fractional interest in a single good or in a number of goods that are to remain together makes a **sale of an undivided**

interest. Ownership and risk of loss pass to each buyer at the time of the sale of each undivided interest.

AUCTION

An **auction** is a public sale to the highest bidder. When an auctioneer decides that no one will bid any higher for the goods on sale, the bidding is closed, usually by the pounding of the auctioneer's gavel. In doing so, the auctioneer accepts the bid on behalf of the owner of the goods. Ownership passes to the buyer at that time. Risk of loss passes whenever the auctioneer acknowledges the buyer's right to possess the goods which generally follows payment. In

NETBookmark

Access lawxtra.swlearning.com and click on the link for Chapter 13. Once in the NCCUSL web site, find and evaluate a copy of the original UCITA. Click on "Final Acts and Legislation" on the right side. Then click on "Computer Information Transaction Act" under "Select an Act Title." Note the original proposed statute's positions on shrink-wrap and point-and-click contracts. Do you agree with these positions? Why or why not?

lawxtra.swlearning.com

What's Your Verdict?, as Tom and Angelina had not paid, they did not have the right to possess the mattress. Therefore, the risk of loss remained on the seller.

Auction sales are "with reserve" unless specifically announced in advance to be "without reserve." "With reserve" means that if nothing to the contrary is stated, an auctioneer may withdraw the goods anytime before announcing completion of the sale. If "without reserve" the goods must be sold to the person who makes the highest bid—even if it is the first and only and ridiculously low.

BULK TRANSFER

A **bulk transfer** is the transfer, generally by sale, of all or a major part of the goods of a business in one unit at one time. Such goods include materials, supplies, merchandise, and equipment if sold with the inventory.

The law protects creditors of the occasional dishonest merchant who would otherwise sell out secretly, keep the proceeds, and disappear. The UCC requires notice to the seller's creditors before the bulk transfer is made. The seller is required to list all creditors. The buyer is required to notify those creditors of the forthcoming transfer of ownership and to pay their claims or to make other arrangements with them. If the buyer does not do this, creditors of the seller may make claims against the inventory and equipment after the buyer takes possession.

An innocent third party who in good faith buys some or all of the goods from a bulk transferee gets good title. But if such third party pays no value or knows the buyer failed to comply with requirements of the bulk transfer law, the creditors can retake the goods.

CHECKPOINT

What is the most common type of transaction for low-priced items such as groceries, and when does risk of loss pass from a merchant to a buyer for these sales?

ECONOMIC IMPACT

IMPACT OF UCITA ON LIBRARIES

The proposed UCITA legislation would have a potentially damaging economic impact on libraries and educational institutions around the country. This potential impact comes in several main areas. Two are most important: first of all, electronic self-help allowed to software companies. In effect, these companies can leave a back door in their program through which they may monitor data on usage and, if necessary, pull the plug on availability of the program to uncooperative institutions. It also leaves open a hacker's dream of access for installing viruses and the like that can destroy systems. Secondly, the original proposed act would allow software firms to waive liability for known defects in their software even if they knew of them and yet failed to disclose them to their customers. This could leave institutions without legal recourse for the damage caused by such defects.

THINK CRITICALLY

Which of these two potential impacts do you think is more serious, and why?

THINK ABOUT LEGAL CONCEPTS

1. The transfer of the risk of loss from seller to buyer always occurs when title transfers. **True or False?**

2. If a buyer properly rejects faulty goods, the risk of loss stays with the seller until the defects are corrected. **True or False?**

3. An insurable interest is acquired by the seller when the goods are identified to the contract. **True or False?**

4. Risk of loss always transfers upon goods being identified to a sales contract. **True or False?**

5. The buyer does not have the right to inspect the goods in which of the following sales situations? (a) cash-and-carry (b) auction (c) COD (d) The buyer can inspect the goods in all of the above situations.

THINK CRITICALLY ABOUT EVIDENCE

Study the situation, answer the questions, and then prepare arguments to support your answers.

6. Sondaya bought a camper trailer at a garage sale. The seller said that Sondaya could take the trailer home at any time. Sondaya went home to get a pickup with a trailer hitch. Upon returning, Sondaya was told that during her absence, an unidentified person had backed into the trailer, causing extensive damage to it. If the person cannot be found, who will have to bear the loss?

7. Donatti, of California, ordered 400 pounds of fresh blueberries from Margeson, a produce broker in New Zealand. The terms called for shipment by airfreight, FOB, to Donatti's cold-storage plant in Los Angeles. The blueberries were properly packed and shipped by airline common carrier, but they were mishandled upon arrival at the Los Angeles International Airport. Delivery was delayed, and when the fruit was finally delivered, it was not edible. Who must suffer the loss?

8. To finance a trip for the high school band, the director bought "safe and sane fireworks" priced at $4,000 wholesale. The director paid cash in a sale-or-return contract. Band members took turns as salesclerks in the Fourth of July booth provided by the distributor. Several items did not sell at all. The wholesale price of those fireworks sold by midnight on July 4 was only $1,286.50. What should the director do?

PREVENT LEGAL DIFFICULTIES

To protect yourself in the actual sales transaction...

1. Remember that ownership of goods will not necessarily prevent transfer of title to them contrary to your wishes when (a) You have authorized others to sell the goods for you. They may violate your instructions. (b) You have been defrauded in a sales transaction and have given a voidable title to the wrongdoer. Before you cancel the contract and try to get your goods back, the wrongdoer can transfer good title to a good faith buyer. (c) You have allowed the person who sold to you to keep possession of your goods. The person who sold them to you might sell them again.

2. Act promptly in identifying goods to the sales contract and in completing performance.

3. In important sales contracts, specify precisely in writing when title to goods and risk of loss of goods are to transfer.

4. As a buyer or a seller, carry adequate insurance when appropriate to cover any insurable interest you may have in goods that are the subject matter of the sales contract.

5. Assure yourself of the integrity and financial responsibility of buyers before selling goods to them on credit, on sale or return, or on approval.

6. When the buyer's credit is questionable, sell for cash or on a COD basis.

CONCEPTS IN BRIEF

13-1 Transfer of Ownership

1. Generally the owner of goods is the only one who can legally transfer title to them. Exceptions are made for a party who
   - is authorized by the owner to sell the goods
   - has obtained good title to the goods by fraud and sells them to a good faith purchaser
   - is the holder of a negotiable document of title
   - is a merchant seller who has retained possession of previously sold goods.

2. Before ownership in goods can pass, goods must be both existing and identified.

3. In determining when ownership and risk of loss pass in a sales transaction, the terms of the sales contract are given top priority. If those terms do not provide an answer, then trade customs and usage may provide the determining customary rule. If not, UCC rules are used to make the determination.

13-2 Risk of Loss and Insurable Interest in Sales

4. The buyer obtains an insurable property interest when goods are identified to the contract.

5. In cash-and-carry sales, title passes at the time of the transaction. If a check is used, the payment is conditional until the check is paid by the bank on which it is drawn.

6. COD terms by a seller do not affect the time of transfer of ownership or of risk of loss. But the terms do reserve control of the goods to the seller until payment is received.

7. In a sale or return sale, ownership and risk of loss generally pass to the merchant buyer upon delivery.

8. At an auction, title passes when the auctioneer signifies acceptance of the bidder's offer. Unless otherwise announced, the auctioneer may refuse all bids and withdraw the goods.

9. Notice of a bulk transfer of the inventory and equipment of a business must be given to creditors of the seller before the sale takes place.

YOUR LEGAL VOCABULARY

Match each statement with the term that it best defines. Some terms may not be used.

1. Completed sale in which the buyer has an option of returning the goods
2. Goods that are not both existing and identified
3. Goods specifically earmarked for a particular sales contract
4. To place the goods at the buyer's disposal
5. Sale that, by agreement, calls for payment for the goods at a later date
6. Public sale to the highest bidder
7. Collect on delivery
8. Innocent third party to a fraudulent transfer of goods who gives value to and acquires rights in the goods
9. The transfer, generally by sale, of all or a major part of the goods of a business in one unit at one time
10. Goods delivered to the buyer "on trial," or "on satisfaction"

- a. auction
- b. bulk transfer
- c. CIF
- d. COD
- e. credit sale
- f. existing goods
- g. FOB
- h. future goods
- i. good faith purchaser
- j. identified goods
- k. sale on approval
- l. sale or return
- m. sale of an undivided interest
- n. tender of delivery

REVIEW LEGAL CONCEPTS

11. Why should an innocent purchaser from a thief receive only possession whereas an innocent purchaser of another's goods from a repairman of those goods obtain good title?

12. What are the advantages and disadvantages to allowing ownership to be transferred by the passage of documents of title?

13. Why should the buyer rather than the seller have to notify creditors in a bulk sale?

14. Why should the courts give priority to the actual sales contract when determining when the ownership of goods passes from seller to buyer?

15. Why should the risk of loss to fungible goods pass at the time of the agreement instead of when the goods are existing and identified to the contract?

WRITE ABOUT LEGAL CONCEPTS

16. Should checks be considered "legal tender?" Write a paragraph stating arguments for both sides of the issue.

17. Are COD sales still useful? Make a list of instances in which they fill a need.

18. **HOT DEBATE** Write a paragraph contrasting the ethical positions of the church versus the owner from whom the laptop was stolen. Ethically, who should be allowed to have the laptop?

MAKE ACADEMIC CONNECTIONS

19. **FOREIGN LANGUAGE** Interview businesses in your area that buy and sell internationally. Prepare a report on problems they have encoun- tered in making their orders and billings clear to their trading partners. Try to find trading partners who speak a variety of different languages.

THINK CRITICALLY ABOUT EVIDENCE

Study the situation, answer the questions, and then prepare arguments to support your answers.

20. Trina, a computer programmer, had her laptop computer stolen. She reported it stolen and gave the police its serial number. Three months later, the police recovered a laptop that was the same make and model as Trina's, but the serial number had been removed. Trina tried to obtain the computer from the police, but they declined her request. They put the computer up for sale at the next police auction. Trina sued to recover what she thought to be her computer. Who won and why?

21. Shortly after her lawsuit against the police department was resolved, Trina decided to buy a new laptop from a 1-800 phone order seller. As Trina and the seller agreed, the seller shipped Trina's new computer to a warehouse near Trina's home. The warehouse then notified Trina to come and pick up the computer. Through no fault of the warehouse, the computer was drenched with water and rendered inoperable during a minor fire. Trina tried to return the computer to the seller for a new one, saying that the seller had to bear the loss. The company refused to accept the return. Trina sued the computer company for her money back or another computer. Who won and why?

22. Shortly after her lawsuit against the computer company was resolved, Trina took her new laptop into a computer store for needed repairs. When Trina returned to pick it up, she found it had been sold by one of the store's salespeople to an innocent purchaser. Evidently, due to a bookkeeping error and its mint condition, Trina's laptop had been shelved with the store's regular stock and was snapped up by the first customer that saw it. Before Trina's attorney could bring suit against the shop, it went out of business. She then sued to recover the laptop from the customer who purchased it from the store. Who won and why?

23. Trina wanted to be able to use her laptop throughout her house and on her deck. As a consequence, she bought a wireless card for it "on approval" from a local manufacturer. Unfortunately, the very day that she installed the card, Trina left the laptop out on the deck while answering the front door. A rainstorm came up and destroyed the laptop and the card. Who has the risk of loss in the sales transaction? Why? Who must bear the loss? Why?

24. When his company developed financial trouble, Pais, a member of the legal staff, was suddenly transferred from Houston, Texas, to company headquarters in New York City. As a consequence, he bought for cash $30,000 worth of new Danish furniture for his apartment on Park Ave. When the furniture was tendered by the seller before the apartment was ready, Pais had to ask them to keep it in their warehouse in the Bronx. In the meantime, his employer had to suspend salary payments for a month. Pais sought to use the furniture as collateral for a loan. Did he have title to it even though he had not taken possession?

ANALYZE REAL CASES

25. Lane had a boat dealership in North Carolina. In February, he sold a new boat, a 120-HP motor, and a trailer to a man who represented himself to be "John Willis." Willis gave Lane a check for $6,285 and left with the goods. The check proved to be worthless. Less than six months later, Honeycutt bought the three items in South Carolina from a man whom he had known for several years as "John R. Garrett." In fact, this was Willis, using an alias. Later, while searching for Willis under the alias of "John Patterson," the Federal Bureau of Investigation contacted Honeycutt. Honeycutt said that (a) he had paid a full price of only $2,500; (b) Garrett had nothing to show he was the owner; (c) he did not know from whom Garrett got the boat; (d) Garrett said he was selling the boat for someone else; (e) Garrett signed what he called a "title" (the document was nothing more than a "Certificate of Number" issued by the state Wildlife Resources Commission, not the "certificate of title" required by statutes); (f) Garrett forged the signature of the purported owner, John F. Patterson, on the so-called title. Plaintiff Lane now claims that defendant Honeycutt was not a good-faith purchaser and therefore should return the boat to him, with damages for a wrongful detention. Who has title to the boat? You decide. (*Lane v. Honeycutt*, 188 S.E.2d 604, N.C)

26. Consolidated Chemical Industries purchased three heat exchangers from Falls Industries in Cleveland. The contract specified that after identification the machines were to be crated securely. They were then to be delivered, without breakage, to the Consolidated plant in East Baton Rouge. Because the machines were not crated securely, the exchangers were badly damaged in transit. Consolidated refused to accept them, and Falls sued. Falls claimed that risk of loss had passed when the goods were delivered to the carrier. Do you agree? (*Falls Industries, Inc. v. Consolidated Chemical Industries, Inc.*, 258 F.2d 277)

27. The plaintiff, a Los Angeles manufacturer of men's clothing, sold a variety of clothing to the defendant, a retailer in Westport, Connecticut. The plaintiff prepared four invoices covering the clothing and stamped them "FOB Los Angeles," and added the words "goods shipped at purchaser's risk." The plaintiff delivered the goods to the Denver-Chicago Trucking Company. When the truck arrived in Connecticut with the goods, the defendant's wife was in charge of the store. She ordered the driver to unload the cartons and place them inside the store. The driver refused and left with the goods. The defendant complained to the plaintiff, who filed a claim against the trucking company. No reimbursement was obtained by the plaintiff, and the defendant never received the goods. Now the plaintiff seller sues the defendant buyer for the purchase price. Who wins? You decide. (*Ninth Street East, Ltd. v. Harrison*, 259 A.2d 772, Conn.)

28. In June, plaintiff Multiplastics, Inc., contracted with defendant Arch Industries, Inc., to make and to ship 40,000 pounds of plastic pellets, which were to be delivered at the rate of 1,000 pounds a day after Arch gave "release instructions." Multiplastics produced the pellets within two weeks. Arch refused to give the release orders, citing labor difficulties and its vacation schedule. On August 18, Multiplastics wrote, "We have warehoused these products for more than 40 days . . . however we cannot warehouse . . . indefinitely, and request that you send us shipping instructions." Multiplastics followed this with numerous telephone calls seeking payment and delivery instructions. In response, on August 20, Arch agreed to issue the release orders but never did. On September 22, the Multiplastics factory, including the 40,000 pounds of this order, was destroyed by fire. The pellets were not covered by Multiplastics' fire insurance policy. Therefore Multiplastics sued Arch for breach of contract and also claimed that the risk of loss had passed to the buyer. You decide. (*Multiplastics, Inc. v. Arch Industries, Inc.*, 348 A.2d 618, Conn.)

CASE FOR LEGAL THINKING

PREWITT V. NUMISMATIC FUNDING CORPORATION
U.S. COURT OF APPEALS, EIGHTH CIRCUIT, 745 F. 2D 1175

FACTS Numismatic Funding Corporation sold rare collectible coins by mail throughout the United States. In general, buyers would request specific coins and Numismatic would ship them on the terms discussed below. Early one year, Numismatic mailed a sizeable shipment of such coins to Frederick Prewitt. Prewitt was a commodities broker in St. Louis, Missouri, with whom the Corporation had done business on at least two other occasions. The shipment of rare gold and silver coins was valued at over $60,000. The would-be sales transaction was governed by the terms set down in the documents that were enclosed with the coins. These terms stated that Prewitt could buy part or all of the shipment which was available to him on a "14-day approval basis."

The accompanying invoice stated that the title did not transfer until the seller was paid in full. Also the buyer was given 14 days from the receipt of the goods to settle the account in full. No directions were provided as to how to return the unwanted coins. After examining the coins, Prewitt told his wife to send them back to Numismatic by certified mail. She did so within the 14-day period. She insured each of the two packages the coins were returned in for $400.

Numismatic Funding Corporation never received the coins. Prewitt then sued to be declared free of responsibility for the loss.

REASONING At trial in Federal District Court it was noticed by the Court that Numismatic's sales technique was to not only mail out coins requested by a prospective retailer, but also to send out unsolicited merchandise at the same time. The Court then found for Prewitt, in effect, deciding that Prewitt had acted properly under the laws and, in doing so, avoided legal responsibility for the loss. Numismatic then appealed to the Eight Circuit Court of Appeals.

PRACTICE JUDGING

1. Who must bear the loss for the rare coins?

2. What legal theory prompted you to answer question 1 as you did?

3. What is the status of the unsolicited merchandise? What is the source of the law that decides the issue of the unsolicited merchandise?

Consumer Protection

14-1 Protection through Governmental Action

14-2 Protection through Action by the Consumer

© GETTY IMAGES/PHOTODISC

Edison buys a lawnmower from a department store. Because of a defect in design, a protective plastic flap binds the lawnmower whenever the lawnmower is pulled backwards. For efficiency's sake Edison removes the flap. Later, as his son is pulling the mower backwards, he trips and falls backwards. Due to the lack of the protective flap, his foot shoots upwards into the mower blade. Edison's son, who was only wearing tennis shoes, loses half his foot. Later, Edison brings suit against the manufacturer on behalf of his son.

Where Do You Stand?

1. List and discuss the legal reasons supporting Edison's suit.

2. List and discuss the legal reasons supporting the manufacturer.

Protection through Governmental Action

▼ GOALS
- Explain the need for governmental involvement in the marketplace
- Identify protections against substandard goods
- Recognize unfair trade practices

GOVERNMENTAL PROTECTION IN TODAY'S MARKETPLACE

WHAT'S YOUR VERDICT?

Eliza had just purchased a classic sports car but did not like the color. He saw a newspaper advertisement for "car painting, $99.99 complete." He went to the place of business, contracted for the service, and selected a dark blue metallic finish. However, when the paint job was completed and Eliza examined the car, the color was obviously light blue. Eliza complained, but the manager claimed the color was close enough to the color selected and refused to make any correction.

How can Eliza resolve the problem in his favor?

A **consumer** is an individual who acquires goods that are intended primarily for personal, family, or household use. Consumers are protected in the marketplace through actions they may take on their own behalf as well as through actions the government takes to protect them.

CONSUMER CAVEATS

The phrase that traditionally guided consumers in the marketplace was *caveat emptor*, meaning "let the buyer beware." Consumers were thought to be adequately protected by their own ability to judge a product's safety and utility. The forces of supply and demand in a competitive marketplace were to keep product makers and sellers committed to producing the best product for the money. Consumers also could (and still can) seek help or advice from the state attorney general's office, the local Better Business Bureau, and, if appropriate, the customer service department of the company involved.

Unfortunately, relying mainly on consumers' individual initiative and resources has proved to be inadequate. In our affluent, technology-oriented society, it is very difficult for consumers to judge properly the quality or advantages and disadvantages of a product. The products often are offered by huge corporations which are not always responsive to consumer complaints.

Local, state, and federal governments have passed legislation to help put consumers on an equal footing with sellers in the marketplace. These laws fund agencies that add to the common-law based contract, tort, and

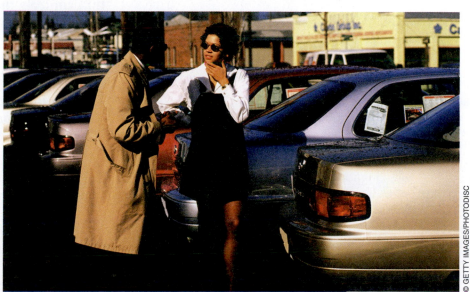

What would the phrase *caveat emptor* mean to this woman who is considering buying a used car?

© GETTY IMAGES/PHOTODISC

criminal protection against such abuses. Today any seller who has deceived a consumer while contracting may be sued by the individual consumer as well as be subject to charges by a governmental agency. This has led to the use of the phrase *caveat venditor*, meaning "let the seller beware."

CLASS ACTIONS

The law also has recognized the fact that if the product in question costs little or the potential damage claims are low, court action by a consumer often is not worth the effort and expense. To help overcome this problem, **class actions** have been authorized by court rules. A class action allows one or several persons to sue not only on behalf of themselves, but also on behalf of many others similarly wronged. This ability to combine individual causes of action in one suit provides incentive for law firms to handle such cases. In *What's Your Verdict*, Eliza should try to solve his problem through individual measures including resort to a small claims court suit. Should those fail, he should notify the appropriate governmental agency and consider the option of a class-action suit.

GOVERNMENTAL PROCEDURE

When a governmental agency acts on behalf of the injured consumer, it may investigate and issue a **cease-and-desist order** to a company. This is an order requiring the company to stop the specified conduct. If the defendant violates the order, heavy civil penalties may be imposed. Often a defendant will sign a consent order rather than resist the charge in a long legal battle. A **consent order** is a voluntary, court-enforceable agreement to stop an illegal or questionable practice. An agency also may order **restitution**, the return to customers of money wrongfully obtained.

LEGAL RESEARCH

Current class actions include suits against: 33 banks for funding Saddam Hussein, a union for collecting dues from non-union workers, alcohol companies for marketing to minors, airlines for cockpit doors that would not withstand hijackings, suppliers for tainted blood, and many more. Prepare a two-to-five page report on class actions in the United States today to include information on how they are generated and conducted, and their success rate.

CHECKPOINT

Define the terms *caveat emptor* and *caveat venditor*.

PROTECTION AGAINST INFERIOR SERVICES AND GOODS

WHAT'S YOUR VERDICT?

The Annihilator Pest Company developed and sold thousands of robot cockroach traps called the Terminator. The human user of the trap simply placed it on the floor of the room and the device would pursue, kill, and consume any roaches on the surface it occupied. Recent consumer reports have shown that the computer chip that controls the trap is too sensitive to vibration and causes the Terminator to go out of control and attack mice, house pets, and even furry house slippers.

What could the government require the Annihilator to do?

LICENSING

Protection of consumers by government often begins with licensing suppliers of consumer services. This is particularly true for those who provide health services, such as doctors, nurses, laboratory technicians, and pharmacists. Also, teachers, lawyers, accountants, construction professionals, realtors, insurance agents, and beauticians, among others, are licensed in most jurisdictions.

Certain businesses and institutions also must pass inspection before they receive operating licenses. Examples include hospitals, rest homes, private schools, check-cashing services, and insurance companies. Failure to maintain minimum standards may cause suspension or cancellation of the license.

Businesses offering repairs on cars, electronic equipment, watches, and the like often are required to give written estimates and detailed bills for all work performed. Similarly, states regulate special sales by retail businesses, such as bankruptcy sales and going-out-of-business sales. Often a special license is required and the businesses must shut down after the sale or be guilty of fraud.

UNSAFE PRODUCTS

Large numbers of people are injured or killed each year by products in use around the home. As a response, in 1972 the Consumer Product Safety Act was enacted. This law created the Consumer Product Safety Commission (CPSC) and gave it authority to issue and enforce safety standards for most consumer products.

The CPSC requires any manufacturer, distributor, or retailer discovering the failure of its products to comply with safety regulations to report that fact to the commission. The CPSC

Why do you think retailers must, in some cases, obtain a special license from the state in order to hold a "going-out-of-business sale"?

also receives reports from the nation's hospitals on product-caused injuries. If the CPSC determines that a product is substantially hazardous, the manufacturer, distributors, and retailers of the product must notify purchasers about the hazard and then either recall and repair the product, replace it, or refund the purchase price.

Often the mere threat of CPSC action causes responsible parties to recall their product "voluntarily." In *What's Your Verdict?* Annihilator could be required to notify those concerned and implement an appropriate remedy. Failure to comply could lead to a fine and imprisonment. If necessary, the CPSC has the power to seize the hazardous product and ban it from the marketplace.

The CPSC recently responded to the publication of conclusive research that the CCA in treated lumber used in decks and children's play sets to preserve the wood leaks out of the wood for years. (CCA is 22% arsenic. One 12-foot section of such pressure-treated lumber contains about an ounce of arsenic, or enough to kill 250 people.) The CPSC noted in its response that it is currently performing studies of wood sealants to keep the arsenic off children's hands—and out of their mouths. They also have removed CCA from the list of approved pesticides and negotiated a phase-out of CCA in wood treatment.

NETBookmark

Access lawxtra.swlearning.com and click on the link for Chapter 14. Click on one of the federal agencies' Recall Press Releases or Recall Announcements. Prepare a short oral report to the class that describes the nature of the product recall as explained in the announcement.

Note that you can sign up on this web site to be notified by e-mail of new product recalls and class-action suits.

lawxtra.swlearning.com

Consumers who think the CPSC is not taking action where needed may sue in federal district court to have a protective rule established. If victorious, consumers may be awarded an amount to cover reasonable attorney's fees, as well as their court costs.

The CPSC maintains a toll-free telephone service. Consumers can call the CPSC and they also may report claims concerning unsafe products, find out about product recalls occurring in the last few months, and get information about unsafe children's products.

Additional protection is afforded to consumers in indirect ways. For example, laws govern the type of construction, location, accessibility, occupancy rate, and type of use of buildings where the public gathers. Detailed regulations apply to fire escapes, elevators, parking, sprinkler systems, exit location and marking, and sanitary facilities. All of these safety laws are designed to protect consumers and to assist them in deciding which products and services best meet their needs.

What do you think would be the issues included in the regulation of a fire escape?

© GETTY IMAGES/PHOTODISC

ADULTERATED FOOD, DRUGS, AND COSMETICS

The federal Food and Drug Administration (FDA) requires that the production facilities for cosmetics, food, and drugs be clean. It also requires that the products be prepared from ingredients fit for human use or consumption. A product that does not meet the minimum standards for purity and quality set by the FDA is considered *adulterated*. Such a product may be confiscated, or seized, by the government.

The U.S. Department of Agriculture also inspects canners, packers, and processors of poultry and meat entering interstate commerce. Their actions help ensure that the products are free of disease and are processed under sanitary conditions.

In addition, the FDA requires that labels on regulated products give the name and address of the manufacturer, packager, or distributor, and reveal the quantity, such as the weight or the fluid ounces. Nutritional labeling also is required. Labels include information such as the fat, sodium, carbohydrate, and protein amounts provided by a serving.

States and localities usually provide for the inspection of businesses where food is handled.

Meat markets, bakeries, restaurants, hotels, and other businesses are rated on their cleanliness and are required to display their ratings. Food handlers may be subject to periodic health examinations. Laws also regulate the purity and quality of such products as milk, meat, fruit, and vegetables sold in such businesses.

Drugs are regulated by the FDA to ensure their safety for users and to be certain of their effectiveness for the purpose sold. Without FDA approval, new drugs cannot be marketed in this country. The FDA also determines which drugs are prescription and which may be sold "over-the-counter." The FDA has been criticized for its extremely cautious approach to granting new drug approval. Its procedures have led some Americans to go beyond the U.S. borders for certain drugs alleged to be life-saving and pain-easing.

IMPROPER WEIGHTS AND MEASURES The U.S.
Constitution gives Congress the power to set standards for weights and measures. Currently the Weights and Measures Division of the National Institute of Standards and Technology promotes uniformity in U.S. weights and measures laws, regulations, and standards. With proper inspection, testing, and enforcement at state and local

levels, the measurement of a gallon of gasoline, pound of bananas, or foot of rope is uniform throughout the country. Most states inspect and test weighing and measuring devices at least once a year. Seals certify the accuracy of such devices as gasoline pumps, supermarket scales, and taxicab meters. Violations of the weights and measures laws are punishable by fine, imprisonment, or both. The goods involved may be confiscated.

CHECKPOINT

What commission sets safety standards for most consumer products?

PROTECTION AGAINST UNFAIR TRADE PRACTICES

WHAT'S YOUR VERDICT?

A national magazine planned to increase subscriptions by giving away prizes of up to $1 million in a drawing. People contacted in a huge mail campaign could enter the drawing by return mail, whether or not they actually subscribed to the magazine. Instructions on how to enter would be placed in the text of the promotional material so a person contacted would have to read about the magazine in order to find out how to enter the drawing. A senior officer of the magazine canceled the plans because she thought it was an illegal lottery.

Was she correct?

Generally, an **unfair trade practice** is any method of business that is dishonest or fraudulent or that illegally limits free competition. To protect consumers, the federal and state governments have enacted numerous laws prohibiting such practices. Chief among these are federal antitrust laws and the Federal Trade Commission Act. They are designed to prevent unfair trade practices in interstate commerce (business con-

ducted between or among two or more states). States have similar laws for intrastate commerce (business conducted wholly within one state). Unfair trade practices take many forms including those discussed in the following sections.

AGREEMENTS TO CONTROL OR FIX PRICES

The part of the free market system that serves the consumer best is *competition*. Competition is the force that drives efficient businesses to create new and better products and services. Competition also drives inefficient firms out of business. Some individuals and companies enter into agreements to control or fix prices and thereby try to ensure their survival by eliminating competition. Such agreements are illegal and unenforceable. Violators are subject to criminal penalties.

FALSE AND MISLEADING ADVERTISING

False and misleading advertising intentionally deceives, makes untrue claims of quality or effectiveness, or fails to reveal critically important facts. Claiming that a mouthwash prevents and cures colds and sore throats when it does not is one example of such advertising.

A store practices another form of improper advertising when it uses an understocked, low-priced "come on" to lure prospective buyers into the store. Once there, the would-be buyers find that the advertised item has been sold out and the customers are then redirected to a more expensive product. This practice is referred to as **bait and switch**.

The advertisement is not considered deceptive if it states how many of the advertised items are available or states that the supply of the item is limited. Many stores that want to maintain customer goodwill give rain checks when even reasonably stocked items are exhausted. Rain checks permit customers to purchase the items later at the advertised price.

The *Federal Trade Commission (FTC)* has the main responsibility for preventing false and misleading advertising. If necessary, the FTC may order an advertisement terminated. If the advertiser has created a false impression that will persist when the advertisement is no longer being run, the FTC may order corrective advertising. *Corrective advertising* requires the advertiser to admit the wrongdoing and state the truth in a prescribed number of future advertisements.

Sending mass, unsolicited advertisements over the Internet is a practice known as *spamming*. Many receivers do not appreciate receiving these unsolicited e-mails. However, spammers say they have a First Amendment right to send e-mails and pop-up ads. Many states have bills before their legislatures to regulate spamming. These bills would either prohibit it altogether or require spammers to provide toll-free phone numbers and return e-mail addresses so recipients can ask to be removed from the e-mailer's list.

THINK ABOUT IT

How would you distinguish Internet spam from the junk mail that is delivered to you at discount postage by the U.S. Postal Service? Is the contrast significant to resolving the issue of spam?

ILLEGAL LOTTERIES AND CONFIDENCE GAMES

As mentioned in Chapter 10, to be a lottery, a gambling scheme or game must have three elements:

1. a required payment of money or something else of value to participate
2. the winner or winners to be determined by chance rather than by skill
3. a prize to be won

Holding or participating in such a gambling scheme is illegal and violators are subject to fine and imprisonment. However, many states have exempted by statute certain religious and charity groups from the lottery prohibition. These groups are allowed to run bingo and other games to produce revenue for their activities. Also, some states hold their own lotteries to generate revenue for state projects.

The use of lotteries by businesses to promote sales remains an unfair method of competition. However, in *What's Your Verdict?* the promotion was legal because no payment was required to participate. Even so, the FTC would monitor such a game to ensure that all promised prizes are awarded.

Other prohibited schemes often are disguised as legitimate business undertakings. These are sometimes referred to as *confidence* games. Such games typically involve a fraudulent device whereby the victim is persuaded to trust the swindler with the victim's money or other valuables in hopes of a quick gain. One example of the confidence game is the pyramid sales scheme. A chain letter is one such pyramid scheme.

UNFAIR PRICING AND SERVICE

Some of the more common unfair pricing methods include intentionally misrepresenting that goods are being sold at a considerable discount and stating that the price charged for the goods is a wholesale price. Both of these unfair pricing schemes are illegal.

Representing goods or services as being free when purchased with another good that is sold at an inflated price to cover the cost of the first also is an unfair pricing method. Merchants may have legitimate "two-for-one" and "one-cent" sales as long as the cost of the main item is not artificially raised for the sale.

Consumers of repair services may have problems related to unfair pricing. These problems may occur when the estimated price of a repair is significantly less than the actual price. They may also occur when the repair service charges the consumer for repairs that were not authorized. Most states require businesses to provide consumers with written estimates of repair costs before the work is performed. As noted earlier, many service providers are required to obtain a license from a government body to further assure consumers of their legitimacy.

MISLABELED GOODS

Mislabeling a good to make it more marketable is an unfair method of competition prohibited by law. Even the shape or size of a container must not mislead the consumer into thinking the package contains more than it does.

The law also requires that certain products carry warning labels. Poisons and insecticides must have appropriate "Danger" labels. Cigarette packaging and advertisements must carry warnings indicating the danger smoking poses to the health of the user and to others.

Mislabeling also involves selling used articles as if new or in a better condition than they actually are. The most common instance occurs when no indication is given that the goods are secondhand. For example, in used cars, odometers (which show the total miles a car has traveled) are sometimes turned back, and the cars are then sold for a much higher price. This activity is illegal.

OTHER UNFAIR TRADE PRACTICES

There are many other forms of unfair trade practices and competition.

- Using a brand name or trademark so similar to a competitor's that it confuses the public.

- Sending unordered merchandise and demanding payment for it or its return. According to federal law, when someone deliberately sends unordered merchandise through the mail, the recipient is under no obligation to return it or to pay for it.

- Giving a corporation's purchasing agent money "under the counter" in exchange for an order from the supplier or paying a retail salesperson "push money" for extra effort in promoting the manufacturer's product.

- Conducting "industrial espionage" to find out a competitor's secrets.

- Conducting fraudulent telemarketing and Internet schemes.

- Figuring finance charges improperly.

- Failing to provide written warranties when required.

- In door-to-door *home solicitation sales,* failing to notify purchasers that they have three days to cancel contracts for purchases of $25 or more.

CHECKPOINT

List at least six forms of unfair trade practices.

Xtra! Study Tools
lawxtra.swlearning.com

14-1 Assessment

THINK ABOUT LEGAL CONCEPTS

1. Legally, a person buying goods for her or his business is not a "consumer." **True or False?**

2. Is restitution a remedy used by consumer protection agencies? **Yes or No?**

3. Local governments do not have any consumer protection laws. **True or False?**

4. The elements of a lottery are _ ? _ , chance, and consideration. (a) price (b) money (c) luck (d) none of the above

5. Which of the following is regulated by the CPSC? (a) drugs (b) firearms (c) toys (d) cosmetics

6. The part of the free market system that best serves the consumer is (a) government regulation, (b) informed consumer, (c) competition.

7. Consumers have three days to cancel home solicitation sales. **True or False?**

THINK CRITICALLY ABOUT EVIDENCE

Study the situation, answer the questions, and then prepare arguments to support your answers.

8. You properly terminated your membership in a CD club four months ago, yet you receive a compact disc through the mail from the club. It is the new release of your favorite artist. You play it repeatedly for more than a month before you receive a letter from the club stating that it made a mistake in sending the disc to you and asking that you either return the disc unused or pay for it. Do you have an

ethical obligation to do so? Do you have a legal obligation to do so?

9. In a national television advertising campaign, FunTime fruit drink was said to contain "natural food energy." The FTC discovered that the "natural food" providing the energy was sugar and held that the advertisement therefore created a false impression. What remedy would you recommend that the FTC use to correct the situation?

Protection through Action by the Consumer

▼ **GOALS**

- ■ **Describe the protection afforded consumers by the law of product liability**
- ■ **Identify the various warranties that may apply to a sales transaction**

WHAT IS PRODUCT LIABILITY?

WHAT'S YOUR VERDICT?

Barsteel ran a lawn mowing business to earn money for college. To make her weed trimmer work faster, she removed the back shield from it. She also refused to wear safety goggles while operating the trimmer. One day, a piece of trimmer line broke and hit her in the cornea of an eye blinding her permanently in that eye. The remainder of the trimmer line was tested and shown to be only half as strong as advertised. Barsteel sued.

Can she recover for the injury caused by the defective product?

In *What's Your Verdict?* do you think that Barsteel's removal of the safety guard and her failure to wear safety goggles will affect her chances of winning the lawsuit against the trimmer manufacturer?

Instead of leaving consumers to rely on governmental agencies to prevent or remedy harm, today many states give consumers rights allowing them to protect themselves. Using these rights in situations where an agency may or may not have acted, the victim may sue for damages and get a court order preventing future injuries.

Product liability means the affixing of responsibility to compensate buyers, users, and even those standing nearby for injuries caused by a defective product. A product liability suit may be based on the torts of fraud, negligence, or *strict liability*. Recall that strict liability is liability that exists even though the defendant was not negligent. A product liability suit also may be based on a breach of **warranty**, which is an assurance that the seller makes about the product's qualities or performance. Because they involve sales of goods, warranties are governed by the Uniform Commercial Code (UCC).

EXPANSION OF PRODUCT LIABILITY

The legal rules for affixing liability for injuries caused by a defective product have been relaxed in recent years in order to protect injured plaintiffs and enable them to recover. This has been especially effective in the areas of privity of contract and damages.

PRIVITY OF CONTRACT At common law, warranty liability depended on the contract between the buyer and seller, who were said to be in privity of contract. **Privity of contract** is the relationship that exists between or among the contracting parties as a result of their legally binding agreement.

In the past only the immediate contracting buyer was permitted to sue, and suit could be brought only against the immediate contracting seller. Thus, an injured consumer could sue the retailer, but not the wholesaler or the manufacturer. This was true even if the wholesaler or manufacturer were primarily responsible for the defect and better able to pay. Now, however, the UCC broadens the common law rule so that all injured persons who are the buyer's family, household, or guests may sue. Moreover, courts in most states now permit the injured party, even a nonuser, to sue retailers, intermediate sellers, and manufacturers.

Today, a manufacturer or producer that makes inaccurate or misleading statements in advertising or labels is liable for resulting injuries to consumers. If the goods are defective and therefore dangerous, the maker is similarly liable for resulting harm. In either case, not only the manufacturer or producer but also intermediate sellers and the immediate supplier may be liable.

If this teenage girl would be injured somehow as a result of proper use of the cooktop her family just purchased, could a lawsuit on her behalf be brought against the manufacturer? Why or why not?

RECOVERING DAMAGES A product liability suit may be based on a breach of warranty or on the torts of fraud, negligence, or strict liability. Regardless of which of these can be used as a basis for recovery, the injured consumer still may have difficulty recovering damages.

For example, a person injured by a defective product might find that there is no warranty, that the warranty is not applicable, or that the warranty has expired. A defrauded person might discover that the seller's misbehavior is difficult to prove. Finally, negligence, even if present, is difficult to prove because the defective product may have been designed and made many months or years before in some distant factory by workers who cannot be identified or located.

Today, a person injured by a defective product is most likely to recover damages by relying on strict liability. The trend in many states is to hold the manufacturer, wholesaler, and retailer strictly liable if someone is injured because of a defective condition in the product that caused it to be unreasonably dangerous to the user or consumer. The liability is imposed without reliance on warranties or on the presence or absence of fraudulent intent or negligence.

There is no liability if the injury was suffered while the product was used for a purpose for which it was not intended, for example, using gasoline to clean clothes. Likewise, there is no strict liability if the product is used for a purpose which could not reasonably be foreseen, for example, trying to climb a mountain using ropes made for tying packages. Liability may be barred if the product has been altered by the user, for example, lengthening a ladder by nailing extensions to its legs.

Liability also may be barred if the injured person is found guilty of improper conduct that causes the accident. Examples of this include driving on a defective tire after discovering the defect, failing to service or to maintain an engine, or taking an overdose of medication. Finally, there generally is no liability if one is hurt when improperly using a product, such as a knife or firearm, which may be dangerous when misused.

In *What's Your Verdict?* Barsteel's removal of the safety guard and the failure to wear safety goggles bar her recovery. Legally, the injury was the result of her choices, not the defect in the trimmer line.

CHECKPOINT

Under what product liability approach is a person injured by a defective product most likely to recover damages?

ECONOMIC IMPACT

PUNITIVE DAMAGE AWARDS

Unlike Japan and other western countries, the U.S. legal system allows the recovery of punitive damages for various intentional torts such as fraud and for medical malpractice, drunk driving, and other injurious behaviors. In response, backed mainly by insurance companies, a tort reform movement has gained momentum to limit the amount of such punitive damage awards. This movement has emphasized the arbitrary and unfair costly nature of such awards. As a consequence, more than 19 states now have passed legislation that typically limits such awards to three times the amount of compensatory damages. A recent Department of Justice study, however, pointed out that punitive damage awards only occur in 3.3 percent of the cases won by plaintiffs with a median award of $38,000. This is a far cry from the millions awarded in a few highly publicized cases.

THINK CRITICALLY

Would the amount of money typically awarded in punitive damages influence your decision to sue a manufacturer for an injury you received while using a product? Why or why not?

HOW IMPORTANT ARE WARRANTIES?

WHAT'S YOUR VERDICT?

Bligh, a sales agent employed by Total Environments, persuaded the Fletchers to install a central air conditioning system. Bligh assured them that "this unit will keep all rooms at 68 degrees even on the hottest summer days and the coldest winter mornings." The unit failed to perform as promised.

Do the Fletchers have any rights against Total Environments?

Although strict liability often provides the best alternative for a cause of action in product liability cases, breach of warranty, if applicable, can be just as good. Warranties may be either express or implied. An assurance of quality or promise of performance explicitly made by the seller is an express warranty. An example is, "Use our brand of oil and you won't need to change your engine oil for 10,000 miles."

In *What's Your Verdict?* Bligh made an express warranty. Bligh's employer, Total Environments, is liable because the warranty was breached. A breach of warranty is a breach of contract. If there is no intent to deceive, it is not the tort of fraud for which punitive damages might be claimed and collected.

An express warranty may be oral or written. It may even be implied by conduct. If the contract is written, the warranty must be included in the writing, or it probably will be excluded from the agreement by the parol evidence rule. However, if the warranty is given after the sale, it may be oral even though the sales contract was written. A warranty or any other term may be added to a sales contract later by mutual agreement, and no new consideration is required.

REQUIREMENTS OF EXPRESS WARRANTIES

Under the Magnuson-Moss Warranty Act, the Federal Trade Commission has established certain minimum standards that must be met by sellers who give written warranties on consumer products that cost more than $15 and that normally are used for personal, family, or household purposes. Note that sellers are not required to give warranties. If sellers do give warranties, however, they must make them available to consumers prior to the sale in a single document, written in simple, understandable language. The following information must be included:

1. to whom the warranty is extended (for example, if it is limited to the original buyer)

2. a description of the product and any excluded parts

3. what the *warrantor* (one who makes a warranty) will and will not do in the event of a breach of warranty

4. when the warranty begins (if different from purchase date) and when it ends

5. the step-by-step procedure to obtain performance of warranty obligations

6. the availability of any informal methods of settling disputes

7. any limitation on how long implied warranties last

8. any exclusion or limitation on incidental or consequential damages

9. the words "This warranty gives you specific legal rights, and you may also have other rights which vary from state to state."

An express warranty that obligates the seller to repair or to replace a defective product without cost to the buyer and within a reasonable time is a **full warranty**. Any warranty that provides less protection than a full warranty is a **limited warranty**, and the seller must identify it as such.

OPINIONS V. WARRANTIES

A positive statement about the value of goods or a statement that is just the seller's opinion does not create a warranty. Sellers often enthusiastically overstate the merits of the goods they are trying to sell. Making statements such as "superb quality," or "best on the market," is exaggerated sales talk called **puffing**. Such words are not warranties or statements of fact. They are merely personal opinions. Buyers should not—and generally do not—accept such opinions at face value. *Caveat emptor* or "let the buyer beware" provides the only measure of protection when sellers make such statements.

Sometimes, however, the buyer has good reason to believe that the seller is an expert. If a buyer asks for the seller's opinion as an expert, the seller's word as to the quality of the

article becomes part of the basis of the bargain. In such a case, it may be taken as a warranty. This is particularly true with merchants. For example, a statement by a jeweler that a diamond is flawless may be relied on as a warranty.

EXPRESS WARRANTIES MADE BY ALL SELLERS

Every seller is bound by any express statement of fact or promise that is part of the bargain. It is desirable to have such statements in writing. When a description of the goods or a sample or model is made part of the contractual agreement, there is an express warranty that all the goods shall conform to the description, sample, or model used. This is true even if the words "warrant" or "guarantee" do not appear in the contract. It also is true even if the seller had no intention to give such a warranty.

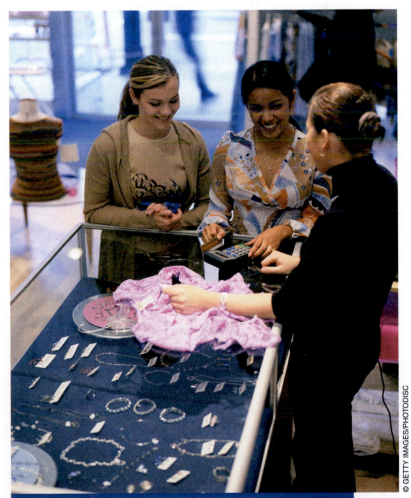

If you ask this jewelry counter salesperson if a certain necklace is sterling silver, and she replies that it is, can you rely on her statement as a warranty? Why or why not?

IMPLIED WARRANTIES GIVEN BY ALL SELLERS

Sellers are free to decide whether to give any express warranties. However, the law compels all sellers to honor certain implicit, or unstated, warranties, in order to ensure minimal standards of contractual performance. This rule applies whether or not explicit warranties are given by the seller. An implicit warranty obligation imposed by law on all sellers is called an **implied warranty**.

The three warranties discussed in the following sections are made to all purchasers by all sellers, including both casual sellers and professional merchants. These warranties are implied by law and need not be mentioned in the contract. Only if the parties specifically agree is any one or more of these warranties excluded.

WARRANTY OF TITLE Implicit in the act of selling, the seller warrants that he or she has title to the goods and the right to transfer them. This warranty is implied by law. Note, however, that it is excluded when it is obvious that the seller does not have title, such as when a sheriff, by court order, sells a debtor's goods to satisfy a judgment.

WARRANTY AGAINST ENCUMBRANCES Also implicit in the act of selling is the seller's warranty that the goods shall be delivered free of all **encumbrances** (claims of third parties, for example, for an unpaid balance) of which the buyer is not aware at the time of contracting.

A QUESTION OF ETHICS

Donnell found a gold ring on a busy downtown street. The ring had no identifying marks. He gave it to the local police, but they returned it after their customary search procedure had failed to locate the owner. Donnell then sold the ring to Leesen. They agreed that because Donnell had found the ring, there would be no warranty of title. Is Leesen ethically obligated to return the ring if the true owner appeared and could prove ownership? Is he legally obligated to do so?

This warranty does not ensure that the goods are free of encumbrances at the time of the sale, but rather that they will be free at the time of delivery. This distinction enables the seller to comply with the warranty by paying off any third-party claimants before transferring ownership.

IN THIS CASE

Kresge sold a portable copying machine to Nansen and promised delivery in two weeks. Kresge did not mention that he owed $850 to the bank, with the machine as security. Kresge can avoid breaching the implied warranty against encumbrances by paying off the loan before delivering the machine.

WARRANTY OF FITNESS FOR A PARTICULAR PURPOSE A buyer who needs goods for a specific purpose often tells the seller about that purpose. Then the buyer relies on the seller's skill and judgment for a selection of appropriate goods.

In such circumstances, the seller makes an implied warranty that the goods delivered to the buyer are reasonably fit for the stated purpose. If they prove to be unfit, the buyer has a right of action for breach of warranty.

This warranty does not arise when the buyer

- personally selects the goods
- orders the goods according to the buyer's own specifications
- does not rely on the skill and judgment of the seller, because of independent testing or for other reasons.

The warranty could arise even when the buyer asks for goods by patent or brand name. However, this variation applies only if the seller knows the purpose for which the goods are required and if the buyer relies on the seller's selection. For example, the buyer might ask for a "Buzzer" brand name chain saw to fell a stand of 30 trees with trunks two feet in diameter. When the seller selects the proper model, the buyer is relying on the seller's judgment, expertise, and implied warranty of fitness for a stated purpose.

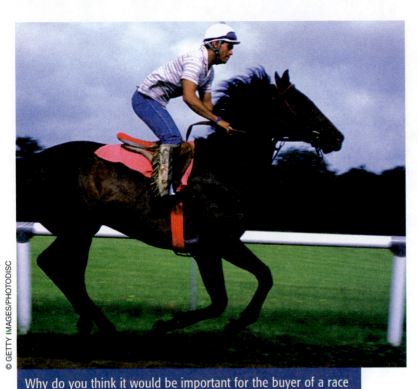

Why do you think it would be important for the buyer of a race horse to receive documentation of the lineage of the horse?

IMPLIED WARRANTIES GIVEN ONLY BY MERCHANTS

Merchants typically are held to higher standards in their dealings with consumers than are casual sellers. This is certainly true in the area of warranties. In addition to the warranties made by all sellers, as previously discussed, the following warranties are, by law, also made by merchants.

WARRANTY AGAINST INFRINGEMENT A merchant makes an implied warranty that the goods in which she or he normally deals shall be delivered to a buyer free of any third party's claims for patent, copyright, or trademark infringement (unauthorized use). This warranty may be excluded by agreement between the parties. If the buyer furnishes specifications to the seller that lead to a claim of infringement against the seller, the buyer is obligated to indemnify the seller for any loss suffered because of the infringement.

WARRANTY OF MERCHANTABILITY Every merchant who customarily deals in goods of a particular kind makes an implied warranty of merchantability to all buyers of the goods. Basically, a **warranty of merchantability** requires that the goods be fit for the ordinary purposes for which such goods are used.

All goods sold must pass without objection in the trade under the sales contract description. Buyers must not refuse to accept them. If the goods are fungible, like grain, they must be at least of fair, average quality within the description. Within variations permitted by the contract, goods must be of even kind, quality, and quantity. If required by the contract, they must be adequately contained, packaged, and labeled. Finally, they must conform to any promises or statements of fact made on the label or on the container.

This implied warranty of merchantability greatly increases the merchant's duties of care and performance beyond those of the casual seller. It extends, for example, to food sold, which must be wholesome and fit for human consumption. It includes foods and drinks that are sold and served to be consumed elsewhere or on the premises, as in restaurants and fast-food shops. Drugs for human use also must be safe and wholesome.

Merchantability requires that any warranty protection that is customary in the trade be extended to all buyers. For example, the seller of a pedigreed animal, such as a dog or horse, is expected to provide documentation of the lineage of the animal because such proof is customary in the trade.

The warranty of merchantability may be expressly excluded by agreement of the parties. Also, when a buyer has examined the goods or a sample or model before contracting, there is no implied warranty of merchantability as to those defects that a reasonable examination would have revealed. This also applies if the buyer refused to examine the goods, sample, or model before contracting.

EXCLUSION OF WARRANTIES

A seller may offer to sell goods without any warranties. This is most likely to occur if the goods are known to have defects or if they are a new design or model. To sell goods without a warranty, the seller must refrain from making any express warranties, and use appropriate language that will exclude implied warranties.

For example, to exclude or modify the broad warranty of merchantability or any part of it, the

Many businesses enter into contracts via the Internet that under the Statute of Frauds would require a "writing." Without such a paper representation of the contract—for example, for a sale of goods valued at more than $500—the agreement basically is unenforceable. Under UCITA such contracts are explicitly held to be valid as long as a record or authentication is available. Other issues that remain unresolved are the validity of electronic signatures, the effect of minority, and the requirements for proof of conditions that invalidate assent, such as intoxication, insanity, etc. Finally, under UCITA, tie-in sales using silence as acceptance would be legal unless a state's consumer protection statute renders them illegal. The terms in tie-in sales essentially state, "you bought our original version of the software, so we'll send you updates and charge you for them until you tell us not to."

THINK ABOUT IT

Elements of the Statute of Frauds and the UCC conflict with the terms suggested by the UCITA. Does knowledge of these conflicts affect your decision to make purchases over the Internet?

---

seller must mention "merchantability" in a disclaimer. A **disclaimer** is a notice of exclusion. To exclude or modify any implied warranty of fitness, the exclusion must be in writing and be easily noticed. A statement such as the following would cover both merchantability and fitness: "There are no warranties of merchantability or fitness that extend beyond the description on the label." Unless otherwise indicated, all implied warranties are excluded by such expressions as "with all faults," "as is," or other similar words.

LEMON LAWS

Warranties are augmented by consumer self-help laws called *lemon laws*. Typically, these laws protect consumers of vehicles but they may extend to other consumer products in certain jurisdictions. Lemon laws are so-called because chronically defective vehicles are referred to as "lemons." Lemon laws exist at both state and federal levels.

Lemon law protection works like this: A consumer returns a vehicle with a major defect to an authorized dealership for repair within the warranty period. If the dealership tries unsuccessfully to fix the vehicle several times (the number varies by statute—typically three visits are required), the consumer should then, in writing, request a refund or a replacement vehicle. If the request is not met, the consumer should seek the help of an attorney.

CHECKPOINT
Distinguish express and implied warranties.

Xtra! Study Tools
lawxtra.swlearning.com

14-2 Assessment

THINK ABOUT LEGAL CONCEPTS

1. A warranty that obligates the seller to repair or replace the defective product with only a labor cost to the buyer is still a full warranty. **True or False?**

2. Laws directed at problems caused by chronically defective automobiles are called "imperfection correction" laws. **True or False?**

3. The warranty of _ ?_ is implied against merchants of food products to be sure those products are fit for human consumption.

4. An express warranty may be given orally and still be legally effective. **True or False?**

5. *Caveat emptor* is Latin for (a) let the buyer beware (b) let the seller beware (c) let the ruler beware.

THINK CRITICALLY ABOUT EVIDENCE

Study the situation, answer the questions, and then prepare arguments to support your answers.

6. When Winslow decided to install a brick walk in front of his home, he bought three sacks of standard Pyramid-brand mortar mix from the U-Can-Do store. Instructions on the bags warned against direct contact with skin. Although Winslow had sensitive skin, he repeatedly touched the wet mix with his bare hands because he was not skilled in using a trowel. This burned his hands and he developed an allergic rash. Is either U-Can-Do or Pyramid liable to him under any theory of product liability?

7. When the Grandiose Motor Car Company introduced its new model, sales lagged. After three months, only 7,500 cars had been sold. To stimulate sales, Grandiose added four years to its standard one-year warranty. It also extended the warranty on the cars already sold. Is Grandiose legally bound to the early buyers for the extra four years even though no new consideration was paid?

8. Kent was critically injured when he dropped a running lawnmower on his foot. At the time he dropped it, Kent was using the lawnmower to trim the top of a three-foot-high hedge. He sued the retailer, wholesaler, and manufacturer of the lawnmower on a product liability theory. Kent claimed an automatic shutoff should have been built into the lawnmower for times when it was not in contact with the ground. Will Kent win? Why or why not?

9. While in Florida, Van Loon decided to go fishing for tarpon. Visiting Stanton's Sports Shop, Van Loon explained his specific need to the salesperson. Van Loon then bought the fishing gear the salesperson recommended. During the first trip out, Van Loon had repeated strikes, but the line was too light for the weight of the fish. The line broke every time even though handled properly. What legal rights, if any, does Van Loon have against Stanton's?

PREVENT LEGAL DIFFICULTIES

For your protection as a consumer...

1. Be wary of companies that conduct fraudulent schemes by telephone or on the Internet Also be cautious with offers to "get-rich-quick." Such offers often involve real estate or precious metals. Fraudulent offers of free gifts and travel also are common.

2. Be cautious of "bargains." Usually they are authentic, but occasionally they are a part of a bait-and-switch scheme or they are loss leaders surrounded by overpriced goods.

3. Do not gamble. Remember that even in free and honest gambling contests, the vast majority of participants receive nothing.

4. When you have a valid complaint about a fraudulent or unfair business practice, take action. Complain to the business involved, the Better Business Bureau, the local prosecutor, the state attorney general, the FTC, the CPSC, and any other governmental body with jurisdiction. If all else fails, consider taking legal action.

5. Try to stay informed about product defects. Watch the stores where you shop for recall announcements. Pay special attention to recall notices you receive in the mail.

6. When in doubt about a product, consult the CPSC. Sign up to receive notices about banned products.

7. Be aware that not every assurance of quality or performance made by a seller is a warranty.

8. Know the implied warranties for goods you buy and watch for sellers' statements of limitation.

9. Make certain that any express warranty you receive is in writing to avoid later disputes as to its meaning or existence.

10. Use special care in buying goods "as is." Inspect the goods to be sure that you are willing to take them without the benefit of warranties.

Chapter 14 Assessment

CONCEPTS IN BRIEF

14-1 Protection through Governmental Action

1. The Latin phrase *caveat emptor* has long urged buyers to beware. The complexity of today's products and the inaccessibility of their makers now require consumers not only to beware but to be aware of the various federal, state, and local laws designed to inform and protect them.

2. Federal agencies and state and local governments work together to ensure safe products, services, and sanitary facilities for consumers.

3. Unfair trade practices include price fixing, false advertising, illegal lotteries, improperly labeling goods, and selling used articles as new.

4. Reports of substandard goods or services can be made to licensing authorities at the state and local levels.

14-2 Protection through Action by the Consumer

5. Generally, any person injured by a defective product may bring suit against any manufacturer or merchant in the distribution chain for that product. Depending on the circumstances, the suit may be based on warranty, fraud, negligence, or strict liability.

6. Warranties may be express or implied. Express warranties are oral or written promises by the seller about product quality or performance. Implied warranties are imposed by law and are effective even when not mentioned by the seller.

7. Merchant sellers normally are bound by the important implied warranty of merchantability unless explicitly disclaimed.

YOUR LEGAL VOCABULARY

Match each statement with the term that it best defines. Some terms may not be used.

1. Notice of exclusion of warranty
2. Return of improperly obtained money or property
3. Individual who buys primarily for personal, family, or household use
4. Greatly exaggerated sales talk
5. Let the buyer beware
6. Let the seller beware
7. Obligation implicitly imposed on all sellers
8. Dishonest, fraudulent, or anti-competitive business method
9. Lawsuit made possible by the procedural joining of similarly situated plaintiffs
10. Explicit assurance of quality or performance by seller
11. Affixing of responsibility to compensate buyers, users, and others for injuries caused by a defective product.
12. Claims of third parties, for example, for an unpaid balance
13. The relationship that exists between or among the contracting parties as a result of their legally binding agreement

a. **bait and switch**
b. *caveat emptor*
c. *caveat venditor*
d. **cease-and-desist order**
e. **class action**
f. **consent order**
g. **consumer**
h. **disclaimer**
i. **encumbrances**
j. **express warranty**
k. **full warranty**
l. **implied warranty**
m. **limited warranty**
n. **privity of contract**
o. **product liability**
p. **puffing**
q. **restitution**
r. **unfair trade practice**
s. **warranty**
t. **warranty of merchantability**

REVIEW LEGAL CONCEPTS

14. What are the normal sanctions available to a consumer protection agency?

15. How would you prove a bait and switch had occurred?

16. Why is it a good idea to leave to local governments the inspection of restaurants and other establishments where food is handled? Why would more centralized state or federal standards not be a good idea?

17. Who can bring suit for product liability under the UCC?

18. Should a written contract include all express warranties?

19. Why are sellers not required to give warranties in every transaction?

20. How do the terms "puffing" and *caveat emptor* relate to one another?

WRITE ABOUT LEGAL CONCEPTS

21. Make a list of the reasons that *caveat emptor* does not work as well now as it once did in protecting consumers.

22. Write a paragraph stating your opinion on what is the most important implied warranty.

23. Would a company selling software that enabled the copying of movie DVDs be committing an unfair trade practice? Why or why not?

24. **HOT DEBATE** Write a persuasive opening statement that emphasizes the legal and ethical points in support of Edison's case. Or, write a persuasive opening statement that emphasizes the legal and ethical points in the manufacturer's favor.

MAKE ACADEMIC CONNECTIONS

25. **PSYCHOLOGY** Research and write a one-page paper on whether the use of subliminal (subconscious) techniques in advertising in movies, print, and television should be outlawed as false and misleading. Bring examples to class, if possible.

THINK CRITICALLY ABOUT EVIDENCE

Study the situation, answer the questions, and then prepare arguments to support your answers.

26. After an hour of persistent persuasion by a door-to-door salesperson, the Arnos signed a contract to buy magazine subscriptions. The next morning, the Arnos did some quick calculating and were appalled to discover that they had agreed to spend $257.40—a sum they could not afford—for magazines. Can the Arnos cancel the contract without being liable for damages?

27. The Motleys entered Penn's Nursery and asked for a 50-pound sack of ZAP, a brand-name weed killer, to kill the narrow-leafed devil grass in their lawn. ZAP was advertised as "effective, when properly used, against crabgrass and other broadleafed weeds and grasses." The Motleys applied the chemical according to directions, but the devil grass survived. They sued the manufacturer, claiming a breach of warranty. They also sued Penn's for failure to give them proper advice as to what kind of weed killer to buy. Will the Motleys win their suit against the manufacturer? Will they win their suit against Penn's?

28. Gallo, an experienced glider pilot, rented a glider at a commercial glider port. While in flight, she lost control because of a defect in the tail assembly. The glider crashed while landing, and Gallo was permanently disabled. Although several years old, the glider had been properly maintained. There was no warranty in effect on the glider. Does Gallo have any legal recourse?

29. Singer-Moser was thirty-nine years old when she had her first cavity. Unfortunately, the dentist treating her for the cavity had to do a root canal procedure. At the conclusion of the procedure, Singer-Moser was left with the shell of her tooth and a filling inside it. A week later, she was eating a hamburger at Carnivoracious, a franchised restaurant in her home town. She bit down on a piece of bone that shattered the remnants of her tooth and dislodged the filling. Now the dentist tells her she must have a cap that will cost $2,500. Her attorney tells her that Carnivoracious should pay for the work. Why?

30. Every week for a year and a half, Newmark was given a shampoo and set by employees of Gimbel's. Then a new product ("Candle Wave," made by the Helene Curtis company) was applied to Newmark's hair. As a result, Newmark suffered contact dermatitis of the scalp, with substantial hair loss. Newmark sued Gimbel's for breach of the implied warranty of fitness for a particular purpose. Gimbel's argued that it was providing a service and not selling goods in this transaction. Therefore it could not be held liable for breach of warranty with reference to the product of Helene Curtis. It could only be held liable, it claimed, if its own employees were proved negligent. Could a jury find Gimbel's liable if the wave solution was defective and caused the injury? (*Newmark v. Gimbel's Inc.*, 258 A.2d 679, N.J.)

31. Mahaney purchased a used car from Perry Auto Exchange. Mahaney was told that the car was in "perfect, A-1, and first-class condition." A written statement given to Mahaney at the time of the sale described the car as being in "good operating condition." Mahaney had no opportunity to investigate the truth of these statements. Later, it was determined that the car had a problem in the differential and had no brakes at the time of the sale. Mahaney sued for rescission. Were Perry's statements merely puffing or were they warranties upon which the rescission could be based? (*Mahaney v. Perry Auto Exchange*, 85 N.E.2d 558, Ohio)

32. On January 1, plaintiff Werner bought the *White Eagle*, a wooden sloop, from defendant Montana, and the parties signed a bill of sale. The previous October they had signed an intent to purchase and sell. During their negotiations, the seller had assured the buyer orally that the hull would "make up" from swelling when placed in the water and would be watertight. At the end of June, Werner put the boat in the water. He allowed more than six weeks—a sufficient time—for the planking to swell to form a watertight hull. But the hull still leaked. The boat could not be sailed. Werner then checked the hull and for the first time discovered extensive dry rot which required substantial repairs. In a letter in September, he demanded that Montana take the boat back and refund the purchase price of $13,250. The defendant refused, and so Werner sued for rescission. Montana argued that the oral assurances he had given that the boat was water-

tight could not be admitted at the trial because of the parol evidence rule. Who should win? (*Werner v. Montana*, 378 A.2d 1130, N.H.)

33. Through radio and television, the defendant's stores advertised a "top quality . . . Queen Anne Console Magic Stitcher" sewing machine, along with a sewing chair, for the "close-out price of just $29.50." Under the sales plan, a "lead person" would accept the customer's order, taking a deposit as small as 25 cents. After that, a demonstrator would visit the customer and "kill the sale" by having the machine jam in use. The demonstrator would also say that the customer could lose an eye if the machine jammed. Then the demonstrator would attempt to "step-up" the sale and persuade the customer to buy a higher-priced machine. In about 19 months, only 26 of the advertised machines were sold, although 10,951 customers entered into conditional sales contracts for such machines. The 26 advertised machines were sold at a time when the defendants had received complaints from a television station and the Better Business Bureau. The defendants were prosecuted for conspiring to sell merchandise by means of deceptive and misleading advertising. The prosecutor gave evidence that the defendants never intended to sell the advertised machines, which actually cost them $45 each. Are the defendants guilty as charged? (*People v. Glubo, Exelbert, Epstein, and Atlantic Sewing Stores, Inc.*, 158 N.E.2d 699)

34. Registration of a "MONOPOLY" trademark for use on clothing was sought by a New York-based corporation named Tuxedo Monopoly, Inc. The makers of the "MONOPOLY" board game, General Mills Fun Group, opposed the application. The Patent and Trademark Office Trademark Trial and Appeal Board sustained the opposition and would not allow the registration. On appeal to the U.S. Court of Customs and Patent Appeals, Tuxedo's attorneys argued that *monopoly* was a common term and that, regardless, there was very little likelihood of confusion between a trademark used on a game and one used on clothing. They also pointed out that the court had previously allowed the registration of the famous "DIXIE" cup mark by a company using it as its mark on waxed paper. If the court finds a likelihood of confusion exists, it will affirm the Board's decision. How should the court rule? (*Tuxedo Monopoly, Inc. v. General Mills Fun Group, Inc.*, 648 F.2d 1335)

CASE FOR LEGAL THINKING

BLEVINS v. CUSHMAN MOTORS
SUPREME COURT OF MISSOURI, 551 S.W. 2D 602

FACTS Maxwell and Blevins teed off on hole number 13, and then hopped into their golf cart and motored out to Maxwell's ball. Maxwell fired his second shot, then drove the cart toward Blevins' ball. As the car approached the ball at approximately 5 mph, it entered a shady area of the course on which a light dew lay. At that point the cart went into a 10- to 15-foot skid. It was like "being on ice." The cart then tipped over. Maxwell was thrown free. However, Blevins, who failed in his attempt to jump from the cart, was pinned under it when it came to rest. Blevins brought suit on product liability grounds based on strict liability in tort, not negligence. He sued for his personal injuries. In addition, his wife brought suit for loss of consortium (the fellowship of husband and wife in companionship and sexual relations).

TRIAL COURT'S DECISION The court found for Mr. and Mrs. Blevins. Both received very substantial awards.

APPELLATE COURT DECISION The Missouri Court of Appeals upheld the decision of the trial court and maintained the amount of the awards. An appeal was taken to the Missouri Supreme Court.

MISSOURI SUPREME COURT'S DECISION
Cushman Motors, manufacturer of the cart, approached the Missouri Supreme Court arguing that although Missouri courts had used strict liability in tort to decide cases involving a defect in manufacturing, the courts of the state should not use such a standard to decide a case involving a defect in design. Instead, the negligence theory should be used to determine whether the maker of the product was liable.

The Supreme Court decided, "There is no rational distinction between design and manufacture in this context, since a product may be equally defective and dangerous if its design subjects protected persons to unreasonable risks as if its manufacture does so."

CONCLUSION Judgment affirmed.

PRACTICE JUDGING

1. What arguments can you make to justify Cushman's distinction between design and manufacture?

2. What arguments can you make against such a position?

3. According to the excerpted text of the Supreme Court's decision quoted above, was it correct to use strict liability in tort to determine the result in this case?

Entrepreneurs and the Law

PROJECT 3 THE LAW OF SALES

SELLING THE DEVICES

After receiving the go-ahead from his attorney, with his patent application in the works, and with the use of Amber's savings, JJ created more DataDarts and tested them in Stinson Adamski's two stores and pick-up route. After the hardware and software bugs were ironed out, JJ bought booth space at a major trade show for dry cleaners. Amber went along to help him demonstrate the product. Word of the product spread quickly and the DataDart received the "major innovation" award at the show. Several stores and a couple of chains placed orders, even though JJ could not promise a delivery date. These orders were accepted on a handshake basis by JJ as

he had not conceived that anyone would buy the DataDart at this stage. In addition, JJ was amazed that the buyers had not blinked an eye when he had named the selling price of $5,000 for each DataDart system. He had intended to sell them for $2,000 each, which was double his cost. Amber had suggested that he start asking far more, as they were such labor-saving items, and he was going to have a patent-based monopoly.

LOCATION AND SHIPPING

JJ looked for a location for his business. He found a small factory in an industrial park several miles from town and leased it. He acquired a business license and a tax number for his business. JJ then moved his equipment and supplies into the structure and started setting up for his first production run. JJ's immediate goal was to be able to fill the many orders he had, and those that soon would be on his way. He also needed to devise a way to get the finished product to the buyers. JJ knew he would have to be careful in packaging as well as in choosing a transport company.

ACTIVITIES

Divide into teams and perform one or more of the following activities, as directed by your teacher.

Prepare Legal Documents

Sales Contract Draft a sales contract for the orders for DataDarts. Be sure to include terms (such as COD, FOB, etc.) that would protect him from loss or damage to the goods.

Prenuptial Agreement JJ has fallen in love with Amber and wants to tell her and ask her to marry him. However, her parents, who have a sizable fortune, were not impressed by JJ's background and level of affluence when they met him. Amber is an only child and would stand to inherit their estate upon their deaths. As a team, brainstorm the terms of a prenuptial agreement that might satisfy Amber's parents. They are concerned about protecting Amber's sizable inheritance. Also consider terms that might protect JJ's interest in the business should the couple divorce, with or without children. Have a group member record each idea. Draft a prenuptial agreement based on the team's ideas.

© GETTY IMAGES/PHOTODISC

COMMUNITY ACTION

Become a Consumer Activist

In 1773 a group of patriots decided to take action against English taxation without representation by throwing a shipload of tea overboard into Boston Harbor. They were consumer activists. This long-standing tradition of citizen action aimed at influencing corporate and governmental decisions is taking on new and unprecedented power. The most popular forms of consumer activists include boycotts (not purchasing products for political reasons), buycotts (purchasing products for political reasons), and socially conscious investing. It also includes politically oriented shareholder tactics such as proposing a resolution, testifying at a shareholder meeting, disrupting a shareholder meeting, protests directed at corporate or governmental organizations, and protests that target businesses directly. Whether conservative or liberal, all political agendas have found their way into consumer activism.

Do Your Part

1. Make a list of three consumer-related concerns that you have about your community or the world. Research to find an organization that matches your concerns. For example, if you are concerned about the use of CCA in treated lumber, you could research the Consumer Product Safety Commission. If your concern is harvesting the world's rain forests or old-growth forests for lumber, you might research Greenpeace.
2. Join the organization and participate in any local activities.
3. Gather a group of your friends to make eye-catching posters that identify and explain your cause. Call for students at your school to participate in a rally, boycott, or buycott.
4. Write letters to the editor for your school and local paper, state representatives, and any other governmental or corporate figures who could help your cause.

Public Speaking I

This event gives FBLA members the opportunity to demonstrate leadership through effective speaking skills.

The topic for your speech is Marriage, Divorce, and Prenuptial Contracts. Your business speech should be four minutes in length and must be developed from one or more of the nine FBLA-PBL goals found at the FBLA web site. Five points will be deducted for any time under 3:31 or over 4:20 minutes. A lectern will be available, but no microphone will be used. The participant may use notes or note cards when delivering the speech. However, no visual aids may be used.

Each participant's speech must be the result of his/her own efforts. Facts and working data may be secured from any source. Speeches must be well organized, contain verified statements, and written in an acceptable business style.

Performance Indicators Evaluated
• Understand the latest trends about marriage, divorce, and prenuptial contracts.

• Describe the role of contracts in marriages.
• Explain the latest marriage and divorce trends.
• Thoroughly defend/oppose prenuptial contracts with valid facts.

For more detailed information about performance indicators, go to the FBLA web site.

Think Critically
1. What is the current divorce rate in the United States?
2. What is a prenuptial agreement?
3. Why have more married couples opted to sign prenuptial agreements?
4. Does a prenuptial agreement contradict the sacred vows of marriage ('til death do we part)? Explain your answer.

http://www.fbla-pbl.org/

UNIT 4

PROPERTY LAW

CHAPTERS

IN PRACTICE PROFILE
Mary Beth Wilker ■ Graphic Designer

Growing up in Cincinnati, Ohio, Mary Beth Wilker considered herself a creative type. After high school she enrolled in the Art Academy of Cincinnati where she focused her studies on graphic design. No one was surprised when she remained in her hometown and established Wilker Design. "I always wanted to own my own design firm," she says.

Mary Beth set up shop in a quaint building in a well-kept neighborhood in Norwood, Ohio, a Cincinnati suburb. Once a family residence, the location seemed ideal: on the corner of a busy intersection next to a major highway. She and her husband Nick "poured our blood, sweat, and tears into creating the ideal space. We spent six months landscaping, painting, laying carpet, installing a new driveway, and getting the building up to city code standards." In the 17 years since, Mary Beth has never needed to make sales calls or advertise her business. "Nearly all of my clients found me as they were driving by."

Today, at age 38, Mary Beth says, "My business is my dream."

Unfortunately others have a different dream for Mary Beth's property. Using the power of eminent domain, Jeffrey R. Anderson Real Estate persuaded Norwood leaders to try to force Wilker Design out of its location. The developer wants to tear down Wilker Design, along with 70 other properties, in order to build office space, retail stores, restaurants, and condominiums. Citing an urban renewal study—paid for by Anderson Real Estate—that designates the area as "blighted," Norwood leaders agreed to the plan. The leaders believe the project will bring badly needed tax revenue to Norwood.

Most homeowners have agreed to sell their property to Anderson, who has offered them 25 percent above fair market value. But the remaining property owners, including Mary Beth Wilker, want to stay. Because Anderson won't purchase any property until all have agreed to sell, the neighborhood's future remains uncertain. Home and business owners who wish to update their property are afraid to invest their time and money. Others are anxious to sell their property to Anderson and move, but are unable to do so.

"Eminent domain should be used for roads and police stations, not for Crate and Barrel and condominiums," Mary Beth believes. That's why she and four other property owners are challenging the decision in court. "In a free country the government does not take from the small to give to the big; it doesn't take my business for a wealthy real estate developer."

While she waits for a court decision, Mary Beth continues the hard work necessary to keep her business—her dream—thriving.

> "Eminent domain should be used for roads and police stations, not for Crate and Barrel and condominiums. . . . In a free country the government does not take from the small to give to the big; it doesn't take my business for a wealthy real estate developer."

CHAPTER 15

Property and Its Acquisition

15-1 Types of Property

15-2 How Property Is Acquired and Held

© GETTY IMAGES/PHOTODISC

When he was 57, Neerow won $20 million in a state lottery. Upon receiving the first of 20 promised annual payments, he went on a spending spree. He had extensive plastic surgery, including a face lift. Then he bought a condominium in Florida, a new car which he soon wrecked, clothes he never even wore, and a mink coat for a casual friend. He staged many parties including a wild New Year's Eve party on a yacht for 50 new friends. While pursuing his new lifestyle, Neerow totally neglected his business, which employed 10 people. The business weakened to the point of near bankruptcy.

Where Do You Stand?

1. Give the legal rationale as to why Neerow should be allowed to continue to waste his resources.

2. From society's standpoint, should his wastefulness be stopped? Why or why not?

15-1 Types of Property

PROPERTY AND ITS CLASSIFICATION

WHAT'S YOUR VERDICT?

Needing a vacation after finishing a new edition of his book, Jon rented a house in Beach Haven, New Jersey, for a couple of weeks. He looked forward to relaxing and getting away from it all during that period.

Did Jon acquire property under the lease?

WHAT IS PROPERTY?

When you hear the term *property*, you probably think of tangible things you can see or touch. Tangible things include this book, clothing, diamond rings, buildings, land, cars, and boats. However, property also includes intangible things, or things you cannot see or touch.

For example, both the goodwill of a brand name and the secret formula by which a product is made are intangible property. Other examples include patents for inventions, the copyright of this book, the franchise to open a particular business in your town, and the right to collect money under an automobile insurance policy.

According to the law, **property** is (1) a thing, tangible or intangible, that is subject to ownership, and (2) a group of related legal rights. For example, suppose you own some land with a house that you correctly call property. Ownership of the land and house gives you a number of legal rights. These include rights to (1) possess, use, and enjoy it; (2) dispose of (by gift or sale), consume, or even destroy it; and (3) give it away by will after death.

You also have the right to transfer possession of your property. Because he acquired possession of the beach house for two weeks by renting it,

in *What's Your Verdict?* Jon acquired property in the transaction.

CLASSIFICATIONS OF PROPERTY

Property can be classified as real or personal. **Real property** is defined as land, buildings and those things permanently affixed to them (*fixtures*). **Personal property** is basically anything that is not real property and can be either tangible or intangible.

REAL PROPERTY Real property (sometimes called *realty*) includes not only the surface of the earth, but also the water and minerals on and below the surface. Real property in the form of land extends down to the center of the earth and, with certain limits, includes the airspace above the land. Real property also includes buildings and anything that becomes permanently attached to buildings and land. The rights to possess, use, profit from, and destroy such things also are considered real property.

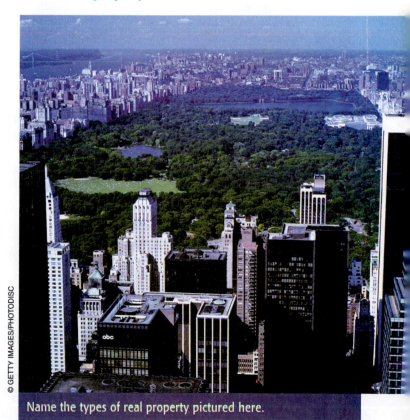

Name the types of real property pictured here.

PERSONAL PROPERTY Tangible personal property (sometimes called *personalty*) is something that has physical form. Intangible personal property comprises anything that does not have a physical form and includes rights in those things. Examples include the goodwill associated with a business and rights in intellectual property.

Intellectual property is intangible property created by the intellect and includes copyrights, service marks and trademarks, patents, and trade secrets. The creation, use, and transfer of interests in intellectual property generally are governed by federal statutes.

COPYRIGHTS A **copyright** protects the *expression* of a creative work, such as the work of an author, artist, or composer. Owners of the copyright have the exclusive right to reproduce, sell, perform, or display the work. Copyrights owned by the creator of the work last for the life of the creator plus 70 years. After a copyright period expires, the work can be used by anyone without cost or obtaining permission. An author can transfer ownership of the copyright to others.

Copyrighted works can include songs, books, computer programs, and architectural plans. The expression must be *fixed* and *original*. Fixed means it is expressed in a permanent way others can understand, for example in writing, painting, computer language, or a blueprint. It is the fixed expression, not the idea, that is protected. If you wrote a book about the Civil War, it is only the way you used the words that would be protected.

Copyright protection is afforded by the common law from creation of the original work until it is spread to those outside of the author's circle. At that time the copyright will be lost unless the work has been registered with the U.S. Copyright Office. Damages may be collected for **infringement**, which is the unauthorized copying, sale, display, or performance of a copyright protected work.

Under the federal copyright law not all unauthorized uses of copyrighted works are infringements. **Fair use** is the very limited use of copyrighted works by critics, researchers, news reporters, and educators. The most important factor in determining whether the defense of fair

Cyberlaw

You probably view the e-mail you send as your own personal property. But what about the e-mail you send at work? Many companies now have e-mail policies about who owns the e-mail correspondence and whether the company considers the messages to be confidential. The courts have ruled that e-mails are the property of the company. In *Shoars v. Epson,* the judge found in favor of the company and stated that it had the right to tap into, read, and print employees' e-mails. The court reasoned that the company's property right in the computers prevailed. The company's ethics were not of consequence, according to the current law. In most cases involving e-mail, the judges have marked their opinions as "Not For Publication," which indicates they feel the statutes need updating. The bottom line: Be careful before you press the Send button. E-mail messages are neither confidential nor your private, exclusive property.

THINK ABOUT IT
Should you be able to send personal messages on your employer's computer system? What are the arguments for and against? Would it matter if you did so on your break time? What about searching the web or playing video games on the employer's computers? If you did any of these things would you have an expectation of privacy?

use is available is the economic impact of the use.

Another factor is the quantity of the copied material in relation to the size of the whole copyrighted work. One novelist might quote a paragraph from another novelist's 300-page book. That would be fair use because it does not injure the first novelist by causing reduced sales of the quoted novel. Also, the paragraph is a small portion of the original, copyrighted novel. Teachers may reproduce very limited portions of copyrighted materials for use in their classes.

TRADEMARKS AND SERVICE MARKS Business firms may acquire property rights known as trademarks. A **trademark** is a word, mark, symbol, or device that identifies a product of a particular manufacturer or merchant. The mark must be unique and identify and distinguish the product. For example, the word "Kodak" is a trademark. It is included in the name of the owner, the Eastman Kodak Company, and it identifies products made by that company. However, descriptive words, such as "35mm camera," are not trademarks, and they may be used by any company. A **service mark** is a unique word, mark, or symbol that identifies a service as opposed to a product.

Registration of trademarks in the United States officially began in 1870. Internationally, the Paris Convention of 1883, along with subsequent amendments led the way. The Convention is an international treaty organization. It requires nations that have signed it to recognize the trademark rights of citizens of the other signatory nations. The Lanham Act, enacted in 1946, is the current U.S. trademark law.

Trademarks have been used for centuries. Ancient Chinese potters and medieval sword makers used pictures and symbols as their trademarks. The American patriot and silversmith Paul Revere marked his work with his initials. Nonetheless, the rights of trademark owners were not clearly established until the nineteenth century with passage of the Lanham Act.

All states and the federal government have trademark registration laws. Registration is not essential. However, if a trademark is registered it is easier to prove ownership of the mark. Common law protection lasts forever if a unique trademark establishes the product in the minds of the public and the trademark is used continuously. The originating company loses its exclusive property right to the trademark if either of the following occurs:

1. the company permits competitors to refer to similar products by the unique trademark, or

2. the trademark is used generally as a descriptive generic term.

Examples of terms that have become generic are "shredded wheat" and "cellophane." In contrast, the terms "Xerox," "Levi's," and "Scotch Tape" remain the property of the original owners.

PATENTS A **patent** is the grant of the exclusive right to make, use, import, sell and offer a novel or new, non-obvious, useful product or process. Novel and non-obvious mean no one has ever thought of the product or process before. Useful means the product or process can help people do things. Like copyrights, patents can be transferred to others. A patent is good for up to 20 years and is not renewable.

An inventor will sometimes patent improvements to the original product and thereby extend the practical life of the initial patent. Patents are given for original designs, such as a unique chair, or original processes, such as one for refining oil into rubber. Patents also are given for certain new and distinct varieties of plants and other biological creations.

TRADE SECRETS Sometimes a business firm will have important ideas or knowledge that cannot be copyrighted or patented. These ideas can still be protected as trade secrets. A **trade secret** is commercially valuable information that the owner attempts to keep secret. If an employee leaves a company and sells a secret formula, process, or customer list, the former employee and the buyer of the trade secret will be liable to the employer.

CHECKPOINT
What are the two main classifications of property?

FEATURES OF INTELLECTUAL PROPERTY

	What is protected?	Registration required?	Duration?	Examples
Patent	Ideas, designs, or processes that are novel, non-obvious, and useful	Yes	20 years	Industrial chemical manufacturing processes, prescription drugs
Copyright	Fixed expressions of creativity	No, but recommended	70 years past the death of the creator	Novels, poems, songs, photographs
Trademark	Distinctive mark, word, or symbol associated with a particular product	No, but recommended	Indefinite	Logos, emblems, catch phrases

15-1 Assessment

Xtra!
Study Tools
lawxtra.swlearning.com

THINK ABOUT LEGAL CONCEPTS

1. The ability to profit from real property is a property right. **True or False?**

2. Intellectual property is (a) tangible, (b) intangible, (c) not capable of ownership.

3. To be protected by law, a trade secret (a) must be copyrightable (b) must be patentable (c) must be commercially valuable (d) must have had efforts to keep it secret (e) both c and d

4. Copyrights held by authors are protected by federal law for the life of the author plus 70 years. **True or False?**

5. Patents are only available for new, useful, non-obvious products or processes. **True or False?**

6. A unique word, protected by federal law, that identifies a business's product is called a(n) _ ?_.

THINK CRITICALLY ABOUT EVIDENCE

Study the situation, answer the questions, and then prepare arguments to support your answers.

7. Stephanie wrote an epic poem about teenage life for her English class. The idea was so novel that her teacher urged her to read it at a school assembly. Stephanie did so. Later, she noticed that large sections of the poem were being published on several web sites. Did Stephanie have the right to stop such publications?

8. Mary developed a hair dye, from natural ingredients, that could be washed with hot water without changing the color. She took the dye to a chemist who said that most chemists were aware of the dye's properties. Which approach is most likely to help Mary protect her formula—a patent, copyright, or trade secret?

9. Steven was president of a successful chemical company. He developed a nonpatentable process for making soap better. At first, he treated his process as a secret. Later, however, his pride caused him to disclose the technique to a number of people. When one of these people started a competing business using his process, he sued claiming theft of a trade secret. Will Steven prevail?

How Property Is Acquired and Held

WAYS OF ACQUIRING PROPERTY

WHAT'S YOUR VERDICT?

Five friends were discussing how they each had acquired their watches. Appleton bought his with earnings from his job at the local fast-food restaurant. Baird received hers as a graduation gift. Cameron inherited hers from an aunt who had died. Dawson, a skilled watchmaker, made his own. Engler found hers on the street. She had not been able to find the owner.

Did each of the friends have the same rights in his or her wristwatch?

Real or personal property is acquired most commonly by contract, gift, or inheritance. In addition, personal property legitimately may be acquired by accession, intellectual labor, finding, or occupancy. Real property may be acquired by adverse possession, dedication, and eminent domain. (See Chapter 17 to read about these means of acquiring real property.) In *What's Your Verdict?* even though each friend acquired a watch through a different means, each had the same ownership rights in his or her own wristwatch except Engler. She only had the rights of a finder—mainly possession and use.

ACQUIRING OWNERSHIP BY CONTRACT

Any kind of property may be acquired and transferred, or bought and sold, by contract. People acquire most of their property by earning money and using it to purchase property.

ACQUIRING OWNERSHIP BY GIFT

To create a valid and binding gift, three things must occur. The person making the gift, the donor, must do two of them: (1) show an intent to transfer ownership, and (2) deliver the property. Delivery is a shift of physical possession of the property to the new owner, the donee. The donee must then (3) accept the gift either by not rejecting it within a reasonable time or expressly or impliedly showing acceptance by conduct.

Often the law allows a symbol of the subject matter of the gift to be substituted in delivery. Thus, the keys to a car or a deed to real property could be used in place of the car or realty itself. This is referred to as **constructive delivery**. Note that a mere promise to make a gift creates no legal obligations.

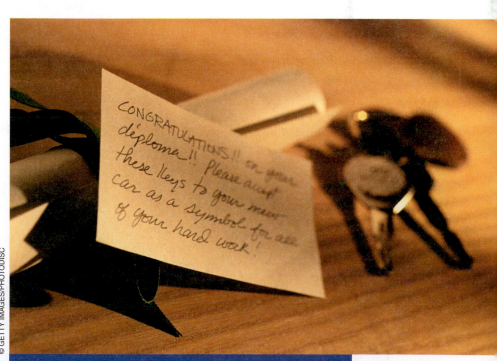

© GETTY IMAGES/PHOTODISC

CONGRATULATIONS!! on your diploma!! Please accept these keys to your new car as a symbol for all of your hard work!

Imagine that your parents give you the keys to a car as a graduation gift. What type of delivery are they employing in giving you the car as a gift?

Sometimes a gift is conditional, as when a man gives his fiancée an engagement ring. If the two mutually agree not to get married after all, or if the woman breaks the engagement, the man generally may reclaim the gift. In most states, if the man breaks the engagement the woman is entitled to keep the ring.

Another type of conditional gift is made when a donor expects to die soon. This is referred to as a gift *causa mortis* (in anticipation of death) and is distinguished from other gifts given *inter vivos* (during life). If the donor of a gift *causa mortis* recovers or dies of another cause or simply revokes the gift before death, the gift is not legally valid.

INTERNATIONAL VIEWPOINT

The Domesday Book

In 1086, King William I of England ordered a survey done of all the lands in his kingdom. William wanted to definitively determine who owned every acre of land in England in order to collect property taxes more efficiently.

The king appointed several commissioners, each of whom conducted their survey in a specific circuit, which was separated into different counties. The commissioners' decisions on ownership were considered as final as the biblical "day of doom." The survey then became known as the Doomsday or Domesday Book.

The survey of land ownership conducted more than 900 years ago still survives today. It is an important source of historical and genealogical information.

IN THIS CASE

Sturgeon Hamilton was diagnosed with a rare form of disease. His doctor told him he would have to be hospitalized immediately and would probably die in 48 to 72 hours. Sturgeon, knowing that he had not made a will, gave away his property to his friends from his hospital bed. He wrote Susie a check for the $34,000 in his banking and savings accounts and gave Tomee the keys to his brand new Jaguar. They thanked him profusely and left. An hour later, as Sturgeon was picking out the wording for his tombstone, his doctor came in and informed him that there had been a mistake at the lab. He really just had the flu and would probably live to be 100. Sturgeon will be able to void the gifts and get his money and car back.

ACQUIRING OWNERSHIP BY INTELLECTUAL LABOR

You can acquire personal property rights by original production of intellectual property. As discussed in the preceding lesson, creators may take legal steps to acquire exclusive property rights in such property in the form of patents, copyrights and the like.

ACQUIRING OWNERSHIP BY INHERITANCE

Personal and real property can be acquired by inheritance. The legal methods involved in such an acquisition are discussed in Chapter 19.

ACQUIRING OWNERSHIP BY ACCESSION

Personal property also may be acquired by accession. **Accession** is the right of an owner of property to a significant *increase* in that property. The increase may be natural or manmade.

Thus, farm crops and the offspring of animals belong to the owner of the land or the animals. When new parts are put into an item of property, they generally become part of the property.

On this sheep farm, by what means does the farmer acquire ownership of the newborn lambs?

coat on a coat rack in a restaurant while you ate, and then walked out without your coat, it would be mislaid. The finder of the coat would be required to turn it over to the restaurant. Because you may come back looking for the coat, this law helps owners find mislaid property.

Generally, the location and situation in which the items are discovered are used to infer whether they are lost or mislaid. Most states have statutes that detail how someone may become the owner of lost or mislaid property upon publication of the find and after a suitable waiting period passes for the true owner to appear.

For example, if a modem is installed in your computer, it becomes part of the computer. If, by mistake, someone improves another's property, courts seek to do justice by letting the improver keep the property after paying fair value for the original item.

ACQUIRING OWNERSHIP BY FINDING

Anyone who loses property has the right to recover it from any finder. One must simply prove true ownership. When a finder of property knows who the owner is, the finder must return the property. Under some laws, a finder must try (for example, by newspaper advertising) to locate the property owner. If the owner is unknown, either the finder or the owner of the place the property was found may keep the property until the true owner appears. Which one has this right depends on whether the property is lost or mislaid.

Finders keep lost property and owners of the place where the property was found keep mislaid property. **Lost property** is created when the owner does not know when or where it disappeared from the owner's possession. If a $100 bill falls from your pocket as you are pulling out your keys and you don't notice it, the money is lost property.

Mislaid property is placed intentionally somewhere but then forgotten. If you hung your

ACQUIRING OWNERSHIP BY OCCUPANCY

Occupancy means acquiring title by taking possession of personal property that belongs to no one else. A common example is personal property that has been abandoned or discarded by the owner. In such a case, the finder who takes possession becomes the owner.

A QUESTION OF ETHICS

Jerry saw another customer in a local restaurant place his overcoat on a coat hook but walk out without it. He also saw the customer drive away from the restaurant. Jerry picked up the coat and found $160 in one pocket. What are Jerry's ethical obligations in this situation? What are Jerry's legal duties in this situation?

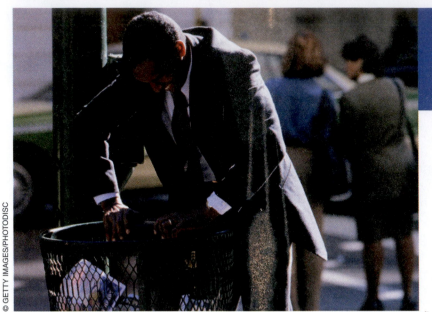

A salesperson has just lost a huge account, and, in disgust, throws his briefcase into a public waste can. Another person notices this, and fishes it out. By what means does the finder acquire ownership of this briefcase?

Like discarded or abandoned property, wildlife is considered to belong to no one. A properly licensed person who takes possession of a wild animal on public lands by killing or capturing it becomes the legal owner. Similarly, one may become the owner of shells by picking them up on a public beach. However, property on private lands belongs to the owner of the real property and may not be acquired by occupation.

CHECKPOINT
Name the three most common means of acquiring property.

HOW IS OWNERSHIP OF PROPERTY HELD?

WHAT'S YOUR VERDICT?

Beth and Maureen inherited a 12-acre tract of land from their parents. Beth moved onto the property, and Maureen stayed in her former home. Beth decided Maureen could have the back six acres and she would keep the front six acres.

Can Beth exclude Maureen from part of the tract of land they co-own?

There are two basic ways to own property—in severalty or by co-ownership. In either case, ownership rights are not absolute but limited as discussed below.

OWNERSHIP IN SEVERALTY
Ownership in **severalty** exists when one person owns all of the property involved. This is the most common form of ownership for personal property.

CO-OWNERSHIP
Co-ownership exists when two or more persons have ownership rights in the same property. Co-ownership may take one of several forms: joint tenancy, tenancy in common, tenancy by the entireties, or community property.

All forms of co-ownership have two attributes in common. The first is that all co-owners have equal rights of possession. Equal rights of possession means that no co-owner can exclude any other co-owner from any physical portion of the property. This is the most basic attribute of co-ownership.

The second attribute common to co-ownership is the right of partition. The **right of partition** allows any co-owner to legally compel the division of the property among the co-owners. Sometimes the partition is physical, as when a co-owned farm is divided into two parcels. Usually partition is financial. For example, a co-owned airplane could be sold and the proceeds of sale divided pro rata among the co-owners.

In *What's Your Verdict?* Beth had no right to exclude Maureen from the front six acres of their tract. They could, however, agree on a division, or ask a court to divide the property.

JOINT TENANCY Joint tenancy is the equal co-ownership of the same property with the *right of survivorship*. Each joint tenant must always have an equal ownership interest, for example 50/50 with two owners or 25 percent for each of four owners. The **right of survivorship** means that if one of the joint owners dies, the deceased co-owner's interest is divided equally among the remaining joint tenants. If the right of survivorship conflicts with provisions of a will, the property passes via the right of survivorship, not the will.

Because the interest in a joint tenancy passes automatically on death, joint tenants often use this form of co-ownership to leave property to the other joint tenant(s). In this way, they do not have to incur the costs and delays of probate.

A joint tenant's interest may be transferred while the joint tenant is alive. However, the transfer would end the joint tenancy. The previous owners and the new co-owner would hold the property as tenants in common.

TENANCY IN COMMON In **tenancy in common** the shares may be unequal and there is no right of survivorship. Upon the death of any tenant in common, that person's interest passes to the heirs (relatives entitled to inherit) or to the beneficiaries designated in the will, if there is one. The heirs or beneficiaries then become tenants in common with the other owners. Any number of co-owners may be tenants in common of a particular piece of property. Tenants in common also may transfer their interest at any time without the other owners' consent.

TENANCY BY THE ENTIRETIES In some states, tenancy by the entireties is a form of co-ownership between husband and wife. A tenancy by the entireties can only be entered into by married couples, carries the right of survivorship, and one tenant cannot sell or mortgage the subject property without the spouse's consent. As a consequence, the claims of one spouse's creditors cannot be exercised against property held jointly in this form unless the other spouse consents. As in a joint tenancy, the interests must be equal.

A divorce or separation usually transforms a tenancy by the entirety into a tenancy in common. This exposes the property previously held in tenancy by the entireties to the claims of the creditors of the individual spouses. Both joint tenancy and tenancy by the entirety must be created with special language so the nature of the right of survivorship is communicated adequately.

COMMUNITY PROPERTY In some states, all property acquired by husband and wife during their marriage is presumed to be community property. With **community property**, each spouse owns a one-half interest in such property. Generally, while the spouses are alive, both must consent to disposal of community property. In some states, there is a right of survivorship. In other community property states, the spouse who dies may dispose of his or her half through a will.

Property owned by either spouse at the time of marriage or received as a gift or inheritance during the marriage is separate property. Such property becomes community property only if the owner formally or informally treats it as community property and mixes it with other community assets.

LEGAL RESEARCH

Research to determine whether your state is a community property state or a non-community property state. Compare the differences in the procedures for transferring the ownership of a home in a community property state and a non-community property state in the event of a sale, a divorce, or the death of an owner.

LIMITATIONS ON OWNERSHIP

Ownership rights are not absolute. An owner of property is not permitted to use that property in an unreasonable or unlawful manner that injures another. The government may adopt laws to protect the public health, safety, morals, and general welfare. All such laws limit the owner's ownership and freedom of use.

Thus, a city may require that buildings be maintained at a certain level of livability. Cities or counties also may enact laws that prohibit the keeping of livestock or other animals in certain sections. Governments may regulate the purity of food and drugs sold to the public. Governments even may destroy private property, such as shipments of canned fish that are infected with deadly botulism.

Some local governments have laws that would prevent a property owner from keeping items such as this on the property. What is your opinion of such laws?

© GETTY IMAGES/PHOTODISC

CHECKPOINT

What are the two basic ways to hold property?

TYPES OF CO-OWNERSHIP

Type of Co-ownership	May any number co-own?	Must interests be equal?	Is consent of co-owners required for sale?	Is there a right of survivorship?	Must co-owners be married?	Can a will replace survivorship?
Tenancy in common	Yes	No	No	No	No	N/A
Joint tenancy	Yes	Yes	No	Yes	No	No
Tenancy by the entireties	No, just 2	Yes	Yes	Yes	Yes	No
Community property	No, just 2	Yes	Yes	Yes*	Yes	In some states

*In some states a deceased spouse's one-half interest in community property passes automatically to the surviving spouse. In other states it can pass via a will to someone other than the surviving spouse; however, if there is no will, it then passes to the surviving spouse.

Assessment

THINK ABOUT LEGAL CONCEPTS

1. The donee must accept the gift for it to be legally complete. **True or False?**

2. The right of an owner of property to a significant increase in that property is _ ?_ .

3. A gift of an engagement ring would typically be a (a) gift *causa vivos*, (b) gift *causa mortis* (c) gift *inter vivos* (d) none of the above.

4. Who has the right to possession of lost property when the true owner cannot be found? (a) the owner of the place where the property is found (b) the finder

5. If you were sailing off the coast of California and left a fishing line streaming behind the boat for three hours, and then you hooked a tuna and reeled it in, under which legal process would you become the owner of the fish? (a) accession (b) gift (c) occupancy (d) intestacy

6. When there is only one owner of property, that person is said to own it in _ ?_.

7. Which form(s) of co-ownership have the right of survivorship? (a) tenancy in common (b) joint tenancy (c) tenancy by the entireties (d) b and c

8. The right of survivorship allows property to pass on an owner's death to co-owners without a will. **True or False?**

9. Which form(s) of co-ownership require that the co-owners be married? (a) tenancy in common (b) joint tenancy (c) tenancy by the entireties (d) b and c

THINK CRITICALLY ABOUT EVIDENCE

Study the situation, answer the questions, and then prepare arguments to support your answers.

10. While on a ski trip in Vermont, you (a) find a $50 bill in a parking lot, (b) pick up a worn pair of ski boots that someone has discarded, and (c) shoot two rabbits you plan to eat for dinner. What property rights have you acquired in each of these goods. Name the method by which you have done so.

11. Yvette gave her nephew, Jake, 100 shares of stock in Gold Stake Oil Co. for his sixteenth birthday. She handed the shares, worth about $2,000, to Jake right after Jake successfully blew out all his candles. Two days later, Gold Stake discovered a large oil field. The value of the stock increased 100 times to $200,000. As a result, Yvette demanded the return of the shares. Must Jake return the stock?

12. Dani worked as a server at Shift's Place, a restaurant and bar. Patrons frequently left things in the bar or cloakroom. Dani was responsible for closing Shift's. Closing required her to clean all the rooms and tables and lock the windows and doors before leaving. In closing, she discovered a full length fur coat in the cloakroom and one diamond earring under a bar stool. The fur coat had a label sewn into it with the name, address, and phone number of Tonya. Who is entitled to possession of the fur coat? The earring? Dani, Shift's, or Tonya?

PREVENT LEGAL DIFFICULTIES

Manage and use property wisely . . .

1. Do not misuse your property in a way that injures others.

2. Use public property with care. Vandalism, destruction, and theft deprive innocent persons of the benefits of use and also cause higher taxes.

3. Do not infringe upon the copyright, trademark, or patent of another.

4. If you become a co-owner, be sure to take title appropriately. Use tenancy in common with strangers, associates, and friends. Use joint tenancy with a spouse or other person whom you want to have full ownership by right of survivorship when you die.

5. In community property states, keep separate property separate with clear records if you do not want it to become community property.

CONCEPTS IN BRIEF

15-1 Types of Property

1. Property is a group of rights or interests in tangible and intangible things recognized by society and protected by law.

2. Real property is land, including surface and subsurface water and minerals, the airspace above, buildings, and fixtures.

3. Personal property is any intangible or movable tangible property.

4. Intangible personal property includes copyrights, patents, service marks, trademarks, and trade secrets.

15-2 How Property is Acquired and Held

5. Rights in personal property may be acquired by contract, gift, inheritance, accession, intellectual labor, finding, or occupancy.

6. Rights in real property may be acquired by contract, gift, inheritance, adverse possession, dedication, and eminent domain.

7. The true owner of property is entitled to it over anyone who finds it. However, if the owner is not known, a finder is entitled to possession of lost property.

8. The owner of the property on which mislaid property is found is entitled to temporary possession.

9. Ownership by one person is ownership in severalty.

10. Co-ownership may take the form of joint tenancy or tenancy in common. In some states, husband and wife hold property by tenancy by the entireties. In other states, property acquired during marriage is community property.

YOUR LEGAL VOCABULARY

Match each statement with the term that it best defines. Some terms may not be used.

1. An item that is intentionally placed somewhere but then forgotten
2. Co-ownership of property without the right of survivorship
3. Ownership of property by one person alone
4. Right of an owner of property to an increase in the property
5. Exclusive, monopolistic right to make, use, and sell a novel, nonobvious, useful product or process
6. Means of acquiring title by taking possession of personal property that belongs to no one else
7. Exclusive right to produce, sell, copy or publish a creative work
8. Land, buildings, and fixtures
9. Co-ownership of property with the right of survivorship available to persons who are not husband and wife
10. Very limited use of copyrighted material allowed in certain circumstances
11. Unique word, mark, or symbol that identifies a service of a particular company or person
12. A thing subject to ownership and the related legal rights
13. Unique word, mark, or symbol that identifies a product
14. Legal ability of a co-owner to require the physical or financial division of the property among the co-owners

a. accession
b. community property
c. constructive delivery
d. co-ownership
e. copyright
f. fair use
g. infringement
h. intellectual property
i. joint tenancy
j. lost property
k. mislaid property
l. occupancy
m. patent
n. personal property
o. property
p. real property
q. right of partition
r. right of survivorship
s. service mark
t. severalty
i. tenancy by the entireties
v. tenancy in common
w. trademark
x. trade secret

REVIEW LEGAL CONCEPTS

15. Identify items of property you can see in or from your classroom and classify them as real or personal.

16. Write a paragraph about how you would protect an original song you wrote.

17. Explain how the patent office distinguishes patentable and non-patentable inventions.

18. Describe the right of survivorship in joint tenancy.

19. List the various means of acquiring ownership of personal property. Give examples of how you have acquired or might acquire property in each case.

20. Identify and distinguish between the various forms of co-ownership of real property.

WRITE ABOUT LEGAL CONCEPTS

21. Write a paragraph describing tenancy in common.

22. Write a paragraph describing joint tenancy.

23. Write a paragraph describing tenancy by the entireties.

24. **HOT DEBATE** Through court action, relatives now seek to stop Neerow from using his money and goods so wastefully. Should they be allowed to do so?

MAKE ACADEMIC CONNECTIONS

25. **ARCHITECTURE** Research how various structures are attached to the ground so as to be able to determine when they actually become real property. Compare high-rise buildings, houses, mobile homes, yard buildings, fences, and various ground coverings.

THINK CRITICALLY ABOUT EVIDENCE

Study the situation, answer the questions, and then prepare arguments to support your answers.

26. Your mother operates a small lumber business. She owns a tract of land with a stand of trees on it. She cuts down the trees, saws them into construction lumber, and sells the wood to builders. She also is building a house as a business venture. The house is about one-third finished, and one-half of the framing for the walls is completed. Your mother is concerned about her insurance coverage because it covers only personal property. Which parts of her property are real property and which are personal property?

27. Jeff's school has a computer laboratory. Jeff also has a computer at home and decides to copy the school's word processing program for his personal use. The program is copyrighted by its developer. Is it legal for Jeff to make a copy for himself? Would it be ethical for Jeff to make a copy if he first obtains permission from the school's principal?

28. Michael carves and fashions furniture out of cherry wood. One day while walking on what he thought was a part of his forested acreage south of the city, he saw and then cut down a beautiful cherry tree. Later, his neighbor had a survey done of their communal property line and discovered that the cherry tree, which Michael had since fashioned into a magnificent cherry cabinet and sold for $10,000, actually was on his land. She sued Michael. Will the neighbor recover the value of the felled tree (approximately $750) or the value of the cherry cabinet?

29. Kurt and his best friend bought a motorcycle when they were 17 years old. Because they were such good friends they decided to co-own the bike as joint tenants. Five years later, Kurt married. He wrote a will which stated that upon his death all of his personal property should go to his wife. While driving to work one day he crossed some railroad tracks and was hit by a train. Kurt's car was crushed, and he was killed. Who owns Kurt's interest in the bike?

30. You combine your savings with five friends to buy a large sailboat. What form of ownership makes the most sense for your group?

31. Foxx, Flynn, and Fish had equal shares as tenants in common in a drag racer. Foxx wants to get out of the arrangement. She proposes that she keep the engine as her share of the commonly owned racer. Is she entitled to it?

32. Joseph's aunt sent him $5,000 as a gift. Later, she sent a letter stating that upon her death the money was to be distributed among Joseph and his brothers and sisters. After the aunt died, Joseph kept the money and was sued. Joseph defended himself by claiming that a valid gift of the money occurred before the letter was sent, so the letter is of no legal significance. Is Joseph correct? (*In re Gordon's Will,* 27 N.W.2d 900, Iowa)

33. Betty Dolitsky was in a booth of the safe deposit room of the Dollar Savings Bank when she discovered a $100 bill in an advertising folder that the bank had placed in the booth. She turned the money over to the bank. A year later after the money had not been claimed by its true owner, Betty asked for it. The bank refused. Betty sued. Who prevails? (*Dolitsky v. Dollar Savings Bank,* 119 N.Y.S.2d 65)

34. Hamilton and Johnson were tenants in common of a parcel of land. Hamilton wanted to end the relationship and brought suit for partition of the property. A forced sale of the property would be inconvenient for Johnson and would cause him some loss. Must the court, nevertheless, divide the property? (*Hamilton v. Johnson,* 137 Wash. 92, 241 P. 672)

35. Alejo Lopez was a married man. Without divorcing, he married a second time. He and his second wife, Helen, purchased property and tried to take title as tenants by the entireties. Later Alejo divorced his first wife and then remarried Helen. When he died, a question arose as to whether the property was owned in tenancy by the entireties. Is it? (*Lopez v. Lopez,* 243 A.2d 588, Md.)

36. Bernice Paset went into the Old Orchard Bank to gain access to her safe deposit box. Once inside the vault, she went into an examining booth, which contained a small table and a chair. The chair was partially under the table. When Bernice pulled the chair out she discovered $6,325 in cash on the seat of the chair. Is this property abandoned, lost, or mislaid? Who, between Bernice and the bank, is entitled to possession of the property? (*Paset v. Old Orchard Bank,* 378 N.E.2d 1264)

37. On his wife's birthday, Leopold Cohn wrote, in the presence of his entire family, the following:

    West End, N.J., Sept. 20, 1911

    I give this day to my wife, Sara K. Cohn, as a present for her (46) forty-sixth birthday (500) five hundred shares of American Sumatra Tobacco Company common stock.

    Leopold Cohn

    That writing was immediately delivered to his wife. Six days later, Leopold died. At that time, Leopold owned 7,213 shares but the stock was in the name of and in the possession of his firm, A Cohn & Co., in which he was a partner. Is this a valid gift? (*Matter of Cohn,* 176 N.Y.S. 225)

38. E. I. DuPont de Nemours & Co. (DuPont) developed a new process for production of methanol. Although it had not patented the process, it had taken steps to keep the process secret. In order to implement the discovery, DuPont began construction of a refinery. During the construction process an aircraft was observed circling low above the construction site. When DuPont traced the aircraft by its numbers, they discovered that the occupants were photographers who had taken aerial pictures of the plant for an undisclosed client. DuPont believed the photographs might communicate the nature of its trade secret. Accordingly, it sued the photographers to obtain the identity of their client. DuPont then planned to sue the client for misappropriation of a trade secret. Would DuPont prevail in such a suit against the client? (*DuPont v. Christopher,* 621 F.2d 1012)

39. Roberts had an above-ground swimming pool installed on his land. It was not permanently attached to the realty and could be easily disassembled and moved to another location. Then Roberts received a real estate tax assessment bill with an increased assessed value because of the pool. Roberts sued for a deduction, claiming that the pool was personal property. Will he prevail? (*Roberts v. Assessment Board of Review of the Town of New Windsor,* 84 Misc. 2d 1017, N.Y.)

CASE FOR LEGAL THINKING

MARCUS v. ROWLEY
695 F2D 1171

FACTS This is an appeal from a suit for copyright infringement. The plaintiff is a public school teacher who owns a registered copyright to a booklet on cake decorating. The defendant, also a public school teacher, incorporated a substantial portion of the copyrighted work into a booklet which she prepared for use in her classes.

Plaintiff, Eloise Toby Marcus was employed by San Diego Unified School District ("District") as a teacher of home economics. Plaintiff wrote a booklet entitled "Cake Decorating Made Easy." Plaintiff's booklet consisted of 35 pages of which 29 were her original creation. Plaintiff properly registered the copyright for "Cake Decorating Made Easy," and 125 copies of the booklet were published.

Defendant, Shirley Rowley ("Rowley"), teaches food service classes in the District. She enrolled in one of plaintiff's cake decorating classes and purchased a copy of plaintiff's book. During the following summer, Rowley prepared a booklet entitled "Cake Decorating Learning Activity Package (LAP)" for use in her food service classes.

Rowley admits copying 11 of the 24 pages in her LAP from plaintiff's booklet. Rowley did not give plaintiff credit for the 11 pages she copied, nor did she acknowledge plaintiff as the copyright owner with respect to the pages. The lower court entered an order in favor of the defendant.

REASONING In determining whether the use made of a work in any particular case is a fair use, the factors to be considered shall include:

© GETTY IMAGES/PHOTODISC

1. the purpose and character of the use, including whether such use is of a commercial nature or is for non-profit educational purposes
2. the nature of the copyrighted work
3. the amount and substantiality of the portion used in relation to the copyrighted work as a whole
4. the effect of the use upon the potential market for or value of the copyrighted work.

The facts that Rowley used the LAP for a nonprofit educational purpose and the LAP was distributed to students at no charge were not disputed.

These facts necessarily weigh in Rowley's favor. Nevertheless, a finding of a nonprofit educational purpose does not automatically compel a finding of fair use.

[Another] factor to be considered is the amount and substantiality of the portion used in relation to the copyrighted work as a whole. In this case, almost 50 percent of defendant's LAP was a verbatim copy of plaintiff's booklet and that 50 percent contained virtually all of the substance of defendant's book. This case presents a clear example of both substantial quantitative and qualitative copying.

[Also] to be considered with respect to the fair use defense is the effect which the allegedly infringing use had on the potential market for or value of the copyrighted work. Under these circumstances . . . the fact that plaintiff suffered no pecuniary damage as a result of Rowley's copying supports a finding of fair use.

CONCLUSION The order of the lower court is reversed. Summary judgment is entered for the plaintiff.

PRACTICE JUDGING

1. If only a page had been copied, would this be fair use?

2. If Rowley had given Marcus credit, would this be fair use?

3. If the 11 pages had been copied and credit given, but the plaintiff suffered financial injury, would this judge have concluded that the usage was fair?

Bailments

16-1 Bailments

16-2 Bailor and Bailee Duties

HOT DEBATE

© GETTY IMAGES/PHOTODISC

The wind picked up as Abrahms turned into the discount store parking lot, as she had many times before. A big storm was approaching, and there were few cars in the huge lot surrounding the store. She pulled into a parking space near the front door of the store and locked her new car. Abrahms had to dodge wind-blown shopping carts that were sailing across the parking lot. She watched a cart hit a nearby car leaving dent marks in it. Forty-five minutes later, Abrahms pushed her full shopping cart out of the store to find the rain had stopped, but the wind was still howling. She put her purchases in the trunk of her car. Then, wanting to avoid stepping in a water puddle, she left her cart at the rear of her car rather than putting it in the cart corral some distance off. As she walked towards the driver's door, she saw the pattern of squares where a cart had obviously hit her car. Angrily, she glanced up at the store only to spy in the store window the large sign, yellowed with age: "NOT RESPONSIBLE FOR SHOPPING CART DAMAGE".

Where Do You Stand?

1. Ethically, who do you believe should be responsible for the damage to Abrahms car? Why?

2. Legally, does Abrahms have a claim? Why or why not?

▼ GOALS
■ Discuss the ways in which bailments are created and ended
■ Identify common real-life bailments

HOW ARE BAILMENTS CREATED AND ENDED?

WHAT'S YOUR VERDICT?

Posighdon was vacationing in Key West, Florida. Late one afternoon, she wanted to get a better view of the sunset. She rented a jet ski from Trident Rentals and rode it out beyond the harbor.

What is the legal relationship between Posighdon and Trident?

IN THIS CASE

Ruden was a construction contractor. She leased a scoop loader from Max Power Controls for six months at $2,000 per month to fulfill a subcontract she had been awarded on a new freeway. Unfortunately, three months later, Ruden was killed when her pickup overturned on the way to the construction site. Because the bailment ran for another three months, the bailor could still collect the remaining rental fee of $6,000 against the assets Ruden left behind.

If you lend your pen to a friend, borrow a lawnmower from a neighbor, find a $20 bill, or rent a DVD, you become a party to a legal relationship called a bailment. The transaction is neither a sale nor a gift, because the personal property involved does not change ownership. The only change is one of possession. As defined at law, a **bailment** is the transfer of possession and control of personal property subject to an agreement to return the property or deliver it to a third party. Note that the subject of the bailment can only be personal property. Real property, such as land or buildings, cannot be bailed. Real property is leased under different rules of law which will be discussed in Chapter 17.

The **bailor** is the party who gives up possession of the property. The **bailee** is the party who accepts possession. In *What's Your Verdict?* a bailment was created between Posighdon and Trident, with Trident being the bailor and Posighdon the bailee. The rental agreement they entered into defined the rights and duties of the parties during the bailment and when and how it would end.

TRANSFER OF POSSESSION AND CONTROL

POSSESSION Usually property is bailed by the person who has title to the goods, but property may be bailed by any person in possession. This includes the owner's agent or employee, a finder, or even a thief.

There are two ways to transfer possession and control of goods. In **actual bailments**, bailees

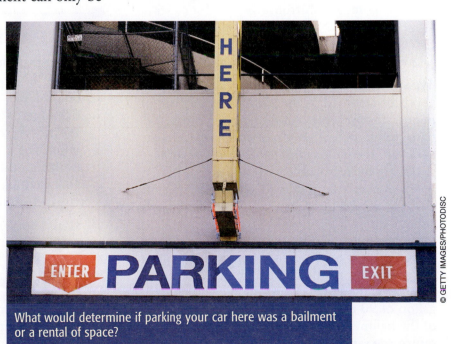

What would determine if parking your car here was a bailment or a rental of space?

receive and accept the goods themselves. When you rent a car, get behind the steering wheel, and drive off, you receive and accept the car in bailment.

Constructive bailments occur when the bailee receives and accepts a symbol of the personal property. If you asked to borrow your neighbor's truck, and received and accepted the keys, you would be entering into a constructive bailment for the truck.

CONTROL In order for a bailment to arise, both possession and control of the goods must shift from the bailor to the bailee. Disputes often arise over cars left in parking lots. Suppose a car owner drives onto a lot, parks the car, but keeps the key. The owner can later drive the car away without permission of an attendant. The owner gave up possession but not control. In this case there is no bailment. There is a bailment, however, if an attendant takes possession of the car and gives the owner a claim check that must be turned in to get the car back. In this situation both possession and control are given to the bailee.

It is possible for a person to have temporary control of another's personal property yet not have a bailment. This occurs with **custody**. A person hired to guard the paintings in an art museum has custody of the art but is not a bailee. The owners of the art do not give complete control of the art to the guard. They authorize the guard to watch over the goods, but the owners retain control.

DISPOSITION OF THE GOODS

Typically, both bailor and bailee agree that the goods be returned to the bailor. In some bailments, however, the bailor identifies another party to whom the goods must be delivered. In addition, the bailee must return the identical goods absent reasonable wear and tear. The goods also may be modified somewhat, as a result of agreed-upon use, repairs, processing, or aging.

Finally, some goods are fungible. *Fungible* means there is no difference between one unit of the goods and another. A gallon of 90-octane gasoline is the same as, or fungible with, another gallon of 90-octane gasoline. When the subject of the bailment is fungible, the bailee need only return the same unit of the goods.

TERMINATION OF THE BAILMENT

The bailment ends when the time agreed upon by the parties has elapsed, when the agreed purpose has been achieved, or when the parties mutually agree to end it. If no termination time is stated, either party may end the bailment. Thus, the bailor might ask for return of the property. Or the bailee may no longer need the property and return it. If the bailed property is destroyed or damaged so badly that it is not fit for the intended purpose, the bailment ends.

Death, insanity, or bankruptcy of one party can end the relation when the bailee's duties cannot be performed by another, or the bailment is one that may be ended at will. Normally, however, if there is a contractual bailment for a fixed period, death or incapacity does not end the relation. The rights and duties of the deceased are transferred to the personal representative of the estate.

CHECKPOINT
What are the three ways in which bailments are ended?

COMMON EXAMPLES OF BAILMENTS

WHAT'S YOUR VERDICT?

Werner owned a retail sporting goods store. A supplier, Irresistible Lures, offered Werner a counter card that displayed a new type of fishing lure. Werner agreed to display the card when the sales agent said, "You pay nothing and return any lures not sold. Just deduct 50 percent of each sale for yourself and send the balance to us."

Was Werner a bailee?

The most common examples of bailments include bailments for transport, hire, services, and sale.

BAILMENTS FOR TRANSPORT

A **common carrier** is an enterprise that agrees, for a fee, to transport goods for anyone who applies, provided the goods are lawful and fit for shipment. Although passengers may be transported by common carriers, only their baggage is governed by bailment law.

A common carrier has the right to do the following:

1. Enforce reasonable rules and regulations for the conduct of its business (for example, it may enforce rules stating how goods must be packed)

2. Charge an amount negotiated with the bailor or, if the carrier is regulated by the government, charge the scheduled rate

3. Charge **demurrage**, that is, a fee for use of the transportation vehicle when it is not loaded or unloaded at the agreed time

4. Enforce a **carrier's lien**, that is, retain the goods until charges for transportation and incidental services are paid.

BAILMENTS FOR HIRE

A bailment for hire arises when the bailor, for a fee, provides personal property (such as a car, truck, tool, machine, or other equipment) for use by the bailee. Under the common law the bailee is required to act with ordinary care. However, most rental contracts modify the duty of care making the bailee strictly liable for property damage.

Typically the rental companies ask the bailee to initial those parts of the contract which modify the duty of care. The bailee must abide by the contract, using the property only for the stated purposes and returning it at the agreed time.

BAILMENTS FOR SERVICES

When a person delivers goods to be serviced, repaired, or made into a finished article, a bailment for services results. For example, the bailor may deliver wool cloth to a tailor to have a suit made. Or a bailor may deliver clothes to a dry cleaner to be laundered or a watch to a jeweler to be repaired.

If the goods are damaged or destroyed, but the bailee has exercised ordinary care in their protection, the loss falls on the bailor who owns them.

Moreover, the bailor must pay for any work done by the bailee before the accident. Of course, the bailee remains liable for harm to the goods resulting from the bailee's negligence.

BAILMENTS FOR SALE

Goods may be sent on consignment by a manufacturer to a retailer. With **consignment**, ownership remains with the manufacturer or wholesaler (the bailor) until the goods are sold. Retailers who display and sell consigned goods (like Werner in *What's Your Verdict?*) are bailees.

A bailment also is created when a merchant sends goods "on approval" to a prospective buyer. In a sale on approval the prospective buyer may use the goods to decide whether to buy them. During this time the prospective buyer is a bailee of the goods.

Ownership shifts if the bailee agrees to buy the goods. At that point the bailment ends. If the bailee rejects the goods, they must be returned. This arrangement is common in merchandising books, cassettes, and compact disks.

CHECKPOINT

Name four common examples of bailments.

NETBookmark

Access lawxtra.swlearning.com and click on the link for Chapter 16. Read the article, which is an advertisement for a book about starting an eBay consignment business. Explain the concept behind starting such a business. Which party is the bailee and which is the bailor in such a business? What do you think of the eBay consignment business owner's chance for success in this business? Explain your answer.

lawxtra.swlearning.com

THINK ABOUT LEGAL CONCEPTS

1. If you rent a locker at an airport, put your luggage in it, and keep the key to the locker, a bailment has been created. **True or False?**

2. If a farmer stores a particular grade of potatoes in a warehouse, the warehouse must return the same potatoes to the farmer. **True or False?**

3. The fees a common carrier receives for use of its vehicle in the event that it is not loaded or unloaded at the agreed time is called (a) incidental charges (b) a carrier's lien (c) demurrage.

4. The situation that occurs when the bailee receives and accepts a symbol of the property is called (a) constructive bailment (b) actual bailment.

5. In a bailment relationship, the party who accepts possession and control of the property is the (a) bailor (b) bailee.

6. A publisher lent one of its authors a computer to use in producing her manuscript. Unfortunately, she suffered a severe personal loss several months into the job and was declared insane. Did the bailment end at that point? **Yes or No?**

7. In a consignment, the retailer is a bailee. **True or False?**

8. A common carrier does not have the right to retain possession of the goods until the charges for transportation and accompanying services are paid. **True or False?**

THINK CRITICALLY ABOUT EVIDENCE

Study the situation, answer the questions, and then prepare arguments to support your answers.

9. Lorant found a watch along the sidewalk. The watch was not accurate, but Lorant thought it was worth fixing. She took the watch to a jeweler's shop, where she left it for repairs. Were bailments created? If so, who were the parties?

10. Hoping to collect a reward, Moriarity stole a rare breed of dog from the fenced yard of a wealthy lady. He placed the dog in a kennel in another town. Were any bailments created?

11. Vernay found an old portrait of her grandparents that had been damaged from moisture and abrasion. She took the portrait to Stockhelm so that he could restore it. Stockhelm thought the process would take him several months, but before finishing the work, he was killed in an accident. What relationship was created between Vernay and Stockhelm? What effect, if any, did Stockhelm's untimely death have on this relationship?

12. Hanson bought and contracted to have delivered a large industrial stamping machine weighing 11,000 pounds. When a common carrier truck arrived with the machine, it took Hanson a week to locate a crane that could lift the stamping machine off the truck. Is he liable for the rental value of the truck while it waited to be unloaded?

13. Wingate took her chair to a local shop, Just Like New, to be reupholstered. Just Like New finished the work on May 22. It notified Wingate that the chair was ready and placed the reupholstered chair in a locked storage room at the rear of its building. Wingate planned to pick up the chair May 23, but on the night of May 22, someone broke into the storage room and stole some items, including Wingate's chair. What relationship existed between Wingate and Just Like New? Who bears responsibility for the loss? Must Wingate pay for the work already performed by Just Like New?

14. NewMark Co. sent Breggler a postal meter with the understanding that Breggler could try it out for 60 days. If at the end of the 60 days Breggler wanted to keep the postal meter, she was to pay for it. If she was dissatisfied or just decided she did not want it, she was to return it to NewMark before the end of the 60-day period. What relationship was created between NewMark and Breggler during the 60-day period? Who owned the postal meter during the 60-day period?

Bailor and Bailee Duties

DUTIES OWED BY THE BAILEE IN A BAILMENT

WHAT'S YOUR VERDICT?

After taking a sailing class at her university, Patricia borrowed her friend Amy's small sailboat for the afternoon. While out on Lake Stockton with it, a strong wind came up unexpectedly and ripped the sail in two.

What type of bailment have Patricia and Amy created? Is Patricia liable for the damage to the sail?

Both the bailor and the bailee owe various duties at law in order to ensure the success of the bailment. However, most legal issues spring from the care or lack thereof that the bailee gives to the bailed property. When the property is damaged, whether or not the bailee is liable is determined by the type of bailment involved and the degree of care owed as a consequence. In general, there are three levels of care: extraordinary, ordinary, and minimal. In a trial, the burden of showing that the required level of care has been met rests with the bailee.

DUTY TO CARE FOR THE PROPERTY

When goods are bailed with common carriers and hotels an **extraordinary bailment** arises. The duty of care required as a result is extraordinary. **Extraordinary care** generally means the bailee will be strictly liable for any damage, loss, or injury to the goods. Thus a common carrier is strictly liable for injury to the bailed goods. The only time such a bailee is not liable is when the loss is caused by an act of war, unforeseeable acts of God, or acts of police.

When only one of the parties benefits from the bailment, a **gratuitous bailment** arises. When the party benefited is the bailee, there is a gratuitous bailment for the sole benefit of the bailee. This applies if you lend your calculator to

a classmate without charge. The bailee's duty of care for this type of bailment is extraordinary care.

In *What's Your Verdict?* Patricia is a gratuitous bailee. The bailment is for her sole benefit, so she must exercise extraordinary care. She is liable for the damage to the boat. High winds are not unforeseeable acts of God. Damage caused by a tornado would have been considered an act of God. In that case, Patricia would not have been liable.

Ordinary care means that the bailee will be liable if negligent in some way. A **mutual-benefit bailment**, in which consideration is given and received by both bailor and bailee, invokes the duty of ordinary care. Assume that you left your car at a repair shop and paid $27.99 for an oil change. You would receive the benefit of the oil change, and the repair shop would receive the benefit of the $27.99. Mutual-benefit bailments result from contracts, whereas gratuitous bailments do not because there is no exchange of consideration.

Minimal care is called for with **involuntary bailments**, which arise without the consent of the bailee. **Minimal care** generally means that the bailee must not ignore, waste, or destroy the bailed property. This can happen, for example, when your neighbor's trash cans blow onto your property. For valuable property, the bailee must make a minimal effort to identify the owner.

Which of the six major requirements of contracts explains the relationship between mutual-benefit bailments and contracts? Use the oil-change example in your answer. (Hint: See Lesson 6-1.)

© GETTY IMAGES/PHOTODISC

In some states courts use the standard of reasonable care rather than the three levels of care. Courts in those states try to determine what degree of care a reasonable person would exercise under the same circumstances. Courts look at such factors as type of goods, nature of the bailment, available facilities, and the bailee's knowledge and skills.

● ●

Research the liability ceilings in your state for hotels, warehouses, common carriers, repair facilities and other bailees. Are the ceilings reasonable? Would the average bailor know of or consider them in the bailment bargain? Do the limits impede or further the businesses involved?

Involuntary bailments also arise when mail is delivered to the wrong addressee.

A bailment for the sole benefit of a bailor also calls for minimal care. This type of bailment would arise if you agree to care for a neighbor's house plants without charge while the neighbor is on vacation. Your duty of care in this case would be minimal.

MODIFICATION OF THE LEVEL OF CARE

There are three common ways to modify the nature of the bailee's duty of care: (1) by legislation, (2) by contract, and (3) by disclaimer.

MODIFICATION BY LEGISLATION An industry may seek to avoid the duty of care established by the common law by lobbying for legislation with a state legislature or regulatory body.

For example, as common carriers, airlines would owe the duty of extraordinary care for passengers' luggage. However, the industry has persuaded the Federal Aviation Administration to adopt a regulation limiting liability for loss, delay, or damage to baggage to a set amount per passenger on U.S. domestic flights.

Laundries and dry-cleaning establishments often have special legislation limiting their duty of care. On the other hand, legislatures may increase the duty or limit the ability of the industry to modify the duty of care.

MODIFICATION BY CONTRACT When the bailor and bailee negotiate a contract, they usually can modify the duty of care. Suppose a large auto

manufacturer negotiated with a transportation company to deliver cars to local auto dealers. The parties could agree in the contract that this bailment for mutual benefit would create an extraordinary duty of care for the transportation company. Or, they could agree that the duty would be minimal. The bailee cannot, however, be relieved of liability for willful or deliberate injury to the bailed property.

MODIFICATION BY DISCLAIMER Often merchants attempt to modify the duty of care with a disclaimer. A **disclaimer** is a sign, label, or warning reducing the bailee's duty of care. Thus, a garage may have a sign on the wall stating that it is not liable for loss of items left in a car. A restaurant may have a sign indicating that it is not responsible

INTERNATIONAL VIEWPOINT

International Air Carrier Liability

The Warsaw Convention of 1929 governs many aspects of international aviation law. This international agreement was adopted in the United States in 1934. It is the law in more than 120 nations.

The Warsaw Convention determines whether an international air carrier can be held liable for personal injury or death of a passenger. It also determines whether the air carrier is liable for damage to luggage and personal belongings. The Warsaw Convention has been amended several times since 1929.

for loss of coats left on coat racks. A parking lot might have a ticket with small print on it stating that it is not liable for any loss or damage to the car.

Usually disclaimers only become a part of the contract when the bailor is aware of the limitation before the purchase. So a limitation in small print on a claim check or parking ticket is insufficient notice, unless the bailor has read it or was specifically told about the limitation in advance. Courts often find disclaimers to be unenforceable.

DUTY TO RETURN THE GOODS

The bailee's duty to return the property requires the bailee to return the bailed property according to the terms of the bailment agreement. A bailee entitled to payment is granted the right under the law to enforce one of several types of **bailee's liens**. These allow the bailee to retain possession of the goods until paid. If payment is delayed unreasonably, the bailee may sell the property to recover the fee and related costs. Note that, if the bailee gives the property back to the bailor without receiving payment, the bailor loses the right to force the sale of the bailed property to pay the amount due. (See also artisan's lien coverage in Chapter 32.)

A QUESTION OF ETHICS

Haybarn Swings was a popular attraction with groups of city school and church children. The "swings" allowed the kids to swing on ropes and fall into piles of hay. The activities were supervised by employees of the Swings. A disclaimer was presented to the parent of each member of a group upon its arrival at the attraction's location. The parent's signature was required before the child was allowed to enter with his or her group. The disclaimer absolved Haybarn Swings of all liability related to the visit and made the parents liable for the injuries of any Swings employee that occurred while supervising the children. Is the disclaimer ethical? Would it be upheld in court?

CHECKPOINT

Name the three levels of care owed bailed goods.

WHAT DUTIES ARE OWED BY THE BAILOR IN A BAILMENT?

WHAT'S YOUR VERDICT?

Hon Qua Viet rented an RV to take his family from Santa Ana, California, to a reunion in Joplin, Missouri. The RV dealer forgot to mention to Hon that there was a small propane leak in the RV's oven and that it should not be used.

What type of bailment is involved here? Will the dealer be liable if the oven explodes and Hon and his family are injured?

Other than those prescribed by a contract or by statute, a bailor generally has duties relating to the condition of the property bailed. These duties depend upon the type of bailment involved.

MUTUAL-BENEFIT BAILMENTS

In a mutual-benefit bailment, the bailor's main duty is to provide goods fit for the intended purpose. In addition, a bailor in a mutual-benefit bailment who fails to inform the bailee of defects which reasonably could be discovered is liable for any resulting injuries. Thus, the RV dealer in *What's Your Verdict?* would be liable to Hon's family for any injuries resulting from the failure to warn of the defective oven.

A bailee who has been told about or discovers a defect cannot collect damages if injured because of the defect. The bailee is held to have assumed the risk. This could happen, for example, if a bailee drives a rented truck with defective brakes after being told of the dangerous condition.

BAILMENTS FOR THE SOLE BENEFIT OF BAILOR

Suppose your friend goes on vacation and leaves her dog, house plants, and car with you to take care of as a favor to her. These are gratuitous bailments for the sole benefit of the bailor. The standard of care that the bailee has to maintain is minimal.

In a bailment for the sole benefit of the bailor, before transferring possession the bailor should examine the goods for possible defects. Failure to inform the bailee of known or reasonably discoverable defects makes the bailor liable for any possible resulting injury. Unless otherwise agreed, the bailee may not use the bailed items unless the use is necessary to preserve or maintain them.

BAILMENTS FOR THE SOLE BENEFIT OF BAILEE

Friends or relatives often borrow equipment and other personal property from one another with-

What kind of bailment is created when you leave your clothes with a dry cleaner? What level of care does the dry-cleaning establishment owe its customers?

© GETTY IMAGES/PHOTODISC

out charge. These transactions are gratuitous bailments for the sole benefit of the bailee. As such, they require that the bailee take extraordinary care of the bailed goods. The bailee-borrower may use the goods, but only as agreed. Note that the bailor-lender is obligated to inform the bailee of known defects. The bailor who knows of a loose rung in a ladder, yet says nothing, may be liable for any resulting injuries suffered by the bailee.

CHECKPOINT

Name the types of bailments in which a bailor has duties.

16-2 Assessment

Xtra! Study Tools
lawxtra.swlearning.com

THINK ABOUT LEGAL CONCEPTS

1. The level of care a bailee must exercise over the goods is determined by (a) the value of the bailed property (b) whether a bailor is a merchant or not (c) the type of the bailment.

2. When both parties benefit from a bailment, it is a mutual-benefit bailment and the bailee's duty of care is ordinary. **True or False?**

3. When the bailment is only for the sole benefit of the bailor, the duty of care is minimal. **True or False?**

4. The bailee in an extraordinary bailment is strictly liable for loss or damage to the bailed goods. **True or False?**

THINK CRITICALLY ABOUT EVIDENCE

Study the situation, answer the questions, and then prepare arguments to support your answers.

5. During the fall harvest, most of the Roman Beauty apples picked at Scott's Orchard were immediately placed in the Kool-Tech Storage Co. warehouse. Scott paid a monthly fee for the storage, and the contract specified that the apples would be stored at temperatures between 40 and 55 degrees. When Scott removed some of the apples three months later, many had begun to rot because Kool-Tech had failed to keep the building at the proper temperature. Who is liable for this loss?

6. Widdington inherited an old 90-foot navy-patrol boat. She delivered it to Ol' Jon Silver's Shipyard, located near the oceanfront. Widdington contracted with Jon Silver for a conversion of the patrol boat into a houseboat for $130,000. After the work was completed, but before Widdington came to get her boat, a tidal wave destroyed the shop and all the boats in the immediate vicinity. Is Jon Silver liable for the loss of Widdington's boat? Or must Widdington pay the $130,000?

7. Cararro rented a car and, because it wasn't his, treated it harshly. He gunned the engine before engaging it in gear, drag raced, and intentionally burned a cigarette hole in the upholstery. When a friend asked why he did it, he said, "The car isn't mine, so who cares? Besides, it's kind of fun. It makes me feel good, and kind of powerful." Is Cararro acting ethically? Why or why not? Is Cararro liable for the damage? Why or why not?

8. Boyd borrowed a lawn edger from her neighbor Enbanks. The edger's circular blade was defective, but Enbanks did not know this. While Boyd was using the edger, the blade snapped. A piece of metal lodged in Boyd's eye, blinding it. Was Enbanks liable for the injury?

9. J. Eric worked in a dry cleaners. While going through some costumes that had been turned in for cleaning, he found an expensive ring in a pocket. He turned the ring over to the shop owner. Shortly thereafter it disappeared even though the shop owner had been keeping it in a locked drawer in his office. The ring's owner has appeared asking for it. Who is liable, and why?

PREVENT LEGAL DIFFICULTIES

For Bailors . . .

1. Although a bailee may be liable for willful or negligent conduct which damages your goods or injures third parties, it is still wise to carry appropriate property and liability insurance to cover possible losses.

2. Spell out the terms of the bailment contract in writing whenever practicable. Always get a receipt for goods transferred to a bailee.

3. If the bailee is to repair or service the goods, be as precise as possible about prices and work to be done.

4. If you rent a car or other equipment that could be dangerous if in faulty condition, inspect it carefully and correct defects before delivering it to the bailee.

5. If it is not feasible to correct a defect, warn the prospective bailee of the defect so that she or he assumes the risk.

For Bailees . . .

1. Before you take possession of or use bailed goods, be sure you have adequate liability and property insurance coverage. You usually are required to pay if you damage or destroy the bailed property or injure someone with it.

2. If you have performed services on bailed goods, utilize the power of your bailee's lien and do not return them until you have been paid for your services or are satisfied that the bailor's credit is good.

3. When you find and take possession of something of value belonging to another person, you become a constructive bailee. Act reasonably in caring for the property and seeking the true owner.

Chapter 16 Assessment

CONCEPTS IN BRIEF

16-1 Bailments

1. To be a bailment, one party must have possession and control of personal property belonging to another.

2. Every bailment has four characteristics: the subject is tangible personal property; the bailor transfers temporary possession to the bailee; the bailor transfers temporary control to the bailee; the goods must be returned to the bailor or to someone the bailor specifies.

3. A bailment may be terminated by agreement, an act of either party, destruction of the subject matter, or operation of law (such as by death of a party).

4. Common types of bailments are those for transport, for hire, for services, and for sale.

16-2 Bailor and Bailee Duties

5. Bailments created for the benefit of both parties are mutual-benefit bailments. Bailments created for the benefit of only one party are gratuitous bailments. Mutual-benefit bailments arise from contracts because there is an exchange of consideration.

6. In a mutual-benefit bailment, the bailee must exercise ordinary care. In a gratuitous bailment for the sole benefit of the bailee, the bailee must exercise extraordinary care. In a gratuitous bailment for the sole benefit of the bailor, the bailee need exercise only minimal care.

7. In a mutual-benefit bailment, the bailor is liable for damages caused by known or reasonably discoverable defects in the property unless the bailee has been informed of such defects specifically.

8. A bailee may by law have a bailee's lien in the subject property to assist in the collection of repair or storage fees from the bailor if such are due.

YOUR LEGAL VOCABULARY

Match each statement with the term that it best defines. Some terms may not be used.

1. Party who accepts possession and control of another's personal property
2. Duty of care when the bailment is involuntary
3. Bailment in which the bailee receives and accepts a symbol of the personal property rather than the property itself
4. Allows a bailee to hold goods until paid
5. Enterprise that undertakes, for hire, to transport goods or passengers for anyone who applies
6. Fee for delay by party shipping goods in loading or by party receiving goods in unloading
7. Control of another's personal property, under the owner's direction
8. Bailment in which one party receives no benefit
9. Bailment that arises without the consent of the bailee
10. Party who gives up temporary possession and control of personal property
11. Bailment in which the bailee is liable for all damage, loss, or injury, such as a bailment with a hotel or a common carrier
12. Sign, label, or warning reducing the bailee's duty of care

a. **actual bailment**
b. **bailee**
c. **bailee's lien**
d. **bailment**
e. **bailor**
f. **carrier's lien**
g. **common carrier**
h. **consignment**
i. **constructive bailment**
j. **custody**
k. **demurrage**
l. **disclaimer**
m. **extraordinary bailment**
n. **extraordinary care**
o. **gratuitous bailment**
p. **involuntary bailment**
q. **minimal care**
r. **mutual-benefit bailment**
s. **ordinary care**

REVIEW LEGAL CONCEPTS

13. Create a factual scenario where property is mislaid.

14. Create a factual scenario where property is lost.

15. Create a factual scenario where the bailee's duty of care is ordinary care.

16. Create a factual scenario where the bailee's duty of care is extraordinary care.

WRITE ABOUT LEGAL CONCEPTS

17. You are headed for the lake pulling your boat. Suddenly your vehicle starts to veer to the right and you realize that your boat trailer tire on that side is going flat. You pull into a station to fix it. You borrow a tire tool from the station owner to take the tire off. As you do not have a spare, you then ask if you can leave the boat in her lot while you go to a nearby garage to have the tire repaired. She says fine. You lock the trailer hitch so that the boat cannot be towed, and then leave. Write a short paragraph about the bailment transaction(s) involved in this scenario.

18. **HOT DEBATE** As Abrahms pulls away from the store, angry and disgusted, the wind drives the cart she has just left into a little old lady using her walker to get to her car. She falls and breaks her hip. A store clerk, who was pushing the lady's cart, has observed Abrahms leaving the cart where she did and gets her plate number. Write a paragraph about who is ethically and legally responsible for the little old lady's injuries.

MAKE ACADEMIC CONNECTIONS

19. **ARCHAEOLOGY** One of the most valuable bailments in history took place when many of the treasures of King Tut were sent to the United States as an exhibit. Other exhibits of priceless artifacts and paintings regularly tour the country. Research the precautions against damage and theft taken, how the pieces are valued, and the type and provider of insurance associated with one such tour. Report your findings to the class.

THINK CRITICALLY ABOUT EVIDENCE

Study the situation, answer the questions, and then prepare arguments to support your answers.

20. Babbitt rented a paint-spraying outfit from Baron. The equipment was in good working condition, and Babbitt knew how to use it properly. However, when Babbitt was shifting position between two buildings, she carelessly sprayed the neighbor's building and the top of the neighbor's car parked below. The neighbor sued Baron. Is Baron liable?

21. Bortez, a sales representative, had a breakfast appointment with a prospective buyer. They were to meet in the restaurant of the Grand Prix Hotel. Bortez left his brief case, which contained almost $30,000 worth of sample watches, with the clerk in the hotel checkroom. The clerk gave him a receipt that stated in fine print: "Not liable for loss or damage from any cause beyond a maximum of $100." Bortez, in a hurry, stuffed the stub into his pocket without reading it. The clerk left his post briefly to go to the restroom. When he returned, the case was gone. Is the Grand Prix liable? If so, for how much?

22. Burg customized and sold new vans and serviced old ones. Jake and Jayne Slinker were trusted employees who had been carefully hired and trained and had worked for Burg for ten years. Jake did metalworking and woodworking; Jayne did upholstering. One holiday weekend, the Slinkers and an accomplice stole three vans and then disappeared. The first van belonged to Adams, who had brought it in to have the engine tuned. The second van belonged to Yates, a friend who had asked Burg if he could leave the van on the lot with a "For Sale" sign. Burg had agreed and did not charge Yates. The third van was a very valuable vehicle, built by Burg, and sold to Mox. Mox had loaned the van to Burg, free, for display in the latter's exhibit at a Civic Auditorium show scheduled for the following week. What is Burg's liability, if any, to Adams? to Yates? to Mox?

23. Mineo was a member of the state highway patrol working a stretch of I-44 near Springfield, MO. Late one night he stopped a brown westbound sedan for not signalling a turn. In interviewing the driver, Mineo became suspicious due to the driver's inconsistent answers to Mineo's questions. Finally Mineo asked if he

could search the vehicle, and the driver consented. Mineo found $500,000 in small, unmarked bills in the trunk. The driver said that she had answered an ad in a Chicago paper wanting individuals to drive cars to Phoenix, and that the property was not hers. A phone call to the number the driver had in her possession, was answered but the party hung up upon Mineo identifying himself. Thereafter, no responsbile party could be reached to claim ownership of the half-millon. Who should retain the $500,000 until the true owner is found?

ANALYZE REAL CASES

24. Plaintiff Wall drove his car into a self-parking lot at O'Hare Airport in Chicago. He entered through an automatic gate and received a ticket bearing the date and time of arrival. He parked, locked the car, and left with the keys. Normally, when ready to depart, he would walk to his car and, using his keys, would enter the car and drive it to the exit. There an attendant would take the ticket and compute and collect the parking fee. This time his car had been stolen. He sued the defendant, Airport Parking Company of Chicago, for damages. Is the defendant liable? (*Wall v. Airport Parking Company of Chicago*, 244 N.E.2d 190, 41 Ill. 2d 506)

25. Mrs. Carter took her fur coat to Reichlin Furriers to be cleaned and stored. She was given a receipt for the coat. On the front of the receipt an employee had written the number "100." On the back of the receipt, the words, "the . . . amount recoverable for loss or damage to this article shall not exceed . . . the depositor's valuation appearing in this receipt . . ." Also on the front of the receipt was a place for the customer's signature, but Mrs. Carter had not signed it. The coat was lost. Is Reichlin liable for its market value of $450 or only for the $100? (*Carter v. Reichlin Furriers*, 386 A.2d 648)

26. A student enrolled in flight school. While 900 feet above the ground on a practice flight in the school's aircraft, the student discovered that the rudder was stuck. As a result of the stuck rudder, the plane crashed into the ground, and the student was seriously injured. Is the school liable to the student for the injury? (*Aircraft Sales and Service v. Gannt*, 52 A.2d 388)

27. Loden shipped a quantity of perishable cucumbers from Yuma, Arizona, to Los Angeles via the Southern Pacific Company Railroad. However, the carrier failed to deliver the goods within the ordinary and usual time. On January 25, a railroad inspector was sent out to check the track structures. The inspector discovered that heavy rainfall had damaged two bridges. Repairs were started on January 26, and the tracks were joined on January 28. The making of these repairs further delayed the shipment of Loden's cucumbers. When the cucumbers finally arrived in Los Angeles on January 29, they were spoiled. Loden sued the railroad for $10,000 in damages. Which party is liable for the damages? (*Southern Pacific Company v. Loden*, 19 Ariz. App. 460, 508 P.2d 347)

28. Armored Car Service, Inc., had its employees pick up at the Miami Springs Junior High School a locked money bag containing $1,511.25. The money was supposed to be deposited in the proper cafeteria-fund account at a certain bank. However, the bag was mistakenly delivered to the First National Bank of Miami. First National provided a receipt for the bag but made no record of the bag's handling or disposition. Presumably, the bag was stolen. Armored Car Service indemnified the high school and now seeks to recover its loss from First National. (a) What kind of bailment was created by the mistake? (b) Is the First National Bank of Miami liable as bailee? (*Armored Car Service, Inc. v. First National Bank of Miami*, 114 So. 2d 431)

29. A woman parked in a parking lot. An attendant asked her to leave her keys in the car. The car was stolen and was later recovered, but it had been damaged. Must the parking lot company be held liable? (*Agricultural Insurance Co. v. Constantine*, 58 N.E.2d 658, Ohio)

30. Allen left his car with the defendant's parking lot. Allen's golf clubs were in the trunk of the car but Allen did not tell defendant of their presence. The car was stolen and later recovered but the golf clubs were missing. Is the defendant liable for the golf clubs? (*Allen v. Houserman*, 250 A.2d 389, Del.)

31. Singer owned air conditioning units. He stored them in Stoda's warehouses. A fire destroyed the air conditioners. Singer sued and showed that Stoda knew the sprinkler system in the warehouse did not operate, the fire alarm would not automatically activate, and no security guards were present. Is Stoda liable? (*Singer Company v. Stoda Corporation*, 436 N.Y.S.2d 508, N.Y.)

FACTS Mark Teller was a partner with Norman Applebaum in Numismatic Enterprises. The business bought and sold rare coins. The partners traveled to Indianapolis, Indiana, for a convention of coin dealers. They brought a large black briefcase with a double lock on it containing rare coins worth more than $300,000.

When they arrived at the Hyatt Regency Hotel, an employee named Ms. Atkinson took them to the safe deposit room and assigned them a box. Atkinson gave them one of the two keys required to open the box. When this occurred, Teller told Atkinson that he was with the coin show. Then Teller signed a Safe Deposit Record form and Atkinson signed as a witness.

Later, when Teller opened the safe deposit box to retrieve the coins, the box was empty. The partners sued, claiming that Hyatt had breached its duty as a bailee.

REASONING The Indiana statute provides: "A hotel, apartment hotel, or inn, or the proprietor or manager thereof, shall not be liable for the loss of or damage to any merchandise samples or merchandise for sale, whether such loss or damage is occasioned by the negligence of such proprietor or manager or his agents or otherwise, unless the guest or other owner shall have given prior written notice of having brought such merchandise into the hotel and of the value thereof, the receipt of such notice shall have been acknowledged in writing by the proprietor, manager or other agent and in no event shall liability exceed the sum of four hundred dollars ($400.00) unless the manager or proprietor of such hotel, apartment hotel or inn shall have contracted in writing to assume a greater liability."

In the present case, there does not appear to be any dispute that the plaintiffs failed to comply with the statute's requirements. Although it might be argued that the hotel had sufficient notice under the statute as a result of its employee's observation of the coins and her conversation with the plaintiff.

The court found persuasive the defendant's argument that the Safe Deposit Record cannot be construed as sufficient notice under the Indiana Innkeeper's statute. It did not inform the Hyatt Regency of the fact that the plaintiffs were bringing their merchandise into the hotel or the estimated value thereof. Although the Hyatt Regency's agent (Atkinson) signed the Safe Deposit Record, thereby wit-

nessing the Plaintiff's execution of the form (and at least implicitly, the fact that Teller had read the "Rules and Regulations Governing Safe Deposit Boxes"), her signature hardly constitutes a written acknowledgment that the Hotel had received sufficient notice under the statute. Even if Ms. Atkinson's signature could somehow be interpreted as the equivalent of a written acknowledgment that plaintiff Teller was bringing merchandise into the Hotel (on the theory that Teller provided Atkinson and her employer with "notice" of that fact when he (1) told her he was with the Coin Show, and (2) proceeded to place the partnership inventory in the safe deposit box while in her presence), it would nevertheless fail to constitute a valid acknowledgement. Under the statute, an innkeeper's agent must acknowledge notice which includes a declaration of the value of the guest's merchandise.

CONCLUSION Judgment for Hyatt Corporation

PRACTICE JUDGING

1. If there were not a special statute in Indiana, what duty of care would Hyatt owe?

2. How would this case have been decided if there were not a special statute for innkeepers in Indiana?

3. Which do you think is more fair, this innkeeper's statute or the bailee's usual duty?

© GETTY IMAGES/PHOTODISC

CHAPTER 17

Ownership and Leasing of Real Property

17-1 Ownership and Transfer of Real Property

17-2 Leasing Real Property

© GETTY IMAGES/PHOTODISC

HOT DEBATE

Sally rented an apartment that had been constructed only a month before she moved in. After she had lived there for a week, she discovered the fan in her bathroom didn't work. Because she was knowledgeable about electrical work, Sally made the repair to the fan herself. Then she told her landlord about the problem and her solution. She asked to be compensated for her work at $35 per hour, the going rate for electricians in her community.

Where Do You Stand?

1. What, if any, are the legal reasons why Sally should be compensated for fixing the fan?

2. What, if any, are the legal reasons why the landlord should not have to compensate Sally for fixing the fan?

Ownership and Transfer of Real Property

▼ GOALS

■ Understand both the rights and limitations associated with ownership of real property
■ Identify the forms of ownership and how they are transferred

RIGHTS AND LIMITATIONS OF REAL PROPERTY OWNERSHIP

WHAT'S YOUR VERDICT?

Durston planted a hedgeapple tree just a foot from the boundary of his land. As the tree grew, its limbs extended across the boundary. Each fall hedgeapples from the tree would fall onto his neighbor's property. One November day, Durston noticed that the neighbor had cut off the limbs of the tree at the boundary of the neighbor's land. Durston summoned the police and accused the neighbor of destruction of property and vandalism.

Was Durston correct in his accusations?

Real property was defined in Chapter 15 as land, buildings, and fixtures. Any piece of personal property that becomes permanently attached to land or a building is called a *fixture.*

For example, if the attachment of a structure is to a foundation set into the land, the structure will be considered a fixture and taxed as real property. If instead the building is merely placed on the land, such as a portable tool shed, it remains personal property. Items built into the walls of realty which cannot be removed without permanent harm to the structure become realty themselves as fixtures.

However, items of business property permanently attached to realty, such as a pizza oven bolted to the floor of a restaurant, are considered *trade fixtures.* These fixtures retain their identity as personal property. Finally, crops growing on land typically are considered personal property if they are harvested at least once a year. Crops harvested less frequently are considered realty until they are separated from the land.

REAL PROPERTY RIGHTS

Ownership of real property entails having claim to a number of rights in these three physical items. With land, for example, the buyer usually acquires surface rights, rights to the air space above the land and, in most states, the rights to the earth beneath the surface.

SURFACE RIGHTS *Surface rights* include the right to occupy the land, develop it with buildings and fixtures, and even to lay waste to it by destroying its resources such as timber or water.

RIGHTS TO THE AIR SPACE ABOVE THE LAND The air space above the surface of the land is also part of the realty. Ownership of that space is called the

© GETTY IMAGES/PHOTODISC

If the apples in this orchard are harvested each fall, would the apples be considered personal property or real property?

right to air space. The ownership power, except for the right to exclude aircraft from flying over, extends to the upper atmosphere. If the branch of a neighbor's tree grows into your air space (as did Durston's tree in *What's Your Verdict?*), you have the right to force its removal. This is seldom done because both property owners generally benefit from the vegetation. However, in *What's Your Verdict?* The neighbor did act legally in cutting the limbs. (Durston should beware of a slander suit by the neighbor against him.)

While surface rights and the right to air space usually are owned by the same party, occasionally one party owns the surface rights and another has rights in the air space. For example, in large cities, a company may acquire the right to build an aerial walkway between two of its corporate buildings from the owner of the land underneath.

MINERAL RIGHTS Realty also includes the earth beneath the surface. The right to dig or mine that earth is called a *mineral right.* In theory, ownership of mineral rights extends down from the land surface to the center of the earth. The extent of the right to extract the resources below the surface, however, varies depending on the physical state of the resource.

SOLID MINERALS Ownership of solid minerals such as coal, iron ore, copper ore, nickel, and uranium usually extends downward from the perimeter of a surface parcel. The owner of the mineral right has the power to remove any mineral located within that area.

FLUIDS Ownership of fluids such as oil (a liquid) and natural gas (a vapor) also usually extends downward from a surface area. However, the **doctrine of capture** grants ownership of these fluid minerals to the party who extracts (or captures) them. Thus, if a person drilled an oil well on a quarter-acre lot and began pumping from a pool of oil that extended beneath a 25-acre area, all the oil could be removed under the doctrine of capture. This is so even though the oil originally was another's property and, because of the pumping, it flowed from one location to another. Note that the well shaft itself may not extend into realty owned by others.

WATER RIGHTS Water on the surface or under the ground is a part of the realty. Control of that water is called a *water right.* Control of water rights is governed by individual states. States use two systems for regulating the use of water. The most-used system grants the water rights to ripar-

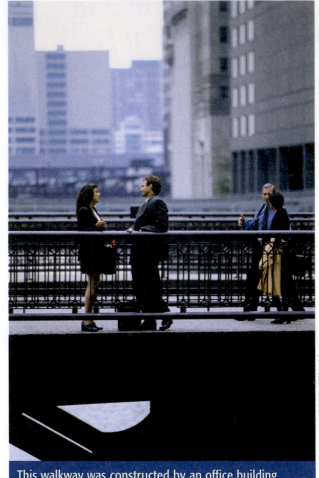

This walkway was constructed by an office building owner to connect the offices to a parking garage belonging to the owner. What rights did the owner have to acquire in order to build it?

ians. A *riparian* is someone who owns land abutting a body of water. Thus, ownership of the adjoining land (or the land beneath the water) carries with it the right to use the water.

The other system, used by a minority of states, is called the *prior appropriation system.* Prior appropriation does not connect the right to use the water with the adjoining land. Rather, it grants the first party to use the water priority in subsequent years over other potential users. The amount of the initial use determines the amount of water that may be used in later years.

LIMITATIONS ON OWNERSHIP

Ownership of real property is at the heart of our economic system. However, some limitations on ownership rights are posed by the rights of others in the form of easements, restrictive covenants, zoning, and those who might simply enter upon it.

Law Brief

Assume you are a judge on your state's circuit court. Decide each of the following cases by determining if the property involved is real or personal. Research to find cases deciding similar issues in your state or nearby states. Write a paragraph that supports your decision for each case, citing the cases you found.

a. A convenience store is moving its location and wants to take along the gas tanks it buried on the property when it began its lease five years ago.

b. The seller of a piece of residential property wants to take along her 9' × 12' metal storage building that is resting on, but not attached to, a concrete pad she had poured specifically for the structure.

c. The seller of a 40-acre tract of farmland wants the right to "harvest" the 1,152 cherry trees he grew around the perimeter of the acreage. Under the sales contract, he is to be allowed to profit through the current growing season from any crops planted before the sales contract was signed.

● ●

EASEMENTS Irrevocable rights to some limited use of another's land usually are called *easements*. Easements generally are given for substantial periods of time—for example, for five years, fifty years, or forever. To comply with the Statute of Frauds, easements should be in writing. Easements may be granted to allow a neighbor to drive across your land, for a utility company to bury a sewer pipe or hang power lines, or to make any other use that does not constitute exclusive possession. Easements may be appurtenant, in gross, by necessity, or by prescription.

EASEMENT APPURTENANT When easements are given to neighboring landowners and the easement benefits the neighbor's land, then it is called an *easement appurtenant*. Appurtenant means attached to the land. Thus an easement to drive farm equipment across a neighbor's land in order to farm an otherwise inaccessible parcel would be an easement appurtenant. Easements for access roads or water ditches are easements appurtenant. These easements are generally transferred when the land benefited by the easement is sold.

EASEMENTS IN GROSS Easements that do not benefit neighboring land, but benefit a person or business are called *easements in gross*. Examples include access to your property for telephone lines and poles or access that you might give to a non-neighbor. The person benefited generally cannot transfer his or her rights.

EASEMENT BY NECESSITY An owner may sell part of her property, and the buyer can only gain access to it by crossing the seller's property. If nothing has been stated about an easement, the law will assume the parties intended the buyer could cross the property of the seller. An *easement by necessity* is created in such a case.

EASEMENT BY PRESCRIPTION If someone makes systematic use of your property for a long period of time, typically 15 to 21 years, then the law will acknowledge an *easement by prescription* arising from the use.

RESTRICTIVE COVENANTS A restrictive covenant is a promise usually made in writing by the buyer to the seller. Usually the promise limits the use of the land in some way. For example, the buyer may contract with the seller, promising not to graze sheep on the land. If the buyer who gave the covenant resells, the new owner is bound only if the covenant is the kind that *runs with the land*. This means that the covenant must be intended to pertain to subsequent owners who are on notice of it and must affect the use or title of the property.

ZONING ORDINANCES The owner's use of his or her realty also can be restricted by zoning ordinances. Zoning ordinances are adopted by cities or counties to regulate the location of residential, business, and industrial districts. If the zoning reduces the value of the owner's land, the owner would bear the loss and could not recover from the local government for the financial injury.

Zoning is not enforceable if it exceeds the constitutional powers of the government. This occurs when the ordinance is clearly arbitrary, unreasonable, or without substantial relation to the public health, safety, morals, and general welfare. In addition, zoning cannot be used unreasonably to eliminate an existing use. Thus a zoning ordinance restricting use of an area to residential could not be used to eliminate an already existing cemetery. (The cemetery in a residential zone is called a *nonconforming use.*) Recently, however, some courts have begun to allow reasonable zoning ordinances that eliminate existing uses.

Spot zoning is the treatment of a single property in a manner inconsistent with the treatment of similar properties in the area. It is usually prohibited. However, a **variance** may be granted by a city or county to allow a landowner to make some use of his or her land that is inconsistent with the general zoning ordinance. Usually the applicant for a variance must appear before a variance board and establish hardship and lack of injury to others.

DUTIES OWED TO ENTRANTS ON LAND

A person who has the right to possess land may owe certain tort duties to others who come on the land. Under the common law, the extent of the duties depends on whether the people are trespassers, licensees, or invitees. Some courts ignore these distinctions and hold possessors liable if they fail to take reasonable steps to prevent harm to those entering their land.

TRESPASSERS A **trespass** occurs when a person is on the land without a right to be there. Thus, when a neighbor walks upon your land without your consent, the neighbor is a trespasser. The only duty a landowner has to trespassers is to refrain from doing them intentional harm.

If the land contains something of particular attraction to children, such as a swimming pool, it is said to contain an *attractive nuisance.* Owners are strictly liable for harm caused to children in such a circumstance.

LEGAL RESEARCH

In some states, real property rights can be divided so as to run independently of one another. In Oklahoma, for example, ownership of mineral rights can be sold separately or retained by a previous owner who has sold the surface realty. Under such a system, having mineral rights means having the right to capture the minerals. The minerals, such as oil and precious metals, are not owned by the holder of the mineral rights until they are actually captured.

LICENSEE A *licensee* is a person whom the possessor of real property has permitted to be on that realty. Social guests and delivery persons are examples of licensees. The possessor of realty has the duty to disclose to the licensee any known non-obvious dangers on the realty and to refrain from doing them intentional harm.

Why is it a good idea to keep sidewalks free of hazards, such as ice and snow build-up?

© GETTY IMAGES/PHOTODISC

INVITEE An invitee is either a public invitee or a business invitee. A *public invitee* is a member of the public invited by the land's possessor to enter or remain on the land for a public purpose. A *business invitee,* such as a shopper or a moviegoer, is invited on the realty to do business with the possessor. The possessor of realty has the duty to invitees to inspect the premises in a reasonable fashion so as to find dangers and correct them. The possessor also has a duty to warn invitees of dangers on the land of which the possessor should be aware and which are not reasonably discoverable by the invitee.

CHECKPOINT

List four potential limitations on the ownership rights of real property.

IN THIS CASE

John Elza and his son, JJ, entered a movie theater after the feature had begun. In the darkness, with JJ leading the way, they moved into a row of vacant seats headed for the middle two. Suddenly, JJ slipped on a box of popcorn that the previous crowd had left. His face collided with the seat back in the row ahead. An inch-long split opened under his right eye. John Elza rushed the child to a doctor who stitched up the cut. John Elza then turned the child over to his mother and returned to the theater to take the names of witnesses to the incident and to the fact of how littered the theater floor was. He then notified the theater of his contention that they owed for his son's treatment and pain and suffering, as he was a business invitee. The theater agreed and its insurer paid. The insurer also required that the theater clean the aisles after each showing after that event.

OWNERSHIP FORMS AND THEIR TRANSFER

WHAT'S YOUR VERDICT?

Susan gave her daughter Emily a deed to a five-acre lot next to her home with the hope that Emily would live there. In the deed, Susan wrote that the property was being deeded on the condition that Emily not keep any livestock on the property. If Emily did so, the ownership of the property would revert to Susan or the current owner of her home. Emily did build a home on the property, and, fifteen years later while Susan was still alive, she also built a stable and kept horses there.

Will Emily lose ownership of the realty because of the horses?

FORMS OF REAL PROPERTY OWNERSHIP

Ownership of realty usually is acquired by the passage of rights via a purchase, gift, or inheritance. Regardless of how rights to real property are acquired, not all owners necessarily receive the same rights. The number of rights received in the transfer is determined by the estate in land that the new owner receives. Each **estate** is comprised of a certain set of ownership rights. The words used in the deed, will, or lease determine which estate and thereby which rights are transferred. The party who transfers ownership powers is called the *grantor.* The party who receives ownership powers is called the *grantee.* When an estate is transferred from a grantor to a grantee by deed, the transaction is called a **conveyance.**

The major types of estates in real property are the fee simple absolute, conditional estates, life estates, and non-freehold estates.

FEE SIMPLE ABSOLUTE A **fee simple absolute** is the estate with all the ownership rights. The owner of this estate exercises all the power allowed by law. If this estate is present, there can be no other estate in the same land as the holder in fee simple has all the powers. Almost all buyers of homes and farms and commercial property purchase the fee simple absolute estate.

CONDITIONAL ESTATE A *conditional estate* makes the ownership conditional on some act or event. For example, ownership may be conveyed to exist only "so long as no alcoholic beverages are served on the premises." Therefore, if beer were served, ownership would shift from the owner of the conditional estate to the grantor who conditionally conveyed the property. Similarly, if a deed made ownership conditional upon not having horses on the property, ownership of the realty would be lost by violating that condition. Thus, in *What's Your Verdict?* Emily would lose ownership of the five-acre lot.

Whenever there is an estate with powers less than fee simple absolute, there must be a second corresponding estate with the remaining powers. In the conditional estates, the second estate is made up of the ownership power retained by the grantor of the conditional estate. This nonpossessory estate is called a *future interest*. An example of a future interest would be the potential right of Susan to reclaim the property she deeded her daughter in *What's Your Verdict?* if livestock were kept on it.

LIFE ESTATE A *life estate* is ownership only for the length of a specified person's life. The owner of a life estate has the right of possession and exercises all the ownership powers except the right to permanently dispose of the property. The length of the ownership period is generally conditioned on the life of the holder of the life estate but does not have to be. For example, a husband might convey his home "to my wife Julia, for life." Julia would own the home only for her lifetime. She could not transfer the property by will upon her death. Upon Julia's death, the property would go back to her husband, or to whomever he specified such as their children.

NON-FREEHOLD ESTATE A *non-freehold estate*, sometimes called a tenancy, involves ownership for a limited period of time. Those who are renting real property own non-freehold estates. The length of ownership is either specified in the rental agreement, indicated by the payment period, or lasts only as long as the landlord desires.

TRANSFER OF OWNERSHIP

Ownership of real property is transferred principally by sale, gift, or inheritance. Ownership also can be transferred by adverse possession, by dedication, and by eminent domain. A deed is the primary evidence of the transfer in most of these transactions.

DEED A **deed** is the legal document used to transfer ownership of real property. The two major types of deeds used to convey realty are the quitclaim deed and the warranty deed. The *quitclaim deed* transfers any interest the grantor may have in the real property. This doesn't guarantee that the grantor owns anything or that the grantee receives anything. A grantee has no legal claim against the grantor based on the quitclaim deed. The *warranty deed,* however, protects the grantee by providing several enforceable grantor's warranties. The principal warranties include the following:

Cyberlaw

You may have heard the phrase "buying swamp land in Florida." That phrase originated with get-rich-quick land deals in the 1920s, when people invested in real estate that turned out to be swamp and wilderness land. Today, the Florida swamp land schemes have been replaced with Internet real estate offers. These offers claim you don't need money to start (or even need a real estate brokers' license) to get rich selling real estate. You just need to say yes—and then send money. These land deals typically don't even involve land. What you receive for your money is either a seminar or book on making money. All you learn is that your investment money now belongs to someone else. If such an e-mail offer comes to you, you may want to simply press the Delete key before trying to make quick money through real estate over the Internet.

THINK ABOUT IT
How would you determine if such a potential good deal is legitimate?

- The grantor has the legal ability to transfer the realty described by the deed.
- There are no undisclosed claims or encumbrances (for example, liens, mortgages, or overdue taxes) against the property.
- The grantee shall have *quiet enjoyment* of the property (no one with superior title will disturb the grantee's possession).

GIFT, SALE, OR INHERITANCE The requirements of an enforceable gift or sale have been discussed elsewhere in the book. The laws of inheritance are discussed in Chapter 19.

ADVERSE POSSESSION In some situations, a person who publicly occupies another's land for a number of years may be treated by the law as the new owner of the realty. Suppose you bought a 600-acre farm and the legal description of its boundary inadvertently included 10 adjoining acres that belonged to an absentee neighbor. If you fenced your farm and included the 10 acres, or otherwise occupied this land for period set by state statute, you could become its owner. This is because of the doctrine of adverse possession.

Adverse possession occurs when you adversely and exclusively possess in an open and notorious way the land of another private person. Possession must be continuous for the statutory period of 5 to 21 years, depending on state law.

- *Adverse* means that the occupation is without the consent of the owner. If an owner said you could occupy the land, either for rent or without charge, you could not become an adverse possessor.
- *Open and notorious* means that the occupation must be visible to the public, including the owners, upon inspection. Erecting fences, planting crops, building barns, and grazing cattle constitute open and notorious occupation.
- *Continuously* means that the occupation is uninterrupted. If a couple occupied your land for two years, then moved away, then returned two years later and occupied it for another six years, they would not satisfy a statutory requirement that the adverse possession occur for seven years.

Many states require the payment of property taxes on the occupied land before adverse possession can be asserted. Some states also require that adverse possessors have a legal basis for concluding that they own the property.

DEDICATION OR EMINENT DOMAIN Dedication typically involves giving real property to the government, such as a city, for use as a park or roadway. As with any other gift, the dedication is effective only if the government accepts the property.

In contrast with dedication, **eminent domain** is the power of the government to take private property for public use in exchange for the fair market price. If the owner is unwilling to sell at a price that the government thinks is fair, the government initiates a condemnation proceeding.

A *condemnation proceeding* is a hearing to determine fair compensation for the owner and acquire ownership for the government. If not satisfied with the price offered, the owner may demand a trial by jury to set a just price.

Property taken under eminent domain must be for a public use, such as for highways, airports, parks, or schools. Privately owned railroads and utilities also may exercise this power for such essentials as land for tracks and switching yards and for telephone and electric lines. Eminent domain may not be used for other private purposes even though the public may benefit and a fair price is offered.

CHECKPOINT
Name the four major types of estates in real property.

NET Bookmark
Sometimes local governments try to use eminent domain to acquire property they then resell to other private parties for redevelopment projects. Access lawxtra.swlearning.com and click on the link for Chapter 17. The Castle Coalition is a group that helps people protect their ownership rights in these situations. What must the government prove in order to acquire property for purposes other than public use? What can you do if you are faced with such a situation?

lawxtra.swlearning.com

Assessment

lawxtra.swlearning.com

THINK ABOUT LEGAL CONCEPTS

1. Land is the only component of real estate. **True or False?**

2. The owner of realty generally owns (a) the land (b) minerals under the surface (c) space above the land (d) all of the above.

3. The water in a river is treated by the law as real property. **True or False?**

4. Which of the following does not have the right of possession? (a) fee simple absolute (b) conditional estates (c) future interests

5. The length of a life estate can be measured by the life of anyone the grantor chooses. **True or False?**

6. Which of the following is the most common and greatest estate? (a) conditional estate (b) life estate (c) nonfreehold estate (d) fee simple absolute

7. The _?_ deed provides the most protection to grantees.

8. Adverse possession can occur in secret. **True or False?**

9. An estate is a particular bundle of legal rights in real property. **True or False?**

10. Taking by eminent domain only can occur when there is a legitimate public purpose for the taking. **True or False?**

11. Easements appurtenant benefit nearby land. **True or False?**

12. The owner of land only owes which of the following duties to a trespasser (a) to refrain from doing the trespasser intentional harm (b) to warn them of known dangers (c) to conduct reasonable searches for dangers.

THINK CRITICALLY ABOUT EVIDENCE

Study the situation, answer the questions, and then prepare arguments to support your answers.

13. Clarence sold Delbert a parcel of land on which there was a house, a barn, unharvested crops, and a house trailer. The house trailer was on a cement foundation, connected to the city electricity line, and plumbed into the water and sewer systems. Delbert protested when Clarence removed the trailer, and Delbert sues to recover it. Who should prevail, Clarence or Delbert?

14. When oil was discovered on his neighbor's property, Slasher brought in a wildcat drilling company to drill on his. The wildcatters suggested that they drill on a slant so that they would stand a better chance of tapping the same pool of oil as his neighbor. Slant drilling would cause the hole to go directly below his neighbor's land. The wildcatters also stated that, even if they drilled straight down and hit the same pool as his neighbor had, they could pump as much as they wanted from it. Are either of these approaches legal? Why or why not?

15. Atushi conveyed a life estate for his lifetime to his niece, Tomomi, with a quitclaim deed.

Three years later Atushi died. What estate is owned by Tomomi after Atushi's death?

16. With a warranty deed, Anistasio conveyed a life estate to his niece, Terresa, for her lifetime. Six months later Terresa died. What estate did Anistasio own during Terresa's lifetime? After Terresa's death?

17. Juan bought a farm and took title with a warranty deed. He then built a fence around the farm. He misjudged the boundary so that his fence ran 25 feet inside the property of his neighbor Swensen. The fence remained in place for 22 years and Juan paid taxes on all the enclosed realty. Then Swensen died without a will. The statutes of his state specified his brother, Phil, would receive his real property in the event Swenson died without a will. Phil had a surveyor check the boundary of the farm and identified the misplaced fence. Phil then hired a bulldozer operator to level the fence. Juan obtained an injunction to halt this action. He filed suit asking a court to determine who owns the disputed land. Who will win, Juan or Phil?

▼ GOALS

- **Compare the various types of leases**
- **Explain the rights and duties of landlords and tenants**

WHAT ARE THE TYPES OF LEASES?

WHAT'S YOUR VERDICT?

Curtis entered into an oral agreement with Kearne to lease Kearne's cabin in the Rockies for three months during the winter ski season. However, skiing was poor that year because there was little snowfall. Therefore Curtis tried to avoid the contract. Curtis claimed that the lease was not enforceable because it was not in writing and because of the poor skiing conditions.

Is Curtis correct?

A **lease** is an agreement in which one party receives temporary possession of another's real property in exchange for rent. **Rent** is the consideration given in return for temporary possession. The lease creates a relationship between the person conveying possession of the realty (called the **landlord** or *lessor*) and the person receiving possession (called the **tenant** or *lessee*). The ownership interest of the tenant is called a leasehold estate. A **leasehold estate** is similar to the other estates in land in that it grants certain rights in the subject property to the tenant.

Most leases constitute a blending of the law of conveyance (that is, transferring ownership of realty) and the law of contracts. The conveyance aspect of the transaction is concerned with transferring a leasehold estate to the tenant. The contract aspects relate to the agreements between the parties on such issues as the amount of the rent, who shall repair the realty, and the amount of security or cleaning deposits.

A lease may be oral. However, under the Statute of Frauds in most states, leases that extend for more than one year must be in writing or courts may refuse to enforce them. Even if a writing is not required, it is a good idea to put the important terms of a lease in written

form to avoid disputes. In *What's Your Verdict?* Curtis is wrong. Oral leases are valid and the lease was not made conditional on the amount of the snowfall.

There are four basic types of leasehold estates that can be created. These estates are a periodic tenancy, a tenancy for years, tenancy at sufferance, and a tenancy at will.

PERIODIC TENANCY

A *periodic tenancy* arises when the leasehold is for a renewable period of time with rent due at stated intervals. Leases that create a periodic tenancy sometimes identify a rental period, such as

One important issue for you to consider in renting an apartment might be whether or not you are allowed to keep a pet there. How can you be sure that your pet would be welcome?

© GETTY IMAGES/PHOTODISC

from "week to week," "month to month," or "year to year." If the lease does not state the period, then the frequency with which rent is paid will be assumed to be the period.

In general, this tenancy continues for the length of the payment period and is automatically renewed unless one party gives adequate notice of termination. If no length of time is set for notice in the lease, then in most states the notice of termination must equal the length of one full payment period. Thus, where rent is paid every month, a one month notice to terminate would be required.

TENANCY FOR YEARS

When a leasehold is for a definite period of time—such as six months, one year, or ninety-nine years—it creates a *tenancy for years.* It has this name even when the period of the lease is less than one year. The feature that distinguishes a tenancy for years from a periodic tenancy is the identification of a date for the ending of the lease. Thus, if a lease states that the rental period is from May 1 to August 15, this is a tenancy for years because August 15 is specified as the ending date. At the end of the lease period, a tenancy for years terminates automatically without a requirement of notice.

TENANCY AT SUFFERANCE

Tenants often have a hard time leaving the rented property before the day when the lease ends. If a tenant remains in possession after a lease has expired, a *tenancy at sufferance* arises. The tenant is then called a *holdover tenant.*

When there is a tenancy at sufferance, the landlord generally has a choice of remedies. The holdover tenant can be evicted—that is, be forcibly removed from the property by the sheriff. Further, the tenant is liable for reasonable rent for the holdover period. In some states the landlord can collect double or triple rent for the holdover period. If the tenant holds over, the landlord may—as alternative to eviction—compel the tenant to pay rent for another lease period.

If the holdover tenant pays and the landlord accepts additional rent, a periodic tenancy is generally created for the same period or term as the prior lease. Therefore, if the prior lease were for one year, the tenant would be liable for another full year's rent. If the old lease were for one month, the landlord would be obligated to provide the premises for another month.

IN THIS CASE

Anne rented an apartment to Clare, a college freshman. The lease was for a nine-month period from September 1 to May 30, and rent was due in advance every month. Clare paid the rent on May 1 for May. Then she decided she wanted to go to a summer school session which lasted two months. She paid a month's rent on June 1 without disclosing her plans. The payment was accepted by Anne. Clare and Anne initially created a tenancy for years because the termination date was identified. When Clare stayed in the apartment after the end of May, a tenancy at sufferance existed. When Anne accepted the rent in June, Clare ceased being a tenant at sufferance and both Anne and Clare were bound to a lease for another nine-month period.

TENANCY AT WILL

If a party possesses land with the owner's permission but without an agreement as to the term of the lease or the amount of the rent, a *tenancy at will* results. Such a leasehold may be terminated at any time by either party with minimal notice.

CHECKPOINT
Name the four types of leaseholds.

RIGHTS AND DUTIES OF THE TENANT AND THE LANDLORD

WHAT'S YOUR VERDICT?

Luis was a writer who often wrote for hours at a time. One Sunday, his landlord, Trip, called to ask if he could show Luis' apartment to some prospective tenants in the next few minutes. Luis knew the interruption would cause him to break the flow of his work. Quickly he checked his lease but there wasn't a term in it that covered the situation.

Can Luis legally deny the landlord's request?

TENANT'S RIGHTS

The tenant in a leasehold has several rights, subject to the terms of the lease. These rights include the rights to the possession and use of the premises and the rights to assign the lease or sublet the premises.

RIGHT OF POSSESSION The tenant has a right to the possession of the real property starting at the time agreed upon in the lease. In addition, unless otherwise provided in the lease, the tenant's possession is to be exclusive of all other persons and is for the duration of the lease. Landlords generally do not have a right to enter leased premises for inspection unless this right is given in the lease.

Luis in *What's Your Verdict?* could legally deny Trip's request to show the apartment to a prospective renter. Even if a landlord is given the right to enter and inspect the leased premises, most states require that the landlord give reasonable advance notice and that the landlord inspect at a reasonable time of the day.

If the landlord blocks the tenant from possession of all the real property, an **eviction** has occurred. The tenant may recover damages from the landlord if the eviction is improper.

Under some circumstances, the tenant may claim a *constructive eviction* and refuse to pay rent. A constructive eviction occurs if the landlord fails to perform certain duties as defined in

In *What's Your Verdict?* Luis is not legally obligated to allow his landlord to show the apartment to a prospective renter. What would you do if confronted by this situation?

© GETTY IMAGES/PHOTODISC

the lease or imposed by statute and if the tenant abandons the premises because of such a breach.

For example, if the landlord fails to heat residential premises and this forces the tenant to move out, there has been a constructive eviction. If the lessor fails to keep residential premises in a condition fit for human habitation for other reasons, perhaps because of infestation by insects or rodents, this also could amount to a constructive eviction if the tenant leaves the premises because of such condition.

INTERNATIONAL VIEWPOINT

In Mexico, a tenant who has been leasing real property for more than five years has preferential rights to the property if the owner decides to sell. What would be the impact of such a law in this country on the length of leases, the ability to sell real property, and the mobility of the population?

RIGHT TO USE THE PROPERTY The tenant is allowed to use the leased property in the manner specified in the lease. If a particular use is not mentioned in the lease, the tenant may use the property for any purpose for which it is designed or customarily used.

RIGHT TO ASSIGN THE LEASE OR TO SUBLET THE PREMISES Unless restricted by the terms of the lease, a tenant may assign the lease or may sublet the premises. An assignment of a lease takes place when the tenant transfers his or her entire interest in the lease to a third person. Although the new tenant becomes liable to the landlord for the rent and performance of other conditions of the lease, the original tenant also remains liable.

Subletting occurs when the tenant does either of the following:

- leases all of the property to a third person for a period of time that is less than that remaining on the lease, or
- leases part of the property to a third person for part or all of the term remaining.

When the property is sublet, the original tenant continues to be directly liable to the landlord for performance of the lease. Leases often require the landlord's prior approval of assignment or subletting. However, courts have held that the landlord must have a valid reason if consent is withheld.

TENANT'S DUTIES

With rights come duties such as the tenant's duties to pay rent, take care of the property, and be responsible for torts that occur on the property.

DUTY TO PAY RENT A tenant's most important duty is to pay the agreed-upon rent when it is due. Although rent usually is expressed as a fixed sum of money, it may consist of a share of the crops of a farm or a percentage of the profits of a business. The tenant may be evicted for failure to pay rent.

Before leasing property in a tenancy for years or a tenancy from month to month, landlords sometimes require the payment of the first and last months' rent. Thus, if the tenant fails to make prompt payment for the next period's rent, the landlord can use the last month's rent for the month during which legal steps are taken to evict the tenant. In residential rentals, a "cleaning" or "security" deposit is almost always required. The amount of this deposit should be refunded at the end of the lease period if the property is left as clean and undamaged as it was when first occupied, less ordinary wear and tear.

DUTY TO TAKE CARE OF THE PROPERTY A tenant owes a duty of reasonable care to return the property in substantially the same condition it was in when the lease began. This ordinarily includes responsibility for making all minor repairs. The tenant is not liable for wear and tear caused by ordinary use. However, the tenant is liable for the destruction, damaging of, or substantial deterioration in value of the estate due to the tenant's unreasonable conduct. This is referred to as *wasting* the estate.

In some states by statute, and sometimes based on the lease, landlords make all repairs. This can include even minor repairs such as replacing faucet washers and electric fuses. The tenant normally is under no obligation—in fact, has no right—to make major structural changes or to make improvements without the consent of the landlord. For example, if the roof leaks, the necessary repair is the responsibility of the landlord.

However, legally the tenant is expected to act reasonably and to take appropriate steps to prevent avoidable damage until the landlord has been notified and can make needed repairs. The tenant also is obligated to notify the landlord when major repairs are needed. In a few states, the tenant may apply up to a full month's rent toward essential repairs if the landlord does not make the repairs after reasonable notice.

A QUESTION OF ETHICS

Morgan entered into a lease agreement for an apartment with Hernandez. Morgan was to pay $535 each month for a two-bedroom apartment, with electricity, water, and cable included in the price of the rent. One month, the power to Morgan's apartment was out for three days. Does Morgan have an ethical duty to pay her entire month's rent even though she did not have electricity for three days? Does Hernandez have an ethical duty to refund part of Morgan's rent payment?

TORTS DUTY A business or residential tenant in possession of leased property has a duty of care to those who enter the property. An injury to a licensee or invitee caused by a tenant's negligence is the responsibility of the tenant in the areas under the tenant's control. The tenant even may be held liable if the landlord had the responsibility under the lease to make repairs, which, if they had been made, would have avoided the injury. A tenant can buy liability insurance to protect against loss from injury claims.

In the majority of states, lessees assume liability for injuries to themselves and to others (torts) that occur on the leased property. An exception to this rule exists when the landlord knows the defective condition but does not disclose it to the tenant, and the tenant would not be able to identify the problem after a reasonable inspection. The landlord is also liable for injuries occurring on portions of the property, such as hallways, which the landlord controls. In general, the landlord controls the common areas. These are areas used by all the tenants. Thus if a tenant's guest is injured because of a defective diving board in the pool area of an apartment complex, the landlord is likely to be liable.

LANDLORD'S RIGHTS

Generally, the rights of landlords find their complements in the corresponding duties of the tenant. The landlord's primary right is to receive the rent agreed upon in the lease. If the tenant fails to pay the rent, the landlord may take legal action to recover the rent and evict the tenant.

If a tenant vacates the property before the end of the lease, that tenant remains liable for the unpaid rent. In some states, the tenant is liable for the rent even if the landlord allows the property to remain empty. Most states, however, require that the landlord mitigate the damages by making a good-faith effort to rerent the property. If the property still cannot be rerented, the original tenant is liable for the rent remaining on the lease. If it is rerented, but at a lower rental amount, the original tenant is liable for the difference.

If the tenant fails to pay rent and remains in possession, the landlord may sue to evict the tenant. The landlord may include the claim for overdue rent in the same suit. However, the landlord may not take the law into his or her own hands, personally evicting the tenant and placing the tenant's belongings on the sidewalk. If the tenant refuses to leave the premises, a court order directing the sheriff or other official to evict the tenant must be obtained.

At the end of the lease term, the lessor also has the right to regain possession of the real property. If a tenant has added fixtures to the realty, they belong to the landlord. This general rule does not apply to trade fixtures added by business tenants.

LANDLORD'S DUTIES

DUTY TO PROVIDE HABITABLE PREMISES The landlord's duties tend to complement the tenant's rights and reasonable expectations. These duties emphasize the providing and maintaining of a habitable premises for the tenant. In addition, when a number of tenants rent portions of a building, the landlord is responsible for all the upkeep of the exterior and the public, or common, areas. Common areas are those not under the specific control of any one tenant. Public areas include common hallways, stairs, elevators, yards, and swimming pools.

One who is injured because of the faulty condition of common areas could bring suit for damages against the landlord. In addition, a landlord may be held liable for injuries that result from defective conditions in the property in the tenant's exclusive possession if the conditions are concealed or are not readily apparent.

DUTY TO CONFORM TO GOVERNMENTAL REQUIREMENTS A landlord is required to provide residential property in a condition fit for human living. This sometimes is enforced by the courts in the form of an implied warranty of habitability. In other instances and especially in many large cities, the law—in the form of a *housing code*—may prescribe in detail the required condition of such properties. A representative city housing code makes provisions such as these:

- There should be no exposed electrical wiring.
- The roof should not leak.
- Every ceiling and wall should be smooth, free of loose plaster and wallpaper, and easily cleanable.
- Outside doors and windows should have tight-fitting screens.
- Every unit should have a private bathroom.
- Gas stoves should be properly vented and connected.

Often, violation of housing codes is a violation of the *warranty of habitability*. If that warranty is violated, the tenant may recover damages, become entitled to a reduction in rent, or terminate the lease.

In addition to conforming to the appropriate codes, the landlord must pay all property taxes and assessments on the leased property. However, long-term leases of commercial property commonly provide that the tenant will pay such taxes and assessments, as well as premiums for fire insurance.

Finally, the Fair Housing Act makes it illegal for the lessor, or the lessor's agent, to discriminate on the basis of race, religion, sex, national origin, handicap, or family status. A lessor must allow a handicapped person to pay for reasonable modification to the property on the condition that the property is returned to its original condition at the end of the lease. In addition, lessors may not discriminate against families with children unless the facility falls within the "housing for older persons" exception.

© GETTY IMAGES/PHOTODISC

Why might a landlord attempt to discriminate against families with children?

CHECKPOINT
Name three rights a tenant has.

17-2 Assessment

Xtra!
Study Tools
lawxtra.swlearning.com

THINK ABOUT LEGAL CONCEPTS

1. Which of the following must be in writing to be enforceable by a court? (a) a lease for a period of two months (b) a lease for a period of six months (c) a lease for a period of 12 months (d) a lease for period of 24 months (e) both c and d

2. If the landlord and tenant do not identify an ending date for the lease, but they do identify a payment period, then the lease is a _?_.

3. If the landlord and tenant identify an ending date for the lease, then the lease is a (a) periodic tenancy (b) tenancy for years (c) tenancy at sufferance (d) tenancy at will.

4. If a party possesses land with the owner's permission but without an agreement as to the term of the lease or the amount of the rent, that party has a tenancy _?_.

5. The landlord does not have the right to enter the premises even if the lease states that right exists. **True or False?**

6. If a tenant transfers her interest in the lease for all but the last month, which of the following has occurred? (a) subletting of the premises or (b) assignment of the lease

7. Which of these is not one of the tenant's duties if a major repair becomes necessary? (a) to notify the landlord of the problem (b) to take reasonable steps to prevent avoidable damage (c) to make the necessary repairs

8. The lessor is responsible for all repairs for (a) common areas (b) the tenant's premises (c) both a and b

9. It is illegal to discriminate on the basis of sex in the rental of housing. **True or False?**

Study the situation, answer the questions, and then prepare arguments to support your answers.

10. The written lease on your apartment specifies December 31 of the current year as its termination date. As required, you plan to move out as of December 31 but do not tell the landlord. Two days before the lease expires, while you are packing, your landlord appears and informs you that because you did not give notice of your intent to leave, you owe rent for an additional month. Is the landlord right?

11. Smith rented a furnished apartment from Jerry on a month-to-month basis for $700 per month. At the time Smith first saw the apartment, there was a large tear in the carpet right behind the entryway door. The carpet there often bunched up and it was easy to trip on if you didn't notice it. On Saturday, Smith was entertaining guests when her boss arrived. The boss rang the doorbell and let herself in when no one answered. She then tripped on the torn rug, fell, and broke her arm. She sued both Smith and Jerry for her medical expenses, lost wages, and pain and suffering. Smith is nearly broke, but Jerry her landlord is a multi-millionaire. Is Jerry liable?

12. Buford moved into a high-rise University dormitory building in August in preparation for school to start. During his first month a hot snap with temperatures over 100 degrees at midday and no lower than 80 degrees at night occurred. When the air conditioning broke, Buford discovered that the windows in the building could not be opened. He thought about leaving but instead stayed in the dorm during the two-week period that the air conditioner wasn't working. When his rent was due, he refused to pay more than for two weeks out of the month saying he had been constructively evicted for the other two weeks by the heat and lack of air conditioning. Do you agree? Why or why not?

PREVENT LEGAL DIFFICULTIES

In dealing with real property...

1. If your personal property is to be attached to real property in any transaction, agree in writing who will retain or receive ownership of it. Put the agreement in writing, whether the contract involved is a sale, lease, or mortgage.

2. When purchasing real property, protect your interest by (a) having the property properly surveyed, particularly if it is irregularly shaped or has uncertain borders (b) requiring a deed containing all possible warranties (c) securing title insurance if it is available (d) being represented in the transaction by a professional. If there is anything distinctive about the transaction, use a lawyer who specializes in real estate.

3. Be sure that any deed to land you have purchased is recorded promptly.

4. To prevent adverse possession, check it periodically—especially if it is raw land—to see if someone is occupying it without your consent.

5. If you are asked to convey property and want to be free of possible future obligations, use a quitclaim deed.

6. If the government seeks to take your land by condemnation under its right of eminent domain, consult a lawyer. You have a constitutional right to a trial by jury to determine the fair price that must be paid.

7. Written residential leases generally are prepared by the landlord or the landlord's attorney. Thus, such leases often contain many clauses that protect the landlord's interests. Read with understanding before you sign. If the terms are unacceptable to you, request a change. If you are refused, go elsewhere.

8. Do not remodel or significantly change premises of a leasehold without the consent of your landlord.

9. You may be held liable if someone is injured because of the faulty condition of the premises if such condition was caused by your negligence. Normally you, the tenant, have the obligation to make necessary minor repairs and to notify your landlord of the need for major repairs. Protect yourself with careful maintenance and with adequate liability insurance.

10. When you move, give your landlord proper notice. Such notice is required in periodic tenancies. Failure to give adequate notice may obligate you to pay additional rent even after you vacate the premises.

CONCEPTS IN BRIEF

17-1 Ownership and Transfer of Real Property

1. The rights that exist in real property include surface rights, rights to air space, mineral rights, and water rights.

2. Personal property becomes realty when it is intentionally and permanently attached to the realty

3. The rights and powers of ownership are determined by the estate in land received by the purchaser. Fee simple absolute is the most common and greatest estate. Other major estates are conditional estates, life estates, nonfreehold estates, and future interests.

4. Real property can be transferred by sale, gift, inheritance, adverse possession, dedication, or eminent domain. The transfer usually is evidenced by a quitclaim deed or a warranty deed.

5. The exercise of the rights of ownership of real property can be limited by licenses, easements, restrictive covenants, and zoning.

17-2 Leasing Real Property

6. A leasehold estate may be a tenancy for years, a periodic tenancy, a tenancy at will, or a tenancy at sufferance.

7. Generally the tenant is responsible for paying the rent, taking reasonable care of the premises, and using the premises only for the agreed purposes.

8. A tenant may assign the lease or sublet the premises unless there is a restriction in the lease.

9. The landlord must make major repairs, see that the tenant is not deprived of the use of the leased property, and pay the taxes.

10. A lease may be terminated by expiration of the lease period, by agreement of the parties, or at the option of either party upon material breach by the other. In a periodic tenancy, either party seeking to terminate must give the other party proper notice.

YOUR LEGAL VOCABULARY

Match each statement with the term that it best defines. Some terms may not be used.

1. Greatest possible bundle of ownership rights in, and powers over, realty
2. Irrevocable rights to some limited use of another's land
3. Method of acquiring title by occupying land belonging to another, without the other's consent, for a certain uninterrupted period of time, under prescribed conditions
4. Document used to evidence transfer of ownership of real property
5. Power of the government to take private property for public use upon payment of the fair market price
6. Consideration given by a tenant
7. One who, through a lease, transfers to another exclusive possession and control of real property
8. Grants ownership of below-ground fluid minerals to the party that extracts them
9. Grants certain rights in the subject property to the tenant
10. Tenant's transfer of partial interest in the leasehold to a third person
11. Legal action taken to remove a tenant from possession of the landlord's real property

a. adverse possession
b. conveyance
c. deed
d. doctrine of capture
e. easement
f. eminent domain
g. estate
h. eviction
i. fee simple absolute
j. landlord
k. lease
l. leasehold estate
m. rent
n. restrictive covenant
o. spot zoning
p. subletting
q. tenant
r. trespass
s. variance
t. zoning ordinance

REVIEW LEGAL CONCEPTS

12. Define the differing duties owed by the owner to a trespasser, a licensee, and a business invitee on real property.

13. Describe the legal features of fee simple absolute.

14. Explain what a future interest is.

15. Describe a situation where an estate at will is created.

16. Describe a situation where a tenancy at sufferance is created.

17. Describe how the room in which you sleep could be rented so that a periodic tenancy would arise.

18. Describe when a lease does not need to be placed in writing yet will still be enforceable in court.

WRITE ABOUT LEGAL CONCEPTS

19. Assume you own a fast-food restaurant with a leasehold in the local mall. Write a paragraph distinguishing the licensees from the business invitees that enter your premises at that location.

20. Write a paragraph describing the parts of a typical apartment complex where the landlord will be liable for injuries to guests.

21. Write a paragraph describing the parts of a typical apartment complex where the tenants will be liable for injuries to guests.

22. Write a paragraph describing the condition of an apartment at the beginning of a lease. Write another paragraph describing the difference between an apartment at the end of a lease after "normal wear and tear" and after deterioration because of willful misuse.

23. **HOT DEBATE** Suppose that Sally had instead made emergency repairs to a skylight in the apartment's living room. The skylight had been improperly installed and began leaking during a fierce rainstorm on her furniture and the apartment's rug and hardwood floor. How would your arguments differ for Sally and the landlord?

MAKE ACADEMIC CONNECTIONS

24. **HISTORY** Research the history of the estate in real property known as the "fee tail." Write a report on the conditions that caused it to come into and then go out of use.

THINK CRITICALLY ABOUT EVIDENCE

Study the situation, answer the questions, and then prepare arguments to support your answers.

25. Brand had been squatting on land adjacent to a local river for over three years. She had moved a mobile home onto it, fenced it, and farmed it. Alioto offered her $10,000 for it. What type of deed would best suit the transfer of "ownership"?

26. Purcey gave a written easement to her neighbor Pitzer allowing Pitzer to run a water ditch across Purcey's property to irrigate Pitzer's land. Purcey sells her property to Riddell, who fills in the ditch because, "it's dangerous for my kids." Pitzer sues. Who prevails?

27. Swit bought a single-family residence and converted it into a halfway house for delinquent teenagers. Neighbors objected to the increased risk of crime in the neighborhood. Then the neighbors filed suit claiming that the residents of the home were not, "a single family," as required by the applicable zoning ordinance. Who prevails, Swit or his neighbors?

28. The city of Westerly maintained an old-fashioned Merry-Go-Round near a beach. All summer both kids and adults would ride it. It was shut down during the winter. Occasionally, kids would climb the fence around the Merry-Go-Round, start the electrical motor, and ride it for free. Shelly, age 12, climbed the fence, started the motor, but had her hand crushed when it was caught between a v-belt and a pulley on the motor. Is the city of Westerly liable to Shelly?

29. Slovin entered into a month-to-month tenancy of an apartment for $450 per month. When he married, his wife moved in with him. The landlord did not discover this until three months later. The landlord told Slovin that he owed an extra $100 per month for the time during which the wife had also occupied the apartment. In addition, he told Slovin that the rent for the next month would be $600. What are Slovin's legal obligations to the landlord?

30. Romero rented a farmhouse under a three-year lease. At the end of the lease, Romero and the landlord walked through the farmhouse to inspect for damage. In an empty upstairs room the landlord found a window that was jammed open. It was obvious that rain and snow had come through the open window and damaged the curtains and carpeting. Who is liable for this damage, Romero or the landlord?

31. Houser opened a hamburger shop in a building that she leased for five years from Livingston. The long hours impaired Houser's health and after one year she sold the business to Todd, assigning the lease as part of the deal. When Todd later defaulted on rent payments, Livingston tried to collect from Houser. Is Houser liable?

ANALYZE REAL CASES

32. W. E. and Jennie Hutton executed a warranty deed conveying their interest in a parcel of land to the local school district. The words of conveyance stated: "This land to be used for school purposes only; otherwise to revert to grantors herein." The property was used for a school for 32 years. Then the property was used by the school district for storage purposes. When this occurred, the heirs of the Huttons filed suit to recover the property from the school district. Who owns the land? (*Mahrenholz v. County Board of School Trustees of Lawrence County*, 417 N.E.2d 138, Illinois)

33. Holmes was engaged in the business of raising and processing chickens. He bought property in Clackamas County, Oregon, on which he planned to erect a chicken-processing plant. To prepare for construction, he spent $33,000 to install a well system, plant special grass, and run soil tests to determine where drain fields for the plant's sewage should be located. Later Clackamas County enacted an ordinance zoning the property Rural Agricultural-Single Family Residential. The zoning prohibited further construction of the chicken-processing plant. Holmes continued work and the county sued. The trial court enjoined defendant from further construction. He appealed. What resulted? (*Clackamas County v. Holmes*, 508 P.2d 190, Oregon)

34. The Wakes operated a cattle ranch in Cassia County, Idaho. During the spring and fall, they drove their cattle over land owned by the Johnsons. Eventually the Wakes sold their cattle ranch to the Nelsons. The new owners continued to use the Johnsons' land as a cattle trail twice a year. This went on for about sixteen years before the Johnsons objected and locked the gates to the cattle trail. The Nelsons sued, claiming an easement by prescription. Is there an easement by prescription here? (*Nelson v. Johnson*, 679 P.2d 662) EOC ch. 21 #32

35. Smith bought two lots along the shore of Lake Pepin and built a cottage, which he mistakenly extended over the boundary line into a third lot, Parcel X8. Smith cleaned all three lots, seeded X8 with grass, and used it in the sporadic and seasonal manner associated with lakeshore property. Burkhardt had a warranty deed to X8 but did not challenge Smith's possession for more than twenty years. Now Smith claims title to X8 by adverse possession. Burkhardt argues that the entire parcel was not actually occupied nor was it usually cultivated. Burkhardt also argues that Smith's possession was not hostile because it was based on a mistaken boundary line and because Smith paid no taxes on X8. Does Smith get title to Parcel X8 by adverse possession? (*Burkhardt v. Smith*, 17 Wis. 2d 132)

36. Wallenberg leased certain property from Boyar in a tenancy from month to month, beginning October 1. The rent was payable in advance on the first of each month. On November 27, Wallenberg left without notifying the landlord. Is Boyar entitled to rent for the month of December? (*Boyar v. Wallenberg*, 132 Misc. 116, 228 N.Y.S. 358)

37. James Kreidel was engaged to be married and planned to attend school. He entered into a lease of an apartment from May 1, 1972, to April 30, 1974. Before the lease period began, Kreidel's engagement was broken. As a student, Kreidel then had no means of support and therefore had no way to pay the rent. On May 19, 1972, he wrote the landlord explaining his situation and stating that he was abandoning the lease. Although the landlord had the opportunity, he did not rerent the apartment until September 1, 1973. Is James liable for the rent from May 1, 1972, to September 1, 1973? (*Sommer v. Kreidel*, 378 A.2d 767, N.J.)

CASE FOR LEGAL THINKING

CHERBERG V. JOSHUA GREEN CORPORATION, ET AL.
564 P.2D 1137

FACTS The Cherbergs leased a portion of the Lewis Building on Fifth Avenue in downtown Seattle and invested approximately $80,000 in the establishment of a restaurant business at that location. Joshua Green Corporation acquired the Lewis Building in February, subject to the Cherberg lease. In April Peoples National Bank of Washington, the owner of the property abutting the Lewis Building on the south, commenced demolition of the existing buildings on its property for the purpose of constructing a high-rise office tower. The demolition work resulted in the exposure of the south wall of the Lewis Building. It was found to be structurally unsafe and in need of substantial repairs to satisfy requirements of the City of Seattle Building Department. The premises here at issue were located within the Lewis Building but did not abut the south wall.

The lease between the parties required the lessee to make necessary repairs to maintain the premises, excepting the outside walls and other structural components of the building, and reserved to the lessor the use of the roof and outside walls of the building.

Upon learning of the problems with the south wall, the lessor contacted the Cherbergs, indicating that the Green Corporation would probably elect not to repair the wall and that the City might order the building closed. The Cherbergs responded that the lessor was obligated under the lease to make repairs and that they would suffer substantial damage should their tenancy be disrupted. James Cherberg and his wife brought suit claiming the tort of intentional interference with business expectations arising from the willful refusal of the Joshua Green Corporation, their landlord, to perform duties owed them under a commercial lease.

The trial court, at the conclusion of testimony, instructed the jury that Green Corporation was liable for damages caused by the failure to repair the outside wall. It further instructed the jury with regard to the elements of the tort of intentional interference with business expectations that, if the jury concluded that the defendant's actions were willful, damages for mental suffering, inconvenience, and discomfort would be compensable. The jury made a special finding of willful action and returned a verdict of $42,000. The defendant then appealed.

REASONING The first issue is the rights and duties of the parties with regard to the unsafe condition of the south wall of the building.

A landlord has a duty to maintain, control, and preserve retained portions of the premises subject to a leasehold in a manner rendering the rented premises adequate to the tenant's use. Failure to fulfill this duty results in liability on the part of the lessor for injury caused thereby, and failure to fulfill this duty, by omission to repair, can in a proper case constitute an actionable constructive eviction.

The willful refusal to adequately maintain retained portions of a building so as to allow the tenant to enjoy the beneficial use of the rented portion of the building is a breach of an implied duty owed by the landlord to the tenant under Washington law. On these facts, this breach of duty was sufficient to constitute an actionable constructive eviction and provides a basis for the conclusion that the landlord was liable for any damages stemming from that breach.

CONCLUSION The judgment in favor of the Cherbergs is upheld. It is so ordered.

PRACTICE JUDGING

1. Can the lease create a duty to repair, which differs from the duty presumed by the law?

2. Who had the duty to maintain the interior of the restaurant, the lessor or lessee? If the lessor had not retained control over the exterior walls, would the court have ruled differently?

Insurance Law

© GETTY IMAGES/PHOTODISC

You start a successful business. To insure against loss due to employee dishonesty, you must have fidelity insurance. You apply for it knowing that Joan, one of your managers, has served a prison term for theft. She has had many opportunities to take money from your business, but she has not done so. If you tell the insurance company about Joan's record, your rates would be so high that you would have to fire her to stay in business. Two years after you take out the policy, another employee steals $50,000. The insurance company performs a background check on all your employees. It finds out you knew about but did not report Joan's record and refuses to pay the claim.

Where Do You Stand?

1. If you sue to force the insurance company to adhere to the policy, what are the legal reasons supporting your suit?

2. What are the legal reasons in favor of the insurance company?

▼ **GOALS**

- Discuss the rationale for insurance
- Identify the common types of insurance
- Recognize when an insurable interest is present

WHY HAVE INSURANCE?

WHAT'S YOUR VERDICT?

Eric has a successful dry-cleaning business. His main competitor is about to be forced to move from its present location to one several miles away due to the sale of the building in which it is located. Eric wants to open another store near the competitor's soon-to-be-closed location. However, he is worried about the risks involved in expanding his business. Eric approaches his insurance agent to take out coverage for any losses he might suffer due to the expansion.

Will the agent be able to sell him a policy that insures against this risk of doing business?

Insurance is a contractual arrangement that protects against loss. One party—usually an insurance company—agrees to pay money to help offset a specified type of loss that might occur to another party. The loss may be the death of a person, property damage from earthquake, or injury resulting from exposure to many other risks.

When one party pays to compensate for such harm, that party is said to **indemnify**, or make good, the loss to the suffering party. The party who agrees to indemnify is called the **insurer**. The party covered or protected is the **insured**. The recipient of the amount to be paid is the **beneficiary**. In some cases, notably under life insurance contracts, the insured will not be the beneficiary.

Insurance makes an important contribution to society. By collecting relatively small premiums from many persons, an insurer builds a fund from which to pay insureds that suffer a covered loss. This process spreads losses among a greater number of people.

The written contract of insurance is called a **policy**. The **face value** of a policy is the stated maximum amount that could be paid if the harm a person is insured against occurs. However, a person who suffers a loss covered by insurance recovers no more than the actual value of the loss, even if this amount is less than the face value of the policy.

The consideration for a contract of insurance is called the **premium**. The possible loss arising from injury to or death of a person or from damage to property from a specified peril is called the **risk**.

The risk of most financial losses can be covered by insurance. Certain risks, however, cannot be covered. In *What's Your Verdict?* Eric cannot be insured against a business loss. This illustrates one of the most important risks for which a policy of insurance cannot be written. The risk of

What specific risks can you think of that this business owner might want to insure against?

© GETTY IMAGES/PHOTODISC

doing business is too unpredictable and too subject to the control of the would-be insured. If he were insured, Eric could simply neglect the business and still collect on the insurance when the store failed. The best protection against the risk of doing business is found in hard work, good products, and excellent service.

CHECKPOINT

What is the purpose of insurance?

COMMON TYPES OF INSURANCE

WHAT'S YOUR VERDICT?

To raise funds for a trip to the New Year's Day Parade in New Orleans, the Band Boosters planned a fall festival complete with contests and games. Some of the planned events involved a risk of injury to participants and spectators alike.

What kind of insurance would protect the Band Boosters against liability for negligence or other torts that might result in injury to individuals at the fundraiser?

There are seven major types of insurance. These are (1) life insurance, (2) fire insurance, (3) casualty insurance, (4) social insurance, (5) marine insurance, (6) inland marine insurance, and (7) fidelity and surety bonding insurance. These types will be discussed in the following paragraphs.

LIFE INSURANCE

Insurance that pays the beneficiary a set amount upon the death of a specified person is life insurance. There are three common types of life insurance: term, whole or ordinary, and endowment. In addition, insurance companies have developed combination policies to meet the changing needs of their customers. Life insurance will be discussed further in Lesson 18-3.

TERM INSURANCE *Term insurance* is written for a certain number of years—generally one, five, or ten years. If the insured dies within the policy term, the beneficiary receives the face value of the policy. If the term ends before the insured dies, the contract ends with no further obligation on the insured or the insurer. Term insurance is a relatively inexpensive type of life insurance.

WHOLE LIFE INSURANCE *Whole life insurance,* sometimes called *ordinary* or *straight life insurance,* provides for the payment of premiums for as long as the insured lives or until age 100. The premiums remain constant and a portion of the premium goes into a savings program against which the insured can borrow at a relatively low interest rate. If the insured dies, the face value less any outstanding loans against it is paid to the beneficiary.

A variation of whole life insurance is *limited pay life.* The policyholder pays premiums over a shorter period of time (usually 10, 20, or 30 years) and at a higher amount. Coverage extends beyond the period of making payments. The beneficiary receives the face value of the policy when the insured dies, whether the death occurs during the period when premiums are being paid or after all payments have been made. Limited pay life has the advantage of enabling the insureds to pay premiums during their high-earning-power years.

ENDOWMENT LIFE INSURANCE *Endowment life insurance* requires the insurer to pay the beneficiary the policy's face amount if the insured dies within the period of coverage, usually 20 years or until the insured reaches retirement age. If the insured lives to the end of the coverage period, the owner of the policy (usually the insured) is paid the face value. Premiums for endowment policies are high. However, this type of policy has been attractive to people who need a large lump sum available at a set point in time. For example, this money could be used to buy a retirement home.

FIRE INSURANCE

Insurance that indemnifies for loss or damage due to fire (and usually smoke as well) is *fire insurance.* The typical fire insurance policy coverage may be increased to cover losses due to perils such as rain, hail, earthquake, and windstorm.

CASUALTY INSURANCE

Casualty insurance provides coverage for a variety of specific situations in which the intentional, negligent, or accidental acts of others or mere chance may result in loss. Some of the most important types of casualty insurance include the following.

BURGLARY, ROBBERY, THEFT, AND LARCENY INSURANCE
Such insurance protects against losses resulting from identifiable criminal behavior. In addition, this form of insurance may also protect against the mysterious disappearance of property, that is, when the reason the property disappeared cannot be determined.

AUTOMOBILE INSURANCE
This type of insurance indemnifies for losses arising from or connected to the ownership and operation of motor vehicles. This important insurance coverage will be discussed in detail in Lesson 18-2.

LIABILITY INSURANCE
Such insurance provides protection against claims of parties who suffer injury or other loss as a result of negligence or other torts committed by the insured. In *What's Your Verdict?* if the Band Boosters were insured under a suitable liability policy, the organization would be protected against claims arising from the fundraiser.

DISABILITY, ACCIDENT, OR HEALTH INSURANCE
These policies protect the insured from the financial consequences of hospital bills and loss of income stemming from accident or illness.

SOCIAL INSURANCE

Under the provisions of the Social Security Act and related acts, millions of Americans insure themselves against unemployment, disability, poverty, and medical expense problems. This form of insurance is covered in Lesson 18-3.

MARINE INSURANCE

Marine insurance indemnifies for loss of or damage to vessels, cargo, and other property exposed to the perils of the sea. It is perhaps the oldest type of insurance, dating back to ancient times.

INLAND MARINE INSURANCE

Inland marine insurance covers personal property against loss or damage caused by various perils where the property is located. The property is also covered while it is being transported by any means other than on the oceans.

FIDELITY AND SURETY BONDING INSURANCE

Fidelity insurance provides coverage against financial loss caused by dishonesty. Such dishonest acts include embezzlement or failure of one person to perform a legal obligation to another, such as constructing a building as promised. Contracts of fidelity insurance are often known as surety bonds.

CHECKPOINT
Name the seven major types of insurance.

The oldest known marine insurance policy written in English covered the voyage of a ship called the Santa Crux which sailed from Calicut, India, to Lisbon, Portugal, around 1555. What does the existence of marine insurance in ancient and medieval periods suggest about trade in those times?

© GETTY IMAGES/PHOTODISC

WHAT IS AN INSURABLE INTEREST?

WHAT'S YOUR VERDICT?

While the kids were in their teens, Iris Nelson took out an insurance policy on her husband, Clyde, naming herself as beneficiary. The policy was for a quarter of a million dollars. Now, seven years later, the kids are out of college and leading their own lives, and she and Clyde are divorced. Nonetheless, she has continued paying the premiums on the policy.

If Clyde dies, can she legally collect the $250,000?

A person with contractual capacity can acquire insurance if he or she would suffer loss if the insured property is damaged or destroyed or if the insured person is injured or dies. This potential to sustain loss is referred to as an **insurable interest**.

INSURABLE INTERESTS IN PROPERTY

Any person who would suffer a direct and measurable monetary loss if property were damaged or destroyed has an insurable interest in that property. Note, however, for the insurer to be legally obligated to pay, an insurable interest in property must exist at the time of the loss. A person may not insure property, then sell it, and expect to be paid if the property is later damaged or destroyed.

A person need not hold all the property rights (title, possession, use, a security interest, or some future interest) in the insured property in order to have an insurable interest. Just one of these rights would be sufficient. Many individuals

IN THIS CASE

Canteleone drove a taxi that he leased from the Cab Company. The Cab Company owned the vehicle, but it was financed through the local bank. All three parties—Canteleone, the Cab Company, and the bank—have insurable interests in the vehicle.

may therefore have an insurable interest in the same property at the same time.

INSURABLE INTERESTS IN LIFE

A person has an insurable interest in her or his life. Everyone who meets the insurance company's requirements and is legally competent may acquire a life insurance policy on herself or himself. Would-be beneficiaries seeking to take out a policy on another person's life must demonstrate that they would suffer direct financial loss if the insured died.

Could this woman have had an insurable interest in her husband before he died? Why or why not?

© GETTY IMAGES/PHOTODISC

Creditors may insure their debtors, business people may insure their partners or key employees, and husbands and wives may insure one another. Courts frequently rule against adult children having insurable interests in their aging parents. Brothers and sisters ordinarily do not have insurable interests in each other.

Unlike property insurance, the insured has to demonstrate only an insurable interest at the time the policy is taken out, not at the time of the death of the person whose life is insured. Therefore, in *What's Your Verdict?*, Iris could legally collect the $250,000 upon the death of her ex-husband.

CHECKPOINT
What is an insurable interest?

18-1 Assessment

THINK ABOUT LEGAL CONCEPTS

1. The party who agrees to indemnify another is termed the (a) insurer (b) insured (c) beneficiary.

2. The face value of a policy is always paid whenever the covered loss is sustained. **True or False?**

3. The consideration for a contract of insurance is called the _?_.

4. The risk of any and all financial losses can be covered by insurance. **True or False?**

5. The party taking out the life insurance policy does not have to be the beneficiary nor the party whose life is insured. **True or False?**

6. Which type of insurance covers loss of or damage to property while it is being transported? (a) marine (b) surety (c) fidelity (d) none of the above

7. The three common types of life insurance include term, whole or ordinary, and _?_.

8. _?_ insurance provides coverage for a variety of specific situations in which the intentional, negligent, or accidental acts of others or mere chance may result in loss.

9. An insurable interest in property must exist at the time of loss for a fire insurance policy to pay. **True or False?**

THINK CRITICALLY ABOUT EVIDENCE

Study the situation, answer the questions, and then prepare arguments to support your answers.

10. Bentson's house was covered by an extensive fire insurance policy. One day Bentson had a grease fire in his kitchen. Thanks to the quick response of the fire department, the only damage from the fire itself was to the stove. However, several windows were broken by the fire department and much of the home's furnishings were damaged by water and smoke. Will the fire insurance policy cover these losses?

11. Your parents are concerned about the advancing age of their parents. They apply for life insurance on the lives of each of your grandparents, to be used to pay for funeral expenses. Will the applications be accepted?

12. Lampson sold Stark a large recreational vehicle for $52,500. However, Lampson forgot to cancel the insurance he held on the vehicle. One month after Stark bought the recreational vehicle, it was totally destroyed by fire. Shocked by the occurrence, Lampson then remembered the policy and immediately filed a claim for the loss of the recreational vehicle with his insurance company. Will he be able to collect?

13. Buck and Shannon formed a partnership to market a new type of computer memory device that Buck had developed. Shannon, who was in poor health, had all the business contacts that would make the venture a success. Buck worried that she would lose her $250,000 investment if Shannon died. Therefore, Buck insured Shannon's life for $250,000. A year later, Shannon quit the partnership and retired. Buck decided to keep the insurance in force, however. When Shannon died eight months after she retired, Buck sought to collect the $250,000 from the insurance company. Will she be successful?

Property and Casualty Insurance

PROPERTY AND CASUALTY INSURANCE

WHAT'S YOUR VERDICT?

When he noticed that his home's fire insurance policy from his regular carrier, Farmer's Mutual Aid, did not have coverage from loss due to earthquake, Worriare bought a second fire policy from West Coast Fire Insurance Co. that did. When the house burned down, Worriare tried to collect the full amount of the loss, some $450,000, from both companies.

Is he legally entitled to do so?

The general type of insurance intended to indemnify for harm to the insured's personal or real property brought about by perils such as fire, theft, and windstorm is **property insurance**. The type of insurance that indemnifies for losses resulting from accident, chance, or negligence is **casualty insurance**. There is some overlap between these two. Certain types of casualty insurance (for example, automotive policies) are written to indemnify for both casualty and property losses. Examples of casualty insurance include workers' compensation, disability insurance, and health insurance.

Liability insurance, which protects the insured against other parties' claims of negligence or other tortious conduct, also is a type of casualty insurance.

The purpose of all property and casualty insurance is indemnification for loss. This means that a person who experiences a loss recovers no more than the actual value of the loss. In *What's Your Verdict?* Worriare's total recovery from both insurance companies could not exceed $450,000.

Although property and casualty insurance can be obtained to indemnify for almost any peril that might cause a loss, certain exceptions to coverage relieve the insurance company from paying. These exceptions, known as **exclusions**, are expressly stated in the policy.

Many states make certain that all exclusions are easily noticeable within a policy. States may require that exclusions be set in a different style and larger size of type, in a different color of print, or both. Examples of common exclusions include losses due to war, invasion, rebellion, nuclear disaster, depreciation, and pollution.

What general type of insurance would you need to purchase to protect yourself from damage caused by a hurricane?

© GETTY IMAGES/PHOTODISC

FIRE INSURANCE

The type of property insurance that covers the direct loss to property resulting from fire, lightning strike, or removal from premises endangered by fire is known as **fire insurance**. Any fire insurance contract written to cover these risks is composed of a basic or standard fire policy and one or more forms that modify the standard policy to make it apply to the specific type of property being insured.

STANDARD FIRE POLICY The standard fire policy itself is composed of basic policy provisions required by the law of the state in which the policy is written. All the states have such provisions. Some forms include a Dwellings and Contents Form for homes and a Mercantile Building and Stock Form for businesses. For those who have no need for policies to cover the building itself, such as renters and tenants, there are special forms covering only the contents and other personal property.

ENDORSEMENTS TO THE STANDARD FIRE POLICY

The standard policy and forms may be modified by **endorsements**, also known as *riders*. Endorsements are attached to the policy and forms to provide for special and individual needs. Endorsements help, for example, in clarifying whether a loss was caused by fire, lightning, wind, explosion, or some other peril.

To illustrate this, suppose that a truck crashes into a building and explodes, causing a fire. In such a case, it would be hard to tell how much of the loss was caused by the impact of the truck, how much by the explosion, and how much by the resulting fire. To avoid this difficulty, a fire insurance policy may be issued with an extended coverage endorsement. This endorsement adds coverage for damage by windstorm, hail, explosion, riot, smoke, aircraft, and vehicles. Therefore, it would not be necessary to determine the exact cause of the damage, because all possible causes would be covered. Because of the frequency of the losses covered by an extended coverage endorsement, such an endorsement usually is added routinely to the Dwellings and Contents Form.

PROVING A LOSS SHOULD BE INDEMNIFIED

Regardless of the particular forms or endorsements added to the standard fire policy, three steps must be taken to prove that a particular loss should be indemnified.

1. The insured must show that there was an actual fire. A glow or a flame is required. Damage to an item resulting from scorching, blistering, or smoke due to being too near to a heat source is not enough.

2. The actual fire has to be hostile. A *hostile fire* is either (a) a fire started by accident, negligence, or a deliberate act uncontrolled by the insured or (b) a *friendly fire* (a fire in its intended place) that becomes uncontrollable.

3. The hostile fire has to be the natural and foreseeable cause of the loss. This cause is referred to as being the proximate cause of the harm. Generally, a hostile fire is considered the proximate cause of damage produced not only by the burning, but also produced by scorching, smoke, techniques used in extinguishing the fire, and actions in removing goods endangered by the fire.

"Wildfire" is the term used to describe any unwanted and unplanned fire burning in a forest, shrub, or grass. Nine out of ten "wildfires" are caused by humans. Explain, then, why most wildfires can be considered hostile.

© GETTY IMAGES/PHOTODISC

As the capability of fire departments to respond to alarms and quickly suppress fires has increased over the years, the number of structures totally lost to fire has decreased markedly. In recognition of this fact and the needs of their insureds to keep premiums low, insurance companies developed coinsurance.

COINSURANCE

Coinsurance is a clause in a fire insurance policy that requires the insured to maintain coverage equal to a certain percentage of the total current value of the insured property. The coverage amount, therefore, must be increased as the property value increases. In the event of loss, the insurance company will fully indemnify up to the face amount of the policy unless the insured has failed to keep that face amount at the proper level.

INLAND MARINE INSURANCE

Modeled after insurance covering goods being transported on the high seas, *inland marine insurance* was developed by fire insurance companies to indemnify for loss to most personal property while it is being transported across land or inland waterways. However, the carrier, such as the automobile, airplane, or railroad car, is not covered by this insurance. In response to the changing needs of insureds over time, the basic inland marine policy was altered to produce a second type, called a *personal property floater*. This was issued to cover any and all of an insured's personal property against practically any peril regardless of the location of the property. The term *floater* means that the protection floats with, or follows, the property.

Rather than have the policy written to cover all the insured's personal property, it also is possible to contract for coverage of scheduled (specifically identified) property, such as jewelry, furs, stamp collections, musical instruments, livestock, athletic equipment, wedding presents, computer and photographic equipment. One also can arrange to insure a single piece of personal property, such as an antique vase or a neon sign. Mail-order dealers frequently take out a blanket policy to cover all losses, including breakage and mysterious disappearances of shipped goods. Laundries and dry cleaners may take out policies covering possible losses to customers' property in their possession. Such a policy is known as *lessee insurance*.

Although the application of the personal property floater is quite broad, some losses are excluded from coverage. Examples include losses caused by wear and tear, repair efforts, dampness, temperature, war, confiscation, and dishonesty of a party to whom the goods have been entrusted.

LIABILITY INSURANCE

Liability insurance is a type of casualty insurance that indemnifies against personal injury or property damage claims for which the insured is legally responsible. Generally, liability coverage is limited to harm accidentally caused by the insured. Intentional infliction of harm by the insured is not covered.

Liability coverage is a major part of most automobile insurance policies. Coverage for liability claims not arising out of the operation of a motor vehicle often is offered as part of a homeowner's or an apartment dweller's insurance policy.

Many persons engaged in providing personal services, such as beauty salon operators, and most businesses usually carry liability insurance. Persons rendering professional services, such as hospital operators and physicians, usually purchase coverage for malpractice through liability

Why would surgeons need to purchase malpractice insurance?

insurance. Television and radio broadcasting companies also carry liability insurance to protect against liability for defamation.

CHECKPOINT

What general type of insurance indemnifies for losses resulting from accident, chance, or negligence?

AUTOMOBILE INSURANCE

WHAT'S YOUR VERDICT?

Kim drove to work early in the morning. She had a favorite shortcut across a mall parking lot. One spring morning she was cutting across the mall lot when the sun came up over one of the large department store buildings. Momentarily blinded, she drove into a concrete pillar supporting a handicapped sign. Kim was uninjured thanks to her seatbelt. The pillar was not damaged but Kim's small sports car was totaled.

What type of insurance would cover Kim for the loss of her vehicle in this situation?

A variety of coverages may be provided by the typical **automobile insurance** policy. These include liability coverage, medical payments coverage, collision and comprehensive coverage, and uninsured and underinsured coverage.

LIABILITY COVERAGE

An automobile insurance policy's liability coverage obligates the insurer to represent and provide for the insured's defense if the insured is accused of or sued for negligent ownership, maintenance, or use of the motor vehicle. In addition, if necessary, the coverage indemnifies for the payment of damages resulting from such negligence.

Automobile liability insurance coverage may be augmented by an *omnibus clause*. An omnibus clause extends similar coverage to all members of

NETBookmark

Access lawxtra.swlearning.com and click on the link for Chapter 18. Many web sites are available to help you become a wise consumer of automobile insurance. Click on "Auto Insurance Articles" under the Auto Insurance tab on the Insurance.com home page. Read one of the articles. Then prepare a one- to two-minute presentation to the class on what you learned.

lawxtra.swlearning.com

the named insured's household and to any person not in the household who is given permission to drive the insured's car.

Automobile liability insurance usually also provides coverage for the insured and members of the insured's family when such persons are operating non-owned vehicles with the owner's permission. This coverage applies to all borrowed or substitute automobiles. Examples include automobiles used when the car described in the policy has broken down or is being repaired or serviced. Also, if one purchases another automobile to replace the insured car, generally all the coverage under the policy applies to the replacement car for a limited time as specified in the policy.

When one becomes liable for damage or injury while driving a vehicle he or she does not own, the car owner's policy provides the primary coverage. The driver's policy then provides coverage up to its face amount for any excess liability.

Insurers are contractually liable for legitimate claims against their insureds. Therefore, the insurers have the right either to settle such claims out of court or to defend their insureds in court. Because the insurer has potential liability under the policy, only the insurer can make a settlement with claimants against the insured. If the insurer requires the presence of the insured as a witness at any legal hearings, most automobile insurance policies provide for payment of lost wages to the insured.

Liability claims against the insured that the insurer may have to pay include bodily injury or death of third parties and damage to the property of third parties. Third parties are persons other than the insured or insurer.

MEDICAL PAYMENTS COVERAGE

Medical payments coverage pays for the reasonable medical claims of occupants of the insured's vehicle who are injured in an automobile accident. An *occupant* is one who is in, upon, entering, or leaving a vehicle. The coverage also applies to the insured and the insured's family members while such persons are driving or riding in another's vehicle. This kind of coverage is mainly for vehicle occupants. However, it also covers the named insured and the family members if a vehicle strikes those persons while walking, riding bikes, roller skating, or sledding.

Imagine this woman was driving her sister's car when it collided with another car. What type of insurance would pay for any reasonable medical claims she might have as a result of the accident? Who would need to have this insurance?

© GETTY IMAGES/PHOTODISC

IN THIS CASE

Spielman was disabled due to the loss of his leg to diabetes. When his car broke down, Spielman borrowed a friend's. Unfortunately, when he went to hit the brake while approaching a stop sign, he mistakenly hit the accelerator and the car ran the stop sign and hit another. Two occupants of the other car were seriously injured and the other car totaled. The friend's auto policy limit for liability was $100,000. Consequently, the friend's insurance company would have to pay up to that amount. Spielman's auto insurance company would pay everything over that amount up to the limit of his policy. He would be personally responsible for any excess.

COLLISION AND COMPREHENSIVE COVERAGE

Two types of automobile insurance coverage indemnify insureds for damage to their own vehicles. The first, **collision insurance**, protects against direct and accidental damage due to the vehicle caused by (a) colliding with another object, such as a tree or bridge abutment, and (b) overturning (upset). Kim in *What's Your Verdict?* would be covered for the loss of her vehicle by collision insurance because she collided with the concrete pillar.

Collision coverage pays only the actual cash value (the cost new minus an allowance for age and use) of the vehicle or its damaged parts less any deductible. Thus, for each loss the insured pays up to the amount of the deductible. The insurer pays the rest up to the policy limit.

The second type of automobile insurance coverage indemnifying insureds for damage to their own vehicles is **comprehensive insurance**. (Sometimes it is called *other than collision insurance*.) Comprehensive insurance indemnifies against all damage to the insured's car except that caused by collision or upset. The causes covered by comprehensive insurance, include fire, theft, water, vandalism, hail, and glass breakage. Theft includes loss of the car and any part of the car, such as hubcaps. However, loss of clothing and other personal property left in the car generally is not covered unless the loss is by fire. Similarly, most policies require extra premiums to cover compact disc players, radios, and stereos. Any damage done to a car, such as broken locks, is covered.

Law Brief

Vehicular homicide is the unlawful killing of another with the use of a vehicle. Unlike the crime of murder, vehicular homicide does not require intent. Under a typical state statute, the punishment depends on the severity of the incident. First-degree vehicular homicide usually is a felony punishable by five to fifteen years in prison. Such a charge stems from events where a death has been caused by the defendant who unlawfully passed a stopped school bus, left the scene of the accident, was driving under the influence, was trying to flee from a police officer, etc.

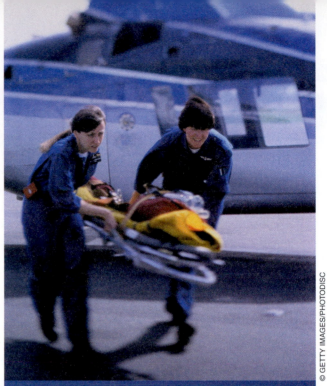

Imagine that this car accident victim does not survive the emergency airlift to the hospital. If the driver of the other car had been driving under the influence, what crime will he or she be guilty of, and what would the punishment likely be?

UNINSURED AND UNDERINSURED COVERAGE

An accident may be caused by the negligence of a driver who is uninsured and potentially insolvent or one who leaves the scene and cannot be found. In these situations, innocent parties involved in the accident may have to bear their own losses. Certainly their collision and medical payments coverage may help, but significant amounts of loss, for example, lost wages and the medical payments that exceed the limit of their policy, may not be indemnified.

Consequently, many vehicle owners carry a supplemental coverage to a regular policy. This additional coverage, called *uninsured motorists coverage,* allows the insured to collect damages from his or her own insurance company when they are not collectible because the person who caused the harm is uninsured. In most states, the coverage is limited to compensation for bodily injury, death, lost wages or support, and pain and suffering. Indemnification for property damage generally is excluded from this coverage. A similar type of coverage is *underinsured motorists coverage,* which compensates the insured when the negligent driver may be insured but does not have sufficient insurance to cover damages. Like uninsured motorists coverage, underinsured motorists coverage excludes payment for property damage.

NO-FAULT INSURANCE

To cut back on the growing number of cases in our court systems, some states have instituted no-fault insurance systems. **No-fault insurance** requires that parties to an automobile accident be indemnified by their own insurance company regardless of who is at fault. Therefore, a court trial to determine who is at fault in an accident may be avoided. The indemnification of the losses by the insurance company takes the place of the damages that might have been awarded. However, if the medical claims of an injured person exceed a set amount or the injuries are permanent, a suit can be brought for all alleged damages, including pain and suffering.

Generally, property damage is not covered at all by a no-fault system. This is because it is not likely that people will sue for the amounts involved. Insurance companies tend to resolve such claims fairly and efficiently without court involvement.

CHECKPOINT

What four major types of coverage are found in a typical automobile insurance policy?

ECONOMIC IMPACT

NO-FAULT INSURANCE

The basic idea behind no-fault insurance was to lower premiums by saving the expenses and delays of court trials. However, today in most of the states that have adopted the idea, no-fault policies actually cost more than regular policies. In a true no-fault system, the driver's insurance company would pay for all their insured's losses in an auto accident up to the policy limits. No state has seen fit to adopt such a system, however. In the 12 states plus the District of Columbia that have no-fault systems at the current time (DC, FL, HI, KS, KY, MA, MI, MN, NJ, NY, ND, PA,), the legislatures only adopted a part of the no-fault concept (called PIP for personal injury protection) into law. Typically these states have retained the right to sue the other driver under certain conditions. These conditions are based on the severity of the accident or the dollar level of the potential loss. As a consequence, liability insurance is mandated in all the no-fault states in addition to the no-fault policy.

THINK CRITICALLY

Why do you think the states did not adopt a pure no-fault system? Why might the costs be higher for no-fault in the states that have adopted it, than for a regular insurance policy?

18-2 Assessment

Xtra!
Study Tools
lawxtra.swlearning.com

THINK ABOUT LEGAL CONCEPTS

1. Automobile insurance may be written to indemnify for both casualty and property losses. **True or False?**

2. Which of the following is not a common exclusion in a property and casualty policy? (a) loss due to depreciation (b) loss due to pollution (c) loss due to war (d) All of the above are common exclusions.

3. Which of the following is not covered in the standard fire policy? (a) losses due to fire (b) losses due to lightning strikes (c) losses due to inept attorneys (d) none of the above are covered

4. A friendly fire that becomes uncontrollable is considered a hostile fire for fire insurance purposes. **True or False?**

5. A(n) _?_ clause extends auto insurance coverage to members of the insured's household.

THINK CRITICALLY ABOUT EVIDENCE

Study the situation, answer the questions, and then prepare arguments to support your answers.

6. Scandinavian Fire Insurance Company insured Carnes against fire. One day while ironing, he left the room to answer the telephone and negligently forgot to turn off the iron. The iron fell from the ironing board, and the carpet caught fire. The fire then spread to the drapes. As flames engulfed the room, smoke damaged the remainder of the house. Will the loss be covered by the policy?

7. To protect her inventory, Olivet, owner of an appliance store, carried a coinsurance fire policy. The policy required that Olivet carry insurance in the amount of 80 percent of the current inventory value. Late one night, fire totally destroyed the inventory, which was valued at $100,000 when the loss occurred. The face value of Olivet's policy was $80,000. For how much of the $100,000 loss will the insurance company pay?

Life and Social Insurance

LIFE INSURANCE

WHAT'S YOUR VERDICT?

Edmonton was the beneficiary of her uncle's term life insurance policy. When her uncle, a Navy pilot on active duty, was killed in a terrorist bomb explosion overseas, the insurance company refused to pay the policy's face value of $100,000.

Can the insurance company legally be forced to pay the policy?

Life insurance is a contractual arrangement under which an insurer promises to pay an agreed-upon amount of money to a named party upon the death of a particular person. Given the uncertainties of today's fast-paced world, such insurance is crucial to families, businesses, and responsible individuals throughout our society. The insurer of life agrees to pay to a named beneficiary or to the insured's estate the amount stated in the policy, in accordance with the policy provisions.

EXEMPTIONS

Life insurance policies sometimes contain provisions that exempt (or excuse) the insurer from liability when death is due to certain causes, such as the crash of a private airplane. These provisions are called *exemptions*. Policies also may provide for exemption from liability in case of the policyholder's death during military service abroad or at home.

In cases where death occurs under an exemption, the insurer is liable for return of the premiums paid or cash value (less loans against the policy), instead of the proceeds. In *What's Your Verdict?* if such an exemption were in Edmonton's uncle's policy, the insurance company legally could not be forced to pay the $100,000.

INCONTESTABILITY CLAUSE

In addition to exemptions, a life insurance policy usually contains an *incontestability clause*. Such a clause prohibits the insurer from refusing to perform due to misrepresentation or fraud after the policy has been in effect for a specified period of time—usually one or two years. However, if the misrepresentation or fraud involves the age of the insured, the policy is not voided regardless of the length of time it has been in effect. Instead the insurer provides the face amount of insurance that the premium would have bought if the insured's correct age had been known.

A similar clause requires the insurer to pay even if the insured commits suicide after one or two years from the date the policy was issued. If the suicide occurs before the one- or two-year limit, the insurer is required to return only the premiums paid.

Why might a life insurance policy contain an exemption for a policyholder's death due to the crash of a private airplane?

© GETTY IMAGES/PHOTODISC

GRACE PERIOD

By statute, most life insurance contracts must also provide for a period of time, called the *grace period,* during which an overdue premium can be paid to keep the policy in force. Typically, this period is one month. If an insured fails to pay the premium before the grace period expires, the policy terminates, or lapses. A policyholder in good health who pays the back premiums can revive or reinstate a lapsed policy.

ADDITIONAL COVERAGES

In addition to these common provisions, it is possible to write additional coverage into a life insurance policy. One way is through *double indemnity coverage,* which requires the insurer to pay twice the face amount of the policy if the death of the insured is accidental. Triple or quadruple coverage also may be purchased, if desired. Such coverage usually excludes certain causes of death, such as suicide, illness or disease, wartime military service, and certain airplane accidents. It also is inapplicable after a certain age, such as 65 or 70.

The second additional coverage, disability coverage, provides for protection against the effects of total permanent disability. At a minimum, it cancels the requirement for payment of policy premiums while the insured is totally disabled. It often provides money to replace lost wages.

IN THIS CASE

Elton's life insurance policy was for $500,000 when he died of pneumonia at the age of 57. His policy contained a triple indemnity clause. As a consequence, his wife anticipated a payout of $1.5 million dollars. However, as the death was by natural causes the company only had to pay the face amount of $500,000.

CHECKPOINT

To whom is a life insurance policy face amount paid when the insured dies?

WHAT'S YOUR VERDICT?

Johnny contracted diabetes late in life. After several years fighting the disease, he lost first one leg and then another to the point where he was unable to work at all.

What social insurance program would assist him?

The primary source for social insurance coverage in this country is the federal government's Social Security Act. Coverage provided under the act frequently is labeled RSDHI (for Retirement, Survivors', Disability, and Health Insurance). Unemployment compensation, which is designed to lessen the financial hardship of losing one's job, also is provided indirectly through programs under the act. Unemployment compensation programs, however, are controlled by the individual states.

RETIREMENT INSURANCE

An eligible person may elect to begin receiving social security retirement insurance checks as early as age 62. The amount of these checks, however, is just a percentage of the full retirement check available between 65 and 67 years of age. (65 is the full retirement age if you were born in 1937 or before. The age gradually increases to 67 if you were born in 1960 or later.) Regardless of when you retire, the checks are meant to provide supplemental income only.

LEGAL RESEARCH

Unemployment benefits are a vital part of social insurance. However, they vary widely in eligibility, duration, and amount. Research unemployment law of your state and a state in a different region and report your findings to the class. How well could you live on what your state provides?

Too often, individuals rely solely on these checks for their retirement income. This is not the purpose of the program.

During the working years, each individual is responsible for accumulating savings. These savings should provide enough income that, when added to the social security retirement amount, will allow an adequate standard of living during the retirement years. All too often, people retire only to find that they have to return to some form of employment to make ends meet.

SURVIVOR'S INSURANCE

Survivors of a person eligible for benefits under the system also may receive benefits if they are

- a widow or widower age 60 or older (or, if disabled, age 50 or older)
- a widow or widower of any age if caring for a child under age 16 or a child that is disabled
- a dependent child.

© GETTY IMAGES/PHOTODISC

What do you think about working during what are traditionally thought to be "the retirement years"? Should the federal government be responsible for paying for your entire livelihood when you retire through the social security program? Why or why not?

DISABILITY INSURANCE

A severe, long-lasting disability is one that prevents the eligible person from being able to do "any substantial work." Before any payments can be made, it must be established that the condition is physical or mental, and is expected to continue indefinitely or result in death. The disabled person must have earned a certain number of work credits within a specific time period. The eligible person must not refuse reasonable medical treatment.

The following conditions ordinarily are considered severe enough to meet the test of disability:

- Loss of both arms, both legs, or a leg and an arm. In *What's Your Verdict?* the loss of both his legs to diabetes would make Johnny eligible for assistance under the disability coverage of the social security system.
- Heart and lung diseases that cause pain or fatigue on slight exertion
- Progressive cancer
- Brain damage that results in loss of judgment or memory
- Loss of vision, inability to speak, deafness

HEALTH INSURANCE

In the last two decades, the costs of medical care have risen so dramatically that a major illness involving extended hospitalization and treatment threatens not only the physical well-being but also the financial livelihood of the patient and the patient's family. As a consequence, health insurance, which indemnifies against the cost of medical care necessary to regain physical well-being after an illness, has become very important. Medicare provides such coverage primarily for those age 65 and older. Private insurance com-panies provide similar coverage for those not protected by the Social Security Act.

MEDICARE Medicare consists of two basic pro-grams. The first, hospital insurance, helps pay for hospital expenses and the costs of follow-up treatment. To receive payments under this program, an eligible person must enter a hospital for necessary treatment. Persons with enough work credits and who are age 65, those with permanent kidney failure, or those covered for extensive periods by the disability program if under age 65 are eligible.

Medical insurance, the second basic Medicare program, helps pay for items not covered by hospital insurance. These include services of physicians and surgeons. Also included are services such as ambulance charges, X-rays, radium treatments, laboratory tests, surgical dressings, casts, and home visits by nurses or therapists. The patient pays relatively small yearly deductibles, and then medical insurance generally pays either a large percentage or all of the costs of the covered services.

Unlike hospital insurance coverage, financed primarily from the social security tax, contracting and paying premiums for medical insurance coverage are voluntary. Each person enrolled in the medical insurance plan pays a monthly premium. The federal government pays an equal amount out of general revenues.

CHECKPOINT
What does RSDHI stand for?

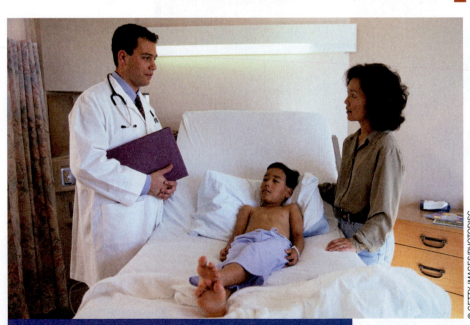

© GETTY IMAGES/PHOTODISC

In 2003, an estimated 15.6 percent of the U.S. population was without health insurance coverage. Do you think that the U.S. government should be responsible for providing health insurance coverage for all U.S. citizens? Why or why not?

THINK ABOUT LEGAL CONCEPTS

1. Which of the following indemnifies against the cost of medical care necessary to regain physical well-being after an illness? (a) survivor's insurance (b) disability insurance (c) health insurance (d) life insurance

2. Unemployment programs under the Social Security Administration are controlled directly by the federal government. **True or False?**

3. Which of the following types of social insurance provides health insurance and hospital insurance for people age 65 and older? (a) retirement insurance (b) survivor's insurance (c) disability insurance (d) Medicare

4. A(n) _?_ clause prohibits an insurer from refusing to perform due to fraud or misrepresentation after a policy has been in effect for one or two years.

5. Double-indemnity coverage requires the insurer to pay half the face amount of the policy if the death of the insured is accidental. **True or False?**

THINK CRITICALLY ABOUT EVIDENCE

Study the situation, answer the questions, and then prepare arguments to support your answers.

6. When Henecker took out his life insurance policy, he misrepresented his age as 27. In reality, he was 34. Will the insurance company be required to pay on the policy when Henecker dies?

7. When she turned 62, Shirly filed for her social security retirement benefits. Will she receive more money per month because she filed early?

8. Shuster had a $100,000 life insurance policy. Three years after contracting for it, she committed suicide. Will the insurance company have to pay $100,000?

9. A month after his release from jail, Bill Bravo insured his own life in a double indemnity policy. Two months later, he was killed while attempting to hold up a bank. The insurance company refused to pay the benefits to Bill's wife and son, even though the policy contained no provision excluding liability if the insured died as a result of violating the law. Under what legal grounds can the insurance company refuse to pay this claim?

PREVENT LEGAL DIFFICULTIES

1. Be honest in answering all questions on insurance applications. A false representation or warranty or concealing a material fact may allow the insurance company to void the policy rather than pay for the loss.

2. Carefully read the insurance contract to be familiar with all its terms. Pay special attention to stated exclusions and conditions.

3. Select your potential insurers with caution as to their financial reserves and their reputation for good service in case of loss.

4. Be aware of the expiration dates, cancellation terms, and renewal provisions of your policies. Move quickly to acquire other coverage if a policy lapses or is terminated.

5. One of the most frequently incurred and potentially disastrous liabilities results from a lawsuit based on bodily injury and property damage in an automobile accident. To protect yourself, carry adequate automobile liability coverage.

6. If you are sued as a result of an accident and you have complied with the policy requirements, your insurer is required to defend you. Thus, if you are involved in an accident, no matter how trivial it may seem to you, report it to your insurer immediately.

7. If you are self-employed, report your income fully so as to be eligible for the maximum amount of social security benefits.

Chapter 18 Assessment

CONCEPTS IN BRIEF

18-1   Insurance Fundamentals

1. Although insurance is an excellent way to protect against possible loss, certain risks such as that of doing business cannot be covered.

2. Fire insurance policies can be augmented to cover other risks as well, such as hail, earthquake, and windstorm.

3. An insurable interest in property must exist at the time of the damage or destruction of the subject matter or the insurance will not pay for the loss.

4. An insurable interest in life need only exist at the time the policy was taken out.

18-2   Property and Casualty Insurance

5. Losses covered by a fire insurance policy will be indemnified only upon a showing that they were most likely caused by a hostile fire.

6. A property or casualty insurance policy can be assigned only with the consent of the insurer. The right to recover from an insurer a loss that already has been sustained may be assigned by the insured without consent of the insurer.

7. Coinsurance requires the insured to keep the face value of the policy equal to a certain percentage (usually 80 percent) of the current value of the insured property.

8. The basic purpose of automobile insurance is to provide coverage against liability. It also can provide medical payments coverage, collision and comprehensive coverage, and uninsured and underinsured coverage.

9. No-fault insurance indemnifies the insured for various losses sustained in an automobile accident regardless of who had legal responsibility for the accident. It is now required by some states.

18-3   Life and Social Insurance

10. Life insurance policies may be subject to exemptions for deaths related to military service, private airplane crashes, and others.

11. Federal disability insurance provides monthly benefits for a worker and dependents if a severe, long-lasting disability is suffered.

12. Social security retirement insurance provides monthly benefits for a worker and dependents when the worker retires at age 62 or later.

YOUR LEGAL VOCABULARY

Match each statement with the term that it best defines. Some terms may not be used.

1. To make good a loss
2. Party who will indemnify if loss occurs
3. Stated maximum amount that can be paid under a policy
4. Consideration for a contract of insurance
5. The potential loss that has been insured against
6. Potential to sustain loss due to the covered risk
7. Indemnifies for loss from personal negligence, chance, and accident
8. Exceptions to insurance coverage
9. Modifications to the standard fire policy made to satisfy individual needs
10. Requires that, in the event of loss, insureds be indemnified by their own insurance companies
11. Clause in a fire policy that requires the insured to maintain coverage equal to a certain percentage of the total current value of the insured property
12. Recipient of the amount to be paid under an insurance policy

a. automobile insurance
b. beneficiary
c. casualty insurance
d. coinsurance
e. collision insurance
f. comprehensive insurance
g. endorsements
h. exclusions
i. face value
j. fire insurance
k. indemnify
l. insurable interest
m. insurance
n. insured
o. insurer
p. liability insurance
q. life insurance
r. no-fault insurance
s. policy
t. premium
u. property insurance
v. risk

REVIEW LEGAL CONCEPTS

13. As a seasonal bonus you are planning a trip for your employees to the local casino. Each one is to be given $1,000 in credit and must share half of any earnings with the business. Is insurance available to cover your risk?

14. Why does the insurable interest in property have to be present at the time of loss?

15. What is the purpose of fidelity insurance?

16. The insurable interest in life only has to be present when the policy is taken out. Can you think of situations where this might lead to problems?

17. Why should renters and tenants have fire and liability insurance?

WRITE ABOUT LEGAL CONCEPTS

18. Compose a persuasive written statement for the editorial page of your newspaper as to why flight insurance should be no longer allowed.

19. **HOT DEBATE** Write a persuasive opening statement that emphasizes the legal and ethical points in your favor. Write a persuasive opening statement that emphasizes the legal and ethical points in the insurer's favor.

MAKE ACADEMIC CONNECTIONS

20. **POLITICAL SCIENCE** Research the issues surrounding the funding of the social security system. Note especially how it was treated during the last presidential election and the demograph- ics among seniors regarding which candidate they voted for. Write a paper connecting the prospects for the system with the results.

THINK CRITICALLY ABOUT EVIDENCE

Study the situation, answer the questions, and then prepare arguments to support your answers.

21. An abandoned store surrounded by high, dry weeds stood adjacent to a frequently traveled road near Ashleigh's home. She realized that the store would be destroyed if just one cigarette butt were thrown from a passing vehicle. Therefore, even though she did not own it, she decided to insure the building against loss by fire. After she obtained the insurance, there was a fire that destroyed the structure. Legally, will Ashleigh be allowed to collect?

22. Claudia James took out a $200,000 life insurance policy on her husband and named herself as beneficiary. Three months later they were divorced, and a month after that her ex-husband died in a car accident. Claudia sought to collect on the policy, but the insurance company refused to pay. The company said she lacked an insurable interest both at the time the policy was taken out and at the time of death. Is the company legally obligated to pay the $200,000?

23. McNeely owned a go-cart track on which the public was invited to race the small motorized carts that she provided. Collisions and upsets occurred relatively frequently. What type of insurance would it be advisable for McNeely to have?

24. Dr. Bray performed a tympanoplasty (eardrum replacement) on Azle. The operation appeared to be successful, but one year later the doctor found the ear canal to be completely closed due to the growth of scar tissue from areas where Dr. Bray had drilled improperly. What type of insurance would protect Dr. Bray from a malpractice suit by Azle?

25. Sarnof took a summer job to earn money for his college education. On his way home from work late one evening, a drunken driver ran a red light and smashed into Sarnof's car. Sarnof's medical bills were more than $45,000 and his injuries prevented him from working for the rest of the summer. Unfortunately, the drunken driver had only the minimum state-required liability coverage ($10,000). The driver's other known assets totaled less than $5,000. This will cause Sarnof to exhaust his college fund and take out a loan to pay his medical bills. What type of auto insurance coverage would have helped Sarnof cover the excess costs?

26. Antrell made an offer to purchase a building on the Leech Lake Indian Reservation for $300. He paid $100 in cash at the time he made the offer and received the keys to the structure. Without examining the property, his insurance company issued a policy with a face value of $16,000. Several months later, fire totally destroyed the structure. At the time of the loss, Antrell had not paid the balance of the purchase price nor had the title been transferred. The company claims that the plaintiff did not have the required insurable interest and that, therefore, the company was not liable on the policy. Do you think the company should pay? (*Antrell v. Pearl Assurance Company,* 89 N.W.2d 726)

27. Lakin sued the Postal Life and Casualty Insurance Company for its failure to pay him, as beneficiary, under an insurance policy on the life of his business partner, Hankinson. Evidence presented at the trial showed that Hankinson had contributed neither capital nor skills to the alleged partnership, that he could not issue partnership checks, and that he could not hire or fire employees. In addition, it was disclosed that Lakin paid the policy premiums and had made no settlement of "partnership" interests after Hankinson's death. Should the insurance company be ordered by the court to pay the $25,000 face amount to Lakin? (*Lakin v. Postal Life and Casualty Insurance Company,* 316 S.W.2d 542)

28. In the life insurance policy agreed to by James McElroy was a term that read, "if the insured is over the age of 54 years at the date hereof, this policy is void. . . ." McElroy was indeed over 54 at the time. When he died three years later, his beneficiary sued for the face amount of the policy claiming it should be paid because of a two-year incontestability clause in the same policy. Should the court order the insurance company to pay the policy's face amount? (*Hall v. Missouri Ins. Co.,* 208 S.W.2d 830)

29. Milburn carried automobile damage and theft insurance on his Cadillac sedan as required by the creditor on his car loan. Milburn could no longer make the payments. He turned the car over to an automobile salesperson to sell. The salesperson ultimately disappeared with the car. The insurer, Manchester Insurance Company, refused to pay, and World Investment Company, Milburn's creditor on the loan, sued Manchester. Manchester claimed the policy insured against theft which, as larceny, involved a taking against the owner's will. Because Milburn voluntarily delivered the car to the salesperson, no theft had occurred. World Investment Company claimed that the word "theft" should be given its common meaning of "steal" and so the insurance company should pay. What do you think? (*World Investment Co. v. Manchester Insurance and Indemnity Co.,* 380 S.W.2d 487)

30. When Wilson and his passenger Davison were injured in an automobile accident, the insurance company stated that the policy on Wilson excluded coverage of more than one person in a single accident. Davison sued, contending that because the exclusion of coverage in the policy was not in a different color or type than the rest of the policy as required by state statute, the term was void. The insurance company pointed out that although the exclusion did not appear in a different color or type of print, it was in a section of the policy clearly labeled "exclusions." Should Davison be allowed to collect? (*Davison v. Wilson,* 239 N.W.2d 38)

31. Gary Stallings was on active duty with the National Guard when the three-quarter-ton truck he was driving overturned and caused a fellow Guard member and passenger, Robert Ward, bodily injury. Stallings was the named insured in Michigan Mutual Liability Company's "Auto-Guard" Family Insurance Policy. When Ward sued Stallings for the injuries, Michigan Mutual refused to defend Stallings and denied responsibility to pay any judgment that might result. In addition to other coverages, the policy obligated the company to defend and pay judgments up to the policy limit if the insured was driving a "nonowned automobile." The company maintained that the three-quarter-ton army truck with canvas top and doors was not an automobile. What do you think? (*Michigan Mutual Liability Company v. Stallings,* 523 S.W.2d 539)

CASE FOR LEGAL THINKING

HALL v. WILKERSON
926 F.2D 311

BACKGROUND At the time of the automobile accident that is the origin of this suit, Wayne Wilkerson was residing in the home of Gwendolyn Hall. Before she left for France one spring, Hall gave permission to Wilkerson to continue to reside in her house and to drive her car under certain prescribed conditions. In particular, there were to be no drugs in her car, and she considered alcohol to be a drug just like any other.

FACTS Unfortunately, Wayne Wilkerson liked to drink—and he drank a lot. So after having consumed a large quantity of beer one day, he was involved in an accident. The accident involved only one vehicle. In the accident both of Wilkerson's passengers, Susan Kilmer and Richard Schock, were seriously injured. The car Wilkerson was driving in the accident was Gwendolyn Hall's.

LOWER COURT Gwendolyn Hall's insurance company and the injured parties brought this suit seeking a determination of whether or not Wayne Wilkerson was an insured at the time of the accident.

The lower court concluded that Wilkerson's use of alcohol was indeed a violation of the conditions imposed on his being able to use Hall's vehicle with permission. Therefore, he was not an "insured" under Hall's policy.

APPEALS The state law where the accident occurred requires that insurance coverage be maintained under such permissive use clauses in a policy if the driver's deviation is slight and inconsequential. It will not be permissive use if the deviation is substantial.

ISSUE Gwendolyn Hall's automobile insurance policy read:

"Who is an insured (under this policy)?"

The policy then answered its own question as follows:

"For YOUR car—YOU, any RELATIVE, and anyone else using YOUR CAR if the use is (or is reasonably believed to be) with YOUR PERMISSION, are INSUREDS.

PRACTICE JUDGING

1. Should the policyholder have the power to eliminate insurance coverage by imposing conditions on permission to drive, as Gwendolyn Hall did in this case? For example, what if Hall had granted Wilkerson permission to drive on the condition that he neither damage the car nor involve it in an accident?

2. If Wilkerson is not an insured, the injured parties lose a major source of funding to pay for the expenses of recovering from their injuries. This may prevent them from receiving treatment that would enable them to engage in gainful employment and/or may force them into conditions of financial hardship. On the other hand, holding that they are unable to recover from their injuries because Wilkerson is not an insured may send a warning to others to be careful about the persons from whom they accept rides under similar circumstances. From a societal standpoint, which alternative do you think should be chosen? Why?

3. How do you think the appellate court should hold? Why?

CHAPTER 19

Wills, Trusts, and Estates

19-1 Property Distribution Upon Death

19-2 Trusts

Jewell Marie was 83 when she suffered her first stroke. She recovered well and went back to living on her own about three blocks from her son and his family. Two years later she had another, more serious, stroke. Her son then moved her into his home. The burden of caring for Jewell increased. She would seldom eat and usually threw the food on the server. She had little control of her bodily functions and had to be cleaned each evening by her son. Finally, she suffered a massive stroke and was placed in intensive care in a local hospital. Jewell remained in a coma-like state for a week. Her doctor approached the son and suggested "off the record" that he could put Jewell to sleep peacefully but permanently before the hospitalization expenses ate up her financial resources.

© GETTY IMAGES/PHOTODISC

Where Do You Stand?

1. Discuss the legal and ethical reasons in favor of keeping Jewell alive.

2. List the legal and ethical reasons for putting her to "sleep."

Property Distribution Upon Death

LEGAL ALTERNATIVES IN PROPERTY DISTRIBUTION

WHAT'S YOUR VERDICT?

Ethel had lived within 10 miles of her birthplace her entire life. She never married and worked in a local factory until retirement. Then she lived on her social security checks. Ethel was an avid and conservative saver. When she died the value of her property totaled more than $800,000 but she had never made a will.

How will her property be distributed?

When a person dies, the law looks for his or her instructions to resolve some basic legal issues that arise. These issues include how the debts of the person who dies, called the **decedent**, are to be paid and what is to be done with the remaining property. The necessary instructions are found either in the wishes of the decedent as expressed in a will, in statutes (especially if the decedent did not leave a will), or both.

DEATH WITHOUT A WILL

Those who die without a valid will are said to have died **intestate**. When a person dies intestate, as Ethel did in *What's Your Verdict?,* a special court has the power to settle the affairs of the decedent. This court, generally called a *probate court* or *surrogate's court,* appoints a personal representative known as an **administrator** to take charge of the intestate's property. This representative uses the property of the deceased, called the **estate**, to pay all debts, including the costs of administering the estate. The remainder of the property will then be distributed in accordance with the state's intestacy statute. Dying without a professionally drafted will can cause the beneficiaries to pay considerable administrative expenses and needlessly large estate taxes.

Intestacy statutes vary from state to state. Generally, intestacy statutes call for a surviving spouse to receive one-third to one-half of the estate with the remainder divided equally among the children. A representative division of an intestate decedent's assets is presented in the Law Brief on page 345.

DEATH WITH A WILL

All concerned usually benefit if the decedent dies **testate**, or leaving a valid will. A **will** is a legal expression, usually in writing, by which a person directs how her or his property is to be distributed after death. (See the example on the next page of the "Last Will and Testament of Rebecca Birk Faulstich.") The maker of the will is called the **testator**. A will allows a person to direct his or her estate's resources to where they can do the most good. This contrasts with the intestacy

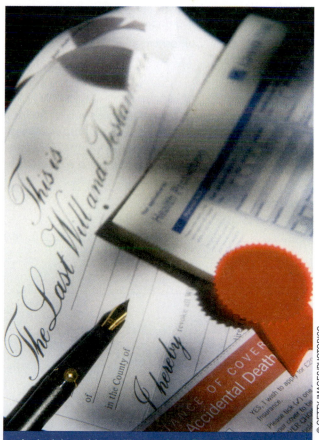

Why is dying with a will more beneficial to a person and his or her heirs than dying without a will?

LAST WILL AND TESTAMENT
REBECCA BIRK FAULSTICH

I, Rebecca Birk Faulstich, of 1875 El Rey Way, San Francisco, California, declare that this is my will. I revoke all wills and codicils that I have previously made.

FIRST: I am married to Kevin Alan Faulstich and we have one child, Jeffrey Michael, born March 12, 2001.

SECOND: After payment of all my debts, I give my estate as follows:

(A) To my twin sister, Rachel Ann Wilson, I give my personal clothing, jewelry, and sporting equipment, if she should survive me.

(B) To my beloved husband, Kevin, I give all the residue if he should survive me for thirty (30) days.

(C) To our son, Jeffrey Michael, I give all the residue if my husband should not survive me for thirty days and if my son should survive me for thirty days.

(D) To the Regents of the University of California (to provide student scholarships and awards without reference to financial need, in order to encourage excellence of effort and achievement), I give all the residue if neither my husband nor my son should survive me for thirty days.

THIRD: I nominate my husband as the executor of this will. If for any reason he should fail to qualify or cease to act as such, I nominate my sister, Rachel, as executrix. If for any reason she should fail to qualify or cease to act as such, I nominate the Central City Bank, a California corporation, to act as executor. I direct that neither my husband nor my sister be required to post bond as executor or executrix.

IN WITNESS WHEREOF, I have hereunto set my hand this ___18th___ day of __January__, 2006, in San Francisco, California.

Rebecca Birk Faulstich
Rebecca Birk Faulstich

The foregoing instrument was subscribed on the date which it bears by the testatrix, Rebecca Birk Faulstich, and at the time of subscribing was declared by her to be her last will. The subscription and declaration were made in our presence, and being present at the same time; and we, at her request and in her presence and in the presence of each other, have affixed our signatures hereto as witnesses:

Diana P. Davis residing at _432 Third Street_
San Francisco, California

Adam T. Price residing at _1644 Prospector's Point_
San Francisco, California

statutes, which distribute a decedent's estate without regard for need.

A will also allows its maker to name his or her own personal representative, called an **executor**, to carry out the directions in the will. The testator can specify that the executor be exempted from *posting bond,* or paying the court a sum of money to insure the duties are properly performed. A will also may be used to name a guardian for minor children of the testator. Through the will, the named guardian also can be exempted from posting a bond.

Living will is a term used for a document directed to attending physicians regarding a person's choices about the use of life-support systems in treatment for terminal illness or vegetative state. Be sure to distinguish living wills from the wills described in this chapter. The term *living will* is a poor label. A more descriptive term for living will would be "Directive to Physicians." An alternative to achieve the same end would be using a *durable power of attorney,* which confers on a chosen or court-appointed individual the right to make health-care decisions, such as removal of life support.

CREATION AND EXECUTION OF A VALID WILL

To counteract the possibility of forgery, the law has strict requirements regarding the preparation and execution of valid wills. To be valid, a will must conform to the state laws regarding creation and execution. The most basic requirements in almost every state are the following:

1. The testator must have the clear intention to make a will. This is called *testamentary intent.* A person must not be pressured into signing the document against his or her desires by the undue influence of others. Likewise, the signer must not be misled into thinking that the document is something other than a will.

2. At the time the will is executed, the testator must have testamentary capacity to make the will. *Testamentary capacity* means the maker must know, at least in a general way, the kind and extent of the property involved, the persons who stand to benefit, and that he or she is making arrangements to dispose of his or her property after death. Lapses into senility by the maker may bring the will of an elderly person into question due to the possible lack of capacity. In most states a person under age 18 does not have testamentary capacity.

3. Ordinarily the will must be in writing and, in most states, signed at the end of the document to prevent unauthorized additions. The signing must be witnessed by at least two adults. In some states, three witnesses must sign. These witnesses should not be individuals who will inherit under the will. The witnesses must be advised that they are watching the testator's will being signed as they do so.

AMENDMENT OF A VALID WILL

A will takes effect only upon the death of the maker. Therefore, it can be changed or canceled at any time during the maker's life. However, this ability to change the document as often as desired, coupled with the fact that the contents of a will are proved only after the death of the maker, opens the way to potentially false claims under forged documents.

Regardless of the potential problems in making changes, it is, nonetheless, important that the maker of a will keep it current. Marriage, divorce, the birth of children, and other significant changes in a person's life should be reflected in the document by periodic amendments or by a new will. In states requiring a formal will, changes must be made using a **codicil**, which is a formal, written, and witnessed amendment. A codicil must be executed with the same formalities as a will.

SPECIAL TYPES OF WILLS

There are exceptions to the rules for the creation, execution, and altering of a valid will. For example, many states recognize a **holographic will** as valid even without witnesses. A holographic will is one that was written entirely by the decedent's own hand and signed by him or her. Where a valid holographic will is used, changes require appropriate additions or deletions before witnesses, if necessary, in the handwriting of the maker.

A **nuncupative will**, or oral will, is recognized in some states if proclaimed during the maker's last illness or by service personnel on active duty. However, the will must be witnessed and often is limited to controlling the distribution of personal property.

IN THIS CASE

While cleaning her rifle, Charleson accidentally shot herself. As she lay dying, she told the paramedics and the responding police officer that she was making an oral will. She then stated that she wanted her valuable collection of dolls to go to her only granddaughter, Annabelle. Charleson's state allowed nuncupative wills if the witnesses' recollections of the will agreed and were properly and promptly reduced to writing. Therefore, Charleson's dying wish would be carried out.

REVOCATION OF A WILL A will is subject to partial or total change at the desire of the testator. A will is only intended to take effect upon the testator's death. Anytime before that moment, as long as the testator has testamentary intent and testamentary capacity, the will can be amended. A will also can be completely revoked. A will may be completely revoked, rather than being amended, in several ways. Doing something to the will that clearly indicates intent to revoke it, such as destroying it or defacing it, will accomplish this end.

According to some state statutes, the marriage of the maker or the birth or adoption of a child by that individual works an automatic termination of the will. Divorce, on the other hand, does not produce such an automatic revocation. However, a divorce settlement does revoke the parts of a will with which the settlement conflicts once the divorce occurs.

Finally, a will may be revoked by a written revocation in a later will. Such a document must either explicitly state, "I hereby revoke all prior wills," or contain provisions that conflict with the prior will so that it impliedly revokes the preceding document.

CHECKPOINT

What does it mean to die intestate?

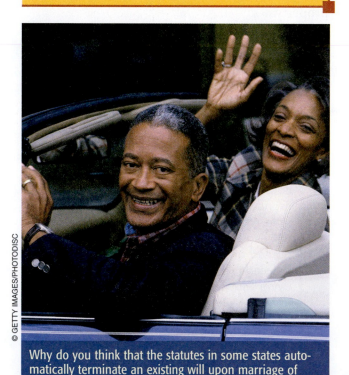

© GETTY IMAGES/PHOTODISC

Why do you think that the statutes in some states automatically terminate an existing will upon marriage of the testator?

DISTRIBUTION OF THE DECEDENT'S ESTATE

WHAT'S YOUR VERDICT?

Strontiumm made a personal loan to his old business school buddy, Burser. The money, $45,000, was for Burser to start a frozen custard business in his hometown. The loan was due and payable in a year. Although he lived in another state, Strontiumm attended the grand opening of the business two months later. Unbeknownst to Strontiumm, however, Burser was killed a week later while picking up trash in the business's drive-through. When, at the end of the year, Strontiumm tried to contact Burser to collect on the loan, he discovered Burser's death and that the six-month period for filing claims against Burser's estate had elapsed.

Can Strontiumm still collect the $45,000?

PROCEDURE PRIOR TO DISTRIBUTION

Regardless of whether a person dies testate or intestate, the first item of business on the executor's or administrator's list is to offer proof of death to the appropriate court. This proof may be in the form of a death certificate, official notification of death from an armed service, or even testimony of the deceased's presence in a disaster that resulted in unidentifiable or irretrievable bodies. In the last case, the court can take judicial notice of the situation and issue a declaration of death.

If a person simply vanishes without a trace, after several years he or she can be declared dead under the "Enoch Arden laws." (These laws were named for a poem by Tennyson about a seaman who returns home after a long absence to find his "widow" married to another.) Almost without exception, the time required under such laws is either five or seven years of absence.

After proof of death is established, the personal representative's duties include the following:

1. assembling, preserving, inventorying, and appraising the assets of the estate and collecting the debts owed to it
2. giving public notice of the estate and the necessity for filing claims against it within the statutory period
3. paying valid claims against the estate
4. distributing the remaining property according to the will or statute

The personal representative will be liable for failure to reasonably carry out her or his duties. Depending on the size and types of property in the estate, the task can be quite complex. As indicated above, the personal representative must properly give public notice that all creditors of the estate have a set time, typically six months, to file a claim or go unpaid. He or she must then determine which claims are valid and pay them where possible. In *What's Your Verdict?* because Strontiumm did not file within the proper period, he cannot collect the loan from the estate. Note, however, that although six months are given to file such claims, the full procedure of settling an estate can take several months beyond this. This is true especially if the validity of the will is challenged or contested or if the meaning of the will is unclear in some of its provisions.

DISTRIBUTION

WITHOUT A WILL As mentioned previously, intestate distributions are determined by the appropriate state statute. See the Law Brief feature in the next column.

WITH A WILL Where there is a valid will, its terms are to be followed as closely as possible by the executor. The probate or surrogate's court will supervise this procedure. Regardless, the personal representative often is assisted by an attorney whose reasonable fees are paid out of the estate. Following the will's directives frequently is complicated by paying valid claims from creditors against the estate for which the maker did not allow.

There also may be statutory provisions allowing certain relatives to override the will's terms and receive more of the estate than the will provided. For example, in most states the surviving spouse is able to elect to receive a set percentage of the decedent's property instead of what was allocated under the will. Usually this *right of election* is for one-third to one-half of the decedent's property.

Law Brief

Typical Intestate Distribution

f a person dies without a will…

- With no spouse but one or more children surviving, the children inherit equal shares in the real and personal property.

- With a spouse and one or more children or grandchildren surviving, the spouse gets one-half of the real and personal property and the children share equally in the remainder. If a child is deceased but has surviving children, those children share equally in the deceased child's share.

- With a spouse and no children or grandchildren surviving, the spouse gets one-half of the real and personal property and the deceased's parents receive the remainder. If the deceased's parents are not alive, the deceased's brothers and sisters receive equal shares in the remainder.

- With no spouse, no children, and no grandchildren surviving, the deceased's parents each receive one-half of the real and personal property or, if only one parent survives, he or she receives it all. If both of the deceased's parents are dead, the brothers and sisters of the deceased share equally.

Another complex issue has to do with how the testator has decided to split the property among the lineal descendants. The testator may specify that the living lineal descendents split the property equally, be they children, grandchildren or even further down the lineal tree. This is referred to as a *per capita* distribution. Or the testator may specify that the lineal descendants split equally what a deceased parent would have received but receive nothing if the parent still lives. This latter is referred to as a *per stirpes* distribution. These are illustrated in the charts below.

IF THERE ARE NO INHERITORS If there are no inheritors, the property of the deceased **escheats** (or reverts) to the state.

Per Stirpes Division of a $1,800,000 Estate

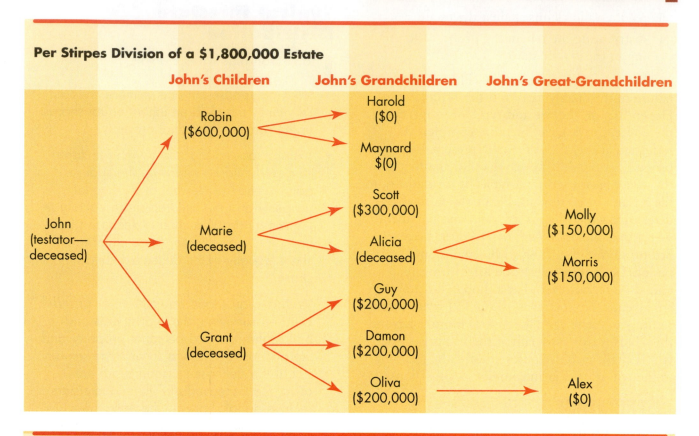

Per Capita Division of a $1,800,000 Estate—the 10 lineal living descendants all share equally

Assessment

Xtra!
Study Tools
lawxtra.swlearning.com

THINK ABOUT LEGAL CONCEPTS

1. Those who die without a valid will are legally termed to have died intestate. **True or False?**

2. If there are no inheritors of the decedent's estate, the property _?_ to the state.

3. The maker of a will is called (a) an administrator (b) an executor (c) a decedent (d) a testator.

4. A will can be amended at any time as long as the maker has testamentary intent and testamentary capacity. **True or False?**

5. The legal term for an oral will is a(n) _?_ will.

6. The execution of a codicil on a will does not have to be witnessed. **True or False?**

7. If the person making a will decides to split the property equally among all his or her living lineal descendents, he or she is specifying a _?_ distribution.

8. The typical time allowed for all creditors of the estate to file a claim against it is (a) four months (b) six months (c) ten months (d) twelve months

9. If a person vanishes without a trace, the person's estate can be probated after a year. **True or False?**

THINK CRITICALLY ABOUT EVIDENCE

Study the situation, answer the questions, and then prepare arguments to support your answers.

10. Sid went to his attorney's office and described in detail how he wanted his estate distributed upon his death. The lawyer made extensive notes and prepared a 12-page will. He called Sid and read it to him over the phone. Sid made a few minor changes. The lawyer then prepared a final copy. On his way to the lawyer's office to sign the document, Sid died of a heart attack. Was the final copy a valid will? Why or why not?

11. Toa was ill. She did not think she could afford an attorney, so she sat down and wrote on notebook paper what she wanted done with all of her property upon her death. She signed at the end and dated the document in front of four neighbors, who also signed as witnesses. Will Toa's estate be distributed according to her wishes or in some other manner?

12. Hilda executed a will on the first day of January. On the first day of June in the same year she executed a second will, which contained many provisions in conflict with the first will. She died on the first day of December. Which will governs the distribution of her estate?

13. Eric executed a valid will dividing his property among his wife, Amber, and their five children. The will was not altered for 22 years. Then Eric separated from his wife but did not divorce her. He wrote a second will, which left all his property to their children. Eric passed away before making any further changes. What can his wife do to receive a portion of Eric's estate?

14. Evangel Smith was appointed the personal representative to settle the estate of Everett Smith. Evangel provided the appropriate public notice necessary to give creditors a fair chance to file their claims against the estate. Unfortunately, due to the negligence of the staff he hired, some of the claims were lost. Evangel settled the estate and distributed the proceeds without discovering the lost claims. Now the unpaid creditors want their money. Can Evangel be held personally liable for the debts of the estate? Why or why not?

15. Evander was the lineal descendant through his father, Eston, of his grandfather, Elias Fieldstone. When Elias died he left an estate worth $5,000,000. Elias' will called for the estate to be distributed per capita among his lineal descendants. These included four children and seven grandchildren, of which Evander was the youngest. Regrettably, Evander's father had died during the time between when the will was made and Elias' death. All the other lineal descendants were alive and well. How much will Evander receive from the distribution of Elias' estate (not considering taxes and administration charges)?

▼ GOALS
■ Recognize the value of the trust instrument
■ Identify the various types of trusts

19-2 Trusts

PURPOSE AND CREATION OF TRUSTS

WHAT'S YOUR VERDICT?

Jan loved getting his family of five grown children together. As a consequence, he bought an estate in Key West that was large enough to accommodate him, all the children, and their families. He then extended an open invitation to them to visit any time but especially at Christmas. As he entered his seventies, he worried that the family would gradually grow apart if they didn't have the estate as a rallying point at which to come together. He wanted to be sure the children did not sell the property and split the proceeds after his death.

What legal device can Jan use to prevent that from happening?

NETBookmark

Access lawxtra.swlearning.com and click on the link for Chapter 19. Read "The Will versus Trust Debate" and then answer the questions.

1. Does life insurance go through probate?

2. When an estate goes through probate, does the public have access to information about how it is to be distributed?

3. Can trusts ever be open to public view? If so, under what circumstances?

4. Are the actions of a trustee supervised by a court?

lawxtra.swlearning.com

erty in the trust in such a way as to accomplish the trust's objectives.

The creator of a trust is known as the **settlor**. The party for whose benefit the trust is managed in accordance with the settlor's wishes is the **beneficiary**. The trustee has a fiduciary duty

For various reasons, people may wish to transfer the immediate control of some or all of their property to another party with instructions on how it is to be managed for the benefit of the transferor or a third party. When the transferee of the property is a separate entity under law, a **trust** has been created.

A trust can be created for any conceivable legal purpose. The legal entity that has the title to the subject property is known as the **trustee**. The trustee must utilize the prop-

Assume that the man in this photo has created a trust for his wife and daughters and their families. Identify the settlor and the beneficiaries in this photo.

© GETTY IMAGES/PHOTODISC

(requiring the highest care and loyalty) to the beneficiary. The trustee cannot cause the beneficiary to acquire liability to third parties through the trust management. In addition, the trust does not usually terminate at the death of the trustee. Another person simply is appointed to fulfill the trustee's role, and the operation of the trust continues.

Finally, even if it is not mentioned in the trust document, trustees have the right to be paid for their services. The probate court or state law will determine just how much the trustee's fee might be in such a case. However, the settlor also may detail in the trust document how much the trustee will receive for her or his services. If the pay is inadequate, it is wise for the settlor to keep in mind that the person nominated for the trusteeship is free to decline it. In *What's Your Verdict?* Jan should create a trust to manage the property with the objective of prolonging his family's contact with one another.

CHECKPOINT

What is the legal term for the creator of a trust?

IN THIS CASE

Rensch loved a radio show concerning automobile problems that was broadcast weekly on National Public Radio (NPR). As a consequence, he placed $100,000 of his considerable estate into a trust to be managed by a trustee in the trust department of his local bank. The trust was to pay its proceeds to NPR as long as the show was broadcast by the network. After the show left the air, the trust property would revert back into Rensch's estate.

A QUESTION OF ETHICS

Marie's 82-year-old father, Isaac, mentioned that he wanted to see the western part of the United States before he died. Marie, his only child, didn't hesitate to help him fulfill this request. Late in May, they headed out from Maine in a recreational vehicle he purchased for the trip. Marie found it easy to drive and things went well at first. Then Isaac suffered a heart attack walking some miles through rough terrain to a cliff dwelling in northern New Mexico. Although the paramedics did their best to revive him, Isaac died. Marie arranged to fly his body back home and left the RV with a car dealership to be sold on commission. In going through Isaac's things, Marie found a valid holographic will that left half of his considerable estate to Estelle, his housekeeper of more than 35 years. The will was dated two days before the trip had begun. As far as Marie knew, no one else knew of it. She always had thought Estelle had too much influence over Isaac, and now this. Marie felt she had been a good daughter, doing things for Isaac, staying near his home all her life, and leaving her family behind for this tour. She felt she deserved the full measure of the estate. Still, she wanted to respect her father's wishes. She wondered why he had not made the will public before leaving. Perhaps he was still considering whether or not to put it into effect, or maybe he was waiting until the end of the trip to tell her about it. Now she sat in her seat in the airplane, her father's casket in the hold below. She had to make a decision by the end of the flight. Should she probate the will or not?

Trusts basically are named according to the timing and purpose of their creation. A trust may be created during the lifetime of the settlor. This type of trust is known as an ***inter vivos trust***. A trust created after the death of the settlor in accordance with directions in her or his will is labeled a **testamentary trust**.

A trust created for the fulfillment of an altruistic purpose is known as a **charitable trust**. Alternatively, a trust created for a private purpose is known as a **private trust**. One type of private trust is called a **spendthrift trust**. This trust protects the beneficiary's interest in the subject property from the beneficiary's creditors. The beneficiary can have no control whatsoever in such a trust arrangement, so creditors cannot reach the property in the trust. In *What's Your Verdict?* a testamentary spendthrift trust could be formed around Gleason's estate with his children as beneficiaries. The trustee, a local bank's trust department, could be instructed to pay the children's reasonable expenditures for their necessities and provide them some disposable income. Also, in most states, the children's creditors could not reach the income-generating assets of the estate.

The trusts mentioned above usually are created by a written or oral statement in which the terms are clearly stated by the settlor. As a consequence, they are all properly labeled **express trusts**. The law, however, also makes provisions for at least two types of *implied trusts*. The first implied trust is known as a **resulting trust**. This trust is formed when the entity intended to receive the benefit of an express trust cannot do so. In such a case a resulting trust is formed to hold the property for its original owner.

The other type of implied trust is known as a **constructive trust**. Such a trust is created to require a person holding property to transfer it to another because retention of the property would be a wrongful and unjust enrichment of the holder. Property obtained through fraud, duress, or like means is deemed to be held by the wrongdoer in constructive trust for the person wronged.

Assessment

lawxtra.swlearning.com

THINK ABOUT LEGAL CONCEPTS

1. A trust terminates at the death of the trustee. **True or False?**

2. Every type of trust terminates upon the death of the settlor. **True or False?**

3. A resulting trust may be created due to the death of a trust's beneficiary. **True or False?**

4. A trust created by the will of a deceased settlor is known as a(n) (a) *inter vivos* trust (b) end of *vivos* trust (c) testamentary trust (d) none of the above

5. A charitable trust is created for a(n) _?_ purpose.

6. In a spendthrift trust the beneficiary's creditors can utilize the trust's property to satisfy the debts owed them by the beneficiary. **True or False?**

7. Is a resulting trust an express trust? **Yes or No?**

8. The trustee has a responsibility requiring the highest degree of care and loyalty to the beneficiary. This is referred to as a (a) fiduciary duty (b) legal caretaker's duty (c) lawful caretaker's duty (d) none of the above

THINK CRITICALLY ABOUT EVIDENCE

Study the situation, answer the questions, and then prepare arguments to support your answers.

9. Terry was named in his parents' will as the trustee of the family farm. He does not want the position as he has little or no interest in farming. His brother, Harold, has worked the farm for the last five years and would be a far better trustee. His parents chose Terry, however, because he was older. What can Terry do in this situation?

10. If Terry does take the position described in exercise 9, he will lose time that he could spend working on his new insulation business. Worse, the will does not mention the possibil-

ity of any pay for Terry. What can he do to help the situation?

11. Terry decides to repair the farmhouse. He solicits bids from different contractors and chooses the low bidder. However, when it comes to the contract to insulate the farmhouse, he has his firm do it and sends the estate a bill that is $1,000 more than the cost if other firms had bid the job. When his brother discovers what Terry has done, Terry merely states that the extra charge was to help pay for his time as trustee. Has Terry acted legally? Why or why not?

PREVENT LEGAL DIFFICULTIES

In making provision for the distribution of your assets...

1. Be sure to make a legally proper and clear will. Dying intestate will result in the needless payment of various taxes and fees. Plus it will bring about the distribution of the assets of the estate in accordance with the state intestacy statute.

2. Keep your will updated. An unclear or out-of-date will may cause conflicts among your potential beneficiaries. This may leave lifelong hard feelings and cost a great deal in legal fees.

3. A will can be changed or canceled at any time during the maker's life. Avoid confusion as to

which is the effective will by using an attorney. Be sure that any subsequent changes are properly executed and, if appropriate, nullify any existing will.

4. Consider utilizing a trust to insure fulfillment of your wishes for the management of your assets; both before and after death (*inter vivos* and testamentary trusts). Trusts are flexible, professional management can be utilized, and they can outlast the settlor.

CONCEPTS IN BRIEF

19-1 Property Distribution Upon Death

1. An individual either dies testate (with a valid will) or intestate (without a will). An intestate death requires that the estate of the deceased be distributed in accordance with the state's intestacy statute. A testate death allows the distribution of the estate according to the will of the decedent.

2. The basic requirements for a valid, formal will are testamentary intent and capacity, a general knowledge of what is being done, and a signed writing with witnesses.

3. A will can be revoked or changed at any time prior to the testator's death.

4. Creditors' rights against the estate and the rights of a surviving spouse to a share of the estate may not be defeated by a will that attempts to give the property to others.

19-2 Trusts

5. In essence, a trust can be created to accomplish any conceivable legal purpose.

6. Trusts may either be created *inter vivos* (during the life of the settlor) or testamentary (through the execution of the provisions of a decedent's will).

7. *Inter vivos* or testamentary trusts may either be charitable or private, express or implied.

8. A resulting trust is formed when the entity intended to receive the benefit of an express trust cannot do so. The resulting trust is intended to hold the property for its original owner. Note that it differs from a constructive trust, which is imposed on someone wrongfully holding the property of another but which is also imposed to benefit the true owner.

YOUR LEGAL VOCABULARY

Match each statement with the term that it best defines. Some terms may not be used.

1. A deceased person
2. To die without a will
3. Intestate's personal representative appointed to settle the estate
4. Property of the deceased
5. To die with a valid will
6. Maker of a will
7. Orally made will
8. Creator of a trust
9. Trust created by the will of the settlor
10. A reversion of estate property to the state
11. Trust created for the fulfillment of an altruistic purpose
12. Trust in which the terms are explicitly stated by the settlor
13. Will written and signed entirely by the maker
14. Legal vehicle used to transfer the immediate control of property to another party
15. Trust created during the lifetime of the settlor

a. administrator
b. beneficiary
c. charitable trust
d. codicil
e. constructive trust
f. decedent
g. escheat
h. estate
i. executor
j. express trust
k. holographic will
l. *inter vivos* trust
m. intestate
n. nuncupative will
o. private trust
p. resulting trust
q. settlor
r. spendthrift trust
s. testamentary trust
t. testate
u. testator
v. trust
w. trustee
x. will

REVIEW LEGAL CONCEPTS

16. What changes in the settlor's life should cause the updating of a will?

17. Why would a holographic will be disallowed?

18. What is the difference between a per stirpes and a per capita distribution?

19. Is a spendthrift trust fair to the creditors of the settlor? Why or why not?

20. Why do some states require a formal will?

21. Does a resulting trust carry out the wishes of the original owner? Why or why not?

22. Could a constructive trust be used in situations in which the property is not wrongfully obtained from the true owner? Why or why not?

WRITE ABOUT LEGAL CONCEPTS

23. Is it fair for individuals under age 18 not to have testamentary capacity? Write a comparison of "legal ages" such as to drive and to consume alcoholic beverages and identify the traits necessary for capacity in each instance. What trait is more important for testametnary capacity than for the others? Should the age level be increased?

24. Draft a will for yourself.

25. How could you use a trust in your life? Draft a document to set it up.

26. What qualities would you want in the trustee of your estate? List them in order of importance.

27. **HOT DEBATE** Write a letter to your legislative representative taking a stand either for or against the government taking control of such situations and deciding when people in Jewell Marie's situation can be removed from life support and allowed to die. Consider especially the long-term potential of allowing the government to determine who, among law-abiding citizens, may live or die.

MAKE ACADEMIC CONNECTIONS

28. **MEDICINE** Read recent articles in medical journals to determine just how we currently define a vegetative state from a medical standpoint and, therefore, the medical evaluations the courts use to determine who may be removed from life support. Report your findings to the class.

THINK CRITICALLY ABOUT EVIDENCE

Study the situation, answer the questions, and then prepare arguments to support your answers.

29. Tim had a considerable estate. He also had three children whom he loved dearly. He did not want to show any favoritism in the distribution of his estate after his death. Therefore, he decided not to make out a will and let the state handle the matter according to its rules. Is this a good idea? Explain.

30. On his deathbed, Tim's youngest child Paula finally persuades him to make a will. The other two children are rushing to be at Tim's bedside but have not arrived yet. A nurse overhears Paula telling Tim that the other two children died several years ago and that they should, therefore, receive nothing. Tim, nodding his head in agreement, then signed the will leaving everything to Paula. Two friends of Paula then signed as witnesses. Will the will stand up in probate court?

31. Not only was Tim's will attacked by the other two children as soon as it was filed in probate court but Tim's wife suddenly reappeared. She had been thought to have drowned two years before when a golf cart she was driving veered into a canal near their Florida home. She is extremely upset that Tim has willed away all the property. Does she have any rights in the matter?

32. Suspicious of the validity of the will, the probate court appointed a neutral party rather than Paula as executor. The executor discovered that, about two months before his death, Tim had set up a spendthrift trust for Paula. Tim had set it up with more than $500,000 in principal. Should the amount in the trust be included in the estate for distribution? Why or why not?

33. Paula has a number of creditors mainly because of her gambling problem. Will these creditors want to have the $500,000 included in the estate if Tim's will is held to be valid? Will they want the amount to be included in the estate if the will is invalidated?

34. Ralph Mangan was wounded by a gunshot in 1971. He was hospitalized and later moved to a nursing home. There, he executed a will dated February 23, 1972. After his release from the nursing home, he was cared for by his brother for a short time. Because of Ralph's advanced age and medical problems, he was again hospitalized. In May 1972, he returned to the nursing home and in June was adjudicated incompetent. He died in August 1972. His will was filed for probate and was contested on the grounds that Ralph was disoriented because of his advanced age, heart disease, and the gunshot wound. The will left property to someone described as a nephew when there was no such nephew. Witnesses testified that during Ralph's first stay in the nursing home he was self-reliant and was able to handle his own business affairs. Ralph's attorney testified that Ralph appeared to be of sound mind at the time he executed the will. Ralph had discussed the details of the will with the attorney and had mentioned a number of nephews, cousins, and other distant relatives. Ralph's physicians testified that Ralph had periods of disorientation and periods of lucidity. Is Ralph's will valid? (*Edward L. Mangan v. Joseph J. Mangan, Jr.,* 554 S.W.2d 418)

35. Joyner wrote out her will and took it to the neighbors to type and sign as witnesses. She only told them that it was a "piece of paper" that she wanted "fixed up so as I can sign it so that [her son] could have a place to live." The neighbors knew that she was asking them to sign the paper so her property would be properly disposed upon her death. Did Joyner's failure to announce that it was her "last will and testament" render the will invalid? (*Faith v. Singleton,* 692 S.W.2d 239)

36. When the administrator of Courziel's estate opened the safe deposit box that contained a copy of Courziel's will, he found the will was missing the last page. Unfortunately this page contained Courziel's signature and those of the witnesses to the document. Courziel had sole control over the box. Should the "will" be enforced? (*Board of Trustees of the University of Alabama v. Calhoun,* 514 So. 2d 895)

37. Gillespie, during a visit to his bank, dictated a codicil to his will. It was typed and signed by Gillespie before he left the bank. However, it was not until later that two bank employees signed the document as witnesses. They were not present to see Gillespie actually sign the document. Would the probate court treat the codicil as valid? (*Brammer v. Taylor,* 338 S.E.2d 207)

38. Mr. Suarez purchased a $50,000 insurance policy on himself from Liberty National Insurance Company. As beneficiary, he designated his mother, Guarina Cardona. Months later Suarez met with his insurance agent to change the beneficiary on his policy from Cardona to Zeigler. At the meeting Suarez indicated that he wanted the policy payoff to be used for the benefit of his two children, Ebony and Antonio. After Zeigler agreed to carry out Suarez's wishes, Suarez changed the beneficiary to Zeigler. However, when the insurance agent submitted the change of beneficiary form to Liberty National, the company never actually changed the beneficiary. Not knowing this, Zeigler faithfully paid the premiums on the policy until Suarez's death. Afterwards this suit was brought to correct the matter. What sort of trust device could be used by the court to see that Suarez's wishes would be carried out? Why? (*Ziegler v. Cardona,* 830 F. Supp. 1395)

39. When Edwin Fickes died his will provided that a trust should be established and that it should be split "in equal portions between the grandchildren then living" upon the death of his last surviving child. When that occurred, there were eight surviving grandchildren. Four of these were adopted. Two of the adopted grandchildren had been adopted before Fickes died. The other two were adopted afterwards. Which grandchildren should receive a portion of the estate? (*Connecticut National Bank v. Chadwick,* 217 Conn. 260)

MORSE V. VOLZ
164 CAL. APP. 3D 1001 (1985)

BACKGROUND The plaintiff, John Morse, son of the decedent, Marvin, brought this action to contest his father's will. He alleged that his father lacked testamentary capacity and was under the undue influence of his second wife when he made out the contested document. The Lower Court decided in favor of the son and ruled that it was not the father's legitimate last will and testament. Barbara Volz, the personal representative of the estate of John Morse's second wife, now deceased, brought this appeal.

FACTS When the father's first wife lay dying, he began to exhibit behavior that seemed questionable. He drank more and refused to visit her in the hospital. He would isolate himself in his study with a bottle of scotch and take long solitary walks. He was so irritable that he struck his granddaughter and yelled and screamed at family, friends, and neighbors.

This behavior struck his son, John, as exceptional as he had never seen his father act in such a way. After the death of his first wife, the father refused to make the funeral arrangements or attend the visitations. To John, he had always been a kind and understanding man. John and his wife, Claire, decided to live permanently near the father and had a caring relationship with him for several years after the first wife's death. Then the father's eyesight began to fail and he became depressed and reclusive. He began to drink heavily.

Obsessed with money, the father moved into the basement of his house and slept on a cot to save on utilities. He also experienced memory lapses and could not recall the events of past days or even hours. After his house was burglarized, the father began to prowl it at night carrying a .20 gauge shotgun.

Then he began seeing Inga, the woman who would become his second wife. Inga was at the time seeing another man named Eldon Zion. Following a luncheon with her friend Zelma and Marvin, Inga telephoned Zelma and said that, although she loved Eldon, she was going to date Marvin because Eldon "had no money and was not a Mason."

When Marvin announced his impending marriage to Inga, his son noted that the date for the wedding was during the time the son and his wife would be in Italy. At the same time, the father also said that he had been to an attorney and "everything has been taken care of to protect all of our children."

After the wedding, the father made out the new, contested will. "At the time there was nothing at all unusual about him," testified the attorney chosen to craft the will and who took the decedent through it "rather carefully" afterward. The attorney also said "He was quite capable of making a will."

The will in question left everything to Inga, if she survived him, and to her children, if she predeceased him. The will expressly stated that the decedent left nothing to his son as "he does not have the need for what I may leave in my estate."

Various experts testified to the possibility that the decedent may have been subject to early senile degeneration or Alzheimer's Disease at the time of the making out of the will.

PRACTICE JUDGING

1. Did the decedent have testamentary capacity?

2. Did the decedent act of his own free will in cutting out his son and the son's family or was Inga's influence too great?

3. How should the court rule in this case?

Entrepreneurs and the Law

PROJECT 4 PROPERTY LAW

A month after beginning production, the number of sales and the size of his profit staggered JJ. Even with the lease payments and paying for supplies to create new inventory, he would be able to pay Amber back in full plus interest within a few months.

PATENT PROTECTION

JJ had hired an engineer and a patent lawyer with the funds Amber provided him. They immediately set about the tasks necessary for filing the patent application. The drawings were done and the lawyer began identifying the claims (the characteristics that set JJ's invention apart from all others) that would be made on the DataDart to obtain the patent.

POTENTIAL LIABILITY

JJ then heard that Stinson Adamski, without consulting him, had sold one of its DataDarts and a pirated copy of the DataDart software for $10,000. The purchaser, a dry-cleaning store in another urban area, had improperly installed it and ruined several thousands of dollars worth of garments by processing them improperly. As a consequence, JJ was concerned as to his potential liability stemming from the situation. Soon his fears were realized when he was served with a complaint and summons. *Grayson v. Stinson Adamski Inc. and JJ Adamski, DBA DataDart Systems, Inc.*, the process read. The purchaser was bringing suit and had named all parties potentially responsible.

JJ was worried and immediately called Amber. She assured him that her firm would defend him and that the cost would not be prohibitive. "It's not your fault, and we'll be able to show that with just a deposition or two," she commented. "So don't worry about it. Just get busy on those new orders."

INSURANCE NEEDS

Before she hung up, Amber reminded JJ to set up a meeting with a local business insurer. "You need some insurance protection—for you and the business. There's too much riding on it now to take any further risks."

© GETTY IMAGES/PHOTODISC

JJ felt snowed under for a moment, but then rebounded when Amber said, "I know you're worried, JJ. But, I'll be there to help, if you want me." JJ smiled, "You can count on that. Thanks. Love you." JJ's mind raced as he waited for her reply. Amber paused, "I'm proud of the way you are handling things, JJ, and I love you too." JJ immediately asked Amber to meet him for dinner that evening, proposed, and cried when she accepted. When he showed her the prenuptial he had prepared, she tore it apart saying that they'd be married and if her parents didn't like it, too bad.

ACTIVITIES

Divide into teams and perform one or more of the following activities, as directed by your teacher.

Prepare Legal Documents

Consider your team to be the firm of intellectual property attorneys Amber worked for and that has been hired by JJ to protect the hard and software involved in the DataDart system. Draft a patent application that includes the following sections:

1. Background of the Invention
2. Detailed Description of the Invention
3. Claims

Divide the team into three groups, and have each group work on a different section. Assemble the sections and submit the completed application to your teacher.

Argue

Divide the team into three groups, each representing a party in the lawsuit. Consider the possibility, grounds, and likelihood of success of a countersuit by JJ. Each group should prepare an opening argument to use in the event of a trial. After each side presents its argument the class should vote on which party is liable for the injury.

Demonstrate

Divide the team into five groups. Each group should choose one of the following types of insurance JJ will need: liability insurance, property insurance, fidelity insurance, life insurance, and disability insurance. Discuss JJ's needs for each type of insurance.

COMMUNITY *ACTION*

Protect Your Environment

Did you know the nations' leading environmental protection club has youth programs that encourage young people to become actively involved in protecting the environment? The Sierra Club—nature's advocate in the United States—in partnership with Youth Services, has provided more than 500,000 young people nationwide with the opportunity to experience wilderness outings, learn about environmental issues, and engage in grassroots activism. Youth programs include Inside the Outdoors, Denver-based Peaks and Plains, Chicago Wilderness, Sierra Scholarships, Inner City Outings, and Sierra Student Coalition.

Do Your Part

1. Research to find out about a local environmental problem through local newspapers, radio and television news programs, and on the Internet.
2. Use the Internet to find the closest chapter of the Sierra Club. Contact them to see if they are already working on the problem.
3. Working either through the Sierra Club, another environmental protection organization, or with a group of your classmates, research the issue thoroughly to be certain of the facts.
4. Make up a fact sheet.
5. Write a speech that you can give to groups in the community. Your speech should include the facts and what action needs to be taken.
6. Ask to speak to local organizations, which may include the PTO, Rotary Club, Lions Club, and other organizations. Contact your local government to learn the procedure for speaking at a council meeting. Pass out your fact sheet to people at the meeting.

Presentation Management

This event will assess your use of current desktop computing technologies and software to prepare and deliver an effective multimedia presentation.

You will design a computer-generated multimedia presentation. You have fifteen (15) minutes for preparation and setup. The presentation will last a minimum of seven (7) minutes and a maximum of ten (10) minutes. Up to five (5) minutes will be allowed for questions from the judges. The contestant must make effective use of current multimedia technology in the presentation. In preparation of the presentation, contestants should use space, color, and text as design factors. No VCR or laser disc may be used in the presentation. Charts and other graphics should be used in the presentation. The student is responsible for securing a release form from any individual whose name, photograph, and other information is included in the presentation.

You are an attorney who specializes in wills and estates. Many individuals recognize the need for wills; however, they just don't seem to take time to create a will. Individuals without wills have not exercised their right to tell the government how to distribute their property when they die. You must prepare a multimedia presentation for young parents with children. The presentation must emphasize the importance of wills and discuss what happens to estates when individuals die.

Performance Indicators Evaluated

- Understand wills and estate planning.
- Explain strategies for developing a will.
- Explain what happens to property not covered by a will.
- Discuss the importance of a will to carry out the wishes of individuals.

For more detailed information about performance indicators, go to the BPA web site.

Think Critically

1. What is a will?
2. Why is it important for a young, healthy family to have a will?
3. What can happen to an estate when no will exists?
4. Why should an individual consider hiring an attorney when drawing up a will?

http://www.bpa.org/

AGENCY AND EMPLOYMENT LAW

IN PRACTICE PROFILE

Chris Reynolds ■ Senior Associate Athletic Director
Indiana University

Chris Reynolds not only worked hard in academics during his four years at Indiana University in Bloomington. He also was a standout on the school's basketball team. During his playing career the team posted a 105 to 27 record, won two Big Ten titles, and went to the NCAA Final Four. Chris's dedication to his sport won him the job of co-captain of the 1992–93 team. His dedication to academics won him a 1993 Academic All-Big Ten selection.

After graduating with a Bachelor of Arts degree, Chris stayed at IU to earn a law degree. "Initially I had dreams of working in a big law firm," he remembers. But during his second year of law school he decided to use his talents in a different way.

"When I was a student athlete, living four hours from home, I had several mentors who helped me along and kept me focused on what was important. During law school I realized I wanted to return the favor by mentoring young people. I wanted to make a positive difference in their lives just like others had done for me."

Today, Chris regularly interacts with students, providing them the same support others provided him. As Senior Associate Athletic Director at Indiana University, he's the primary human resources

director for the athletic department. Chris also is the school's administrative liaison for many of the school's sports teams including women's basketball; baseball; and the men's and women's swimming, diving, soccer, tennis, and water polo teams.

Chris puts his law degree to work on a regular basis. He is responsible for the employment contracts for many of the school's coaches and provides consultative support for game contracts.

Securing sponsorship for IU sports teams also involves legal work. "I am involved in the process of sending out Requests for Proposals to all possible sponsors." He helped to secure a sponsorship with Adidas which, among other things, means every student athlete is provided Adidas apparel and shoes for practice and competition.

Prior to employment at IU, Chris worked with the athletic staff, coaches, and student athletes at the University of Notre Dame. Before that, he was an assistant athletic director at Western Michigan University. Chris also has conducted leadership workshops for Nike Inc. and the NCAA. Although he has enjoyed all of his career opportunities, Chris is happy to be at his alma mater. "I really enjoy my job."

© INDIANA UNIVERSITY

> "When I was a student athlete, living four hours from home, I had several mentors who helped me along and kept me focused on what was important. During law school I realized I wanted to return the favor by mentoring young people."

Agency Law

20-1 Creation and Operation of Agencies

20-2 Agency Duties

HOT DEBATE

After two years of courtship, Alexis, the widow of a famous American diplomat accepted an engagement ring from Osiris, a billionaire Russian businessman. Osiris desired not only Alexis, but also the prestige a marriage to her would bring. Alexis called in her attorneys to negotiate the prenuptial agreement with Osiris' attorneys. After a week of negotiations, the agreement was signed by both parties. The couple then said their vows of love and devotion in a simple ceremony at a Black Sea resort.

Where Do You Stand?

1. Should agents (the lawyers) be used in such an intimate setting to put a price tag on feelings? Does not this disrupt the basic concept of marriage of "from two, one?" Justify your answer.

2. Given the disruptive effects of "blinding" love on individuals, should any such prenuptial agreement be enforceable? Why or why not?

WHAT IS AN AGENCY?

WHAT'S YOUR VERDICT?

Ortiz, a minor, had a huge CD collection. In order to raise funds for college, she downloaded them onto her computer. Then she agreed to pay Stems, a local shopkeeper, a 10 percent commission if he would sell them for her. After he found a buyer, however, Ortiz's computer hard drive crashed, and she decided not to sell. She claimed that, as a minor, she could avoid both the agency contract and the sales contract even though it was made by an adult merchant.

Is she correct?

An **agency** is a relationship between two parties that allows one of the parties to act so as to legally bind the other. The person who authorizes another to enter into legal relationships in his or her behalf is the **principal**. The party so authorized is the **agent**.

The most common form of agency occurs when a salesperson in a store makes a contract with a customer on behalf of the store's owner. Note that the same salesperson who acts as an agent in a sales transaction may then turn around and perform other duties that do not involve agency such as putting goods on shelves and cleaning the store. These tasks are performed by the person in her or his role as an *employee* under the supervision and control of an employer.

Agency is consensual. Even if you contract to make someone your agent, both parties always have the power to terminate the agency relationship. While there may be liability for breach of contract for ending the agency, no one can be forced to continue in an agency relationship.

PRINCIPALS

Generally, almost anyone can be a principal. Minors and others who lack contractual capacity can be principals and act through agents. However, they retain their rights flowing from a lack of contractual capacity. Thus they may disaffirm contracts made with their agents for nonnecessaries. In *What's Your Verdict?* Oritz may avoid her contract to pay Fischer the 10 percent commission. As a minor, she also can avoid the contract with the buyer of her CDs because contracts made through agents can be avoided by those who lack capacity.

As a general consequence of this potential for avoidance, the law tries to protect third parties with a warranty of capacity. A **warranty of the principal's capacity** is imposed by law on the agent. The law assumes that the agent promised the third party that the principal had capacity. If the principal lacked capacity, avoided the contract, and thus injured the third party, the third party can recover from the agent.

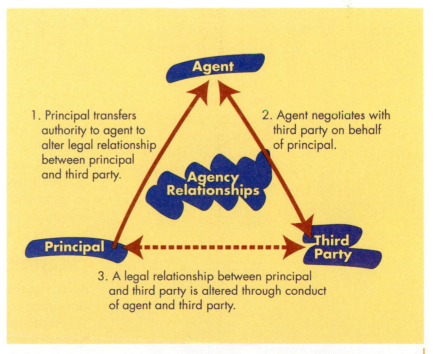

1. Principal transfers authority to agent to alter legal relationship between principal and third party.

2. Agent negotiates with third party on behalf of principal.

Agent

Agency Relationships

Principal

Third Party

3. A legal relationship between principal and third party is altered through conduct of agent and third party.

AGENTS

As far as who can qualify to be an agent is concerned, the general requirement is that an agent must be able to understand the transaction entered into on behalf of the principal. As a consequence, those who lack contractual capacity themselves still may be agents. Thus, minors who lack legal capacity to act for themselves generally can act for and bind adults in contracts. An adult principal cannot later avoid the resulting contract simply by showing the minority of her or his agent. Instead a principal must show that the individual agent lacked capacity due to an inability to understand that particular transaction.

To protect the public, all states require that agents in certain occupations be licensed. This usually requires passing a professional examination. Licensing often is required of auctioneers, insurance agents, lawyers, stock brokers, and real estate brokers.

CHECKPOINT
Define the agency relationship.

LEGAL RESEARCH

Contact several literary agents for copies of their standard contracts. Annual listings can be found in commercial publications, such as *The Literary Marketplace*, at your local library or bookstore. Compare the contracts you obtain to see who—author or agent—is most favorably treated. Do you think a best-selling author such as John Grisham would receive the same contract from such an agent as a first-time author? Why or why not?

SCOPE OF AN AGENT'S AUTHORITY

WHAT'S YOUR VERDICT?

Jared was shopping for a new car. One morning, while admiring a new Thunderhawk sedan on a dealer's lot, he was approached by Arnold, a salesperson for the dealership. After considerable negotiations, they arrived at an agreement for the sale of the car to Jared. However, Jared said he wanted to think about it overnight. Arnold then wrote down the terms of the deal they had agreed upon including a statement that the deal was good until 5 P.M. the next day. He signed the paper and gave it to Jared. When Jared returned the next day to take the deal, he found that Arnold had been fired for wrecking a dealership car that he had driven out to lunch.

Is the dealership bound by the terms of the deal for the sale of the Thunderhawk?

An agent must act within the granted **scope of authority** in order to bind the principal. The scope of authority is the range of acts authorized by the principal. If the agent has acted outside the scope of authority, the principal is not bound.

Generally, agents are not personally liable for the contracts that they negotiate on behalf of their principals. However, when the agent acts outside the scope of authority and the third party suffers an injury as a result, the third party can recover from the agent. Of course a person who is not an agent has no authority and cannot bind another party. In *What's Your Verdict?* Arnold was an agent and did bind the dealership to the agreement by his signature as it was well within his scope of authority.

CREATION OF AUTHORITY

Agency authority is created when a principal authorizes an agent to represent the principal. When the principal agrees to pay the agent, the agency relationship arises from a contract between the agent and the principal. In other instances, there is no contract. One person may simply agree to help another in altering legal relationships with third parties. In cases where the agent receives no consideration and there is no contract, the agency is called a **gratuitous agency**.

Agency authority may be created in a variety of ways. These include an express grant of authority, an implied grant of authority, creation by apparent authority, and ratification.

EXPRESS GRANT OF AUTHORITY **Express authority** is communicated directly by the principal to the agent. It may be oral or written. If written, the grant may be in an informal letter or a carefully drafted document. Any writing that appoints someone as an agent is called a **power of attorney**. See the sample power of attorney document on page 364.

IMPLIED GRANT OF AUTHORITY **Implied authority** is the power to do anything that is reasonably necessary or customary to carry out the duties expressly authorized. Thus, an agent's implied authority flows out of the express authority. Implied authority may be expanded in an emergency. For example, suppose Taylor asks Logan to run an errand for her and gives Logan the keys to her car. If Taylor's car catches on fire while Logan is driving it on the errand, Logan would have implied authority to promise money to someone to assist in putting out the fire. Taylor would be liable to pay for this help.

NETBookmark

Access lawxtra.swlearning.com and click on the link for Chapter 20. Read the Power of Attorney FAQ, and then answer the following questions.

1. Which type of power of attorney gives the person you choose the power to manage your assets and financial affairs while you are alive?

2. Which type of power of attorney stays valid even if you become unable to handle your own affairs?

3. Which type of power of attorney allows the principal to give only specific powers to the agent?

lawxtra.swlearning.com

APPARENT AUTHORITY Agency authority may sometimes result from the appearance created by the principal. This does not create a conventional authority because there has been no agreement between the principal and the agent. **Apparent authority** is created when a principal leads the third party to reasonably believe that a particular person has agency authority. The apparent authority must always come from the principal's words or conduct. It can never arise from the words or conduct of the agent alone.

IN THIS CASE

Bob owned a hi-tech home theater business. One day the store, which had several suites where the prospective customers could preview the various screens and projectors, was especially busy. As Bob's salespeople were out doing installations, he was handling the customers himself. Bob recognized Jameel, a customer that he had been working with for several days, pulling into the parking lot. He knew he would have to deal directly with Jameel so as to close the sale. As a consequence, Bob went into the back of the store and pulled Doris, an employee he had hired the day before, away from her job of assembling new displays. He told her to keep showing the customers more equipment until he had closed the sale with Jameel. He then introduced Doris to the other customers and in so doing said, "She'll be able to help you." Before Bob could return, Doris had sold a $23,000 home theater system to the Pushkins for half the normal price. Because he had clothed Doris in apparent authority, Bob had to go through with the contract.

RATIFICATION As previously mentioned, if a person acts outside the scope of his or her authority, the principal is not bound. However, a principal who later agrees to the transaction can be bound. This approval of a previously unauthorized act, or an act outside the agent's scope of authority, is called **ratification**. A principal impliedly ratifies an agency transaction by knowingly accepting its benefits.

POWER OF ATTORNEY
GENERAL

Know All Men by These Presents: That I, _____

_____

the undersigned (jointly and severally, if more than one) hereby make, constitute and appoint _____

_____

as a true and lawful Attorney for me and in my name, place and stead and for my use and benefit:

(a) To ask, demand, sue for, recover, collect and receive each and every sum of money, debt, account, legacy, bequest, interest, dividend, annuity and demand (which now is or hereafter shall become due, owing or payable) belonging to or claimed by me, and to use and take any lawful means for the recovery thereof by legal process or otherwise, and to execute and deliver a satisfaction or release therefor, together with the right and power to compromise or compound any claim or demand;

(b) To exercise any or all of the following powers as to real property, any interest therein and/or any building thereon: To contract for, purchase, receive and take possession thereof and of evidence of title thereto; to lease the same for any term or purpose, including leases for business, residence, and oil and/or mineral development; to sell, exchange, grant or convey the same with or without warranty; and to mortgage, transfer in trust, or otherwise encumber or hypothecate the same to secure payment of a negotiable or non-negotiable note or performance of any obligation or agreement;

(c) To exercise any or all of the following powers as to all kinds of personal property and goods, wares and merchandise, choses in action and other property in possession or in action; To contract for, buy, sell, exchange, transfer and in any legal manner deal in and with the same; and to mortgage, transfer in trust, or otherwise encumber or hypothecate the same to secure payment of a negotiable or non-negotiable note or performance of any obligation or agreement;

(d) To borrow money and to execute and delivery negotiable or non-negotiable notes therefor with or without security; and to loan money and receive negotiable or non-negotiable notes therefor with such security as he shall deem proper;

(e) To create, amend, supplement and terminate any trust and to instruct and advise the trustee of any trust wherein I am or may be trustor or beneficiary; to represent and vote stock, exercise rights, accept and deal with any dividend, distribution or bonus, join in any corporate financing, reorganization, merger, liquidation, consolidation or other action and the extension, compromise, conversion, adjustment, enforcement or foreclosure, singly or in conjunction with others of any corporate stock, bond, note, debenture or other security; to compound, compromise, adjust, settle and satisfy and obligation, secured or unsecured, owing by or to me and to give or accept any property and/or money whether or not equal to or less in value than the amount owing in payment, settlement or satisfaction thereof;

(f) To transact business of any kind or class and as my act and deed to sign, execute, acknowledge and deliver any deed, lease, assignment of lease, covenant, indenture, indemnity, agreement, mortgage, deed of trust, assignment of mortgage or of the beneficial interest under deed of trust, extension or renewal of any obligation, subordination or waiver of priority, hypothecation, bottomry, charter-party, bill of lading, bill of sale, bill, bond, note, whether negotiable or non-negotiable, receipt, evidence of debt, full or partial release or satisfaction of mortgage, judgment and other debt, request for partial or full reconveyance of deed of trust and such other instruments in writing of any kind or class as may be necessary or proper in the premises.

Giving and Granting
unto my said Attorney full power and authority to do and perform all and every act and thing whatsoever requisite, necessary or appropriate to be done in and about the premises as fully to all interests and purposes as I might or could do if personally present, hereby ratifying all that my said Attorney shall lawfully do or cause to be done by virtue of these presents. The powers and authority hereby conferred upon my said Attorney shall be applicable to all real and personal property or interests therein now owned or hereafter acquired by me and wherever situate.

My said Attorney is empowered hereby to determine in his sole discretion the time where, purpose for and manner in which any power herein conferred upon him shall be exercised, and the conditions, provisions and covenants of any instrument or document which may be executed by him pursuant hereto; and in the acquisition or disposition of real or personal property, my said Attorney shall have exclusive power to fix the terms thereof for cash, credit and/or property, and if on credit with or without security.

The undersigned, if a married women, hereby further authorizes and empowers my said Attorney, as my duly authorizes agent, to join in my behalf, in the execution of any instrument by which any community real property or any interest therein, now owned or hereafter acquired by my spouse and myself, or either or us, is sold, leased, encumbered, or conveyed.

When the contest so requires, the masculine gender includes the feminine and/or neuter, and the singular number includes the plural.

WITNESS my hand this _____ day of _____, 20_____

_____   _____

_____   _____

State of _____, ⎫
                             ⎬ SS.
County of _____ ⎭

On _____, before me, the undersigned, a Notary Public in and for

said State, personally appeared _____

_____

known to me to be the person _____ whose name _____ subscribed

to the within instrument and acknowledged that _____ executed the same.

(Seal) _____

Witness my hand and official seal.   Notary Public in and for said State

For a valid ratification, the following conditions must be met:

- The third person must have believed that by dealing with the principal's agent, he or she was making a contract with the principal.
- Before ratification, the principal must have full knowledge of all material facts.
- The principal must show an intent to ratify.
- The principal must ratify the entire act, not just one part of the transaction.

- The principal must ratify before the third person withdraws from the unratified transaction.

CHECKPOINT

List the ways in which agency authority can be created.

Assessment

Xtra! Study Tools
lawxtra.swlearning.com

THINK ABOUT LEGAL CONCEPTS

1. Every employee who is authorized to bind the employer to a contract is an agent. **True or False?**

2. If an agent acts outside the agent's authority, then (a) the principal is not bound (b) the agent is liable to the third party for any injury caused by acting outside the scope of authority (c) both a and b.

3. Apparent authority arises out of the principal's conduct toward the agent. **True or False?**

4. Minors who act through agents have the same rights they would have if they acted directly. **True or False?**

5. Which of the following are types of authority? (a) express authority (b) implied authority (c) apparent authority (d) all of the above

6. When someone acts outside the scope of express authority, but the principal accepts the benefits of the transaction with knowledge of all its terms, this is called _?_.

THINK CRITICALLY ABOUT EVIDENCE

Study the situation, answer the questions, and then prepare arguments to support your answers.

7. Alonzo hired Lawrence to help him sell a valuable Persian rug. He authorized Lawrence to sell it for $400,000 cash. Lawrence did so. Later, Alonzo discovered that the rug was worth more than $600,000. Because Alonzo was a minor, he disaffirmed the contract, returned the $400,000 to the buyer, and got the rug back. The buyer sued Lawrence for $200,000—the difference between the $400,000 contract price and the $600,000 value. Will she collect?

8. Sweet Store, Inc., hired Li to work in the store. Mrs. Sweet, the owner, asked Li to be in charge of the vegetable displays. This involved spraying the vegetables with water periodically and sorting out vegetables that no longer looked fresh. Another employee was in charge of ordering and taking deliveries of the vegetables. Cash register clerks were in charge of selling the vegetables. One day, Li was taking a break on the loading dock when a load of vegetables arrived. He signed the shipping receipt, although he was not authorized to do so. Unfortunately, the order was short and about $600 worth of vegetables were missing. Is the store liable for the loss because of Li's signature?

9. Jane asked Kroger to represent her in selling her farm. She signed a power of attorney authorizing Kroger to negotiate a sale and to execute all necessary documents to transfer title to her real property. Then Jane left for vacation. When she returned, she learned that Kroger had sold the farm at an attractive price. He also sold two tractors and a truck. Is Jane bound by Kroger's conduct in selling the farm? In selling the tractors and the truck?

20-2 **Agency Duties**

▼ **GOALS**
- List the duties of an agent
- List the duties of a principal
- Identify when an agency is terminated

WHAT ARE AN AGENT'S DUTIES?

WHAT'S YOUR VERDICT?

Medici placed an ancient Italian urn up for sale through an agent in New York City. It was to be sold at the highest possible price. Without informing Medici, the agent sold the urn to her boyfriend at half the market price.

If Medici discovered what occurred, could she recover the rest of the urn's value from the agent?

DUTIES OWED THE PRINCIPAL

In many respects, the agent's duties to the principal are the same as those of an ordinary employee. However, the agent has the additional ability to bind the principal in dealings with third parties. Therefore, agents must be exceptionally honest and show good faith. The law encourages this by requiring fiduciary duties of the agent. **Fiduciary duties** in general require an agent to put the best interests of the principal ahead of her or his own.

The specific fiduciary duties owed by agents to principals are loyalty, obedience, care and skill, confidentiality, and accounting. If an agent violates a fiduciary duty and that injures the principal, the agent will be liable for the injury. In *What's Your Verdict?* Medici could recover the shortfall from the sale from the agent.

LOYALTY AND OBEDIENCE The agent's core duties are those of loyalty and obedience. The **duty of loyalty** means that the agent may not secretly benefit from the agency transaction. Thus, agents may neither buy from nor sell to themselves, their relatives, or their friends without prior approval from their principals. In addition any profits the agent earns in performing the agency duties belong to the principal, unless otherwise agreed.

The agent also owes the **duty of obedience** to the principal. This means that the agent must carefully obey the instructions of the principal. Of course an agent should not follow instructions to do an illegal or immoral act. For example, a sales agent may not lie about a product even if the principal has ordered such fraudulent conduct. If a principal orders an agent to do something illegal or immoral, the agent should resign from the agency relationship.

REASONABLE CARE AND SKILL In representing one's principal, an agent must satisfy the **duty of reasonable care and skill**. This requires the agent to exercise the degree of care and skill that a reasonably prudent person would use in a similar situation. Failing to satisfy the fiduciary duty of reasonable care and skill renders the agent liable to the principal for the resulting loss or injury. At a minimum, reasonable care and skill requires the agent to communicate to the principal any information that would affect the principal's decisions.

Law Brief

In late September of 2004, President Bush signed into law a bill imposing higher standards on sports agents. The new law imposes much stiffer penalties on agents who unethically sign amateur athletes in high school or college. The law requires that the agent disclose in writing that the athlete may lose NCAA eligibility after signing with an agent. The agent and the athlete also are required to notify the athlete's school so that it will not use an ineligible athlete and have to forfeit games. The law also bars giving anything of value to the athlete or the athlete's family or friends. Penalties up to $11,000 per day can be levied for each offense.

When his company asked him to find a real estate broker through which to purchase a location for a new plant, Larry Steward contracted with Tom Rancour, his brother-in-law. Rancour was a licensed real estate broker but up until that time had only sold residential properties. Neither Steward not Rancour informed the company of their relationship as they were afraid the company wouldn't allow it. Steward then saved the company money by securing a lower commission percentage from Rancour, 3.5 percent instead of a full 6 percent. Ultimately, Rancour found an optimal location for the new plant at a low cost. Did Rancour and Steward act ethically?

CONFIDENTIALITY The **duty of confidentiality** requires the agent to treat information about the principal with great caution. Information that is obviously confidential must be kept confidential. Some information obviously is not confidential. If a principal asks an agent to treat any information as confidential, however, the agent must do so. This duty of confidentiality survives the agency relationship. The duty may bind the agent years after the agency relationship has ended.

ACCOUNTING Agents owe the **duty of accounting** to the principal. It requires an agent to account to the principal for all money and property of the principal that comes into the agent's possession. The agent must promptly notify the principal of the receipt of money from third parties and must make an accounting within a reasonable time. An *accounting* is a formal statement, usually in writing, that tells the principal what happened to all of the principal's money or property.

The duty of accounting prohibits the agent from commingling. **Commingling** is mixing the funds or property of the principal and agent. If commingling occurs and there is a loss, the agent bears that loss.

Money of the principal held by the agent usually must be deposited in a bank, in an account separate from that of the agent. The separate accounts for the funds of principals are called **trust accounts**. Professional agents such as lawyers, accountants, real estate brokers, and stockbrokers maintain trust accounts that are separate from their personal and office checking accounts. If an agent places a client's funds in the agent's personal or office account, it would be commingling. Such action would subject the agent to both professional sanctions, such as disbarring a lawyer, and liability to the principal for any loss.

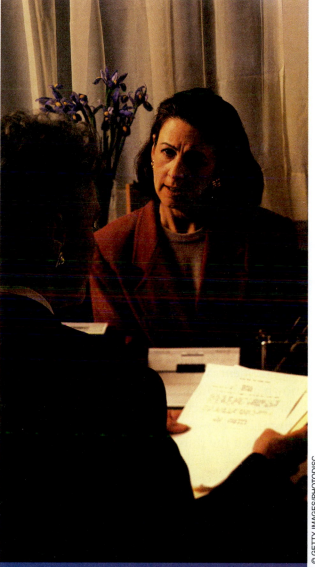

The woman on the right (the principal) hired the woman on the left (the agent) to represent her in the sale of her business. The principal emphasized that it was important to her to keep the terms of the sale secret. Which fiduciary duty of the agent does this situation call for?

© GETTY IMAGES/PHOTODISC

DUTIES OWED TO THIRD PARTIES

An agent owes two main duties to third parties. First, the agent must not act outside the scope of authority given him or her by the principal. Second, the agent must insure that the principal has capacity. A breach of either of these duties may result in the agent being liable to the third parties dealt with under the agency.

EXCEEDING THE SCOPE OF AUTHORITY

If an agent acts without authority from the principal, the agent becomes personally liable to the third party for resulting injury. That is because the agent implies the promise that he or she has appropriate authority. This usually arises when an agent exceeds the authority given by the principal.

In some cases, a person will act as agent for an alleged principal when absolutely no authority has been given for any action. Again, only the "agent" is liable to the third party unless the "principal" ratifies or has given apparent authority.

PRINCIPAL'S LACK OF CAPACITY

An agent warrants the principal's capacity to the third party. If it turns out that the principal does not exist, or that the principal is able to avoid the contract for lack of contractual capacity, the agent will be liable. Normally, to bind the principal and to avoid personal liability an agent will sign the name of the principal to a contract and add words to indicate that the signature is by an agent.

LIABILITY DUE TO AN UNDISCLOSED PRINCIPAL

Sometimes under the terms of the agency an agent is not allowed to reveal the principal's existence or identity. The principal in such a case is known as an **undisclosed principal**. The agent is liable on a contract entered into under such circumstances. However, in most contractual situations, when the third party learns the identity of the principal, the third party generally may elect to hold either the principal or the agent to the agreement. The third party may not enforce the agreement against both, however.

CHECKPOINT

What are the duties of an agent to the principal?

WHAT ARE THE PRINCIPAL'S DUTIES?

WHAT'S YOUR VERDICT?

Thompson had owned a small but profitable boat and jet ski sales dealership for more than 30 years. Finally, he decided it was time to retire and contracted with a business broker to sell the business for $750,000. The broker was to receive a 15% commission for producing a buyer. As Thompson had seriously undervalued the business, the business broker was able to find a ready, willing, and able buyer within a week. In the meantime, Thompson had discovered his error and refused to sell.

Is the broker entitled to the commission?

In an agency relationship, a principal has duties to both the agent and third parties. A failure to fulfill these duties can result in liability for the principal.

DUTIES OWED THE AGENT

The principal's main duty is to pay what was promised for the agency services. In addition, if an agent properly incurs expenses, the principal must reimburse the agent. If the agent suffers any loss because of the principal's instructions, the principal must indemnify, or repay, the agent the amount lost. In *What's Your Verdict?* Thompson must fulfill his duty to compensate the broker for his services as the broker fulfilled his duty under the agency agreement.

Finally, after a principal gives an agent certain tasks to perform, the principal has a duty to cooperate with the agent so that the tasks can be performed. Failure of the principal to fulfill her or his obligations gives the agent the right to quit and recover any damages.

DUTIES OWED THIRD PARTIES

As long as agents act within the scope of their authority, principals are bound by the agreements with the third parties. Even when the agents exceed their authority, principals are bound when they ratify the unauthorized acts.

Principals also have a duty not to authorize or permit improper acts in carrying out the agency. If torts or fraud are committed by an agent, the agent is liable. The principal also will be liable if the principal directed the agent to engage in the illegal activity, or the agent was acting to advance the interests of the principal. For example, if a sales agent defrauds a customer in order to make a sale, the principal is liable for any damages that result.

Usually, the principal is not liable for an agent's crime unless the crime itself has been authorized or ratified. As an exception to this rule, the principal generally is liable for the illegal sale, by the agent, of intoxicating liquor or adulterated foods. Thus, a bar owner, the principal, would be liable if the agent, a bartender, illegally served liquor to a minor.

IN THIS CASE

Reepou, the credit manager for Suburban Motors, thought that Bently had fallen behind in her payments on her SUV. Early one Sunday morning, Reepou had Bently's vehicle towed back to the dealership. In reality, Bently had married and her new checks bore her married name. She had, in fact, informed the dealership of the change. Even though her account had not been credited with the amounts of the payments, the checks had been received exactly on time and had been cashed by the dealership's credit office. Reepou committed the tort of conversion and would be personally liable to Bently, as would Suburban Motors, her principal.

CHECKPOINT
What is a principal's main duty?

HOW IS AN AGENCY TERMINATED?

WHAT'S YOUR VERDICT?

Daisy entered into a one-year written contract with the Sweet Magnolia Nursery as its sales agent in North and South Carolina. After six months, company sales dropped far below expectations. Daisy was the last to be hired, and so she was the first to be fired—even though her manager admitted that her performance had been satisfactory.

Did the nursery have a legal right to terminate the agency?

BY UNILATERAL ACTION OF A PARTY

Generally, both the agent and the principal have the power, but not the right, to terminate the agency at any time. The principal terminates by revoking the agent's authority. If the termination violates the agency agreement the principal must pay damages for doing so.

In *What's Your Verdict?* the nursery could revoke Daisy's authority. As a result, Daisy could no longer bind the nursery. This illustrates that the nursery had the power to terminate the agency, but it did not have the right. It would be liable in damages for breach of the one-year agency contract.

In a similar way, the agent has the power to quit at any time. However, he or she may lack the right to do so unless the principal has breached the contract. If an agent wrongfully terminates the agency before the contract expires, the principal is entitled to damages. Note that in a gratuitous agency, which exists when it is agreed that the agent will not receive any consideration, the agent cannot recover any damages if the authority is revoked. Likewise, a principal normally cannot recover any damages from a gratuitous agent who abandons the agency.

BY AGREEMENT

An ordinary agency expires at the time provided in the contract that created it. This may be after a particular length of time, upon the occurrence

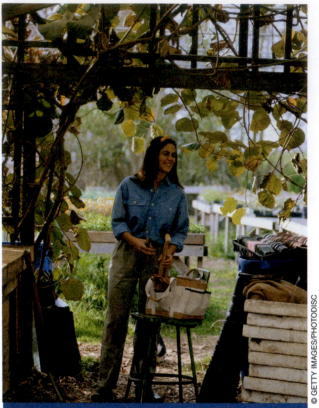

In *What's Your Verdict?* could Sweet Magnolia Nursery be liable for damages if the agency termination were improper?

of an event, or at the completion of certain tasks. If nothing is specified in the agency contract, the agency continues for a reasonable time. An agency can be ended at any time if both the principal and agent agree to terminate it.

BY OPERATION OF LAW

An agency ordinarily is terminated upon the death, insanity, or bankruptcy of either the principal or the agent. Also, if it becomes impossible to perform the agency, such as if the subject matter of the agency is destroyed or if a change of law makes the agent's required actions illegal, the agency is ended.

When the authority of an agent is terminated by the principal's voluntary act, the principal should notify promptly each individual third party who has previously dealt with the agent. If the principal does not give individualized notice, the agent is likely to have apparent authority to make binding contracts between the principal and third persons as long as the third persons do not know of the termination. Others who may have heard of the agency also are entitled to notice. This can be given by publishing the fact

INTERNATIONAL VIEWPOINT

Export Employees and Agents

Companies engaged in direct exporting—selling directly to overseas companies—may hire full-time employees. These employees include full-time export managers and international sales specialists. Their duties include developing new products for overseas markets, pricing, and packaging and labeling products for export, among others.

Instead of hiring its own employees to do so, companies also may conduct business with overseas companies through foreign sales agents. These are agents of the companies who work on commission, earning a percentage of the sales they make.

They also may conduct overseas business using independent contractors, such as foreign distributors or export management companies. Foreign distributors usually are located in the country with which the company is doing business. They assume the risks of buying and warehousing the goods. They typically also service the products they sell, train end users to use the product, extend credit to customers, and advertise the products.

Finally, an exporter may employ an export management company. These companies are consultants that advise manufacturers and other exporters. They conduct research targeted to specific countries, exhibit goods at foreign trade shows, prepare export documentation, handle language translations, and make shipping arrangements.

of the termination in a newspaper of general circulation in the area.

CHECKPOINT

Name the three general ways in which an agency may be terminated.

THINK ABOUT LEGAL CONCEPTS

1. Fiduciary duties are owed to the agent by the principal. **True or False?**

2. Which of the following is the most basic duty of an agent? (a) loyalty and obedience (b) reasonable care and skill (c) confidentiality (d) accounting

3. The duty of confidentiality lasts even after the agency relationship is terminated. **True or False?**

4. If an agent acts outside the scope of authority, the principal will still be bound if the principal _?_ the agent's unauthorized acts.

5. Both principals and agents have the ability to terminate the agency even before the contracted-for period, but they may be liable for damages if they do so. **True or False?**

THINK CRITICALLY ABOUT EVIDENCE

Study the situation, answer the questions, and then prepare arguments to support your answers.

6. Jeff hired Sally, a real estate broker, to help sell his home. While she was trying to sell the home, a buyer asked Sally what Jeff's bottom price was. She told the buyer without Jeff's permission and the house sold. Has Sally done anything wrong legally?

7. Anita retained Lynn as her lawyer. When Lynn settled Anita's lawsuit for more than $200,000, the check was mailed to Lynn at her law office. Lynn deposited the check in her personal account and she used the money to pay monthly bills. When Anita asked about the money, Lynn stalled her saying it might take another month to arrive. Anita eventually became suspicious and checked with the defendant only to learn the judgment had been paid. What should Anita do?

8. Kathy was Jon's agent in selling cattle. In the course of a sale Jon lied about the health of a herd. He denied that the cows had hoof and mouth disease when he knew they suffered from it. Is Kathy liable for Jon's conduct?

9. Susan, a minor, hired an attorney to represent her in the sale of her car. The lawyer did not disclose to the buyer that Susan was a minor. Later Susan disaffirmed the sale. Will the lawyer be liable to the buyer?

PREVENT LEGAL DIFFICULTIES

1. If you are a third person dealing with an agent you should verify the extent of the agent's authority directly from the principal. If you are uncertain about the authority or honesty of the agent, make payment by a check payable to the principal.

2. If you are an agent, when you sign anything for your principal, make it unmistakably clear that you are signing as an agent. Always write the name of the principal first, and then add "by" and your signature followed by the word "agent." If you exceed the scope of your authority and that injures the third party, you may be liable for that injury.

3. If you are a principal, remember that your agent's acts become your acts. Use care in selecting agents. If you discharge your agent, protect yourself against apparent authority by notifying those the agent dealt with in your name.

4. You must be loyal to your principal and exercise reasonable care and skill in obeying all proper instructions.

5. If you handle your principal's money or other assets, you should keep them separate from your own.

Chapter 20 Assessment

CONCEPTS IN BRIEF

20-1 Creation and Operation of Agencies

1. An agency is a relationship between two parties that allows one of the parties to act so as to legally bind the other.

2. In order to have capacity as an agent a person must be able to understand the transaction entered into on behalf of the principal.

3. Generally, if the agent has acted outside the scope of authority granted by the principal, the principal is not bound.

4. Agency authority may be created by an express grant of authority, an implied grant of authority, apparent authority, and ratification.

5. An action taken by an agent that is outside the scope of authority still may be ratified and thereby made effective against the principal.

20-2 Agency Duties

6. An agent owes a general fiduciary duty to the principal to put the best interests of the principal ahead of the agent's.

7. The specific fiduciary duties owed by agents to principals are loyalty, obedience, care and skill, confidentiality, and accounting.

8. The principal's main duty is to pay what was promised for the agency services and to reimburse the agent for reasonable expenses and losses involved in carrying out the agency.

9. Either the principal or the agent has the right to terminate the agency at any time. If the termination violates the terms of the agency agreement, however, the terminating party may be liable.

YOUR LEGAL VOCABULARY

Match each statement with the term that it best defines. Some terms may not be used.

1. Requirements that an agent act in the principal's best interests

2. Agency that is not based on a contract

3. A written grant of agency authority

4. A person who authorizes another to alter one of his or her legal relationships

5. A person who authorizes an agency but does not allow the revealing of his or her existence or identity

6. Mixing together the property of the agent and the principal

7. Principal's assent to unauthorized acts of an agent

8. Separate repository for the money of the agent's principal

9. Requirement that the agency respect the private nature of the information received from the principal

10. The range of acts authorized by the principal

11. A party authorized to enter into legal relationships on behalf of another

12. Means that the agent may not secretly benefit from the agency transaction

13. At a minimum, requires the agent to communicate to the principal any information that would affect the principal's decisions

a. agency
b. agent
c. apparent authority
d. commingling
e. duty of accounting
f. duty of confidentiality
g. duty of loyalty
h. duty of obedience
i. duty of reasonable care and skill
j. express authority
k. fiduciary duties
l. gratuitous agency
m. implied authority
n. power of attorney
o. principal
p. ratification
q. scope of authority
r. trust account
s. undisclosed principal
t. warranty of the principal's capacity

REVIEW LEGAL CONCEPTS

14. Distinguish the effect of minority on the position of principal versus the position of agent.

15. Describe a transaction where a principal creates apparent authority. Describe a transaction where an agent acts outside the scope of authority.

16. Describe the fiduciary duty of confidentiality.

17. Explain the rationale for trust accounts.

18. Describe the fiduciary duty of loyalty.

WRITE ABOUT LEGAL CONCEPTS

19. Create a one-paragraph scenario where a principal ratifies conduct outside the scope of authority.

20. Create a one-paragraph scenario where the fiduciary duty of reasonable care and skill has been violated.

21. Create a one-paragraph scenario where the fiduciary duty of confidentiality has been violated.

22. **HOT DEBATE** Five years later, Osiris was killed in the crash of his private jet. Alexis then sought to enforce her rights under the prenuptial agreement. Amile, Osiris' son, who stood to inherit Osiris' fortune, realized that the contract contained provisions that would result in a long legal battle. Such a battle would delay his being able to exercise control over his father's empire. He therefore offered to buy out Alexis' rights for 100 million dollars, but she held out for more. Finally, they settled on a quarter of a billion dollars. Does such a result justify the use of attorneys as agents to negotiate a prenuptial agreement? Write a short paragraph supporting your answer.

MAKE ACADEMIC CONNECTIONS

23. **ATHLETICS** Read a book on the marketing of athletes, such as *The Business of Sports Agents* by Shropshire and Davis. Then report to the class on the ethics and legalities of sports agency.

THINK CRITICALLY ABOUT EVIDENCE

Study the situation, answer the questions, and then prepare arguments to support your answers.

24. Susan celebrated her sixteenth birthday. Two weeks later she went shopping for a car using money she inherited. She became frustrated with the process and asked her father to select and purchase an appropriate car on her behalf. She trusted her dad to know what she would like and also thought he was more knowledgeable. He found a car and purchased it, signing as her agent. Unfortunately dad bought a large gray four-door sedan and Susan wanted something sporty. Can Susan disaffirm?

25. When Kraus discharged his purchasing agent, Stacey, and terminated their agency relationship, Stacey became angry. To get even, Stacey made two contracts that included terms that were unfavorable to Kraus, yet were reasonable in the competitive market. The first contract was with an old customer, A, who thought Stacey was still the purchasing agent for Kraus. The second contract was with a new customer, B, who had never heard of Stacey or Kraus before. Is Kraus liable on either of these contracts?

26. Bud was a real estate broker. He was acting as the agent in finding a buyer for Crib's home. A seller made an offer of $250,000 for the property but said, "If Mr. Crib doesn't accept this offer, I will raise it by $15,000." Bud knew that the duty of loyalty compelled him to tell Crib of the buyer's statement. Is this fair to the buyer? Why or why not? What could Bud do in future transactions to allow him to treat buyers more fairly.

27. Baroni asked her boyfriend, Sid, to help her sell her car. She promised to pay Sid 10 percent of the sales price. Sid agreed. Later, when trying to sell the car, Sid stated that a rebuilt engine had just been installed. This was not true. Kate bought the car. When she discovered the deception, she sued Baroni. Is Baroni legally responsible?

28. Nissan Motor Corporation appointed McKnight as its Denver area agent and dealer for the sale of its automobiles. McKnight purchased automobiles and parts from Nissan. He then sold them as he desired and at prices he set without any control from Nissan. The question arose as to whether an agency existed. What is your judgment? (*United Fire and Casualty Company v. Nissan Motor Corporation*, 164 Colo. 42, 433 P.2d 769)

29. Serges owned a retail butcher shop. One of his managers borrowed $3,500 from David for use in the butcher shop. Serges claimed that the manager had no authority to borrow money. Nevertheless, Serges made payments of $200. Serges also told David on several occasions that the full sum would eventually be paid. Was Serges liable? (*David v. Serges*, 373 Mich. 442, 129 N.W.2d 882)

30. Mrs. Terry is dealing with Alice, a clerk in Peters Department Store. Mrs. Terry sees a cashmere sweater she likes, but she notices it is slightly soiled. Alice, pushing for a sale, agrees to mark it down from $25 to $15, which she has no authority to do. Mrs. Terry says, "fine," asks that the sweater be delivered, and promises to pay C.O.D. The manager of Peters sees the item being wrapped, corrects the bill, and sends it out to Mrs. Terry. On seeing her sweater accompanied by a bill for $25, Mrs. Terry calls the store. She is told by Peters that Alice had no authority to mark down the price. Mrs. Terry also is told that she should either pay the bill or return the sweater. Is Mrs. Terry entitled to her bargain? Why or why not? (From Mearns, "Vicarious Liability for Agency Contracts," 48 Virginia Law Review 76.)

31. Smith and Edwards operated a sporting goods shop in Brigham City, Utah. Sponsors of the Golden Spike Little League made arrangements with the store to purchase, at a substantial discount, the players' baseball uniforms and equipment. The sponsors picked up $3,900 worth of merchandise without making any payments. After a demand for full payment, Smith and Edwards sued the sponsors. The sponsors defended by asserting that they were agents of Golden Spike Little League, acting within the scope of their authority, and thus were not personally liable. The trial judge found that Golden Spike Little League was a loosely formed voluntary association and thus not a legal entity upon which liability could be imposed. Are the sponsors liable? If the sponsors avoided liability, do you think this would be ethical? (*Smith and Edwards v. Golden Spike Little League*, 577 P.2d 132, Utah)

32. MBank hired El Paso Recover Services to repossess the Pontiac Trans-Am owned by Sanchez because she was late on her loan payments. The repossessor went to Sanchez's home with a tow truck and tried to hook the car to the tow truck. Sanchez, who was cutting her grass at the time asked what they were doing. The repossessors didn't respond. Sanchez then locked herself in the car to try to stall them until the police arrived. The repossessor finally towed the Trans Am on a high-speed trip, with Sanchez inside, to a repossession lot where they left the car in a fenced and locked yard. Police later rescued Sanchez. She sued MBank. Will she recover? (*MBank of El Paso v. Sanchez*, 836 S.W.2d 151, Tex.)

33. Margaret Berry was admitted to the hospital in February. In March, she executed a power of attorney designating her niece, Irene Montanye, as her agent. In April, Margaret suffered a stroke. She remained in a comatose or semi-comatose condition until her death in June. On April 30, Mrs. Montanye, acting under the power of attorney, transferred some $109,000 of the decedent's funds into a trust account in the name of the decedent in trust for Ann R. Scully, administrator of this estate. Heirs of the decedent maintained that the transfer of the funds was void because at the time of the transfer and thereafter the decedent was mentally incompetent by reason of being in a comatose or semi-comatose state and, therefore, the agency was revoked. Is the transfer valid? (*In re Estate of Berry*, 329 N.Y.S.2d 915)

PERKINS V. RICH
415 N.E.2D 895 (MASS. 1980)

FACTS The First Parish Unitarian Church of East Bridgewater hired Rich as its minister. At this time a Church Committee ran the church. As Rich's role in the Church expanded, he began to perform many of the duties of the Committee. The Church also expanded, from 12 families to more than 400. After about 10 years the Committee stopped meeting. Rich then ventured into real estate and other unrelated business ventures. To finance these, he gave mortgages on the church property which he, but not the Church Committee, executed. When the businesses he established failed, the creditor sought to foreclose on the mortgages. Church members claimed the mortgages were invalid because the Committee did not authorize them. The lower court found for the mortgage holders and the Church appealed.

The Committee claims that it did not know of the existence of the mortgages. Thus its failure to repudiate the mortgages resulted not from a ratification of the transactions but from ignorance of essential facts. Generally, in order to establish ratification of unauthorized acts of an agent, a principal must have "knowledge of all material facts . . ." However, a qualification to this rule is that one cannot "purposefully shut his eyes to means of information within his own possession and control." This is especially true of the Committee that functioned as the "business center" of the Church and had a duty to keep itself informed of Church business.

Further, the Committee was not totally ignorant of Rich's actions. From the many indications of the radical physical and structural changes to the Church and surroundings, it should have been obvious to the Church that "something was afoot." The very nature of the construction and renovation indicated that large expenditures were being made. Although Rich was far from candid in his disclosures, he did inform Church members of various projects at Church events through annual reports and publications.

REASONING We conclude that the Committee's knowledge of substantial and costly physical changes at the Church should have provoked an investigation by the Committee which would have led to the discovery of the mortgages. In these circumstances, the Committee's failure to act "will be deemed to constitute actual knowledge." By failing to disavow the mortgages, the Church ratified the transactions, a ratification that may be inferred without a vote by the Committee.

VERDICT The mortgages are valid. The decision of the lower court is affirmed.

PRACTICE JUDGING

1. Do you think the Church or the mortgage holders should pay?

2. What specific conduct does the court point to as constituting the ratification?

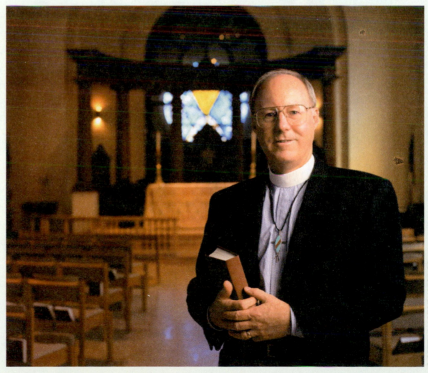

Employment Law

21-1 Making and Terminating Employment Contracts

21-2 Duties of Employers and Employees

HOT DEBATE

Justin wanted to be a chef. He was considering joining the Army to get training and experience in that field. A friend pointed out that in combat cooks often are made to take up their rifles and fight like infantry. Justin, who was strongly against killing under any circumstances, said that it was just a job. If ordered to fight in combat, he said he would refuse to do so and quit the service.

© GETTY IMAGES/PHOTODISC

Where Do You Stand?

1. Would Justin's proposed course of action be ethical? Who might be harmed by his refusal?

2. Would Justin's proposed course of action violate his contract with the Army? Why or why not?

21-1 Making and Terminating Employment Contracts

HOW ARE EMPLOYMENT CONTRACTS MADE?

WHAT'S YOUR VERDICT?

Andrewski hired on as a machinist in Zinton's fabricating shop. Her supervisor told Andrewski she would have to provide her own protective gloves, goggles, and protective apron. Andrewski complained to Zinton, saying that providing these items was not covered in the employment contract.

Can Andrewski supply these items to stay employed?

Employment is a legal relationship based on a contract that calls for one individual to be paid for working under another's direction and control. The parties to this contract are the employer and the employee. The party who pays someone in order to direct and control that person's activities is the **employer**. The party who is paid by the employer to serve under the employer's direction and control is the **employee**.

If there is no contract to pay for work, or if there is no direction and control, the relationship between the parties is not one of employment. If you hire someone merely to produce a result in the manner they see fit, you have hired what the law terms an **independent contractor**. In general, an independent contractor agrees to produce a finished job without being supervised. An example would be an independent contractor who is hired to write one issue of a company's newsletter. On the other hand, an employee agrees to do a range of tasks under the direction and control of the employer. An example of this would be a public relations specialist hired as an employee to write all of a company's newsletters and press releases.

TERMS OF THE EMPLOYMENT CONTRACT

Employment contracts are unusual because their terms can come from a variety of sources. The terms can be derived from

■ express agreements between the employer and employee
■ implied agreements between the employee and employer
■ state and federal laws

EXPRESS AGREEMENTS Express employment contracts are oral or written documents. Detailed written contracts are used with sports professionals, entertainers, top-level managers, and union members. These written contracts expressly

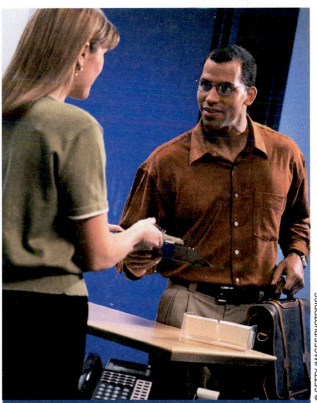

This man has just been hired as a customer service representative at a large consumer products company. The woman in the photo will be his supervisor, and he will work under her direction. Is he an employee or an independent contractor? Explain.

© GETTY IMAGES/PHOTODISC

describe all of the elements of the employment relationship. A party who violates an express term is liable for breach of the contract.

Only a small percentage of employment contracts are completely in writing. Most express contracts are partly written and partly oral. Compensation is almost always an express term. So are fringe benefits. Often the employer and employee also expressly agree upon the duration of the job or the time required for advance notice of termination.

IMPLIED AGREEMENTS When hiring hourly workers, custom or trade practice determines whether length of employment is expressly stated. Generally, hourly wage jobs are impliedly considered to come under the doctrine of **employment at will**. This means that an employee can be discharged at any time for any cause because there has been no agreement about the length of the employment. It also means an employee may quit a job at any time without being liable for breach of contract. Employment contracts can always be identified as either "at will" or "for a specific period."

Frequently, other terms also are implied from the way individual employers supervise their employees. For example, in a particular restaurant there may be an implied term that requires waiters and waitresses to pool their tips and to share them with the people who clear tables. Factory workers may be required to provide their own safety shoes and gloves. Andrewski in *What's Your Verdict?* can be fired if she does not provide the items required by her employer.

TERMS IMPOSED BY LAW State and federal laws impose many important terms into each employment contract whether or not the employer and employee want them included. Terms requiring the payment of a minimum wage and the hiring of racial and other minorities over other more qualified applicants are examples.

CHECKPOINT

Name three sources of the terms in employment contracts.

HOW ARE EMPLOYMENT CONTRACTS TERMINATED?

WHAT'S YOUR VERDICT?

As Jin was unloading a truck on the dock of his employer, a fellow employee moved a box that had been holding the truck door in place. The door swung down and hit Jin in the side of the head and knocked him off his feet. Groggy, his eyesight blurred, Jin kept working. Finally, as the symptoms would not go away, he went to see his doctor. His doctor told Jin than he had a concussion. When Jin filed a workers' compensation claim based on the incident, his employer fired him.

In a state that allows employment contracts to be terminated at will, does Jin have any legal recourse against his ex-employer?

Generally, contracts of employment are terminated either by performance of a specific job or performance for a specific period, by termination at the will of one or both of the parties, or as the result of a material breach. Terminated employees may be eligible for government assistance during their subsequent unemployment.

NETBookmark

Many federal laws have been passed to protect employees from wrongful termination. Access lawxtra.swlearning.com and click on the link for Chapter 21. Read the article "Employment at Will: U.S. Federal Laws Limiting Employment at Will." Then click on one of the laws listed and read about it. Write a paragraph that explains how this law protects an employee from wrongful termination by his or her employer.

lawxtra.swlearning.com

BY PERFORMANCE

Most contracts of employment are terminated the way all other contracts are—by performance. Completion of the job or the running of the period of employment defined in the contract terms is the key to such performance. As mentioned previously, the courts will look at the express, implied, and terms defined by laws to determine the obligations owed by the parties to one another. If these obligations have been fulfilled, the employment contract is terminated.

BY TERMINATION AT WILL

As discussed, many employment contracts are terminable at the will of either the employer or the employee. This occurs because the employer and employee generally do not specify a length of time for the employment relationship. The law then assumes that either party may terminate employment at any time without liability.

For example, if an automobile repair shop hired a mechanic for $27 per hour and a competitor later offered the mechanic $35 per hour, there generally would be no liability for quitting the $27 per-hour job. On the other hand, the repair shop manager could fire the mechanic without giving any reason for doing so.

WRONGFUL DISCHARGE

There are limitations on this power to terminate without cause. Firing because of race, religion, gender, age, disability, pregnancy, veteran status, or national origin is job discrimination and illegal. Federal law also prohibits an employer from dismissing an employee for engaging in union activities. Further, most states now deny the power to terminate at will when it is used to retaliate against those who

- refuse to commit perjury at the request of the company

- insist on filing a workers' compensation claim
- report violations of law by the company
- urge the company to comply with the law

When an employer fires an employee for one of the above reasons, it commits the tort of **wrongful discharge**. Jin in *What's Your Verdict?* would be able to sue his ex-employer for such a wrongful discharge.

VIOLATION OF CONTRACT TERMS Employers who make promises orally or in company documents such as employee handbooks to "treat employees fairly" may cause this promise to become a part of the employment contract. When such terms are part of the employment contract, the employer cannot fire an employee without a fair reason.

GOVERNMENT EMPLOYEES In general, employees who work for the government, often referred to as *public employees,* are entitled to due process before being discharged. This means that they are entitled to notice of the reasons for the discharge along with a hearing. In a hearing, they are given the opportunity to present their own evidence and to challenge the claims of the governmental employer. For this reason, it is more difficult to discharge public employees than private sector employees.

The Pregnancy Discrimination Act is a federal law that outlaws discrimination against employees based on pregnancy, childbirth, or related medical conditions. Do you think such protection for pregnant women is necessary? Why or why not?

© GETTY IMAGES/PHOTODISC

BY MATERIAL BREACH

If the obligations of the employment contract are not fulfilled, breach of contract occurs. As mentioned, if the breach is material, it extinguishes the obligations of the other party to the contract.

Suppose an employer fails to pay the employee an agreed-upon monthly check. This would be a breach of the contract. Because it is material, the employee would be justified in quitting or in abandoning the job without liability for breach of contract. Similarly, if the employee fails to live up to the material obligations of the job, the employer may treat the contract as terminated and discharge the employee without liability.

UNEMPLOYMENT COMPENSATION

Workers who have been terminated despite having complied with all the terms of their employment contract are said to have been **discharged without cause**. This means the cause of the discharge was not the employee's conduct. An employee who is discharged without cause is entitled to unemployment compensation benefits.

Unemployment compensation is money paid by the government or a private insurance fund to workers who have lost their jobs through no fault of their own.

If an employee has been discharged because of violating an employment obligation, then the employee is said to be **discharged for cause**. The worker discharged for cause generally is not entitled to unemployment compensation.

Unemployment compensation payments are made by the states in cooperation with the federal government under the Social Security Act of 1935. There usually is a period of one or two weeks after termination before payments begin. Then a percentage of the regular wage is paid to the unemployed person every week for a limited period of time. Unemployment compensation generally is not available to those who quit voluntarily, strike, or refuse to accept similar substitute work. It often is available to part-time workers.

CHECKPOINT

What are the three main ways in which an employment contract is terminated?

Upon graduating from college later in life with a chemistry degree, Alexandra took a job as a lab technician. The job bored her, and she began to arrive late for work or not show up at all. Would the lab be justified in terminating her? What would be its justification?

© GETTY IMAGES/PHOTODISC

THINK ABOUT LEGAL CONCEPTS

1. Someone who is paid to perform a job but is not supervised or controlled in so doing is a(n) _?_.

2. Federal law is likely to supply which of the following terms in employment contracts? (a) job title (b) minimum wage (c) job location

3. When no length of employment is specified, the employer–employee relationship is known as employment _?_.

4. Wrongful discharge is always committed by the employer. **True or False?**

5. Unemployment compensation will be denied if the employee was fired for cause. **True or False?**

6. Most _?_ employees are entitled to due process (notice and a hearing) before they can be discharged.

THINK CRITICALLY ABOUT EVIDENCE

Study the situation, answer the questions, and then prepare arguments to support your answers.

7. Susan was hired to park customers' cars at a local restaurant. All her pay was in the form of tips and she worked whenever the restaurant was open. She had no direct supervisor and parked the cars in a lot nearby. When she was unable to work, the restaurant placed a sign at their entrance telling customers to self-park. Is Susan an employee?

8. Darrell, a high school student, was friends with an adult neighbor, Bill. Bill operated an auto tune-up business from his garage. Darrell often helped out. At first he would drop by for an hour in the evening and just watch. Then he started handing tools and parts to Bill. Occasionally Bill would give Darrell a $5 bill or take him to dinner. Darrell showed up about twice a week, but there was never any advance notice. Is Darrell an employee?

9. Amit was the night clerk at the India Inn. He had several duties besides working at the main desk. Therefore, he was not allowed to sleep while on the job, even if business was slow. On several occasions, the manager of the inn found Amit sleeping and warned him not to do so. If Amit continued to fall asleep on the job, would the manager be justified in discharging him? If discharged, could Amit collect unemployment compensation?

10. Belly T. Buckle, a famous rodeo bull rider, signed on for a rodeo tour of 15 shows. His employer, In the Dirt, Inc., featured him in all their advertisements. Halfway through the tour, Belly fell in love with an emergency room nurse. As a consequence, he quit the tour. In the Dirt had to hire a replacement rider on short notice at a premium of $75,000 over Belly's pay. At the close of the tour, In the Dirt sued Belly for the extra $75,000, $23,000 for the expense of changing its ad campaign, and more than $200,000 in projected attendance revenue lost due to Belly not being on the tour. Will Dirt recover? How much?

© GETTY IMAGES/PHOTODISC

Duties of Employers and Employees

▼ GOALS
■ List an employer's duties
■ Name an employee's duties

WHAT ARE AN EMPLOYER'S DUTIES?

WHAT'S YOUR VERDICT?

Armstrong was a nurse at the local hospital and an Army reservist. When her unit was called to active duty for service in the Middle East, Armstrong left her job and family to serve her country. After she was honorably discharged from the Army she sought to reclaim her job at the hospital. Upon her return, however, she found the job had been filled by another person.

Is she entitled to regain her job?

Employers owe a variety of duties to employees and others. Some of these duties arise out of the express terms of the contract of employment. Others are implied by law. Following are the principal duties that employers owe employees.

DUTIES OWED TO EMPLOYEES

REASONABLE TREATMENT An employer is required to treat workers in a reasonable manner. If the employer commits an assault or battery upon an employee, the employee may quit the job without liability. The injured employee also may sue for damages.

SAFE WORKING CONDITIONS An employee is entitled by law to reasonably safe working conditions, including safe tools, equipment, machinery, and the building itself. The working conditions must not be harmful to the employee's health, safety, morals, or reputation. If the employer does not provide safe working conditions, the employee may quit without breaching the contract.

FAIR LABOR STANDARDS The federal government has enacted the Fair Labor Standards Act to establish the minimum wage and maximum hours for all employees under the jurisdiction of

the act. Maximum hours that can be worked at regular rates of pay are 40 per week (with no daily maximum). If more than 40 hours are worked in a week, overtime must be paid at one and a half times the regular rate.

Not all workers are covered by this act. The minimum wage and overtime requirements of the law do not apply to executives, administrators, and professional workers. In addition, the hourly provisions apply only partially to workers in seasonal industries. Special rules apply to trainees, apprentices, student workers, and handicapped workers. In certain circumstances they may be paid at 85 percent of the minimum wage.

PAYROLL DEDUCTIONS Certain governmental programs are financed by payments made by employees. Typically the employer deducts money from the employee's paycheck. These are sometimes called **payroll deductions**. Thus, the employer is legally obligated to withhold a percentage of the paycheck to cover the employee's federal and state income tax obligations. Similarly, the employer must withhold certain amounts for the employee's portion of social

This metal-cutting tool was supplied by the employer of the man who is using it. If it malfunctions, the man is burned, and he quits his job over the incident, will he have breached his employment contract? Why or why not?

security payments. The abbreviation FICA, which stands for Federal Insurance Contributions Act, on an employee's paycheck stub refers to these social security payments.

Other payments often are made from the funds of the employer. **Workers' compensation** is an example. This is a payment into an insurance fund that compensates employees for their injuries on the job. It eliminates the need for employers to compensate employees directly for on-the-job injuries.

Similarly, employers must make payments for unemployment insurance. Unemployment insurance provides short-term income, or unemployment compensation, for people who have recently lost their jobs. This topic was discussed in Lesson 21-1.

MILITARY SERVICE The Military Selective Service Extension Act of 1950 requires that certain military persons be re-employed by their former employer after honorable discharge from the service. Persons who have been drafted, enlisted, or called to active duty receive this protection. To qualify for reemployment veterans must still be able to perform the work. In *What's Your Verdict?* Armstrong is legally entitled to her get old job back.

VOTING More than one-half the states provide that workers must be given sufficient time off with pay, at a time convenient to the employer, to vote in regular primary and general elections.

DUTIES OWED TO MINORS

Both state governments and the federal government have prescribed employer duties aimed at protecting minors from overextended working hours and dangerous working conditions.

Although the federal and state laws vary, they are all based on the following principles:

- A person's early years are best used to obtain an education.
- Certain work is harmful or dangerous for young people.
- Child labor at low wages takes jobs from adults.

STATE LAWS Every state government regulates the conditions and types of employment permitted for persons under age 18. These are often termed child-labor laws. When state child-labor laws have stricter standards than federal laws, the state laws control.

The states usually specify a minimum age for employment. All states place a limit on the number of hours a young person may work. In calculating the maximum number of hours, the school hours often are combined with the hours on the job while school is in session. For example, a common maximum is 48 hours (school and outside work combined) in one week. Most states maintain controls over those hours, and most require a work permit if the individual is under the age of 18.

INTERNATIONAL VIEWPOINT

Child Labor In Mexico

Child labor in Mexico for children under the age of fourteen is illegal. Nevertheless, millions of children are employed, often in hazardous jobs. In the state of Guanajuato, for example, shoe manufacturing is an important industry. In the Mexican shoe industry, it is customary to employ young boys. These boys are called *zorritos*, meaning "little foxes." Conditions for the *zorritos* often are hazardous. They are exposed not only to dangerous machinery but also to toxic substances. One particularly toxic substance is the glue that holds the shoes together.

In addition, some states have child labor laws that

- set the maximum number of working hours in one day
- prohibit night work
- prescribe the grade in school that must be completed before being able to work
- set the required age for certain hazardous occupations and
- restrict the hours of work to between 5 A.M. and 10 P.M.

FEDERAL LAW The Fair Labor Standards Act sets the minimum protection for young workers. This law makes it illegal for people under fourteen years old to work, except in entertainment and agriculture. Fourteen- and fifteen-year-olds are only permitted to work limited hours after school in non-hazardous jobs. Unless modified by state law, sixteen- and seventeen-year-olds can work unlimited hours in non-hazardous jobs.

Child labor laws in this country are written essentially to discourage child labor. Do you see any benefits of children working? If so, what are they?

© GETTY IMAGES/PHOTODISC

Law Brief

Hazardous Occupations Not Available To Minors

- Mining
- Manufacturing explosives, brick, or tile
- Operating power-driven hoists
- Logging and saw milling
- Driving motor vehicles or acting as an outside helper on such vehicles (except for incidental, occasional, and school bus driving)
- Slaughtering or meat packing
- Operating circular saws, band saws, or guillotine shears
- Wrecking or demolishing buildings or ships
- Roofing and excavating

DUTIES OWED TO THOSE INJURED BY EMPLOYEES

If an employee, acting within the *scope of employment,* commits a tort (injures persons or property), the employer is liable for the damages. It is immaterial that the employer did not authorize the act. If an employee commits a tort but is not acting within the scope of the employer's business, the employee alone is liable for any resulting injuries. Even if an employee intentionally causes damage, the employer may be held liable if the employee has acted with the intention of furthering the employer's interests

Generally, if a person is an independent contractor rather than an employee, the person who hired the contractor is not liable for the contractor's torts. If the job is inherently dangerous, such as blasting with dynamite, the party who hired the independent contractor may be liable to those injured.

CHECKPOINT

Name the duties owed by employers to their employees.

WHAT ARE AN EMPLOYEE'S DUTIES?

DUTY TO FULFILL THE EMPLOYMENT CONTRACT

An employee has a duty to fulfill the express terms of the employment contract and other implied agreements made with the employer. In addition to the duties acquired by personal consent to the employment agreement, the employee also has duties imposed by state law. These duties include the following:

DUTY OF OBEDIENCE

Each employee is bound by the **duty of obedience**. This means the employee has a duty to obey the reasonable orders and rules of the employer. This duty exists whether or not the employee has expressly agreed to it. However, an employee cannot be required to act illegally, immorally, or contrary to public policy.

IN THIS CASE

Ash was the assistant to the president of Pinos Point Properties. She had confidential information that her company was going to make an offer on a certain piece of land for $250,000 but would be willing to pay as much as $350,000 for it. Ash told this to the owners of the land, who agreed to give her one-half of any amount over $250,000 that they received. After the purchase was made for $350,000, Pinos Point learned of Ash's action. Pinos justifiably dismissed Ash and sued her for damages.

A QUESTION OF ETHICS

Tuchbach was a coach at the University of Southern Missouri. In his third season of a five-year contract, he led his football team to an 10-1 record and a Division I-AA bowl bid. Two weeks after the game, Tuchbach received an offer from another school at double his current salary plus a weekly interview show and endorsement rights. Is it ethical to break his contract even if he pays damages?

DUTY OF REASONABLE SKILL

The **duty of reasonable skill** requires that those who accept work possess the skill, experience, or knowledge necessary to do it. The employer need not keep the employee, nor pay damages for discharging the employee, if the employee does not perform with reasonable skill. Thus, a welder whose welds keep breaking could be fired for the lack of reasonable skill.

DUTY OF LOYALTY AND HONESTY

An employee owes the **duty of loyalty and honesty** to the employer. The employee is obligated to look out for the employer's best interest. By committing a fraud upon the employer, or by revealing confidential information about the business, an employee may be justifiably discharged. Such a worker also may be liable for damages.

DUTY OF REASONABLE PERFORMANCE

Employees owe the **duty of reasonable performance** to employers. This is the obligation to perform the job tasks with competence. An employer is justified in discharging an employee who fails to perform assigned duties at the prescribed time and in the prescribed manner. Occasional minor failure to perform as expected ordinarily is not sufficient grounds for dismissing an employee.

On the other hand, any employee may be discharged if unable to do the work because of illness or injury. Poe's termination as an employee of Kleerglass in *What's Your Verdict?*, although regrettable, was legal.

21-2 Assessment

lawxtra.swlearning.com

THINK ABOUT LEGAL CONCEPTS

1. Which of the following is not a duty owed by the employer to the employee? (a) duty of reasonable treatment (b) duty to provide safe working conditions (c) duty to follow Fair Labor Standards (d) all of the above are employer duties

2. If state laws designed to protect minors have stricter requirements than federal laws, the federal laws still prevail. **True or False?**

3. An employer is liable for the torts of an employee if the employee was acting within the _?_ when the tort occurred.

4. Any party who hires an independent contractor may be liable for the independent contractor's torts if the work (a) involves overtime (b) is inherently dangerous (c) requires professional skill

5. Which of the following is not a duty owed by employees to employers? (a) duty of obedience (b) duty of reasonable performance (c) duty of reasonable skill (d) duty of loyalty and honesty (e) all of the above are employee duties

6. Generally, an employee may be discharged if unable to do the work because of illness or injury. **True or False?**

THINK CRITICALLY ABOUT EVIDENCE

Study the situation, answer the questions, and then prepare arguments to support your answers.

7. Socow's father was an operator of a backhoe. For three summers, the father trained his son to operate backhoes. When Socow turned 14 years old, he applied for a job with a local construction firm as a backhoe operator but was turned down because of his age. Was the construction company's conduct legal?

8. Your friend is hired as a ride operator with a traveling carnival. At a county fair, he carelessly fails to secure the safety bar over the seat on a small roller coaster. Two riders are thrown out and seriously injured. Who is liable for the injuries?

9. Holtz entered into a contract with Acme Pool Company for the construction of a pool in the back yard of his new country estate. As the pool was to be located on a rock bluff, Acme had to do a considerable amount of dynamiting. During one blast, a large portion of the bluff accidentally fell away and severely injured a neighbor below. The neighbor sued Acme and Holtz for $1,000,000. Acme's assets and insurance coverage equalled no

more than $150,000. Is Holtz liable for the remainder?

10. Sharp worked as a machinist building models of new products. His firm was working on a contract for a new doorknob for Costcorp, Inc. Sharp approached one of Costcorp's competitors and showed them a design that his firm had developed. Is this grounds for firing Sharp?

11. Francis was hired as a cook at a local restaurant. He said he was experienced in cooking breakfast items and could handle lunch, too. In fact, his only experience was as a dishwasher, although he had carefully watched cooks work. On the first day, he was fired because he was too slow. Was the employer acting legally?

12. Inez worked as a cashier in an all-night cafeteria. One night two men followed her home from the swing shift. They assaulted her at her home demanding "the money and the deposits." They thought she took money home from the cafeteria to deposit in the bank the next morning. Inez filed a claim for workers' compensation. Was she injured on the job?

As an employee...

1. Realize that you and your employer are parties to a contract in which you both have rights and duties.

2. Before you go to work, learn as much as you can about the job. Find out about hours, pay, duties, dress, fringe benefits, and any other related matters.

3. Avoid tardiness and absenteeism.

4. Remember that in addition to reasonable skill and performance, you owe your employer loyalty, honesty, and obedience. However, the duty of obedience does not require employees to engage in illegal, immoral, or unsafe activities.

5. Remember that you are personally responsible for your own negligent acts. This is true even though the injured party may also be able to recover from your employer.

As an employer...

1. Remember to treat your employees reasonably and provide them with safe working conditions.

2. Be aware of and comply with applicable federal and state laws governing the work environment.

© GETTY IMAGES/PHOTODISC

Chapter 21 Assessment

CONCEPTS IN BRIEF

21-1 Making and Terminating Employment Contracts

1. In an employment relationship, an employee is paid for working under the direction and control of an employer.

2. If there is no contract to pay for work, or if there is no direction and control, the relationship between parties is not one of employment.

3. Express employment contracts may encompass oral and written documents. These may be augmented by terms implied from the work setting and environment.

4. Many employment contracts are terminable at the will of either the employer or the employee. This applies primarily to those without a set duration or job to complete. Employment contracts also may be terminated by performance or material breach.

5. If they are discharged without cause, employees may be eligible for unemployment compensation.

21-2 Duties of Employers and Employees

6. An employer's primary duties are to treat the employee reasonably, provide safe working conditions, and comply with applicable laws and the contract of employment.

7. Both state and federal governments have child-labor laws that regulate conditions and types of employment for persons under age 18.

8. An employee must adhere to the fiduciary duties prescribed by law and comply with the contract of employment. Employees have duties to fulfill the employment contract, of obedience, of reasonable skills, of loyalty and honesty, and of reasonable performance.

YOUR LEGAL VOCABULARY

Match each statement with the term that it best defines. Some terms may not be used.

1. Governmental payments to those who recently lost their jobs

2. Payment for injuries that occur on the job

3. Party who engages another to work for pay under the former's control and direction

4. One who contracts to do something for another but is free of the latter's direction and control

5. Contractual relationship in which one party engages another to work for pay under the supervision of the party paying

6. Party who works under the supervision of another for pay

7. The obligation to look out for the best interests of the employer

8. The obligation to perform the job tasks with competence

9. Firing an employee in retaliation for reporting violations of law by the company

10. Obligation to obey the reasonable orders of the employer

11. Employment relationship whereby employee may be discharged at any time because no agreement was made about length of employment

12. Money withheld from an employee's paycheck

a. **discharged for cause**
b. **discharged without cause**
c. **duty of loyalty and honesty**
d. **duty of obedience**
e. **duty of reasonable performance**
f. **duty of reasonable skill**
g. **employee**
h. **employer**
i. **employment**
j. **employment at will**
k. **independent contractor**
l. **payroll deductions**
m. **unemployment compensation**
n. **workers' compensation**
o. **wrongful discharge**

REVIEW LEGAL CONCEPTS

13. Describe the difference between an independent contractor and an employee.

14. Evaluate the employer's exposure to liability due to employee and independent contractor activities.

15. Explain how courts will decide whether an employment contract is terminable at will.

16. What are the basic provisions of the Fair Labor Standards Act?

WRITE ABOUT LEGAL CONCEPTS

17. Write a short description of a job you know about. Next write two or three sentences describing an employment contract for that job that makes it terminable at will. Last, write another two or three sentences describing an employment contract for the job that makes it not terminable at will.

18. Write a short comparative essay on the origins and evolution of your state's unemployment compensation programs and the federal unemployment compensation programs. Include the social, economic, and political pressures that caused the enactment of each.

19. Write a short essay comparing the purpose, history, work, and effectiveness of your state's gov-

ernmental job training and job search program to that of another state's program, such as the Texas Workforce Commission.

20. Contact the embassies of several foreign countries, being sure to include at least one country from each populated continent. Ask for a list of employee and employer rights and protections in the country. Compare them with the rights and protections of workers and employers in the United States. State your conclusions as to which countries provide better conditions, and where the United States both excels and falls short.

21. **HOT DEBATE** What sanctions would the Army impose on Justin if he reacted in combat as he planned? Would these be ethical?

MAKE ACADEMIC CONNECTIONS

22. **ENGLISH** Consider how conditions of employment have changed since the turn of the twentieth century by reading *The Jungle* by Upton Sinclair. Sinclair, one of the famous authors dubbed

"muckrakers" by President Theodore Roosevelt, investigated the working conditions of immigrants in the Chicago meat packing industry. Prepare a report for the class on the changes.

THINK CRITICALLY ABOUT EVIDENCE

Study the situation, answer the questions, and then prepare arguments to support your answers.

23. Chin interviewed Caroline for a position as a cashier in her grocery store. She described the job responsibilities, the days and hours Caroline would work, the attitude she wanted Caroline to communicate to customers, and the hourly pay. After the interview, Chin said she would hire Caroline and they shook hands. Describe three terms of this employment contract that are express and three that are imposed by law.

24. Myron owned Crossroads Service Station. He directed Pat, an employee, to put re-refined oil into the unlabeled oil jars displayed for sale. Pat knew that the law required re-refined oil to be labeled "re-refined." Therefore, Pat refused to fill or display the jars. Was Pat's disobedience grounds for discharge? If discharged, could Pat collect unemployment compensation?

25. Harrison was hired as an electrical engineer but there was no agreement about the length of the employment period. At the time he was hired he was told that he would not be fired unless he failed to perform his job. The employee's handbook said the same thing. Later when the company changed product lines, it fired Harrison. Can Harrison recover for breach of the employment contract?

26. Cerney operated a computer programming business. Sharon began working for Cerney after school because she could program in a useful language. When she was hired, she was told she would be paid $14 dollars per hour. However, her first paycheck had a third of the pay taken out for federal and state taxes, social security (FICA) taxes, and other deductions. Are the deductions legal?

27. Thomas P. Finley worked for Aetna Life Insurance. Aetna had a company personnel manual that stated that employees would "not be terminated so long as their performance is satisfactory." Finley was fired. He sued and asserted that the language in the personnel manual meant that he was not terminable at will but rather entitled to employment as long as he performed satisfactorily. Can a personnel manual supply such terms of the employment contract? (*Finley v. Aetna Life and Casualty Company,* 202 Conn. 190)

28. Gale, an umpire, was a member of the Greater Washington Softball Umpires Association. During a game which Gale was officiating, a player objected to his decision on a play. The player then struck Gale with a baseball bat, causing injuries to Gale's neck, hip, and leg. Gale claimed that he was an employee of the association and, as such, sought workers' compensation for his injuries. The association asserted that its members were independent contractors. It based this assertion on the fact that the umpires had full charge and control of the games, and that the association did not direct the worker in the performance or manner in which the work was done. The evidence presented showed (a) that the umpires were paid by the association from fees collected from the teams; (b) that the umpires, while assigned to the games by the association, were not obligated to accept the assignments; (c) that the association conducted clinics, administered written examinations, and required members to wear designated uniforms while officiating; and (d) that the umpires had to meet with the approval of committees of the association who observed a member officiating during a probationary period. Under these circumstances, do you believe Gale was an employee of the association or an independent contractor? (*Gale v. Greater Washington Softball Umpires Association,* 311 A.2d 817)

29. Whirlpool operated a manufacturing facility that used overhead conveyors to transport parts around the plant. Because the parts sometimes fell from the overhead conveyor belt, Whirlpool installed a wire screen below the conveyor belts to catch them. Maintenance workers were required to retrieve fallen parts from the screen, which was about twenty feet above the floor of the plant. On two occasions, maintenance workers fell through the screen onto the floor. One of the workers was killed by the fall. Shortly thereafter, Vergil Deemer and Thomas Cornwell asked that the screen be repaired. When repairs were not made, these men complained to OSHA. The next day they were told by their supervisor to climb out onto the screen to retrieve fallen parts. When they refused, they were sent home without pay. Was their refusal a violation of their duty of obedience? (*Whirlpool v. Marshall,* 445 U.S. 1)

30. Lucky Stores, Inc., owned a building with a large sign spelling out "ARDENS" on it. Lucky hired Q.R.I. Corporation as an independent contractor to remove the sign. The removal work was inherently dangerous because each letter was about six-feet high and two and one-half feet wide and weighed between fifty and sixty pounds. Q.R.I. workers safely removed the letter "A" and loaded it on their truck. They also safely removed the letter "R" and leaned it against the truck. Then, for a moment, one worker negligently released his hold on the letter. A gust of wind blew the letter into contact with 79-year-old Smith, injuring her seriously. Is Lucky liable to Smith for damages? (*Smith v. Lucky Stores, Inc.,* 61 Cal. App. 3d 826, 132 Cal. Rptr. 628)

31. Central Indiana Gas Co. hired Frampton. Later Frampton was required to serve on a jury. Because he missed work for jury duty, he was fired. He sued. Will he win? (*Frampton v. Central Indiana Gas Co.,* 297 N.E. 2d 425, Indiana)

32. Walgreen Company planned to open a restaurant in Duluth, Minnesota. A.J. Gatzke, a district manager for Walgreen, was sent to Duluth to supervise the opening. Gatzke obtained a room—paid for by Walgreen—in a motel owned by Edgewater Motels, Inc. One day after work, Gatzke and another Walgreen employee went to a bar near the motel. There Gatzke drank four brandy Manhattans in about one hour. Then Gatzke went back to his motel room where, apparently, he smoked several cigarettes after completing an expense account report. The butt of one cigarette was apparently thrown into a wastebasket in the room. The room caught on fire and the fire spread to the entire motel. Gatzke escaped uninjured, but the damage to the motel was more than $330,000. Edgewater Motels sued both Gatzke and his employer, Walgreen Company. Who is liable? (*Edgewater Motels, Inc. v. Gatzke,* 277 N.W.2d 11)

PROGRESS PRINTING CO. v. NICHOLS
421 S.E.2D 428 (VIRGINIA SUPREME CT.)

FACTS At the time Nichols began work as a pressman for the Progress Printing Company he was given a copy of the Employees' Handbook. The handbook stated that Progress would not discharge or suspend an employee "without just cause" and that the company "shall give at least one warning notice in writing" before termination. Later, the company's personnel director gave Nichols a form that stated in part:

I have received a copy of the Progress Printing Employee Handbook. . . . I agree to follow the procedures and guidelines it contains. . . . The employment relationship between Progress Printing and the employee is at will and may be terminated by either party at any time.

Nichols and the personnel director both signed the form. Nichols became upset over Progress's failure to correct a recurring defect in a print job, and he refused to complete that job. Nichols was fired on the following day without the prior written notice promised by the Employee Handbook. Nichols then sued for wrongful discharge in a Virginia trial court. After that court ruled in his favor and awarded him $9,000 in damages, Progress appealed.

REASONING In Virginia, as in a majority of jurisdictions, the employment relationship is presumed to be "at will," which means that the employment term extends for an indefinite period and may be terminated for any reason. This presumption may be rebutted if sufficient evidence is produced to show that the employment is for a definite, rather than an indefinite, term. Progress argues that Nichols failed to rebut the presumption because the handbook did not constitute an enforceable employment contract and, even if it did, the subsequent execution of the acknowledgment form created an at-will employment relationship.

A number of jurisdictions have held that termination-for-cause provisions contained in employee handbooks can bind the employer if those provisions are communicated to the employee in a sufficiently specific manner. We have held that an employment condition that allows termination only for cause sets a definite term for the duration of the employment. We nevertheless agree with Progress that the acknowledgment form specifically superseded and replaced the [just cause] provision with the agreement that the employment relationship was at will.

We base this holding on a number of grounds. The termination-for-cause language of the handbook and the employment-at-will relationship agreed to in the subsequent acknowledgment form are in direct conflict and cannot be reconciled in any reasonable way. If the documents are considered a single contract, this conflict fails to provide sufficient evidence to rebut the presumption of employment at will. In any event, the acknowledgment form was not a part of the handbook and was executed 13 days after Nichols began work. Under these circumstances, the form reflects an understanding between the parties separate from that contained in the handbook. Execution of the form memorialized reciprocal commitments that satisfy the requisites of a contract; that is, there was an offer of employment at will; the employee continued service, which constituted the consideration; and the employee accepted by performance.

CONCLUSION Progress did not breach the employment at will contract when it terminated Nichols. The trial court decision is reversed.

PRACTICE JUDGING

1. Would the decision have been different if the acknowledgment had been signed first and the handbook later provided to Nichols?

2. Which do you think is better evidence of the understandings of the parties, the signed agreement or the statement in the handbook?

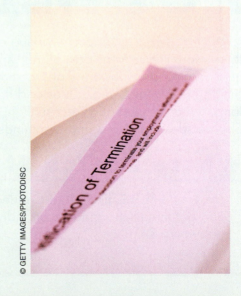

© GETTY IMAGES/PHOTODISC

Unions and the Employment Relationship

22-1 Establishment of Unions

22-2 Employment Relations in a Unionized Workplace

© GETTY IMAGES/PHOTODISC

Charlee Brawn is a laborer working at harvesting various crops throughout the western part of the United States. Her employer hires thousands of laborers and contracts their labor out to various farmers to pick vegetables and fruit. The hours are extremely long, typically spent in direct sunlight, and the pay is minimal. She decides to try and improve things.

Where Do You Stand?

1. Do you think it is likely that Charlee can get things changed as an individual worker?

2. Identify the problems Charlee might encounter in trying to form a union. Does such an action seem possible?

Establishment of Unions

HISTORY OF LABOR LAW

WHAT'S YOUR VERDICT?

Tron, a news desk anchor for the Channel 39 news team, wanted to form a union for the employees of the station.

Would the process be governed by the National Labor Relations Board?

The current state of labor law in the United States is best understood through a brief look at relevant history. The early labor organizations in this country did not engage in strikes until the 1800s. When these labor stoppages began to occur, the law responded with hostility.

EARLY LABOR LAW

Initially the law held that union activities were the result of criminal conspiracies. Unions were held to be organizing their members to extort higher wages at the expense of the consuming public. The courts supported this claim until about 1842. After that time, the courts ceased classifying unions as criminal conspiracies.

After union activities were decriminalized, the legal attack on them shifted to the civil law. Courts reasoned that, as employment contracts already existed between employers and workers, strikes were attempts to pressure employers into accepting terms they otherwise would reject. Courts therefore held that strikes, boycotts, and similar tactics were actions in breach of the employment contract. Consequently, companies felt justified in firing any employee suspected of sympathizing with unions. In most states, companies could do this because employment contracts were terminable at will.

In other states, companies made employees agree as a condition of employment not to join a union. Therefore, union membership could legally justify immediate dismissal. Employment

contracts that contained this term earned the name **yellow-dog contracts**. In addition, court-issued injunctions often were used to hinder union organization efforts aimed at employees already working under such contracts.

These and similar injunctions often were issued by a judge after hearing only one side of an argument, typically the employer's. An injunction issued in this manner is termed an **ex-parte injunction**. If the employer could show potential injury flowing from a strike, many judges would issue an injunction prohibiting the strike. If employees struck or continued to strike in the face of the injunction, they could be arrested and imprisoned for contempt of court.

In 1890, Congress passed the Sherman Antitrust Act, which prohibited restraints of trade and made business monopolies illegal. Federal judges came to interpret this act as making unions illegal as they monopolized the supply of labor. For example, in the Danbury Hatters case, the U.S. Supreme Court held that the Sherman Antitrust Act did apply to unions. Eventually, in a portion of the Clayton Act, Congress responded by exempting unions from the Sherman Antitrust Act.

NETBookmark

Access lawxtra.swlearning.com and click on the link for Chapter 22. Read the details surrounding the Danbury Hatters Case, and then answer these questions:

1. What was the situation that prompted the suit against the hatters' union?

2. When did the U.S. Supreme Court decide the case?

3. What punishments did the Supreme Court hand down to the hatters' union?

lawxtra.swlearning.com

THE DEPRESSION ERA

When the pro-business climate of the post-World War I economy disintegrated in the wake of the Great Depression, unions came more into favor. As a part of its sweeping economic reforms under the leadership of President Franklin Roosevelt, the federal government solidified the status of unions in this country by assuming regulatory responsibility for labor relations.

As a consequence, today most labor relations are governed by a federal administrative agency instead of through the courts and Congress. That agency, the National Labor Relations Board (NLRB), administers the rights and duties given to workers, employers, and unions. The NLRB was created by the National Labor Relations Act (also known as the Wagner Act) in 1935. The NLRB supervises and controls all the aspects of labor relations from the formation of a union, through representative bargaining, to the implementation and carrying out of the collective bargaining agreements. Representatives of the union, employers, and individual workers are entitled to file charges and to take part in hearings before the NLRB. A party that is dissatisfied with the board's order may seek review in the federal courts, but that review power is limited.

Although the potential jurisdiction of the NLRB is quite broad, reaching to any business that directly or indirectly affects interstate commerce, it restricts itself to larger enterprises. Control of labor relations in smaller businesses is left to the states. (See the Law Brief feature on this page for a sample of current guidelines.) Whether or not Tron's efforts in *What's Your Verdict?* to unionize the station would be governed by the NLRB would be determined by the gross volume of the station's business. As most of the guidelines were set many decades ago and have not been adjusted for inflation, there is a great likelihood that the answer is yes.

Law Brief

Currently the NLRB will claim jurisdiction over labor relations only when the business involved exceeds a certain dollar amount in gross volume. In addition, the NLRB has refused to exert any jurisdiction over certain industries such as horse and dog racing. Some examples of NLRB jurisdictional minimums are

Non-retail businesses	$50,000
Radio, TV, telegraph and telephone companies	$100,000
Newspapers	$200,000
Hospitals	$250,000
Public utilities	$250,000
Retail business	$500,000
Taxicab companies	$500,000
Symphony orchestras	$1,000,000
Private education institutions	$1,000,000

HOW IS A UNION ESTABLISHED?

WHAT'S YOUR VERDICT?

John worked on the dock for Right of Way Truck Lines Company. When union organizers gathered enough signatures to force a vote, the NLRB conducted an election at the company. The majority of employees, John being a major dissenter, voted for union bargaining representation. John now finds that the contract negotiated by the union is lacking, especially where it creates an agency shop and requires union dues deducted from every worker's pay whether or not they join the union. Consequently, John wants to negotiate his own contract with the employer.

What are John's rights in this situation?

CHECKPOINT

What federal agency currently exercises control over labor relations?

The formation of a union can be a long and difficult process. The following sections discuss the steps in this process.

DETERMINING THE BARGAINING UNIT

To establish union representation, a series of steps needs to be taken. One step involves determining which employees should be represented together. Within a unionized company, any group of employees whose employment contract is negotiated together is called a **bargaining unit**. The NLRB may determine the appropriate unit in accordance with statutory requirements.

Common employment interests such as training are important considerations in who should be included in the bargaining unit. Employees who have supervisory responsibilities or those who have a confidential role in creating management-labor policies cannot be in a bargaining unit.

Sometimes one union represents several bargaining units in negotiating with a single employer. Each unit is entitled to create its own union to bargain with the employer or to select an existing union to represent them.

ATTEMPTING VOLUNTARY RECOGNITION

To establish a union, the organizers obtain employee signatures on authorization cards. An **authorization card** indicates the worker wants to be represented by a particular union. If a sizable percentage of workers sign authorization cards for a particular union, it may approach management and ask to be recognized as the exclusive bargaining representative.

HOLDING A CERTIFICATION ELECTION

If management denies voluntary recognition, the union can ask the NLRB to conduct a **representation election**. If at least 30 percent of the employees in the proposed bargaining unit have signed authorization cards or a petition, the NLRB will conduct hearings to determine who is in the bargaining unit and who is eligible to vote. To select a bargaining representative (a union), workers in the bargaining unit vote secretly in an election conducted by the NLRB. Majority vote governs. If a union is selected, it becomes the exclusive negotiator for all the employees in the bargaining unit. The NLRB will then acknowledge that union as the exclusive bargaining agent. This is called **certification**.

CERTIFICATION CAMPAIGNS Often management is hostile to the possibility that a union will represent workers. So labor law makes certain conduct illegal during organizing campaigns. Thus, it is illegal for an employer to fire or to threaten to fire union sympathizers to discourage unionization. Similarly, employers may not threaten to

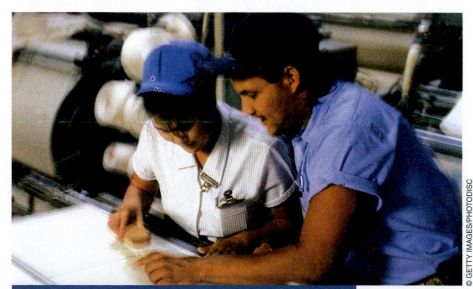

The man in this photo is the woman's supervisor, and he is training her to do a job task. Is he eligible to be in a bargaining unit?

© GETTY IMAGES/PHOTODISC

close a plant, to automate the workplace to reduce the number of workers, or to move work out of the country just to avoid unionization. In addition, management may not support one union over another. Labor unions are similarly regulated. During certification campaigns they may not picket, make threats, or engage in violence.

DECERTIFICATION If a union has been certified and later 30 percent of the employees decide they want different or no representation, they can petition the NLRB to conduct a **decertification election**. At this election, employees can reject union representation or select a different union. If a majority rejects representation, workers will negotiate individually with the employers. An employer cannot file a decertification petition. Managerial employees are not permitted to vote in certification or decertification elections or to be represented by a union.

NEGOTIATING THE EMPLOYMENT CONTRACT

Once a union has been certified, it is the exclusive bargaining representative for everyone within the unit. Whether or not they are union members, all workers in each bargaining unit are bound by the collective agreement reached between the union and the employer. In *What's Your Verdict?* John could not negotiate an individual employment contract with his employer. Whether or not he must join the union depends on the type of shop that has been authorized in the negotiation process.

A QUESTION OF ETHICS

Peresight worked in a furniture plant in a state that had passed right-to-work laws. Because of the collective agreements entered into by the union at her plant, Peresight was making 30 percent more than she would in similar non-unionized plants nearby. Nevertheless, she refused to pay union dues or in any other way support the union. Is she acting ethically?

UNION AND AGENCY SHOPS Workers are not required to join a union unless the employer has agreed to have a union shop. In a **union shop**, non-union employees may be hired, but they must join the union within a stated maximum period, usually 30 days. The **agency shop** is a variation of the union shop. In the agency shop, employees are not required to join the union, but if they do not, they must nevertheless pay union dues as a condition of employment.

OPEN AND CLOSED SHOPS In the **open shop**, employees are not required to belong to a union or to pay dues. The union bargains collectively with the employer and agrees to an employment contract binding union and nonunion workers.

In a **closed shop**, the employer agrees that workers must belong to the recognized union before they can be hired. The closed shop was outlawed by the Labor Management Relations Act (also known as the Taft-Hartley Act) of 1946. The Taft Hartley Act also allows individual states to pass right-to-work laws.

Right-to-work laws prohibit compulsory union membership and ban the union shop, closed shop, and agency shop. In states with right-to-work laws, unions may function, but only with open shops.

CHECKPOINT
What is a bargaining unit?

These employees are working in an open shop. Some of them belong to the union, but others do not. Which employees are bound by the collective bargaining agreements reached by the union with management?

Xtra! Study Tools

lawxtra.swlearning.com

22-1 Assessment

THINK ABOUT LEGAL CONCEPTS

1. Employment contracts that make not joining a union a condition of continued employment are termed ex-parte contracts. **True or False?**

2. The group of workers for whom a union negotiates a common contract is called the _?_.

3. Who conducts the certification election? (a) the union (b) management (c) the petitioning workers (d) the NLRB

4. Who determines the membership in the bargaining unit? (a) the union (b) management (c) the petitioning workers (d) the NLRB

5. What percentage of workers in a bargaining unit must vote in favor to create a union? (a) 10% (b) 20% (c) 30% (d) a majority

6. What percentage of workers in a union must petition the NLRB to get it to conduct a decertification election? (a) 10% (b) 20% (c) 30% (d) a majority

7. In right-to-work states, unions may function but only with closed shops. **True or False?**

THINK CRITICALLY ABOUT EVIDENCE

Study the situation, answer the questions, and then prepare arguments to support your answers.

8. It is in the late autumn of 1852. Your textile plant in northern Massachusetts is working you 14 hours a day, 6 days a week, producing clothing for the upcoming winter. Several of your fellow employees are getting hurt due to the fatigue caused by the extended hours. In addition, word has reached you that several plants in Boston are paying their employees almost half again what yours is paying because they have unionized. You and three of your friends decide to try and form a union at your plant. When the owners of the plant discover this, they file for and receive an ex-parte injunction against your organizing activites. Nonetheless, you continue to recruit for the union. By doing so you (a) are likely to be sued by the company for breach of the employment contract (b) are likely to be fired by the company (c) are likely to be fined and imprisoned for contempt of court (d) all of the above

9. You are working as a printer at a small town newspaper which grosses about $185,000 per year in sales. You lead a unionization drive and file a petition with the NLRB for a certification election. What will happen?

10. At Alta Corporation, 5 of the 20 machinists and 20 of the 30 assembly workers favored unionizing. Describe how the petition for certification and the votes on certification would fare if the bargaining unit(s) were defined as (1) the machinists and the assembly workers as separate units, or (2) a combination of both.

Employment Relations in a Unionized Workplace

HOW IS A LABOR CONTRACT NEGOTIATED WITH A UNION?

WHAT'S YOUR VERDICT?

Ace Inc. manufactures automobile parts for several U.S. car companies. The same union represents all of its manufacturing employees. Historically, labor and Ace management negotiated five-year contracts. The current round of negotiations was unsuccessful. During one session, union and management representatives became very angry with each other, and someone threw a chair across the bargaining table. Because of such incidents and the unlikelihood of reaching an agreement, Ace refused to continue negotiating. It said it was prepared to continue paying workers under the old contract but that it was unwilling to negotiate with the current leaders of the union.

What alternatives are available to solve this problem?

Collective bargaining is the process whereby the union and the employer negotiate a contract of employment that binds both sides. Unions choose their own negotiators. Management and/or company lawyers typically represent the company. Pay and fringe benefits are the most commonly negotiated issues. However, grievance procedures, hours, overtime, pensions, health care, working conditions, and safety issues also are frequently negotiated.

An employer is not required to bargain over such issues as product prices or designs, plant location, or quality of products. These are strictly management matters even though they do affect the company's ability to pay wages.

Many factors influence the relative bargaining power of labor and management. These include the company's profitability, availability of substitute workers, prevailing labor rates, the competitiveness of the industry, and foreign competition.

Should the union and management fail to reach an agreement, the union employees may choose to strike and the employer, to hold a lockout. A **strike** is a collective work stoppage intended to force an employer to alter its position on an issue. A **lockout** occurs when an employer temporarily closes down operations to induce the workers and their representatives to alter their position on an issue.

Great economic pressure results on both sides if either a strike or a lockout occurs. Employee wages usually cease and production often stops. This economic pressure is reinforced by the legal requirement that both management and labor bargain with each other. Failure to bargain is a violation of NLRB rules. In *What's Your Verdict?* Ace committed such a violation by refusing to continue negotiations. The union could file a complaint with the NLRB, which might issue an

LEGAL RESEARCH

Contact the NLRB and the EEOC. Inquire about collective bargaining agreement terms that, when included in a negotiated contract, indicate the intent to comply with the legislated requirements of the ADA, affirmative action, and the various anti-discrimination laws. Ask about the current issues in these areas as well as the rates of actual compliance that the agencies find in their inspections, dispute resolution actions, and prosecutions. What conclusions can you draw from the results of your research?

order compelling management to negotiate in good faith.

When collective bargaining negotiations become *deadlocked* (stalemated) and a strike is imminent or in progress, the government may intervene. When this happens, a representative may be appointed by the government to try to bring the parties together and settle their differences. In **mediation** (also known as *conciliation*), a mediator (conciliator) talks with both sides and attempts to achieve a compromise. However, the result of mediation is not enforceable against the bargaining parties.

In other situations, the parties may submit their deadlocked dispute to binding arbitration if allowed under their labor contract. The arbitrator holds a hearing and then makes a determination that is enforceable at law against both employer and union.

CHECKPOINT

Who are the parties to a collective bargaining agreement?

The signs these union employees are wearing indicate that they are on strike. What issues might their bargaining unit have failed to settle with management?

IN THIS CASE

The management of Serfbored, a video game manufacturer located in Malibu, California, was secretly evaluating a move of its design and manufacturing operations to the northern part of that state. Their union, Local 1101, found out what was going on and wanted to negotiate concerning the prospect of the move. When Serfbored refused to bargain on the matter, Local 1101 went on strike claiming it was an unfair labor practice not to negotiate on that term. Serfbored then replaced all the strikers with workers in San Jose and moved its operations there. The NLRB noted that by law the company did not have to negotiate over location and had made no threats to move. The NLRB concluded that the union's actions were illegal under its contract, and that the workers could therefore be replaced.

WHAT ARE UNFAIR LABOR PRACTICES?

WHAT'S YOUR VERDICT?

Kiersten worked in a factory that manufactured uniforms. Upset by the low wages and poor working conditions at the plant, Kiersten began collecting certification petition signatures during her lunch hour and after work. Kiersten's employer noticed what she was doing. He met with her and stated that, since he paid better-than-union wages and the plant's working conditions were better than those in other plants in the area, he did not want to deal with unions. Nonetheless Kiersten continued her organizing efforts and was fired as a consequence.

Can Kiersten's employer legally fire her because of her organizing activities?

The Wagner Act and other federal and state statutes require that employers treat unions fairly by allowing them to organize. These statutes also require that management engage in good-faith negotiations (collective bargaining) with unions. Such laws seek to ensure unions are fairly treated in these matters by prohibiting certain actions of employers. In other labor situations, unions are prohibited from taking certain actions against employers or their own members. In either case, these prohibited actions are referred to as **unfair labor practices**.

What are management's responsibilities with regard to negotiating with union representatives?

MANAGEMENT'S UNFAIR LABOR PRACTICES

For employers the list of unfair labor practices includes (1) interfering with employees' efforts to form, join, or assist unions (2) dominating a union or giving it financial or other support (3) encouraging or discouraging union membership, and (4) refusing to bargain in good faith with the union.

INTERFERING WITH EMPLOYEES' EFFORTS TO FORM, JOIN, OR ASSIST UNIONS Such interference can take a variety of forms. For example, it would be an unfair labor practice to refuse to deduct union dues for union members, to disrupt organizing meetings, or to threaten to fire employees to keep them from organizing a union. In *What's Your Verdict?* Kiersten's employer was guilty of an unfair labor practice. The employer could be required to rehire Kiersten and to pay her the wages lost while barred from the job. Similarly, employers may not threaten to stop operations, replace workers with machines, or move the factory just to avoid unionization.

DOMINATING A UNION OR GIVING IT FINANCIAL OR OTHER SUPPORT Laws that prohibit management from dominating a union or giving it financial or other support preserve the ability of unions to represent the interests of employees. In the past, some companies tried to influence certification elections. Sometimes they wanted the least aggressive union to win. Other times they tried to win favor with union leaders by contributing money to their election campaigns.

ENCOURAGING OR DISCOURAGING UNION MEMBERSHIP Employers may not threaten to blacklist employees who join unions. Employers blacklist employees by placing their names on a list of pro-union persons and sending it to other employers with the purpose of making it difficult for the employees to find work.

REFUSING TO BARGAIN IN GOOD FAITH WITH THE UNION This means management must participate actively in attempting to reach an agreement. It must make honest and reasonable proposals and must listen to the arguments of the union. Management must attempt to find a common ground with the union. However, the law does not require that management agree to a union proposal. Management must only engage in good faith bargaining. Similarly, it is an unfair labor practice to discharge or otherwise discriminate against an employee for filing charges of labor law violations or for testifying about such charges.

UNFAIR LABOR PRACTICES BY UNIONS

The Taft-Hartley Act and other statutes require that unions treat employees and management fairly. Unfair labor practices by unions include

1. Refusing to bargain collectively in good faith with the employer.

2. Attempting to force an employer to pay for featherbedding. **Featherbedding** is payment for services not performed. If the work is performed, there is no featherbedding even though the work may be unnecessary.

3. **Picketing**, or patrolling near the employer's property with signs, by uncertified unions trying to force the employer to bargain with that union. Certifying elections are the appropriate method for compelling an employer to bargain with a particular union. It is also an unfair labor practice for a union to picket in an effort to force employees to select that union as their representative within 12 months after losing a valid representation election.

4. Engaging in strikes and boycotts prohibited by law. Most strikes are legal, however, if they are conducted without violence.

5. Requiring payment of an excessive or discriminatory fee for initiation into the union.

6. Forcing or attempting to force employees to support a union or to restrain employees from supporting competing unions. A union may, however, try to persuade employees to support it.

7. Causing or attempting to cause an employer to discriminate against an employee because of union-related activities.

After congressional testimony about corruption and violence in a few unions, Congress passed legislation designed to limit union corruption. The Labor-Management Reporting and Disclosure Act (also known as the Landrum-Griffin Act) requires that unions operate in a manner that gives members full voice in decision making. The law was intended to ensure that union members themselves could correct abuses of power by entrenched leadership through free and open elections.

The Union Bill of Rights on this page describes rights that union members have with regard to their unions.

UNION BILL OF RIGHTS

ELECTIONS Union members have the right to equal opportunities for nominating candidates for union offices, and the right to vote by secret ballot in union elections.

MEETINGS Union members have the right to meet with other members to express views about candidates or other business.

DUES Union members have the right to vote by secret ballot on increases in dues, initiation fees, and assessment levies.

LAWSUITS Union members have the right to sue, to testify in court or before any administrative agency or legislative body, and to communicate with any legislator.

DISCIPLINE Union members are protected from union disciplinary action, unless the member is served with written charges, given time to prepare a defense, and afforded a fair hearing. Members may be disciplined for nonpayment of dues without such elaborate due process.

MANAGEMENT Union members have the right to obtain information about union policies and financial matters, to recover misappropriated union funds for the union, to inspect union contracts, and to be informed of provisions of this act.

UNFAIR LABOR PRACTICES IN STRIKES AND BOYCOTTS

STRIKES An *economic strike* is one where the dispute is over wages, hours, or conditions of employment. An employer may respond to an economic strike by giving any striking employee's job to someone else. However, when there is an economic strike, unions commonly refuse to settle unless striking members are rehired.

If the strike is over an unfair labor practice by management, the employer may not permanently give the striking worker's job to someone else. When such an *unfair labor practice strike* is over, the employer must reinstate the striking worker even if this requires transferring or discharging the replacement.

What category of strike would an air traffic controllers' union strike be? Explain your answer.

national emergency strike is one that involves national defense or major industries or would endanger national health or safety. Strikes and lockouts are illegal during the cooling-off period.

BOYCOTTS A **boycott** is a refusal to buy or to use someone's products or services. A *primary boycott* involves the employees' refusals to buy their employer's products or services. Primary boycotts are legal. Typically they are accompanied by a strike and by picketing at the employer's place of business. Usually the striking employees also encourage others, such as customers and suppliers, to boycott the employer.

Sometimes, however, striking employees try to get customers to stop buying the products or services of a third party. Such action against a third party is known as a *secondary boycott*. It generally is illegal. However, picketing is legal if the picketers had urged customers of the stores to stop buying only products made by a particular manufacturer, not all products.

In addition, secondary boycotts are legal when the National Labor Relations Act, or state statutes similar to the NLRA, do not apply. This would be the case with farm labor in most states. Thus, farm workers engaged in labor disputes with farmers have encouraged consumers to not buy anything at grocery stores carrying nonunion grapes and lettuce. This secondary boycott is legal because the farm workers are not covered by the National Labor Relations Act.

Strikes of public employees generally are prohibited even though such workers may unionize and bargain collectively. Sometimes public workers (including police officers, teachers, and fire fighters) strike or stay away from work claiming illness. In such cases, the workers and their leaders are subject to court orders directing them to return to work. If they ignore the court order, they may be fired or jailed.

The President of the United States has the power to obtain an injunction in federal court forcing a *cooling-off period* of 80 days when a national emergency strike is threatened. A

INTERNATIONAL VIEWPOINT

In Mexico, labor relations are regulated by the Federal Labor Law of Mexico. Under this law, labor unions are favored and so are easy to form. If union members decide to strike, the plant will close. This forces the union and company to settle the strike quickly. Mexican law also favors job security for workers. If an employee passes a 30-day trial period, the person may not be terminated for lack of job qualifications.

CHECKPOINT

What is the difference between an economic strike and an unfair labor practice strike?

THINK ABOUT LEGAL CONCEPTS

1. A _?_ occurs when an employer temporarily closes down operations to induce the workers and their representatives to alter their position on an issue. (a) lockin (b) strike (c) shutout (d) none of the above.

2. A compromise achieved by a mediator is enforceable against the bargaining parties. **True or False?**

3. Management's First Amendment rights allow it to say anything in an attempt to defeat the union during a certification campaign. **True or False?**

4. In a collective bargaining session, which of the following is an employer not required to bargain over? (a) wages (b) working conditions (c) plant location (d) the employer must bargain over all of the above

5. Blacklisting an employee is an unfair labor practice. **True or False?**

6. After losing a certification election, a union must wait _?_ months before resuming picketing of a particular employer to be selected as the bargaining representative. (a) 6 (b) 12 (c) it may begin immediately after the loss.

7. In labor parlance, freeloading is payment for services not performed. **True or False?**

THINK CRITICALLY ABOUT EVIDENCE

Study the situation, answer the questions, and then prepare arguments to support your answers.

8. Sharpe was a union leader. In the midst of intense negotiations, a stranger approached her and engaged her in a discussion. The stranger offered her $20,000 if she would support a management proposal. Is this an unfair labor practice?

9. The Electrical Workers Union represented most of the workers in the General TV Plant. In a dispute over wages, the union went on strike and began picketing the plant. They also picketed nearby stores that carried the General televisions, asking that shoppers not purchase them. Is any of this conduct illegal?

10. Alonzo owns his own machine shop and has several close friends among his employees. The NLRB is about to conduct a certification election. Alonzo knows he could persuade his employee friends to spread rumors that if the union is certified, he would move his shop out of the country. He also is certain that such rumors could never be traced back to him. Would this action be legal? Would it be ethical for Alonzo to spread such rumors if they would cause the union to lose the election?

PREVENT LEGAL DIFFICULTIES

In an employment relationship based on collective bargaining, remember....

1. Employees generally have the legal right to organize into unions and bargain collectively with employers.

2. An employer may not legally discharge an employee for engaging in union activities. An employer that does so is guilty of an unfair labor practice.

3. A union member has the right to vote for union officers in secret elections and to see accurate and timely information on union finances and activities.

4. Employers should cooperate with unions that represent their employees in good faith for the common good of all parties involved.

5. Unless there is a legal union shop, employers may not discharge or otherwise discriminate against workers because they join a union or because they refuse to join a union.

6. Employers must bargain collectively in good faith with representatives of any union chosen by a majority of the workers in each bargaining unit.

Chapter 22 Assessment

CONCEPTS IN BRIEF

22-1 Establishment of Unions

1. Labor law in this country has taken about two centuries to evolve to its current state.

2. The National Labor Relations Board (NLRB) is the federal administrative agency that regulates union activity.

3. Organizing a union is an activity protected by law.

4. Steps in organizing a union include securing authorization card signatures from the employees, determination of the appropriate bargaining unit, holding a representation election, and receiving certification as the collective bargaining representative.

5. Right-to-work laws passed by individual states prohibit mandatory union membership.

22-2 Employment Relations in a Unionized Workplace

6. Where a union does represent the employees, they bargain collectively through it in hopes of obtaining better wages and working conditions, and other labor objectives.

7. Over the years, unfair labor practices for unions and employers have been spelled out by the law.

8. Strikes and lockouts may occur where the parties cannot reach agreement in the collective bargaining sessions.

9. Mediation and binding arbitration may result in a compromise settlement in difficult labor negotiations so as to avoid the commonly depleting waste of resources characteristic of a strike or lockout.

YOUR LEGAL VOCABULARY

Match each statement with the term that it best defines. Some terms may not be used.

1. A process by which a union ceases to be the exclusive bargaining agent for employees

2. State laws that ban both the union shop and the closed shop

3. Establishment in which all employees must belong to the union, either when they are hired or within a specified time after they are hired

4. Any group of employees whose employment contract is negotiated together within a unionized company

5. Concerted stoppage of work to force an employer to yield to union demands

6. Patrolling by union members with signs alongside the premises of the employer during a labor dispute

7. Union or employer actions that violate the rights of employees with respect to union activity

8. Attempt by a neutral third party to achieve a compromise between disputing parties

9. Employer's shutdown of operations to bring pressure on employees

10. Establishment in which employees do not have to belong to a union nor pay dues

11. The process whereby the union and the employer negotiate a contract of employment that binds both sides

12. Employment agreements that make employees agree not to join a union as a condition of employment

a. agency shop
b. authorization card
c. bargaining unit
d. boycott
e. certification
f. closed shop
g. collective bargaining
h. decertification election
i. ex-parte injunction
j. featherbedding
k. lockout
l. mediation
m. open shop
n. picketing
o. representation election
p. right-to-work laws
q. strike
r. unfair labor practices
s. union shop
t. yellow-dog contracts

REVIEW LEGAL CONCEPTS

13. Explain the history of labor law.

14. Explain the steps involved in establishing a new union.

15. How can members of a bargaining unit change their selection of the union that represents them?

16. Contrast the various types of "shops" that may result in collective bargaining situations.

WRITE ABOUT LEGAL CONCEPTS

17. Invent four examples of unfair labor practices by a union. Describe each in a separate paragraph.

18. Invent four examples of unfair labor practices by management. Describe each in a separate paragraph.

19. Explain which boycotts are legal and which are not in a short paragraph.

20. **HOT DEBATE** Charlee discovers that the vast majority of the would-be members of her prospective union are not citizens. Write a paragraph analyzing why this should matter or not in forming a union.

MAKE ACADEMIC CONNECTIONS

21. **HISTORY** Research the strike called by John L. Lewis, the head of the United Mine Workers (UAW), during the height of World War II. More than half a million workers went out on strike and stayed out in defiance of government orders to return to work. As a consequence, steel mills stopped production and the war effort was hampered greatly. Write a paragraph analyzing the ethics of this action from both sides.

THINK CRITICALLY ABOUT EVIDENCE

Study the situation, answer the questions, and then prepare arguments to support your answers.

22. When a national union sent organizers to try to persuade Baker's workers to join the union, Baker called three of her most trusted employees to her office. She urged them to organize a new union limited to company employees. She offered to provide the union with office space and time for officers to conduct union business. Baker then gave the three workers money to buy printed notices and refreshments for an organization meeting. Was Baker's action legal?

23. O'Donnell felt that management at the company where he worked was engaging in unfair labor practices. He complained in public and filed charges with the NLRB. Those charges were dismissed. Later he was called to testify about charges filed by the union. O'Donnell's bosses hinted that they would get even. About two months later, the company decided to eliminate O'Donnell's job. Does he have any recourse?

24. Joan and the other members of her union were striking for higher wages. Management made a public announcement that workers who failed to report on the following Monday would be permanently replaced. Can an employer permanently replace striking union members? Can a union continue striking until the employer agrees to rehire the striking employees?

25. A strike at the Titan Stone Works was in its fifth week when Paxton, a federal mediator, was called in. After long discussions with both sides, she persuaded the union representatives to accept certain terms. The terms were a major concession on the part of the union but seemed to her to be fair to all parties involved, including the buying public. Titan rejected the terms even though it was financially able to meet every demand. Can Paxton compel Titan to sign the proposed contract?

26. In August 1981, President Ronald Reagan, confronted by striking federal air-traffic controllers who threatened to shut down the nation's airlines, fired them all. The president justified his actions by noting the striking workers were in violation of the law. Their places were taken in the short term by military air traffic controllers and ultimately, after training, by new personnel. Did President Reagan act legally? Did he act ethically?

27. The United Steelworkers of America, a national union, had a provision in its constitution that imposed requirements to be satisfied before a member could run for leadership positions in local affiliates. The limitation was that to be eligible to be a local officer, the union member must have attended at least one-half of the regular local meetings for the three years prior to the election. Is this restriction legal? (*Local 3489 United Steelworkers of America v. Usery,* 97 S. Ct. 611)

28. Mary Weatherman was the personal secretary to the president of Hendricks County Rural Electric Membership Corporation. One of her friends at the firm was involved in an industrial accident that resulted in the loss of one of his arms. Shortly after the accident, he was dismissed. Mary, concerned about the plight of her friend, signed a petition seeking his reinstatement. Because of this conduct Mary also was discharged. Mary filed a charge with the NLRB alleging an unfair labor practice. The company defended itself by claiming that because Mary was a confidential secretary, she was not covered by the National Labor Relations Act's definition of "employee." Who is right, Mary or the company? (*NLRB v. Hendricks County,* 102 S. Ct. 216)

29. During a union-organizing campaign at Portage Plastics Company, some members began wearing union buttons on the job. Because a button fell into a grinder and caused loss of material and because of the increasing division among the employees, the president of Portage prohibited the wearing of either union or nonunion badges at work. Other jewelry and hair attachments were still permitted even though such ornaments also had fallen into equipment and caused losses on prior occasions. Immediately after the president gave his order, a strike was started in protest. Was the company rule on union badges an unfair labor practice? Would it make any difference if the union agreed, after the order, that its members would not wear badges? (*Portage Plastics Company v. International Union, Allied Industrial Workers of America, AFL-CIO,* 163 NLRB No. 102)

30. Kuebler was a member in good standing of the lithographers union when it struck the Art Gravure Company. Several months after the strike began, Kuebler met in a non-secret meeting with 12 or 13 other strikers. Their purpose was to discuss "the widening gap" between the labor and management bargaining committees and to "try to straighten this thing out to where we could get back to work." Later, a three-person committee from the group communicated its views to the Union Negotiating Committee. Kuebler returned to the picket line. When the strike finally ended, the trial board of the local union charged and found Kuebler guilty of attending "a meeting . . . held for the purpose of undermining the Union Negotiating Committee." Kuebler was suspended from the union for three months and was fined $2,000. He filed a notice of appeal to the membership and requested several items: copies of charges against him, with supporting facts; names of the persons on the executive board who had accused and tried him; a copy of the decision in writing showing how each member had voted; and a copy of the transcript of the evidence and proceedings at his trial by the union trial board. This information was refused, and so Kuebler sued for relief in the U.S. district court. Had the union violated Kuebler's rights? Had Kuebler been denied a fair hearing? (*Kuebler v. Cleveland Lithographers and Photoengravers Union Local,* 473 F.2d 359)

31. The Greenpark Nursing Home hired First National Maintenance to maintain its facilities. First National in turn hired employees to work for it on the premises of the nursing home. These employees of First National formed a union. Shortly after, First National decided, for financial reasons, to cancel its maintenance contract with the nursing home. Anticipating a complete layoff, the union sought to negotiate with management over the decision to terminate this contract. Management refused to negotiate on this issue. Was this refusal to negotiate legal? (*First National Maintenance v. NLRB,* 452 U.S. 666)

CASE FOR LEGAL THINKING

GENERAL INDUSTRIAL EMPLOYEES UNION v. NLRB
951 F. 2D 1908

FACTS Mohawk Liqueur Corporation's collective bargaining agreement with Local 42 (the union) was about to expire, and the parties were negotiating a new contract. The parties disagreed on many issues but talks continued. Then Mohawk submitted its final offer, including a statement that it would not pay the final cost of living adjustment (COLA) due under the old contract, for work already performed. The union declared this an unfair labor practice, and struck. Mohawk unilaterally implemented its final offer and refused to pay the COLA. Negotiations resumed and about two months later Mohawk agreed to make the old COLA payment. It then warned the workers that they would be permanently replaced if they failed to return by August 4.

On August 3, the union met. The workers agreed that the COLA payment was no longer an issue but voted to continue the strike. The employees hoped to force Mohawk to divulge the names of certain workers the company planned to discharge, to offer a general amnesty to all strikers, and to grant certain financial benefits. Mohawk replaced all striking workers. On August 11 the union voted to return to work. Mohawk reinstated some but not all of the strikers, and five months later the parties reached a new contract.

The Board determined that what had begun as an unfair labor practice strike had changed into an economic one, and that Mohawk had lawfully replaced some workers permanently. The union appealed.

REASONING Employees who take part in an economic strike run the risk of permanent replacement by new hires. But unfair labor practice strikers are entitled to reinstatement if they wish to return to work and, if denied reemployment, are also entitled to back pay from the date of denial.

The causes of a strike can, of course, change over time. Sometimes a strike that starts for economic reasons is prolonged by the employer's subsequent unlawful conduct and is thereby "converted" from an economic to an unfair labor practice strike.

The stated purpose for the members' meetings was to decide whether to prolong the strike. The minutes of the meeting, the motion by which the strikers decided not to return to work, and the testimony before the Administrative Law Judge all demonstrate that the reasons for continuing the strike had nothing whatsoever to do with Mohawk's prior violations of the NRLA. The May 31 COLA came into the deliberations only when the Union negotiator and attorney explained why it was no longer a reason to strike. The evidence relating to both the August 11 negotiating session (such as testimony that the parties agreed the COLA issue had been "settled" and the Union's announcement that it was withdrawing its COLA grievance) and the August 12 Union meeting also supports the Board's conclusion that the strike was prolonged for reasons entirely unrelated to Mohawk's unfair labor practices.

CONCLUSION The Board's order, declaring the permanent replacements lawful, is affirmed.

PRACTICE JUDGING

1. What is the unfair labor practice alleged by the union?

2. Would the outcome for fired workers have been different if the union had not made demands unrelated to the COLA?

3. If the COLA questions had not been settled and the additional demands had been made, would this be an unfair labor practice strike or an economic strike?

© GETTY IMAGES/PHOTODISC

CHAPTER 23

Discrimination in Employment

23-1 Legal versus Illegal Discrimination

23-2 Proving Illegal Discrimination

© GETTY IMAGES/PHOTODISC

Phan's parents were born in Vietnam. They spoke Vietnamese in the home. Phan did not learn English until he began kindergarten. Upon graduating from high school, Phan's language skills were still below par. When Phan applied for a job, he was asked to take an English grammar test. He took the test but failed, and therefore was denied employment. Phan contended that his life circumstance caused him to fail the test. The prospective employer said the company didn't care about Phan's life circumstance, only how well he could do the job.

Where Do You Stand?

1. Why did Phan deserve the job?

2. Why did Phan not deserve the job?

Legal versus Illegal Discrimination

WHEN IS DISCRIMINATION ILLEGAL?

WHAT'S YOUR VERDICT?

Clare has been working at Rich Manufacturing for three years. Lisa has been working there for two months. They both operate computerized machine-tooling equipment. The machines perform many operations, such as drilling, cutting threads, turning, deburring, and surfacing metal objects. Lisa is faster. When a promotion opportunity came along, it was given to Lisa. Clare protested, saying that she was being discriminated against. She was angry because Lisa would be earning almost 30 percent more money than she would.

Is Clare correct? Is she a victim of unjustified discrimination?

Everyone discriminates for and against individuals. Choosing a team for a pick-up game of basketball, friends, a mate for marriage, a class officer, or a President of the United States are all actions that require discrimination. In one sense then, discrimination is a normal part of life. However, in the work environment when it is not objectively justified, discrimination is extremely harmful. The harm affects not only the individual discriminated against but all of society, as achieving efficient production and quality products depends on putting the best qualified person in the right job.

As a consequence, the government has become involved in making sure that choices within the workplace are made on the proper bases and do not reflect illegal **employment discrimination**. Such discrimination is defined as treating individuals differently on the basis of race, color, gender and pregnancy, age, religion, disability, and national origin. The law attempts to protect people from being judged on the basis of their membership in these groups. It is unjustified discrimination. Instead of judging people by the groups to which they belong, the law compels employers to judge each person according to their individual abilities to perform the work at hand.

It is a form of discrimination to pay more money to those who are more productive. However, this form of discrimination is justified. An important step in understanding this chapter comes in knowing the difference between justified discrimination and unjustified discrimination.

Justified discrimination is permitted and even encouraged. Workers fairly judged as dependable, skilled, creative, smart, or hard working usually receive more favorable treatment. They earn more money and have more job opportunities. Thus, in *What's Your Verdict?* Clare is being discriminated against justifiably. If the employer has a good reason for the treatment

Do you think it is fair for employers to treat more favorably employees who are dependable, skilled, and hardworking? Why or why not?

© GETTY IMAGES/PHOTODISC

(for example, Lisa works faster), the discrimination is justified.

PROTECTED CLASSES

The law attacks unjustified discrimination in a practical way. It identifies group characteristics that employers may not consider when making employment decisions. The courts have attached the label **protected classes** to people within these groups. Members of protected classes are often, but not always, minorities. Employment discrimination law is designed to ensure that membership in a protected class is not a significant factor in employment decisions. A variety of federal statutes define the criteria that employers cannot consider when making employment decisions. These criteria and the associated protected classes of persons are listed in the following paragraphs.

RACE AND COLOR The protected class based on race or color includes all persons who are not white. So, African Americans, Asians, Filipinos, Hispanics, Native Americans, and others are members of this protected class.

GENDER Employers may not discriminate against females or males based on their gender. In addition, sexual harassment is illegal.

PREGNANCY Employers may not discriminate because of a person's childbearing condition or plans.

AGE People over age 40 are protected against discrimination on the basis of their age.

Although recent studies have shown that mildly obese white women have wage levels 5.9 percent lower than their standard weight counterparts and extremely obese white women were 24.1 percent lower, obesity is not a protected class at the federal level. Of the states, only Michigan prohibits employment discrimination because of weight.

RELIGION People who have religious beliefs of any kind are members of a protected class. This category could include everyone.

DISABILITY The physically and mentally disabled are afforded limited protection against discrimination.

NATIONAL ORIGIN People are protected against discrimination based on their country of origin. Those who do not speak English or who are not citizens of the United States are protected to a limited extent.

SCOPE OF PROTECTION

The most obvious forms of employment discrimination arise out of the hiring decision. In the past, this country's employment advertisements often included such language as "men only," "no black people need apply," and "persons between the ages of 16 and 30 years only, please."

AGAINST UNJUSTIFIED CONDITIONS OF EMPLOYMENT Today the law makes illegal not only unjustified discrimination in hiring, but also unjustified discrimination in any "term, condition, or privilege of employment." This means it is illegal to discriminate against protected classes in any aspect of the job. If the unjustified discrimination is displayed in pay, promotions, training, overtime, educational opportunities, travel requirements, shift rotations, firings, layoffs, post-employment letters of recommendation, or any other aspect of employment, it is illegal.

GOVERNING MOST EMPLOYERS Most employers that have 15 or more employees and are engaged in interstate commerce are subject to federal employment discrimination laws. This means that almost all employers except some small businesses are subject to the laws described in this chapter. Agencies of state governments, employment agencies, and labor unions generally also are subject to anti-discrimination laws.

CHECKPOINT

Name the bases for unjustified discrimination in employment.

LAWS THAT PROHIBIT EMPLOYMENT DISCRIMINATION

WHAT'S YOUR VERDICT?

Jannette was employed in a glass factory. Her job was to inspect and pack glass jars in cartons. Men were employed in the same capacity, and they were required occasionally to lift the packed cartons. The women were paid 10 percent less than the men were.

Is the difference in pay illegal?

The federal government has enacted a number of statutes to prohibit unjustified discrimination in employment. These statutes are described in the following sections.

TITLE VII OF THE CIVIL RIGHTS ACT OF 1964

With some exceptions, Title VII of the Civil Rights Act of 1964 forbids employers, employment agencies, and unions from discriminating in hiring, paying, training, promoting, or discharging employees on the basis of race, color, religion, national origin, or sex. An employer may discriminate in selecting one worker over another if the standard set is necessary for proper performance of the job. For example, a prospective airplane pilot may be required to understand radar and navigation equipment. That person also may be required to react quickly to emergencies and to be free of potentially fatal heart diseases.

Title VII of the Civil Rights Act also created the **Equal Employment Opportunity Commission (EEOC)** and gave it the authority to investigate and settle complaints of job discrimination. If necessary, it also can prosecute offenders. If an employer has discriminated in the past, the courts may mandate an **affirmative action plan** to remedy the past discrimination. The plan must include positive steps aimed at offsetting past discrimination by bringing the percentages of minorities and women in the workforce up to their corresponding percentages

Cyberlaw

Disabilities Under the SSA

The Social Security Administration (SSA) is the government agency that runs the social security program in the United States. The SSA has one of the most extensive web sites of any government agency. When you visit www.ssa.gov you can perform a number of functions. You can learn about the history of the SSA and its plans for the future. You can inquire about all of the benefits that the SSA offers, such as disability and retirement income and Medicare. You also can request many of the services the SSA offers directly from the web site. The SSA accepts requests from the web site for personal earnings and benefits summaries. Companies can download forms they need to report employees' earnings and wages to the SSA.

THINK ABOUT IT

Research the SSA web site to look into the disability status of a specific physical condition or problem, for example, obesity. Research the procedure to be followed for someone who has the condition or problem to establish their entitlement to disability income. Also check the web sites of attorneys willing to represent disability claimants for their fees and specialties.

in the pool of qualified applicants. Most employers that contract with the federal government also must submit affirmative action plans. Because the federal government is the biggest buyer of goods and services in the country, most large employers are directly affected by affirmative action.

EQUAL PAY ACT OF 1963

The Equal Pay Act prohibits wage discrimination on the basis of sex. Women who do the same work or substantially equal work as that of men must be paid at the same rate. This means that when the same skill, effort, and responsibility are required and when the job is performed under similar working conditions, women must be paid the same as men.

Thus, in *What's Your Verdict?* a court would hold that Jannette and the other women were entitled to equal pay for equal work and that "equal work" did not mean identical duties. Differences in pay are allowed if based on any of the following:

1. merit system
2. seniority system
3. system basing pay on quantity or quality of production
4. system based on any factor other than gender

AGE DISCRIMINATION IN EMPLOYMENT ACT OF 1967

The Age Discrimination in Employment Act forbids discrimination against workers over the age of 40 in any employment practice (hiring, discharging, retiring, promoting, and compensating). Exceptions are made when age is a necessary consideration for job performance. Such occupations include bus drivers, fire fighters, and police officers.

AMERICANS WITH DISABILITIES ACT

The **Americans with Disabilities Act (ADA)** requires that employers not engage in unjustified discrimination against disabled persons on the basis of their disability. The act attempts to prevent employers from automatically assuming that disabled persons cannot perform work. A **disability** substantially limits a major life activity. It can be physical or mental. However, current use of illegal drugs is not a disability under ADA. Neither are sex-related traits or conditions such as homosexuality. A person with a contagious disease may be protected under the ADA, although the courts determine this based on individual medical judgments.

The ADA defines a qualified individual with a disability as one who can perform the essential functions of the job or who could perform those functions with a reasonable accommodation. Thus employers must make a reasonable accommodation for the qualified disabled worker. A reasonable accommodation is not required if it would produce an undue hardship for the employer. Factors considered in determining whether there would be undue hardships are the cost of the accommodation and the financial resources of the employer.

PREGNANCY DISCRIMINATION ACT

The Pregnancy Discrimination Act is a statute that makes it illegal to discriminate because of pregnancy, childbirth, or related medical conditions. Accordingly, an employer may not fire, refuse to hire, refuse to promote, or demote a woman because she is pregnant.

The act also makes it illegal to discriminate in the providing of fringe benefits on these bases. Thus, an employer cannot carry an insurance policy that insures all physical conditions except pregnancy.

Federal anti-discrimination laws such as those just discussed have been enacted because of past injustices in the hiring, paying, training, transfer-

LEGAL RESEARCH

Interview the manager responsible for compliance with ADA rules and regulations at a local business. Note and report on the manager's knowledge of the law and attitude towards the law and its enforcers. Then interview an employee who is disabled about the accommodations he or she has received. Note and report on the employee's knowledge of the law and attitude towards the law and its enforcers. Compare your notes on the two interviews. What conclusions can you draw? Compare your conclusions with those of your classmates.

ring, and discharging of workers. Most states and many cities have enacted similar laws. In addition, the Supreme Court has interpreted the Fourteenth Amendment to apply to employment. The Supreme Court also has extended to employment the civil rights laws passed in 1866 and 1870.

These efforts have modified the old common-law concept that an employer has complete freedom in hiring and, subject to liability for breach of contract, freedom in discharging workers. Essentially, current laws, regulations, and court decisions require that job applicants be judged on their merits as individuals, not as members of any group or class.

CHECKPOINT
Name the laws discussed in this section that prohibit unjustified discrimination in employment.

lawxtra.swlearning.com

23-1 Assessment

THINK ABOUT LEGAL CONCEPTS

1. Any discrimination by an employer is illegal. **True or False?**

2. In general, employment law makes it illegal to consider a group characteristic when hiring individuals. **True or False?**

3. "Protected classes" refers to members of groups that are illegal to discriminate against. **True or False?**

4. Which of the following employees would not fit into a protected class? (a) pregnant female (b) 60-year-old white male (c) Buddhist monk (d) All of these would fit into a protected class.

5. Which law prohibits discrimination based on race, religion, sex, or national origin in any term, condition, or privilege of employment? (a) ADA (b) Equal Pay Act (c) Civil Rights Act of 1964

6. The law that protects workers over age 40 is called the _?_.

THINK CRITICALLY ABOUT EVIDENCE

Study the situation, answer the questions, and then prepare arguments to support your answers.

7. Sven immigrated to the United States at age 12 and obtained citizenship at age 18. He speaks with a thick accent. When he applied for a job as a bank clerk, someone else was selected because the other person was more accurate in counting money. Has Sven been the subject of discrimination? Was the discrimination justified or unjustified?

8. "We Wash Windows" is a company that washes windows in a commercial building where many windows are six or seven feet off the ground. Taller people can wash these windows more quickly. Atushi is Japanese. When he applied for a window washer job the company told him they don't hire Japanese because most Japanese people are too short. Atushi is six feet, four inches tall. Has Atushi been the subject of discrimination? Was the discrimination justified or unjustified?

9. When Quality Furniture Manufacturing Company faced financial difficulties it began laying off employees. The majority were over the age of 40, although they constituted only 5 percent of the workforce. Young workers in their twenties were immediately hired to fill the jobs of those discharged. Quality justified this action by noting that increased health insurance costs were the overwhelming reason for its financial problems. As insurance coverage for older employees, especially those 50 and older, costs two to three times what coverage for younger employees costs, it only made common sense to discharge the older employees first. Is this ethical? What statute, if any, was violated?

10. Irene was a Mormon. She believed that other members of her religion were more honest than the general population. When she was asked to hire a bank teller for her employer, she advertised the job as one available only for members of her religion. Is Irene's action legal? Would it be legal if Irene could prove in court that members of her religion were in fact more honest?

Proving Illegal Discrimination

UNEQUAL TREATMENT CASES

WHAT'S YOUR VERDICT?

Geraldo, an Hispanic, had 10 years of experience as a finish carpenter. He applied for a job with a local construction company but was turned down. The company continued advertising the position and eventually hired Jake, who was white. He did not have as much experience as Geraldo. Geraldo filed a discrimination suit against the company. At the trial, the company was not able to justify its decision to hire Jake instead of Geraldo.

Will a court find in favor of Geraldo or the company?

Unequal treatment (sometimes called *disparate treatment*) means that an employer intentionally treats members of a protected class less favorably than other employees.

EVIDENCE OF UNEQUAL TREATMENT

Based on the nature of the evidence, cases based on unequal treatment have taken several forms.

CASES BASED ON DIRECT EVIDENCE In the past, unequal treatment often was both intentional and open. Newspapers carried want ads that listed jobs as "men only." Some firms would refuse publicly to hire African Americans, Asians, Cajuns, Mexicans, mulattos, Puerto Ricans, or women. Flyers would sometimes state, "no Irish" or "no Jews need apply." Sometimes women would receive letters stating, "I am sorry, but we have a policy against hiring women in these positions."

To win a case where the discrimination is admitted, the employee need only prove that she or he was denied employment because of membership in a protected class. Today, most direct-evidence litigation focuses not on the decision to hire, but on decisions related to other aspects of the employment relationship. Thus, if an employer offered life insurance as a fringe benefit but the amount was less for women than for men (on the grounds that women outlive men), this would be intentional unequal treatment.

CASES BASED ON INDIRECT EVIDENCE Today most cases involve situations where the employer denies any intention to illegally discriminate. To establish a case against such an employer, an employee must show the following:

1. The person was a member of a protected class.

2. The person applied for the job and was qualified.

3. The person was rejected.

4. The employer held the job open and sought other persons with similar qualifications.

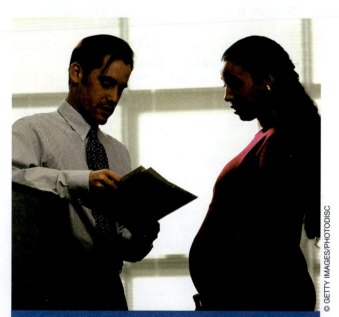

Kari applied for a job for which she believed she was well qualified, but she was rejected. She's not sure, but she thinks the employer objected to the fact that she was pregnant. What must she show in order to establish a discrimination case against this employer?

In *What's Your Verdict?* Geraldo, a member of a protected class, applied for a job for which he was qualified. He was rejected, and the company held the job open and later hired Jake. The court presumed that the discrimination was intentional and Geraldo won the suit.

CASES BASED ON STATISTICS In some cases, the government can initiate proceedings against a company for employment discrimination when there is evidence of a pattern and practice of discrimination. In this type of litigation, the government merely shows a statistically significant difference between the protected class composition of the pool of qualified applicants and the workforce.

IN THIS CASE

Beck wanted to be considered for advanced training at her company's headquarters. Their bosses nominated employees for the training. In Beck's job classification, there were about 80 men and 60 women. Beck's boss nominated her. Of the 20 people nominated for the home-office training, half were men and half were women. Of the 10 people selected for the training, all were men. If she filed a complaint, Beck's employer probably would be liable for employment discrimination due to the statistically significant difference between the protected class in the pool of applicants and those picked for training.

EMPLOYER'S DEFENSES

BUSINESS NECESSITY Once the employee has shown, with either direct or indirect evidence, that unequal treatment occurred, the employer may defend by establishing one of several defenses. These defenses attempt to show that the unequal treatment was justified by a reason that is legal. Thus, in an indirect proof case, the employer's most common defense is that the employee's skills or work history was the reason for not hiring. This general defense is sometimes called business necessity or job relatedness. **Business necessity** means that

the employer's actions were meant to advance the business rather than to create unjustified discrimination.

BONA FIDE OCCUPATIONAL QUALIFICATION

Another defense available to an employer is called the **bona fide occupational qualification (BFOQ)**. A bona fide occupational qualification is a job requirement that compels discrimination against a protected class. Thus, if an employer hired actors to play parts in a stage show, some of the parts would be for men and so the employer justifiably could decide to hire only men for these parts. Similarly, employers could request only male or female models for a fashion show.

To establish the BFOQ, the discrimination must truly be essential to the business. The fact that discrimination is helpful is not enough. When airlines were fighting to preserve female-only flight attendants, they presented surveys showing that a high proportion of their passengers preferred to be served by women. The courts rejected this argument and held that being female is not necessary to perform the job.

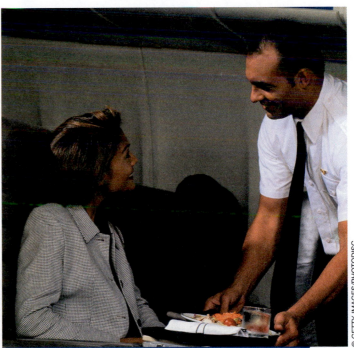

When the airlines were attempting to preserve the tradition of female-only flight attendants, why do you think the courts rejected their argument that female flight attendants were necessary because most passengers preferred to be served by women?

SENIORITY Seniority can be another justification for unequal treatment. A **bona fide seniority system** is one that rewards employees based on the length of employment rather than merit and is not intended to discriminate. In the law, a bona fide seniority system can justify discrimination. If an employer pays union members on the basis of seniority, promotes on the basis of seniority, or lays employees off on the basis of seniority, unequal treatment of protected classes will be tolerated. The Supreme Court will permit seniority to be used even when it perpetuates past discrimination.

PRETEXTS Employers sometimes assert business necessity or BFOQ as a pretext, or a cover, for discriminating. For example, a company hires a male instead of a female, Julie, for a job. The company says the reason is that the job involves a lot of travel. Because Julie is the mother of three children, the company says that would make travel harder for her to schedule. Julie could establish that this reason is not a business neces-

sity but a pretext by showing that men with three or more children had been hired for the job.

CHECKPOINT

What are the three main bases for unequal treatment cases?

DISPARATE IMPACT CASES

WHAT'S YOUR VERDICT?

Sharon's Machine Shop manufactures fire hydrants. When finished, each hydrant weighs approximately 175 pounds. Part of the job description for hydrant assemblers states that a person hired for this job be able to lift 175 pounds ten times in two minutes. This requirement is similar to the actions required to assemble the hydrants.

Is this job requirement a form of illegal employment discrimination?

Many companies have a policy (like the one at Sharon's in *What's Your Verdict?*) that is regarded as **neutral on its face**. This means that the policy makes no reference to a protected class. In *What's Your Verdict?* more men probably will be able to satisfy this job requirement than women. So the policy has a disparate, or different, impact on a protected class. **Disparate impact** indicates that the policy eliminates more members of protected classes than members of the majority. If prison guards are required to be six feet tall, this would eliminate a higher proportion of Asians, Hispanics, and women than white and black males. Agility tests, height tests, weight tests, educational requirements, and tests of clerical abilities all may have a disparate impact on a protected class.

The courts treat cases involving job requirements quite differently from cases involving unequal treatment. To win a suit claiming disparate impact, the employee need not prove an intention to discriminate. However, the employee must identify a specific employment practice and show statistically that the practice excludes members of a protected class. Even then the employee will lose if the employer is able to show that there is a legitimate business necessity for the practice.

In *What's Your Verdict?* Sharon's weight-lifting test is neutral on its face. It can be statistically shown, however, that a smaller proportion of women will pass the test. Therefore, it has a disparate impact. However, the test is justified by business necessity because it is clearly job-related. In the past, such practices as requiring high school graduation, written aptitude tests, height and weight requirements, and subjective interviews have been attacked by employees on the basis of disparate impact.

BY STATISTICAL PROOF

To win a case based on disparate impact, an employee must establish that fewer members qualified for the job when the challenged employment practice is used than when it is not. This involves examining two groups:

1. the **applicant pool** (those qualified for the job without regard to the challenged practice)
2. the **workforce pool** (persons actually in the employer's workforce)

The percentage of protected class individuals in each pool is then compared. If the percentage in the applicant pool is statistically higher than the percentage in the workforce group, this suggests disparate impact. But one other element, *causation,* must be proven. Causation is a linking of the challenged practice and the difference in percentages of protected class persons. After causation is established, the employee has proven disparate impact.

EMPLOYER'S DEFENSES

Employers can avoid liability even after the employee has shown disparate treatment. If the challenged practice is justified by business necessity, there is no liability. Thus, if weight lifting is required on the job, it does not legally matter that the requirement excludes a protected class from the job. In addition, an employer can utilize the defenses of bona fide occupational qualification and seniority.

CHECKPOINT
What does disparate impact mean?

SEXUAL HARASSMENT CASES

WHAT'S YOUR VERDICT?

Ben delivered the internal mail at the headquarters of Antonia's, a national chain of lingerie shops. Everyday when he entered the product design section, several of the female employees would whistle at him and call him "honey doo" and other similar terms of endearment. Occasionally, a female worker in the section would pinch him or caress him. Ben mentioned to their manager that the attention made him uncomfortable, but she refused to correct it.

What form of sexual harassment is taking place here? Would the company be liable for what is done by its employees and manager?

One unique form of sex discrimination is sexual harassment. Sexual harassment takes two forms: quid pro quo and hostile environment.

QUID PRO QUO

Quid pro quo means one thing is exchanged for another. The most vivid illustration of this form of sexual harassment is when a boss threatens to fire a subordinate unless sexual favors are provided. Continued employment is being exchanged for sexual favors. The employer may offer any term, condition, or privilege of employment, such as a raise, or a favorable evaluation.

HOSTILE ENVIRONMENT

A **hostile environment** arises when unwelcome sexual comments, gestures, or contact interfere with an employee's ability to work. In instances where a supervisor sexually harasses a subordinate, the employer is strictly liable.

Generally, the employer is liable for the conduct of non-supervisory employees only when the harassment is either known or should have been known to supervisors and they failed to act effectively to prevent further occurrences. In *What's Your Verdict?* the manager knew about the harassment. Therefore, Antonia's will be liable if Ben brings a hostile environment case.

CHECKPOINT

What are the two forms of sexual harassment?

A QUESTION OF ETHICS

Suzie works in the accounting department of a manufacturing company. Seven other women work in the same room. Men from the plant often walk by and joke with the women. Most of the women enjoy the interaction but it makes Suzie uncomfortable. Should Suzie ask everyone to stop because she finds the flirtation offensive?

ECONOMIC IMPACT

DEFENDING A SEXUAL HARASSMENT LAWSUIT

Business managers unfamiliar with the laws on discrimination and particularly sexual harassment often go into shock when confronted with the costs of defending against such a suit. The business is motivated to stage a good defense due to the potential of compensatory and even punitive damages they might incur. Consequently, the business will not utilize in-house counsel but will, at considerable expense, hire an attorney who specializes in the area. The employer often is ordered to pay the attorney's fees of the employee whereas, should the business win, the employee seldom is given a responsibility to pay those of the business. Also, as a consequence of being involved in a sexual harassment lawsuit, the business often loses the patronage of several of it customers, even if the resolution is in the business's favor. The business also loses the innumerable hours its managers and employees spend in hearings, depositions, searching for evidence, and trials. Finally, the business must face increased charges for its liability insurance.

THINK CRITICALLY

How might a company protect itself from sexual harassment suits?

23-2 Assessment

Xtra!
Study Tools
lawxtra.swlearning.com

THINK ABOUT LEGAL CONCEPTS

1. To win a case where the discrimination is admitted, the employee need only prove that she or he was denied employment because of membership in a(n) _?_.

2. Which of the following are grounds for illegal discrimination? (a) disparate treatment (b) disparate impact (c) pattern and practice (d) all of the above

3. Which type of illegal discrimination is most often concerned with one person? (a) disparate treatment (b) disparate impact (c) sexual harassment (d) none of the above

4. Employers may discriminate against protected classes if it is justified by business necessity. **True or False?**

5. If a member of a protected class proves disparate treatment, the employer will not be liable if it can show the defense of seniority or BFOQ. **True or False?**

6. A job requirement may be illegal although it appears on its face to be neutral towards a protected class. **True or False?**

THINK CRITICALLY ABOUT EVIDENCE

Study the situation, answer the questions, and then prepare arguments to support your answers.

7. Pablo interviewed people to serve as clerks at his dry-cleaning business. Pablo thought that he would get more repeat business if he hired attractive male clerks. He advertised and told females that he was only interested in male clerks so they need not bother with an interview. Would this form of discrimination be proved directly or indirectly? Would the case be one based on disparate impact or disparate treatment?

8. Finance America reimbursed employees for their job-related educational expenses. Janice applied for reimbursement for a course, but was told, "This isn't job related." She learned that another employee, Gail, had been turned down, too. Later, Janice met four men with similar jobs who had taken the same course and had been reimbursed. What type of discrimination occurred? What defense is Finance America most likely to employ in this case?

9. As a condition of employment, Duke Moving required a high school education or a satisfactory score on a general intelligence test. Both requirements were designed to improve the quality of the workforce but neither requirement was shown to improve job performance. Griggs claimed that the test discriminated against him. He said that, as a minority member, he had not had the educational opportunity afforded others. Moreover, he said, the test did not relate to skills and qualifications that were necessary for employment at Duke. Was Griggs legally correct? If he sued, what type of discrimination would Griggs claim?

10. When Debbie won the job of administrative assistant to Toby Main, the president of Condorama, a time share company, she was told the position involved a lot of traveling with the president. Every week, Main flew to various places in the United States and the Caribbean. After a few weeks of this travel, several of her fellow employees started implying that Debbie was being intimate with her boss, which she was not. The gossip, however, made her very uncomfortable, and she was considering quitting her job as a consequence. What options are open to her instead of quitting?

11. The problem eliminated, Debbie decides to stay on. Eventually, Toby Main retires and his son, Randy, takes over the business. On their last trip to Barbados, Toby made it clear that, unless Debbie granted him sexual favors, he would fire her and replace her with someone who would. What would you advise Debbie to do?

PREVENT LEGAL DIFFICULTIES

As an employee . . .

1. Approach every job in a professional manner. Seek to be judged solely on the basis of your potential or actual job performance.

2. Do not create an environment hostile to any protected class.

As an employer . . .

1. Do not ask questions on job applications that require the disclosure of race, religion, sex, national origin, handicap, or pregnancy status.

2. Do not ask questions in job interviews about marital status, maternity plans, child care

3. If you suspect that you are being discriminated against because of your membership in a protected class, contact the Equal Employment Opportunity Commission (EEOC).

abilities, birth control practices, number of children, or other related factors.

3. Carefully train your supervisory employees both to avoid any activity that could be taken as sexual harassment at work and to respond effectively to complaints about like conduct by subordinates.

CONCEPTS IN BRIEF

23-1   Legal versus Illegal Discrimination

1. In the work environment unjustified discrimination harms not only the individual discriminated against but all of society. Achieving efficient production and quality products depends on putting the best qualified person in the right job.

2. Illegal discrimination in employment is defined as treating individuals differently on the basis of race, color, gender and pregnancy, age, religion, disability, or national origin. These categories are referred to as protected classes.

3. A large number of statutes, especially at the federal level, make unjustified discrimination against a member of a protected class illegal.

23-2   Proving Illegal Discrimination

4. Generally, illegal discrimination in employment is proven by showing unequal treatment, disparate impact, or by statistics showing a pattern or practice.

5. Among an employer's potential defenses to charges of illegal discrimination are business necessity, BFOQs, and seniority.

6. An employment policy that has a disparate impact is one that eliminates more members of protected classes than members of the majority.

7. Sexual harassment claims generally take one of two forms: quid pro quo or hostile environment.

YOUR LEGAL VOCABULARY

Match each statement with the term that it best defines. Some terms may not be used.

1. All the people who work for an employer that has been charged with employment discrimination

2. Interference with an employee's ability to work due to unwelcome comments, gestures, or touching of a sexual nature at work

3. Label for a workplace policy that does not seem on the surface to discriminate against any protected class

4. Court order requiring hiring of members of a protected class to remedy past discrimination

5. Employer's defense where actions were meant to advance the business rather than to create unjustified discrimination

6. Exchange of a sexual favor for better work status

7. Groups that employment law protects

8. System that rewards employees for length of employment rather than merit

9. Those qualified for the job

10. Has the authority to investigate and settle complaints of job discrimination and to prosecute suspected offenders

11. Condition that substantially limits a major life activity

12. Employer treats members of a protected class less favorably than other employees

a. **affirmative action plan**
b. **ADA**
c. **applicant pool**
d. **BFOQ**
e. **bona fide seniority system**
f. **business necessity**
g. **disability**
h. **disparate impact**
i. **employment discrimination**
j. **EEOC**
k. **hostile environment**
l. **neutral on its face**
m. **protected classes**
n. **quid pro quo**
o. **unequal treatment**
p. **workforce pool**

REVIEW LEGAL CONCEPTS

13. Explain the difference between justified and unjustified discrimination.

14. Describe the element of disparate treatment and its main defenses.

15. Describe the elements of disparate impact and the way it is proven in court.

16. Describe how disparate treatment cases can still be proven even though there is no direct or indirect evidence.

WRITE ABOUT LEGAL CONCEPTS

17. Write an ad for a job as a server in a restaurant which creates direct evidence of disparate treatment.

18. Write a job description for a high school teacher which contains two types of job requirements. One type might create a disparate impact. Another type will not create a disparate impact.

Which requirements are likely to create a disparate impact?

19. **HOT DEBATE** Write a letter from the employer to Phan explaining the reasons he will not be hired for the job. Write a letter from Phan to the employer explaining why he should be hired.

MAKE ACADEMIC CONNECTIONS

20. **POLITICAL SCIENCE** The passage of the Americans with Disabilities Act was an important event in the political history of the United States. Without great fanfare and little opposition from either party, the ADA became law. Research how the ADA was conceived and passed. Report to the class on the lessons learned.

THINK CRITICALLY ABOUT EVIDENCE

Study the situation, answer the questions, and then prepare arguments to support your answers.

21. When Angela almost miscarried in her sixth month of pregnancy, she was confined to total bed rest. As a consequence of her continuing absence, her employer fired her. Has the employer acted legally?

22. Suppose you were in charge of hiring workers to assemble very small electrical components to make a toy. If you thought that females of Asian ancestry were most likely to do this type of work well, would you limit your interviews to this group of persons only? Would your decision be different if you were certain there would be no legal risk?

23. Peter owned a small restaurant that specialized in Indian food. He had only 8 employees and therefore knew that most employment discrimination laws did not apply to him. Is Peter ethically obligated to follow these laws anyway?

24. Jerry owned a small printing shop. He had medical insurance coverage for all his employees. The policy was periodic, renewable once each year. One of Jerry's employees contracted acquired immune deficiency syndrome (AIDS). As the disease progressed, medical expenses for this employee skyrocketed, but they were covered by the insurance. A clause in the policy allowed the insurance company to raise the premium when the employer renewed the policy. On the annual renewal date, the insurance company presented Jerry with a 1,000 percent premium increase for continued coverage. If he paid the premiums, it would bankrupt his company. Is Jerry ethically obligated to pay the increase to protect his AIDS-infected employee? Has the insurance company acted ethically?

25. Ann Hopkins worked for Price Waterhouse, a large accounting firm. It was a practice to make professional employees partners in the firm after several years. Ann had been distinctively successful in the performance of her job. Of about 600 partners in the firm, only eight were women. When Ann was being considered for partnership, a committee of all male partners evaluated her. Several members of the committee made comments such as the following: "She should go to charm school;" "She needs to learn to dress, walk, and talk like a woman;" and "She should wear jewelry and makeup." Ultimately the committee turned her down for partnership. When she was told the comments of the members of the committee, Ann sued, claiming unequal treatment. Will she prevail? (*Price Waterhouse v. Hopkins*, 109 S.Ct. 1775)

26. Wards Cove Packing Company operated canneries in remote areas of Alaska. The workers in the canneries were primarily Filipinos and native Alaskans. These jobs were unskilled and the pay was low. The workers in non-cannery jobs were primarily white. These positions were highly skilled and highly paid. Antonio was a canner and he sued for employment discrimination. He claimed that the difference in the composition of the cannery and non-cannery workforces established that Wards Cove was illegally discriminating. Will he prevail? (*Wards Cove Packing Company v. Antonio*, 109 S. Ct. 2115)

27. Henderson worked as a radio dispatcher for the Dundee, Florida, police department. The police chief, she alleged, subjected her to repeated sexual comments and requests that she have sexual relations with him. She said that because she refused, the chief refused to allow her to attend the police academy. Further, he suspended her for two days for violating a minor office policy that never before had been enforced. She interpreted the suspension as a threat that she would be fired unless she gave in to her boss's advances. Eventually Henderson quit and then sued the city claiming sexual harassment. Will she prevail? (*Henderson v. City of Dundee*, 682 F.2d 897)

28. United Airlines had certain minimum requirements for the position of flight officer. The applicant had to have 500 hours of flight time, be 21 to 29 years of age, have a commercial pilot's license and instrument rating, and have a college degree. When Spurlock, a black, applied for the position, no one knew his race. At the time, he only had 204 hours of flight time and only two years of college, mostly in music education. His written application was rejected. Therefore Spurlock sued United, claiming racial discrimination in violation of Title VII of the Civil Rights Act. He pointed out that of approximately 5,900 flight officers in United's employ at the time, only nine were blacks. Was United guilty of illegal discrimination? (*Spurlock v. United Airlines, Inc.*, 475 F.2d 216)

29. Shiela Grove and David Klink were both tellers for Frostburg National Bank. Both were high school graduates. They had worked for the bank for the same length of time performing the same duties. Occasionally, Klink performed miscellaneous tasks that were not assigned to Grove. A male supervisor, David Willetts, set the salaries for both tellers. Klink's salary was significantly higher than Grove's. Has the bank violated the Equal Pay Act? (*Grove v. Frostburg National Bank*, 549 F. Supp. 922)

30. Johnson Controls, Inc., manufactures batteries made primarily of lead. Lead is a dangerous substance for pregnant women because exposure to lead can harm the fetus. For this reason, Johnson Controls excluded women who are pregnant or who are capable of bearing children from jobs that involve exposure to lead. Numerous plaintiffs, including a woman who had chosen to be sterilized to avoid losing her job, entered a federal district court class action suit alleging that Johnson Controls' policy constituted illegal sex discrimination under Title VII of the Civil Rights Act. Is this illegal discrimination? (499 U.S. 187, U.S. Sup. Ct., 1991)

HARRIS v. FORKLIFT SYSTEMS, INC.
114 S. CT. 367

FACTS Theresa Harris worked as a manager for Forklift Systems, Inc. During Harris's two and one-half years with Forklift, she was subjected to gender-based insults and unwanted sexual innuendoes from Charles Hardy, the firm's president. Hardy told Harris, for example, "You're a woman, what do you know?" and "We need a man as the rental manager." Once he suggested that he and Harris negotiate her raise at the Holiday Inn. Hardy would also ask Harris and other female employees to get coins from his front pants pocket and to pick up objects that he threw on the ground. Most of these incidents occurred with other employees present.

After Harris complained to Hardy, he apologized and promised to stop. Later however, he inquired whether Harris had promised sex to a customer with whom she had concluded a deal on Forklift's behalf. Shortly thereafter Harris quit. She then sued Forklift for hostile environment sexual harassment in federal district court. Although it considered Harris's claim "a close case" the trial court found for Forklift. It did so in part because it concluded that Hardy's actions were not sufficiently severe to seriously affect Harris's psychological well being. Ultimately, Harris appealed to the U.S. Supreme Court.

REASONING Title VII [of the Civil Rights Act of 1964] makes it "an unlawful employment practice for an employer . . . to discriminate against any individual with respect to his compensation, terms, conditions, or privileges of employment, because of such individual's race color, religion, sex, or national origin." . . . The phrase "terms, conditions, or privileges of employment" evinces a Congressional intent to strike at the entire spectrum of disparate treatment of men and women in employment which includes requiring people to work in a discriminatorily hostile or abusive environment. When the workplace is permeated with discriminatory intimidation, ridicule and insult that is sufficiently severe or pervasive to alter the conditions of the victim's employment and create an abusive working environment, Title VII is violated.

This standard . . . takes a middle path between making actionable any conduct that is merely offensive and requiring the conduct to cause a tangible psychological injury. . . . Conduct that is not severe or pervasive enough to create an environment that a reasonable person would find hostile or abusive is beyond Title VII's purview. Likewise, if

the victim does not subjectively perceive the environment to be abusive, there is no Title VII violation. But Title VII comes into play before the harassing conduct leads to a nervous breakdown. A discriminatorily abusive work environment, even one that does not seriously affect employees' psychological well-being, can and often will detract from employees' job performance, discourage employees from remaining on the job, or keep them from advancing in their careers. We therefore believe the district court erred in relying on whether the conduct seriously affected plaintiff's psychological well being or led her to suffer injury. Such an inquiry may needlessly focus the fact-finder's attention on concrete psychological harm, an element Title VII does not require.

CONCLUSION Reversed and remanded to the District Court.

PRACTICE JUDGING

1. To whom is the court leaving the decision as to whether or not there is a hostile work environment?

2. If Hardy had not made the statements regarding negotiating the raise, "at the Holiday Inn," and had not asked "female employees to get coins from his front pants pocket," would a different decision have been reached?

© GETTY IMAGES/PHOTODISC

Employment-Related Injuries

24-1 Safety on the Job

24-2 Employer's Liability for Work-Related Injuries

© GETTY IMAGES/PHOTODISC

HOT DEBATE

Joaquim worked at a sandwich shop in lower Manhattan. On Halloween, the owner of the shop asked all her employees to wear costumes. Despite a heavy rain, Joaquim, who loved Halloween, came in an elaborate wizard's costume that he owned. He had a long gray wig, a flowing robe, and a tall peaked hat. Unfortunately, while sneaking a cigarette in one of the restrooms during a break, which was against the shop's policies, Joaquim caught the wig on fire. He was unable to get the wig off immediately or to put out the fire, as the shop's fire extinguisher was empty. Instead he ran outside the shop where the rain eventually doused the fire. Joaquim's real hair was burned off and he suffered minor burns to his hands. When a daily newspaper covered the story with color photos shot by a passing tourist under the headline, "Wizard Wigs Out," the shop's business increased twofold. Now Joaquim is considering suing the shop for negligence.

Where Do You Stand?

1. Why should the store be required to pay for Joaquim's injuries?

2. Why should the store not be required to pay?

▼ GOALS
- Recognize the two approaches taken to protect workers from on-the-job injuries
- Distinguish the role of OSHA in the effort to prevent such injuries

REQUIRING A SAFE WORKPLACE

WHAT'S YOUR VERDICT?

Browning Processing Company prepares fruits and vegetables for the market. An OSHA inspector ordered the company to install clutches on the prune-pitting machines and to provide electrical grounding of all electric typewriters and word processors.

Must Browning comply?

The system in place in the United States to protect workers from on-the-job injuries and their consequences utilizes two approaches. The first is a preventive approach used by federal and state agencies that make rules pertaining to safe working conditions. These agencies then make inspections to discover and prosecute dangerous conditions and rule violations. The primary representative of these protective agencies is found at the federal level in the form of the **Occupational Safety and Health Administration (OSHA).**

The second approach involves after-the-fact compensation for injuries sustained on the job. This compensation typically is obtainable through negligence lawsuits and the workers' compensation system and will be discussed in the next lesson. The remainder of this lesson focuses on the positive steps OSHA takes to prevent the injuries in the first place.

LEGISLATIVE BACKGROUND OF OSHA

In 1970, the U.S. Congress enacted the **Occupational Safety and Health Act.** The groundbreaking policy put into force by this legislation was to involve the federal government directly in the preventing of workplace injuries. To this end, the law created the Occupational Safety and Health Administration and empowered it to enact rules and regulations designed to achieve safety in the workplace. Read the provisions of the act on page 427 of this chapter.

The rules and regulations apply to firms with eleven or more employees that are engaged in interstate commerce. The Department of Labor enforces those rules. State administrative agencies

What types of accidents could happen in this factory that would lead to injury? What types of preventive safety measures do these men appear to be taking while working here?

© GETTY IMAGES/PHOTODISC

often apply similar safety laws to smaller organizations or those not engaged in interstate commerce.

OSHA'S RESPONSIBILITIES

ASSURE A HAZARD-FREE WORKPLACE
To comply with the employer's **general duty clause** of its empowering act, OSHA requires that employers provide a place of employment free from hazards that are likely to cause death or serious physical harm. If this general duty requirement is violated, OSHA can fine the company and/or shut down the plant.

DEVELOP AND ENFORCE SPECIFIC REGULATIONS
OSHA also is responsible for making specific workplace safety regulations. Many of these regulations were hastily established shortly after this federal administrative agency was formed. These regulations cover most aspects of work. They spell out safety training requirements; safety clothing and equipment to be worn by workers; and the construction, maintenance, and shielding of equipment.

Minimum standards are established for lighting, ventilation, and sanitation. For example, OSHA specifies that spray paint booths must be vented to the exterior of the building and that they must be constructed of metal rather than wood. Another example is the requirement that hair protection (hairnets) be worn when working near equipment such as drills.

Minor violations of OSHA regulations usually are resolved by bringing the workplace into compliance, although employers can be fined. In *What's Your Verdict?* Browning Processing would be required to comply with OSHA's demands because the lack of clutches and electrical grounding violates specific OSHA regulations. If the company did not comply, it could be fined.

CONDUCT WORKPLACE INSPECTIONS
OSHA uses workplace inspections to ensure compliance with its general duty clause and specific regulations. While an employer may deny OSHA inspectors access to the workplace, inspectors easily can obtain a search warrant giving them authority to inspect.

Employers are required to file periodic safety reports describing work-related injuries. If there is an injury requiring hospitalization of three or more employees or resulting in a death, the employer must notify the Department of Labor within eight hours. These reports often prompt OSHA inspections.

Employees also may anonymously call OSHA to report safety violations. OSHA will then send inspectors to the workplace. Employers may not discriminate against workers who have informed OSHA of safety violations.

DEALING WITH OSHA VIOLATIONS

In most simple cases, employers deal with OSHA officials without a lawyer. The problems usually involve technical engineering and safety issues rather than legal issues. Inspectors and company supervisors are best equipped to deal with these problems. However, some OSHA violations become serious because the cost of compliance can be prohibitive, pushing some companies into bankruptcy. In these situations, the employer needs immediate expert legal help. Unless a company acts quickly, some rights to appeal an OSHA action may be lost.

CHECKPOINT

What are the two approaches taken to prevent on-the-job injuries in the United States?

IN THIS CASE

During an OSHA visit to the St. Louis plant of a large dishwashing soap manufacturer, an inspector noticed that large portions of the production floor were extremely slippery. The company vice president, who was accompanying the inspector, said that the soap product occasionally spilled off the bottling line and caused the problem. She assured the inspector that the spills were cleaned up immediately. The inspector, however, stated that the clean up was not adequate, as it left a slippery film on the floor. He cited the company for a safety violation.

JOB SAFETY & HEALTH PROTECTION

The Occupational Safety and Health Act of 1970 provides job safety and health protection for workers by promoting safe and healthful working conditions throughout the Nation. Provisions of the Act include the following:

Employers

All employers must furnish to employees employment and a place of employment free from recognized hazards that are causing or are likely to cause death or serious harm to employees. Employers must comply with occupational safety and health standards issued under the Act.

Employees

Employees must comply with all occupational safety and health standards, rules, regulations and orders issued under the Act that apply to their own actions and conduct on the job.

The Occupational Safety and Health Administration (OSHA) of the U.S. Department of Labor has the primary responsibility for administering the Act. OSHA issues occupational safety and health standards, and its Compliance Safety and Health Officers conduct jobsite inspections to help ensure compliance with the Act.

Inspection

The Act requires that a representative of the employer and a representative authorized by the employees be given an opportunity to accompany the OSHA inspector for the purpose of aiding the inspection.

Where there is no authorized employee representative, the OSHA Compliance Officer must consult with a reasonable number of employees concerning safety and health conditions in the workplace.

Complaint

Employees or their representatives have the right to file a complaint with the nearest OSHA office requesting an inspection if they believe unsafe or unhealthful conditions exist in their workplace. OSHA will withhold, on request, names of employees complaining.

The Act provides that employees may not be discharged or discriminated against in any way for filing safety and health complaints or for otherwise exercising their rights under the Act.

Employees who believe they have been discriminated against may file a complaint with their nearest OSHA office within 30 days of the alleged discriminatory action.

Citation

If upon inspection OSHA believes an employer has violated the Act, a citation alleging such violations will be issued to the employer. Each citation will specify a time period within which the alleged violation must be corrected.

The OSHA citation must be prominently displayed at or near the place of alleged violation for three days, or until it is corrected, whichever is later, to warn employees of dangers that may exist there.

Proposed Penalty

The Act provides for mandatory civil penalties against employers of up to $7,000 for each serious violation and for optional penalties of up to $7,000 for each nonserious violation. Penalties of up to $7,000 per day may be proposed for failure to correct violations within the proposed time period and for each day the violation continues beyond the prescribed abatement date. Also, any employer who willfully or repeatedly violates the Act may be assessed penalties of up to $70,000 for each such violation. A minimum penalty of $5,000 may be imposed for each willful violation. A violation of posting requirements can bring a penalty of up to $7,000.

There are also provisions for criminal penalties. Any willful violation resulting in the death of any employee, upon conviction, is punishable by a fine of up to $250,000 (or $500,000 if the employer is a corporation), or by imprisonment for up to six months, or both. A second conviction of an employer doubles the possible term of imprisonment. Falsifying records, reports, or applications is punishable by a fine of $10,000 or up to six months in jail or both.

Voluntary Activity

While providing penalties for violations, the Act also encourages efforts by labor and management, before an OSHA inspection, to reduce workplace hazards voluntarily and to develop and improve safety and health programs in all workplaces and industries. OSHA's Voluntary Protection Programs recognize outstanding efforts of this nature.

OSHA has published Safety and Health Program Management Guidelines to assist employers in establishing or perfecting programs to prevent or control employee exposure to workplace hazards. There are many public and private organizations that can provide information and assistance in this effort, if requested. Also, your local OSHA office can provide considerable help and advice on solving safety and health problems or can refer you to other sources for help such as training.

Consultation

Free assistance in identifying and correcting hazards and in improving safety and health management is available to employers, without citation or penalty, through OSHA-supported programs in each State. These programs are usually administered by the State Labor or Health department or a State university.

Posting Instructions

Employers in States operating OSHA approved State Plans should obtain and post the State's equivalent poster.

Under provisions of Title 29, Code of Federal Regulations, Part 1903.2(a)(1) employers must post this notice (or facsimile) in a conspicuous place where notices to employees are customarily posted.

More Information

Additional information and copies of the Act, OSHA safety and health standards, and other applicable regulations may be obtained from your employer or from the nearest OSHA Regional Office in the following locations:

Atlanta, GA	(404) 562-2300
Boston, MA	(617) 565-9860
Chicago, IL	(312) 353-2220
Dallas, TX	(214) 767-4731
Denver, CO	(303) 844-1600
Kansas City, MO	(816) 426-5861
New York, NY	(212) 337-2378
Philadelphia, PA	(215) 596-1201
San Francisco, CA	(415) 975-4310
Seattle, WA	(206) 553-5930

Washington, DC
1997 (Reprinted)
OSHA 2203

Alexis M. Herman

Alexis M. Herman, Secretary of Labor

U.S. Department of Labor
Occupational Safety and Health Administration

This information will be made available to sensory impaired individuals upon request.
Voice phone: (202) 219-8615; TDD message referral phone: 1-800-326-2577

It is now possible to download and file an OSHA complaint online. Such a complaint can be filed anonymously. However, anonymous filings are treated as non-employee complaints and given a lower priority as a consequence. The official form for complaint submission (OSHA-7) along with instructions on how to properly fill it out can be downloaded from the OSHA web site. Access the link through the Xtra! web site.

THINK ABOUT IT

Should someone be able to file such a complaint without being responsible for its allegations? What possible abuses do you think might occur with such a system?

24-1 Assessment

lawxtra.swlearning.com

THINK ABOUT LEGAL CONCEPTS

1. Which of these is not a way the potential for and actual employee injuries are dealt with? (a) negligence suit (b) arbitration (c) workers' compensation (d) job safety requirements

2. OSHA regulations control even very specific conditions of the workplace such as the type of shields that must be on equipment. **True or False?**

3. OSHA can shut down employers who fail to provide a "workplace free from recognized hazards." **True or False?**

4. Even minor violations of OSHA regulations can result in imprisonment of employers. **True or False?**

5. Most employers deal with OSHA violations without involving lawyers. **True or False?**

THINK CRITICALLY ABOUT EVIDENCE

Study the situation, answer the questions, and then prepare arguments to support your answers.

6. Bill operated a bakery with only 16 employees, selling bread in two states. Is the bakery subject to regulation by OSHA?

7. Circo-Pacific manufactured circuit boards—the base on which electrical components are mounted by soldering. Peery worked as a dip solderer, inserting the bare boards into a small tub of molten solder to coat the copper circuits. The building in which he worked leaked. Once when it rained, water dripped into the tub and splashed molten solder onto Peery's arm, causing numerous slight burns. The largest of the burns was about half the size of a pencil eraser. Peery complained to his boss about the problem several times but his boss dismissed the complaints saying,

"Don't be such a sissy." Peery finally complained to OSHA. An inspector arrived at the plant and cited the company. The fine was $500. A month later, Peery was transferred to a job that paid much less than that of dip solderer. He complained to OSHA that he was being discriminated against because of his complaint. Is he correct? What is the result?

8. AB Co. stored trichlorethelene in 55 gallon drums at floor level. A forklift nicked a drum and the liquid spilled out without anyone immediately realizing it. Fumes spread throughout the plant. Five people fainted. The fire department was called and ambulances took the workers to the hospital. The chemical was cleaned up within two hours and production was restored. What legal obligations remain for AB Co.?

Employer's Liability for Work-Related Injuries

▼ **GOALS**

- Recognize the importance of employee negligence suits and workers' compensation
- Describe the procedure for handling workers' compensation cases

NEGLIGENCE LAW AND WORKERS' COMPENSATION

WHAT'S YOUR VERDICT?

Crow was a steelworker working on the fifth story of a fifteen-story apartment project. His employer, Nu-Dimensions, Inc., provided all workers with protective helmets as required by law. One day, because of the intense heat, Crow removed his helmet and worked bareheaded while the supervisor was off-duty. A large bolt fell from the employer's construction crane and hit Crow on the head, fracturing his skull. It was common for objects to fall from the top floor of a construction project.

Could Crow recover any money for injuries due to this on-the-job incident?

If, regardless of OSHA's preventative efforts, worker injuries are sustained, there are two means of providing compensation and rehabilitation. The first and oldest method is a recovery from the employer based on negligence law. The second, covered later in this lesson, is through the system of workers' compensation.

EMPLOYEE NEGLIGENCE SUITS

Under the common-law negligence approach used in this country for centuries, the employees sue the employer for damages. Employees win their negligence suits if they prove in court that the employer's negligence caused their injury. By making employers liable for the injuries caused by their negligence, the common law encouraged employers to protect employees.

Negligence law imposes on employers the general duty to provide reasonably safe working conditions for employees. This duty may be violated in several ways. For example, an employer might fail to provide a safe workspace, safe tools, or safe machinery. Similarly, the employer would violate the duty if there were an insufficient number of co-workers to do a job safely or if employees were given inadequate safety instructions. When the employer violates the duty to provide safe working conditions and this causes injury to workers, the employee has grounds to recover for her or his injuries.

DIFFICULTIES FOR EMPLOYEES IN NEGLIGENCE SUITS

The original common-law system placed many obstacles in the path of an employee seeking to recover from an employer. In particular the injured worker had several reasons for not suing the employer. First of all, the employee had to hire an attorney. Then, the employee who sued also risked being fired. Further, even if an employee proved that the employer's negligence caused the injury, the employee would not collect if the employer proved any one of the following **common-law defenses**:

LEGAL RESEARCH

Contact county, city, state, and federal departments, bureaus, and agencies responsible for overseeing the safety of workers in the workplace. Ask them for a list of the laws, ordinances, or regulations they enforce and what each covers. Compile a composite list. Evaluate your list from the standpoint of effectiveness and from the standpoint of the employer. Are there so many requirements that the employer cannot comply with them all, or has a common-sense balance been reached?

- the employee had assumed the risk involved
- the employee was negligent
- the negligence of a co-worker caused the injury

Assumption of risk occurs when a person is aware of a danger that could cause injury, but voluntarily remains in the dangerous situation. In *What's Your Verdict?* Crow assumed the risk of being hurt by falling objects when he remained on the job after seeing other objects fall.

Contributory negligence means that the employee carelessly did something that contributed to her or his injury or death. This defense can be effective even when the employee's negligence is very slight in relation to the employer's. In *What's Your Verdict?* Crow was contributorily negligent because he removed his safety helmet.

Co-worker negligence means simply that a co-worker is the cause of the injury. It also prevents recovery from an employer. In *What's Your Verdict?* if the employer could show that a co-worker caused the bolt to fall, the employer would not be liable.

THE COMPROMISE OF WORKERS' COMPENSATION

These common-law defenses prevented employees from winning most negligence suits. However, when an employee did win, the size of the recovery often threatened the very existence of the business. Therefore, between 1890 and 1910 state legislatures began enacting compromise laws intended to help more injured employees receive compensation for workplace injuries and be rehabilitated. These laws, which became known as **workers' compensation statutes**, were also intended to limit the exposure of employers to potentially ruinous lawsuits.

Today these statutes require most employers to obtain insurance to pay benefits to injured employees. The benefits are paid without regard to fault. So the insurance pays even when the employer is not a cause of the injury.

The workers' compensation system was created as a substitute for negligence suits. If the injured employee is covered by workers' compensation, no negligence suit ordinarily is allowed against the employer. Also, because the amount an employer must pay for workers' compensation insurance is related somewhat to the firm's safety record, employers still have an incentive to maintain a safe workplace.

RECOVERING IN LIEU OF WORKERS' COMPENSATION

As mentioned, the general rule is that an employee cannot sue the employer for on-the-job injuries if the employee is covered by workers' compensation. However there are several important exceptions. In these exceptional circumstances, an injured employee (or the family of an employee who is killed on the job) can still sue the employer for negligence.

Why do you think it would be a good idea for the employer of these workers to pay for workers' compensation insurance?

© GETTY IMAGES/PHOTODISC

IF EMPLOYER FAILS TO PROVIDE WORKERS' COMPENSATION INSURANCE If state law requires that an employee be covered but the employer has not purchased workers' compensation insurance, the injured employee can sue the employer for negligence. In these cases, the employer generally may not use the employers' common-law defenses of assumption of the risk, contributory negligence, or co-worker negligence. Thus, the employee has the possibility of recovering large sums of money while the employer is almost defenseless. This possibility creates a great incentive for the employer to purchase workers' compensation coverage.

IF EMPLOYEE COVERAGE IS NOT REQUIRED If an employee is not required to be covered by workers' compensation and is injured because of the employer's negligence, the employee may sue the employer. In these cases, the employer usually may use all the common-law defenses.

IF THE INJURY IS NOT COVERED BY WORKERS' COMPENSATION In some cases, the employee is injured because of the negligence of the employer but workers' compensation does not cover the injury. See this lesson's In This Case for an example. In such situations the law would allow the employer to assert the defenses of contributory negligence or assumption of the risk.

EMPLOYER COMMITS AN INTENTIONAL TORT In some states, even when covered by workers' compensation, an employee may sue the employer for intentional actions that the employer knows will cause injury. This most often occurs when the conduct of the employer is criminal, is an intentional tort, or is an intentional violation of a safety regulation.

CHECKPOINT

Name the three common-law defenses utilized by employers against negligence cases by employees.

HOW DOES THE WORKERS' COMPENSATION SYSTEM WORK?

WHAT'S YOUR VERDICT?

Johnson, a jailer for the Tarrant County Sheriff's Department, was cleaning his service revolver at his residence at approximately 9:15 p.m. when he accidentally discharged his revolver into his left leg and foot. Johnson had reloaded the revolver after cleaning it and left the room temporarily. When he returned, he saw oil dripping from the revolver. He then picked it up, spun the cylinder to disperse the oil, and having forgotten that he reloaded it, pulled the trigger.

Can Johnson recover workers' compensation for this self-inflicted injury?

IN THIS CASE

Entertainer Tonight Inc. (ETI) hired performing artists as its employees and booked them for one-night gigs in various cities. It also contracted for private pilots and planes to fly the performers to their various venues. Rapper NoBonzBoutIt was aboard such a plane when it crashed on takeoff. NoBonz was severely injured. The pilot was shown to be well-known for his drinking on the job and had been intoxicated at the controls that evening. ETI could be sued for negligence in its selection of the pilot even though it had workers' compensation insurance.

THE DETERMINATION OF WHICH EMPLOYEES ARE COVERED

Employees are generally protected by workers' compensation insurance if they are injured by accident or disease, including job-related stress, in the scope of employment and from the risks of that employment.

SCOPE OF EMPLOYMENT To recover from workers' compensation, the injured employee must have been acting within the scope of employment at the time of the injury. Scope of employment generally means acting for the benefit of the employer. For example, an auto accident while

You work in a paint booth at a local car body shop. In order to save money, your employer often turns off the ventilation system during the actual painting. She then turns it back on at the conclusion of the job to insure that later paint jobs are not contaminated by a color previously used. Your fellow employee and you often meet after work and while talking spit up orange primer and various top coat colors. You laugh about it until he comes down with lung cancer. Now he is pursuing a workers' compensation claim against the employer. Your employer has called you as a witness and promised you a large increase in pay if you discount your friend's claims about the ventilation system being off during painting. Your husband and two young children need your paycheck and you are worried about being fired if you tell the truth. Are you ethically obligated to tell the truth even if it means your family's future is in jeopardy?

driving to or from work usually would not be within the scope of employment because you do that primarily for yourself. On the other hand, an employee doing an errand for the employer on the way home from work is likely to be within the scope of employment.

The facts in *What's Your Verdict?* were adapted from a Texas case containing typical scope of employment issues. Therein the court wrote:

The Texas Workers' Compensation Act provides a definition of scope of employment: "an activity performed by an employee while engaged in or about the furtherance of the affairs or business of the employer." All county jailers were required to own a weapon, and each officer had the responsibility for cleaning and maintaining his or her own weapon. Because the sheriff's department did not provide an area at the jail for officers to clean their weapons, officers were permitted to clean their weapons at home or "anywhere," as long as they

showed up for work each day with a clean weapon. Johnson is entitled to workers' compensation. (*Esis, Inc. v. Johnson*, 908 S.W.2d 554)

RISKS OF EMPLOYMENT There are risks associated with jobs and these are the risks that workers' compensation generally covers. Thus, while a person assembling heavy fire hydrants could recover for a hernia, a clerical worker who suffered a hernia while picking a piece of paper off the floor might not collect benefits. That is because the injury may not have been caused by the job, but rather by weak abdominal muscles.

EXCLUDED EMPLOYEES Not all workers are required to be covered by a plan of workers' compensation. These include workers for companies with too few employees, casual workers, independent contractors, and those covered by other systems.

WORKERS FOR COMPANIES WITH TOO FEW EMPLOYEES Frequently, companies with three or fewer employees are not required to provide workers' compensation insurance.

What risks of employment do you think would be associated with this job?

© GETTY IMAGES/PHOTODISC

CASUAL WORKERS In most states, casual workers need not be covered. **Casual workers** are those who do not work regularly for one employer.

INDEPENDENT CONTRACTORS Independent contractors need not be covered. An independent contractor is someone hired to accomplish a task, but who is not supervised while doing so. If a dry cleaning company hires an expert to fix the steam mechanism on its dry cleaning system, he or she would be an independent contractor, not an employee.

THOSE COVERED BY OTHER SYSTEMS Rather than being covered by state workers' compensation laws, employees of railroads, airlines, trucking firms, and other common carriers engaged in interstate commerce are governed by special federal laws. Longshore and harbor workers also operate under a different federal law and are not subject to state workers' compensation laws. A special statute also governs the crew on seagoing vessels.

What should independent contractors do to make sure that their medical costs will be covered if they are injured on the job?

THE AWARD HEARING

The decision about whether a person is entitled to benefits is made at a hearing conducted by a state administrative agency. This agency is often called the Workers' Compensation Board or the Industrial Accident Commission.

Hearing procedures for the Workers' Compensation Board and the Industrial Accident Commission are much less complicated than those of a trial. For small claims, the injured worker does not need a lawyer. However, when the claim or injury is significant, a lawyer who is a specialist in the field should represent the person.

THE DETERMINATION OF BENEFITS

If a worker covered by workers' compensation is injured because of the job, the worker becomes entitled to benefits. Sometimes there

is a lump-sum payment to cover such things as pain and suffering involved with injuries such as loss of a hand, or loss of life. All medical expenses usually are covered. Most states also will pay a percentage of lost wages. Compensation for lost wages typically is about 80 percent. In nearly every case, the payment is

NETBookmark

Access lawxtra.swlearning.com and click on the link for Chapter 24. The web site provides links to the Workers' Compensation Boards or Commissions in all 50 states and Washington, D.C. Choose one state and click on the link for its web site. Write a one-page report explaining what an injured employee in that state who is covered by workers' compensation insurance needs to do if he or she suffers an injury on the job.

lawxtra.swlearning.com

In most states both employers and insurers are required by statute to report suspected fraud claims to the local authorities and the state's department in charge of workers' compensation. Note that it is important to distinguish between "abuse" and "fraud." The former is defined as using the system for something other than it was intended. Fraud occurs when there is clear intent to misrepresent one's injuries or fabricate injuries. Criminal penalties for fraud include incarceration for one to five years, fines from $15,000 to $50,000, and repayment of fraudulently obtained benefits.

• •

much less than if the injured party had won a negligence suit.

If an accident makes it impossible for a worker to continue in the former job, most states also pay for vocational rehabilitation.

Vocational rehabilitation is training for another type of job. Often the amount of the benefit is increased if the employer is grossly negligent or reduced if the employee is grossly negligent. A 10 percent increase or reduction is typical.

PAYING FOR THE INSURANCE

Workers' compensation benefits are paid from one of three sources. Employers may purchase a workers' compensation insurance policy from a private insurance company, participate in a state-administered workers' compensation fund, or be self-insured. Insurance companies and state funds charge amounts that reflect the riskiness of the business and each employer's safety history. The amount paid out by those that are self-insured depends on the number and severity of workplace injuries. As a consequence, employers have an incentive to make the workplace safe so as to reduce their costs of workers' compensation coverage.

CHECKPOINT

What employees are generally excluded from the coverage of a workers' compensation system?

24-2

Assessment

Xtra!
Study Tools
lawxtra.swlearning.com

THINK ABOUT LEGAL CONCEPTS

1. Which of the following is not a common-law defense to a negligence suit against an employer? (a) contributory negligence (b) co-worker negligence (c) OSHA violations in the workplace (d) assumption of the risk

2. In general, can an employee who is covered by workers' compensation bring a suit against the employer for negligence. **Yes or No?**

3. When a worker is covered by workers' compensation, it is generally the employee's sole remedy for job-related injuries. **True or False?**

4. Acting for the benefit of the employer is generally referred to as (a) risk of employment (b) scope of employment (c) being an independent contractor (d) none of the above

5. Casual workers generally are covered by workers' compensation. **True or False?**

6. As private insurance companies go out of business often, employers must only purchase workers' compensation insurance policies from the state. **True or False?**

THINK CRITICALLY ABOUT EVIDENCE

Study the situation, answer the questions, and then prepare arguments to support your answers.

7. Suppose you are working at a car wash. One day you are injured when you slip on the wet floor after a fellow worker throws a towel at your head. Which common-law defense would be most useful to the car wash owner in a negligence suit?

8. Wynett was a delivery driver for Express Delivery. One Friday, he departed from his delivery route to see his girlfriend, Latasha. Latasha lived nearly 60 miles away from Wynett's delivery area. As he pulled up to Latasha's home, he was hit in the rear end by a large tractor-trailer truck. This caused whiplash. Was this injury a risk of the employment? Was Wynett acting within the scope of employment? Can Wynett recover workers' compensation for this injury?

9. Lambert hired Mayer, a casual worker, to apply anhydrous ammonia, a fertilizer, to the soil on her farm. Lambert was not required to provide workers' compensation insurance, so Mayer was not covered. Lambert said to Mayer, "Be careful when you handle this stuff; it might burn you." However, Mayer had never used this type of equipment before, and Lambert did not explain to him how to handle the tank or the hose or what to do if he was sprayed on his body. Mayer lost control of the hose and was sprayed in the face with the chemical, blinding him in one eye. He sued Lambert for negligence, claiming that he was not properly instructed in how to handle the equipment. Who wins?

10. Jerold hired a construction worker to install a shake shingle roof on his home. The work was to be completed within 30 days. All the decisions about materials, methods, and time when the work would be done were left to the contractor. Must Jerold purchase workers' compensation insurance for the contractor? Why or why not?

11. A 27-year-old retail store employee was raped twice by a store security guard. The security guard had been convicted of violent sex crimes before the store hired him. In her lawsuit the plaintiff sought $50 million, plus punitive damages. The store has asked a judge to dismiss the woman's lawsuit, contending that her only recourse is to pursue a workers' compensation claim. Is rape a risk of the job? What evidence of negligence by the employer is there here? If there is a negligence suit against the employer, what defenses could the employer assert?

PREVENT LEGAL DIFFICULTIES

As an employee . . .

1. Think about elements of your work that might cause injury to you or a co-worker. If the risks are serious, discuss them in a friendly way with your boss. If your boss is not helpful, consider discussing the situation with the people at OSHA.

As an employer . . .

1. Inspect your workplace to identify and to eliminate risks to the safety and health of your workers.

2. Verify that all your workers are covered by workers' compensation. If some are not covered, ask an attorney who specializes in employment law to review their status.

2. Determine whether you would be covered by workers' compensation insurance before accepting a job involving safety risks.

3. Follow all safety precautions, use all safety devices prescribed for your job, and follow the employer's safety regulations.

3. If you hire servants, agricultural or casual workers, or independent contractors who are not covered by workers' compensation, ask your lawyer for advice on how to limit your liability for injuries to them.

4. Consider asking OSHA inspectors to conduct an informal inspection of your workplace.

Chapter 24 Assessment

CONCEPTS IN BRIEF

24-1 Safety on the Job

1. The U.S. system to protect workers from on-the-job injuries and their consequences currently utilizes two approaches. The first is a preventive approach embodied by OSHA. The second is a negligence law/workers' compensation system.

2. It is the general duty of employers to provide a place of employment free from hazards that are likely to cause death or serious physical harm.

3. OSHA is empowered to develop specific rules and regulations to ensure workplace safety.

4. OSHA is also empowered to conduct inspections and to cite and prosecute violators.

24-2 Employer's Liability for Work-Related Injuries

5. Employees have long been able to sue employers for work-related injuries under the common law of negligence.

6. Unlike the law of negligence, the workers' compensation system is not fault based.

7. Employees are generally protected by workers' compensation insurance if they are injured by accident or disease, in the scope of employment, and from the risks of that employment.

8. Workers can still sue employers for negligence in certain circumstances but, as a general rule, if the business has workers' compensation insurance, a negligence suit is prohibited.

YOUR LEGAL VOCABULARY

Match each statement with the term that it best defines. Some terms may not be used.

1. When a worker knows there is danger on the job but agrees to do it anyway

2. Retraining of an injured worker

3. Laws that provide compensation for workers (or their dependents) when the workers are injured (or killed) in the course of employment

4. Federal agency that administers the Occupational Safety and Health Act

5. Persons who do not work regularly for a certain employer

6. Part of the Occupational Safety and Health Act requiring that employers provide a workplace free from hazards likely to cause serious harm or death

7. Assumption of risk, contributory negligence, and negligence of a co-worker

8. A fellow employee's conduct that is partially responsible for your injury

> a. assumption of risk
> b. casual workers
> c. common-law defenses
> d. co-worker negligence
> e. general duty clause
> f. Occupational Safety and Health Act
> g. Occupational Safety and Health Administration (OSHA)
> h. vocational rehabilitation
> i. workers' compensation statutes

REVIEW LEGAL CONCEPTS

9. Describe when an employee can maintain a negligence suit against an employer.

10. Describe the employer's general duty under the Occupational Safety and Health Act.

11. Invent a situation where an employer would be able to escape liability in a negligence suit by an injured employee by asserting the defense of contributory negligence.

WRITE ABOUT LEGAL CONCEPTS

12. Write a short paragraph describing the reasons why the creation of the workers' compensation system was a good compromise for employers and employees.

13. Write one paragraph describing how the employer's liability for negligence is determined. Write a second paragraph describing how an insurer's liability for workers' compensation is determined.

14. Write a short essay about your state's workers' compensation program. In the essay discuss the program's evolution as well as compare the level of awards the program provides for various injuries with programs of states in other parts of the country.

15. **HOT DEBATE** Write a short paragraph supporting Joaquim's ability to recover under the workers' compensation system. Write another paragraph arguing that he does not have the right to recover under the system.

MAKE ACADEMIC CONNECTIONS

16. **BUSINESS** Select a book advising small business owners about the finer points of the workers' compensation system. Compare the advice it offers with "how to" books on filing workers' compensation claims. Report to the class on the level of compromise and adversarial attitudes found in these publications.

THINK CRITICALLY ABOUT EVIDENCE

Study the situation, answer the questions, and then prepare arguments to support your answers.

17. Blake worked for West Oregon Lumber Company as a wood sorter. In violation of Oregon law, the company did not carry workers' compensation insurance. While sorting wood on a table, Blake knocked a very heavy piece off, and it fell and hit his foot. Blake sued the employer for negligence as the pieces for sorting should have been small enough to handle properly. The lumber company asserted contributory negligence as an employer's defense. Will Blake win?

18. Atlas Warehouse was equipped with an old-fashioned freight elevator that had a manually operated gate on each floor. When the elevator reached a floor, the employee had to raise the gate and then lower it after getting off. Lacey, a supervisor delivering a message to Ritter, stepped off the elevator after raising the gate. She did not lower the gate because she intended to get back on immediately. While she was talking with Ritter, the elevator was moved to another floor. After her conversation, Lacey returned to the elevator. Not noticing it had been moved, she stepped into the shaft and fell to her death. What would be the employer's liability in a negligence suit?

19. Fries and Brack were employed as truck drivers by different companies, and both were covered by workers' compensation. Late one afternoon, Fries was rushing to make a delivery. In haste, Fries negligently rammed into Brack's truck. Brack suffered fatal injuries. Brack's widow later received a lump-sum workers' compensation benefit of $55,000. Is this all she can collect?

20. Randle worked at the Hide Tanning Company, which employed only two people. The company did not carry workers' compensation insurance because the state law did not apply to very small firms. A large wooden vat of acid with an open top was mounted on a wooden stand six feet off the ground. Because the stand was old and rickety, the person working near it was afraid that it would collapse and spill the acid on them. An OSHA inspector cited the company for violation of the general duty clause. Two days after the citation, the vat broke, spilling acid on Randle. Randle sued the employer and introduced the citation as evidence of the company's negligence. The company objected, claiming that OSHA inspections have nothing to do with suits for employer's negligence. Is the company correct?

21. Abell and his brother had been hired as laborers to help prepare the grounds for the county fair. They were to be paid by the hour and were to furnish their own tools. No understanding was reached concerning the length of their employment, but it was understood that it would be "for one or two weeks." The work to be done consisted of "odd jobs," such as cleaning up and making minor repairs. Abell died when he was struck by a tractor while working. In light of these facts, were Abell's survivors entitled to workers' compensation benefits? (*Wood v. Abell,* 300 A.2d 665)

22. Thornton was employed as production foreman with the defendant corporation. On several occasions, Thornton had reprimanded an employee, Sozio, for failure to wear safety glasses and had reported this to the employer. On one occasion, Sozio threatened Thornton, saying, "I'll take care of your eyes later." Nine days after Sozio's employment had been terminated, Thornton saw him in a bar. At that time Sozio said, "Remember me, remember me?" and attacked Thornton, causing him to lose the sight of one eye. Thornton claims that he is entitled to workers' compensation benefits because his injuries arose out of and had their origin in his employment and because the injuries were in the course of the employment. His employer claims that the injuries did not occur on the job even though they did arise out of the employment. Sozio, no longer an employee, had deliberately inflicted the injuries. Therefore, the employer argues, Thornton is not entitled to workers' compensation benefits. Is Thornton entitled to benefits? (*Thornton v. Chamberlain Manufacturing Corporation,* 62 NJ. 235, 300 A.2d 146)

23. Bailey managed a gas station. He was required to use his station wagon to make emergency calls for the station. Tools were carried in the car, and the service station paid for the gas and oil it used. Bailey owned another car that was used as a "family car." One morning while driving to work, Bailey was struck and killed by a train. His wife filed a claim for workers' compensation benefits. The Industrial Commission denied the claim, stating that travel to and from work is not covered by workers' compensation insurance. Was Bailey's death caused by his work? Is his widow entitled to the death benefit? (*Bailey v. Utah State Industrial Commission,* 16 P.2d 208, Utah)

24. Eckis, age 22, was a full-time employee of Sea World, an amusement park. Eckis served as secretary for Burgess, the director of animal training. Eckis, who was an excellent swimmer, had worked as a model. When Burgess asked her to ride "Shamu, the Killer Whale" in a bikini for some publicity pictures, she eagerly agreed. Burgess knew Shamu was conditioned to being ridden only by persons wearing wet suits and had attacked riders in bathing suits. Eckis was warned in general terms of the danger, and she fell off during one practice session while wearing a wet suit. When a trainer told Eckis he would not watch her ride Shamu "because it was really dangerous," Burgess reassured Eckis and she rode Shamu three different times. Each time she wore a bikini instead of a wet suit. During the second ride, Shamu's tail was fluttering, indicating that the whale was upset. During the third ride, Eckis fell off and Shamu bit her on her legs and hips and held her in the tank until she was rescued. As an employee, Eckis qualified for modest workers' compensation payments but had no other insurance benefits. Therefore, she sued for more money in a civil action. She claimed that the employer was negligent, had defrauded her, and was liable for the acts of an animal with dangerous tendencies. The jury awarded Eckis damages of $75,000. Sea World appealed. Was workers' compensation Eckis's only remedy? (*Eckis v. Sea World Corporation,* 64 Cal. App. 3d 1)

25. Barlow's Inc. was an electrical and plumbing contractor. An OSHA inspector appeared at Barlow's place of business and asked to inspect the premises. There had been no injuries at Barlow's and the inspector did not possess a search warrant. Barlow's denied the inspector access to the business. OSHA sued to compel Barlow to admit the inspector without a warrant. Who prevails, Barlow or OSHA? (*Marshall v. Barlow's Inc.,* 436 U.S. 307)

CASE FOR LEGAL THINKING

TOLBERT v. MARTIN MARIETTA CORPORATION
621 F. SUPP 1099

FACTS Deborah Tolbert, a secretary employed by the Martin Marietta Corporation, was raped by a Martin Marietta janitor while on her way to lunch within the secured defense facility where she worked. She sued Martin Marietta, alleging that it had negligently hired the janitor and had negligently failed to make its premises safe for employees. Martin Marietta moved for summary judgment, claiming that Tolbert could not sue in negligence because workers' compensation was her sole remedy.

REASONING The sole issue is whether the Colorado Workmen's Compensation Act covers Tolbert's injury. If it does, workers' compensation is her exclusive remedy and this tort action is barred. Tolbert asserts that her injury is not covered by workers' compensation, presumably because she expects that a tort action would yield a larger recovery. Martin Marietta, on the other hand, apparently is willing to pay the workers' compensation award to avoid risking a large tort verdict. Workers' compensation applies where the injury or death is proximately caused by an injury or disease arising in the course of the employee's employment and is not intentionally self-inflicted. Although her injury did arise in the course of her employment, Tolbert contends that it did not "arise out of" the employment.

Courts have interpreted the "arising out of" language in two different ways: "positional risk" or "increased risk."

The positional-risk doctrine has been defined as follows:

Any injury arises out of the employment if it would not have occurred but for the fact that the conditions and obligations of the employment placed claimant in the position where he was injured. Invoking this rule, Martin Marietta asserts that Tolbert's injury is covered by workers' compensation because: (1) her employment placed her within the building where she was injured, and (2) the assault was a neutral force.

Under the increased-risk test, compensation is awarded only if the employment increases the worker's risk of injury above that to which the general public is exposed. If Colorado presently applies the increased-risk analysis, Tolbert would not be covered by workers' compensation. Certainly her employment as a secretary within a secured defense facility would not be expected to increase her risk of sexual assault above that to which women in the general public are exposed.

The rape was a nonemployment-motivated act directed at the plaintiff because she was a woman. Tolbert was not raped because of the nature of her duties or the nature of her workplace environment, or because of any incident or quarrel growing out of the work. [In Colorado,] an injury arises out of the employment if it would not have occurred but for the fact that the conditions and the employment placed claimant in the position where he was injured.

The workers' compensation statute has not abolished Tolbert's tort claim. Adopting this position has the additional advantage of providing employers an incentive to make reasonable efforts to screen prospective employees so as to avoid hiring rapists or those having the identifiable characteristics of potential rapists.

CONCLUSION Martin Marietta's motion for summary judgment is denied.

PRACTICE JUDGING

1. If the janitor had no prior criminal record, what do you think the outcome of the negligence suit would be?

2. Which test, positional-risk or increased-risk, allows more recovery under workers' compensation?

© GETTY IMAGES/PHOTODISC

Entrepreneurs and the Law

PROJECT 5 AGENCY AND EMPLOYMENT LAW

EMPLOYMENT CONTRACTS

JJ was working night and day and getting more and more behind. It was obviously time to hire some help. Amber realized this and so did JJ. They came up with a plan where they could double production, pay workers almost half again the going rate, and still produce a remarkable profit. JJ also needed help in the office. If he could find an experienced secretary who knew how to set up an efficient front office, he could avoid many start-up mistakes. Suddenly, he had an idea. Pilar Valencia ran the front office for Stinson Adamski extremely well. Perhaps he could lure her away.

ADVERTISING

JJ knew he would have to generate some new business to ensure that his employees had enough to do. His first move would be to place an ad in *Solvent*, the dry-cleaning industry's trade magazine. Some narrative and a decent picture of the DataDart should generate quite a few inquiries. Also, he was considering raising the price of the DataDart to $10,000 per system with three "Dart" guns. The price would include on-site training on the hardware and software and 24-hour access to the "Solution" hot line. Many of his customers had mentioned that the device seemed to be priced too low and the store that paid $10,000 to Stinson Adamski had been a small one. Stores and chains with larger volume would probably pay more. Curiously, a few clients of JJ's business had even commented that the low price of the system had caused them to wonder about the quality of the materials and work used in the DataDart.

© GETTY IMAGES/PHOTODISC

INDEPENDENT SALES AGENTS

JJ also considered contracting with some independent sales agents. These agents traveled around the country selling various items like the DataDart. They typically worked on a commission basis. JJ realized that the creation of such an agency had to be done with care. He had to be sure each salesperson had adequate production information and would convey any unanswered questions back to him.

JOB DISCRIMINATION AND HARASSMENT

Finally, JJ wanted to be sure that his employees were hired without being subject to any form of illegal discrimination. He also wanted to be sure that the job environment was free from all types of harassment.

ACTIVITIES

Divide into teams and perform one or more of the following activities as directed by your teacher.

Prepare Legal Documents

Draft some standard employment contracts for JJ's prospective employees. Consider the following issues: What clauses might you put into the contracts? What should be in the benefit package? What should the rate of pay be in reference to the minimum wage? What legal problem(s) might arise with trying to lure Valencia away from Stinson Adamski? What solutions can you propose? Share your contracts with the class.

Be Creative

Divide the team into two groups. Members of one group should contact trade journals and find out about advertising in the journal. (Ask each trade journal to send a copy of its advertising contract. Be sure to find out how they screen advertisers for legitimacy, the lead time for the ad, and if there are any other constraints.) The other group should prepare various ads to submit to the trade journals. When each group has completed its assignment, the groups should present their results to the team and then to the class.

Role-Play

Divide the team up into student pairs. Each pair should role-play the interview between JJ and an independent sales agent candidate. Students should alternate playing JJ and the candidate.

COMMUNITY ACTION

Homeland Security at School

Do you know the color codes of the Homeland Security Advisory System? If you saw a red alert, would you know there was a severe risk of a terrorist attack? If you saw a green alert, would you know the status was low? The Department of Homeland Security is a federal government agency responsible for protecting the nation against terrorist attacks. Schools can use this system to prepare and respond to national threats and acts of terrorism.

Do Your Part

1. Obtain permission from your school administration to create and display posters that inform students about Homeland Security.

2. Make a poster of the Homeland Security Advisory System to post in the school hallway. Include the following information: SEVERE/Severe risk of terrorist attack (Red); HIGH/High risk of terrorist attack (Orange); ELEVATED/Significant risk of terrorist attack (Yellow); GUARDED/General risk of terrorist attack (Blue); LOW/Low risk of terrorist attack (Green).

3. Make a second poster titled "Terrorism at School: A Guide to Action." Pick up a copy of the information that needs to be on this poster at the National School Safety Center web site. Include information on Precautions to Take, Watch and Report, During an Attack at School, and In the Aftermath.

Human Resources Management

This event will assess interpretation of personnel policies and knowledge of human resource management.

You are the human resources director for a major hotel in a large metropolitan city. You hire employees for all departments of the hotel. Frequently individuals who apply for housekeeping positions are Mexican citizens legally living in the United States who speak only Spanish. You do not speak Spanish. Labor unions are pressuring you not to hire the less expensive labor from Mexico; however, you do not want to be guilty of discrimination. You are challenged to develop a personnel directory that states specifically how employees are selected.

You also must prepare a presentation that will appease the labor union and Mexican citizens applying for positions at your hotel. Your presentation must address the following issues: minimum wages, legal citizenship, and policies against discrimination.

Performance Indicators Evaluated

- Demonstrate understanding of human relations skills.
- Describe why professional development is the responsibility of the business and the employee.
- Demonstrate successful evaluation techniques.

- Discuss compensation, benefits, and incentive programs.
- Recognize how organized labor influences business.
- Demonstrate understanding of policies and procedures manuals.
- Demonstrate effective oral communication skills.
- Demonstrate understanding of policies and procedures manuals.

You have 30 minutes to prepare your event. Your presentation should not last more than seven (7) minutes and judges have three (3) minutes to ask questions about your presentation.

For more detailed information about performance indicators, go to the BPA web site.

Think Critically

1. What is the major purpose for labor unions?
2. Why are more American businesses hiring Mexican citizens?
3. Why is it important for a personnel director to be bilingual?
4. How is training and development affected by a staff that speaks several languages?

http://www.bpa.org/

UNIT 6

LEGAL FORMS OF BUSINESS ORGANIZATION

IN PRACTICE PROFILE
Bert and John Jacobs ■ *Entrepreneurs*

Bert and John Jacobs always thought they would own a successful business someday. There were right. Today, at the ages of 39 and 36, their company's sales exceed $39 million. (That doesn't include sales generated from just-finalized distribution agreements in Canada, Japan, and Mexico.)

Their path to entrepreneurship began in 1989 when they designed their first tee shirt. It combined a clever illustration with one of their grandma's favorite sayings, Life is Good. Although the shirt was attractive, results of their door-to-door sales efforts were dismal, and after five years they had a whopping $78 in savings.

Then they created Jake, an illustrated character who soon would appear on tee-shirts, coffee mugs, backpacks, and other products. Thanks to Jake, the Life is Good brand of products appears in stores internationally, and the Jacobs brothers' dream of a successful company is reality.

The road to success, however, wasn't always easy. The Jacobs brothers didn't know how the process of selling and distributing products worked. "We worked a lot harder than smarter at first, trying to get product into the market," Bert remembers. "We knew we had a viable concept, but we probably could have saved some time by finding an expert in distribution and taking a lesson. What took three years probably could have taken one if we had consulted an expert." Instead, the brothers learned on their own.

Trademarking Life is Good was another obstacle. "I failed four times to trademark Life is Good," says Bert. Unable to afford an attorney, "I was in the Boston Public Library every night trying to figure out what to do." Luck was on his side one evening while playing basketball—he met a trademark attorney who agreed to do the work pro bono. After two more years of work, Life is Good finally was trademarked.

Today the brothers and their attorney spend much time chasing down others who create knock-offs of their products. "As the business grows, it becomes more and more likely that someone is infringing on us," according to Bert.

Selling product direct to consumers online, to 3,500 U.S. retail stores, and to distributors in the United States and abroad involves a diverse set of legal issues. "It's fairly complex, because each segment has its own set of laws, rules, and regulations," says Bert who finds the work interesting. "I'm addicted to business development. As long as I'm learning something, I'm happy with it."

Bert and John's optimism, along with their eagerness to learn and succeed, are the reasons for their success.

They also are the reasons their Life is Good product line continues to expand. Hats, water bottles, boxer shorts, blankets, pajamas, sweats, and items for pets all are available. After years of hard work, Bert and John Jacobs have found that, indeed, Life is Good!

"Bert and John's optimism, along with their eagerness to learn and succeed, are the reasons for their success."

Life is good.®

CHAPTER 25

Forms of Business Organization

25-1 Main Forms of Organization

25-2 Creating and Terminating Partnerships

25-3 Operating Partnerships

HOT DEBATE

© GETTY IMAGES/PHOTODISC

One morning while shaving Bill felt a lump in his neck. The lump seemed to grow over the next few days, so Bill sought treatment in St. John's hospital emergency room. The emergency room physician, Dr. Compton, listened to Bill's worried statement. Then, after nothing more than a visual exam, the doctor told Bill not to worry and started to leave the examining room. Unsatisfied, Bill grabbed Compton's hand and placed it on the lump. The doctor shrugged his shoulders in disapproval but did order a set of X rays to be taken. The X rays ordered by the doctor proved negative, and Bill was dismissed. Months passed, and the lump grew. Seeing the lump one day, a friend recommended Bill see another physician. That doctor and his partners diagnosed the lump as being a malignant growth on Bill's carotid artery and indicated he had but a few months to live.

Where Do You Stand?

1. From an ethical standpoint, identify the parties and organizations that should share blame for what happened to Bill.

2. What parties should be held legally liable for what happened to Bill?

Main Forms of Organization

PRINCIPAL BUSINESS FORMS

WHAT'S YOUR VERDICT?

Shirley wants to open a sporting goods store. She hesitates because she thinks the expenses would be prohibitive. She lists the costs of renting or buying the required space; hiring help; buying a computer to keep records; buying a large inventory; obtaining a charter from the state; and paying for licenses, legal fees, and accounting fees.

Should these costs cause her to drop her plans?

There are three principal forms of business organization:

1. sole proprietorships
2. partnerships
3. corporations

SOLE PROPRIETORSHIPS

Of the three principal forms, the simplest, most flexible, and easiest to start is the **sole proprietorship**, which is owned by one person. The owner of a sole proprietorship has relatively unlimited control over the business and keeps all the profits. However, the sole proprietor also has unlimited personal responsibility for all debts and for other liabilities that the business may incur. If the proprietor is sued for breach of contract or for a tort the proprietor or his or her employees commit, the proprietor's own home, car, and belongings as well as all of his or her business property may be seized to pay the damages awarded by courts. Careful management, along with adequate public liability insurance, limits those risks and makes them tolerable.

Sole proprietorships are by far the most often used form of business organization. Most independent contractors listed in the Yellow Pages of telephone directories are sole proprietors. Many expand their businesses with the help of employees and agents. Corporations are fewer in number, but they have a much larger sales dollar volume and employ many more workers.

There are no particular legal requirements for organizing or conducting a sole proprietorship. When started, many sole proprietorships are conducted out of the owner's home, garage, or van. No help need be hired, no computer is required for the simple records, and inventory may be limited and often purchased on credit. No charter is needed from the state, although a local business license and perhaps a permit to collect sales taxes for transmittal to the state, may be required. Some types of businesses, such as those selling food or securities, are subject to special governmental regulations regardless of the legal form of organization.

Why might the owner of this new coffee shop have chosen to organize the business as a sole proprietorship?

In *What's Your Verdict?* Shirley should not necessarily drop her plans. She should survey her potential market to confirm the need for such a business in that location at the present time. She also should be reasonably sure that she has the necessary knowledge and ability, as well as sufficient capital, for the venture. Usually, it is highly desirable to have prior experience as an employee in a similar business

PARTNERSHIPS

A **partnership** is an association of two or more persons to carry on, as co-owners, a business for profit. This may be referred to as a general partnership. Under the Uniform Partnership Act (UPA), the law that governs partnership in most states, the general partners share all profits equally. They also equally share any losses that are suffered. The partners may agree among themselves to a different distribution. However, just as with a sole proprietor, each partner remains fully responsible for the firm's liabilities. This unlimited liability limits the popularity and utility of the general partnership form of business organization.

The positive feature of the partnership is that it combines the capital, labor, skill, and knowledge of two or more persons. Often the resulting combination serves to multiply the strength of the parties: one plus one equals three or more in talent and productivity. Unique abilities can be better developed and utilized through specialization. Thus bigger projects become manageable.

Because of their close relationship and ability to bind each other legally in contracts and torts involving third parties, partners need to be selected carefully. If possible, partners should be socially compatible, financially responsible, ethical and morally trustworthy, professionally competent, physically fit, and willing to work hard. As with sole proprietors, competence and integrity, coupled with adequate public liability insurance, make the risks of unlimited liability tolerable.

CORPORATIONS

A **corporation** is a legal entity that is treated as an artificial person by the law. It has an existence distinct or separate from the real persons who organize, own, and run it. Therefore, it is the corporation that makes or loses money. The corporation also may injure people and even commit crimes.

As a consequence of the corporation's being treated as an entity in its own right under the law, investors in a corporation only run the risk of losing what they have invested in it, not all their personal wealth. The corporation, but not the investors, may be hit with a large lawsuit. The corporation—not the investors—may lose money and go bankrupt as a consequence. This limit on the owners' potential risk makes the corporate form very attractive. Unlike the partnership the corporate form also features free transferability of ownership. A corporation can have perpetual life as a result. A partnership, however, ends if a partner withdraws, dies, or goes bankrupt.

Corporations have the ability to attract large sums of capital because investors' liability is limited. Efficient corporations generally have greater financial strength than do other forms of business organization. This enables corporations to attract superior workers by offering generous salaries and fringe benefits.

NETBookmark

Access lawxtra.swlearning.com and click on the link for Chapter 25. In the New York Loves Small Business home page, click on the arrow on the drop-down menu under "Starting Your Small Business." Then click on "business organization." Read the information and then answer these questions.

1. If you want to start operating a sole proprietorship in New York under a name other than your own, what document must you file with the state?

2. If you want to start operating a partnership in New York, what document must you file with the state?

lawxtra.swlearning.com

CHECKPOINT

What are the three main forms of business organization?

MAJOR FORMS OF BUSINESS ORGANIZATION

	Sole Proprietorship	Partnership	Corporation
Requirements for Organizing	None	Agreement of the parties	State charter; organizational fees
Legal Status	Owner is the business; not a separate entity	Not a separate entity in many states	Separate entity from owners
Liability	Unlimited liability	Unlimited liability (except limited partnership)	Limited liability of shareholders
Management	Owner decides	Partners have equal say in management unless otherwise specified in agreement	Directors (elected by shareholders) set policy and appoint officers
Dissolution	Owner decides; terminates upon owner's death	Terminates by agreement of partners or upon a partner's death, withdrawal, bankruptcy	Ends when charter terminated
Ease of formation	Just do it	Moderately difficult	Assistance of legal counsel required
Duration	Death or disinterest of proprietor	Death, bankruptcy, or withdrawal of any partner	Can be perpetual
Ability to attract professional managers	Poor	Moderate	Excellent

Assessment

lawxtra.swlearning.com

THINK ABOUT LEGAL CONCEPTS

1. Which form of business organization does not involve unlimited personal liability for its owners? (a) sole proprietorship (b) partnership (c) corporation

2. Which form of business organization does not terminate upon the death of its owner(s)? (a) sole proprietorship (b) partnership (c) corporation

3. Which form of business is the easiest to set up? (a) sole proprietorship (b) partnership (c) corporation

4. Which form of business has the greatest potential to bring together large sums of capital? (a) sole proprietorship (b) partnership (c) corporation

5. Which form of business has the greatest potential for attracting professional managers? (a) sole proprietorship (b) partnership (c) corporation

6. Which form of business organization needs a charter from the state? (a) sole proprietorship (b) partnership (c) corporation

7. The UPA governs (a) proprietorships (b) partnerships (c) corporations.

8. Which form of business organization is looked upon as being an artificial entity, separate from its owners? (a) sole proprietorship (b) partnership (c) corporation

THINK CRITICALLY ABOUT EVIDENCE

Study the situation, answer the questions, and then prepare arguments to support your answers.

9. One day Sol had an idea to make money. He went out and bought large blocks of tickets for the main entertainment attractions in Branson, Missouri, and then called several tour directors to see if they would buy them. When they did, Sol charged them a dollar extra per ticket. What form of business organization does Sol most likely have?

10. Sol hired Nadine to deliver the tickets in his car to the theaters just as the tour buses arrived. If Nadine has an accident on such an errand, what are the potential consequences for Sol's business and his personal assets?

11. After several months of brokering tickets to tour directors, Sol thought it would be a good idea if he offered his ticket service to people on the Internet. His friend Tom was a computer programmer, and Sol made him an offer to join the business. Tom would control computer marketing of the tickets and, rather than a salary, would receive a percentage of the profits. What form of business organization exists between Sol and Tom?

12. If Sol and Tom's employee has an accident while delivering tickets, what might the consequences be for their business and personal assets?

13. As Sol and Tom's business continued to grow, they decided to open a storefront on the main access road into Branson. Unfortunately, their business was still too new to get a loan from the bank, and their personal credit standings would not support a loan the size they needed. They did have some friends who were interested in investing in their business. However, the friends did not want to be exposed to unlimited personal liability. What type of business organization seems ideal in this situation, and why?

14. Sol and Tom decide to go forward with the new storefront and to organize as a corporation. Now the employee is delivering tickets and has an accident. What are the potential consequences for the owners' business and personal assets?

15. Sol and Tom have been running their business as a corporation for a decade. It has grown so much it is difficult to keep up with all the work. One day Sol mentions they could hire professional managers to run the business and live on the dividends from their stock ownership. Tom thought about this and said, "just because we want to hire a professional manager doesn't mean we could find one to work for us." "Actually, we're in the right business form to attract a good one," replied Sol. Is he correct?

Creating and Terminating Partnerships

CREATION OF A PARTNERSHIP

WHAT'S YOUR VERDICT?

Abbie Pinegar and her sister Ashlee wanted to form a partnership to run a hot dog stand at this year's county fair. After talking about what was required, they agreed that each would pay for one half of the supplies and rental of space for the stand. They also agreed that they would alternate days spent running the booth and that the profits would be split equally. Any decisions they could not agree on would be made by their mother.

Does their partnership agreement have to be in writing?

"**S**trong fences good neighbors make" is the old adage. The same is certainly true about "good partners." The strong fences of a partnership are the terms and conditions that the partners agree on to guide them in managing the partnership. These terms and conditions comprise the **partnership agreement**.

FORM AND CONTENT OF THE PARTNERSHIP AGREEMENT

Although best in an explicit written form, the partnership agreement need not be in writing unless required by the Statute of Frauds. As discussed previously, the Statute of Frauds requires a writing signed by the party being sued to make the contract enforceable if it cannot be performed within one year from the date it is made. Therefore, if two persons agree at the time they form their partnership that it is to last longer than one year, their agreement must be in writing and signed by both persons to be enforceable by both. In *What's Your Verdict?* the agreement to operate a booth in this year's fair does not have to be in writing.

If the parties do not agree on a specific length of time for their partnership to continue, their agreement need not be in writing. After all, the contract could be performed within one year, even though it could last for many years. Nonetheless, the time, resources, and detail involved make it highly desirable to put every partnership agreement in writing, preferably with the assistance of a lawyer. This encourages thoughtful review of the many potential problems of the new business. It also helps to avoid future costly controversies by spelling out rights and duties of the partners in advance. A sample partnership agreement with terms addressing common concerns of a partnership is found on page 450.

Why is it a good idea to put a partnership agreement in writing?

© GETTY IMAGES/PHOTODISC

GENERAL PARTNERSHIP AGREEMENT FORMING
"DOWN THE DRAIN"

Date, identity of partners, and purpose of partnership

By agreement made this 18th day of September, 20--, we Amy Brock, Martin Espinoza, and Gerald Hunt, the undersigned, all of Castletown, Kansas, hereby join in general partnership to conduct a plumbing installation and repair business and mutually agree to the following terms:

Name, location, and records availability

1. That the partnership shall be called "Down the Drain" and have its principal place of business at 166 Oak Street, Castletown, Kansas, at which address books containing the full and accurate records of partnership transactions shall be kept and be accessible to any partner at any reasonable time.

Duration and termination procedure

2. That the partnership shall continue in operation for an indefinite time until terminated by 90 days' notice provided by one or more of the partners and indicating his, her, or their desire to withdraw. Upon such notice an accounting shall be conducted and a division of the partnership assets made unless a partner wishes to acquire the whole business by paying a price determined by an arbitrator whose selection shall be agreed to by all three partners. Said price shall include goodwill, and the paying of same shall entitle the payor to continue the partnership business under the same name.

Capitalization

3. That each partner shall contribute to the partnership: $10,000 for initial working capital and the inventory and equipment (including trucks—which shall be marked with the partnership name, address, and logo) of their current individual plumbing businesses.

4. That in return for the capital contribution in item 3, each partner shall receive an undivided one-third interest in the partnership and its properties.

Funding of reserve

5. That a fund of $50,000 be set up and retained from the profits of the partnership business as a reserve fund. It being agreed that this fund shall be constituted on not less than 15 percent of the monthly profits until said amount has been accumulated.

Division of profits and losses, payout schedule

6. That the profits of the business shall be divided equally between the partners, that the losses shall be attributed according to the subsequent agreement, and that a determination of said profits and losses shall be made and profit shares paid to each partner on a monthly basis.

Account location, withdrawal procedure

7. That the partnership account shall be kept in the First National Bank of Castletown and that all withdrawals from same shall be by check bearing the signature of at least one of the partners.

Duties and limitations

8. That each partner shall devote his or her full efforts to the partnership business and shall not engage in another business without the other partners' permission.

Nonroutine decision-making procedure

9. That no partner shall cause to issue any commercial paper or shall enter into any agreements representing the partnership outside the normal conduct of the plumbing business without notice to the remaining partners and the consent of at least one other partner and further that all managerial and personnel decisions not covered by another section of this agreement shall be made with the assent of at least two of the partners.

IN AGREEMENT HERETO, WE ARE

Amy Brock   Martin Espinoza   Gerald Hunt

Signatures

Amy Brock   _Martin Espinoza_   _Gerald Hunt_

LEGAL RESEARCH

Using the Internet or library resources, determine what forms of business organization (for example, joint ventures, partnerships, or standalone entities) are available to U.S. businesses when they do business in the European Union or under NAFTA provisions in Mexico or Canada. What effects do the GATT requirements have on the choice of such business forms?

TYPES OF PARTNERSHIPS

Partnerships may be classified according to their purpose and according to the extent of the liability of the partners.

CLASSIFICATION BY PURPOSE Classified by purpose, partnerships are either trading or non-trading. A **trading partnership** buys and sells goods and services commercially. A **non-trading partnership** provides professional and noncommercial assistance, such as legal, medical, or accounting advice.

CLASSIFICATION BY EXTENT OF LIABILITY Classified by the extent of liability of partners, partnerships are either general or limited.

GENERAL PARTNERS In a **general partnership**, all the partners exercise managerial control over the firm, bind it in contracts, and perform other functions with full legal authority. As a consequence, each **general partner** has full personal liability for debts of the firm. (When the text refers simply to a "partnership," you may assume it means a general partnership. Otherwise the specific type of partnership will be labeled.)

General partners may be classified as silent, secret, or dormant. A **silent partner** may be known to the public as a partner but takes no active part in management. A **secret partner** is not known to the public as a partner yet participates in management. A **dormant partner** is neither known to the public as a partner nor active in management. All such partners, when identified, can be held liable without limit for partnership debts.

Persons determined by a court to be nominal partners also may find themselves liable for the partnership debts. **Nominal partners** hold themselves out as partners, or let others do so, but are not truly partners. Parents sometimes become nominal partners to assist children who have taken over the family business. Consequently, if a partnership liability arises, they are liable as partners. A third party, acting in good faith, may rely on the reputation of the nominal partner and therefore extend credit to the firm. If so, all partners who consented to the misrepresentation are fully liable. If all members consent, the firm is liable as well.

LIMITED PARTNERS In a **limited partnership**, at least one partner must be a general partner, with unlimited liability. However, one or more partners may be **limited partners**. A limited partner's liability for firm debts and losses is limited to the amount of capital the partner invested.

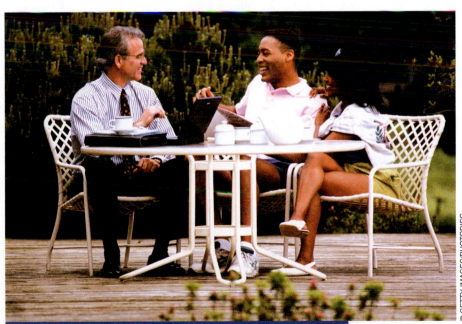

Assume that the man and woman on the right are celebrities and co-owners of a new restaurant with the man on the left. The public knows the couple has an ownership interest in the restaurant. However, the couple is not involved in its management. What type of partner would the couple most likely be?

© GETTY IMAGES/PHOTODISC

The Uniform Limited Partnership Act (ULPA) governs limited partnerships and has been adopted with few amendments in almost all the states. Unlike a general partnership, a limited partnership can be created only by proper execution, recording, and publication of a certificate that identifies the partners and states basic facts about their agreement. Limited partners contribute capital and share profits and losses with general partners.

Why would it be wise for a limited partner to stay clear of any circumstance that might bring her or his status into question?

However, limited partners must not participate in the managerial control of the business. If they do so, they lose their status and become liable without limit as general partners. This rule has been relaxed and redefined of late by the Revised Uniform Limited Partnership Act (RULPA), which has been adopted by a majority of the states. Under RULPA, a limited partner does not participate in the managerial control of the business solely by doing such things as

1. being an independent contractor for, or an agent or employee of, the limited partnership
2. consulting with or advising a general partner
3. attending a meeting of the general partners

IN THIS CASE

Ashlee and Abbie were so successful in running the hot dog stand at the county fair that they wanted to open a small restaurant on a main street in town specializing in hot dog "cuisine." To do so, they needed new capital. As a consequence, they invited their mother to invest in their business as a limited partner. As such she would share in the profits, yet her exposure to loss would be only for the amount of the investment she might make.

4. proposing, approving, or disapproving (by vote or otherwise) the dissolution, change in the nature of the business, admission or removal of a general or limited partner, or amendment to the partnership agreement.

Nonetheless, a limited partner is well-advised to stay clear of any circumstance that might bring her or his status into question.

STATUS OF MINORS

A minor who enters into a partnership agreement generally has special status. In most states, such a partner retains all of the rights and privileges of a minor. Thus, the minor normally can plead minority as a defense and not pay if sued by a creditor of the partnership. The minor may also withdraw and thus dissolve the partnership without being liable for breach of contract. Some states, however, do hold minors liable on contracts made as either an individual proprietor or as a partner in connection with business.

POWERS OF A PARTNERSHIP

Under the UPA, a partnership, in some respects, is legally treated as an entity. This means that it is a distinct, real being in the eyes of the law. A partnership has the power to

1. take title to and transfer property in its own name

2. be regarded as a principal, for which each partner may act as agent, making contracts in the firm's name

3. use its own assets as security for loans and to pay its creditors before any individual partner's assets may be seized.

STATUS OF A PARTNERSHIP

For most purposes, a partnership legally is treated as an aggregation or group of individual partners, with the following results.

1. Each partner must pay income taxes on her or his share of the net profits even if they are retained in the business rather than distributed. The firm pays no income tax but files an information return. This enables the Internal Revenue Service (IRS) to cross-check the accuracy of the partners' individual tax returns.

2. The firm must sue and be sued in the name of all the partners unless there is a state statute allowing such actions as an entity.

3. All debts of the firm not paid out of firm assets are chargeable to every partner. (This reflects the unlimited liability of general partners, which many persons understandably fear.)

4. When any partner drops out of the firm for any reason, the partnership is dissolved. However, prior arrangements can be made to continue the operation of the partnership business without interruption.

5. Because of the uncertain future of a partnership, it is handicapped when it comes to attracting large sums of new capital beyond the amount originally invested.

Note that a partnership is to be distinguished from a **joint venture**. A joint venture occurs when two or more persons or firms combine their resources and skills to do a complex project. Because the joint venture is so similar to a general partnership (which also may be formed to do a single project), many courts, as well as the IRS, treat it as such. However, unlike the rule for general partnerships, death of a participant does not cause dissolution of the joint venture. The joint venture normally continues until the project is completed.

CHECKPOINT

What is the difference between a general partner and a limited partner?

TERMINATION OF A PARTNERSHIP

WHAT'S YOUR VERDICT?

Chris and Chase had a successful manufacturing business in which they were equal and only partners. As they approached retirement age, Chase wanted to move the factory from Missouri to the Florida Keys. Chris, who had many investments in and around the current factory location, did not. After a year of disagreement, their relationship and then their business began to suffer losses. Finally, they brought suit over the issue.

What might a court do in this situation?

When any partner ceases to be associated in the ordinary operation of the business, **dissolution** of the partnership occurs. Dissolution is normally followed by a **winding-up period**, which concludes with the actual termination or ending of the partnership. During the winding-up period, all partnership business in process at the time of dissolution is concluded, creditors of the business are satisfied if possible, and each partner's share is accounted for and distributed. When the winding-up process is completed, **termination** of the legal existence of the partnership actually occurs.

Dissolution of a partnership may be caused by action of one or more of the partners, operation of law, or court decree.

BY ACTION OF ONE OR MORE OF THE PARTNERS

A partnership may be dissolved by agreement of the parties. For example, if the original agreement is for one year, the partnership concludes at the end of that year. Sometimes a firm is organized for a specific purpose, such as the development of a large tract of farmland into a subdivision for houses. Sale of the last lot and house would end the partnership. Also, the parties may unanimously agree at any time to terminate their relationship.

Withdrawal of a partner for any reason dissolves the partnership. The partnership agreement may permit such withdrawal without penalty, preferably after a reasonable advance notice. In such case, the withdrawing partner would not be liable to the remaining partner(s) for any drop in profits that might result. If the withdrawal violates their agreement, the withdrawing partner would be liable in damages for any injury resulting from the breach of contract. If the organization is a **partnership at will**, a partner normally may withdraw at any time without liability to associates. The withdrawing partner could be liable for resulting losses if the sudden withdrawal was unreasonable.

BY OPERATION OF LAW

Death of any partner dissolves the partnership. This is a serious disadvantage of the partnership form of organization. Prudent partners simply anticipate this inevitable

event and specify what action shall be taken when it happens. For example, they may agree that the surviving partner(s) will continue with a new firm and pay for the decedent's share over a period of years.

Bankruptcy, a kind of financial death, also automatically dissolves the partnership. This is true whether the bankruptcy is suffered by any of the partners or by the firm itself. Although rare, subsequent illegality also dissolves the partnership. For example, a professional partnership of doctors would be dissolved if any member lost the license to practice.

BY COURT DECREE

Partners, if living, usually arrange for dissolution privately. If necessary, however, one partner may petition a court to order dissolution if another

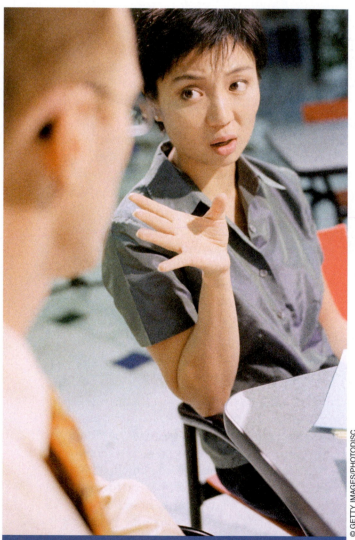

Imagine that this woman is in the process of withdrawing from a partnership. If the business was organized as a partnership at will, what, if any, liability might she face?

partner has become insane, otherwise incapacitated, or guilty of serious misconduct affecting the business.

A court also may act if continuation is impractical or if the firm is losing money continuously and there is little or no prospect for success. This could happen when there are irreconcilable differences between the partners. For example, irreconcilable differences could be the result of decisions to add or drop a major line of merchandise or, as Chris and Chase in *What's Your Verdict?*, to move a factory to another location to reduce labor costs.

CHECKPOINT
Name the three main ways a partnership may be terminated.

25-2 Assessment

Xtra! Study Tools

lawxtra.swlearning.com

THINK ABOUT LEGAL CONCEPTS

1. Which of the following is active in management of a partnership but unknown to the public? (a) silent partner (b) dormant partner (c) limited partner (d) none of the above

2. Which of the following is known to the public but does not participate in management? (a) silent partner (b) dormant partner (c) limited partner (d) none of the above

3. Can a partnership agreement be structured so as to continue the partnership business even if the partnership is dissolved? **Yes or No?**

4. Which of the following does not participate in management and is only potentially liable for her/his investment in the partnership? (a) silent partner (b) dormant partner (c) limited partner (d) none of the above

5. If a partner becomes insane the partnership is dissolved. **True or False?**

6. If you form a partnership to prepare income taxes for businesses over the next five years, does the agreement have to be in writing? **Yes or No?**

THINK CRITICALLY ABOUT EVIDENCE

Study the situation, answer the questions, and then prepare arguments to support your answers.

7. Tole and Hunt orally agreed to sell Christmas trees and share any profits or losses equally. What type of organization have they formed? Must they pay income taxes individually on their profits or will the organization pay as a legal entity?

8. Peterson and Goebel orally agree to fix up a park for the local children. What type of organization have they formed? Could they raise money for the group without changing to a different type of organization?

9. Brooke was 17 years old when he entered into a partnership with Beale, age 22. Their agreement to operate a dog-training school was for three years. After six months, Brooke decided to withdraw. Was he liable for breach of contract? Why or why not?

10. Sanferd and Sontag were partners in a very successful real estate development firm. After all the lots in their latest subdivision were sold they decided to look around for another undeveloped part of town. Acting independently of one another one day, they both bought separate sections of land for the partnership to use for its next subdivision. Neither one had the other sign the contract for purchase. Is the partnership bound to buy both parcels of land? Why or why not?

11. Zeno, Smith, and Cospit were partners in Fly by Night, a small, overnight, parcel delivery service. In forming their partnership, they provided for continuation of the business if the partnership should end for any reason. Their written agreement specified that the business would continue uninterrupted, under the same name, with management and control by a new partnership composed of the surviving partners. The business is now showing a profit of more than $500,000 a year and has net assets valued at more than $5,000,000. If a partner dies, how should the deceased partner's share be valued? How will the partnership be able to pay it?

Operating Partnerships

A PARTNER'S POWERS

WHAT'S YOUR VERDICT?

Jerico customarily bought the cleaning solvent for the Lake Country Cleaners from Solvent Solvers of Camdenton, Missouri. Unknown to Jerico, however, his two other partners in Lake Country Cleaners had voted to stop doing business with Solvent Solvers due to a dispute over a bill. Before finding out about their decision, Jerico contracted to buy five drums of solvent at $500 a barrel from Solvent Solvers.

Will the partnership be bound by Jerico's contract?

A partner's powers are far reaching. They are comprised of specific rights and the implied authority necessary to exercise those rights. In the absence of contrary agreement, each partner has the same rights as every other. Partners may, however, agree as to who shall have particular rights and duties.

A PARTNER'S RIGHTS

The principal rights a partner has include the following:

RIGHT TO PARTICIPATE IN MANAGEMENT Every partner, as a co-owner of the business, has an equal right to participate in its management. Acting alone, a partner may buy, sell, hire, fire, and make other routine decisions in carrying on the ordinary day-to-day activities of the firm. In effect, each partner acts as an agent for the firm and for the other partners. All

partners are bound by the result, unless the partner lacked the necessary authority, and the person with whom the contract was made knew this. In *What's Your Verdict?* the solvent contract resulted from a routine decision by Jerico, a partner with apparent authority. Consequently, the partnership is bound.

In addition to routine decisions, each partner has the right to do the things normally done by managers in similar firms. This includes the right to inspect the partnership books at all times, unless otherwise agreed.

When a difference of opinion arises as to ordinary matters connected with the business, a majority vote of the partners decides the issue. Unless otherwise agreed, each partner has one vote regardless of the amount of capital contributed. If there is an even number of partners and they split equally on a question, no action can be taken. A pattern of such deadlocks can eventually lead to dissolution. To forestall such an outcome, it is often helpful to provide in the partnership agreement that deadlocks over specified matters shall be settled by arbitration.

Unanimous agreement of all the partners is required to make any change in the written

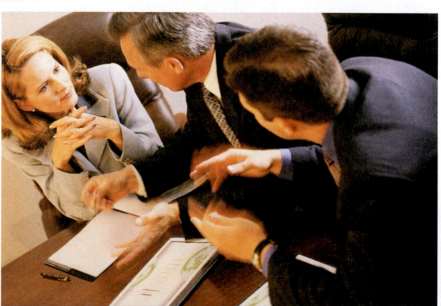

When a difference of opinion among partners arises as to ordinary business matters, how is the issue typically resolved?

© GETTY IMAGES/PHOTODISC

partnership agreement, however minor it may be. All partners also must agree to any fundamental change that affects the very nature of the business (for example, changing its principal activity or location). In addition, under the UPA, unanimous agreement is required for decisions to

- assign partnership property to creditors
- confess judgment (allow a plaintiff to obtain a judgment against the firm without a trial)
- submit a partnership claim or liability to arbitration
- do any act that would make it impossible to carry on the business.

The preceding rules governing the use of managerial authority may be changed by agreement. Often, by agreement, work is divided according to talents and interests. Certain partners have exclusive control over specific activities, such as selling, purchasing, or accounting and finance. By specializing in this way, efficiency and productivity may increase.

RIGHT TO PROFITS Partners are entitled to all profits earned. In the absence of contrary agreement, both profits and losses are shared equally regardless of different amounts of capital contributed or time spent. However, the partners may agree to divide the profits and/or the losses in any percentages desired. Often, profits will be shared equally, but a partner with a large amount of outside income may agree, for tax purposes, to take all the losses. Outsiders, however, are not bound by such internal agreements and may hold any or all general partners liable without limit for all partnership debts. If one partner is

forced to pay an entire debt it is up to that partner to recover from the other partners their rightful share.

RIGHT IN PARTNERSHIP PROPERTY Partnership property consists of all cash and other property originally contributed by the partners as well as all property later acquired by the firm. The property is held in a special form of co-ownership called **tenancy in partnership**. In tenancy in partnership, each partner is a co-owner of the entire partnership property and is not the sole owner of any part of it. For example, if a firm of two partners owns two identical trucks, neither partner may claim exclusive ownership of either vehicle. Therefore, a partner has no salable or assignable interest in any particular item of property belonging to the partnership. However, the interest of a partner in the firm may be sold or assigned to another party. The buyer or assignee is not a partner but is entitled to that partner's share of the profits, and of the assets upon dissolution.

Each partner has an equal right to use firm property for partnership purposes. However, no partner may use firm property for personal purposes unless all other partners consent.

RIGHT TO EXTRA COMPENSATION A partner who invests more capital, brings in more business, or works longer and harder than his or her associates is not entitled to extra pay or a larger share of the profits unless all the partners so agree. Common sense and fairness often dictate that a partner who gives more should receive more, but all partners must agree to this.

A PARTNER'S AUTHORITY

Generally, the law implies to each member the authority necessary to carry on the business. This includes the authority to do the following:

MAKE BINDING CONTRACTS FOR THE FIRM Acting within the scope of the particular business, each partner can make binding contracts deemed by that partner to be necessary or desirable, regardless of the possible folly of the deals. Any internal agreement limiting powers of a partner is binding on the partners, but not on third parties that do not know about the limitation. However, a partner who violates such internal agreement is liable to the other partners for any resulting loss.

IN THIS CASE

When Solvent Solvers presented their bill for $2,500 against the Lake Country Cleaners, the partners who had voted against doing business with Solvent Solvers refused to pay it. Jerico, the partner who had negotiated the contract that led to the $2,500 claim, was then sued by Solvent Solvers and made to pay the bill in full. The partners were to split profits and losses equally under the partnership agreement. Therefore, it will be up to Jerico to recover the other partner's share from them directly.

No partner can bind the firm in contracts that are beyond the scope of the firm's business as publicly disclosed. Partners engaged in an aerial photography business, for example, would not be bound by a contract by one of the partners to use the plane for air ambulance service. Even if a partner has acted beyond authority in making a contract, the other partners may choose to ratify the act. If they do, the partnership is bound, as a principal would be in an ordinary agency.

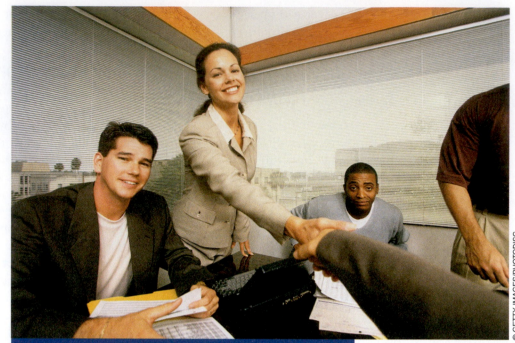

Imagine that this woman is a partner and has just closed a deal with clients on behalf of the partnership. Under what circumstances would the other partners not be bound by the resulting contract?

RECEIVE MONEY OWED TO AND SETTLE CLAIMS AGAINST THE FIRM In the eyes of the law, all partners are assumed to have received any payments to the firm even if the partner who actually received the money disappears. Also, each partner may adjust debts of the firm by agreement with creditors. Each may compromise firm claims against debtors, settling for less than is due. However, a partner may not discharge a personal debt by agreeing to offset it against a debt owed to the partnership.

BORROW MONEY IN THE FIRM'S NAME In a trading partnership, any partner can borrow for partnership purposes. In such borrowing, the partner can execute promissory notes binding the firm and can pledge or mortgage partnership property as security. Partners in a nontrading partnership generally do not have such power.

SELL A partner can sell in the regular course of business any of the firm's goods and give customary warranties. Acting alone, however, a partner may not sell the entire inventory in a bulk transfer because this could end the business.

BUY Any partner can buy for cash or credit any property within the scope of the business.

DRAW AND CASH CHECKS AND DRAFTS A partner can draw checks and drafts for partnership purposes and can endorse and cash checks payable to the firm.

HIRE AND FIRE EMPLOYEES AND AGENTS Each partner has the authority to hire and fire employees, agents, and independent contractors to help carry on the business.

RECEIVE NOTICE OF MATTERS AFFECTING THE PARTNERSHIP When one partner is served with a summons and complaint against the firm, all are deemed to have received the notice, even if they are not informed. Likewise, one partner's declarations and admissions in carrying on the business bind all partners even when contrary to the best interests of the firm.

CHECKPOINT

Name the four principal rights of a partner.

A PARTNER'S DUTIES AND LIABILITIES

WHAT'S YOUR VERDICT?

Fineman was one of five partners in a firm of certified public accountants. Her duties included management of the office. As such, she bought all office equipment. Recently, she purchased an advanced photocopying system for $25,000, a competitive price. Several days later, she met the seller, Fisher, at a dinner party. Fineman convinced Fisher to give her a 5 percent discount on the price because clients of her accounting firm might be inclined to buy similar equipment when they learned of its use from her. Fineman now claims the $1,250 discount belongs to her alone because she obtained it on her own time after the original contract was signed.

Is she correct?

Inherent in the nature of a partnership are certain duties and liabilities. The duties have at their core the fiduciary concept that the interests of the partnership must be placed ahead of personal interests.

A PARTNER'S DUTIES

By law or by agreement each partner has a duty to do the following.

COMPLY WITH PARTNERSHIP AGREEMENT AND DECISIONS
Each partner must comply with the partnership agreement, including later provisions properly added and related decisions properly made.

USE REASONABLE CARE
In performing partnership duties, partners must use reasonable care. However, they are not personally liable for the full loss caused by their own errors in judgment, mistakes, and incompetence. Any resulting financial burden rests on the firm and is shared by all partners. This harsh reality affirms the importance of selecting competent persons as partners.

ACT WITH INTEGRITY AND GOOD FAITH
A partnership is a fiduciary relationship of utmost trust and confidence. Each partner is legally bound to act with the highest integrity and good faith in dealing with the other partner(s). No partner may personally retain any profit or benefit unless the other partners are informed and consent. In *What's Your Verdict?* Fineman was wrong in claiming the discount. All profits or benefits flowing from the firm's business belong to the firm, to be shared by all partners equally or as otherwise agreed.

NOT CONDUCT COMPETING BUSINESS
Unless there is a contrary agreement, a partner may not do any business that competes with the partnership or prevents performance of duties for the firm. A partner may, however, attend to personal affairs for profit, as long as the firm's business is not sacrificed. A partner who withdraws from the firm may compete with it unless validly prohibited by the partnership agreement.

KEEP ACCURATE RECORDS
A partner should keep accurate records of all business done for the firm and give the firm all money belonging to it. Moreover, every partner should disclose to the other partner(s) all important information that concerns the firm's business.

A PARTNER'S POTENTIAL LIABILITIES

Between or among themselves, partners may make any agreements they choose regarding authority to run the business. Outsiders, however, may not be aware of such internal agreements. When this is the case, the partnership firm and all of its members are liable without limit for all obligations of the firm that arise out of contracts made by any partner within the scope of the firm's business.

The partnership and all partners are liable when any partner commits a tort (for example, negligence or fraud) while acting within the ordinary course of the business. The partner who is the wrongdoer would be obligated to indemnify the partnership for any damages it had to pay to the injured party. If the other partners had authorized or participated in the tort, all would share the blame and no indemnity would be payable.

Liability for certain crimes committed in the course of business, such as selling alcoholic beverages to minors, also is imposed on the partnership and all the partners. Generally, however, if the business of the firm does not require the criminal activity, neither the partnership nor the partners who do not authorize or take part in the crime are held criminally liable. Thus, a partner who kills a pedestrian while negligently driving a company car on firm business will alone be criminally liable. However, the wrongdoer as well as the firm and the other partners are civilly liable for damages.

When a judgment is obtained against a partnership, and the partnership assets are exhausted, the individually owned property of the general partners, such as their houses and cars, legally may be seized and sold to pay the debt. Creditors of the respective individual partners, however, have first claim to such property. Any partner who pays an obligation of the firm with personal assets legally is entitled to recover a proportionate share from each of the other partners.

A partner cannot escape responsibility for firm debts by withdrawing from the partnership. One who withdraws remains liable for all debts incurred while a member. A new partner who joins the firm is liable for both existing and new debts of the business. However, creditors with claims that arose before the new partner joined the firm are limited, with respect to the new partner, to action against only the new partner's share of partnership property.

Law Brief

People sometimes join together for social, political, charitable, educational, or general welfare purposes. Examples are churches, private schools, civic clubs, fraternities and sororities, labor unions, and volunteer fire departments. These groups do not conduct business for profit, although they may raise money for activities. Such groups may organize as unincorporated, nonprofit associations. Participating members generally are not liable for debts of the organization. Officers and individual members may voluntarily guarantee the organization's debts. Sometimes such groups organize as nonprofit corporations.

● ●

CHECKPOINT
What are the duties of partners?

25-3 Assessment

Xtra! Study Tools
lawxtra.swlearning.com

THINK ABOUT LEGAL CONCEPTS

1. _?_ agreement of all the partners is required to make any change in a written partnership agreement.

2. Partnership property is held by the partners in a(n) _?_ in partnership.

3. A partner may engage in other businesses, even if they compete with the partnership. **True or False?**

4. Every general partner has an equal right to participate in management of the firm. **True or False?**

5. A partner who invests more time or money in the partnership has a right to a larger percentage of the profits. **True or False?**

6. Any general partner can buy for cash or credit any property within the scope of the partnership business. **True or False?**

7. Which of the following is not a duty of a partner? (a) comply with partnership decisions (b) not conduct competing business (c) keep accurate records (d) All of the above are duties.

THINK CRITICALLY ABOUT EVIDENCE

Study the situation, answer the questions, and then prepare arguments to support your answers.

8. Laird and Ball were partners in an indoor tennis center. Laird, a wealthy surgeon, contributed all the capital. Ball, a former tennis champion with an international reputation, contributed her name and agreed to work full time at the center. They agreed to split the profits equally. The losses, however, were all to be charged to Laird. Can the partners legally receive different proportions of the losses and the profits?

9. Adams, Starnes, and Williams were partners in a burglar and fire alarm service. Adams would mount his own camper cabin on the back of one of the company's pickup trucks every weekend and drive it into the country on overnight fishing trips. Starnes would take the company's laptop computer home every weekend to work on her version of the "great American novel." On weekends, Williams used the company's photocopying machine to run off copies of the weekly bulletins for his church. No partner was aware of any other partner's action. Did each have a legal right to utilize the firm's equipment? Why or why not?

10. Aki, Degas, and Kline were partners in an air-conditioning business. They obtained a $275,000 contract to install units in a candy factory. Long before the job was finished, Kline accepted the final payment of $100,000 and disappeared with the money. Must Aki and Degas absorb the loss and complete the job for the $175,000 already paid to them, without being paid an additional $100,000 by the candy factory?

PREVENT LEGAL DIFFICULTIES

When considering entering into a small business...

1. Carefully evaluate the level of commitment of time, energy, and financial resources necessary for success.

2. Be sure to comply with applicable licensing, registration, and other legal requirements.

3. If you utilize the partnership form, put the partnership agreement in writing with the aid of a qualified lawyer. Include appropriate language covering each partner's

   - duties and authority
   - share of profits and losses, if not intended to be equal
   - salary or right to withdraw earnings (drawing account)
   - vacation and sick-leave rights, and rights to withdraw from the partnership
   - periodic valuation of each partner's interest
   - methods for raising additional capital if needed
   - possible addition or withdrawal of a partner
   - amicable resolution of disputes, as by arbitration
   - possible continuation of the business after dissolution

CONCEPTS IN BRIEF

25-1 Main Forms of Organization

1. The owner of a sole proprietorship has relatively unlimited control over the business and keeps all the profits.

2. The sole proprietor also has unlimited personal responsibility for all debts and for other liabilities that the business may incur.

3. General partners share all profits equally. They also equally share all losses if any are suffered.

4. A corporation is treated as an artificial person by the law. As such it has an existence distinct or separate from the real persons who organize, own, and run it.

5. The major advantage of the corporate form of organization is that its owners risk losing only what they have invested in it. Due to this limited risk, corporations also may attract larger sums of capital than do other forms of business organization.

25-2 Creating and Terminating Partnerships

6. The time, resources, and detail involved make it highly desirable to put every partnership agreement in writing, preferably with the assistance of a lawyer.

7. Partnerships may be classified according to their purpose and according to the extent of the liability of the partners.

8. Under the UPA, a partnership, in some respects, is legally treated as an entity. This means that it is a distinct, real being in the eyes of the law.

25-3 Operating Partnerships

9. A partner's powers are comprised of specific rights and the implied authority necessary to facilitate the exercise of those rights.

10. In the absence of contrary agreement, each partner has the same rights as every other.

YOUR LEGAL VOCABULARY

Match each statement with the term that it best defines. Some terms may not be used.

1. Simplest form of business organization
2. Association of two or more to do business as co-owners for profit
3. Partnership where all partners have full personal liability
4. Partner with limited liability
5. Partner who is publicly known but not actively managing
6. Partner who is not publicly known but is actively managing
7. Form of ownership by which partners hold partnership property
8. Conclusion of a partnership's legal existence
9. Partner who is not publicly known and not actively managing
10. Partnership that provides professional and noncommercial assistance or advice
11. Change in partners' relationship due to a partner's ceasing to be associated with the partnership's ongoing purpose
12. Artificial person created as a legal entity by the authority of federal or state law

a. corporation
b. dissolution
c. dormant partner
d. general partner
e. general partnership
f. joint venture
g. limited partner
h. limited partnership
i. nominal partner
j. non-trading partnership
k. partnership
l. partnership agreement
m. partnership at will
n. secret partner
o. silent partner
p. sole proprietorship
q. tenancy in partnership
r. termination
s. trading partnership
t. winding-up period

REVIEW LEGAL CONCEPTS

13. What are the major problems with the sole proprietorship form?

14. Why would someone want to be a limited partner?

15. What interest does the state have in allowing businesses to adopt the corporate form?

16. If you were a professional manager looking for a lifetime or even a long-term position, under what terms would you consider a partnership or a sole proprietorship as a potential employer?

WRITE ABOUT LEGAL CONCEPTS

17. Design a form of business organization that would be especially useful to a small business owner. What would be its attributes?

18. What protection can you design into your business form in exercise 17 for small investors that have no part in the management of the business?

19. **HOT DEBATE** After experimental surgery saved his life, Bill filed suit against St. John's. He then discovered that the emergency room was not run by the hospital but by a subcontractor, Emergency Physicians, Inc. Bill also found that at the time he was treated there, Dr. Compton was a recovering drug addict and had lost his license to practice in Texas, but he could still practice in Bill's state. The X rays Dr. Compton had ordered only showed Bill's neck from the top of the lump up. St. John's hospital has petitioned the court to be dismissed as a defendant. It contends that only Dr. Compton and Emergency Physicians, Inc., should be held liable. Write a statement supporting St. John's position or one advocating it be held liable as well.

MAKE ACADEMIC CONNECTIONS

20. **ECONOMICS** Research and then write a one-page paper comparing the economic potential of the sole proprietorship to that of the partnership and corporation.

THINK CRITICALLY ABOUT EVIDENCE

Study the situation, answer the questions, and then prepare arguments to support your answers.

21. At the end of the school year, you hire the best students to write comprehensive study guides for the classes they have just completed. Over the summer you then compile these guides, print them on your computer printer, and bind them. When school reopens in the fall, you offer your "Class Busters" for sale. The authors of the guides are paid a percentage royalty on each sale and you pocket the profits. Which form of business organization would you choose for your enterprise?

22. Jonnas and Schmidt entered into a partnership for five years to conduct a catering business. It proved to be very successful. However, after two years, Schmidt's husband's employer offered him a promotion and transfer to corporate headquarters in Los Angeles, 2,000 miles away. Schmidt and her husband decided that he should accept the promotion and they would move. Could she sell out to Topper, a trustworthy, well-qualified assistant, transferring all duties and assigning all her rights, title, and interest in the firm? Could she simply assign her interest to Topper?

23. The written agreement of a professional partnership stated that, during the first year of operations, no partner could draw more than $300 earnings per week, and that no partner could take a vacation. All members would have to rely on personal savings and credit if they needed more funds. The business prospered beyond expectations. After six months, four of the five partners agreed to increase the permitted draw to $500 a week, and three of the five voted to permit up to one week of vacation without pay. Are these modifications legal and binding?

24. Stanton and Tokun agree to work together as partners for a year. Both are experienced in treating wooden shingle and shake roofs to make them fire resistant and waterproof. Stanton puts up the $20,000 capital needed for equipment and supplies. Both agree to work full time, and each draws a salary of $2,500 a month. Stanton does all of the difficult sales work, as well as helping on site. Tokun is slow on the job and repeatedly fails to show up, falsely claiming to be sick. In fact, he goes fishing and hunting on long weekends. At the end of the year, the firm shows a net profit of $25,000 after all expenses and the return of Stanton's capital contribution. How should the net profit be divided? Why?

25. Lewis owned a vacant building. He persuaded Dinkelspeel to open and to conduct a business called The Buffet in the property. Together, they purchased furniture, fixtures, and merchandise. They agreed that Dinkelspeel was to run the business and that profits were to be divided equally. Lewis's interest was not to be disclosed to the public, although he was to raise necessary funds and provide the building space. When the International Association of Credit Men sued both parties for goods sold to The Buffet, Lewis denied liability as a partner. Is he a partner? If so, what kind? If he is a partner, what is his liability? (*International Association of Credit Men v. Lewis*, 50 Wyo. 380, 62 P.2d 294)

26. On January 1 Vernon and Engel became partners in a food brokerage business. Later, they disagreed about the way profits were being divided and expenses were being paid. On August 1 they dissolved the partnership by mutual agreement. Vernon ran the business during the winding-up period. He claimed that Engel had violated their agreement and therefore was not entitled to his share of the profits. Vernon also argued that because he had carried on the business during the winding-up period, Engel was not entitled to any commissions collected during that time. Is Vernon right? (*Engel v. Vernon*, 215 N.W.2d 506)

27. Gast brought suit for back wages against a partnership headed by general partner Petsinger. To improve his chances of recovering a court award, Gast maintained that the limited partners in the business were really general partners and were fully liable along with Petsinger. Gast based his claim on the partnership agreement that gave the limited partners the rights and powers to receive distributions of profits and dissolution funds; prevent the transfer of assets of the firm; examine the books and records; attend meetings; hear reports of the general partner; and transfer, sell, or assign their interests to third parties. Should the limited partners in the agreement be considered general partners? (*Gast v. Petsinger*, 228 Pa. Super. 394, 323 A.2d 371)

28. Cooper and Isaacs were partners in a business that sold and distributed janitorial supplies. Their written agreement provided that the partnership "shall continue until terminated by sale of interests, mutual consent, retirement, death or incompetency of a partner." After eight years, Cooper filed an action seeking dissolution because of irreconcilable differences between the partners regarding matters of policy. He also asked for appointment of a receiver to manage the partnership property until the business was wound up. Isaacs claimed such dissolution was in violation of the partnership agreement. Was Cooper's action a wrongful dissolution? (*Cooper v. Isaacs*, 448 F.2d 1202, D.C.)

29. L.W. Clement and his brother Charles formed a partnership in the 1920s to run a plumbing business. The partnership lasted some 40 years. However Charles ultimately became suspicious of the way L.W., who had total control over the partnership finances, was handling partnership funds. He filed an equity suit maintaining that L.W. had used partnership funds to invest in personal real estate and insurance policies. The chancellor of equity heard the case and awarded Charles one-half interest in the real estate and insurance policies in question. The appellate court reversed the chancellor's decision saying that Charles had no claim as he could not trace the flow of partnership funds into L.W.'s investments. The Supreme Court of Pennsylvania then agreed to hear the case. The issue as perceived by the Pennsylvania Supreme Court was whether L.W. owed to Charles the duty of negating the inference that the source of the funds for the investment was the partnership coffers. Decide. (*Clement v. Clement*, 260 A.2d 728)

30. More than 40 medical doctors held partnership interests in a health club. One of the partners, Dr. Witlin, died. As prescribed by the partnership agreement, the other doctors purchased his share in the partnership. In so doing, they paid his widow a little over $65,000. The amount offered for the share (and originally accepted by Mrs. Witlin) was determined by a committee of the remaining partners and based on the book value of the partnership's assets. The goodwill associated with the health club's name and the intrinsic value of an ongoing business were not included in the valuation because they were not considered part of book value. Also, the partnership was about to sell the club for an amount that would have doubled the widow's payout. This fact was not told to Mrs. Witlin, however. Mrs. Witlin sued to overturn the transaction. Should the court do so? Why or why not? (*Estate of Witlin v. Rio Hondo Associates*, 83 Cal. App. 3d 167)

CASE FOR LEGAL THINKING

LENKIN V. BECKMAN
575 A.2D 273

FACTS The law firm of Beckman and Kirstein was comprised of Robert Beckman and David Kirstein and located in Washington, D.C. Both partners were well schooled and had many years in education and government service between them, including teaching at Harvard Law, serving as counsel to the Civil Aeronautics Board, and working as a trial attorney for the Antitrust Division of the United States Department of Justice. Forming a law practice with another attorney, the resulting partnership signed a 10-year lease for office space in a Washington, D.C., building owned by Melvin Lenkin.

The lease had a clause that stated that the individual partners as well as their successors in interest in the lease could not be held personally liable under its terms. One year after entering into the lease, the partnership was dissolved by the withdrawal of Beckman and Kirstein's other partner. The partnership of Beckman and Kirstein was then formed. A little more than a year after the new partnership began and nearly eight years before the lease was to expire, Lenkin received a letter from Beckman informing Lenkin that the lease was going to be terminated in a month as the partnership of Beckman and Kirstein was to be dissolved. Lenkin then filed suit against Beckman and Kirstein for the balance due on the lease.

Beckman and Kirstein immediately filed a motion to dismiss based on the prohibition in the lease against holding partners individually liable. The lower court granted the motion and also held that, as a partnership cannot be sued in the District of Columbia, Lenkin could not even get a judgment against the partnership of Beckman and Kirstein. As a consequence, Lenkin was left without a remedy. He then appealed.

REASONING The appellate court faced the following issues: 1. Should the assets be retained in the partnership of Beckman and Kirstein to complete the winding-up process for the partnership and before the assets become the personal property of the partners? 2. Should such assets be open to suit by such a creditor as Lenkin even given the prohibition in Washington, D.C., law against suing a partnership?

In resolving these issues the appellate court pointed out that the lower court's holding that the partnership property automatically becomes the personal property of the individual partners upon dissolution was incorrect. Instead, the property of the partnership became the personal property of the ex-partners only after the winding-up process was complete. Secondly, the court noted that although the partnership itself could not be sued under D.C. law, the business entity could be sued by serving both partners.

CONCLUSION Reversed and remanded to the lower court for proceedings according to the above opinion.

PRACTICE JUDGING

1. How would you rule on the first issue and why?

2. If you rule that the property should remain in the partnership until the winding-up process is complete, how would you justify suing the partnership in conflict with D.C. law so that the assets could be properly used to satisfy partnership creditors?

The Law of Corporations

HOT DEBATE

© GETTY IMAGES/PHOTODISC

A large American automobile manufacturer, responding to competition from small, gas efficient foreign cars, rushed a model through production to compete with them. This vehicle had a serious design defect that caused its gas tank to rupture and spray gas and fumes into the passenger compartment upon even a minor rear-end collision. As a consequence, the car would burst into flames almost instantaneously causing grievous burns and death for its occupants.

When initially confronted in a civil case brought by a victim of the car's defect, the manufacturer's executives denied knowledge of any problem. This defense was quickly overcome by the testimony of a surprise witness, the manufacturer's ex-safety engineer. He stated that when he would not sign off on the car for production due to its problems, he was fired. He also presented as evidence memos of the executives' knowledge of and decision to market the car regardless of the defect. After this information became public, a Detroit prosecuting attorney brought criminal charges against the executives.

Where Do You Stand?

1. Which party do you think should be held legally responsible in this situation? How would you punish each?

2. Which parties are ethically responsible?

Founding a Corporation

ATTRIBUTES OF THE CORPORATE FORM

WHAT'S YOUR VERDICT?

Several musicians in Branson, Missouri, formed a corporation, Chariots of Flair, and bought two motorized trolleys. The trolleys were used for tours of the country music theaters and, seasonally, for Christmas light tours. The musicians played, sang, sold CDs of their music, and acted as tour guides. They were the incorporators, officers, employees, directors, and shareholders in the corporation.

If a customer is injured during one of the tours and brings suit, who would have to pay any court judgment that results?

The last chapter introduced the corporate form of business and a few of the reasons many businesses, large and small, utilize it. These businesses obtain the authority to exist in the corporate form by complying with the incorporation statutes of one of the 50 state governments. Congress, by special legislative acts, also creates some corporations (for example, the Federal Deposit Insurance Corporation, or FDIC) to serve specific national interests.

ADVANTAGES OF THE CORPORATE FORM

Although corporations are far outnumbered by sole proprietorships and partnerships, corporations do most of the business in this country. This is because the corporation has advantages that are essential for large-scale enterprises. Some of these attributes are attractive to small business ventures, too. The advantages of corporations are perpetual life, limited liability, transferability of ownership interests, ability to attract large sums of capital, and professional management.

PERPETUAL LIFE Unlike the sole proprietorship, a corporation is a legal entity separate and distinct from its owners and managers. Therefore it can continue to function after they die. Under the law, a corporation may continue indefinitely with new owners, managers, and employees.

LIMITED LIABILITY Creditors normally cannot collect claims against the corporation from persons who own shares in the corporation. The corporation itself is liable without limit for its debts. All of a corporation's assets may be seized under court order to pay delinquent claims. However, individual stockholders stand to lose only the amount they have invested. It is this limited liability that makes the corporation an appropriate form of business organization for investors such as the musicians in *What's Your Verdict?* They are willing to assume risks entrepreneurs face. But they want a ceiling or limit on the amount they might lose if someone successfully sues the business for heavy damages or if the business fails and cannot pay its debts.

Under exceptional conditions, courts may hold the shareholders personally responsible for

IN THIS CASE

Shortly after Chariots of Flair was incorporated, two of its major stockholders received lucrative long-term recording contracts. Because the two artists would have to move permanently to Nashville, Tennessee, they no longer wanted to own shares in Chariots of Flair. This was not a problem as, due to the transferability of ownership of corporate shares, they could sell their stock without causing the business to be dissolved. One of the other stockholders bought their shares to increase her ownership percentage.

corporate debts. This practice is called "piercing the corporate veil." A court may take this extreme action, more likely with small corporations, if shareholders fail to keep corporate assets separate from their own or if they hide behind the corporate form for improper purposes, such as to avoid just debts.

TRANSFERABILITY OF OWNERSHIP INTERESTS
A major advantage of the corporate form over the partnership form is the ease of transferring ownership interests in the firm. Normally, individual owners can sell their interests in the corporation without disturbing the company's operations or getting the consent of other owners. The stock of most large corporations is traded (bought and sold) on the New York Stock Exchange or the American Stock Exchange. By contacting a stockbroker, any person financially able may buy or sell a reasonable number of shares of any listed stock within minutes when the exchanges are open.

ABILITY TO ATTRACT LARGE SUMS OF CAPITAL
Many investors feel comfortable and reasonably secure when buying stock in corporations. This is because their liability as owners of the corporation is limited to the amount they have invested. Moreover, as owners they may readily sell their individual shares, or buy more. Finally, the corporation may have perpetual life, outlasting present owners, directors, and employees, all of whom may be replaced without terminating the business. As a result, large sums of money may be raised. Small and large investments by thousands of persons and institutions are combined to fund giant corporations.

PROFESSIONAL MANAGEMENT Because they can and do raise substantial amounts of capital, efficient corporations generally have greater financial strength than do other forms of business organization. This enables such corporations to attract superior workers by offering generous salaries and fringe benefits. Moreover, because the corporation is not dissolved automatically by the death of any owner or manager, it usually provides better assurance of continued employment.

DISADVANTAGES OF THE CORPORATE FORM
There are some important disadvantages to the corporate form. The federal government taxes net income of corporations when it is earned. What remains after taxes at the corporate level may then be taxed again as part of the income of the owners of the corporation. Some states also tax the corporation income, and then the shareholders, on income received. Certain types of corporations can elect to be given special status under the Internal Revenue Code that allows them to avoid multiple federal taxation. This special status will be discussed in detail in Chapter 27.

In addition to the taxation disadvantage, it is costlier and more troublesome to organize a corporation than it is to organize a sole proprietorship or partnership. Further, large corporations are subject to extensive regulation of the sale of stocks and bonds to the public. Finally, juries tend to favor individuals in legal disputes with corporations. Overall, however, the advantages of the corporation often outweigh its disadvantages, especially for big enterprises.

ECONOMIC IMPACT

SUCCESS OF INCORPORATION STATUTES

U.S. corporate formation laws allow limited liability protection, excellent capital formation potential as a result of easily transferable stock, and perpetual life. These laws have paid off handsomely for the leading U.S. corporations. In the 2003 rankings of the top 1,000 companies worldwide, U.S. corporations occupy the top seven positions in market value and eleven out of the top fifteen. General Electric holds the first position with a market value of $286 billion. Microsoft, Exxon, Wal-Mart follow close (although tens of billions of dollars) behind.

THINK CRITICALLY

What common attributes do these U.S. corporations have? How are they dissimilar?

TYPES OF CORPORATIONS

Corporations are classified according to their place of incorporation and purpose. If a corporation is chartered in a particular state, it is a *domestic corporation* in that state. A corporation doing business in that state but chartered in another state is termed a *foreign corporation*. Finally, a corporation chartered in another nation doing business in the state is an *alien corporation*.

In terms of purpose, a corporation is either public or private. A *public corporation* is established for a governmental purpose. Incorporated cities, state hospitals, and state universities are public corporations. A *private corporation* usually is established by individuals for business or charitable purposes. Note that sometimes a private corporation is said to be "publicly held" because its stock can he owned by the general public and typically is listed on a stock exchange. This availability for public ownership of stock differentiates such a company from a *closely held corporation* which is a private corporation that is owned by just a small number of shareholders. Generally a closely held corporation's stock is held by a family or like grouping of people.

Private corporations are further classified as profit-making, nonprofit, and public service corporations. A *profit-making corporation* is a private corporation organized to produce a financial return on the investment of its owners. Examples include banks, manufacturing and merchandising companies, and airlines.

A *nonprofit corporation* is organized for a social, charitable, or educational purpose. It may have revenues that exceed expenses, but it does not distribute to owners any earnings as profits. If a nonprofit corporation engages in business for profit, it must, like any other business, pay income taxes. Churches, colleges, fraternal societies, and organizations typically are organized as nonprofit corporations.

Finally, a *public service corporation* (also called a *public utility*) generally is a private company that furnishes an essential public service. Electric, gas, and water companies are examples. However, they are regulated closely as to the quality of service they must provide, the prices they can charge, and the profit margin they may earn. Over time it has been shown that competition in providing such services needed by most persons would be wasteful of scarce resources. Therefore such public utilities usually receive monopolistic franchises and special powers of eminent domain to acquire needed real estate.

CHECKPOINT

Explain the corporate advantage of limited liability.

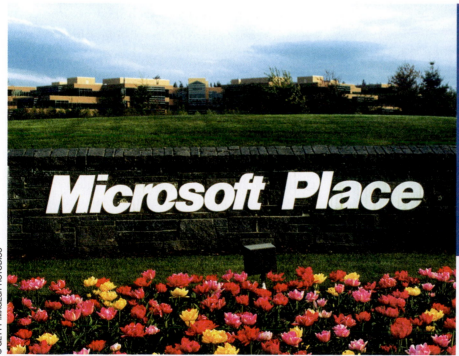

© GETTY IMAGES/PHOTODISC

The Microsoft Corporation was incorporated in the state of Washington in 1975. The company's fiscal 2003 earnings were $32.19 billion. As of October 31, 2004, the company had 10.87 billion shares of common stock outstanding. Based on this information, in terms of place of incorporation, what type of corporation is Microsoft in the state of Washington? In terms of purpose, is Microsoft a public or a private corporation? Is Microsoft a closely held corporation? Why or why not?

HOW IS A CORPORATION FORMED?

WHAT'S YOUR VERDICT?

The Chariots of Flair Company was incorporated in Delaware. It now wants to incorporate a subsidiary in Missouri to build and operate a country music theater.

Can Chariots of Flair be an incorporator of another corporation?

Typically, a corporation is formed as a result of the efforts of one or more persons called **promoters**. These individuals bring together interested parties and take preliminary steps to form a corporation. The resulting corporation is not liable on any contract made on its behalf by them. The promoters cannot bind an organization that is still to be created. Usually, though, once it comes into being the corporation adopts such contracts and is thereby bound by them. The promoters, however, also remain liable on such contracts.

To create a corporation in most states, an application for a corporate charter must be filed with a state. The application is submitted to the proper state official, usually the Secretary of State, in the state in which incorporation is sought. This application is accompanied by or contains the articles of incorporation. The **articles of incorporation** contain the basic facts about the would-be corporation. (See the sample on page 471.)

The articles are signed and submitted by one or more persons called **incorporators**. At least one of the incorporators must have legal capacity to enter into a binding contract. Thus, the incorporators cannot all be minors. A corporation such as Chariots of Flair in *What's Your Verdict?* may, however, be an incorporator.

Articles of incorporation generally contain the following elements:

1. Name of the corporation
2. Duration (definite time period or perpetual)
3. Purpose, or purposes, for which the corporation is organized, which may be broadly stated (for example, "any purposes legal for a corporation in this state")
4. Number and kinds of shares of capital stock to be authorized for issuance
5. Location of the corporation's principal office and the name of its agent to whom legal notices may be given
6. Number of directors or the names and addresses of the persons who are to serve as directors until the first annual meeting of shareholders or until their successors are elected (in some states, the incorporators serve as directors until the shareholders elect their replacements)
7. Name and address of each incorporator
8. Any other provision consistent with the law

If, after reviewing the articles of incorporation, the state approves, it will issue a certificate of incorporation, more commonly called a **corporate charter**. Once the corporation receives the corporate charter, shares of stock are sold. The shareholders (owners) then meet and elect a board of individuals to administer the corporation. This group then hires the managers who will run the company on a day-to-day basis. These managers then use the capital collected in return for the sale of the shares of stock to begin doing business.

INTERNATIONAL VIEWPOINT

Multinational Corporations

Corporations that have a significant investment of assets in foreign countries are called multinational corporations (MNCs). These firms operate production facilities and target markets for their products worldwide. In the late 1990s the largest 500 U.S. corporations earned more than half of their revenues from products sold outside the country. Examples of MNCs are Procter & Gamble, a consumer goods company, International Business Machines (IBM), Coca-Cola, and McDonalds.

CHECKPOINT

What is the difference between a promoter and an incorporator?

THE STATE OF MISSOURI
OFFICE OF THE SECRETARY OF STATE

ARTICLES OF INCORPORATION
(As required by revised statutes of Missouri, Section 351.055)

1. **THE NAME OF THE CORPORATION SHALL BE:** The Checkered Flag Company.

2. **THE ADDRESS, INCLUDING STREET AND NUMBER, IF ANY, AND ITS INITIAL REGISTERED OFFICE IN THIS STATE, AND THE NAME OF ITS INITIAL REGISTERED AGENT AT SUCH ADDRESS:** Omar Bradley Johnson, Agent, at 213 First Street North West, Miller, MO 56707.

3. **THE NUMBER, CLASS, AND RIGHT OF THE HOLDERS OF AUTHORIZED SHARES:** 100,000 common shares each with full ownership rights and voting authority.

4. **A CURRENT SHAREHOLDER'S RIGHT TO PURCHASE SHARES IN A NEW STOCK ISSUE:** Each current shareholder shall have the right to purchase a pro rata share equal to her or his ownership percentage of each subsequent issue at the public offering price of that issue.

5. **THE NAME AND PLACE OF RESIDENCE OF EACH INCORPORATOR:**

   Omar Bradley Johnson, Miller, MO 65707

   Charles Edgar Johnson, Miller, MO 65707

6. **THE NUMBER OF CORPORATE DIRECTORS AND THE NAMES AND ADDRESSES OF THOSE CHOSEN TO FILL THOSE POSITIONS UNTIL THE STOCKHOLDERS CAN ELECT THEIR REPLACEMENTS:** Three (3) directors shall constitute the initial Board of Directors of The Checkered Flag Company. They are:

   Omar Bradley Johnson, 213 First Street North West, Miller, MO 65707

   Charles Edgar Johnson, 1717 E. Delmar, Miller, MO 65707

   Jacqueline Alexis Johnson, 213 First Street North West, Miller, MO 65707

7. **THE NUMBER OF YEARS THE BUSINESS IS TO CONTINUE:** The business is to enjoy perpetual existence.

8. **THE PURPOSE(S) FOR WHICH THE BUSINESS IS FORMED:** The Checkered Flag Company is to involve itself in racing competitions with the hope of profiting thereby.

Assessment

THINK ABOUT LEGAL CONCEPTS

1. Which form of business is most likely to attract large sums of capital? (a) sole proprietorship (b) partnership (c) corporation

2. Can a corporation, unlike a sole proprietorship or partnership, enjoy perpetual life? **Yes or No?**

3. The _?_ sign the articles of incorporation.

4. All corporations are subject to double taxation. **True or False?**

5. In the event of problems, individual stockholders in a corporation generally stand to lose only what they have invested in the corporation. **True or False?**

6. A corporation that furnishes a utility such as water, sewer, etc., is known as a public service corporation. **True or False?**

7. Which of the following is not required to be in the articles of incorporation? (a) name of the corporation (b) period of duration of the corporation (c) purpose, or purposes, for which the corporation is organized (d) all of the above are required

8. When courts take the action of holding shareholders personally responsible for the debts of the corporation, it is referred to as "piercing the corporate veil." **True or False?**

THINK CRITICALLY ABOUT EVIDENCE

Study the situation, answer the questions, and then prepare arguments to support your answers.

9. Several juniors at Metropolitan High School plan to organize a corporation named Teenage Noteworthy Talent, Inc., (TNT for short). Drawing on the talents of high school students, they hope to arrange part-time jobs and full-time summer jobs as tutors, models, playground helpers, keyboard operators, tour guides, and clerks. What will prevent them, acting alone, from incorporating their business?

10. The Lacklands bought 5,000 shares of stock in Space Age Motion Pictures Inc., a speculative company created to imitate the fabulous success of producers of such space dramas as Star Wars. Were the Lacklands correct when they said, "At $25 a share, we can't lose more than $125,000; one big hit and we're millionaires!"?

11. Alibi Corporation, named for the creative suggestion service it provides via an 800 number, earned more than $75,000 last year. It paid income taxes on that amount and was left with an after-tax gain of more than $50,000. $25,000 of that was distributed in the form of dividends to the five shareholders. Will the shareholders have to pay taxes on the dividends?

12. Billy and Brady Anderson have just graduated from the University of Virginia with Masters in Business Administration degrees (MBAs). They are about to begin their careers as professional managers. In their final months in the MBA program they interviewed with some of the largest companies in the country. As graduation approached, they each had narrowed their choices down to two firms. Billy had job offers from a corporation and a large partnership. Brady had offers from a corporation and a sole proprietorship. The two brothers discussed the relative merits of each job offer. Billy said, "For professional managers like we will be, the form of the business does make a difference." What are the advantages and disadvantages of working for each of these business forms (sole proprietorship, partnership, corporation)?

13. Brady Anderson, see exercise 12, noted that he would like to have a share of the ownership in the business he worked for. It would motivate him as a manager. What he did to save or make money for the business would mean more money for him directly. Billy nodded in agreement. Which form of business organization would be the best in this regard? Why?

14. Billy noted that he wanted to put whatever organization he went to work for on the fast track for growth. Expansion into new areas with new stores and/or production facilities would be a necessity. Which form of business organization is best suited to attract the capital needed to fulfill Billy's desires for the future? Why?

Shareholders, Directors, and Officers

▼ GOALS

- **Understand the types of stock shareholders may own**
- **List the rights of shareholders**
- **Explain the roles of corporate directors and officers**

THE ROLE OF SHAREHOLDERS

WHAT'S YOUR VERDICT?

Chariots of Flair's new corporation, County Flair Theater Inc., was capitalized with a $2 million dollar sale of stock to various investors. The money was used to build a theater in Branson, Missouri, and purchase equipment for the performances.

Who owns the theater and the equipment?

Typically, the promoters of a corporation sell not only the business idea but the corporate form for it. As a result of their sales efforts, they secure stock subscription agreements from the various potential investors with whom they have dealt. These subscription agreements require the investors to buy a certain number of ownership units at a set price once the corporation is chartered. These ownership units are known as shares of stock. Usually, the subscription agreements are not put into effect (in other words the corporation chartered and the stock sold) until a sufficient amount of capitalization has been promised. A person who owns one or more shares of stock in a corporation is termed a shareholder (or *stockholder*).

A shareholder might receive a *stock certificate,* which is written evidence of ownership and rights in the business. Stock ownership does not transfer title to specific corporate property to the holder. The corporation, as a legal person, remains the owner of all corporate property. In *What's Your Verdict?* County Flair Theater Inc. owns the equipment and the theater itself.

The corporation uses the money received from the initial sale of stock to buy equipment, supplies, and inventory; to hire labor; and to pay other expenses. As goods and services are produced and sold, more income flows into the business. Often earnings are reinvested. Also more shares of stock may be sold and money may be borrowed to provide for further expansion.

TYPES OF STOCK

Corporate stock comes in many varieties, each combining certain attributes to meet particular needs of the issuing corporation. The main types of stock include par and no-par stock, common stock, and preferred stock. Note the differences in the rights of shareholders with regard to common and preferred stock.

PAR AND NO-PAR STOCK Stock may have a *par value,* which is the face value printed on the certificate. If it does not have a par value, it is *no-par stock* and is originally sold at a price set by the board of directors of the corporation. When either par or no-par stock changes hands in later transfers, the price may be higher or lower. This market price is determined by many factors, including past and anticipated future profits.

What does possession of a stock certificate indicate?

© GETTY IMAGES/PHOTODISC

COMMON STOCK Corporations may have one or more kinds of stock. **Common stock** is the basic type, with the right to vote in corporate elections. Shareholders of common stock typically have one vote per share owned, and they generally receive dividends. **Dividends** are distributions of profits earned by the corporation. If the corporation does not earn a profit, typically it will not pay a dividend to its common shareholders.

PREFERRED STOCK To attract additional funds from investors who want greater assurance of payment of dividends, some corporations also issue **preferred stock**. Owners of preferred stock usually have no voting power, but they legally are entitled to a stated dividend, if it is earned, before the common shareholders get anything. For example, the preferred shareholder may be entitled to receive $7 per share each year before any distribution of profits is made to the common shareholders. If profits are high, the common shareholders may get more money than the preferred shareholders. Preferred shareholders also generally have a priority right to be repaid the face value of their stock from the corporation's funds obtained in a liquidation. **Liquidation** occurs when all of the business assets are sold, all debts are paid, and the corporate existence is ended.

Preferred stock may be *cumulative*. With cumulative preferred stock, if the promised dividend is not paid in a given year, it remains due and payable in the future. Each year the unpaid dividends cumulate (add up) and must be paid in full before the common shareholders receive any dividends.

In some cases, the preferred stock also can be *participating*. For example, in a given year, if dividends are distributed, the participating preferred stock's shareholder receives the basic dividend as contractually agreed, and the common shareholder receives an equal amount per share. Then any remaining profit to be distributed that year is divided between the preferred and common shareholders. This remaining profit can be divided equally or in any agreed-upon ratio.

SHAREHOLDER RIGHTS

Ownership of stock in a company does not give shareholders the right to possess any corporate property or to participate directly in management. It does, however, confer on shareholders the following important rights.

RIGHT TO A STOCK CERTIFICATE

If a corporation issues stock certificates, a shareholder has the right to receive a certificate as evidence of ownership of shares in the corporation. One certificate may represent one or more shares. Many large corporations have an independent trust company serve as registrar and transfer agent for the corporation's securities. Often shareholders give such trust companies, or the corporation, the right to retain possession of the shares for safekeeping.

In most states, corporations may issue *uncertified stock.* These shares are not represented by a piece of paper. Rather, their ownership and transfers are registered on books kept by or for the issuing corporation.

RIGHT TO TRANSFER SHARES

A shareholder generally has the right to sell or to give away any shares owned. This right sometimes is restricted in closely held corporations, where the owners may want to limit ownership to employees or to members of a given family. Accordingly, the corporation's articles of incorporation may provide that an owner who wants to sell shares must first offer them to the corporation or to the other stockholders.

RIGHT TO ATTEND SHAREHOLDER MEETINGS AND TO VOTE

A shareholder may attend shareholder meetings and vote shares owned in any class of stock that has the right to vote. Regular meetings usually are held annually at the place and time designated in the articles or bylaws. Notice of the regular meetings usually is not required. Reasonable notice is required for special meetings.

In a corporate election, a shareholder usually is entitled to the number of votes that equals the number of shares of voting stock held. Having a *minority position* means owning less than 50 percent of the voting shares. To safeguard the interests of such shareholders, many states provide for *cumulative voting* in the election of directors. Under this plan, each shareholder has the right to cast as many votes as the number of shares of stock held, multiplied by the number of directors to be elected. The shareholder may cast all available votes for one candidate or distribute them among two or more candidates with the top vote getters being elected.

A shareholder who does not wish to attend meetings and to vote in person ordinarily has the right to vote by **proxy** (see the illustration at the bottom of the page). Most of the millions of people who individually own comparatively few shares of stock in various corporations cast their votes in this manner. The management, or anyone seeking control of the corporation, mails the necessary proxy forms to all shareholders and solicits their votes. The shareholders may then

---

The County Flair Theater, Inc.
Proxy

The undersigned hereby appoints IRV BERLIN proxy and with the power of substitution (i.e., power to name a replacement) to attend the initial meeting of the shareholders of The County Flair Theater Inc. at the company's main office in Branson, Missouri, on December 30, 20__, commencing at 10 A.M. and any adjournment thereof, and there to vote all the shares of the undersigned for election of Directors, and on any other business that may properly come before the meeting.

Dated _____

Signature _____

Phil J. Sousa
75 Main Street
Indianapolis, Indiana

Proxy #13

Berlin owned 301 of the 1,000 shares issued by County Flair Theater Inc. She wanted to be certain to elect at least one of her people as a director of the corporation out of the three to be elected by cumulative voting. To be certain of doing so, she would only have to concentrate her 903 votes on one candidate (301 shares × 3 positions). Therefore, no matter how the remaining 2,097 votes (699 × 3 positions) were voted, she would be sure one of her candidates would be in the top three vote getters and thereby be elected.

sign and return the forms. Shareholders who are satisfied with the corporation's performance typically give their proxies to incumbent directors, giving them authority to cast the votes. Federal law requires that the proxy form give the shareholder an opportunity to specify by ballot approval or rejection of particular proposals.

RIGHT TO INCREASE CAPITAL STOCK Shareholders alone have the right to increase the capital stock (total shares of stock) of the corporation. This usually is done by majority vote, on the recommendation of the board of directors. In some corporations, when the capital stock is increased, each shareholder may have a right to purchase additional shares to maintain the percentage of interest in the corporation owned before the increase. This is called the **preemptive right**.

RIGHT TO SHARE THE PROFITS Each shareholder is entitled to a proportionate share of the profits that are distributed on the class of stock owned. These dividends usually are paid in money, but they may be paid in shares of stock. Occasionally products of the corporation are distributed as dividends. Even when profits are earned, the board of directors may decide to retain them in the business for future needs of the firm. In effect, the stockholders are thus forced to make an additional investment in the business. Ideally, this should cause the price of stock to go up, and the stockholders can sell out if they so choose. Under unusual circumstances, courts will intervene to compel distribution of dividends at the request of shareholders who claim that there is an unreasonably large surplus of retained and unused or underutilized earnings.

RIGHT TO SHARE IN A DISTRIBUTION OF THE CAPITAL If a corporation is dissolved, its creditors have first claim upon the assets of the business. After their claims have been satisfied, any remaining assets or proceeds from the sale of assets are distributed to the shareholders. Preferred stockholders generally have priority over common stockholders in such distribution.

RIGHT TO INSPECT CORPORATE BOOKS OF ACCOUNT A shareholder has the right to inspect and to make appropriate records of the accounting books of the corporation. However, this inspection right may be denied if it is not made at a reasonable time and place, in good faith, and with proper motive. This restriction is understandable in light of the many thousands of shareholders in large corporations. Without restrictions, competitors could buy shares simply to gain an unfair advantage by inspection of company books.

CHECKPOINT

Name the most significant powers of a common shareholder.

THE ROLES OF DIRECTORS AND OFFICERS

WHAT'S YOUR VERDICT?

Berlin was in Las Vegas when she heard a great new act, Vermillyon or "V" as he was called. V did country rap which Berlin believed to be the coming thing. As a consequence, Berlin, a major shareholder in County Flair Theater Inc., signed V to a year-long contract at the County Flair Theater.

Did Berlin's action legally bind the Theater?

As noted earlier, a corporation is a legal person in the eyes of the law. It must act through human agents elected by the shareholders, appointed by the directors, or hired by the officers. No shareholder, even one that owns most or all the stock, can act for the corporation or bind it by contract merely because of such ownership. In *What's Your Verdict?* Berlin had no authority to represent the corporation and therefore the Theater is not bound. The officers (appointed by directors) and their agents are the only parties that can bind the theater to contracts.

DIRECTORS

Although shareholders have the power to vote on major corporate issues such as changing the corporate articles or merging with another company, they do not directly control the running of the corporation. This is done through the directors whom the shareholders elect.

DIRECTORS AS FIDUCIARIES Directors are responsible for providing general guidance for the corporation. They are fiduciaries and as such are duty-bound to act in good faith and with due care, oversee the corporation, and formulate general policies. They must not act fraudulently or illegally. Most states apply the standard of the Model Business Corporation Act. This requires that directors act in a manner they "reasonably believe to be in the best interests of the corporation, and with such care as an ordinary prudent person in a like position would use under similar circumstances." Failure to do so can make the director liable to the shareholders.

REQUIREMENTS FOR DIRECTORS The number of directors varies among corporations. Most states allow the shareholders to determine the number. Some states require at least three. Other states require only one director, who also can be the sole officer and sole

shareholder. This gives the corporation the attributes of a sole proprietorship while retaining the advantage of limited liability for its owner.

Statutes sometimes require that directors be shareholders. A few states require that directors be adults. Some states require that the president of the company serve as a director, while in many corporations all the directors are officers. This is called an *inside board* and is not considered ideal because the directors naturally tend to approve their conduct as officers. Better results sometimes are obtained from an *outside board,* which has no officers in its membership and which presumably scrutinizes corporate performance more objectively and critically. Probably the best form is a *mixed board,* with some officers to provide information and detailed understanding and some outsiders "to ask the embarrassing questions."

DUTIES OF DIRECTORS The directors are the top officials of the corporation. They set major goals and determine basic policies (for example, whether to sell for cash, credit, or both, and whether to expand or reduce operations in a given area). They appoint and set the salaries of the top officers of the company: typically the president, vice president, secretary, and treasurer. Acting together, the directors have the power to make contracts for the corporation, but they delegate the day-to-day duties of running the business to the officers they have selected.

The directors are expected to exercise their own best judgment in appointing the officers

Why do you think a mixed board of directors, consisting of both corporate officers (insiders) and outsiders, might provide the most effective guidance for a corporation?

© GETTY IMAGES/PHOTODISC

and in overseeing their work. The directors alone may declare dividends and authorize major policy decisions. Therefore they may not have others serve as substitutes at board meetings to deliberate and vote for them.

OFFICERS

Directors generally employ managing officers and delegate to them necessary authority to conduct the firm's day-to-day business. Corporate managing officers commonly include a president, a vice president, a secretary, and a treasurer. However, the duties of two or more of these positions may be combined. Other positions may be created as required. Many states and the Model Business Corporation Act permit one person to hold two or more offices, except that the president may not also serve as secretary. This helps to prevent falsification of records.

The board of directors usually appoints officers, although in some corporations they are elected by the shareholders. Generally there are no restrictions on the selection of officers. Thus, they do not necessarily have to be shareholders or

directors, have certain qualifications, or be a certain age.

Because the officers of a corporation are its agents, they are fiduciaries governed by applicable principles of agency law. The articles of incorporation, the governing rules of the corporation, and the board of directors may impose limitations.

Officers are legally accountable to the corporation for willful or negligent acts that cause loss to it. However, neither shareholders, directors, officers, nor other corporate employees can be held personally to be criminally or civilly liable to parties outside the corporation for honest errors of judgment made in the course of business. This is referred to as the **business judgment rule**.

CHECKPOINT

What is the importance of the business judgment rule?

Law Brief

Two and one half years after the Enron scandal broke and the energy giant collapsed, the ex-CEO, Kenneth Lay, was finally indicted. Lay surrendered at the FBI office in Houston early one morning and was led away to the federal courthouse with his hands cuffed behind his back. There he pleaded not guilty to each of the 11 charges and was released on $500,000 bond. Lay later said that he took responsibility for Enron's collapse but denied that he did anything wrong. "I continue to grieve, as does my family, over the loss of the company and my failure to be able to save it," said Lay, speaking forcefully. "But failure does not equate to a crime." Enron's bankruptcy holds the record as the largest collapse in corporate history.

A QUESTION OF ETHICS

Mammoth Corporation had been one of the success stories of the 1960s. Mammoth was a conglomerate consisting of many unrelated companies in fields from high-tech agriculture to manufacturing children's clothing. Now its stock was at an all-time low. Bill Predator, president of Shark Inc., did some simple math. He figured that if he bought all the shares of Mammoth at their present market value, he would spend little more than $5 billion. Then he could break the company up and sell it in pieces to waiting buyers. The pieces would sell for more than $10 billion. However, this would leave the majority of Mammoth's 30,000 employees without jobs. Are Predator's plans legal? Are they ethical? Should the government allow him to go through with the plans?

Assessment

THINK ABOUT LEGAL CONCEPTS

1. Shareholders will always be paid dividends as long as the corporation makes a profit. **True or False?**

2. Unless a shareholder possesses a stock certificate, there is no ownership interest in the corporation. **True or False?**

3. If a cumulative preferred stock dividend is not paid in a particular period, it remains due and payable in full before the common shareholders receive any additional dividends. **True or False?**

4. No-par stock is sold originally at a price set by the market. **True or False?**

5. Directors have the ultimate control of corporate affairs. **True or False?**

6. Which rule protects corporate officers from being held personally liable (criminally or civilly) to parties outside the corporation for honest errors of judgment made in carrying out the corporate business? (a) immunity rule (b) corporate officer shield (c) business judgment rule (d) none of the above

THINK CRITICALLY ABOUT EVIDENCE

Study the situation, answer the questions, and then prepare arguments to support your answers.

7. Ben invested $1 million in a company making computerized maps. The company was owned by its CEO who had a majority—more than 50 percent—of the stock. Each year Ben waited for dividends to be paid on the shares he owned. However, the CEO increased her pay each year to levels that cancelled out any possible earnings and, therefore, payment of dividends. Are the CEO's actions legal? Why or why not?

8. All directors of the ABC Avionics Corporation also were officers of the corporation. As directors, all were involved in the unanimous decision to follow the advice of De Moreal, the dynamic president. He had presented engineering and marketing studies in support of a proposal to build a small helicopter that also could be used as an automobile on public highways. After further study, the directors, as officers, proceeded with the plan to design, produce, and market the vehicle. Many problems caused abandonment of the project after the corporation had spent more than $25 million developing it. Several stockholders sued the directors/officers for the full amount. Are they liable?

9. Fleener was employed as a director and vice president of Mt. Everest Productions, a manufacturer of outdoor sports equipment. Without informing the other directors of the corporation, she bought control of a small company that manufactured specialty nylon and composite fabrics. It sold large quantities of its products to Mt. Everest Productions, at a profit. Its prices were fair and competitive, and the quality superior. Was Fleener's conduct legal? Was it ethical?

10. The CEO of the Consolidated Hands of Help, a nonprofit New York Corporation, was shown to be using corporate funds to maintain several limos and various houses for himself around the country. He responded that he needed these to enable him to better recruit donors. The board of directors agreed with his position. A shareholder brought suit claiming that more than 12,000 homeless people could be helped for what was being paid for the luxury items. The suit sought to recover the expenditures from the CEO and the board members. Will it be successful? Why or why not?

11. Bridges Inc., a large construction company dealing in federal highway construction contracts, showed earnings of $2 million for its latest fiscal year. The Board of Directors voted to pay out the $2 million in dividends. There are 2,000,000 preferred shares outstanding. Each preferred share has a stated dividend of $.50. There are 2,000,000 common shares outstanding. How much will be paid out in dividends to all the common shareholders?

▼ **GOALS**

■ **Explain the powers of a corporation**
■ **Relate the various ways that the dissolution of a corporation might be brought about**

THE POWERS OF A CORPORATION

WHAT'S YOUR VERDICT?

When a tornado hit Branson one summer, the board of directors of County Flair Theater Inc. voted to open the theater as a shelter for people made homeless by the storm. They also voted to spend $10,000 for clothing, blankets, and food for the victims.

Can a corporation formed for a business purpose make such a charitable gift?

In general, a corporation can be formed for any lawful purpose. The corporation then is allowed to exercise all powers that are necessary, convenient, and lawful in achieving that purpose. As a result powers vary among corporations, but some are inherent in almost every corporation. These powers include the following:

POWER TO CONDUCT BUSINESS

First and foremost, in order to achieve its basic purpose, a corporation may use any legal means to conduct its authorized business. Thus, the corporation has the power, in its own name, to

a. Make contracts.

b. Borrow money and incur other liabilities.

c. Lend money and acquire assets, including all forms of real and personal property.

d. Make, endorse, and accept commercial paper (orders or promises to pay money).

e. Issue various types of stock and bonds. **Bonds** are written promises to pay back money borrowed by the corporation. Bonds usually are secured by a mortgage or deposit of collateral. Unsecured bonds are **debentures**.

f. Mortgage, pledge, lease, sell, or assign property.

g. Buy back from owners its own stock, unless this would make it impossible for the corporation to pay its debts or to pay off any superior class of stock. Such purchases are sometimes made to boost the market price of the stock, to eliminate protesting shareholders, to acquire shares for employee purchase and bonus plans, or to reduce the size of the corporation.

h. Acquire and hold stock in other corporations provided this does not violate antitrust laws.

i. Make reasonable donations or gifts for civic or charitable purposes to promote goodwill in accord with corporate social responsibility. In *What's Your Verdict?* the expenditures for aid of the victims of the tornado was not only legal but commendable.

j. Hire and fire agents, independent contractors, and ordinary employees.

In your opinion, how seriously should a company take its corporate social responsibility?

© GETTY IMAGES/PHOTODISC

k. Establish pension, profit sharing, and other incentive plans for employees.

l. Sue and be sued.

POWER TO CONTINUE INDEFINITELY

In most jurisdictions, the corporation is the only form of business organization that may be granted the power of perpetual succession. This means that regardless of changes in the shareholders (owners), the corporation may continue indefinitely or for whatever period originally requested by the incorporators. During this time, the death or withdrawal of a director, manager, or shareholder has no legal effect on the corporation's continuity.

POWER TO OPERATE UNDER A NAME OF ITS OWN CHOOSING

A corporation can select any name to identify itself unless that name is identical or deceptively similar to the name of another business already operating in that geographical area. Most states require that the name selected indicate that the business is a corporation to alert the public of the owners' limited liability. Corporations do this by including a descriptive word in the name, such as Company, Corporation, or Incorporated (or Co., Corp., or Inc.).

Any business organization has the legal power to use a fictitious name. However, most states require that fictitious names be registered in a designated government office, along with information about the owners of the corporation.

POWER TO MAKE RULES TO GOVERN ITS OPERATION

A corporation can make its own reasonable rules and regulations for the internal management of its affairs. Called **bylaws**, these rules specify times for meetings of shareholders and directors, for example, and define duties of officers.

IMPLIED POWERS

A corporation may do any legal act that is necessary or convenient for the execution of its express powers. This would extend to such matters as doing pure and applied research and development (R & D) work, leasing space and equipment, advertising, and buying life and health and liability insurance for officers and other employees.

CHECKPOINT
What are bylaws?

CAUSES OF CORPORATE DISSOLUTION

WHAT'S YOUR VERDICT?

A decade after its founding and against the objection of many performers who would be put out of work, a two-thirds majority of the stock of County Flair Theater Inc. was voted to terminate its existence. This contradicted the articles of incorporation which claimed a perpetual existence for the corporation.

Is the termination legal?

A variety of causes may bring about the dissolution or termination of a corporation. These include the following:

AT A TIME SPECIFIED IN THE ARTICLES OF INCORPORATION

The lifetime of the corporation can be set by the incorporators in the articles of incorporation for a certain number of years or the occurrence of a particular event.

BY AGREEMENT OF THE SHAREHOLDERS

A corporation can be terminated by a set majority vote of its stockholders even before the time set in the articles of incorporation. In *What's Your Verdict?* the termination vote would legally bring County Flair Theater Inc. to an end.

BY FORFEITURE OF THE CHARTER

The state may bring judicial proceedings for the forfeiture of the charter of a corporation that has been guilty of certain acts. Examples of such acts are

1. fraudulent submission of articles of incorporation
2. obvious misuse of corporate powers, and
3. repeated violation of the law.

Forfeiture is rare because the state does not monitor corporate affairs, and aggrieved persons can seek private relief in court.

IN THIS CASE

When she turned 50, Berlin, who over the years had acquired over 70 percent of the stock in County Flair Theater Inc. decided to retire. She tried to sell her stock but it would only bring approximately 40 percent of her share of the asset value in the corporation. She, therefore, decided to dissolve the corporation, liquidate the assets, and retire on the payout.

BY CONSOLIDATION OR MERGER

A **consolidation** of corporations can occur with the approval of the boards of directors and a majority of the shareholders in each of the corporations involved. The two corporations cease to exist and a new corporation is formed.

In a **merger** one corporation absorbs the other. The surviving corporation retains its charter and identity; the other disappears. Again, approval must be given by the directors and by the shareholders of the merging corporations.

A combination through either consolidation or merger must not violate antitrust laws by interfering unreasonably with free competition. An illegal monopoly occurs when one company controls the supply of goods, excludes competitors, and sets prices. It also is illegal for two or more companies to conspire to set prices or to allocate marketing areas, as this reduces free competition.

U.S. antitrust laws have been amended to permit competing companies to form partnerships for joint research in order to meet global competition. Thus, for example, it is legal for General Motors, Ford, and Chrysler to do joint research on materials, oil and reformulated fuel, batteries, and electronic systems for control of vehicles.

AS A RESULT OF BANKRUPTCY

Bankruptcy of a corporation does not in itself cause dissolution. However, some bankruptcy proceedings leave the corporation without assets with which to do business. In addition, some state statutes provide that when a corporation is insolvent, its creditors may force dissolution.

BY COURT ORDER

Occasionally a corporation's assets are seriously threatened with irreparable harm because the board of directors or the shareholders cannot resolve an internal dispute. In some states a court can order dissolution if interested parties petition for dissolution.

CHECKPOINT

What is the difference between a consolidation and a merger?

26-3 Assessment

THINK ABOUT LEGAL CONCEPTS

1. A rule adopted by a corporation's board of directors that calls for a stockholder meeting every six months properly would be termed a corporate bylaw. **True or False?**

2. Corporate debentures are (a) secured, (b) unsecured, (c) government guaranteed

3. When two corporations merge, they both disappear and a new corporation is formed. **True or False?**

4. A corporation with perpetual life according to its articles of incorporation could still be dissolved by a vote of an appropriate majority of its shareholders. **True or False?**

5. Which of the following may result in a corporate dissolution? (a) corporate bankruptcy (b) irresolvable internal corporate dispute (c) state-ordered forfeiture of the corporate charter (d) all of the above

THINK CRITICALLY ABOUT EVIDENCE

Study the situation, answer the questions, and then prepare arguments to support your answers.

6. In order to attract a top manager away from another company, Scavengerr Corporation offered her a salary, profit sharing, and pension package that would cut deeply into prospective dividends to most shareholders for at least two years. Is this legitimately within the corporate powers?

7. Baccarat Groceries, Inc., (BGI) was chartered in Delaware in 1995. As the years wore on, the management of BGI neglected to pay the annual registration fees to the state as required by law. The state has warned BGI of its deliquent status numerous times. What action might the state take as a consequence?

8. BGI (see exercise 7) was a solvent corporation until it lost its contract with a large warehouse. As a consequence, it became unprofitable and operated as such for three years. Now, it has virtually no assets and many creditors. If the creditors force BGI into bankruptcy, will that terminate the corporation's existence?

PREVENT LEGAL DIFFICULTIES

1. Directors should be extremely careful to obey all laws, study the corporate records, and use independent judgment on policy decisions. To "rubber stamp" management proposals is to invite lawsuits by disgruntled shareholders if losses occur.

2. Corporate officers should be selected with great care because they make most of the day-to-day management decisions. Directors tend to rely on the advice of the officers.

3. Shareholders should not casually sign proxies that give directors continued control. Shareholders should try to exercise their voting rights after studying the annual reports and comparing the corporation's progress with that of similar corporations.

4. Shareholders with a minority position have a better chance to be represented on the board if the company uses cumulative voting.

5. It is usually risky to buy stock in new or small, once closely held corporations because they are more likely to fail. The majority of shareholders may favor themselves with high salaries as officers and pay low or no dividends, and it may be difficult to sell the shares to others.

6. The buyer of preferred stock who desires greater assurance of receiving dividends should seek cumulative and participating shares.

CONCEPTS IN BRIEF

26-1 Founding a Corporation

1. A corporation can be created only by government grant available under incorporation statutes in all states or by special legislative acts of the U.S. Congress.

2. In some states, corporate existence begins when properly prepared articles of incorporation are filed with the office of the Secretary of State. In some states, charters or certificates of incorporation are issued.

3. Corporations are a favored form of business organization because of advantages of potential perpetual life, limited liability of shareholders, easy transferability of shares, better access to capital, and professional management. A major disadvantage is double taxation.

26-2 Shareholders, Directors, and Officers

4. Although status as a shareholder does not give one the right to possess any corporate property or to participate directly in management, it does convey many other rights.

5. Shareholder rights include the right to see the corporate books, the right to vote and the right to share in whatever profits the corporation might develop.

6. The shareholders elect the directors who then select the officers of the corporation. The directors also create the bylaws of the corporation and monitor the day-to-day running of the business by the officers.

26-3 Corporate Powers and Termination

7. Corporate powers are many as a corporation is treated as an artificial person in our society. These powers such as the powers to buy and sell, sue and be sued, mortgage and donate, all basically allow the corporation to carry out its mission to make a profit.

8. Corporate existence can be terminated in a number of ways. Usually a corporation ends as specified in the articles of incorporation or when a majority of the stockholders vote to dissolve it.

YOUR LEGAL VOCABULARY

Match each statement with the term that it best defines. Some terms may not be used.

1. Signers of the articles of incorporation
2. Non-voting stock conveying the right to receive a stipulated dividend before any common shareholders receive their dividends
3. Application to a state for a corporate charter
4. Units of ownership in a corporation
5. Power to vote shares for shareholders
6. Distributions of corporate earnings
7. Rules for the internal organization and management of a corporation
8. Combination of two companies into one new one
9. Basic stock in a corporation conveying the right to vote and to receive dividends to its owner
10. Rule that protects management from being personally held criminally or civilly liable for a business decision made within the scope of power and authority granted by the corporate charter and applicable laws
11. Individuals elected by the shareholders to be responsible for the general guidance of the corporation

a. **articles of incorporation**
b. **bond**
c. **business judgment rule**
d. **bylaws**
e. **common stock**
f. **consolidation**
g. **corporate charter**
h. **debentures**
i. **directors**
j. **dividends**
k. **incorporators**
l. **liquidation**
m. **merger**
n. **preemptive right**
o. **preferred stock**
p. **promoters**
q. **proxy**
r. **shareholder**
s. **shares of stock**

REVIEW LEGAL CONCEPTS

12. What other uses can profits be put to instead of paying dividends?

13. Why is it important to pay dividends in the first place?

14. Are preemptive rights more important in a small corporation or a large publicly held corporation? Why?

15. Must dividends be paid to preferred shareholders regardless of whether or not the corporation has made a profit? Why or why not?

16. Why should preferred shareholders have priority over common shareholders in a corporate liquidation?

WRITE ABOUT LEGAL CONCEPTS

17. Devise a better way than cumulative voting of ensuring minority opinions are represented on a corporate board. Write an outline that sums up your plan.

18. Write an essay stating your opinion about whether it is ever appropriate for the courts to violate the business judgment rule and punish individual officers for their criminal actions on behalf of the corporation.

19. **HOT DEBATE** Write a letter to the editor of one of the Detroit papers discussing the business judgment rule and either supporting the prosecuting attorney's filing of charges or arguing against the action. Read the letter to the class. The letter should give the justification for the business judgment rule regardless of the side taken.

MAKE ACADEMIC CONNECTIONS

20. **HISTORY** Read a book on the development of the corporation, for example, Bruce Brown's *The History of the Corporation*, in which he cites the Benedictine Order of the Catholic Church, founded circa 529 A.D., as being the oldest surviving corporation. Draw conclusions and give a report to the class on your findings.

THINK CRITICALLY ABOUT EVIDENCE

Study the situation, answer the questions, and then prepare arguments to support your answers.

21. Hull organized a corporation to manufacture antibiotics for cattle. She owned most of the capital stock. All went well until a faulty batch of the drugs caused the serious illness or death of more than 3,000 cows. After a series of lawsuits, the corporation was forced into bankruptcy with some $200,000 in debts unpaid. Could Hull be held personally liable for these debts?

22. In its press release, Able Products, a Virginia corporation, announced that it was forming a joint venture with Hyallah, Inc., a toy-making corporation chartered in South Korea. In the release, Hyallah was referred to as a public, foreign corporation. Lin, the CEO of Hyallah, pointed out the terms "public and foreign" were legally incorrect. Is he correct and why or why not?

23. Charlene Bertram owned 98 percent of the stock of Traces of Beauty, Inc. The company had been founded in the 1920s by her maternal grandmother. The company had been run by professional managers after the grandmother died and left Charlene her stock. Traces imported cosmetics from France, England, and Sweden. The products were then sold directly to consumers by mail, 800 numbers, and on the Internet. While on a trip to Italy, Charlene found a new line of cosmetics that dazzled her. Without consulting any of the company officers, Charlene negotiated an exclusive distributorship for Traces with the Italian cosmetic maker. Upon her return to the states, Charlene met with the company president and told her about the deal. The president was shocked and noted that carrying the Italian line would breach an existing contract with the French cosmetic firm. This contract had made Traces millions of dollars over the last 10 years. The president then consulted the corporate legal staff to see if there was any way out of the contract with the Italian firm. Assume you are the company attorney. How would you answer the question posed by the president? Explain your answer.

24. As the testing of its new anti-arthritis drug showing results that exceeded anyone's expectations, JointEase Corporation bought back more than one third of its outstanding, publicly traded,

stock. As a consequence, because of the decreased supply, when the company announced the test results its stock price increased to more than double what would have been expected without the buyout. Feeling that they had been defrauded, the ex-shareholders who had sold their stock back to JointEase picketed outside company headquarters and complained to the media. Has the drug company done anything wrong?

ANALYZE REAL CASES

25. Pillsbury believed that the U.S. involvement in the Vietnam War was wrong. When he learned that Honeywell, Inc., had a large governmental contract to produce antipersonnel fragmentation bombs, he became determined to stop such production. Pillsbury learned that a trust set up by his grandmother for his benefit owned 242 shares of the stock, but these shares were voted by the trustee. Therefore Pillsbury bought just one share in his own name. As a shareholder, he petitioned the court to order Honeywell to produce its shareholder ledgers and all records dealing with weapons manufacture. He wanted to communicate with other shareholders to change the board of directors and then to have the corporation stop making munitions. Should the court grant his request? (*Pillsbury v. Honeywell, Inc.*, 291 Minn. 322, 191 N.W.2d 406)

26. A group of shareholders of the Manganese Corporation of America sued the corporation and four officers who also were directors. The group of shareholders sought to recover damages for the corporation and all its shareholders. Evidence indicated that the officers and directors negligently had caused the corporation's assets to drop from $400,000 to $30,000 in less than two years by being wasteful, careless, and unwise. Are the officers and directors liable for the losses? (*Selheimer v. Manganese Corporation of America*, 423 Pa. 563, 224 A.2d 634)

27. General Telephone Company of Florida owned more than 1 percent of the stock of Florida Telephone Corporation. General sought to examine the latter's stock records in order to make a list of the names, addresses, and holdings of all shareholders. Florida refused, claiming that General intended to use this information in order to buy more shares and thus get control of the corporation. Can General get a court order to compel the disclosure? (*Florida Telephone Corporation v. State ex ref. Peninsular Telephone Company*, 111 So. 2d 677, Fla.)

28. Years before lights were installed in Wrigley field in Chicago, Schlensky, a minority stockholder in the Chicago National League Ball Club (Inc.), owner of the Chicago Cubs, sued the corporation and its board of directors, including Philip K. Wrigley. Wrigley also was president and owned about 80 percent of the voting stock. Schlensky alleged negligence and mismanagement for failure to install floodlights to permit night games. He claimed that funds for the installation could be obtained and would be far more than recaptured by increased ticket sales. Allegedly Wrigley thought that baseball was a daytime sport and that night games would have a negative effect on the neighborhood surrounding the ball park, and the other directors gave in. The trial court dismissed the complaint, and Schlensky appealed. How should the appellate court rule? (*Schlensky v. Wrigley*, 237 N.E.2d 776, Ill.)

29. Two attorney-shareholders in Ched Realty sought to buy out the shares of two recently deceased shareholders in the company. The attorneys cited a clause in a shareholder agreement that allowed them to buy the shares at "book value or $200 per share, whichever was greater." At the time, the book value of the shares was negative, as the assets of the longstanding corporation had been depreciated to nothing. However, the market value of the shares was well over $40,000 per share. The estates of the two deceased shareholders sued to block the sale for $200 per share claiming that the deceased shareholders were not fully aware of what they were signing because they were older and had not completed high school. The lower court disallowed the shareholder agreement. The two attorneys appealed. Should the appeals court overturn the lower court's ruling? Why or why not? (*Rosiny v. Schmidt*, 587 N.Y.S.2d 929)

30. After decades of operating as a partnership, the Bay Minette Flower Shop was incorporated in the early 1970s. Prior to its incorporation it had opened an account with a wholesaler, M & M Wholesaler Florist, Inc. M & M continued to supply Bay Minette and was never told of the incorporation. Finally, in the early 1990s, M & M sued the Bay Minette Flower Shop and its owners personally for an overdue debt. Should the court allow the piercing of the corporate veil to attach liability to the stockholders of Bay Minette because they did not inform M & M of the change in status? Why or why not? (*M & M Wholesale Florist, Inc. v. Emmons*, 600 So.2d 998)

CASE FOR LEGAL THINKING

K. C. ROOFING CENTER v. ON TOP ROOFING
807 S.W. 2D 545

FACTS On Top Roofing, Inc., was incorporated in 1977 as Russell Nugent Roofing, Inc., but changed its name to On Top Roofing, Inc., in 1985. Russell and Carol Nugent were the sole shareholders, officers, and directors of the corporation. On Top ceased doing business in 1987 when RNR Inc., was incorporated with Russell and Carol Nugent as the sole shareholders, officers, and directors of the corporation.

RNR went out of business in 1988 and RLN Construction, Inc., was incorporated in its stead with Russell and Carol Nugent again the sole shareholders, officers, and directors of the corporation. RLN Construction went out of business in 1989 and Mr. Nugent then formed Russell Nugent Inc.

All the companies were located at the same address, 614 Main in Grandview, Missouri, which was owned by the Nugents and used the same business telephone number. Although three directors were required, only Carol and Russell Nugent had been directors for several years.

Mr. Nugent's corporations did not produce records of any annual meetings in 1988 or 1989. In 1987, K. C. Roofing Center (the plaintiff) advanced about $45,000 in roofing supplies to On Top, which went unpaid, and fostered this suit.

Mr. Nugent testified that he stopped buying materials from suppliers when they refused to advance any more materials on credit.

Finally, it was shown that Carol and Russell Nugent received rent for 614 Main in amounts varying with the success of the corporations they owned and in 1986 included a $99,290 rent payment in addition to their $100,000 salaries for that term.

REASONING Alleging the debtors (Nugents) used the corporate form for improper purposes and acted in a manner showing they themselves disregarded the corporate form except for its limited liability protection, the creditors brought suit to "pierce the corporate veil" of On Top Roofing, Inc., and thereby go beyond corporate limited liability to affix full personal liability on its owners.

LOWER COURT HOLDING The court with original jurisdiction denied the creditors' request, and they appealed.

PRACTICE JUDGING

1. Have the Nugents used the corporate form for its proper purposes? Why or why not?

2. Should the corporate protection of limited liability be pierced here to make the Nugents fully personally liable for the debts of On Top Roofing?

3. Should the suppliers of On Top Roofing and the other Nugent corporations have any blame allocated to them for their being in their current position?

© GETTY IMAGES/PHOTODISC

Organizational Forms for Small Business

27-1 Traditional Small Business Forms

27-2 New and Evolving Small Business Forms

© GETTY IMAGES/PHOTODISC

HOT DEBATE

Earl opened his recreational vehicle repair garage, Snowbird's Nest, in Florida in the late 1970s. He incorporated the garage as a C corporation. As the years wore on, Earl retained this status although his CPA told him he was losing money due to the double taxation. Now that his children are out of college and settled down, Earl has decided to take more risks. He plans to expand his garage operation into a couple of other locations, start selling accessories for RVs, and open an RV park. He also is considering taking a new business form. His CPA has advised him that he can elect to be taxed as a subchapter S corporation just by filing a one-page form with the IRS. The CPA even offered to do it for Earl for free. The CPA also told Earl that for around $750, an attorney could move his company into an LLC form.

Where Do You Stand?

1. List and discuss the reasons that Earl might want to assume the subchapter S form.

2. List and discuss the reasons that Earl might want to assume the LLC form.

Traditional Small Business Forms

▼ GOALS

- Contrast the roles of general partners and limited partners in a limited partnership
- Explain why the owners of a C corporation would elect the S corporation status

LIMITED PARTNERSHIPS

WHAT'S YOUR VERDICT?

Melbourne, a wealthy financier, decided to invest as a limited partner in a business that manufactured a new form of collapsible luggage. The business did well. One day, when he was at the main office, the general partner mentioned that she was going to move the business into another field of manufacture. Melbourne, who had invested 80 percent of the capital to start it, blurted out, "Oh no, not with my money you're not." The general partner, in front of all the front office personnel, immediately retracted her decision. Later, one of the front-office secretaries, Jim, won his suit against the partnership for sexual harassment. He could only collect $500,000 of the $1,000,000 damage award from the business. Therefore, he went after Melbourne's private fortune. Jim cited the incident in the front office as proof that Melbourne was a general partner and, as a consequence, fully personally liable.

Will Jim be able to recover the remaining damages from Melbourne's private fortune?

Because today's economic giants all have their origins in small ventures, organizational forms have been created to help similar small businesses develop. These forms evolve constantly but have their roots in the limited partnership and the subchapter S corporation forms. This lesson discusses these two older forms, and the next lesson covers those more recently developed.

ATTRIBUTES OF THE LIMITED PARTNERSHIP

In a limited partnership, there must be at least one general partner with unlimited liability. All the other partners may be limited partners. Limited partners are liable only to the extent of their investment in the business. The general partners in a limited partnership have full managerial control over running the business. They are the ultimate decision-makers about such factors as who has what responsibilities in making the business a success.

As with a general partnership, if the terms of the partnership agreement are not set out by the partners themselves, the law will impose its own terms. However, the government intrudes further into the domain of the partners in a limited partnership than it does in a general partnership. In the eyes of government, this additional intrusive behavior is warranted due to the limited liability provisions afforded the limited partners.

IN THIS CASE

Fresh out of business school, Maltese formed a limited partnership with Dr. Falcon, a noted surgeon, as the limited partner who supplied the capital. After five years of intense work by Maltese, during which she acquired many personal assets, the business was a roaring success. Finally, Maltese decided that it was time to do something she had put off for too long—to change the business from a limited partnership to the corporate form. Such a move would eliminate the full personal liability to which she had been exposed as the general partner since the business began. Dr. Falcon would continue to enjoy a limited liability protection.

FORMING A LIMITED PARTNERSHIP

Unlike a general partnership, a limited partnership can only be created by following the procedures set forth in the controlling state statute. Although most states originally enacted a controlling statute modeled after the Uniform Limited Partnership Act (ULPA), the majority have now amended their statutes to conform to the provisions of the Revised Uniform Limited Partnership Act (RULPA). Regardless, unlike the general partnership, a limited partnership can be created only by proper execution, recording, and publication of a certificate that identifies the partners and states basic facts about their agreement.

The sample limited partnership certificate shown below is based on the RULPA requirements. Note that the limited partnership is legally formed at the time of the filing, usually with the Secretary of State. If the filing requirements of the controlling statute are not met, all business participants are treated as general partners.

RECORD KEEPING FOR A LIMITED PARTNERSHIP

In addition to the information contained in the Certificate of Limited Partnership, the RULPA requires certain records to be kept at the office specified in paragraph 2 of the certificate. These records include

1. A list of the last known addresses of the general and limited partners with each properly identified as general or limited

2. Copies of the certificate of limited partnership and its amendments

3. Copies of the limited partnership's local, state, and federal income tax returns for the three most recent years

4. Copies of any currently effective partnership agreement and any financial statements issued for the three most recent years

5. Unless contained in the partnership agreement, a listing of the amount of cash and property contributed or pledged by any partner, times of any future contributions by any partner, and agreed-to circumstances that might require the limited partnership's dissolution and winding up

Any of these records are obtainable by subpoena and are subject to inspection and copying by the reasonable request of any partner during ordinary business hours.

STATUS OF THE PARTNERS

Under the ULPA, limited partners who participate in any managerial decisions lose their status and become liable without limit as general partners. This rule was relaxed and redefined by the Revised Uniform Limited Partnership Act (RULPA). Under the provisions of the RULPA, a limited partner does not participate in the managerial control of the business solely by doing such things as consulting with the general partner(s), acting as an agent or employee for the partnership, attending meetings of the general partners,

---

CERTIFICATE OF LIMITED PARTNERSHIP

1. **Name** (must contain without abbreviation the words "Limited Partnership")—Burnin' Hot Charcoal, A Limited Partnership

2. **Address of Office** (need not be a place of business but must be located in the state where records required by RULPA are kept)—350 BarBQ Lane, Westown, NM

3. **Agent for Service of Process** (must be either a natural resident, domestic corporation, or foreign corporation authorized to do business in New Mexico)—Howard Fernandez, 1339 Savory Street, Liberty NM

4. **Name and Address of Each General Partner**—Margaret Whitaker, 1313 Hideaway Haven, Bluffton, NM

5. **Latest Date Upon Which the Limited Partnership is to Dissolve**—March 13, 2013

6. **Any Other Matters the General Partners Determine to Include Therein**—N/A

Filed with the Secretary of State, March 13, 2006,
and effective as of that date

---

or by participating in the restructuring of the partnership.

In *What's Your Verdict?* the answer would depend on the state that had jurisdiction over the case. In a state that has not adopted the RULPA, Jim would be able to recover the remaining $500,000 against the private fortune of Melbourne. If the RULPA were in place, however, Melbourne would probably be able to keep his private fortune intact. This is because the RULPA does allow limited partners to participate in decisions that pertain to the structuring of the partnership. Consequently, if the lawyer for Melbourne could show how the move into another field of manufacture would necessitate such restructuring, his private fortune would be safe.

Under almost all controlling statutes, if a limited partner knowingly allows her or his name to be used in the name of the limited partnership, that limited partner is liable to creditors who extend credit without actual knowledge that she or he is a limited partner.

CHECKPOINT

How do general partners differ from limited partners in a limited partnership?

SUBCHAPTER S CORPORATIONS

WHAT'S YOUR VERDICT?

Juwon and Ennis founded a business partnership to remanufacture alternators for automobiles. After several successful years, they adopted the C corporation form and have operated under it for almost a decade. Recently Juwon bought Ennis' stock and is now the sole owner of the corporation. Juwon wants to become a subchapter S corporation and avoid the double taxation.

Can Juwon elect the subchapter S corporation form?

Several decades ago, Congress authorized a new corporate form. It was intended to give small business owners a tax break by allowing them to choose an alternative to the traditional corporate form governed by subchapter C of the Internal Revenue Code. This was important as subchapter C corporations are subject to double taxation.

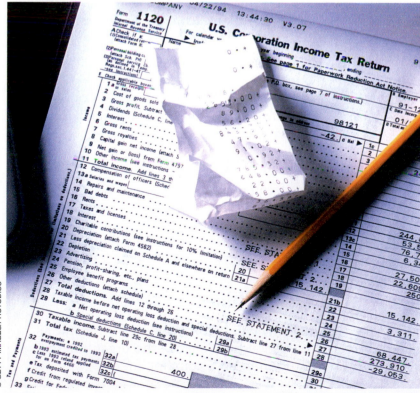

Explain why the earnings of C corporations are said to be subject to double taxation.

© GETTY IMAGES/PHOTODISC

Double taxation means that the corporation is taxed on corporate income and corporate shareholder owners are taxed on dividends. This alternative form provided by Congress is the **S corporation**, governed by subchapter S of the Internal Revenue Code. By making the owners of small corporations exempt from double taxation, Congress hoped to leave them with more funds to grow their businesses.

ATTRIBUTES OF THE SUBCHAPTER S FORM

An eligible corporation need only elect to be taxed as an S corporation. When it does so, corporate earnings are treated the same as a gain (or loss) from a partnership and only taxed at the individual owner's level. The elimination of double taxation in this manner resulted in many businesses adopting this form. Even though newer business forms with more attractive corporate and partnership attribute mixes are now available (see the next lesson), businesses still choose the subchapter S form due to its ease of entry from the C corporate form. Juwon in *What's Your Verdict?* could take advantage of this ease of entry by simply filing the one-page election form with the IRS before March 15 of the year in which he wants the business to be classified as a subchapter S corporation.

Electing to be taxed as an S corporation will allow Juwon to treat his business income or loss as personal income or loss on his taxes. In addition, the best elements of the corporate form, such as limited liability, perpetual life, and free transferability of ownership interests will be retained for his business.

ELIGIBILITY REQUIREMENTS FOR AN S CORPORATION

In order to qualify as an S corporation under the IRS code, the business must satisfy several requirements.

1. *Timely filing* A corporation wanting to be taxed as an S corporation must file the appropriate form indicating such an election with the IRS before March 15 of the tax year in which the election is to be effective. The election must reflect the unanimous choice of the stockholders. Any election of an S-qualified company to resume being taxed as a C corporation also must be the unanimous decision of shareholders.

2. *Domestic corporation* The S corporation status is reserved for businesses incorporated in the United States.

3. *Identity of shareholders* Only natural persons, estates, or certain types of trusts can be shareholders in an S corporation. Other corporations, partnerships, and non-qualifying trusts cannot. In addition, nonresident aliens cannot be shareholders.

4. *Number of shareholders* The corporation must have 75 or fewer stockholders.

5. *Classes of stock* The corporation can have only one class of stock. Shareholders do not have to have the same voting rights.

FORMATION OF AN S CORPORATION

The S corporation is not so much a corporate form as it is a tax status. To form such an entity, one needs only to be in the form of a corporation and then make a qualified filing with the IRS.

CHECKPOINT

Why would the owners of a C corporation elect to change the organizational form to an S corporation?

THINK ABOUT LEGAL CONCEPTS

1. There could be ten or more general partners in a limited partnership. **True or False?**

2. Which uniform act is more flexible in the governing of key issues of limited partnerships? (a) ULPA (b) RULPA

3. A limited partner might be held personally liable to the firm's creditors by letting her/his name be used in the limited partnership's name. **True or False?**

4. Which of the following records do not have to be kept in the limited partnership's designated office within the certifying state? (a) tax records for the last five years (b) names and addresses of all the general partners (c) names and addresses of all the limited partners (d) all of the above

5. A subchapter S corporation can include as a stockholder a venture capitalist living in Kyoto, Japan. **True or False?**

6. What is the maximum number of stockholders in a subchapter S corporation? (a) 15 (b) 50 (c) 75 (d) unlimited

7. All a corporation's shareholders must assent before the subchapter S status can be assumed. **True or False?**

THINK CRITICALLY ABOUT EVIDENCE

Study the situation, answer the questions, and then prepare arguments to support your answers.

8. Judith's brother, a famous actor, left her a fortune. She wanted to invest part of it in a start-up business venture. At a party, Judith met Hector, an electrical engineer with an invention that he wanted to market. Judith liked the idea and wanted to capitalize the venture with $150,000. However, she wanted to be able to maintain control over who had an ownership interest in the business and all the business losses for tax purposes, and keep her liability limited to what she had invested in the concern. Hector had no money to invest but did have the rights to the invention and some managerial skills. What business form would you recommend? Why?

9. In a state in which only the ULPA is in effect, Dee was a limited partner in a small manufacturing business. One day she insisted that the general partner hire her sister as his administrative assistant. Did her action make her as liable as a general partner for the debts of the business?

10. In exercise 9, if RULPA is in effect, would Dee be liable as a general partner for the business debts?

11. Eriq wanted to start a tennis court repair business. To get the supplies and capital equipment needed, he decided to form a corporation and issue stock. Some 83 investors, including a closely held corporation owned by his dad, bought stock. Later, Eriq wanted to elect the subchapter S form of corporation. Can he do so? Why or why not?

12. Tracy wanted to start a company to make Christmas ornaments. Her mother agreed to help fund the company by buying stock in it. Tracy's attorney suggested that she utilize the subchapter S form for the business. Tracy knew that the subchapter S form only had one class of stock. She worried that if she and her mother both had the same level of ownership, her mother might try to manage the company. Tracy thought it might be a better idea to form a regular corporation and sell her mother preferred stock with no voting rights. The lawyer shook her head. "That means you'll likely have to pay thousands more in taxes. Instead, let me tell you some good news about the subchapter S stock." What was that good news?

13. Tracy (in exercise 12) mentioned to her lawyer that she wanted to be sure that, if her company were successful, she could pass its ownership on to either or both of her two daughters. She mentioned that she was worried that, like a partnership, the subchapter S corporation would end when she died. Is this correct? Why or why not?

New and Evolving Small Business Forms

▼ GOALS

- Explain the attributes of the LLC that make it ideal for small businesses
- State why the LLP form is so useful to professional partnerships

THE LIMITED LIABILITY CORPORATION

WHAT'S YOUR VERDICT?

Jose wanted a business form that had the limited liability protection of the corporation, no double taxation, and no restrictions on ownership.

Which form should he choose?

For years, the best forms of business organization for small businesses were the limited partnership and the subchapter S corporation. These forms, however, had flaws and limitations that needed to be improved upon. These improvements began to appear in the American West in 1977. The Economic Impact feature on this page explains the introduction of the limited liability corporation (LLC) form of business organization in the United States. This form offers limited liability, taxation as a partnership, and few of the restrictions encountered in the S corporation or limited partnership.

FORMATION OF AN LLC

Similar to a corporation or limited partnership, a limited liability corporation (LLC) must be formed and operated in accordance with the law in the state in which it was organized. In most states, an LLC is formed by filing articles of organization in an appropriate state office (usually the Secretary of State's office). A typical "articles of organization" submission is shown on page 495.

The owners of an LLC are known as members. Their liability is limited to the amount that they have invested in the business, and the earnings of the LLC are taxed as a partnership. However, some states allow certain members to declare themselves as fully personally liable at the time of organization. This often is a plus with potential creditors who want someone's personal assets at risk in addition to the corporation's.

ECONOMIC IMPACT

BIRTH OF THE LIMITED LIABILITY CORPORATION

In 1977 legislators in Wyoming took a bold step toward providing the ultimate in small business organization alternatives to Americans by passing a statute that authorized creating Limited Liability Corporations (LLCs) in their state. They based their statutory creation on forms of business organizations that existed in Europe and South America. In essence, the LLC offered limited liability protection and taxation as a partnership, but lacked the limitations of the subchapter S or limited partnership alternatives. For more than a decade, however, the LLC remained an alternative only in Wyoming and Florida. (Florida imitated Wyoming's creative action by passing a similar statute in 1982.) Interest in LLCs mushroomed in 1988, when the Internal Revenue Service ruled that LLCs would be taxed as partnerships at the federal level. By late 1997, every state in the union had an LLC-empowering statute. Today, small businesses throughout America are better protected and capitalized as a result.

THINK CRITICALLY

Why do you think it took so long for the United States to allow LLCs when they had been in existence in Europe and South America for an extended time?

ARTICLES OF ORGANIZATION

1. **Name*** —The Moot Point LLC

2. **Nature of Business** —Retailer of fine accessories for the successful attorney

3. **Office Address** —1339 W. Synchronicity Blvd., Coincidence, Colorado

4. **Agent for Service of Process** —Ben Acausal, 1339 W. Synchronicity Blvd., Coincidence, Colorado

5. **Name and Address of Organizers** —Ben Acausal, 1339 W. Synchronicity Blvd., Coincidence, Colorado

6. **Names of Initial LLC Members** —Ben and Susan Acausal, 1339 W. Synchronicity Blvd., Coincidence, Colorado

* Note that the business's name must include the LLC designation or the full Limited Liability Company title.

THE OPERATING AGREEMENT

After the articles of organization, the most necessary document for an LLC is its **operating agreement**. This document is somewhat like the bylaws of a corporation but more far reaching. An operating agreement is required by many states but, whether required or not, is a good idea even in an LLC with just one member. When there is only one member, the operating agreement protects the LLC from appearing as a sole proprietorship and thus possibly being stripped of its limited liability protection in a court action.

An operating agreement should cover the following:

1. *Assignment of percentages of ownership* Most states have a "default" statute that will assign percentages of ownership according to the value of capital contributions. However, this statute only comes into play if the members do not assign the percentages in the operating agreement. Oftentimes, one member may not be able to contribute much in capital but deserves—and needs to be motivated by—a large ownership interest. The LLC form allows such an assignment regardless of capital contribution percentages.

2. *Assignment of distributive shares* Although most often assigned in the same percentage as capital contributions in the state's default statute, the members can allocate each

When drawing up the operating agreement, what do the members of an LLC need to consider in assigning percentages of ownership?

© GETTY IMAGES/PHOTODISC

member's shares of profits and losses as they see fit. These **distributive shares** do not have to be equal percentages for profits and for losses. Many times a person with outside income will want to take a much larger percentage of the LLCs losses than profits for tax purposes. It also is wise to note in the operating agreement if and when the distributive shares will be paid.

3. *Voting rights* The operating agreement should reflect the members' choice between whether each has a vote on important matters (called per capita voting) or if they have voting power proportional to their capital investment percentages.

4. *Member rights and duties* The operating agreement can specify which members have the power to bind the LLC to contracts of various kinds and which do not. Possession and use of LLC property also can be covered.

5. *Prohibitions on sale of interest* Any restrictions on members selling their interests should be explicitly stated in the operating agreement.

6. *Termination of ownership interests* Procedure on how to value and buy out the interests of

members who die, retire, or withdraw for other reasons should be specified in the operating agreement.

Other stipulations can be included in the operating agreement. If the members do not formulate provisions for their agreement themselves, the state of organization likely will have a default statute to provide missing terms. These terms probably will not be as desirable as those the members could have created for themselves.

Cyberlaw

Today a number of companies provide services that allow a business to be incorporated via the Internet. Basically, the provider of the service does the paperwork and filing of the documents. It also typically acts as the long-term representative, called a registered agent, for the new company in the jurisdiction awarding the charter. Of course, it has long been possible for a business of one state to incorporate in another—it has just not been this easy. Because of revenue generated, states vie for the position of "most hospitable" to foreign (out of state) incorporators. Delaware and Nevada are the most utilized jurisdictions at the moment. However, the Internet brings an international set of options to such a decision. Through the Internet it is possible to exercise the option of incorporating "offshore" with relative ease. Offshore typically refers to "safe financial havens" where privacy is as much the currency as the dollar and means out of the jurisdiction of the United States and the easy reach of its legal process. Currently a major shift in the availability of "safe havens" is underway. Many old havens associated with Great Britain, such as the Cayman Islands, Anguilla, Bermuda, British Virgin Islands, Montserrat, Turks and Caicos, the Isle of Man, and the British Channel Islands have had the privacy protection diminished by international accords. New havens, such as the Caribbean Island of Nevis, and assistance by the Internet, have moved in to take their place.

THINK ABOUT IT

One such Internet site offering offshore incorporations offers protection from "litigious attorneys, employers/employees, ex-spouses, ex-business partners, big brother and others" that might invade the privacy of their users. Are these ethical reasons for choosing the corporate form? For incorporating offshore?

ADVANTAGES OF LLCS

The most significant advantages that make LLCs more attractive than other small business forms are the following.

1. No limitation on the number of members (the S corporation currently limits the number of stockholders to 75).

2. No limitations as to whom or what can be a stockholder in an LLC. Therefore, foreign nationals, corporations, and other business entities can be shareholders.

3. Members are allowed to participate completely in managing the business. There are no worries of losing the limited liability status for those who do manage, as might be the case even under RULPA.

DISADVANTAGES OF THE LLC

After several decades of modification, the LLC has become the ideal form for most small businesses. Tests imposed on it in the mid-1990s by the IRS to determine if it should be afforded limited liability status have been swept away. The only relative disadvantage to the form impacts those who encounter tax problems in transferring assets from a partnership or other type of corporation to the LLC. A partial solution to this remaining problem exists in the recently created form of the limited liability partnership which will be discussed in the next section.

Today, however, the attributes of the LLC are so suitable to small businesses that, unless a business entity is either a corporation formed under a state incorporation statute (not an LLC statute), a publicly traded corporation, or particular types of foreign-owned corporations, it will be presumed by the IRS to want to be taxed as an LLC. If the business entity wants to be taxed as a corporation, it can achieve this end by simply checking a box on the appropriate IRS form. With all this in mind, Jose in *What's Your Verdict?* would do well to choose the LLC form.

CHECKPOINT

What are the most significant advantages of the LLC for small businesses?

NETBookmark

Access lawxtra.swlearning.com and click on the link for Chapter 27. Read the article about Limited Liability Companies (LLCs). Then select your state or another state on the left side of the home page. Read the "Details Specific to [state name] Incorporation." Prepare a short oral report on what you learned from this material about starting a LLC in the state you chose.

lawxtra.swlearning.com

THE LIMITED LIABILITY PARTNERSHIP

WHAT'S YOUR VERDICT?

Drs. Bryant, Rico, and Ferrar wanted to form a partnership. Dr. Rico, however, was concerned about the possibility of being held personally liable for any malpractice claims against her partners.

What business form could protect Dr. Rico from such claims?

With all the advantages of the LLC, it is hard to imagine a need for any other small business form. However, as mentioned above, already-existing business entities might find it difficult to convert to an LLC form due to tax and asset appreciation issues. In addition, especially for partnerships constructed for professionals, the difficulty is not limited to these taxation problems but extends to the complexity of ending the partnership, valuing the interests, and then fairly reestablishing the concern as an LLC.

As a consequence, in 1991 Texas created the **limited liability partnership (LLP)**. This form offered ease of conversion from an existing partnership, avoidance of double taxation, and partial limited liability protection. Barely more than a decade later, almost all the states have enacted LLP statutes, mostly by simply amending already-existing partnership statutes.

Under the majority of the LLP statutes, the limited liability protection extends only to shield against the consequences of conduct involving the torts of others in the partnership. The Texas statute, for example, protects innocent partners from the consequences of errors, omissions, negligence, incompetence, or wrongdoing stemming from partnership operations.

Therefore, if a partner commits professional malpractice and the recovery from it exceeds the amount of liability insurance coverage the partnership or that individual carries, the other partners will not have their personal fortunes endangered. In *What's Your Verdict?* Dr. Rico would be protected from personal liability for malpractice claims against Drs. Bryant and Ferrer if they formed an LLP. The partners remain responsible for other debts such as wages or loans.

Imagine that one of these doctors is a member of an LLP with other doctors. The doctor makes a mistake on the operating table, and the patient dies because of it. The patient's family sues the doctor, and they are awarded an amount that exceeds the LLP's liability insurance coverage. What is the extent of the other partners' liability for the mistake?

© GETTY IMAGES/PHOTODISC

CHECKPOINT

What limited liability protection does an LLP offer?

LEGAL RESEARCH

Compare and contrast the information required by your state for the formation of a sole proprietorship, a general partnership, a limited partnership, a corporation, a limited liability corporation, a limited liability partnership, and any other hybrid business form legally available. What does the information you find tell you about the state's regulatory emphasis in the area of forms of business organization?

Law Brief

Medical malpractice is a form of professional malpractice in which a professional breaches his or her duty of ordinary care. An example of medical malpractice would be a surgeon amputating the wrong limb of a patient. Medical malpractice also may apply to misdiagnosing patients' medical problems. In the United States, about 80,000 people die each year due in part to medical malpractice. Only 2 percent of the patients who are victims of medical malpractice seek compensation through filing a lawsuit. Doctors are not required to purchase medical malpractice insurance.

THINK ABOUT LEGAL CONCEPTS

1. LLCs are modeled on a type of business form that has existed for many years in Europe and South America. **True or False?**

2. The members of an LLC can define the ownership percentages as they see fit regardless of capital contributions. **True or False?**

3. The members of an LLC can define the _?_ shares of the profits for the members.

4. The operating agreement is the same as the articles of organization of an LLC. **True or False?**

5. An LLC can have no more than 75 members. **True or False?**

6. Which of the following could not be an LLC member? (a) corporation (b) partnership (c) foreign, nonresident, national (d) all of the above can be members

7. LLCs are still subject to double taxation. **True or False?**

8. For professional partnerships, the main advantage of an LLP over an LLC is the ease of transferring to the LLP form. **True or False?**

THINK CRITICALLY ABOUT EVIDENCE

Study the situation, answer the questions, and then prepare arguments to support your answers.

9. Phil Rosato and his three brothers formed a business to manufacture baseball mitts. A minor league baseball club, the Carolina Copperheads, wanted to invest in the business so as to have specialty gloves made for it by the Rosatos. Also, due to the depreciation of their newly purchased equipment, the Rosatos were sure to have losses for the first two years. Thereafter, the profits should be substantial. As far as the Copperheads are concerned, why would the LLC form be better for the Rosatos than the S corporation?

10. All four Rosato brothers plan to continue working at their current jobs for the first year or so after the business starts up. How will the LLC

form help them tax-wise? Once the Rosatos' business starts to show a profit in the third year, how will the LLC form help them even more?

11. If the Rosatos' business grows, the likelihood of marketing their gloves in Japan seems great. The Rosatos feel that, should they decide to penetrate the Japanese market, they would want to bring in as a member their long-time friend, Mickie Hosaido. Mickie is a Japanese national living in Tokyo. How would the LLC form facilitate bringing Mickie into the business better than the S corporation form?

12. To facilitate going international, the Rosatos will probably have to "go public" and list their stock on a major stock exchange. How will this affect their choice of business form?

PREVENT LEGAL DIFFICULTIES

In choosing a form for a small business . . .

1. Carefully evaluate the advantages and disadvantages of each of the forms discussed in this chapter before making your choice.

2. In evaluating the limited partnership form, note that the death, disability, or withdrawal of a partner may place the business in serious jeopardy due to the necessity of dissolution.

3. If you already are in the corporate form, the most convenient way to avoid double taxation is to elect the subchapter S corporate form.

4. If you are not in the corporate form, the LLC is highly recommended. Compare the various LLC statutes in order to select the best state in which to organize.

5. Remember the limited liability inherent in the LLP is typically a protection against financial loss stemming from conduct involving a tort, not other potential sources of liability.

Chapter 27 Assessment

CONCEPTS IN BRIEF

27-1 Traditional Small Business Forms

1. The primary advantages of most small business forms are the avoidance of double taxation and limited liability.

2. The limited partnership form requires one partner with full personal liability but this is often required by lenders of LLCs as well.

3. Limited partnerships, like all partnerships, do not have perpetual life.

4. The subchapter S business form, while easy to assume, comes with several eligibility requirements.

27-2 New and Evolving Small Business Forms

5. The LLC has evolved from an obscure beginning to become the most chosen and optimal small business form in the United States.

6. The LLC has the desirable attributes of the subchapter S form but without the limitations.

7. The operating agreement is vital to the legal status of the LLC.

8. Tax problems encountered by professional partnerships trying to assume the LLC form have been alleviated by the LLP form.

YOUR LEGAL VOCABULARY

Match each statement with the term that it best defines. Some terms may not be used.

1. Owners of an LLC

2. Form of business organization that offers limited liability only to the consequences of conduct involving torts

3. Form of business organization offering limited liability and the elimination of double taxation but limiting the number and types of permitted shareholders

4. Document filed with the state to organize an LLC

5. Taxation of a corporation as an entity based on its earnings and then of the shareholders on corporate dividends

> a. articles of organization
> b. distributive shares
> c. double taxation
> d. limited liability corporation (LLC)
> e. limited liability partnership (LLP)
> f. members
> g. operating agreement
> h. S corporation

6. Form of business organization that avoids double taxation, affords limited liability protection, and is without limits imposed on other forms

7. The equivalent of corporate bylaws but for an LLC

8. Agreed-to percentage split of LLC profits and losses

REVIEW LEGAL CONCEPTS

9. What records are limited partnerships required by law to keep?

10. Why is there a prohibition against ownership of a subchapter S corporation by another corporation?

11. What is the financial effect for a business of organizing as an LLC?

12. Why is the operating agreement so important for an LLC?

WRITE ABOUT LEGAL CONCEPTS

13. Fill out an articles of organization form for an imaginary business or one that you are familiar with.

14. For the business in exercise 13, make up an operating agreement covering each of the suggested areas mentioned on pages 495 and 496. Presume there are at least two members.

15. Suppose you and a friend decide to start a business writing and selling computer programs. Make a list of the pros and cons of each form of business organization you are considering.

16. **HOT DEBATE** Discuss the disadvantages that the S and LLC forms pose for Earl. Choose the form you think Earl should utilize and justify your choice in a short paper.

MAKE ACADEMIC CONNECTIONS

17. **POLITICAL SCIENCE** The acceptance of the LLC business form by the IRS came after a power struggle between the states and the federal government. The federal government saw the potential for business growth in the new status. The states stood to lose large amounts of corporate tax revenue without any compensating funding from the federal level. Research the development of this conflict and how it was resolved within the political and legal systems.

THINK CRITICALLY ABOUT EVIDENCE

Study the situation, answer the questions, and then prepare arguments to support your answers.

18. West Virginia Tank and Tower Inc. bought and sold used water towers. One of its 75 stockholders was a Canadian living in Chicago; the remainder were United States citizens. When the company filed its corporate tax return on April 15, it elected to be taxed as an S corporation for the previous tax year. Will the IRS allow their election? Explain your answer.

19. Della Octaves, a well-known opera singer, was a limited partner in "Octaves and Clark, a limited partnership." The Florida real estate development concern's only project was the construction and management of Octaves Area, a residential retirement complex for senior citizens. When the partnership approached a group of local banks for an expansion loan, it did not mention that Octaves was just a limited partner. The loan was for $1.5 million and is now in default. Can the banks collect what is due from Octaves' personal fortune?

20. Three doctors were in a limited liability partnership with Dr. S. Kay Bell. The practice's offices were in Dallas, Texas. During a minor plastic surgery, one of Dr. Bell's partners severed an artery of a patient and the patient died. The family brought suit and recovered more than $4 million dollars. The financial resources of the negligent surgeon are financially exhausted after paying nearly $1.5 million dollars of the recovery. The partnership's liability policy has covered all but $1 million of the rest. Now the other doctors want to take out a loan in the partnership's name to cover the remaining million. Dr. Bell has come to you for advice as to whether or not she should go along with the idea. How would you advise her? Why?

21. Quiet Running, a closely held LLC, produces electric cars. It recently secured the rights to a patent that will allow it to produce such cars with a cruising range of nearly 500 miles. In order to meet the anticipated demand, it needs a large amount of capital to set up a new factory. You are the corporate counsel and are attending a board meeting when one of the company's financial advisors suggests that the company "go public" with their stock. What advice would you give as to the potential impact of doing so on the company's organizational form?

22. A limited partnership was formed to promote a boxing match between professional football player Lyle Alzado and an ex-boxing heavyweight champion, Muhummad Ali. The limited partner in the deal was to be the firm of Blinder, Robinson and Co. with Alzado and others joined together in an organization known as Combat Associates to be the general partner. Alzado personally guaranteed that if the proceeds of the match were to be less than $250,000 he would make up the difference. In preparation for the match, Blinder, Robinson and Co.'s president participated in interviews and a promotional rally. In addition, the company allowed one of its offices to be used as a ticket office and also held parties. When the proceeds came to less than $250,000, Blinder sued Alzado for the shortfall. Alzado counterclaimed contending that Blinder, Robinson and Co. had acted in such a way that it had become a general partner. How should the court rule on the general partner issue? Why? (*Blinder, Robinson and Co. v. Alzado*, 713 P. 2d 1314)

23. Ward Parkway was a wholly owned subsidiary of Kroh Brothers Development Company. Ward Parkway was also the general partner in West Tech, a limited partnership. Boatmen's Bank made a $1.3 million loan to West Tech but deposited it in the Kroh Brothers Development Company accounts. Section 620.60(2) of the ULPA states that an act of a partner that is not apparently for the carrying on of the business of the partnership in the usual way does not bind the partnership unless authorized by the other partners. No such authority was forthcoming from any partner when Jacob D. Mondahein, executed the note for the loan as vice president of West Parkway. Mondahein also directed Boatmen's to put the money in the Kroh Brothers account. Should Boatmen's be able to collect its money from West Tech? Why or why not? (*West Tech, Ltd. v. Boatmen's First National Bank of Kansas City*, 882 F. 2d 323)

24. Allright Missouri, Inc. (Allright), a Missouri corporation, was a limited partner in Downtown Development Associates, Ltd. (Downtown). The limited partnership was formed to develop two city blocks located in an area known as Lacledes Landing in downtown St. Louis, Missouri. When questions arose as to the transfer of some of Downtown's land to another limited partnership, Allright and many other limited partners sought to sue Downtown. Should limited partners be allowed to sue the partnership they are a part of? Why or why not? (*Allright Missouri, Inc. v. Billeter*, 829 F. 2d 635)

25. American National Insurance Co. had a foreclosure sale on a limited partnership's property to recover an amount owed. The proceeds fell short by almost $1.5 million. To recover the shortfall, American National sought to recover against individuals who became partners after the obligation was undertaken by the limited partnership. Can it do so? Why or why not? (*American National Insurance Co. v. Gilroy, Sims and Associates*, 874 F. Supp. 973)

26. Ramsey Homebuilders was a limited partnership that constructed residential properties in the state of Alabama. Ramsey was the general partner in the firm while two others were limited partners. Ramsey had a bad credit history. So, when funds were needed to increase the partnership business, his signature alone often was not enough. Flanagan Lumber Company at first denied credit to the partnership. Pitman was one of the two limited partners and the possessor of a longstanding credit account with Flanagan. Pitman contacted Flanagan's credit manager and was able to get an account opened in Ramsey Homebuilders' name. When the partnership failed to pay off its account, Flanagan sued Pitman, alleging that his vouching for the partnership's credit made him responsible for the partnership's debt. The trial court found that Pitman had exercised control of the business by securing credit for it. Therefore, Pitman was held personally liable for the Flanagan debt. Pitman appealed to the Supreme Court of Alabama. Control is defined as "the power or authority to manage, direct, superintend, regulate, govern, administer, or oversee" according to Black's Law Dictionary. Did Pitman exercise control and therefore become liable for the debt? Why or why not? (*Pitman v. Flanagan Lumber Co.*, 567 So.2d 1335)

UNITED STATES V. DORMILEE MORTON
U.S. DISTRICT COURT FOR THE EASTERN DISTRICT OF MISSOURI
682 F. SUPP. 999

FACTS Until his death, Cody Morton, deceased husband of the defendant, operated a construction business out of the family home. Upon Cody's death, Dormilee Morton succeeded to her husband's ownership interest in the business.

In the years before the construction company finally ceased doing business, it became liable for at least 16 unpaid quarters of withholding taxes for its laborers. The Internal Revenue Service then brought suit.

Dormilee Morton contends that she should not be held liable for the overdue taxes because she was not a general partner in the business but, at most, a limited partner.

The evidence showed that from time to time Mrs. Morton would sign bank notes and supporting documents granting security interests in the business equipment. The signatures would be in the form of "Dormilee Morton and Steven Morton (son) d/b/a Morton Construction Company. Mrs. Morton also provided funds for the business, kept the telephone listing for the business in her home, and received the business mail.

Partnership tax returns signed by Steven Morton listed Dormilee as a partner and she received her share of the profits and losses on the Partner's tax form each year.

Mrs. Morton contributed all the capital assets to the Morton Construction Company. She granted the Bank of Salem, as lender of money, a security interest in the machinery and equipment of the business. She paid the assessed penalty for failure to file a partnership return for the period ending the year 1980. She also acknowledged that she owed the taxes assessed for the business in 1981 and 1982. Mrs. Morton also took advantage of the 50 percent distribution share of the 1984 business loss on her 1984 individual return.

In her defense, Dormilee notes Steven Morton's indication on the appropriate tax forms that the Morton Construction Company was a limited partnership and that Steven was the general partner. Dormilee was referred to only as a "silent" partner on one of the forms.

ISSUE Were Mrs. Morton's actions indicative of a general partner or was she merely a limited partner and therefore not liable for the back taxes, interest, and penalties sought by the Internal Revenue Service.

COURT DECISION After a failure to make the required deposits of federal withholding and FICA taxes or to otherwise pay the amounts of these taxes over to the United States, a delegate of the Secretary of the Treasury properly and timely made assessments against Dormilee Morton and Steven D. Morton, partners, Morton Construction Company. The amount determined to be due and payable for said delinquent taxes, penalties and interest was $44,460.52. Notices of federal tax liens under the Internal Revenue Code for the assessments were promptly filed with the recorder of deeds of Dent County, Missouri.

PRACTICE JUDGING

1. In your opinion, should Dormilee be held liable for the back taxes as a general partner?

2. What facts were most persuasive in causing you to reach your judgment in deciding the issue in question 1?

3. What rule of law was most significant in reaching your decision on that issue?

© GETTY IMAGES/PHOTODISC

Entrepreneurs and the Law

PROJECT 6 LEGAL FORMS OF BUSINESS ORGANIZATIONS

JJ watched as the crane lowered the new DataDart sign onto the top of the steel pedestal in front of his factory. The last 18 months had been amazing. Orders from the trade journal ads were coming in steadily. Even the $10,000 unit price hadn't deterred buyers. The independent salespeople also were producing. Sales were at an all-time high, even though the economy was in recession. Pilar Valencia had created an efficient front office. And the production line had yet to miss a deadline.

BUSINESS ORGANIZATION

On a personal level, Amber and JJ were in love. They planned to have a summer wedding. Her family was coming around to approving of him. JJ invited Amber's dad to tour the plant and inspect the books. He was impressed and only made one comment with a negative ring. He felt JJ's business should not be in the sole proprietorship form. "Even with insurance," he commented, "one bad mistake

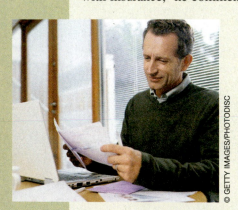

© GETTY IMAGES/PHOTODISC

by a company driver or defective DataDart and you are in serious trouble." JJ only nodded when the comment was made. He had just settled the Grayson suit for less than $1,000. Nevertheless, JJ decided to listen to his future father-in-law and took the matter up with his attorneys. JJ called and explained that he wanted to look into alternative forms of organizing his business.

JJ also had realized that the DataDart had many other applications outside of the dry-cleaning industry. One that seemed especially pertinent was in luggage handling for airlines. He thought that setting up another company to handle the development and marketing of like equipment in this related field would be the best idea, but he wasn't sure.

GOVERNMENT AGENCIES

JJ also asked his attorneys if there were any other potential problems that he could avoid by adequate legal review and preparation. The attorneys commented that there were a lot of government agencies just waiting to make JJ's life more complex. They promised to draw up a list and detail what each agency would be looking for and to brief JJ on what to do when contacted by the agencies.

ACTIVITIES

Divide into teams and perform one or more of the following activities, as directed by your teacher.

Brainstorm

Make a list of all the different forms of businesses JJ should consider both for DataDart Systems and for his potential entry into luggage tracking with the newly christened "SmartDart." Then record the advantages, disadvantages, duties, and responsibilities of each form. As a group, decide which form of organization JJ should choose for each situation and how they should be related. Present your decision to the class, explaining the reasons you chose each particular form of organization.

Prepare Legal Documents

Assume that JJ has chosen the LLC form of business organization for both enterprises. Prepare the articles of organization and operating agreement for each business. (Each team member should prepare a different section, especially of the operating agreement. Then assemble the documents and submit them to your teacher.)

Research and Present

Each team member should prepare a report about a different government agency that JJ will need to deal with. The report should detail the types of regulations that the agency imposes on businesses. Members should then present their reports to the team. (Agencies to report on include the Interstate Commerce Commission, Federal Trade Commission, Securities and Exchange Commission, Federal Communications Commission, National Labor Relations Board, Equal Employment Opportunity Commission, Occupational Safety and Health Administration, and the Environmental Protection Agency.)

COMMUNITY ACTION

Ethical Business Conduct

Reality shows are big hits on television. But what are these shows teaching viewers about ethics and the way to treat others? One reality program about business rewards the team that earns the most money for their project. However, it rarely discusses the ethics of how the money was obtained.

Ethics give you a system of moral principles that govern appropriate conduct, but not everyone agrees on what conduct is appropriate. One business owner might think it is ethical to lock out a renter who is late with the rent. Another business owner might think that is unethical. Your own moral code will help you determine what you think is ethical conduct.

Do Your Part

1. Interview a businessperson you admire who is in a position to set the ethical tone for his or her company. This could be the owner or someone in upper-level management.
2. Before the interview, write a list of questions that concern the ethics of the company. You might ask: What are the ethical issues you confront in your business? How do ethics play a role in the success of your company?
3. Call for an appointment. Explain to the person you want to interview that you are doing a research project on business ethics.
4. Write a report on your interview. Comment on whether you agree with the person's business ethics, and why or why not.

Business Plan

Business plans are the key to acquiring finances for a start-up business. The business plan allows entrepreneurs the tool for evaluating, organizing, and selling a new business concept.

After conducting the appropriate research, select a business to start in your community. Your business plan should include an Executive Summary (brief synopsis of the key points and strengths included in the plan), Company Description, Industry Analysis, Target Market, Competitive Analysis, Marketing Plan and Sales Strategy, Operation, Management and Organization, Long-Term Development, and Financials. *Pay special attention to the legal form of business ownership and the legalities involved with the form of ownership.*

Include attachments such as certifications, licenses, and tax requirements. The business plan can be single- or double-spaced but cannot be more than 30 pages in length. The oral presentation will include five minutes for set up and ten minutes to present your business plan. Visual aids may be used during the presentation. Following each oral presentation, the judges or class may ask questions for five minutes.

Performance Indicators Evaluated

• Understand the complete business plan.

• Describe the form of business ownership and legal agreements.
• Present the business plan with confidence and authority.
• Reinforce the business plan with appropriate research.
• Reinforce the presentation with appropriate visual aids.
• Produce a clear and concise written document that follows grammar, punctuation, spelling, and business style rules.
• Demonstrate understanding of policies and procedures manuals.

For more detailed information about performance indicators, go to the FBLA web site.

Think Critically

1. Why is the business plan so important for an entrepreneur?
2. Why is the form of business ownership important to a lending institution?
3. Why does a financial institution want to know the long-term goals for a business?
4. Why should an entrepreneur consider hiring an attorney when writing a business plan proposal?

http://www.fbla-pbl.org/

BORROWING MONEY AND PAYING BILLS

IN PRACTICE PROFILE

Amida Mehta ■ Director of Marketing
Consumer Credit Counseling
Services of America

When an individual or family is sinking into credit card debt, filing for bankruptcy may seem the only way out. Amida Mehta's job is to offer an alternative.

As Director of Marketing for Consumer Credit Counseling Services of America (CCCSA), Amida's job is to find people who are one step away from bankruptcy. Her co-workers, credit counselors, then work with them to resolve their crisis and restore their financial well-being. "Many of our clients don't realize how difficult it is to recover their credit after filing Chapter 7 (liquidation of assets) or Chapter 13 (wage earner payment plan). We want them to avoid those options if possible." To do so, the counselors evaluate all of their client's expenses, and then help them create a working budget, called a Debt Management Program.

The counselor contacts each creditor who is owed money, and negotiates a payment plan. Ultimately, the client makes one payment each month to CCCSA, which in turn makes payments to the clients' creditors.

That's not all they do for their clients. "We leverage all of the federal and state laws to protect our clients and ensure they can repair their damaged credit," Amida explains. Some are federal laws, others are state laws. All are in place to protect consumers, including the Credit Repair Organization Act, the Equal Credit Opportunity Act and the Truth in Lending Act. Thanks to the Fair Debt Collection Practices Act, once a client's Debt Management Program is in place, they will no longer receive phone calls from companies to whom they owe money.

As a non-profit organization, the CCCSA retains its non-profit status by following all related Internal Revenue Service laws. For example, education must be the primary focus of the business. "One of my responsibilities is making sure we are focused on keeping consumers informed," Amida explains.

Helping people to help themselves is "extremely rewarding," Amida says. "A person's financial strife can disrupt his or her life and the lives of their loved ones. Every time we are able to reach someone who can benefit from our services, that person is one step closer to changing a stressful, burdensome situation."

As Director of Marketing, Amida's primary responsibility is finding the people who need their services. "That's the fun part," Amida explains, "because I know once we find them, we can make a difference in their lives." The process involves getting a true understanding of a potential client, and what they are going through.

Amida began her career at a business strategy consulting firm servicing online businesses. Today, she enjoys the challenge and the personal satisfaction of making a difference in the lives of others.

"A person's financial strife can disrupt his or her life and the lives of their loved ones. Every time we are able to reach someone who can benefit from our services, that person is one step closer to changing a stressful, burdensome situation."

Commercial Paper

© GETTY IMAGES/PHOTODISC

HOT DEBATE

When your sister returned home from college for Thanksgiving break, she brought her boyfriend with her. The boyfriend was given your room, and you slept in the den. Sunday after the holiday, after they had returned to school, you retook possession of your room. Later that evening you looked for your checkbook, but it was not in the usual drawer of your desk. Finally you found it behind the dresser where you normally place it while undressing. Curious, you run through your check register and compare check numbers. It seems as though two are missing. However, you often forget to record them so you do nothing. When your next bank statement arrives, you find that two checks have been written on your account that you do not believe you wrote. You call the bank and they retrieve the photocopies of the checks. The signatures on the checks are not even close to yours, yet the bank, in violation of its contract with you, has paid them. When the bank refuses to credit your account, you bring suit against it requesting the court to order the amounts of the checks credited to your account.

Where Do You Stand?

1. List the legal reasons supporting your demand that the bank credit your account for the amount of the checks.

2. State any justification the bank may have for not doing so.

Basic Types of Commercial Paper

▼ GOALS
■ Recognize the need for commercial paper
■ Identify the various types of commercial paper

WHAT IS COMMERCIAL PAPER?

WHAT'S YOUR VERDICT?

It is 1789, London. Lord Bennington has just received word that his ne'er-do-well son, Anthony, had once again overspent his allowance and now had several creditors hot on his heels. Bennington shook his head in disgust. Still he had to appease the creditors before they did in his only son. Anthony had been sent to University in Edinburgh, Scotland, both for the quality of the education and to get him away from the temptations in London. Instead he'd just gotten wilder. Now Bennington had to get enough gold sovereigns to a solicitor in Edinburgh to allow him to pay the creditors directly without Anthony getting his hands on it.

How can Lord Bennington get the necessary money safely to the solicitor?

Throughout history, there always has been a need for a safe way of transferring things of value without exposing them to loss. Gold, silver, jewels, and currency all were and are invitations to thieves to come and help themselves. As a consequence, commercial paper and the banking system were created. A person could deposit money in a banking institution at one location and then order it paid to another by an affiliated institution in another location. This was done by a written instrument validated by the signature of the depositor.

In *What's Your Verdict?* Lord Bennington would simply write an order to a bank in Edinburgh to pay to the solicitor the appropriate number of gold sovereigns. He would sign and probably seal the order, and then send it by messenger to the solicitor in that faraway city. The solicitor would take it to the bank and collect the amount of gold sovereigns necessary to keep the son out of debtor's prison. The Edinburgh bank would then collect the amount of the order from its London affiliate.

Today, unconditional written orders or promises to pay money are collectively defined as **commercial paper**. Most of the laws governing the legitimacy and use of commercial paper are in the Uniform Commercial Code (UCC).

Law Brief

You may be familiar with the horrible legends of debtor's prisons in England and the United States. These were places of indefinite imprisonment where those unable to meet their debts often wasted away their lives. Charles Dickens' father almost died in a debtor's prison in England. This gave Dickens the idea for several of his works centered on poverty in England in the early 1800s. Now there are serious articles and appeals to bring debtor's prisons back. In Canada, several protestors against the incarceration of those behind on their support checks suggest they already are in existence. One among many cases involved a Toronto man, a self-employed consultant. He went to a default hearing for failure to make his support payments with his financial records but without a lawyer. He intended to show the judge how the economic downturn made it impossible to meet the level of payments that had been set for him when he was riding high. The judge arrested him on the spot and hauled him off for a 90-day stretch. The consultant says it was an odd experience. He was a non-convict in a prison, and, as a result of not being convicted of anything, he was not afforded the same rights as a convict.

However, other laws are important to commercial paper as well. For example, commercial paper is not valid if used in illegal transactions, such as gambling, as defined in criminal codes.

In the new revision of the UCC, the term *negotiable instrument* is used in place of *commercial paper*. However, due to its historical significance and the possibility of confusion with other negotiable instruments, such as documents of title and stocks and bonds, we shall mainly use the term commercial paper in this text.

The check is the most common form of commercial paper. As implied above, like other forms of commercial paper, it was developed centuries ago to serve as a relatively safe substitute for money. In those times, a bank could tell if an order was authentic by comparing the signature on the order with the depositor's signature that it had on file. The bank then complied with the order because, once an individual had deposited the currency—gold or silver—the bank became the depositor's debtor. Consequently, if the depositor appeared and demanded the gold or silver, the bank had to give it back.

This is still true today. Banks are the debtors of their depositors. They compete with one another to borrow funds from their depositors and then lend what they have borrowed to others. Checks are called *demand instruments* because they enable depositors to withdraw their money or have it paid in accordance with their order.

CHECKPOINT
Why are banks debtors of their checking account depositors?

TYPES OF COMMERCIAL PAPER

WHAT'S YOUR VERDICT?

In order to take a two week pre-Christmas vacation in the Florida Keys, John borrowed money from his friend, Patrick. In exchange, John gave Patrick an IOU for that amount. He signed the IOU and dated it.

Is the IOU commercial paper?

Commercial paper can be grouped into two categories. The first consists of unconditional orders to pay money. The second category is composed of unconditional promises to pay money.

"Unconditional," as used to define commercial paper, means that the legal effectiveness of the order or promise does not depend on any other event. Accordingly, an instrument that reads in part "Pay to the order of Sam after he delivers the bike to me" would not be commercial paper because its enforceability is conditional upon delivery of the bike.

Unlike unconditional orders or promises to pay a sum of money, an IOU (such as the one John gave to Patrick in *What's Your Verdict?*) only acknowledges the debt. The law holds that such an acknowledgment is far short of a promise or order to repay. Therefore, an IOU is not enforceable as commercial paper.

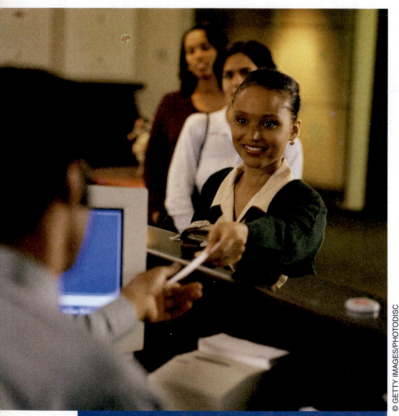

© GETTY IMAGES/PHOTODISC

In the depositor-bank relationship with regard to checking accounts, who is the debtor and who is the creditor?

Of the four main types of commercial paper, two—the draft and the check—are unconditional orders to pay money. The other two—the promissory note and the certificate of deposit—are unconditional promises to pay money. These four main types are discussed in the following sections.

DRAFTS

A **draft** or **bill of exchange** is an unconditional written order by one person that directs another person to pay money to a third. The person directed to pay may be a natural person or an artificial "legal" person, such as a corporation.

If it is not necessary to specify that a particular person receive the money, the order may be made payable to "cash" or to "bearer." Then the person in legal possession of the order may collect on it. However, the order must be either effective upon demand or at a definite date, such as the "thirty days after sight" as shown in the illustration.

The person who executes or "draws" the draft and orders payment to be made is the **drawer**. The **drawee** is the party ordered to pay the draft. The **payee** is the party to whom commercial paper is made payable. The drawee is usually the debtor of the drawer. Refer to In This Case where Jay Minton is the drawer, Margaret Sanford is the drawee, and Downtown Audio is the payee.

Drafts are sometimes classified in terms of the time of payment. A draft may be payable "at sight" (also termed being payable "on demand"). This is called a **sight draft**, and is presented to the drawee by the one holding the draft. The drawee on a sight draft is expected to pay immediately.

If a draft is payable on a set date, at the end of a specified period after sight, or at the end of a specified period after the date of the draft, it is a **time draft**. Minton's draft in the example is a time draft. When a time draft is payable a number of days or months after sight, it must be presented to the drawee for acceptance in order to start the running of the specified time.

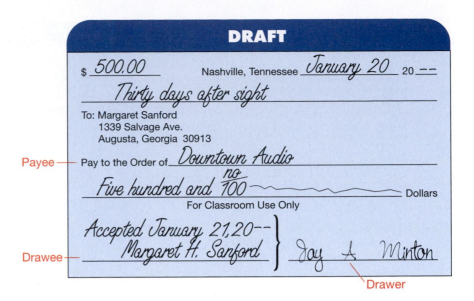

Acceptance is the drawee's promise to pay the draft when due. Such a promise usually is evidenced by the signature of the acceptor on the face of the instrument along with words indicating the acceptance. When a draft states it is payable a number of days or months "after date," the time starts running immediately from the date of the draft.

IN THIS CASE

Margaret Sanford bought a used amplifier for her electric guitar from Jay Minton for $600. She paid Minton $100 down and promised to pay the remaining $500 by her next payday. A few days after the sale, Minton bought a state-of-the-art, low-distortion speaker system for $750 at a clearance sale at Downtown Audio. As partial payment to Downtown Audio, Minton drew a draft (see the illustration above) on the $500 Sanford owed him. To be sure Sanford had enough time to get the money, Minton made the draft payable to the order of Downtown Audio thirty days after sight. Upon receiving the draft, Downtown immediately presented it to Sanford who indicated her willingness to pay in 30 days by writing the date and her signature on the front of the paper along with the word "accepted."

CHECK

PB PROGRESSIVE BANK & TRUST CO.
PROVIDENCE, RHODE ISLAND

No. 165

57-7325
2115

May 17 20__

Pay to the Order of *Honest John's Auto Repair* $385.00

Three hundred eighty-five and 00/100 ———— Dollars

For Classroom Use Only

Frank Hubble

⑈2115⑈7325⑈ 65⑈855⑈038⑈

Drawee
Payee
Drawer

CHECKS

A **check** is a type of draft by which a bank depositor orders the bank to pay money, usually to a third party (see the illustration above). Checks usually are written on special forms that are magnetically encoded to simplify check processing for the banking system. However, checks may be written on blank paper, on forms provided by the depositor, on rawhide, or on other materials and still be legally effective. The drawee, though, must always be a bank for the instrument to qualify as a check.

HONOR AND DISHONOR The bank, according to the contract between it and the depositor, agrees to **honor** (pay when due) each check as long as sufficient funds remain in the depositor's account. The bank owes that duty as a debtor of the depositor in return for being able to use the depositor's funds until the depositor demands their return. This means that the bank must retain a sizable percentage of the deposited funds so that it can pay properly drawn checks when presented. The remainder of the deposited funds is loaned at interest or invested to pay for the bank's operations and to return a profit to the bank's owners.

A person who deliberately issues a check knowing that there are insufficient funds in the account to pay the check when it is presented at the drawee bank is guilty of a crime. The bank will **dishonor** (refuse to pay when due) the instrument and the payee or current owner of the check will not get money for it from that source. In addition, if a check is issued to pay a

NETBookmark

Access lawxtra.swlearning.com and click on the link for Chapter 28. Read the article on the Federal Reserve Bank of San Francisco's web site entitled "How Are Checks Processed?" Then answer the following questions:

1. What is the first step in the check-processing system used at the Los Angeles Branch Check Processing system?

2. What is the name of the control document that accompanies the items through the process?

3. What step lists information from all the block tickets for a particular entry and shows anything that is out of balance?

lawxtra.swlearning.com

A QUESTION OF ETHICS

John Effriham is out of money. However, he will be paid in two days. John knows that he can cash a personal check with his employer at any time. He also has figured out that if he folds the check he's about to write many times and wets the crease over the electronic coding, the automatic check-routing machines will kick it out to be handled manually. Manual handling will cause at least another day's delay before the check gets to his bank. Therefore, he could write a check late today and, in effect, use his employer's money to live on until payday. Is this ethical? Would anyone be injured by John's action? Is it illegal?

debt, the payoff is not effective until the check is presented to and honored by the drawee bank.

STOP-PAYMENT ORDERS When a check has been lost or stolen, the drawer should direct the bank not to pay it. Such an instruction is called a **stop-payment order**. If the drawee bank still pays the check, the bank must re-credit the account. The bank, not the depositor, must bear any loss. Oral stop-payment orders are good for only two weeks unless they are confirmed in writing. Written stop-payment orders are good for six months, but lapse at the end of that time unless renewed.

PRECAUTIONS AND CARE Care must be taken to prevent checks from being altered. When writing a check, do not leave space for someone to insert figures and words that would change the amount of the instrument. Certainly, never sign a blank check. Do not give anything of value in return for a check that appears to have been altered in any manner. In addition, be wary of a check that may have been issued in connection with illegal activities, for example, gambling. Courts usually consider such instruments void.

PROMISSORY NOTES

A **promissory note** is an unconditional written promise by a person or persons to pay money according to the payee's order or to pay money to the bearer of the instrument. The payment may have to be made on demand or at a definite time according to the stated terms on the face of the note (see the illustration). The person who executes a promissory note is the **maker**. (If two or more persons execute the note, they are termed "co-makers" and also may be liable for payment.)

Many financial institutions will not lend money unless some personal or real property is offered as security by the would-be borrower.

What is one precaution you can take to make sure that another party does not alter a check you have written?

The security ensures that the loan will be paid when due. If the debtor fails to pay, the creditor can force the sale of the property and then take the proceeds of that sale to cover the amount the debtor owes. When personal property is offered as security and so indicated on the face of the note, the paper is a **collateral note**. When real property is the security for payment, the paper is a **mortgage note**.

CERTIFICATES OF DEPOSIT

A **certificate of deposit** is an instrument bearing a bank's written acknowledgment of the receipt of money, together with an unconditional promise to repay it at a definite future time (see the illustration on the next page). A certificate of deposit often is called a CD.

PROMISSORY NOTE

$ *3,000.00*   Las Vegas, Nevada *December 20* 20 *--*

Sixty days _____ after date *I* promise to pay to

— Payee

the order of *First National Bank* _____

Three thousand and ^no^/*100* ~~~~ Dollars

For Classroom Use Only

Payable at *First National Bank, Building, Las Vegas, Nevada*

with interest at *9* % a year.

No. *6* Due *February 18, 20--*   *Eric Gordon*

— Maker

28-1 Basic Types of Commercial Paper 513

Federal law prohibits banks from paying out CDs and other long-term deposits before maturity without a penalty to the depositor. Usually the penalty is a sharp reduction in the amount of interest payable on the funds. This inhibits depositors from withdrawing funds before maturity and permits the banks to lend the funds to others on a long-term basis. Consequently, interest rates on CDs usually are significantly higher than the rates on savings or checking accounts (from which the depositor is far more likely to withdraw funds).

CHECKPOINT

What is the difference between a check and a draft?

28-1 **Assessment**

THINK ABOUT LEGAL CONCEPTS

1. Unconditional written orders or promises to pay money are collectively known as (a) commercial promises (b) IOUs (c) ICIs (Intentional Credit Instruments) (d) none of the above

2. The Uniform Commercial Code controls the use of most commercial paper. **True or False?**

3. With checking accounts, banks are the creditors of their depositors. **True or False?**

4. A note secured by land is a mortgage note. **True or False?**

5. A depositor's instruction to his or her bank not to pay a particular check is referred to as a(n) _?_.

6. An instrument bearing a bank's written acknow-ledgment of the receipt of money, together with an unconditional promise to repay it at a definite future time, is a(n) (a) check (b) note (c) CD (d) promissory note

THINK CRITICALLY ABOUT EVIDENCE

Study the situation, answer the questions, and then prepare arguments to support your answers.

7. Hubble paid Honest Horace's Auto Repair $385 by check for the repair of his car's transmission. When the job proved defective, Hubble telephoned his bank and ordered it to stop payment on the check. Three weeks later, however, the bank honored the check and paid Honest Horace's the $385 out of Hubble's account. Did the bank make a mistake?

8. Burger was the owner and president of a small surfboard manufacturing company. She also owned the land and building the company occupied. When she needed to raise cash to finance a major expansion, her financial advisers told her that the best way to do so was by using the building and land as a source of funds. How could Burger do this?

9. Carl's son, Jared, wanted a new sports car. He convinced Carl to sign a promissory note in favor of the car dealership for the $47,000 purchase price. Jared also signed the note. Four months later, Jared stopped making payments and drove the car to Mexico and sold it. Jared has taken up permanent residence in Juarez, Mexico. Is Carl nonetheless obligated to pay off the balance of the note?

Specialized Types of Commercial Paper

SPECIALIZED TYPES OF COMMERCIAL PAPER

WHAT'S YOUR VERDICT?

Dr. Pugh, of Santa Ana, California, needed expensive drugs to treat a patient with a rare nerve disease. Drugtek, the supplier of the drug, was a New York corporation. It would not ship COD, extend credit, or accept personal checks from customers outside the state.

What other means of payment could Dr. Pugh use to satisfy Drugtek?

The four types of commercial paper described in the previous lesson are the most frequently used. However, certain forms of commercial paper are available to meet specialized needs. Typically, these forms provide for an extremely safe, non-cash means of transfer of monetary value. Specialized forms that meet this need include those described in the following sections.

CERTIFIED CHECKS

A person offered a personal check as payment may fear the bank will not honor the check because of insufficient funds in the drawer's account. However, if the bank already has agreed to pay the check, only if the bank fails will the payee or current owner of the check not receive the money due.

A personal check that has been accepted by a bank before payment is a certified check. At the time of certification, the bank draws funds from the depositor's account and sets them aside in a special account in order to pay the check when it is presented. In addition, the bank marks the front of the check with either the word "accepted" or "certified," along with the date and an authorized signature of the bank. In *What's Your Verdict?* Dr. Pugh could use a certified check if Drugtek will accept it.

TELLER'S CHECK

A draft drawn by a bank on funds that it has on deposit at another bank is a teller's check. Such a document is a draft drawn by one bank on a second bank. Individuals and business firms also may use these instruments when a substantial sum is involved. A teller's check is another possibility open to Dr. Pugh.

CASHIER'S CHECK

A check that a bank draws on itself is a cashier's check (see the illustration below). Banks use such checks to pay their own obligations. Persons who wish to pay others but who do not have checking accounts or find it impractical to use their personal checks also may purchase them from a bank. Because it is relatively risk-free (only the bank may stop payment on the check), a payee usually is willing to take such a check. This could be the most appropriate type of check for Dr. Pugh.

CASHIER'S CHECK

First State Security Bank
Santa Ana, CA 92703

1203

December 15 20 ——

Pay to the Order of *Drugtek* $ 1,375.50

Thirteen hundred and seventy-five and 50/100 —— Dollars

For Classroom Use Only

CASHIER'S CHECK

⑈08 20⑈00 13⑈

Martha C. Todd
as ASSISTANT MANAGER of First State Security Bank

Drawee — Payee — Drawer

Letters of credit are specialized types of commercial paper used in international transactions. The letter of credit is issued by a bank on behalf of an account holder. It represents the bank's promise to pay, accept, or negotiate the beneficiary's draft up to a certain amount of money, in the stated currency, and within a prescribed time limit. The two types of letters of credit are documentary letters of credit and standby letters of credit. *Documentary letters of credit* are used in transactions involving the sales of goods. *Standby letters of credit* are used to guarantee that a party will fulfill monetary obligations involving construction, service, or sales contracts.

MONEY ORDERS

Persons who do not have checking accounts often use money orders. A **money order** is a draft issued by a post office, bank, express company, or telegraph company for use in paying or transferring funds for the purchaser. Dr. Pugh also could use a money order.

TRAVELER'S CHECKS

Travelers are rightfully wary of carrying a lot of cash. Retailers and hotelkeepers worldwide are understandably reluctant to take checks from people from other regions and other countries. The traveler's check was devised to overcome

LEGAL RESEARCH

Interview several banks in your area to determine if they deal in letters of credit and, if so, how. Make a list of those that do. Also list the typical business transactions and regions/industries of the world in which letters of credit are used.

these problems and meet the needs of both groups. A **traveler's check** is a draft drawn by a well-known financial institution on itself or its agent.

The buyer signs the traveler's checks when purchased. Later, when used to pay for a purchase, the traveler writes in the name of the payee and then signs again, in the presence of the payee. The payee then deposits and collects the traveler's check in the same manner as other checks. The payee's ability to compare the two signatures, coupled with the reputation of the financial institution that issued the instrument, usually reduces the risk to the point where businesses worldwide accept traveler's checks.

CHECKPOINT

What is the difference between a certified check and a cashier's check?

Cyberlaw

Services are now available online to allow the sending of money orders via the Internet. These services stem from the need to be able to eliminate fraud and forgeries in paying for purchases made during cyber auctions. Online auction houses now offer the successful bidder the alternative of sending a money order. This is done by going to the auction house's web site and entering the auction details and payment information. The amount is debited against whatever credit or debit card is on file for the bidder. The auction house will then send payment to the seller by mailing a Western Union® brand money order. It's quick, efficient, and the seller quickly has cash in hand as a result.

THINK ABOUT IT
Can you think of other transactions that this technique might facilitate?

THINK ABOUT LEGAL CONCEPTS

1. A check that a bank draws on itself is termed a certified check. **True or False?**

2. Only the drawer of a cashier's check can stop payment on it. **True or False?**

3. The type of check that requires the owner to sign twice on its face is a (a) cashier's check (b) certified check (c) traveler's check

4. When a bank accepts liability on a personal check before it is presented for payment, the check is said to be certified. **True or False?**

5. A(n) _?_ draft is a draft drawn by a bank on favorable monetary balances it has in other banks.

6. Individuals who do not have checking accounts often use money orders. **True or False?**

THINK CRITICALLY ABOUT EVIDENCE

Study the situation, answer the questions, and then prepare arguments to support your answers.

7. Garrett owes Nosmada $250. Nosmada is driving through a subdivision one day when he spots a garage sale. At the sale, a nearly new titanium bicycle is marked for sale at a price that is one-fifth of its retail. Unfortunately, the price is still $200 more than Nosmada has. Luckily, the seller knows commercial paper law and the creditworthiness of Garrett. As a consequence Nosmada writes out an order to Garrett to pay the seller the $200 needed to close the deal. What form of commercial paper has Nosmada utilized? Who are the drawer, drawee, and payee?

8. Howard ordered a new pair of running shoes from a discount 800 number. He paid by cashier's check. When he finds out that his new shoes are defective, he calls the bank to stop payment on the check. Can he stop payment? Who is liable on the instrument?

9. Homer's sister Henrietta has just moved to New York City. She doesn't have a bank account as yet and does not want to carry around much cash. She does have a check made payable to her by a car dealership to which she sold her car upon arriving in New York. What could she do with the check to make sure it will be honored when she cashes it?

10. Several months pass. Henrietta has become adjusted to the big city and wants to return home to Wisconsin to visit. She does not want to carry cash with her. What kind of commercial paper would you recommend that she use to carry her funds with her? It must be usable to pay many small amounts and be trusted by merchants in Wisconsin.

PREVENT LEGAL DIFFICULTIES

In dealing with commercial paper

1. Be focused when you are drawing or making commercial paper. Giving in to distractions can lead to mistakes that invalidate the paper or make it subject to forgery.

2. Specific errors in issuing commercial paper include leaving enough blank space for someone to insert figures and words that would change the face amount of an instrument or failing to have one portion of the paper agree with another, such as the amount in numbers with the written amount.

3. If you lend a significant amount of money, get a promissory note in return.

4. If practical, ask for security for a loan and identify the collateral on the face of the instrument.

5. Use traveler's checks and credit cards on long trips. Do not carry a lot of cash.

6. Never sign a blank piece of commercial paper. Take care not to let your blank checks be stolen. Any negligence you contribute to the theft may make you liable for any forgeries that occur.

7. Remember that an oral stop-payment order is good for only 14 days unless confirmed in writing. A written stop-payment order is good for six months and can be renewed.

Chapter 28 Assessment

CONCEPTS IN BRIEF

28-1 Basic Types of Commercial Paper

1. Commercial paper was developed centuries ago to serve as a relatively safe substitute for money.

2. A promissory note is an unconditional written promise by a person or persons to pay money according to the payee's order or to pay money to the bearer of the instrument.

3. A certificate of deposit is an instrument bearing a bank's written acknowledgment of the receipt of money, together with an unconditional promise to repay it at a definite future time.

4. A draft or bill of exchange is an unconditional written order by one person that directs another person to pay money to a third.

5. A check is a type of draft by which a bank depositor orders the bank to pay money, usually to a third party.

28-2 Specialized Types of Commercial Paper

6. Specialized forms of commercial paper are available to provide for an extremely safe, non-cash means of transfer of monetary value.

7. A personal check that has been accepted by a bank before payment is a certified check.

8. A check that a bank draws on itself is a cashier's check.

9. A draft drawn by a bank on funds that it has on deposit at another bank is a teller's check.

10. A money order is a draft issued by a post office, bank, express company, or telegraph company for use in paying or transferring funds for the purchaser.

11. A traveler's check is a draft drawn by a well-known financial institution on itself or its agent that has attributes created to offer overwhelming assurance that it is a legitimate instrument.

YOUR LEGAL VOCABULARY

Match each statement with the term that it best defines. Some terms may not be used.

1. Unconditional written promise or order to pay money
2. Person to whom commercial paper is made payable
3. Drawee's promise to pay draft when due
4. Draft written on bank by depositor
5. Bank's promise to pay check when due
6. Person who executes a promissory note
7. Check drawn by bank on itself
8. Draft drawn by a bank on funds it has on deposit with another bank
9. Written instrument acknowledging a bank's receipt of money and promising to repay it at a definite future time
10. Draft issued by a post office, bank, or express company for use in transferring funds for the draft's purchaser
11. An unconditional written promise by a person or persons to pay money according to the payee's order or to pay money to the bearer of the instrument

a. **acceptance**
b. **bill of exchange**
c. **cashier's check**
d. **certificate of deposit**
e. **certified check**
f. **check**
g. **collateral note**
h. **commercial paper**
i. **dishonor**
j. **draft**
k. **drawee**
l. **drawer**
m. **honor**
n. **maker**
o. **money order**
p. **mortgage note**
q. **payee**
r. **promissory note**
s. **sight draft**
t. **stop-payment order**
u. **teller's check**
v. **time draft**
w. **traveler's check**

REVIEW LEGAL CONCEPTS

12. Why was commercial paper created?

13. Could you cash a check made out to you but written on an ordinary piece of paper?

14. What is the difference between a check and a draft?

15. Would a check or other piece of commercial paper be legally effective if written in pencil?

16. What is the purpose of having the purchaser sign the traveler's checks when buying them?

WRITE ABOUT LEGAL CONCEPTS

17. If a good customer comes into a bank and wants to stop payment on a cashier's check she had purchased and had the bank issue, how could the bank protect itself in doing so?

18. Would you rather hold a promissory note from a local retailer or a certificate of deposit from a local bank?

19. **HOT DEBATE** Write a persuasive opening statement that emphasizes the legal, ethical, and economic points in favor of your petition. Or, write a persuasive opening statement for the bank that encompasses the economic and legal reasons why the loss should fall on the depositor in this situation.

MAKE ACADEMIC CONNECTIONS

20. **ECONOMICS** Survey the Federal Reserve Board explanations, charts, and aggregate data to form an opinion as to how important commercial paper is to the U.S. economy. Compose a paragraph summarizing your findings and then read your paragraph to the class.

THINK CRITICALLY ABOUT EVIDENCE

Study the situation, answer the questions, and then prepare arguments to support your answers.

21. Joseph McReynolds gave the following signed instrument to Helen Harrison after borrowing $5,000 from her: "IOU Helen Harrison $5,000." It was dated and signed by McReynolds. Is the instrument commercial paper?

22. Chen wanted to order skis that she had seen advertised in a national magazine. The advertisement expressly said, "Do not send cash or personal checks. No COD orders accepted." How could Chen pay?

23. Thruster owns Discovery Electronic Works, a small company that manufactures portable computers. The company is doing well but needs to expand and update its product line. Thruster plans to use credit to do both. What specific types of commercial paper will be used if:

    a. Discovery Electronic Works borrows $15,000 out of the $20,000 needed to pay for a shipment of integrated circuit chips and uses the chips as security for payment?

    b. Discovery Electronic Works borrows $65,000 out of the $100,000 needed to buy a building for a new assembly line and uses the real property as security for payment?

24. You are working as a checkout clerk at Surprise Discount, Inc., a local department store. Sarah Johnson, an elderly lady, comes through your line with what she describes as "the perfect gift for my great-grandson." She says that she never expected to find it for under $200 much less the $110 that it is marked at. She writes out a check for the purchase. After she has left the store, you realize that she has written the check for $15.50 rather than the $115.50 purchase price plus tax. However, there is plenty of room to alter the amount to the correct figure. Should you do so?

25. While in Shreveport, Louisiana, Claypool wanted to play poker for money stakes at the Crystal Bar. He persuaded Parker to stand good (pay) for any losses he might have. Before the night was over, Claypool's losses amounted to $6,000. Afterwards, Claypool gave Parker a promissory note for $10,473.14 to cover the $6,000 in gambling losses and a legitimate previous loan. When the note came due, Claypool refused to pay. Parker sued, and Claypool defended on the grounds that the note was illegal and void, because it originated in a gambling debt. Will Parker recover? (*Parker v. Claypool*, 78 So. 2d 124)

26. Purchasers of land developed by Holiday Intervals, Inc., signed writings in which they promised to pay a certain sum of money at a definite time in the future. However, according to the signed instruments, the payments were due only if specified structures were built in the complex within two years of the signings. Some of these instruments were labeled "promissory note." Were any of the writings commercial paper? (*In re Holiday Intervals, Inc.*, 94 Bankr. 594)

27. Gunn contracted to sell Tak, a broker from Hong Kong, 60,000 metric tons of UREA, a fertilizer, at $400 a ton. In connection with this $24 million sale, Gunn entered into another contract agreeing to pay Tak a commission for all Tak's sales of the fertilizer. After 10,000 tons of UREA had been sold, paid for, and delivered, Gunn bought and delivered to Tak a cashier's check from the Empire Bank of Springfield for $150,000 payable to Tak's order. Shortly after, Gunn learned that the balance of the order for the remaining 50,000 tons of UREA had been canceled by Tak. Consequently, Gunn went to court and obtained an injunction from the court to the bank to stop payment on the cashier's check. Shortly after the court acted, the cashier's check was transferred by Tak to Lai, who now claims the right to collect the face amount. Should the court order the bank to honor the stop-payment order, or must the bank pay Lai the face amount of the check? (*Lai v. Powell*, Judge, 536 S.W.2d 14)

28. In a Missouri circuit court, Kleen was convicted of issuing an insufficient funds check. He appealed, pointing out that he had merely signed a blank check form in Missouri and then given the form to his truck driver. The truck driver carried the signed blank check form to Memphis, Tennessee, where someone at the Herring Sales Company filled in the company name as the payee and also filled in the amount. Herring kept the check in return for a truckload of meal that was transported by Kleen's truck and driver back to Kleen's business in Nevada, Missouri. Kleen therefore contended that even though the check was drawn on the Citizen's Bank of Nevada, the alleged criminal act occurred in Tennessee, where the signed blank form was made a check and was issued. Consequently, Missouri had no jurisdiction, and his conviction should be overturned. You decide. (*State v. Kleen*, 491 S.W.2d 2)

29. General Motors Acceptance Corporation (GMAC) financed the purchase of a Jeep by Azevedo. It then held the positon of lienholder on the vehicle and was noted as such on the vehicle's title and car insurance policy. The policy was taken out by Azevedo but listed GMAC as the beneficiary. Therefore, if the vehicle was involved in an accident and damaged, the insurance company, Abington Casualty, was to pay GMAC the value of the loss. Later, after the Jeep was damaged in an accident, Azevedo submitted a claim on the policy. After suitable appraisals of the loss, Abington issued a check with joint payees, Azevedo and GMAC. Abington then delivered the check to Azevedo who deposited it in his bank with his indorsement but without GMAC's. The bank paid on the check in full to Azevedo even without the indorsement. GMAC never received the benefit of the funds. Now it has brought suit against Abington to recover for its loss. Is GMAC entitled to the insurance money? (*General Motors Acceptance Corporation v. Abington Casualty Insurance Co.*, 602 N.E.2d 1085)

BACKGROUND Rick Means and Fred Barry owned an apartment building which they wished to sell. On July 18, 1980, they entered into a contract for deed with respondents, Joan and Gary Doerhoff. The agreement provided that the Doerhoffs would receive the apartment building and would give in exchange 6.81 acres of land in Maries County, Missouri, and a note purportedly executed almost a year earlier by Nancy Clardy, respondent Bruce Clardy's mother. At the time Means and Barry took the note in partial payment for the apartment building a required $5,000 payment had been made but several of the monthly installments were in arrears. Nonetheless the note's balance had been reduced to approximately $22,000 from its original $31,000. Curiously, the monthly payments according to the terms of the note had been and were to be in cabinets made in the Clardy cabinet shop with value "figured at the prevailing builders price for Jefferson City . . . until October 12, 1981, at which time the entire balance thereof is due and payable in cash . . ." When the note was not paid by Oct. 12, Means and Barry brought this lawsuit to collect the $22,000 still due plus interest and charges.

During the lower court trial, Nancy Clardy testified that she did not sign either the note or the bill of sale accompanying it. She alleged that her son, Bruce, had done so and had drawn $5,000 from a "remodeling" fund to make the initial payment on the note thereafter making payments in cabinets. Bruce took the Fifth Amendment (protection against self-incrimination) when asked about this at the trial.

Nancy Clardy's signature on the documents was notarized by John Gross. Gross later testified that Nancy Clardy had not signed any documents in his presence but that as a favor to Bruce he notarized them after Bruce told him that Nancy Clardy had signed them.

Under oath, Nancy Clardy stated that her son, Bruce, told her that he had signed her name to the documents. She did not remember exactly when he told her this. Mrs. Clardy testified that she did not contact Mr. Doerhoff or plaintiffs when she learned that Mr. Clardy had signed her name. She also testified that she had learned, after-the-fact, that Bruce Clardy used $5,000 from a remodeling fund in order to pay the initial $5,000 due on the note. Mrs. Clardy had authorized Mr. Clardy to draw upon the fund to remodel an investment property which she owned. She did not authorize him to use the money to pay the note for the cabinet shop.

The trial court held that Bruce Clardy had indeed signed the note for both parties. As a consequence, the trial court held that Nancy Clardy was not liable. Means and Barry then brought this appeal.

REASONING Means and Barry ask that the decision of the lower court be overturned and they be allowed to recover from Nancy Clardy because she had ratified her signature on the commercial paper by doing nothing to correct the situation. Means and Barry also ask that they be allowed to collect against the Doerhoffs as well because, on commercial paper, the UCC holds that "(2) Any person who transfers an instrument and receives consideration warrants to his transferee . . . that (b) all signatures are genuine or authorized." Therefore the Doerhoffs had breached the warranty and Means and Barry should be able to collect for the loss they suffered as a consequence.

CONCLUSION The appellate court ruled that Nancy Clardy did not ratify her signature and was not liable on the instrument. The court also determined that the note was not commercial paper and that, therefore, the UCC section upon which Means and Barry relied in their appeal did not apply. As a consequence they could not collect.

PRACTICE JUDGING

1. Do you agree with the court's conclusion that Nancy Clardy did not ratify the note? Why or why not?

2. Why did the court determine that the note was not commercial paper and that, consequently, Means and Barry could not recover?

3. Could Means and Barry recover on any other theory?

Negotiability and Negotiation of Commercial Paper

29-1 Requirements of Negotiability

29-2 Proper Indorsement and Negotiation

HOT DEBATE

Souquer is president of his own company, SpringGen. Earlier this morning his secretary, Elizabeth, placed a stack of checks to pay the monthly bills on his desk for his signature. As he glanced through them he spotted a $5,000 check for electronic items to his old friend Bill Hutton's company. Later that week, he ran into Bill who mentioned that he hadn't sold SpringGen anything in ages and who expressed concern that his company had done something wrong. Souquer investigated and found that, over the last year and a half, Elizabeth had him sign more than $125,000 in checks made out to suppliers for goods they didn't provide. She then took the checks, forged the payee's signature to indorse them in blank, and deposited them in her account to be used to cover gambling debts. Subsequent to the discovery, the company attorney sues both Elizabeth and the bank that cashed the checks against the company account over her forgeries. It is discovered that Elizabeth has few assets. She just sold her home and gambled away those proceeds as well.

Where Do You Stand?

1. From an ethical perspective, who besides Elizabeth is at fault for SpringGen's losses?

2. What legal right does SpringGen have to seek compensation for the losses from the bank?

Requirements of Negotiability

▼ **GOALS**
- ■ **Explain the importance of negotiability**
- ■ **Distinguish negotiable from non-negotiable instruments**

THE IMPORTANCE OF NEGOTIATION

WHAT'S YOUR VERDICT?

Dwaynette was preparing to open her new business, a sub shop. However, in talking with her accountant, Dwaynette indicated that she wanted to do business on a cash-only basis because taking checks or promissory notes is too risky.

Is this advisable?

If commercial paper is to be accepted instead of cash, the person or business firm receiving it must be assured that there is a very great chance the instrument will be paid. The UCC provides that assurance. It empowers a qualified owner of commercial paper to overcome many of the legal defenses the person who is obligated to pay the instrument might raise to keep from paying.

To enable the owner to overcome most common defenses and collect on commercial paper, the instrument bearing the promise or order to pay money must be negotiable. **Negotiable** means that it must be in writing, contain an unconditional promise or order payable in a sum certain, be payable on demand or at a definite time, and be payable to the bearer or to someone's order. (These requirements are prescribed by statute and are discussed in the following section.) An instrument must be negotiable in order to be classified as commercial paper. As mentioned in Chapter 28, another term generally meaning commercial paper is **negotiable instrument**.

The parties trying to secure the maximum number of rights to enable collection on pieces of commercial paper they hold must acquire the subject instruments in the correct manner. **Negotiation** means the proper transfer of a negotiable instrument so that the person receiving the instrument has the power to collect on it by overcoming certain defenses of the person who must pay it off. If an instrument is not negotiated, it is considered to have been only assigned. In the case of assignment, the parties' rights are governed by contract law rather than the law of negotiable instruments. This means in most cases that the owner of commercial paper is subject to many defenses the obligor on the paper can raise against being forced to pay. Therefore, a person would prefer to hold a negotiable instrument than an assigned instrument because the chances of collection are greater.

In *What's Your Verdict?* the accountant would probably advise Dwaynette that significant protection would be afforded her by the UCC if she were to take properly transferred negotiable instruments. Such protection would drastically reduce the risk of not being able to collect. Refusing to accept commercial paper would probably mean losing customers. If they were

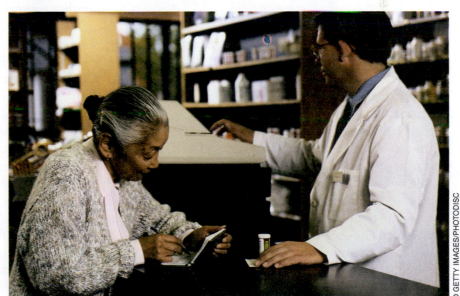

Why is it in this pharmacy's best interest to accept commercial paper from customers?

denied the safety and convenience of using checks and notes in her store, they might not shop there at all.

CHECKPOINT

Why would you prefer to hold a negotiable instrument rather than an assigned instrument?

WHAT MAKES AN INSTRUMENT NEGOTIABLE?

WHAT'S YOUR VERDICT?

As mayor of his small town, a position that paid $400 per year, Adamson also had to hold down a normal job. Thus he often could not be present to sign checks when needed. As a consequence, he had a signature stamp made up and gave it to the town clerk to be used at her discretion. The signature stamp read "by John Adamson, Mayor."

Were the checks signed in such a manner legal?

According to the UCC, whether or not an instrument is negotiable is determined by what appears on its face at the time it is issued. However, negotiability does not require that the instrument state that something of value has been given for the paper. Identifying such value given often is a good idea, however, and will not defeat negotiability.

Likewise, the ability to negotiate (but not the ability to collect on) an instrument is not affected by the fact that it is **antedated** (dated earlier than the date of issuance), **postdated** (dated later than the date of issuance), or even undated. If a date is not present, any owner who has possession and who knows the date on which the paper was issued may enter it.

In particular, to be negotiable according to the UCC requirements an instrument must

1. be in writing and be signed by the maker or drawer
2. contain an unconditional promise or order to pay
3. be payable in a sum certain in money
4. be payable on demand or at a definite time
5. be payable to the bearer or to someone's order.

IN THIS CASE

St. Benet received a check in the mail for payment of a debt. When she went to cash the instrument she noticed that the drawer had not entered a date on it. St. Benet, knowing the check was issued a week previous, wrote that date on the instrument and cashed it. Her action did not defeat the negotiability of the instrument.

IN WRITING AND SIGNED BY THE MAKER OR DRAWER

To be negotiable, commercial paper must be in writing and signed by the maker or drawer with the intent that it create a legal obligation. Because of the writing, commercial paper is subject to the parol evidence rule when its terms are challenged at law. (Under the parol evidence rule, oral testimony cannot be used to contradict terms in a complete, final, written contract.) However, oral evidence may be used to show fraud, incompleteness, forgeries, or illegalities, or to clarify ambiguities.

The writing may consist of a printed form with the terms typed or written in. Or, the paper may be totally handwritten. The law is very flexible in this regard. An ink pen, a typewriter, even a pencil may be used, although a pencil is not recommended because it invites alteration. Any medium is satisfactory as a writing surface as long as the result is recognizable as a writing.

If there are conflicting terms within the writing, those written in by hand prevail over both typewritten and printed form terms. Similarly, typewritten terms prevail over printed form terms. Further, an amount expressed in words prevails over an amount expressed in figures.

Law Brief

As passports today are valid for 10 years, be very aware of your signature sample that they contain. When overseas and purchasing items with commercial paper, especially traveler's checks, a merchant usually will refer to the signature that appears on your passport for validity. This applies whether the checks have an initial signature on them or not. It is a good idea to practice your "passport" signature before traveling or while you are overseas.

• •

As far as the signature is concerned, the form it takes does not alter its legal effectiveness as long as the writer placed it there with the intent to authenticate the instrument. For example, a legally effective signature may be made with a rubber stamp, as in *What's Your Verdict?*

A trade or assumed name may be used in signing if it is intended as one's signature. Also, one person may legitimately sign another person's name if authorized to do so as an agent. A manager may sign commercial paper as an agent for a corporation. Any individual who is unable to write her or his name because of illiteracy or a physical handicap may sign with a mark, typically an "X." However it is an advisable practice to have another person then insert the name of the signer next to the mark and sign as a witness.

The location of the signature generally is immaterial as long as it appears on the face of the instrument. Thus, the signature may appear scrawled diagonally across the face or even in the body of the instrument as long as the signer's status as maker or drawer is clear.

UNCONDITIONAL PROMISE OR ORDER

To be negotiable, a promissory note or a certificate of deposit must contain an unconditional promise to pay money. Similarly, a check or a draft must contain an unconditional order to pay money. Simply acknowledging a debt as

in "I owe you $100" is not enough. There is nothing in such a statement to indicate that the money will ever be repaid.

The use of the word "unconditional" means that the promise or order to pay money must be absolute, that is, free of any limits or restrictions. "I promise to pay Ann Kiersten $1,000 if my mare foals in the next year" would be conditional upon an event that might not occur. Therefore, the instrument that included the statement would not be negotiable.

Making payment subject to another agreement would make the obligation conditional on the agreement being properly performed. Such conditions would restrict the free flow of commercial paper. Conditions would require a prospective purchaser of the paper to deal with the uncertainty that the condition might not have been satisfied. This would mean that collection might not be legally possible. However, instruments that merely acknowledge the source of the obligation, as in "pay to the order of Merrick Miller as per contract," are negotiable.

A phrase entitling the holder to reasonable attorney's fees upon default or enhancing the possibility of collection, such as "secured by a mortgage," would improve the potential for negotiation by reducing the uncertainty of collection. Finally, courteous or considerate language, such as "please pay to the order of" or listing the obligor's bank account number (without the word "only" following) for the convenience of others, does not affect negotiability.

PAYABLE IN A SUM CERTAIN IN MONEY

To be negotiable, commercial paper must call for the payment of a sum certain in money. **Money**, for this purpose, is any official currency or coin acceptable as a medium of exchange either in the United States or in any foreign country at the time the commercial paper is written. Thus, commercial paper that is collectible in the United States but that has the amount expressed in an acceptable foreign currency is negotiable.

Often the foreign currency is simply changed into U.S. dollars on the day the paper is payable. However, if the paper requires that the foreign currency be used as the medium of payment, the commercial paper is payable in that currency.

Payment must be solely in money and not money plus a good or service. On the other hand, paper that gives the obligee (creditor) a choice of money or something else, for example, "I promise to pay to the order of Vera Spielman $10,000 or thirty-five ounces of gold at the obligee's option" would be negotiable because the obligee could choose money as payment. If the choice to pay in money or a good or service was the obligor's (debtor's), the instrument is not negotiable. In such a case the obligor could choose to make payment in something other than money.

An instrument still is negotiable if it requires that the amount be paid

- with interest or a discount. (The interest rate may vary. For example, if the instrument reads "interest to be set at the usury limit less 2%" the instrument would still be negotiable.)
- by installment, perhaps with an **acceleration clause** that makes the entire balance due and payable upon the happening of a certain event (for example, the obligor's default by missing an installment payment)
- with bank charges for exchanging one national currency into another
- with costs of collection and reasonable attorney's fees in case the paper is not paid

Most of these provisions usually tend to make the commercial paper more attractive to prospective owners.

INTERNATIONAL VIEWPOINT

Hard vs. Soft Currencies

Hard currencies are those freely traded on world markets. Currencies considered "hard" are those of the United States, Europe, and Japan. The value of hard currency is set on the open market—that is, by what buyers and sellers will pay for it at any given time. Values of hard currency may be affected by government intervention, interest rates, or other market factors.

Soft currencies, on the other hand, have fixed exchange rates. Examples are the Russian ruble, the Indian rupee, or the Chinese renminbi. These currencies are purchased at the rates the countries' governments establish for them.

NETBookmark

Commercial paper may be collectible in the United States even if the amount is expressed in a foreign currency. Often the foreign currency is changed into U.S. dollars on the day the paper is payable. Find the exchange rates for foreign currency by accessing lawxtra.swlearning.com and clicking on the link for Chapter 29. Find today's exchange rate with the U.S. dollar for the currency of five different countries.

lawxtra.swlearning.com

When is commercial paper payable in a foreign currency in the United States?

PAYABLE ON DEMAND OR AT A DEFINITE TIME

Negotiability also requires that an instrument be payable on demand or at a definite time. **Payable on demand** means that the commercial paper is written so as to be payable immediately upon presentment (demand for payment) or at sight. If no time of payment is specified, an instrument is interpreted as being payable on demand.

Payable at a definite time means that the commercial paper is written payable on or before an identified calendar date. It is also acceptable for an instrument to be payable within a set period after an identified calendar date or a fixed period, such as 90 days after sight. An instrument is not negotiable if it is payable at or after an event that is sure to occur but whose date cannot be determined beforehand. For example,

a note payable "30 days after the death of Sam Larue" would not be negotiable. Such a promise might be honored by the person making it or it might be legally enforceable as part of a contract. However, that has nothing to do with whether the instrument is commercial paper and can therefore be negotiated.

PAYABLE TO BEARER OR TO SOMEONE'S ORDER

The final requirement is that the paper contain the words of negotiability by being made payable to bearer or to a specified person's order. When commercial paper is legally collectible by the party in possession of it, it is referred to as **bearer paper**. The party in possession of bearer paper is called the **bearer**. To qualify as bearer paper, the face of a piece of commercial paper can read "pay to the order of bearer," "pay to bearer," "pay to (a named party) or bearer," "pay to cash," or any other way that does not identify a specific payee, such as a fictitious character like Superman or Santa Clause.

In contrast, when commercial paper is made payable to the order of a specified payee, it is called **order paper**. Such phrasing shows the intent of the maker or drawer to have the paper payable to the named payee or to anyone to whom the paper is subsequently negotiated by order of that payee. Order paper may read "pay to the order of Charles Blevins" or whatever specific party the maker or drawer intends. It also may read "pay to Charles Blevins or order." However, if it only reads "pay to Charles Blevins," it is not negotiable. An exception under the 1990 version of the UCC is a check. A check may be negotiable without being payable to order or bearer. However check forms ordinarily contain the preprinted words "Pay to the order of."

Order paper may be made payable to the order of more than one party. These parties can be named either jointly ("pay to the order of Jeannette Edwards and

© GETTY IMAGES/PHOTODISC

Would a note payable "on Christmas of next year" be negotiable? Why or why not?

Anthony Edwards") or individually ("pay to the order of Emilio Morales or Daniel Elliott"). In the first example, both Jeannette and Anthony have to sign the instrument to negotiate it further. In the second example, either Emilio or Daniel acting alone can sign and cash it.

CHECKPOINT
What requirements must be met for an instrument to be considered negotiable?

29-1 Assessment

Xtra! Study Tools
lawxtra.swlearning.com

THINK ABOUT LEGAL CONCEPTS

1. Is a check that fulfills all the other requirements of negotiablity but is written in pencil still negotiable? **Yes or No?**

2. A negotiable instrument dated later than the date of issuance is said to be _?_.

3. If there is a conflict between the amount of a check written in numerals and a different amount written out in words, the amount written in numbers will prevail, as numbers are easier to read. **True or False?**

4. A promissory note is physically issued on June 6 of this year. Which of the following dates, if actually entered on the face of the instrument as the date of issue, would make it antedated? (a) June 5 (b) June 7 (c) July 7 (d) June 6

5. A signature can be written anywhere on the face of an instrument. **True or False?**

6. A(n) _?_ in a negotiable instrument makes the entire balance due and payable upon the happening of a certain event.

7. Commercial paper cannot be signed with an "X." **True or False?**

8. Which of the following wordings would not result in the paper being payable to the party in possession of it? (a) pay to bearer (b) pay to cash (c) pay to Sherlock Holmes (d) All of the above would result in the paper being payable to the possessor.

9. If the indorsement on a negotiable instrument reads "pay to the order of Michelle Holley" it is called _?_ paper.

THINK CRITICALLY ABOUT EVIDENCE

Study the situation, answer the questions, and then prepare arguments to support your answers.

10. C.W. Bean wrote a check payable to Christopher John for the full purchase price of Christopher's used pickup. Bean put "$7,500" in numerals on the payee line for the amount of the check but wrote out "seven thousand eight hundred dollars" below it. If no other evidence were presented as to the sale price, what would a court hold as to the amount of the check?

11. On April Fool's Day, a friend gives you a $25 check that she has deliberately antedated to April 1 of the previous year. If she has adequate funds in her account when you present the check, can you still collect on it?

12. On August 7, you sell your car to pay for your college tuition. The buyer asks that you

not cash the payoff check until his payday on the first of September because he needs the money in his account for family expenses. You promise not to cash it, but when you go to register for classes you find that the tuition amount must be paid immediately or else you cannot enroll. Your only source of funds is the check, and you did tell the buyer that the money was to go for your tuition. You know that by law a check is a demand instrument. Can you cash it? Should you cash it?

13. Campbell wrote the following by hand: "I, Gary Campbell, promise to pay to the order of Allison J. Nagy $2,500." Campbell then delivered it to Nagy. In a dispute that arose later, it was argued that because the instrument lacked Campbell's signature, was not dated, and was without a time of payment, it was not negotiable. Do you agree?

Proper Indorsement and Negotiation

▼ GOALS
- ■ Describe how commercial paper is transferred
- ■ Compare the functions of the various indorsements

HOW IS COMMERCIAL PAPER TRANSFERRED?

WHAT'S YOUR VERDICT?

After being paid every week, Rainquest drove to a nearby grocery store and cashed her paycheck. Each time the store clerk would ask her to sign the back of the check. Finally, Rainquest complained to the store manager about having to do so, saying that her signature is private and others shouldn't see it as they might forge it later. The store manager just said if she didn't sign the check they couldn't give her the funds due on it.

Is Rainquest's signature necessary legally or is the store just being overbearing?

Commercial paper usually is transferred by negotiation. As discussed previously, negotiation may give the transferee greater rights than if the paper is merely assigned. This is true because, in an assignment, the transferee receives only the rights of the transferor. In negotiation, the transferee, if qualified, may receive additional rights granted under the UCC.

In particular, negotiation for value may be to a party who has no knowledge of defects in the original transaction in which the paper was created. This could give that innocent transferee the power to overcome many defenses against payment that the party obligated to pay might have used otherwise. These defenses include breach of contract and failure of consideration, which are explained in the next chapter.

If the transfer of commercial paper does not qualify as a negotiation, it is legally considered as having been assigned. As such, it is subject to contract law. To enable a transferee to receive rights available under the UCC, it is critical to know the proper way to transfer commercial paper. The proper method of transfer in a specific instance depends on whether the instrument is order or bearer paper.

If the instrument is order paper (payable to the order of a named person), the named person or her or his agent must sign the paper on its reverse side. In *What's Your Verdict?* the store clerk and manager properly requested that Rainquest sign the back of the check. If she did not sign the check, the store could not collect the money due on it. After the signature is applied the paper must be delivered to make the negotiation complete and proper.

A signature on the back of an instrument is termed an **indorsement**. (Indorsement is the spelling used by the UCC and in the law of negotiable instruments, and so will be used in this text. The popular spelling of this word is endorsement.) An owner of commercial paper who signs on its reverse indorses the paper and is an **indorser**. The party to whom the paper is indorsed is the **indorsee**. A party who has physical possession of commercial paper that is payable to his or her order or who is in possession of bearer paper is a **holder**. Therefore, a bearer is a holder, as is a person in possession of paper payable to his or her order.

LEGAL RESEARCH

Search the law literature for descriptions of fraudulent schemes that have been committed against financial institutions. Report these to the class and discuss how businesses and individuals can protect themselves from similar problems.

If the paper is bearer paper, it may be negotiated by delivery alone. The bearer simply may hand the paper to the transferee. Many transferees, however, will require the bearer to indorse the paper. This generally allows the future holders to pursue the transferor for payment of the paper's value if there are problems collecting it from the maker or drawee.

CHECKPOINT

How does the proper way to negotiate order paper differ from that required to negotiate bearer paper?

INDORSEMENTS AND THEIR FUNCTIONS

WHAT'S YOUR VERDICT?

Gordon Marshall paid his ex-wife, Gloria Marshall, her monthly alimony by indorsing a weekly paycheck with his name only and handing it to her. While shopping, Gloria had her purse stolen. The thief found the check and promptly bought goods with it at the Penny-Ante Quick Shoppe, which accepted it in good faith. Penny-Ante can legally collect on the check.

What kind of indorsement might have protected Gloria from this loss?

Indorsements are classified by whether any words, other than the indorser's signature, have been added to them and, if so, what those words are or what they direct.

BLANK INDORSEMENTS

A **blank indorsement** consists of just the indorser's signature (see Gordon Marshall's signature in the illustration on this page.) Because it is quickly written, the blank indorsement is the most common. It does not specify a particular person to whom the paper is being transferred. Therefore, it will transform order paper into bearer paper. Even a finder or a thief may

negotiate an instrument with a blank indorsement. A blank indorsement is satisfactory and safe for the indorser if

1. value is immediately received for it, or
2. the paper is deposited in a bank at the time of indorsement.

SPECIAL INDORSEMENTS

A **special indorsement** makes the paper payable to the order of a designated party. Recall that, unless the instrument is a check, the words "Pay to the order of" must be used on the face of the instrument to achieve the same result. With an indorsement, the more concise wording "Pay to Gloria Marshall" is as effective as "Pay to the order of Gloria Marshall." The paper will be order paper as a result of either wording.

To be properly negotiated, order paper requires the signature of the party named in the indorsement. A forged signature used as an indorsement cannot transfer title. Therefore, unlike the situation with paper having a blank indorsement, a thief or a finder of the paper could not legally cash it.

Transferees who receive commercial paper with blank indorsements may protect themselves by writing that the paper is payable to them above the indorser's signature. This is perfectly legal and restores the order character of the instrument. For example, as shown in the illustration at the top of the next page, Gloria Marshall could have taken the blank indorsement of Gordon Marshall and written above it "Pay to the order of Gloria Marshall" or "Pay to Gloria Marshall." Then the thief would have had to forge her signature to pass the instrument. The law states that the loss generally falls on the person who takes from the forger. Therefore,

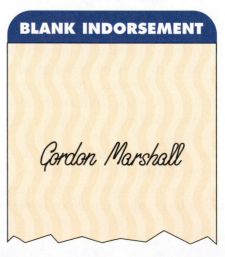

BLANK INDORSEMENT

Gordon Marshall

SPECIAL INDORSEMENT

*Pay to the order of
Gloria Marshall
Gordon Marshall*

if Penny-Ante had accepted the check with a special indorsement, it would have been unable to collect.

It is important to note that there are exceptions to the above rule. Innocent holders may be allowed to collect despite the forgery. These exceptions require negligence on the part of the maker or drawer. For example, suppose that a dishonest employee fraudulently gets an employer to sign a check made payable to a frequent supplier of the business but for a non-existent shipment. The employee then takes the check, forges the supplier's indorsement, and cashes it. The employer must pay it, because it was the employer's negligence that placed the employee in a position to commit the forgery. The employer can then try to recoup the loss from that dishonest employee.

Another exception occurs when an impostor tricks the maker or drawer of commercial paper into giving the impostor an instrument that is made payable to the person who is being impersonated. The impostor then forges the indorsement of the party being impersonated and cashes the check. The instrument is effective against the maker or drawer, who was negligent in not properly identifying the party to whom the paper was given.

QUALIFIED INDORSEMENTS

If the maker or drawee of an instrument fails to pay it, the indorsers may be required to pay it. Adding "without recourse" or equivalent words such as "not liable for payment" over a blank or special indorsement can eliminate this potential secondary liability based on signature. The result is a **qualified indorsement**. A qualified indorsement eliminates the indorser's secondary liability because of his or her signature appearing on the instrument. If the maker or the drawee does not add such wording, the result is an **unqualified indorsement**, and the indorser may be liable to subsequent holders.

Even though secondary liability is avoided by qualifying the indorsement, certain warranties still may bind a transferor. These warranties are implied by law against all transferors and may still require the indorser to pay if the instrument cannot be collected. The warranties guarantee that

1. the transferor is entitled to enforce the paper
2. all signatures are genuine
3. the instrument has not been altered
4. the transferor has no knowledge of a bankruptcy proceeding against the maker, drawer of an unaccepted draft, or an acceptor
5. there are no defenses of any type good against the transferor

The warranty liability of a qualified indorser is the same as the warranty liability of an unqualified indorser. The warranties are very broad in coverage.

The transferor of bearer paper who does not indorse it (and therefore does not acquire secondary liability on her or his signature as an indorser) still is accountable for these warranties. However, warranty liability runs only to the immediate transferee if not indorsed. If the transferor does indorse the bearer paper, the implied warranties are extended to protect the transferees beyond just the immediate transferee.

IN THIS CASE

To pay Barrington back for a loan, Bill Austin made out a check to "cash" for the amount due and gave it to her. Barrington then drove to her bank and sought to receive funds for the check. When she passed it to the teller, the teller returned it and asked that she indorse the instrument. Barrington at first thought it strange as the check was a piece of bearer paper and could be negotiated by just a transfer of possession. Then she realized that the bank wanted her indorsement for warranty purposes.

A QUESTION OF ETHICS

When Cindy Reich returned to her car after shopping at the outlet mall, she noticed a piece of paper trapped under her front driver-side tire. It looked important. She pulled her car forward and then retrieved a check for $1,750. It had been indorsed with the payee's signature and the words "For Deposit Only."

Glancing around, Cindy saw that the check likely had blown out of the deposit tray at the drive-through of a bank located across the street from the mall. From a business law class that she had taken, Cindy knew that the finder or even the thief of such bearer paper could convey good title to such an instrument. She could deposit the money in her account and use it until the true owner showed up. Then she would return it. However by not walking across the street to the bank and simply returning it, she was depriving the loser of the use of his or her money until that time. Then again, how could she be sure that the bank personnel would handle it correctly and get it to the true owner? What should Cindy do?

of the instrument, would destroy negotiability, but this is not true if included in an indorsement. However, a future holder is bound by the condition and cannot collect the instrument against the restrictive indorser until the condition is satisfied.

ACCOMMODATION PARTIES

Sometimes a person who desires to borrow money or to cash a check is not well known in the community or has not established credit. To make her or his commercial paper acceptable, the person might arrange for someone who is known and has a good credit rating to join in signing the paper. Such a cosigner is an **accommodation party**. Under such circumstances, a person who signs as an indorser, maker, drawer, or acceptor becomes primarily liable in that role. It is as though they received the value from the transfer of the instrument. The obligee of the instrument does not have to try to collect from the accommodated party before proceeding against the accommodation party.

However, if the accommodation party is collected against, he or she has the right to seek compensation from the accommodated party. On the other hand, if the party accommodated is collected against, he or she has no legal right to any contribution from the accommodation party simply because the latter was a cosigner.

To be totally without potential liability on a piece of commercial paper, a qualified indorser might add "without warranties" and thus eliminate all warranty liability. However, it will be extremely difficult to find a transferee that will give significant value for the instrument to a potential transferor under such circumstances.

RESTRICTIVE INDORSEMENTS

A **restrictive indorsement** directs the use of the proceeds from the instrument or imposes a condition upon payment of the instrument by the indorser. For example, "Pay to Chase Larue to be held in trust for his oldest son, Tommy," would be a restrictive indorsement, because it directs what is to be done with the proceeds of the paper. "For deposit only" and "for collection" also are restrictive indorsements.

In addition, a restrictive indorsement might impose conditions on payment such as "Pay to Kiersten Alexis upon her delivery of her 1965 Mustang to me." Such a condition, if on the face

CHECKPOINT

List the four main types of indorsements.

Assume the man on the right is serving as an accommodation party for the woman sitting to his left. What is the extent of his liability for the instrument for which he is cosigning?

© GETTY IMAGES/PHOTODISC

Xtra! Study Tools
lawxtra.swlearning.com

THINK ABOUT LEGAL CONCEPTS

1. A check made out to cash does not have to be indorsed in order to be negotiated. **True or False?**

2. The only two types of indorsements that determine how the instrument is to be negotiated are (a) blank and qualified (b) blank and special (c) qualified and blank (d) qualified and restrictive.

3. An instrument that is payable on presentment is termed a _?_ instrument. (a) liquid (b) collateral (c) demand (d) none of the above

4. "Pay to Matt Jones" is a restrictive indorsement. **True or False?**

5. Would you use a restrictive indorsement to direct the use of the proceeds from the instrument. **Yes or No?**

THINK CRITICALLY ABOUT EVIDENCE

Study the situation, answer the questions, and then prepare arguments to support your answers.

6. An impostor came to Jean's door and stated he was the campaign chairman for Senator Walton Knudson's reelection. Without asking for identification and as she was a Knudson supporter, Jean made out a check to the "Walton Knudson Campaign Fund" for $500. The impostor forged the fund's indorsement and cashed the check at a dealership as partial payment for a new car. Can the car dealership enforce the instrument against Jean's checking account?

7. Lisa Pratt received a promissory note for $1,000 payable to bearer. She indorsed it "Pay to Vince Leonard, Lisa Pratt" and delivered it to him. Later Vince simply delivered the note to the Renaissance Record Shop for a laser disc player and a collection of greatest hits of the Sixties, Seventies, and Eighties. Was Vince's action a proper negotiation?

8. In return for repairing their car, you take a check from a couple in an old station wagon. The car is packed with what looks like all their worldly goods. You have a feeling that either the account is closed or that the check will not be paid or, most likely, both. What indorsement can you use to limit your liability to subsequent holders of the instrument?

9. If you also wrote in "without warranties" above your indorsement in exercise 8, would that help limit your liability?

10. Your friend wants to buy a car but his credit rating is poor. He asks you to cosign the note with him so that the transaction will go through. If you do so, could you later be required to pay the full amount of the note?

PREVENT LEGAL DIFFICULTIES

In dealing with commercial paper . . .

1. Remember that even if an instrument is not negotiable commercial paper, it still may be a valuable contract or creditor's claim and be freely transferable by assignment.

2. If you issue commercial paper that is payable on demand, be ready to pay at any time. Civil and even criminal penalties may result from your failure to do so.

3. Learn and utilize the various indorsements. They have been created to fulfill vital purposes.

4. Only issue bearer paper or create it by indorsement if you immediately deposit it or immediately transfer it and receive value in exchange. Otherwise unauthorized persons may misuse the bearer paper with the loss falling to you.

5. If you are the payee of commercial paper, try to include a clause for the payment of reasonable attorney's fees and collection costs by the issuer in case of default.

6. Do not sign as an accommodation party unless you are prepared to pay the full amount of the instrument or have your credit standing damaged by it going into default before you are requested to pay it.

Chapter 29 Assessment

CONCEPTS IN BRIEF

29-1 Requirements of Negotiability

1. To be negotiable, an instrument must
   - be in writing and signed by the maker or drawer
   - contain an unconditional order (if it is a draft or a check) or promise (if it is a note or a CD)
   - call for payment of a sum certain in money
   - be payable on demand or at a definite time
   - be payable to the bearer or to the order of a specified person
2. In conflicts between terms written by various means, the handwritten version prevails over the typewritten version, and the typewritten version prevails over the printed version. Amounts expressed in words prevail over amounts expressed in figures.
3. Although the order or promise given in commercial paper must be unconditional, certain terms may be added to an instrument without destroying negotiability. An example is a provision for the recovery of collection costs and reasonable attorney's fees in case of default.

29-2 Proper Indorsement and Negotiation

4. Commercial paper payable to order may be negotiated only by the proper indorsement and delivery. Commercial paper payable to the bearer may be negotiated by delivery alone.
5. The four basic types of indorsements are blank, special, qualified, and restrictive.
6. Qualified indorsers have some potential liability on an instrument unless they add the words "without warranties" above their signatures, along with "without recourse."
7. An accommodation party is liable to all subsequent holders of the paper who give value for it, but an accommodation party is not liable to the party accommodated.

YOUR LEGAL VOCABULARY

Match each statement with the term that it best defines. Some terms may not be used.

1. Paper that is to be paid on presentment or at sight
2. Dated later than the date of issuance
3. Indorsement that eliminates the indorser's secondary liability to pay if the primarily liable party does not
4. Indorsement consisting only of the signature of the indorser
5. Person who signs as maker, drawer, acceptor, or indorser to lend name and credit to another person
6. Indorsement that directs the use of the proceeds from an instrument or imposes a condition on payment
7. Indorsement that makes a paper payable to a particular party or to his or her order
8. Dated prior to the date of issuance
9. Official medium of exchange in the United States or a foreign country at the time a piece of commercial paper is issued
10. A signature rendered on the back of a piece of commercial paper
11. Commercial paper legally collectible by the party in possession

a. acceleration clause
b. accommodation party
c. antedated
d. bearer
e. bearer paper
f. blank indorsement
g. holder
h. indorsee
i. indorsement
j. indorser
k. money
l. negotiable
m. negotiable instruments
n. negotiation
o. order paper
p. payable at a definite time
q. payable on demand
r. postdated
s. qualified indorsement
t. restrictive indorsement
u. special indorsement
v. unqualified indorsement

REVIEW LEGAL CONCEPTS

12. In interpreting conflicting terms that appear on the face of commercial paper, why are handwritten terms given precedence over printed terms?

13. Explain why a finger or thumb print would be effective as a signature on a piece of commercial paper.

14. List and explain the importance of the necessary elements of a negotiable instrument.

15. Why are "reasonable attorney's fees" acceptable as part of a "sum certain"? Surely nothing can be less certain.

16. Why is it so important that the face of commercial paper bear the words "payable to order" or "payable to bearer?"

WRITE ABOUT LEGAL CONCEPTS

17. Why are holders allowed to eliminate their signature-based liability to future holders by using a qualified indorsement?

18. Why are warranties extended to all subsequent holders by a holder who indorses the paper?

19. **HOT DEBATE** Write the bank's attorney's opening statement to persuade the court that the loss should not fall on the bank.

MAKE ACADEMIC CONNECTIONS

20. **ART** Commercial art takes many forms, from the classic movie poster to the design of an ad showing a superhero endorsing cereal. Andy Warhol raised the common soup can to a level of consideration no one but its designer had given it. Collect several samples of checks and evaluate the background art on each. Formulate the requirements for such art and then create your own. Compose a report on the guidelines that should be used in these efforts and show a sample of your work to the class.

THINK CRITICALLY ABOUT EVIDENCE

Study the situation, answer the questions, and then prepare arguments to support your answers.

21. Parnell was the maker of a promissory note payable to LaSalle. The note was complete and legally correct in all respects but contained the following additional terms. Do any of the added terms destroy the negotiability of the note?

    • "This note is prepared as a result of a service contract between the parties dated 3/13/—"

    • "This note is secured by a mortgage on the maker's residence at 67 Park Central West, Pierre, South Dakota."

    • "This note is payable in Canadian dollars, with exchange."

22. Lasorda paid $7,500 for a $10,000 promissory note payable on the day the Chicago Cubs next win the World Series. Is the note negotiable? Can it still be collected?

23. Anton drew a check for $750 payable to bearer. Anton gave the check to Brewster. Brewster negotiated it by delivery to Charlois. Charlois negotiated it by delivery to Deltoid. Deltoid tried to collect but found that Anton's bank account lacked the necessary funds for payment. May Deltoid collect from either or both of the prior holders, and if so, under what circumstances?

24. Krosby was starting a new business and needed cash. He convinced the Finance Bank to lend him $10,000 against his new equipment. However, the bank insisted that his prominent friend, Hopper, or someone of equal financial means indorse the note as well. What would be the extent of Hopper's potential liability from such an act?

25. Associates Discount Corporation sought court enforcement of a note it held. The note stated that Fitzwater owed a large sum of money for a tractor that had been delivered to him. Fitzwater, the signer and obligor on the note, wanted to testify to the effect that the tractor was never delivered. May he do so? (*Associates Discount Corporation of Iowa v. Fitzwater,* 518 S.W.2d 474)

26. On May 8, 1957, Brookshire was convicted of issuing a check with intent to defraud. On January 1, 1957, Brookshire had given a check dated December 31, 1957, to pay his taxes for 1956. On January 7 or 8, 1957, Brookshire's bank dishonored the check due to insufficient funds. Under these circumstances, should an intent to defraud be inferred from Brookshire's issuing a postdated check? If not, should the conviction be overturned? (*State v. Brookshire,* 329 S.W.2d 252)

27. In May 1963, Ferri executed a note promising to pay $3,000 to Sylvia's order "within ten years after date." Two years later, Sylvia demanded payment. When refused, Sylvia sued Ferri. Is the note due at a definite time? If so, when? If not, why not? (*Ferri v. Sylvia,* 214 A.2d 470)

28. A $10,000 certificate of deposit (CD) "payable to the Registered Depositor hereof" was issued to John D. Cox by Commercial Bank of Liberty. Cox then used the CD as security for a loan made by the Kaw Valley Bank. When Cox defaulted on the loan, Kaw Valley sought to collect on the CD but Liberty refused to pay. Kaw Valley brought suit but could only collect if the CD was negotiable. Was it? (*Kaw Valley Bank Etc. v. Commercial Bank of Liberty,* 567 S.W.2d 710)

29. Haas, a trusted employee of a firm by the name of Trail Leasing, Inc., used her access to her employer's blank checks to defraud Trail Leasing of almost $40,000. She did this by making checks payable to the firm's bank, Drovers First American. She then had the checks signed by an authorized officer of the firm when she obtained cash for them. Once it discovered the fraud, Trail Leasing sued the Bank to recover its losses. Decide. (*Trail Leasing, Inc. v. Drovers First American Bank,* 447 N.W.2d 190)

30. When an employee of Epicycle cashed a payroll check at Money Mart Check Cashing Center, Inc., the instrument was deposited with others into Money Mart's bank account. Regrettably the check was subsequently returned marked, "payment stopped." When Money Mart attempted to collect on the check at a later date, Epicycle defended against the collection efforts by maintaining that Money Mart could not do so as it failed to even inquire about the validity of the check before taking it. Decide. (*Money Mart Check Cashing Center, Inc. v. Epicycle Corp.,* 667 P. 1372)

FEDERAL DEPOSIT INSURANCE CORPORATION V. CULVER
640 F. SUPP. 725

FACTS When Texan Nasib Ed Kalliel entered into a business deal with the Rexford State Bank of Rexford, Kansas, the bank was in excellent financial shape. Kalliel suggested that he had a plan to rescue several farmers from the financial disaster that many in the farming industry at that time were experiencing. He suggested that if the bank would loan its money to farmers in trouble, he would guarantee the loan repayment through one of his companies. Unfortunately, the bank did not have enough capital to make adequate loans to all the farmers who needed them. Consequently, the bank agreed to take deposits from a New Jersey firm in the form of high-yield large certificates of deposits. Most of the new deposits went directly to farm loans. However, about 20 percent were "farmed out" to Kalliel himself and his companies.

Kalliel and a Missouri farmer, Gary Culver, agreed to a working relationship in which Kalliel would manage the business end and Culver the production end of the Culver farm. When Culver told Kalliel that he must have $30,000 to prevent foreclosure, the Rexford Bank provided the money. Shortly thereafter a Bank representative approached Culver and induced him to sign a blank promissory note form. The Bank's representative maintained to Culver that the note was nothing more than a receipt for the money. Later the amount, interest rate, and due date on the note were filled in. However $50,000 was entered as the amount instead of $30,000. When the Rexford Bank later became insolvent, the FDIC bought the note as it did the remaining outstanding Rexford Bank notes. The FDIC then sought to collect on the note as it was mature and no collection efforts had ever been started on it.

REASONING The FDIC moved for summary judgment. Culver defended that the circumstances surrounding the issuance of the note provided him with the defense of fraud which would be good even against the collection efforts of the FDIC. The FDIC maintained its right to collect, as under the UCC the defense of fraud is available only as long as there has not been "reasonable opportunity to obtain knowledge of its character or its essential terms" provided to the maker of the note. The FDIC maintained that Culver's failure to take notice of the nature of the form of the instrument that he was presented as a "receipt" was negligence and that, therefore, it could collect to the full value of the face of the note.

PRACTICE JUDGING

1. Should the FDIC's request for summary judgement against Culver be granted? Why or why not?

2. If Culver had just signed a blank piece of paper after being told that the bank would make a receipt out of it by printing the appropriate words around his signature, would he be able to avail himself of the defense of fraud? Why or why not?

3. If the Bank had made the note payable for an unreasonable amount, such as $1,000,000, could the FDIC have collected?

© GETTY IMAGES/PHOTODISC

CHAPTER 30

Discharge of Commercial Paper and Electronic Fund Transfers

30-1 Discharge of Commercial Paper

30-2 The Law of Electronic Fund Transfers

© GETTY IMAGES/PHOTODISC

HOT DEBATE

Buanna Myers sat at her desk at the Commerce Bank of Statusville. She was deciding whether or not to buy a promissory note from Alyssia Thomas, the proprietor of Alyssia's Autos. The maker of the note was Televangelist Robert Shore, as president of Mercyland, a not-for-profit corporation that managed low-cost rental properties. Buanna knew that many of the transactions originating with Alyssia's Autos had resulted in lawsuits, mainly because the vehicles Alyssia sold were substandard. The note from Mercyland was for $78,000 for a bus just purchased. Buanna knew that her higher ups at the bank would insist on collecting, even from Mercyland. She also knew that if she didn't buy the note, someone else would.

Where Do You Stand?

1. Assume Buanna buys the note and the bus is defective. Should the bank be able to collect? Why or why not?

2. As the attorney for Mercyland, what arguments can you make to allow the cost for repairs to be offset from the amount due on the note?

Discharge of Commercial Paper

▼ **GOALS**

- List the ways commercial paper can be discharged
- Recognize the importance of the status of a holder in due course
- Identify the limited and universal defenses

HOW IS COMMERCIAL PAPER DISCHARGED?

WHAT'S YOUR VERDICT?

Sapper held a promissory note for $10,000 on which Albertson was the maker. As he left his desk one evening, he accidentally brushed against the edge of the note. The note fell to the floor and was trashed by the cleaning service.

Did this discharge Albertson's debt?

The obligations assumed in commercial paper transactions may be discharged in a variety of ways.

BY PAYMENT

The vast majority of commercial paper is paid and discharged according to its terms. The maker usually pays a note or a certificate of deposit. A check usually is paid upon demand by the bank on which it is drawn. Other types of drafts usually are paid by the drawees who have accepted the drafts. Without such reliability the commercial paper system would not function.

By law the commercial paper terms must dictate that payment be made in money. At maturity or on demand, however, the holder (obligee/creditor) may agree to some form of substitution. For instance, the holder may agree to take different kinds of property, such as other commercial paper or anything else of value, instead of money.

When an obligor pays a holder the amount due on commercial paper, the obligor should obtain possession of the paper. Otherwise, a dishonest holder who retains the paper might falsely claim that it had not been paid and

IN THIS CASE

Hofstra owed $7,700 on a note held by Duvall. On the due date Hofstra offered Duvall a prize quarter horse worth more than $7,700 as payment instead of cash. At that point, the holder, Duvall, had the right to demand payment in money or to consider the obligor, Hofstra, in default. Recognizing the value of the quarter horse, however, Duvall agreed to the substitution, and the note was discharged.

demand a second payment. Such a dishonest holder also could negotiate it wrongfully to an innocent third party, who then also might be entitled to payment. Even if the amount due on paper is paid only in part, this fact should be shown by appropriate notation on the paper itself. Mistakenly marking a note paid and returning it to the maker does not discharge the obligation by itself. However, it is very difficult evidence for the obligee to overcome in order to be still allowed to collect.

© GETTY IMAGES/PHOTODISC

What is the most common method of payment and discharge for commercial paper?

BY CANCELLATION

The obligation to pay commercial paper also may be discharged by cancellation. **Cancellation** in this context consists of any act by the current holder that indicates an intent to end the obligation of payment. Knowingly tearing up the paper, burning it, or just drawing a line through the name of a potential obligor, like an indorser, would be excellent evidence of an intent to discharge one or all obligations arising from the instrument. If the cancellation was the result of fraud, an accident, or a mistake, as in *What's Your Verdict?*, the action does not discharge the obligation.

BY ALTERATION

A fraudulent change to or fraudulent completion of commercial paper by a party to the instrument will discharge the obligation of the other party. For example, suppose that it is shown to the satisfaction of a court that the holder of a note fraudulently changed the rate of interest due from 7 to 17 percent. In such a case, the maker would not be obligated to pay it. However, the original parties to the paper still might be bound to make payment in accordance with the original terms under certain circumstances. These circumstances will be discussed in the next section.

BY IMPAIRMENT OF COLLATERAL

If a holder extends the time of payment, releases the principal debtor, or impairs collateral provided as security for payment of the negotiable instruments, any party whose rights are affected and who did not consent is discharged.

AS A CONTRACT

A negotiable instrument may be discharged in the same ways as an ordinary contract for the payment of money. For example, a discharge could occur by novation, by accord and satisfaction, or by operation of law, such as in bankruptcy or because of the running of the statute of limitations.

CHECKPOINT

Name four means of discharging commercial paper.

COLLECTION OF COMMERCIAL PAPER OBLIGATIONS

WHAT'S YOUR VERDICT?

Donna paid Alanna $500 for a promissory note with a face value of $10,000. The note was bearer paper, and Alanna refused to indorse it, saying that she had to leave town and therefore her indorsement would not do any good. Donna knew Alanna recently had been indicted for participation in a blackmail scheme. When Donna tried to collect on the note, the maker refused to pay claiming he had signed it only because Alanna had threatened to reveal certain incriminating facts to the Internal Revenue Service.

Is Donna a holder in due course and thereby able to overcome the obligor's defense and collect?

If payment of commercial paper according to its terms is not voluntarily forthcoming, the obligee must try and collect what is due. Standing in the way may be one or more of a variety of defenses raised by the obligor. These defenses may be effective or not depending on their validity and the status of the obligee. To maximize the chances of collection, an obligee should try and attain the status of a holder in due course.

HOLDER IN DUE COURSE

As defined in the last chapter, a *holder* is a person who has physical possession of bearer paper or order paper payable to the order of that person as a payee or indorsee. All holders have the right to assign, negotiate, enforce payment, or discharge the paper, with or without payment in return. However, when trying to collect on an instrument, a party who qualifies as either a holder in due course or a holder through a holder in due course is legally placed in a much better position than a mere holder or an assignee.

To be a **holder in due course** (HDC), a person must qualify as a holder and, in addition, take the commercial paper in good faith, give value for it, and not have knowledge of any defense, adverse claim to, or dishonor of the instrument.

Sometimes, for example if the instrument is overdue and the acquirer knew or should have known of its status, a person cannot be an HDC. Such a person could still qualify as a **holder through a holder in due course** (HHDC). An HHDC is a holder who takes commercial paper anytime after an HDC. An HHDC normally has the same rights as an HDC. Note, however, that according to the Uniform Commercial Code (UCC), persons cannot improve their position on commercial paper through reacquisition.

If an individual had been a mere holder the first time she had an instrument and she then sold it to a person who qualified as an HDC, reacquiring the instrument from that HDC would still leave her with only her original rights as a mere holder, not those of an HHDC. In collecting, either an HDC or an HHDC can overcome more of the defenses that the obligor on an instrument might raise against payment than a mere holder can overcome.

Defenses that are good against everyone except an HDC or an HHDC are termed **limited defenses**. (These were labeled *personal defenses* under pre-UCC law, but this term may still be used in some jurisdictions.) Defenses that are good against all plaintiffs suing on a negotiable instrument are called **universal defenses**. (These were known as *real defenses* under pre-UCC law, and this term also may still be used in some jurisdictions.) These defenses will be discussed in detail later in this section.

QUALIFICATIONS OF AN HDC

For a holder to be considered an HDC and thereby able to overcome limited defenses, the holder must take the paper in good faith and give value without notice of defense or dishonor.

TAKE IN GOOD FAITH AND GIVE VALUE Taking paper in good faith requires that the holder act honestly, not just in the immediate transaction, but in relation to the complete set of circumstances surrounding the paper. In addition, although the courts generally do not consider the adequacy of the value given for commercial paper, the amount given may affect the court's judgment as to the good faith of the parties

involved. For example, if the value given is small in relation to the face value of the instrument, fraud or some other unconscionable act that would prevent the holder from being considered an HDC may be implied by the court.

In *What's Your Verdict?* Donna's knowledge of Alanna's alleged criminal activities and the small value given probably will disqualify her from being an HDC. There was an implied lack of good faith in the situation.

WITHOUT KNOWLEDGE OF DEFENSE OR DISHONOR
Besides giving value in good faith, an HDC must not know the paper is overdue. For example, a time instrument is overdue the day after the maturity date. If payments are to be made in installments, the paper is overdue if even a single installment is late. If an instrument is due on demand, it is overdue a reasonable time after it is issued. However, the UCC specifies that a check is overdue 90 days after issue. Also every holder is charged with knowledge of what is on the instrument, so failing to notice the date is no excuse. Similarly, if the date has been altered, as from May 5 to May 15, and if the alteration is

not recognizable by a reasonable person, an innocent holder is accountable only for the date as altered (May 15).

Finally, to qualify as an HDC a holder must not know of any defenses against enforcement of the paper, any claims of ownership from third parties, or any previous dishonors of the paper. Any such knowledge attributable to the holder when he or she acquired the paper would prevent that holder from being considered an HDC. As a consequence, that holder legally might be unable to overcome an obligor's limited defenses against payment of the paper.

CHECKPOINT

What must a mere holder do to be considered an HDC?

WHAT ARE THE LIMITED AND UNIVERSAL DEFENSES?

WHAT'S YOUR VERDICT?

Santana owned "Hello, Cleveland!" a business that provided touring rock groups with transportation from one concert to another. He bought a large used recreational vehicle (RV) to convert for such a purpose from Trail's Used Car and RV Center. Trail assured Santana that the odometer reading of 25,275 on the RV was correct. Santana paid for the vehicle with $15,000 in cash and by issuing a $45,000 promissory note payable to Trail's order. Santana later learned from state authorities that the true odometer reading was 125,275 miles. Santana wanted to avoid the contract because of the fraud. In the meantime, Trail had negotiated the note to the Continental Bank, an HDC, for $41,000.

Must Santana pay Continental the $45,000 as promised?

NETBookmark

Access lawxtra.swlearning.com and click on the link for Chapter 30. If a holder in due course of a social security check somehow loses or destroys the check before depositing it, that party can receive the funds by following a specific procedure. Read the Social Security Administration's policy regarding reimbursing for checks that are not physically returned to the Federal Reserve Bank. Which agency will reissue a social security check to the holder in due course if it is a legitimate claim and a proper request is received within 14 months from the issue date of the check?

lawxtra.swlearning.com

Even though the emphasis in this section is on defenses, it is once again important to realize that most commercial paper is enforceable according to its terms and is promptly paid. Only in the exceptional case do defenses to collection come into play. In such instances, however, the holder's risk of not being able to collect is greatly reduced if he or she is an HDC and thereby is able to overcome the limited but not the universal defenses that might be raised against such collection.

THE LIMITED DEFENSES

Limited defenses are good against all holders except an HDC or an HHDC. Against ordinary holders they are just as effective in barring collection as the universal defenses discussed later in this section. The following are the limited defenses.

BREACH OF CONTRACT OR FAILURE OF CONSIDERATION
Often commercial paper is issued as a result of a contractual agreement, as in *What's Your Verdict?* Ordinary or mere holders are subject to defenses that arise when the terms of such a contract are not fulfilled or the consideration (or partial consideration) is not given as bargained for by the person who issued the instrument. In *What's Your Verdict?* for example, if Trail had failed to deliver the RV on time, it would have been a breach of contract or, if the RV were defective, a failure of consideration. In

either instance only an HDC or an HHDC could have collected on the note. An ordinary holder, like Trail, could not have overcome the defenses.

FRAUD IN THE INDUCEMENT

If a person uses fraud to induce another to issue commercial paper, as Trail did to Santana in *What's Your Verdict?,* the party defrauded has a limited defense to use against holders who try to collect. However, in *What's Your Verdict?* Continental Bank is an HDC. Therefore, Santana must pay the note. Santana can then seek to recover from Trail.

Fraud in the inducement occurs when the issuer is aware that an obligation based on commercial paper is being created and knows the essential terms. However, the person is persuaded to issue the paper because of fraudulent statements. This should not be confused with fraud in the execution, where the issuer is unaware that an obligation based on commercial paper is being created or is unaware of the nature or essential terms of the commercial paper. Fraud in the execution is a universal defense covered later in this section.

TEMPORARY INCAPACITY TO CONTRACT— EXCLUDING MINORITY

Contractual obligations made when a person is experiencing a temporary loss of capacity, such as through insanity or intoxication, are voidable. The law establishes a limited defense against commercial paper issued during such periods of temporary loss of capacity.

ORDINARY DURESS

Duress can be either a limited or a universal defense depending on its severity. Ordinary duress, typically from severe economic threat or a legitimate threat of criminal prosecution, does not strip away a person's capacity to contract. It does force the person to enter into a contract improperly. As a consequence, ordinary duress provides a limited defense against collection of any commercial paper that originates in such a contractual setting.

PRIOR PAYMENT OR CANCELLATION

If the obligee pays the amount due on a piece of commercial paper but does not obtain the instrument or at least have it marked "paid," the instrument could continue circulating. If it does, and it ends up in the hands of an HDC, that party could then enforce it against the obligor a second time because prior payment or cancellation only produces a limited defense.

CONDITIONAL DELIVERY OR NONDELIVERY

Assume that a check or a note is delivered under a separate agreement that the instrument is to be negotiated only upon the occurrence of a certain event. Before the condition is satisfied, the paper is negotiated regardless. The resulting defense of conditional delivery is good only against ordinary holders.

Nondelivery also is merely a limited defense. In such a case, an instrument is prepared or indorsed properly but only circulated as a result of theft or negligence. If the instrument is in bearer form, a later HDC could enforce it, but a mere holder could not.

UNAUTHORIZED COMPLETION

A maker or drawer who signs a negotiable instrument but leaves the amount blank runs a great risk. In such an instance, someone else typically is authorized to complete the paper when, for example, a final price is negotiated. If the amount actually entered is not within authorized limits and the instrument is transferred to a holder in due course, the amount would have to be paid to the HDC because unauthorized completion is only a limited defense.

THEFT

A mere holder cannot collect on the instrument if the holder or a person through whom she or he obtained the instrument acquired it by theft. An HDC can require payment in such circumstances, however.

THE UNIVERSAL DEFENSES

Defenses that are good against all kinds of holders, including HDCs and HHDCs, are universal defenses. They include the following.

PERMANENT INCAPACITY TO CONTRACT AND MINORITY

If a person is declared permanently insane or a habitual drunkard by judicial proceeding, the person is not responsible for any obligation incurred thereafter on commercial paper. Either status poses a universal defense to the making, drawing, accepting, indorsing, or accommodating of another party on an instrument.

Just as a minor may avoid contractual responsibilities, her or his refusal to pay on a piece of commercial paper is a universal defense. This is true whether the minor signs as maker, drawer, acceptor, indorser, or in any other capacity.

ILLEGALITY Commercial paper issued in connection with illegal conduct, such as illegal gambling or prostitution in most states, is unenforceable even by an HDC or an HHDC.

FORGERY OR LACK OF AUTHORITY When one person signs the name of another with the intent to defraud, a forgery has been committed. Such an act is a crime. Forgery on commercial paper produces a universal defense for the person whose signature has been forged. If the intent to defraud is lacking, but a person signs another's signature without authorization, the signer does not commit forgery. However, the effect on an HDC would be the same unless the person whose name was signed later ratified (approved) the signing. Both the forger and the unauthorized signer would be liable for the instrument regardless.

ALTERATION An **alteration** is a party's unauthorized change to or completion of a negotiable instrument intended to change the obligation of a party. If the alteration was made fraudulently, the person whose obligation is affected no longer has liability on the instrument. Other alterations do not discharge a party, and the instrument may be enforced according to its original terms.

Even if the alteration was fraudulent a payor bank, a drawee, or a person taking the instrument for value, in good faith and without notice of the alteration can enforce the instrument according to its original terms. These parties also can enforce the terms as filled in on an incomplete instrument altered by unauthorized completion. If the $15 amount payable on a check is altered to read $150, an HDC or HHDC could collect on the instrument, but only $15. If, by negligence, the person sued on the check substantially contributed to making the alteration possible, that person cannot use the defense of alteration.

FRAUD IN THE EXECUTION OF THE PAPER OR AS TO THE ESSENTIAL TERMS Sometimes trickery is used in such a way that even a careful person who signs does not know and has no reasonable opportunity to learn of the nature or essential terms of the document. Such a person has a defense of fraud against even an HDC or an HHDC. For example, a celebrity signs an auto-

graph on a blank sheet of paper. The "fan" then prints or writes a promissory note around the signature. Or suppose the signer of the paper is not able to read because he or she is illiterate in English or has broken glasses, and the person planning to defraud gives a false explanation of the essential terms or substitutes one paper for another before the signing. Not even an HDC or an HHDC can collect in these cases.

DURESS DEPRIVING CONTROL While ordinary duress is a limited defense, duress that deprives a person of control is a universal one. For example, a person who signs a note or draft because another person is threatening to shoot him with a gun has a defense good against even an HDC or an HHDC.

CLAIMS AND DEFENSES STEMMING FROM A CONSUMER TRANSACTION Although not defined as a universal defense by the UCC, by Federal Trade Commission (FTC) rule any defense a consumer could raise against the seller of a good or service can be raised against commercial paper originating in the same transaction. Defenses such as breach of contract, failure of consideration, and fraud in the inducement are thereby made good even against an HDC or HHDC in the proper circumstances. A **consumer transaction** is one in which a party buys goods or services for personal

Imagine this woman has asked the celebrity to sign his autograph on a blank piece of paper. If she then creates a promissory note around the signature, what defense does the celebrity have?

or household use. A notice stating that a piece of commercial paper originated in a consumer transaction and that the debtor's defenses are good against holders must be given in bold print on the instrument.

Prior to the "consumer revolt" of the 1960s, the holder in due course doctrine allowed collection in both consumer transactions and business transactions. For example, if you purchased a defective car whose transmission fell out on the way out of the used car lot, you would still have to pay off in full any promissory note that you signed in order to buy the car if the note was held by an HDC. You could seek compensation only from the used car dealer.

CHECKPOINT
What is the difference between a universal and a limited defense?

lawxtra.swlearning.com

30-1 Assessment

THINK ABOUT LEGAL CONCEPTS

1. Can a mere holder of a note who cannot qualify as an HDC sell it to a party who qualifies as an HDC and then by reacquiring it have the rights of an HDC? **Yes or No?**

2. Which of the following would not discharge an instrument? (a) payment (b) alteration (c) unintentional destruction (d) All of the above would discharge the instrument.

3. A holder who takes paper in good faith, gives value, and does so without notice of defense or dishonor can become an HDC. **True or False?**

4. Can a mere holder discharge a potential obligor such as an indorser before the instrument is paid? **Yes or No?**

5. The vast majority of commercial paper is paid and discharged according to its terms. **True or False?**

6. Permanent incapacity to contract is a limited defense. **True or False?**

7. Fraud in the inducement is a universal defense. **True or False?**

THINK CRITICALLY ABOUT EVIDENCE

Study the situation, answer the questions, and then prepare arguments to support your answers.

8. On December 1, Sven Bollinger took a third-party check from Tim Wallace in partial payment for a used stereo Sven sold Tim. The check was made out on August 31 payable to Tim. He indorsed it in blank upon transfer. Can Sven be a holder in due course on the instrument?

9. Ficklin was an unqualified indorser on a note for $10,000. Dixon, the holder of the note, mistakenly believed that Ficklin was in financial ruin. Thinking that she could not collect on the note, Dixon struck out Ficklin's indorsement. Is Ficklin still potentially liable on the instrument?

10. A 17-year-old student contracts to pay $3,000 for a 12-month modeling course. She pays $500 down and gives a note for the balance, payable in 23 monthly installments. Advertisements for the course promise "exciting, high-paying jobs." However, it becomes clear that the only jobs offered are to model clothes at local schools. The student decides to avoid the contract but is told that the note has been transferred to a bank that is a holder in due course. Must she pay as promised?

11. You contract for aluminum siding to be installed on the building of your skateboard manufacturing business. You sign a promissory note for $10,000 payable to the order of the siding company. Later, although the siding company has gone out of business without doing the job, a bank demands payment of the note. The bank purchased the instrument from the siding company for $9,500 and is a holder in due course. Are you legally required to pay the note?

30-2 The Law of Electronic Fund Transfers

▼ **GOALS**

- Distinguish the financial transactions that are electronic fund transfers
- State the rules controlling electronic fund transfers

ELECTRONIC FUND TRANSFERS

WHAT'S YOUR VERDICT?

As Snyder used her ATM card at her bank's drive up machine, her PIN was observed by a man parked nearby using binoculars. He then followed Snyder and, later in the day, while she ran into a convenience store to pay for gas, stole her purse with the card in it. Snyder immediately notified the police of the theft but she did not notify her financial institution for three days. During that time the thief took out $2,100 in cash advances using the card.

Who is liable for the loss?

To prevent what happened to Snyder in *What's Your Verdict?* from happening to you, what safety precautions can you take when using an ATM machine?

A transfer of funds that requires a financial institution to debit or credit an account and that is initiated by the use of an electronic terminal, computer, telephone, or magnetic tape is an **electronic fund transfer (EFT)**.

Law Brief

A new law, called Check 21, went into effect in late 2004 to eliminate the problems caused by the grounding of airlines during the 9/11 crisis. What did that tragic incident have to do with checks? It prevented the quick transfer by air of tens of millions of paper checks. As a consequence millions of consumers got the use of hundreds of millions of dollars for a few more days of "float time" (the time between writing a check and when it is deducted from your account). Check 21 eliminates that ever occurring again by allowing such checks to be immediately taken electronically (as a debit card expenditure is) against an account. This will result in the elimination of "float time" and, according to consumer groups, result in seven million more checks being returned for insufficient funds each year. The law also allows the destruction of cashed paper checks as long as an electronic image of the check is retained. This will cause problems not only in identifying forgeries but also, because of the lack of fingerprint identification, in catching the forgers. In addition Check 21 will not speed up the time in which the funds from deposited funds become available to you.

EFTs basically are conducted without such paper instruments as checks or drafts. Automated teller machines, point-of-sale terminals in stores, pay-by-phone systems that eliminate check writing, and automated clearinghouse networks that credit payroll checks directly to accounts are examples of devices that facilitate EFTs.

ELECTRONIC FUND TRANSFERS ACT

Commercial paper law, due to its emphasis on the need for a writing, was generally inapplicable to EFTs. Therefore, the federal government enacted the Electronic Fund Transfers Act (EFTA) to protect consumers making such transfers. The EFTA emphasizes that the use of such transfers is to be purely voluntary. When an EFT is used, the consumer must immediately receive a written receipt and later must receive a statement of all transfers during a particular period. If the consumer detects an error of overbilling, it must be reported within 60 days of the date the statement was sent. The error is reported to the institution responsible for the EFT. The institution then has 10 business days to investigate and to report the results in writing. If the institution needs more time, it can use up to 45 days, but during this time the funds must be made available to the consumer.

In the case of unauthorized transfers, Congress rejected the idea present in commercial paper law

requiring full liability on the part of a depositor who negligently allows such a transfer (by losing a check, for example). Instead, Congress chose to divide the risk of unauthorized transfers between the consumer and the financial institution, even if the depositor is negligent. As a consequence, as long as the financial institution is notified within

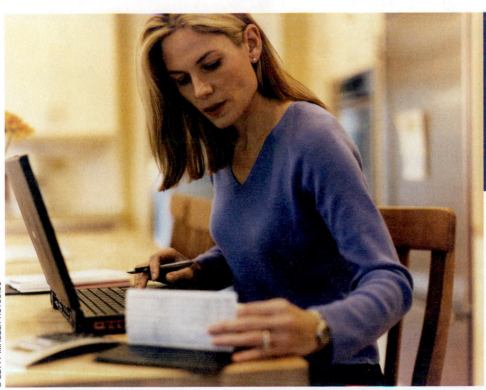

In your opinion, do the safeguards provided by the EFTA provide adequate protection for consumers who transfer funds electronically? Would you feel safe transferring funds electronically from your bank accounts? Why or why not?

© GETTY IMAGES/PHOTODISC

LEGAL RESEARCH

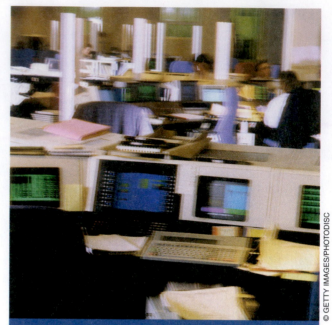

What are the basic differences between consumer EFTs and business EFTs?

© GETTY IMAGES/PHOTODISC

two business days of learning of the loss or theft of the card, the consumer is responsible only for the lesser of $50 or the value obtained in unauthorized transfers prior to the notification. However, if more than two days have elapsed before notification, the consumer may be responsible for up to a maximum of $500.

In *What's Your Verdict?* because three days went by before Snyder gave notification of her loss, she will probably have to pay $500 and the financial institution will have to absorb the other $1,600.

UCC ARTICLE 4A

While consumer electronic fund transfers are governed by the EFTA, electronic fund transfers by businesses are governed by Article 4A of the UCC. These transfers generally involve large sums of money between highly sophisticated parties. Speed in making the transfer often is very important.

CHECKPOINT

Name the laws that govern consumer EFTs and business EFTs.

Cyberlaw

A form of electronic fund transfer used widely in international transactions is *electronic data interchange (EDI)*. With EDI, transport documents such as bills of lading, and others, such as import-export papers and invoices, are sent via computer to their destinations. Use of EDI helps to speed up international transactions for multinational corporations and other companies that do business internationally. Rules governing the EDI transfer of bills of lading and other transport documents have been adopted by an international trade organization, the Comite Maritime International (CMI). The rules govern the problem of negotiating the transport documents. The party who has the right to control and transfer the goods is designated as the "holder" in the computer records. According to CMI, EDI can be used for transport documents only upon agreement of all parties involved in the transaction.

THINK ABOUT IT

What are the incentives for businesses to use this method of transfer of documents?

THINK ABOUT LEGAL CONCEPTS

1. Checks are not covered by the Electronic Fund Transfers Act. **True or False?**

2. When an EFT takes place the consumer must immediately receive a(n) _?_.

3. If, upon receiving an account statement, an error of overbilling is detected by a consumer in an EFT, it must be reported within _?_ days from the date the statement was sent. (a) 15 (b) 30 (c) 60 (d) none of the above

4. Electronic fund transfers by businesses are covered by state law. **True or False?**

5. If negligent, the consumer can be held liable for up to $5,000 of the losses that result from a lost or stolen ATM card. **True or False?**

THINK CRITICALLY ABOUT EVIDENCE

Study the situation, answer the questions, and then prepare arguments to support your answers.

6. In one day, Barbara bought a new couch and paid by check, bought lunch and paid with her credit card, took out cash from an ATM at her bank, and transferred funds by phone from her savings to her checking account. Which of these transactions are EFTs?

7. When she bought lunch, Barbara was double charged. When she received her statement, she noted what had happened and notified the credit card company. Barbara reported the overbilling the day she found the overbilling. Her financial institution took 44 days to investigate the matter and recredited her account on the 45th day. Has the institution acted properly?

PREVENT LEGAL DIFFICULTIES

Be careful in dealing with commercial paper...

1. When you acquire commercial paper, try to do so in a manner that qualifies you for the rights of a holder in due course. Do this by giving value in good faith for it and by taking only paper that is not overdue or subject to any defense, claim, or dishonor of which you have knowledge. If that is impossible, become an HHDC by acquiring the paper from an HDC.

2. When you are acquiring commercial paper, require the transferor to give an unqualified indorsement in your presence. Verify the transferor's identity carefully. If the signature is a forgery, the loss would generally fall on the party who took from the forger.

3. When you receive commercial paper, work to minimize defenses that can be used against you if you try to collect.

4. If you pay your obligation on commercial paper in full, have the paper so marked and signed by the holder, and then obtain possession of it immediately. Have partial payments noted on the paper as well.

5. When using EFT, retain your receipts and use them to verify your statements. Immediately report any lost or stolen EFT cards or any other breach of security surrounding your use of EFT to the financial institution that issued your card. This will minimize your potential losses.

6. When you issue checks realize that the "float" time—the time between writing a check and when it is deducted from your account—has been reduced drastically. Enter and subtract checks immediately in your check register.

CONCEPTS IN BRIEF

30-1 Discharge of Commercial Paper

1. The vast majority of commercial paper is paid and discharged according to its terms.

2. Discharge of commercial paper obligations can occur as a result of payment, cancellation, alteration, impairment of collateral, and in the manner of contracts.

3. When trying to collect on an instrument, a party who qualifies as either a holder in due course or a holder through a holder in due course is legally placed in a much better position than a mere holder or assignee.

4. Limited defenses are good against all holders except an HDC or an HHDC.

5. Universal defenses are good against all kinds of holders, including HDCs and HHDCs.

30-2 The Law of Electronic Fund Transfers

6. An electronic fund transfer (EFT) is a transfer of funds that requires a financial institution to debit or credit an account and that is initiated by the use of an electronic terminal, computer, telephone, or magnetic tape.

7. Congress chose to divide the risk of unauthorized EFTs between the consumer and the financial institution, even if the consumer is negligent in the matter.

YOUR LEGAL VOCABULARY

Match each statement with the term that it best defines. Some terms may not be used.

1. One who takes commercial paper after an HDC and thereby acquires the same rights

2. Holder who takes commercial paper in good faith without knowledge of any defect or overdue status and who gives value for it

3. Defenses good against all obligees

4. Defenses good against all obligees except HDCs and HHDCs

5. An act, such as drawing a line through an indorser's signature, done with the intent to discharge that person's obligation on a negotiable instrument

6. A debit or credit to an account that is initiated by the use of a terminal, computer, telephone, or magnetic tape

7. A party's unauthorized change to or completion of a negotiable instrument intended to change the obligation of a party

> a. **alteration**
> b. **cancellation**
> c. **consumer transaction**
> d. **electronic fund transfer (EFT)**
> e. **holder in due course (HDC)**
> f. **holder through a holder in due course (HHDC)**
> g. **limited defenses**
> h. **universal defenses**

REVIEW LEGAL CONCEPTS

8. Why would a holder be able to cancel the obligation of an indorser on an instrument but not be required to cancel the obligation of the primary obligor at the same time?

9. Why should the payment of a nominal amount for an instrument relative to its face value effect the holder's chances of becoming an HDC?

10. Why does an HHDC have the same rights as an HDC?

11. In what ways can electronic transfers benefit (a) consumers and (b) the banking industry? Do you see any disadvantages to using electronic transfers rather than commercial paper?

WRITE ABOUT LEGAL CONCEPTS

12. Explain the importance of the status of holder in due course.

13. Why should a holder be denied the chance to acquire the rights of an HDC by reacquisition?

14. What is the purpose of the Electronic Fund Transfers Act, and how does it accomplish that purpose?

15. **HOT DEBATE** Write a persuasive letter from the Reverend Robert Shore to the president of the Commerce Bank of Statusville asking for more time to pay the note.

MAKE ACADEMIC CONNECTIONS

16. **ETHICS** A remarkably high percentage of commercial paper is paid off on time. Such instruments and their electronic substitutes have become the backbone of our commerce. Cash, once the unquestionable medium of exchange, has become suspect, requiring all manner of reports to the government if used in only moderate amounts. Do you feel that this shift has occurred because of the legal protections (such as those discussed in this chapter) provided those who take commercial paper in return for goods and services? Or is the shift grounded in an ethical basis? Write a paragraph answering this question and supporting your answer.

THINK CRITICALLY ABOUT EVIDENCE

Study the situation, answer the questions, and then prepare arguments to support your answers.

17. Abbiatti operated her own computer repair business. To work on the newer models, she purchased a set of advanced instruments for $2,300 from CompRepare, Inc. She paid $300 down and signed a 180-day negotiable note payable to CompRepare for the balance. After using the tools, she realized they were not of the precision required or promised. She refused to pay. In the meantime, the note had been sold to the People's Commercial Bank, an HDC, for $1,850. Can the bank overcome Abbiatti's defense and collect?

18. When Rebel T. Clef, a rock star, landed at the local airport, a young woman persuaded him to sign his autograph on a blank sheet of paper. The woman was a skilled typesetter. She went home and printed all the essential language of a promissory note around the signature. After filling in the amount of $15,000 and inserting her name as payee, she sold the note to an HDC. Is Rebel legally obligated to pay the $15,000?

19. Eaton owed Fobair $1,500 for supplies he purchased the year before for his business. Fobair had sold the supplies to Eaton on credit even though he knew that Eaton's business was on the ropes and he would likely not be able to pay. Months later Fobair met Eaton in a restaurant and loudly demanded either cash or a signature on a promissory note with an extremely high interest rate or he would "haul you into court and sue you for all you've got." Eaton signed, and Fobair promptly sold and assigned the note to Livingston. Now Eaton refuses to pay the note, claiming it was signed under duress. Will this be a valid defense to payment?

20. If, in exercise 19, Livingston sold the note to the Hometown Bank, Inc., an HDC, and then Fobair bought it from the Bank, could Fobair collect on the note?

21. Tilly needed another freezer for her ice cream store. She purchased a used one from Worth and paid with a check for $1,275. Worth had assured her that the freezer was in good working order. However, when the unit was installed in Tilly's business, it did not work. Upon removing the back panel, Tilly found that the motor was defective and had not been in working order for several years. What is her defense against collection of the check by Worth? Would Tilly's defense be good against an HDC?

22. On May 2, as part of the $96,500 purchase price of some real estate, Collins issued a 30-day note for $66,500. Just before the due date, Collins ordered his attorney, Sanders, to have money available from Collins' account to pay the note. The attorney had the money and did pay the note, but directed the payees to indorse the instrument in blank rather than mark the note paid. Sanders then, without Collins' knowledge, took the note and, on June 3, pledged it as security to the Oswego Bank for a loan the bank had made to the attorney. When Sanders defaulted on the loan, the bank tried to collect against Collins. Was the Oswego Bank an HDC and therefore able to overcome Collins' defense of prior payment? (*Collins v. First National Bank of Oswego, Kansas,* 746 S.W.2d 424)

23. The Pierces purchased siding for their home from the Globe Remodeling Company, Inc. They gave a promissory note for $3,044.40 in payment. In exchange, they were to receive sufficient siding for the job, properly installed, together with $1,200 in cash. Globe indorsed the note to the Gramatan Company, Inc. Gramatan then sold it without indorsement to its affiliate, the plaintiff, Gramatan National Bank, for $2,250. The bank had previously placed Globe on its "precautionary list" because it knew that in other sales, Globe had not performed as promised. The bank also knew that similar Globe notes were being litigated and that federal law enforcement officials had been investigating Globe's activities. In this case, only about $400 had been paid to the Pierces. In addition, only about one-half the siding had been delivered, and none had been installed. The Pierces refused to pay the note, and the bank sued. Is the bank a holder in due course? (*Gramatan National Bank and Trust Co. v. Pierce,* 159 A.2d 781)

24. A vacuum cleaner sales representative approached the Charltons and offered them a deal called the "club plan." Under its terms, the Charltons were to make appointments in their area for sales representatives to demonstrate the cleaners. For each appointment leading to a sale, the Charltons were to receive $25. After some discussion, the couple read and signed the club plan. Then the sales representative mentioned that because they were to be agents for the company, he wanted to leave a vacuum cleaner with them. He then had them sign a "receipt" for the cleaner. Taking his word for the nature of the document (although they could have read the instrument), the Charltons then signed the receipt. Only later, when approached by the Local Finance Company for payment, did the Charltons find out that the receipt was actually a promissory note. Can they successfully defend against payment by claiming fraud in the execution? (*Local Finance Co. v. Charlton,* 289 S.W.2d 157)

25. Cameo State Bank mistakenly believed that a credit life insurance policy had paid an $8,000 note it held. Consequently, it marked it "paid" and returned it to the heirs of the maker. Having discovered the mistake, the bank now asks the court to void the release and enforce the note against the estate. Has the note been discharged? (*Cameron State Bank v. Sloan,* 559 S.W.2d 564)

26. Ognibene withdrew $20 at an automated teller machine (ATM) through the use of his Citibank card and the entry of his confidential personal identification number. As he did so, he was evidently observed by an individual who was using a telephone between Ognibene's ATM and an adjacent ATM. The individual was seemingly reporting to the bank that the adjacent ATM was not working. The person, speaking into the telephone said, "I'll see if his card works in my machine." He then borrowed Ognibene's card and inserted it in the other ATM several times, finally stating, "Yes, it seems to be working." Then he returned Ognibene's card. Later, Ognibene discovered $400 had been withdrawn from his account by the person. Ognibene then sued the bank to have the $400 recredited to his account claiming it was an unauthorized transaction under the EFTA. The bank refused, stating that by giving the other person the card, Ognibene had "authorized" the transaction and was fully liable even though Ognibene had obviously not benefited from the transaction at all. Do you agree with the bank or with Ognibene? (*Ognibene v. Citibank N.A.,* 446 N.Y.S. 2d 845)

CASE FOR LEGAL THINKING

KRAEMER V. LEBER
267 S.W. 2D 333

FACTS The Kraemers needed money. They owned certain pieces of real estate in Jefferson County, Missouri, and decided to use it as collateral for a loan. To accomplish this, they went to the office of George Pickles, a real estate dealer in the area. There they executed a negotiable promissory note in the principal sum of $50,000, payable five years after date. The note bore the interest rate of 8 percent. They then executed a deed of trust on their real estate as security for the loan.

The promissory note and the deed of trust were in favor of Grace A. Wheeler, the daughter of George Pickles. Ms. Wheeler was merely acting as a "straw party" for her father. As a consequence, she claimed no interest in the notes and indorsed them without recourse to her father, George Pickles. The note provided that payments thereon were to be made at the office of George Pickles. The deed of trust also allowed that the debtors could make payments in multiples of $1,000 at any time on the note.

During the next three years, plaintiffs made more than $12,000 in payments on the notes. Whenever these payments were made, Mr. Pickles would hand to the plaintiffs a printed form of receipt showing the date of payment, the amount paid on the principal, and the amount of the principal remaining to be paid. No indorsement of payment on the note itself was ever made.

Ultimately, Mrs. J. C. Leber purchased the note for $45,000. At that time no notice was given to her of the payments rendered by the Kraemers. Later Mr. Pickles received two other payments on the note but did not remit them to Mrs. Leber.

When Mr. Pickles died before the note matured, Mrs. Leber contacted the Kraemers and for the first time advised them that the note had been purchased by her and that she had been advised by Mr. Pickles' business associate that now "she could do her own collecting."

When the Kraemers and Mrs. Leber could not agree on the amount due on the note, she began foreclosure proceedings. Ultimately, the property was sold and the proceeds deposited in the office of the circuit clerk for disposition by the court. The lower court then refused to give the Kraemers full credit for their payments. They appealed.

REASONING The note was a negotiable instrument of such a character that plaintiffs were bound to have known that it could and probably would be negotiated and passed into the hands of a third party. As a consequence plaintiffs in making payments on this note should have ascertained that the person to whom payment was made either owned the note or had possession thereof for the purpose of collection.

CONCLUSION Judgment of the lower court is affirmed as to the Kraemers not receiving credit for their payments against the face of the note.

PRACTICE JUDGING

1. Should the Kraemers have to pay the full face amount to Mrs. Leber? Why or why not?

2. What other alternatives do the Kraemers have in this situation?

3. Who could the Kraemers sue for their losses in this matter if they must pay the full amount on the note to Mrs. Leber? What legal barriers might they have to overcome to successfully recover their funds in each instance?

© GETTY IMAGES/PHOTODISC

Secured and Unsecured Credit Transactions

31-1 What Is a Secured Credit Transaction?

31-2 How Are Security Interests Perfected and Terminated?

HOT DEBATE

© GETTY IMAGES/PHOTODISC

Zenobia owned several rental properties in Walnut Grove. When they were unoccupied, she had to mow their yards. If she didn't, the city would mow them and bill her. As a consequence, she bought a $3,500 riding lawnmower from the local hardware store. She financed $3,000 of the purchase price, and the hardware store took a security interest in the lawnmower and properly filed their financing statement to perfect it. A year later, Zenobia still owed $2,400 on the lawnmower but had sold her rental properties. Just before moving out of state, she held a garage sale and sold the lawnmower for $2,000 to her neighbor, Susan, who bought it in good faith and without knowledge of the lien against it. Susan intended to use it to mow her home's one-and-a-half acre lawn. Zenobia then stopped making payments and left no forwarding address. Two months later the hardware store repossessed the lawnmower from Susan.

Where Do You Stand?

1. As Susan was not a businessperson, but a consumer, should the hardware store legally be able to repossess the mower? Why or why not?

2. Ethically, is it right to favor an experienced commercial entity over an inexperienced consumer?

31-1 What Is a Secured Credit Transaction?

IMPORTANCE OF SECURED CREDIT TRANSACTIONS

WHAT'S YOUR VERDICT?

The First National Bank of Bassland held a security interest in Sinquer's fishing boat. When Sinquer spent too much time on the water and lost her job, the bank repossessed the boat. Unfortunately, the boat sold for $5,000 but the amount of the debt secured by it was $7,000.

How can the bank collect the remaining $2,000?

In the U.S. economy, all purchases are made either with cash or credit. No debt is involved in a cash transaction. In a purchase on **credit**, however, whole or partial payment is delayed and whatever is owed as payment is referred to as a **debt**. A **debtor** is a person or a business that owes money, goods, or services to another as a consequence of such a credit transaction. The **creditor** is the one to whom the debt is owed.

Law Brief

A bad check is a check written when the amount of money in a checking account is not enough to cover it. Writing a bad check is a crime in all states. Under typical bad-check statutes, it is a crime to write a check with intent to defraud, knowing that the funds are not sufficient to cover the check when presented for payment.

In a sale on credit, the seller is understandably concerned about getting paid in full and on time, as promised by the buyer. The more reassurance society can offer possible extenders of credit, the more business activity and general prosperity in the economy. One legal device that encourages such performance by buyers and is used frequently by sellers on credit is called a secured transaction.

A **secured transaction** is a contractual exchange that creates a security interest in personal property or fixtures. As discussed in the chapters on property, *fixtures* are items of personal property that have become permanently attached to realty. A **security interest** is the interest in or claim against the debtor's property created for the purpose of assuring payment of the debt. **Collateral** is the term given to the property that is subject to the security interest of the creditor.

For what types of purchases do you think consumers should be willing to enter into a secured transaction?

© GETTY IMAGES/PHOTODISC

In a secured transaction, if the debtor-buyer defaults by failing to pay as promised, the creditor-seller, or lender, may exercise the legal **right of repossession**. This means the seller on credit (or the finance company that has provided money for the purchase) takes the goods back, resells them, and uses the net proceeds (after expenses of the repossession and resale are taken out) to pay against the balance due. If there is any excess, it is returned to the original debtor-buyer. If there is still a remaining balance due, as in *What's Your Verdict?*, the seller can sue the original debtor-buyer to collect against her or his other assets. Creditors, be they sellers on credit or lenders of money, are thus more likely to be paid if they are secured parties. A **secured party** is a person who has a security interest in collateral owned by the debtor.

In contrast, a creditor holding a defaulted unsecured claim must first sue, get a court judgment, and then execute (enforce) that judgment against the debtor's property. Other creditors of the debtor may have equal or superior rights in that property. If the debtor's financial obligations are discharged in bankruptcy, the unsecured creditor may receive nothing or only a few cents for each dollar of the unpaid debt rightly claimed. A secured creditor typically will be able to repossess the collateral, sell it, and keep the proceeds up to the amount of the debt. If the proceeds do not extinguish the debt, the secured creditor can then file for the remainder as an unsecured creditor.

A QUESTION OF ETHICS

In the Middle Ages it was unethical for anyone to loan money at interest. The practice was forbidden by the Church and punished in the Church's courts. Why do you think charging interest was considered unethical? Do you agree? Why is charging too much interest (as with usury or loan sharking) considered illegal today? Do you think these practices should be illegal? Why or why not?

IN THIS CASE

When Phil Slither of Debtor Dogs Inc. showed up to repossess Altous Hammond's pickup truck, Altous drove it into his garage, slammed the garage door, and locked it. Altous then stood in front of the door and told Phil that he wouldn't give him the truck until they pried the keys from his cold, dead fingers. Slither then called the local sheriff's office and had a deputy report to the scene. The deputy inspected Slither's credentials and documents, and then ordered Altous to peacefully allow the repossession, which he did.

CHECKPOINT

What is collateral?

CREATION OF SECURITY INTERESTS

WHAT'S YOUR VERDICT?

Earl needed new false teeth but had a bad credit standing. The Smile Center made a new set for Earl but, under an agreement with him, kept possession of them until Earl had paid in full.

What kind of a secured transaction was this?

Before the Uniform Commercial Code (UCC) was enacted, many types of legal transactions gave creditors special rights in the property of debtors. Each type had distinct rules for its creation, maintenance, and execution. These rules varied from state to state. Their number and technical nature created a situation that enabled unscrupulous individuals to take advantage of the unsuspecting or the uninformed.

The UCC, however, solved many of the problems by making secured transactions the only legal means of giving a creditor a security interest in another's property. These UCC provisions apply only to personal property and fixtures. Contracts involving real property as security, such as mortgages and deeds of trust, are still governed by a variety of other state laws.

A security interest under the UCC can be created only with the consent of the debtor. Such consent usually is given if suitable collateral is available, because otherwise the creditor simply refuses to deal.

A security interest is created when three things take place. First, there must be an agreement between the debtor and creditor by which the debtor creates in the creditor a valid security interest. Second, the creditor must give value. Third, the debtor must have rights (either ownership or possession) in the collateral. These three things can occur in any order but when all three have occurred, the security interest becomes enforceable against the debtor. Note that the agreement may be expressed orally or in writing, depending on which of two basic types of secured transactions is used.

WHEN THE CREDITOR HAS POSSESSION OF THE COLLATERAL

In the first type of secured transaction, the creditor obtains possession of the collateral. This transaction, which may be based on an oral or written agreement, is called a **pledge**. The debtor may be buying the collateral, or the debtor already may own or have possession of it. To be a pledge, the creditor must have possession of the collateral until the loan is discharged. Earl's teeth were the collateral for a pledge in *What's Your Verdict?*

Should the debtor default, the creditor has a legal right to sell the property and apply the proceeds of the sale to the debt. Any surplus is returned to the debtor. Any deficit remains an obligation of the debtor and is collectible as an unsecured claim through a lawsuit.

WHEN THE DEBTOR RETAINS POSSESSION OF THE COLLATERAL

In the second type of secured transaction, the debtor retains possession of the collateral under written contract with the secured party. This contract, which must explicitly create or provide for a security interest in the creditor, is termed a **security agreement**. The security agreement must contain sufficient information to clearly identify the collateral, and the debtor must sign it.

It is this second type of secured transaction that enables a consumer to buy an automobile, major kitchen appliance, or other costly item on credit. The debtor gets immediate possession and use of the goods. But the seller (or the bank or finance company) that lends money needed for the credit sale has the right to take the goods back if a payment is missed or if the contract is breached.

In a similar manner, a retail merchant can buy a shipment of goods on credit from a wholesaler or manufacturer. The retailer then routinely sells the goods to customers who get clear title. When the goods are sold to such consumers, the merchant gets paid and in turn pays the supplier. The supplier continues to be protected by the security interest that remains in all of the goods in the shipment that are still unsold.

This second type of secured transaction also is used in lending money, because a lender often demands the security of collateral. Suppose you want to borrow $1,000 from a bank. By giving the bank a security interest in your car or other valuable personal property, such as your personal computer, your promise to repay the loan is

© GETTY IMAGES/PHOTODISC

Assume that this homeowner purchased the appliances for this newly remodeled kitchen by borrowing money from a finance company. What likely will happen to the appliances if the homeowner misses several payments?

strengthened. This is true because the bank has the legal right to repossess the collateral in case of default and then to sell it and apply the proceeds of the sale to repay the loan. If the bank approves the loan, which it is likely to do with this added security, you obtain the desired money and still have the use of your property.

When the borrower retains possession of the collateral, the secured party may have problems repossessing the goods in case of default. Repossession must be accomplished without committing a breach of the peace (that is, without violence, actions likely to produce violence, or other violation of the law). Also the secured party may find that the collateral has been improperly maintained, subjected to the claims of other creditors, or even sold. Even so, the UCC gives the secured party maximum protection against most such occurrences, provided the security interest has not only been properly created but also has been "perfected." How a security interest is perfected is discussed in the next lesson.

CHECKPOINT

What types of property can be collateral for secured transactions under the UCC?

31-1 Assessment

THINK ABOUT LEGAL CONCEPTS

1. A security interest is the interest in or claim against a credior's property, created for the purpose of assuring payment of the debt. **True or False?**

2. A *secured party* is a person who has a security interest in collateral owned by the debtor. **True or False?**

3. When collateral is legally repossessed, the creditor has a legal right to sell the property and apply the proceeds of the sale to the debt and the costs involved in the repossession and sale. Any surplus is returned to the (a) obligee (b) state (c) creditor (d) none of the above

4. In a pledge does the debtor retain possession of the collateral? **Yes or No?**

5. Repossession must be accomplished without committing a breach of the peace. **True or False?**

THINK CRITICALLY ABOUT EVIDENCE

Study the situation, answer the questions, and then prepare arguments to support your answers.

6. When Dodrill started her own copying and duplicating business, she entered into several contractual arrangements. First, she bought $900 worth of paper from Springfield Business Supply, promising to pay the money within 30 days. Then, using her bank credit card, she purchased spreadsheet and word processing software. In addition, she bought several desktop-copying units from the manufacturer on a 24-month installment purchase plan. The plan permitted the seller to repossess the machines if Dodrill defaulted on payments. Finally, Dodrill borrowed $2,000 from the Ozark Region National Bank to meet current expenses, giving a U.S. Treasury bond as security for repayment. Which of the transactions entered into by Dodrill involved a debtor-

creditor relationship? Which relationships were secured? Which were unsecured?

7. Fanno pondered the pros and cons of buying versus leasing a costly computer system for his business. "There are so many improvements coming along," he said, "that I could be stuck with an obsolete white elephant if I buy. On the other hand, leasing eventually costs more because the lessor earns a profit too." Finally he bought the needed machine under a five-year secured transaction. He told a friend, "If something better comes along while we're still making payments, I'll simply default and let the seller repossess the obsolete equipment. Could Fanno legally default as planned? Would it be ethical if this shifted the loss on the obsolete gear to the seller? How would the seller "have the last laugh" in this situation?

How Are Security Interests Perfected and Terminated?

PERFECTING A SECURITY INTEREST

WHAT'S YOUR VERDICT?

When Horton defaulted on his loan to the Zuesstown Bank, the bank repossessed the collateral, Horton's collection of rare musical instruments. When they did so, they discovered that another bank also had a security interest in the instruments, and it had perfected before Zuesstown.

When the collateral is sold, how will the proceeds be used?

It is possible for a debtor to agree to give many different creditors, each unaware of the others, a security interest in the same goods. As a consequence, the sale of the collateral upon default and repossession might not produce enough proceeds to satisfy all the secured parties. The UCC therefore specifies that the first creditor to perfect a security interest is able to satisfy the entirety of her or his debt before the other creditors receive a penny of any left over proceeds. In *What's Your Verdict?* the Zuesstown Bank would only receive what proceeds, if any, that were left over after the other bank had its loan completely paid.

If it were somehow guaranteed there would be only one creditor, there would no need to perfect the security interest. A security interest is valid against a debtor whether or not it has been perfected. A **perfected security interest** exists whenever the secured party has provided sufficient notice to other potential creditors of the existence of his or her secured position in particular collateral.

NOTICE THROUGH POSSESSION

A perfected security interest results when the creditor gives proper notice of the existence of her or his security interest to all other potential creditors. Such notice may be given in a number

ECONOMIC IMPACT

"CHIPPED" PASSPORTS AND IDENTITY THEFT

By the end of 2005, the federal government plans to begin issuing a new type of passport with an embedded microchip containing a facial image and current data on the passport holder. The microchip will emit radio waves with the data that can be read from as far as 30 feet away. Privacy advocates expressed concerns about the ability of anyone in the vicinity to read the chips' signals and collect data on the owners. The Bush administration, however, dismissed these concerns. Suggestions that the information be protected by PIN numbers, as are debit and credit cards, also were dismissed. Privacy advocates cited potential problems including the ease with which terrorists could spot American tourists abroad as well as a means for identity theft. The identity theft potential seems especially alarming. In 2002, 9.9 million Americans fell victim to this problem. Costs to victims of identify theft totaled $5 billion while costs to businesses and financial institutions reached $48 billion.

THINK CRITICALLY

Is the government doing the right thing by not taking steps to safeguard the passport data? What, if any, costs are involved in doing so?

of ways. For example, a creditor in possession of the collateral, as in a pledge, needs to take no additional steps for protection. Possession alone is notice to any possible subsequent buyer or creditor of the debtor that a security interest may exist. The creditor who has possession, thereby, has a perfected security interest. If a creditor is able to repossess collateral upon default, the act of retaking possession also perfects the security interest even though the interest had not been perfected previously.

NOTICE THROUGH FILING A FINANCING STATEMENT

When the debtor has the goods, it may be necessary for the creditor to file a financing statement to perfect the creditor's interest. A **financing statement** is a brief, written notice of the existence of a security interest in the identified property. (See the example below.) It must, to comply with UCC requirements, include the following:

1. the names and addresses of both the debtor and the creditor
2. the signature of the debtor (although the creditor also may sign and commonly does)
3. a statement describing the items of collateral

NETBookmark

Access lawxtra.swlearning.com and click on the link for Chapter 31. Read the article entitled "Revised Article 9 of the Uniform Commercial Code: An Introduction" by Lech R. Kalembka. Then answer the following questions about Revised Article 9 (which relates to the perfection and maintenance of security interests in collateral other than real estate):

1. The effective date in all 50 states of Revised Article 9 was July 1, 2001. True or False?

2. The scope of Revised Article 9 is substantially more narrow than the original. True or False?

3. Under the revision, security interests in deposit accounts and letter-of-credit rights will be subject to automatic perfection. True or False?

4. In the revised article, a very generic description of collateral will be allowed for filing purposes. True or False?

5. Under Revised Article 9, the "location" of most types of debtors is deemed located at its "chief executive office." True or False?

lawxtra.swlearning.com

UNIFORM COMMERCIAL CODE—FINANCING STATEMENT—UCC-1

This FINANCING STATEMENT is presented to a filing officer for filing pursuant to the Uniform Commercial Code. 3 Maturity date (if any):

1 Debtor(s) (Last Name First) and address(es)	2 Secured Party(ies) and address(es)	For Filing Officer (Date, Time, Number, and Filing Office)
Daley, John C. and Ava G. 116 Seashore Drive Biloxi, MS 39534	Adam Cranston 485 Magnolia Street Gulfport, MS 39501	

4 This financing statement covers the following types (or items) of property:

"Smooth Sailin" Houseboat

Check ☒ if covered   ☐ Proceeds of Collateral are also covered   ☐ Products of Collateral are also covered   No. of additional sheets presented

Filed with _____

By: _John C. Daley_ _Ava G. Daley_   By: _Adam Cranston_
    Signature(s) of Debtor(s)   Signature(s) of Secured Party(ies)

Filing Officer Copy—Alphabetical

This form of financing statement is approved by the Secretary of State.

STANDARD FORM—UNIFORM COMMERCIAL CODE—UCC-1

If crops or things attached to buildings or land are involved, the land where such property is located also must be described. If the security agreement extends to products to be derived from the original collateral, such as the calves of cows, or proceeds from the resale of such collateral, these facts must be stated. The security agreement itself may be filed instead of the financing statement if it meets the necessary requirements.

On the financing statement, any description that identifies the collateral reasonably well suffices even though it might be necessary to ask questions to determine exactly what property was intended. Of course, a debtor who possesses two automobiles, a motorcycle, a racing bicycle, and a mountain bicycle should be more specific than listing an unspecified one of these vehicles as "my favorite wheels."

Filing a financing statement with the required governmental office gives **constructive notice** that a security interest in specific property exists. This means that the law presumes everyone has knowledge of the facts on file. Anyone sufficiently concerned may get actual notice by checking the public records. The place of filing varies from state to state and is specified in the state's version of the UCC. Depending on the type of collateral, filing may be required centrally in the office of the secretary of state, or locally in the office of the clerk in the county where the collateral is located, or both.

As explained in the following paragraphs, there are special provisions for perfecting the security interest that depend on whether the property in question is tangible or intangible.

TANGIBLE PROPERTY

When tangible property is used as collateral, the procedure for perfecting the creditor's security interest depends on whether the goods are

- *consumer goods* used primarily for personal, family, or household purposes
- *farm products* crops, livestock, unmanufactured products of the farm, and farm supplies
- *inventory* business goods that are intended for sale or lease, or if they are raw materials, work in process, or materials used or consumed in a business
- *equipment* goods used by a business in performing its function, such as telephone equipment or computers

Goods can be in only one of these four classes at a given time. Their classification may change, however, if their use changes. For example, a television is classified as inventory if held by a dealer for resale. If used as a closed-circuit system in the store for security, it is equipment. If installed in the buyer's home for entertainment, it is a consumer good.

CONSUMER GOODS Filing is not required to protect a seller's security interest in consumer goods against other creditors of the buyer. This is known as a **purchase money security interest** and relieves retail merchants, who sell many thousands of articles on installment plans, of what would be a heavy burden in paperwork and in payment of filing fees. In case of default in payment, the creditor may repossess the goods from the original buyer. Although not legally obligated, most creditors tolerate late payment for perhaps ten or more days. They typically impose a penalty charge for use of this privilege.

Filing would be required for consumer goods if the consumer already owned the goods and was simply borrowing against them as security. Filing also is necessary, even in initial purchases, if the seller wants protection against a third person who might innocently buy the good for personal, family, or household use from a dishonest debtor. Such a buyer of consumer goods, who gives value and does not know of the security

What type of goods would the instruments these professional musicians are playing be considered?

LEGAL RESEARCH

Contact local retailers and see if they file a financing statement on purchase money security interests. Ask each about their loss record, the frequency of repossessions, and improvements they would like to see in the UCC secured transaction provisions in their state. Prepare a report on your findings for the class and send a copy to your local state representative.

IN THIS CASE

Furrow, a Missouri farmer, took out a loan to buy seed from the Urbane Bank in a nearby city. In the security agreement with Urbane, he gave the creditor bank a security interest in his thresher and farm tractor. Because the Urbane Bank was not used to dealing in farm equipment, it misfiled the financing statement pertaining to the security interest by filing it only with the Secretary of State of Missouri and not with Furrow's county clerk. As a consequence, when Furrow took out another loan from a local bank to buy a stock car so as to live out his childhood dream of racing, the local bank just checked the records at the county courthouse. When no lien against Furrow's tractor and thresher was found, the local Bank took a secured interest in them. The local bank then filed properly with the appropriate county clerk. When Furrow crashed the stock car on the first turn of his first race and later defaulted on both loans, the local bank had the only perfected security interest in the tractor and thresher. Whatever proceeds that might have been left after the local bank forced the sale of Furrow's equipment and satisfied its lien fully, if possible, would go to the Urbane Bank.

interest, acquires clear title if there has been no filing.

On the other hand, if a filing is in the public records, the third party is bound by the filed security interest due to the constructive notice it provides. Therefore, the television set that was installed in the buyer's home for entertainment and then sold to a good-faith purchaser for value must nevertheless be returned to the unpaid creditor who had filed a financing statement.

Because there are so many motor vehicles on the roads, most states provide that instead of filing as described above, a special office and procedure are utilized. Thus, the security interest in motor vehicles often is perfected by noting its existence on the certificate of title to the vehicle that is registered in the proper state office. The certificate of title is then held by the creditor until paid.

An exception to the filing requirement also is made when fixtures are sold on credit. Fixtures are items of personal property that are permanently attached to real property in a manner that makes the law treat them like real property. A filing to protect a security interest in fixtures must include in the financing statement a description of the real property involved.

FARM PRODUCTS A security interest in farm products is perfected by filing or by taking possession of the products upon default. This applies to farm products bought on credit and to those used as security for loans. Most states require filing a financing statement for farm products with

© GETTY IMAGES/PHOTODISC

What does the In This Case scenario suggest about the importance of filing the financing statement with the correct governmental office?

the clerk at the courthouse of the county where the products are stored.

INVENTORY A security interest in inventory is perfected by filing or by taking possession of the inventory upon default. This is true whether the inventory is bought on credit or is put up as security for a loan. However, because inventory generally is purchased by business firms for the very purpose of reselling, a person buying from such a debtor in the ordinary course of business gets clear title to the goods even if aware of the security interest. For example, if you buy a stove at an appliance store, you get title to it free of the security interest held by the unpaid manufacturer or wholesaler who originally sold it to the store on credit.

EQUIPMENT A security interest in equipment is perfected by filing or by taking possession of the equipment upon default. This applies whether the equipment is bought on credit or is put up as security for a loan. If the equipment is a motor vehicle, a notation on the certificate of title may substitute for filing in perfecting the interest. As with inventory, perfection of a security interest in equipment requires filing with the state government, usually in the office of the secretary of state.

INTANGIBLE PROPERTY

The second major classification of collateral—**intangible property**—represents value in rights to money, goods, or promises to perform specified contracts. Legal documents or other writings are generally evidence of intangible property. Intangible property includes the accounts receivable of a business, the rights to performance under a contract, bills of lading or airbills, warehouse receipts, commercial paper, and bonds or stocks.

The procedure used in perfecting a security interest in intangible property depends on the classification of that property. A security interest

If inventory that has been put up as security for a loan is sold to a consumer, does the consumer get clear title to the goods if aware of the security interest? Why or why not?

© GETTY IMAGES/PHOTODISC

in accounts receivable or contractual rights that cannot be possessed in a physical sense must be perfected by filing unless the transaction does not cover a significant part of the debtor's accounts receivable or other contractual rights.

For documents used in bailments, such as bills of lading, airbills, and warehouse receipts, the creditor may either file a financing statement or take possession of the goods upon default. To perfect a security interest in commercial paper (promissory notes, stock certificates, or bonds), possession by the creditor, upon default of the debtor, is essential.

CHECKPOINT
What is a financing statement?

TERMINATING A SECURITY INTEREST

WHAT'S YOUR VERDICT?

The Nosmans bought a new flat-screen wall television for their recreation room for $2,000 including the credit carrying charge. They paid $400 down and agreed to pay the balance in eight monthly installments of $200 each. The seller, Silitech, Inc., retained a security interest in the television. After making six payments, the Nosmans defaulted. Silitech repossessed the television.

What must Silitech do to be able to legally keep the set in settlement of the unpaid $400 balance?

Most secured transactions are routinely terminated when the debtor pays the debt in full and the creditor releases the security interest in the collateral. If the creditor has filed a financing statement, this release is made when the creditor files an acknowledgment of the full payment, called a **termination statement**, with the governmental office that has the financing statement. Filing the termination statement informs potential buyers and creditors that the property is no longer collateral. For consumer goods, the termination statement must be filed within 30 days of the payoff or within ten days of a written request by the debtor. Otherwise the creditor must pay $100 plus damages to the debtor.

If the debtor defaults by failing to pay as promised, the secured creditor who does not have possession of the collateral may take possession of it. This may be done without legal proceedings, provided it does not involve a breach of the peace. The creditor may then sell, lease, or otherwise dispose of the collateral. This right of sale also applies after default for the benefit of the secured creditor who has retained possession of the property. The proceeds at disposition are applied to the reasonable expenses of retaking, holding, preparing for resale, and reselling. They also are applied to payment of reasonable attorney's fees and other legal expenses incurred. What remains of the proceeds then goes to pay off the secured debt. In some cases, other creditors may have subordinate or secondary security interests in the collateral, and these are now paid off if proper claims have been made. Finally, if any surplus remains, it goes to the debtor. If there is any deficiency, the debtor is obligated to pay it unless otherwise agreed.

Even when in default as to payment or other performance of the security agreement, the debtor does not forfeit all rights. For example, the debtor may pay the balance due and the expenses of the creditor and redeem the collateral any time before the creditor has disposed of it or contracted for its disposal.

As an alternative to resale, the secured creditor may retain the collateral in full settlement of the debt. Written notice of the creditor's intention to keep the collateral must be given to the debtor. If the debtor (or any other person entitled to receive notice) objects in writing within 21 days, the creditor must dispose of the collateral in a commercially reasonable manner by a public or private sale.

Additional protection is given to consumers who have paid 60 percent or more of the debt. In these situations, the creditor may not keep the collateral in satisfaction of the debt unless the consumer agrees in writing. In the absence of such a written agreement, the creditor must sell the collateral within 90 days after the repossession. This law seeks to protect consumers in situations where the value of the goods exceeds the amount of the debt.

In *What's Your Verdict?* the Nosmans paid $400 down and $1,200 in monthly installments. The total ($1,600) was more than 60 percent ($1,200). Therefore, Silitech must obtain the Nosmans' written consent before Silitech can keep the television. Without that consent, the television must be resold in a commercially reasonable manner.

CHECKPOINT

What significance does the termination statement have for the debtor?

Assessment

THINK ABOUT LEGAL CONCEPTS

1. A perfected security interest exists whenever the secured party has provided sufficient notice to other potential debtors of the existence of his or her secured position in particular collateral. **True or False?**

2. A _?_ is a brief, written notice of the existence of a security interest in the identified property. (a) statement of perfection (b) termination abatement (c) repossession agreement (d) none of the above

3. Computers used by a business in performing its function would be classified as equipment by the UCC. **True or False?**

4. Computers purchased for resale or lease by a business also would be classified as equipment by the UCC. **True or False?**

5. A termination statement is filed by the _?_. (a) debtor (b) creditor (c) obligor (d) none of the above

6. If a consumer has paid _?_ percent or more of the debt before having the collateral repossessed, the creditor may not keep the collateral in satisfaction of the debt unless the consumer agrees in writing. (a) 15% (b) 18% (c) 20% (d) 60%

THINK CRITICALLY ABOUT EVIDENCE

Study the situation, answer the questions, and then prepare arguments to support your answers.

7. Taft borrowed $50 from a friend, agreeing to repay $5 each week. Although the agreement was informal and oral, Taft gave the friend her high school class ring to hold until the debt was paid in full. Did the friend have a perfected security interest in the ring?

8. The Hunts need money for corrective surgery for their young son. They decided to borrow the money from Desperation Finance, from whom they had taken another loan three years before. As in the previous instance, the Hunts put up their boat and cars for collateral. Desperation, however, said that, although the previous loan was paid off, a termination statement had not been filed on it and demanded $100 to file the appropriate paperwork in addition to the loan charges for the new loan. Do the Hunt's have to pay the $100?

9. Cuisine International sold kitchen equipment on credit to the Shoreline Resort. In the security agreement and in the financing statement the collateral was identified as "food service equipment delivered to the Shoreline Resort." When Shoreline was unable to pay its creditors, including Cuisine, some creditors claimed that the collateral description was too vague to create a valid security interest. Were they correct?

PREVENT LEGAL DIFFICULTIES

If you are a borrower or buyer in a secured transaction...

1. Be sure you understand the entire security agreement before you sign it. If you have any doubts, have your lawyer, banker, accountant, or other trustworthy counsel, examine the form and explain it to you.

2. Never sign any security agreement that has blank spaces to be filled in later. Draw lines in any blank spaces not used.

3. Know what any charges are for, especially service charges. Ask for a detailed listing if it is not offered.

4. Find out if there are any penalties for late payment of installments or if there are any discounts for making payments before they are due.

5. Include express warranties or other promises of the seller in the written contract to avoid later difficulty of proof under the parol evidence rule.

6. Always get a copy of the agreement, signed by the other party.

7. After payment in full, check to be sure that a termination statement has been properly filed.

Chapter 31 Assessment

CONCEPTS IN BRIEF

31-1 What Is a Secured Credit Transaction?

1. A secured transaction is one in which a security interest in personal property or fixtures is created.

2. In a secured transaction, upon default by the debtor, the creditor may obtain the collateral, sell it, and use the net proceeds (after expenses of the repossession and resale are taken out) to pay against the balance due.

3. A creditor holding a defaulted unsecured claim must first sue, get a court judgment, and then execute (enforce) that judgment against the debtor's property.

4. In a pledge, the creditor obtains possession of the collateral.

5. If the debtor is to retain possession of the collateral, a creditor must obtain a security interest from the debtor evidenced by a written security agreement.

31-2 How Are Security Interests Perfected and Terminated?

6. The first creditor to perfect a security interest is, upon default, able to repossess and sell the collateral and satisfy the entirety of her or his debt before the other creditors receive a penny of any left over proceeds.

7. A perfected security interest exists whenever the secured party has provided sufficient notice to other potential creditors of the existence of his or her secured position in particular collateral.

8. A creditor in possession of the collateral, as in a pledge, needs to take no additional steps for protection as possession alone should be notice to any possible subsequent buyer or creditor of the debtor that a security interest may exist.

9. When the debtor has the goods, it may be necessary for the creditor to file a financing statement to perfect the creditor's interest.

YOUR LEGAL VOCABULARY

Match each statement with the term that it best defines. Some terms may not be used.

1. Contract that creates or provides for a security interest

2. A person or business that owes money, goods, or services to another

3. An interest in or claim against specified property of the debtor, such interest being created in favor of the creditor to assure payment of the debt

4. Secured party's right to take back collateral to use in satisfying a debt

5. The property that is subject to the security interest of the creditor

6. A filing by a creditor releasing a security interest in collateral

7. A legal filing that makes subsequent creditors aware of a lien against potential collateral

8. Transfer of possession of property to a creditor to insure payment of a debt

9. Rights to money, goods, or promises to perform specified contracts

10. Document filed to provide notice of an established security interest to other potential creditors

a. collateral
b. constructive notice
c. credit
d. creditor
e. debt
f. debtor
g. financing statement
h. intangible property
i. perfected security interest
j. pledge
k. purchase money security interest
l. right of repossession
m. secured party
n. secured transaction
o. security agreement
p. security interest
q. termination statement

REVIEW LEGAL CONCEPTS

11. Why is the law of secured transactions so important to prospective debtors?

12. Why is an unsecured creditor at a disadvantage?

13. Why is possession alone a suitable notice to other creditors who might take a security interest in the collateral.

WRITE ABOUT LEGAL CONCEPTS

14. Why is a debtor allowed to force a sale in a commercially reasonable manner by objecting to the creditor's intent to retain the collateral as full settlement of the debt?

15. Why is it important to have a termination statement filed promptly?

16. **HOT DEBATE** Write a paragraph justifying the difference between a neighbor's purchase of a mower without a filing and a like purchase by a neighbor of a mower on which the seller holds only a purchase money security interest.

MAKE ACADEMIC CONNECTIONS

17. **SCIENCE** What could secured transactions have to do with the advancement of science, you ask. Research the availability of startup loans for companies wanting to develop marketable technology or research and development loans to established companies. Write a report on how the potential lenders evaluate their prospective investment opportunites and what they want to receive in return for a loan.

THINK CRITICALLY ABOUT EVIDENCE

Study the situation, answer the questions, and then prepare arguments to support your answers.

18. D'Artole, an accountant, bought for her personal use a new SUV for $47,500. She paid $10,000 down and then paid $1,250 per month for several months under a security agreement she had signed with the dealer, Where the Pavement Ends, Inc. Finally, she paid off the remaining balance with her Christmas bonus. The next May she needed a $25,000 loan to take advantage of a business opportunity. She offered the SUV as collateral, but the lender refused, saying there was a financing statement showing a security interest in the vehicle in favor of the Where the Pavement Ends still on file. D'Artole did not get the loan as a result. What are her rights in this situation?

19. At a county fair in southwest Nebraska, Gull used cash to buy two cows and a bull, all pure-bred Holsteins. The seller was Spane, who had just moved to the area from another corner of the state bringing his livestock with him. Soon after, Gull was surprised and annoyed when he discovered that Spane had defaulted on a loan given to Spane in a secured transaction in his previous county. The bank in that county had a perfected security interest in the animals. When it repossessed them, Gull protested: "How was I supposed to know that? I never had any notice of the bank's interest. Where's the proof?" Did Gull actually have legal notice of the bank's interest in, and prior claim to, the animals? Did Spane act ethically in their deal? What can Gull do now?

20. You buy a new 25" flat screen monitor for your computer under a contract that permits the seller to repossess it if you miss a payment. The seller has filed a financing statement evidencing its security interest. If you sell the monitor to a friend before you have paid in full for it, does your friend get clear title?

21. Burney loaned Sampson $4,000 to buy a car. Sampson issued a promissory note in favor of Burney for that amount. Also, when he registered the new car, Sampson had Burney's name entered on the title as lienholder. Later Sampson took out a loan from the First National Bank of Pennsboro. After a few months, he defaulted on both the bank loan and the promissory note. The bank filed suit and obtained a judgment against Sampson that it sought to execute against the car. Burney maintained his security interest in the car took precedence over the Bank's claim. Who won?

22. Shelton purchased an automobile on credit from Erwin. Both Shelton and Erwin clearly intended to create a security interest in the car in favor of Erwin. As a consequence, they signed a bill of sale that set out the terms of payment of the balance due and that also required that Shelton insure the auto until paid for in full. Shelton later obtained a title certificate from the state that clearly showed Erwin as the holder of a first lien on the car. Did these actions and documents give Erwin a security interest in the car? (*Shelton v. Erwin,* 472 F.2d 1118)

23. Speigle fell behind in his car payments to Chrysler Credit Corporation. He had made 14 monthly payments on a 36-month contract, and Chrysler had accepted several late payments. Then Speigle was out of work and money. He was almost a month in default on a current payment. Speigle went to the Chrysler office to negotiate a solution to his problem. While there, a Chrysler employee parked a car behind Speigle's car, blocking it so it could not be moved. Another employee told him it was repossessed. Speigle sued, claiming Chrysler's conduct was inequitable and in breach of the peace. Do you agree? (*Speigle v. Chrysler Credit Corporation,* 56 Ala. App. 469, 323 So. 2d 360)

24. The Uniform Commercial Code excludes "money" from its definition of goods. As a consequence, a perfected security interest cannot be obtained in money merely by the creditor's taking possession of it. Midas Coin Company transferred possession of some rare U.S. coins to the St. John's Community Bank as security for a loan. Did the bank have a perfected security interest? (*In re Midas Coin Co.,* 264 F. Supp. 193)

25. The Franklin State Bank repossessed the Parkers' automobile because of the Parkers' delinquency in payments. At the time, Mr. Parker and his son were giving the engine of the car a tune-up in their garage. The vehicle was not mechanically operational because the spark plugs, points, condenser, and air filter had been removed. Franklin State Banks did not try to determine why the car was not mechanically operational. Instead, after a three-day notice to the Parkers, the bank sold the car at a private sale to an auto parts dealer for $50. The bank then sued the Parkers to recover the substantial balance of the purchase price remaining and unpaid. Which party should win the suit? Why? (*Franklin State Bank v. Parker,* 136 N.J. Super. 476, 346 A.2d 632)

26. When Ziluck submitted the application for his Radio Shack credit card, he signed an application that had the following statement about the signature line: "I have read the Radio Shack Credit Account and Security Agreement, including the notice provision in the last paragraph thereof. . . . And I agree to the terms of the Agreement and acknowledge receipt of a copy of the agreement." The Security Agreement referred to was on the back of the application and read in part: "We retain a security interest under the Uniform Commercial Code in all merchandise charged to your Account. If you do not make payments on your Account as agreed, the security interest allows us to repossess only the merchandise that has not been paid in full." Ziluck later filed for bankruptcy. The bankruptcy court had to determine whether or not this was a valid security agreement. It decided that it was not because (1) the signature was on the opposite side of the form from the "Agreement," and (2) any collateral subject to the agreement would be improperly described. Radio Shack appealed the decision of the bankruptcy court. Does Radio Shack have a case? Why or why not? (*In re Ziluck,* 139 Bankruptcy Reporter 44)

27. Calcote bought a car using a loan from Citizens & Southern National Bank. The bank obtained a security interest in the car. Calcote later defaulted on the loan and the bank repossessed the car. The bank then sent notice of the repossession, the bank's plans to sell the repossessed car at a private auction, and Calcote's right to demand a public sale to her at the last known address that the bank had. Calcote did not get the certified letter, yet the car was thereafter sold at a private sale with more than 150 dealers invited to participate. Calcote then brought suit against the bank due to its failure to properly notify her and dispose of the vehicle in a commercially reasonable fashion. Do you think the bank acted improperly? Why or why not? (*Calcote v. Southern National Bank,* 345 S.E.2d 616)

28. The Fishes bought some very expensive jewelry from Odom's Jewelers. They were to pay monthly installments on the purchase price until it was fully paid. When they fell behind in their payments, they orally agreed to return the jewelry to Odom's to hold until the purchase price was paid. While Odom's held the jewelry, the Fishes filed for bankruptcy. Did Odom's have a security interest in the jewelry? (*In re Fish,* 128 Bankruptcy Reporter 468)

CASE FOR LEGAL THINKING

In Re Holiday Intervals, Inc.
931 F.2d 500

FACTS Holiday Intervals sold "time share" deeds for the Holiday Shores resort it was developing at the Lake of the Ozarks, Missouri. These deeds entitled buyers to spend one week per year at one of Holiday's units. Many of the buyers agreed to pay the purchase price through installment contracts. Some of these installment contracts contained a separate promissory note section that repeated the buyer's installment obligations in the form of a promissory note, while other contracts contained no promissory note section. Holiday obtained financing for construction of the units by assigning its copies of the installment contracts and promissory notes to the banks. The banks did not seek to perfect their security interests in these installment contracts and promissory notes. Instead they assumed that they had perfected their security interests by possession of the buyers' installment contracts and promissory notes.

© GETTY IMAGES/PHOTODISC

After Holiday ran into financial difficulties, Holiday Owners (one of Holiday's creditors) and various other creditors filed an involuntary bankruptcy petition against Holiday. Holiday Owners took over operation of the resort afterwards.

When a bankruptcy petition is filed, claims against the debtor's estate are automatically stayed. In order to obtain the installment contract proceeds, the banks separately moved for relief from this automatic stay.

REASONING The banks sought relief on the ground that they held perfected security interests in the installment contracts through possession of the contracts. In the alternative, the creditors claimed that even if they had not perfected their security interests as to all installment contracts, they had at least done so to those installment contracts containing promissory notes. The bankruptcy court rejected both arguments and denied the banks' motion for relief from the automatic stay. The banks then appealed to the Federal District Court.

CONCLUSION OF THE FEDERAL DISTRICT COURT DECISION The district court affirmed the bankruptcy court's decision in part and reversed in part, holding that the banks had perfected their security interests in those installment contracts which contained promissory notes, but not in the other installment contracts which did not. All parties then appealed to the Federal Court of Appeals.

PRACTICE JUDGING

1. In reaching its decision, the federal appeals court noted the rule that the seller's interest in a land sale contract is a general intangible. If this is so, how is perfection to be achieved?

2. Given your answer to the above question, have the creditors perfected or are their interests to be treated the same as any other unsecured creditor and, therefore, subject to the stay?

CHAPTER 32

Creditors, Debtors, and Bankruptcy

32-1 Legal Protection of Creditors

32-2 Legal Protection of Debtors and Credit Card Users

32-3 Bankruptcy

© GETTY IMAGES/PHOTODISC

HOT DEBATE

Norm was a foreign correspondent for a large national television network. One afternoon he took his expensive watch to a jewelry shop to be repaired. The jeweler recognized Norm and told him he watched his network. The jeweler said the watch would be ready the next day. Norm left the store. He then received a call telling him to pack and head for Western Russia. When he went to get his watch, almost four months later, the jeweler told him he had sold it after sending Norm ten reminders. Norm responded that there was no mail service where he had been. The jeweler shrugged and said he was just following the state's artisan's lien laws. Norm's attorney ultimately brought suit against the jewelry store for damages.

Where Do You Stand?

1. What are the jewelry store's reasons for selling the watch?

2. What legal reasons support Norm's suit?

Legal Protection of Creditors

LAWS THAT PROTECT CREDITORS

WHAT'S YOUR VERDICT?

To finance her divorce, Quinlan pawned her engagement ring for $300. Three months later, when she and her husband made up, she went back to redeem the ring and was told that she now owed almost $350. Shocked, she realized that the interest rate she was being charged was nearly 72 percent a year.

Is this legal?

The primary concern of a typical creditor is that the loan be paid promptly when due. If it is not paid, and especially if costly efforts to collect it prove fruitless, the creditor usually suffers a financial loss. When feasible, such bad debt losses are shifted to other borrowers through higher fees and charges. Thus, it is in the interest of all society that fair and honest loans be collectible with minimum difficulty and expense. Laws that protect creditors will be discussed in the following sections.

LAWS ALLOWING SECURED DEBTS

Taking a security interest in personal property and fixtures or a mortgage on real property are common ways the law allows creditors to protect themselves. If a default occurs the creditor may then exercise the right under a mortgage to obtain a court order for sale of the property or, if the secured property is personal or a fixture, the creditor may peacefully repossess it, if possible, and sell it to satisfy the loan.

PLEDGES Some secured debt arrangements permit the creditor to have possession of the property until the debt is paid. In the pledge, for example, personal property is given to a creditor as security for the payment of a debt or for the performance of an obligation. The property may be either goods or documents representing property rights (for example, corporate stock). The **pledgor** (debtor) voluntarily gives up possession of the property. The **pledgee** (creditor) gets possession. Normally, the debt is paid when due or the legal obligation is performed. Then the property is returned to the pledgor.

While the pledge lasts, the pledgee must treat the property with reasonable care. The property may, however, be repledged to a third party on terms that do not prevent the pledgor from getting the property back when the debt is paid.

A **pawn** is a legally regulated pledge of tangible personal property, usually of small size and comparatively high value. Collateral for this type of pledge includes such durable and readily resalable items as jewelry, cameras, and musical instruments. It excludes intangible property rights, stocks and bonds, as well as other valuable documents. A pawnbroker lends money at interest and takes possession of tangible personal property from the borrower as security for repayment. The borrower who pawns goods gets a

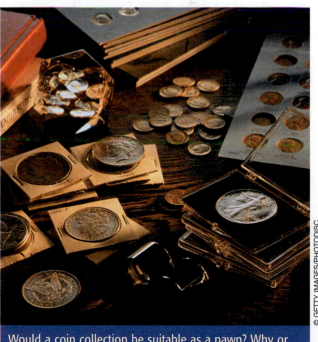

Would a coin collection be suitable as a pawn? Why or why not?

© GETTY IMAGES/PHOTODISC

receipt known as a pawn ticket. When the borrower repays the debt together with interest due and turns in the pawn ticket, the pawnbroker returns the goods. As a pawn shop operation faces many risks, the law allows what would otherwise be a very high interest rate to be charged. In most states, as in *What's Your Verdict?*, this rate is between 5 and 6 percent per month or between 60 and 72 percent per year.

Because thieves sometimes convert stolen goods into cash by pawning them, special statutes regulate the business. These laws require that the pawnbroker be licensed, post a bond, and keep accurate records open to police inspection. If stolen goods are found in the pawnshop, they may be seized without compensation to the pawnbroker. Also, maximum limits are imposed on the rate of interest pawnbrokers may charge.

Goods that are pawned must be held by the pawnbroker for a time prescribed by law (four months is typical) before they can be sold. In most states, the rights of the parties to the proceeds of the sale are the same as for ordinary pledges. In some states, the pawnbroker automatically gets title to pawned and unclaimed goods at the end of a specified time.

INVOLUNTARY LIENS A lien gives the creditor the right, in case of default on a payment that is due, to sell the property and to use the proceeds from the sale to pay the debt. Although most liens are created with the consent of the debtor-owner, statutes in many states create liens in favor of the creditor without such consent. These involuntary liens include the mechanic's lien and the artisan's lien.

The **mechanic's lien** allows a person who has not been paid for labor or materials furnished to build a home, building, or other real property improvement to file a legal claim against the property. If the debt is not paid, the realty may be sold. The holder of the mechanic's lien gets the amount owed from the proceeds. Thus, such a lien holder is entitled to the amount owed from the sale proceeds even before other claimants, such as a bank with a mortgage on the property, gets any money.

The **artisan's lien** allows persons who have not been paid for services, such as repairing a car or providing a hotel room, to retain possession of the car or the luggage that has been brought onto the premises until they are paid. If payment is not made, these retained goods may

be sold to pay the debts that are due. A lien holder who gives up possession of the property before the debtor pays for the services loses the artisan's lien.

If this carpenter does not receive the contractually agreed-to payment for the deck he is building, what kind of lien would be placed on the homeowner's real property?

© GETTY IMAGES/PHOTODISC

LAWS INVOLVING THIRD PARTIES

In addition to liens, other means of protection are available to creditors. These means involve third parties and are known as suretyship and guaranty.

SURETYSHIP A creditor who wishes assurance beyond the debtor's promise to pay may demand that a creditworthy third party assume the liability. This is **suretyship**, a contractual relation in which a third party agrees to be primarily liable for the debt or obligation if payment or performance becomes overdue. Three parties are involved. The **principal debtor** owes the debt or obligation. The *creditor* is the one to whom the obligation is owed. The **surety** is the third party who promises to be liable in case of default by the principal debtor. The surety may be bound by an oral contract because a suretyship is a primary obligation. Nevertheless, such agreements usually are put in writing.

Suretyship contracts are discharged in much the same way as other contracts. If the debtor pays, the surety is discharged. The surety also is discharged if the creditor releases the debtor or alters the obligation, as by extending the time of performance, without the surety's consent. But a surety who is required to pay the creditor has a legal right to collect from the principal debtor.

If there are cosureties, any cosurety who pays the full debt may get a judgment against the other cosureties for their proportionate share of the debt. This is called the *right of contribution*.

GUARANTY The guaranty relationship protects the creditor. In it, the third party, the **guarantor**, agrees to pay if the principal debtor fails to do so. Unlike a surety, therefore, the guarantor is only secondarily liable. In effect, the guarantor merely promises that the debtor will pay when the debt comes due. However, this means that the creditor must first sue the defaulting debtor and get a judgment that proves to be uncollectible.

In contrast, in a suretyship, such a suit is not necessary. The surety has primary liability equal to that of the debtor. Also unlike the suretyship the contract creating the guaranty relationship must be in writing and signed by the guarantor to be enforceable under the Statute of Frauds.

LAWS CONCERNING UNSECURED DEBTS

When the debt is small or the credit standing of the borrower is very good, the creditor may be willing to take an **unsecured debt**. This is a debt based only on the oral or written promise of the debtor.

Upon default, an unsecured creditor is in a much weaker position than a secured creditor, because in order to collect, the unsecured creditor must sue the debtor for breach of contract. Then, upon obtaining judgment, the creditor must take legally prescribed steps to collect. This is costly and time-consuming. Moreover, some debtors may prove to be dishonest and may move without leaving a forwarding address. Or they may have no assets that the creditor can take.

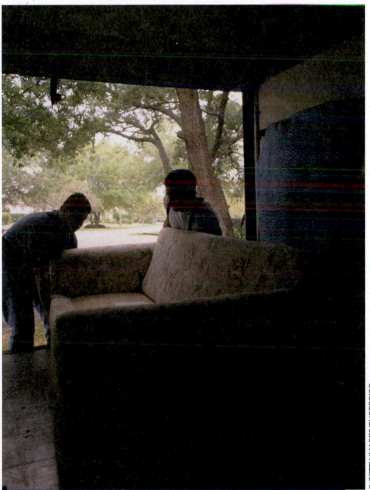

© GETTY IMAGES/PHOTODISC

Imagine that the man on the left owes at least 100 creditors amounts between $250 and $500. Because he cannot pay them, his solution is to move to another state and not give anyone a forwarding address. Would the creditors likely pursue this man for payment of his outstanding balances? Why or why not?

In other instances, debtors may discharge their obligations by going through bankruptcy. In a bankruptcy proceeding, secured creditors may sell the collateral and satisfy their entire claim with the proceeds before any unsecured creditor gets a dime.

LAWS ALLOWING GARNISHMENT OF WAGES

One other method for creditor protection is the garnishment of wages. Once a creditor's claim is shown to be legally valid and fair in a court hear-ing, the creditor may receive a portion of the debtor's wages directly from the debtor's employer. The amount that can be garnished by all creditors, however, generally is limited by the Consumer Credit Protection Act to 25 percent of the debtor's take-home pay.

CHECKPOINT
What is the primary difference between a surety and a guarantor?

Xtra!
Study Tools
lawxtra.swlearning.com

32-1   Assessment

THINK ABOUT LEGAL CONCEPTS

1. While the pledge lasts, the pledgee must treat the property with reasonable care. **True or False?**

2. A pawn is a legally regulated type of pledge. **True or False?**

3. In a bankruptcy proceeding, unsecured creditors generally stand a better chance of being paid in full than secured creditors. **True or False?**

4. In a surety relationship, before the debt can be collected, a creditor first must sue the defaulting debtor and get a judgment that proves to be uncollectible. **True or False?**

5. The amount that can be garnished by all creditors generally is limited by the Consumer Credit Protection Act to _?_ percent of the debtor's take-home pay. (a) 10% (b) 15% (c) 25% (d) none of the above

THINK CRITICALLY ABOUT EVIDENCE

Study the situation, answer the questions, and then prepare arguments to support your answers.

6. After graduating from high school, Jack Tern decided to become a truck driver. The A-OK Truck Driving Academy offered a two-week, intensive, one-on-one (instructor-student) course with training on two- and three-axle tractors and on 45-foot single and double trucks, for $4,000 cash. Because Jack had no money, A-OK agreed to take his written promise to pay the tuition fee in monthly installments of $130 for four years provided he could get a surety or guarantor to promise to pay if he defaulted. Jack's Uncle Joe signed a guaranty agreement, and Jack enrolled and completed the course. After six months, however, he lost his job as a truck driver and could not continue making the monthly payments. Can A-OK immediately demand payment from Jack's Uncle Joe?

7. Gary Meter took his very expensive watch in for repair to Mike's service center. The bill for the repair came to more than $375. When Gary heard how much it was, he told Mike that he could pay him at the first of the month. Gary also informed Mike that the watch had been given to him by his grandmother who was celebrating her hundredth birthday in two days. Gary then asked if he could take the watch with him without paying, so that he could wear it to his grandmother's birthday party. Mike sympathized with Gary and let him do so. When the first of the month came around, Gary did not pay. Mike waited until the end of the month. Then he decided to try and collect by legal means. Does Mike still have an aritsan's lien he can enforce against Gary? Why or why not? What are his other alternatives? Are they as effective as the lien?

8. Garrett took several items into the HiDollar Pawn Shop to get a loan. The items were an expensive guitar, 100 shares of stock in a large auto maker, and a large horseshoe-shaped ring set with diamonds. Which of these items would the pawn shop loan on?

Legal Protection of Debtors and Credit Card Users

DEBTOR PROTECTION

WHAT'S YOUR VERDICT?

Bill complained that he was not getting his cell phone bill in time to pay for it. As a consequence, the cell phone company was charging him a $20 late fee each month. Thomas asked him what date his account came due. Bill replied that it was the first of each month. Thomas then had Bill look at the date the cell phone company mailed the last bill. Thomas noted that it was the 25th of the month. "Aha!" said Thomas.

What is Thomas about to say about the dates?

The law tries to protect debtors from unfair practices and situations by

1. setting maximum interest rates
2. requiring clear and complete advance disclosure of loan terms
3. changing the terms of unconscionable contracts
4. correcting specific abuses of the credit system
5. requiring the creditor to record a public notice when certain debts have been paid
6. canceling most debts and giving the debtor's financial life a fresh start

LAWS SETTING MAXIMUM INTEREST RATES

Usury laws that set maximum interest rates were discussed in the chapters on contracts. Usually such laws apply only to loans of money. They do not govern carrying charges imposed on credit purchases of goods and services "on time." A few states do regulate such charges as interest. They

do this on the theory that the store, in effect, borrows money and re-lends it to the customer-debtor to finance the purchase on credit.

LAWS REQUIRING DISCLOSURE OF TERMS

A consumer loan arises when a person borrows money primarily for personal, family, household, or agricultural purposes. It often is called a personal loan to distinguish it from a business or commercial loan.

The federal Truth in Lending Act (part of the Consumer Credit Protection Act) was designed to protect consumers when they become debtors. This law requires complete and clear disclosure of loan terms. In particular, it requires creditors to furnish debtors with certain information. The law does not limit the percentage amounts that may be charged. However, it requires creditors to make a full disclosure of interest and finance charges whenever the consumer loan is repayable in four or more installments or carries a finance charge.

A **finance charge** is the total added cost when one pays in installments for goods or services. The creditor also must declare the true equivalent annual interest rate or annual percentage rate (APR). Thus, 1 1/2 percent a month must be stated as 18 percent a year. Under the law, a credit sales contract also must state such details as the cash price of the item; the down payment or trade-in allowance, if any; an itemized list of finance charges; and the total amount to be financed.

The Truth in Lending Act does not apply to first mortgage loans on homes. Fortunately, interest rates on home loans usually are comparatively low. No doubt this is true because the security behind such loans, namely the houses, tends to be high and can be protected by insurance.

Any creditor who willfully and knowingly violates the Truth in Lending Act may be fined, imprisoned, or both. The violator also must pay the debtor twice the finance charge (but no less than $100 nor more than $1,000) plus court costs and attorney's fees.

An increasing number of consumers lease automobiles and other equipment instead of buying the items. A big advantage of leasing for some persons is that it requires no down payment. However, in the end, the total price paid in leasing usually is higher than a cash or credit purchase would be. This is especially true for those who maintain their automobiles properly and keep them for perhaps five or more years.

The federal Consumer Leasing Act extends the protection of the Consumer Credit Protection Act to consumer lessees. Before the contract is signed, the lessor must comply fully with the disclosure requirements in the act.

LAWS CHALLENGING UNCONSCIONABLE CONTRACTS

The UCC provides that a court may find that a contract or a clause of a contract is unconscionable, that is, grossly unfair and oppressive. An unconscionable contract or clause offends an honest person's conscience and sense of justice. The terms need not be criminal nor violate a statute. They may simply be unethical. Contracts of adhesion are more likely to be unconscionable because one of the parties dictates all the important terms and the weaker party either must take it as offered or not contract. An example is a contract for emergency repairs in which a dishonest mechanic may take unfair advantage and grossly overcharge a motorist who is unfamiliar with automobiles and their maintenance and repair. If the contract is challenged in court, a judge who decides that a clause of the contract is unconscionable may

- refuse to enforce the contract
- enforce the contract without the unconscionable clause, or
- limit the clause's application so that the contract is no longer unfair

The law is not designed to relieve a person of a bad bargain. One still may be legally bound by the purchase of overpriced, poor quality, or unneeded goods.

LAWS PROHIBITING ABUSES IN THE CREDIT SYSTEM

Laws have been enacted to correct specific problems such as the relative inability of women to get credit, unfair debt-collection practices, and inaccurate credit reports.

FEDERAL EQUAL CREDIT OPPORTUNITY ACT This act makes it unlawful for any creditor to discriminate against an applicant because of sex or marital status. In the past, women had difficulty obtaining credit. This was true even for women who had jobs. It was especially true for married women who worked as homemakers. The act was created to make such discriminations illegal. Major provisions of the act are the following:

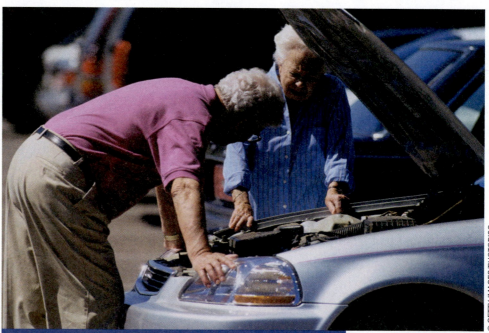

This couple has just had an emergency repair made to the transmission of their car. After paying for the repair work and traveling only five miles, the car freezes up again. If they take the case to court, and a judge refuses to enforce the contract, what, at a minimum, do you think the repair company will be required to do?

1. A creditor may not refuse, on the basis of sex or marital status, to grant a separate account to a creditworthy applicant.

2. A creditor may not ask the applicant's marital status if the applicant applies for an unsecured separate account.

3. A creditor may not prohibit a married female applicant from opening or maintaining an account in her maiden name.

4. A creditor shall not request information about birth control practices or childbearing intentions or capability.

5. Married persons who have joint accounts have the right to have credit information reported in both their names in order to provide a credit history for both. In the past, upon divorce or upon death of the husband, the wife often would be denied credit because the joint account had been listed in the husband's name only.

FEDERAL FAIR DEBT COLLECTION PRACTICES ACT

This act makes abusive and deceptive debt-collection practices illegal. The act applies to professional bill collectors or agencies that regularly try to collect consumer debts for clients. Prohibited practices include

1. harassment of debtors (as with a series of letters that contain menacing or threatening language, or with repeated telephone calls, especially at night)

2. abusive and profane language

3. threats of violence

4. contact with third parties (relatives, neighbors, friends, and employers)

5. communication with the debtor at work

The act is aimed at aggressively insensitive and irresponsible professional collection agencies. It does not apply to individual creditors who personally try to collect money due them. Nor does it apply to "in-house" debt collection efforts of the creditor or of employees of the creditor. However, a seriously abused debtor may sometimes succeed in a civil action against any debt collector for damages. The legal basis could be the tort of defamation, assault, invasion of privacy, or intentional infliction of mental suffering.

FEDERAL FAIR CREDIT BILLING ACT
This act provides the following protections to credit card holders:

1. Creditors must mail bills at least 14 days before the due date, must acknowledge billing inquiries within 30 days, and must settle any complaints within 90 days. In *What's Your Verdict?* Thomas is about to tell Bill that the cell phone company is violating the Fair Credit Billing Act and that he should report it. Complaints in such matters should be taken to the nearest FTC Regional Office. If they concern national creditors, they should be sent in writing to the Correspondence Branch, Federal Trade Commission, Washington, D.C., 20580.

2. Creditors may not send repeated, insistent letters demanding payment until disputes over the billing are settled.

3. Credit card holders may withhold payment for items that prove defective without being held liable for the entire amount owed. This applies only in case of purchases of more than $50 made in the buyer's state or within 100 miles of the buyer's home.

The Fair Credit Billing Act also permits merchants to offer discounts to customers who pay cash instead of using credit cards. Thus, gasoline service stations often charge a few cents less per gallon to customers who pay cash. This is fair because extending credit is costly for sellers even though it may increase sales volume.

NETBookmark

Access lawxtra.swlearning.com and click on the link for Chapter 32. Read the Federal Trade Commission press release about the provisions of the new Fair and Accurate Credit Transactions Act that address the problem of identity theft. Choose the provision that you think will be especially helpful in dealing with identity theft. Then write a paragraph about the provision explaining why you think it is helpful.

lawxtra.swlearning.com

FEDERAL FAIR CREDIT REPORTING ACT

This act regulates credit-rating service companies that review personal financial records of credit applicants. Aided by computers, these companies or agencies maintain voluminous files covering pertinent information about millions of individuals and business firms that buy goods and services on credit. Retailers, wholesalers, and manufacturers routinely supply such credit-rating agencies with data about their experience with customers. In turn, credit-rating agencies relay relevant information to cooperating member firms that request it when someone asks them for a credit purchase.

The Retailers Credit Association, composed of retail merchants who sell on credit, is an example of a credit-rating agency. It determines the prospective buyer's credit rating. A **credit rating** reflects the evaluation of one's ability to pay debts. Under the law, if credit is denied because of information in a credit report, the company denying credit must tell the applicant. The applicant then may demand that the reporting agency disclose the general nature of the contents of its file (except medical information) and the names of parties who were given this information. However, names of those who provided the information need not be disclosed.

If there is any demonstrated error in the report, the credit-reporting agency must correct it. Upon request, it must notify the inquirers who had been misinformed. The agency must make the disclosures and reports without charge if the applicant acted within 30 days of getting notice of a denial of credit. Similar rules apply when an individual is denied an insurance policy or employment contract because of an unfavorable credit report.

CREDIT REPAIR ORGANIZATIONS ACT

The Credit Repair Organizations Act (CROA), passed in April 1997, governs companies that help consumers "repair" their credit histories. By law, these organizations must notify you of your rights (by providing a copy of the government document entitled "Consumer Credit File Rights Under State and Federal Law") before you sign a contract with them. The law states that a credit repair company cannot

- make false claims about its services
- charge you until they complete the promised services

- perform any services until you have signed a written contract and completed a three-day waiting period

Any contract you make with a credit repair service must specify

- the payment terms for services, including the total cost of these services
- a detailed description of the services they will perform
- how long it will take them to achieve the results
- guarantees they offer
- repair company's name and business address

Individuals who have been injured by violations of the CROA can sue to recover the greater of the amount paid to the credit repair company or actual damages, punitive damages, costs, and attorney's fees.

LAWS REQUIRING NOTICE OF DEBT PAYMENT TO BE RECORDED

As a practical matter, debtors should always request receipts, especially when paying in cash. In some states, a debtor is not required to pay a debt unless such a receipt is given. Financial institutions either return paid and cancelled checks to the drawers (writers) of the checks or keep an electronic image of them in their database. In either form, such canceled checks can serve as receipts. It often is helpful to indicate on the face of each check the purpose for the payment. Even without such notation, it can serve as evidence of payment. When a secured debt is paid in full, the law generally permits the debtor to require the creditor to record that fact in the public records.

LAWS ALLOWING DEBTORS TO CANCEL DEBTS AND START OVER

Bankruptcy laws have been enacted to help debtors who have become overburdened with debts. These laws are described in detail in the next lesson.

CHECKPOINT

Name at least four of the six approaches the law takes to protect debtors.

PROTECTIONS FOR CREDIT CARD USERS

WHAT'S YOUR VERDICT?

When Beatrice's purse was stolen by a purse snatcher late Monday morning, she immediately notified her four credit card companies using a list she kept at home. Later that day, each card was charged up to its limit in stores around town. The unauthorized use totaled more than $4,000.

How much of the $4,000 in losses is Beatrice responsible for?

Millions of consumers buy goods and services by using credit cards. A credit card identifies the holder as a person entitled to obtain goods or services on credit. The issuer of the card specifies the limit of available credit, and before a large sale is made, the seller can contact the issuer to determine if this limit has been exceeded.

Usually a credit card is made of plastic, is embossed with the holder's name and identification number, and has a space on the back for the holder's signature. As further protection against misuse, the card may have the holder's picture or other identification material on it as well. Annually, billions of dollars of credit purchases are made with this "plastic money." Some credit cards are intended for specialized purchases such as gasoline or oil. Some are limited to use in specific retail outlets, such as department stores or gas stations. Some are all-purpose cards, usually issued by banks, and intended for purchases from any cooperating seller. Examples are MasterCard, Visa, and Discover cards. A credit card usually is issued in response to a consumer's written application. The consumer who signs the card is bound in a contractual relation with the issuer and is liable for all purchases made with the card by the holder or by others with the holder's permission.

IN THIS CASE

Because of a recent divorce, Allee Mony's credit standing had slipped to such a low point that she knew she could not get a mortgage loan. The situation seemed hopeless as it would likely take years to rebuild her creditworthiness. Then LifeRing Credit Repair Services called and promised that they would repair her credit practically overnight to a point where it would be better than ever—for a price tag of more than $1,000 up front. Even though she was suspicious of their claims, Allee agreed to let them try. Three months later her credit had not improved, and she sorely needed the $1,000 she had given LifeRing. Frustrated and angry, she sought legal counsel. She was told that LifeRing had violated a number of provisions of the Credit Repair Organizations Act (CROA) by taking payment up front, working without a written contract, and not advising her of her rights in the situation. As a consequence she could sue to recover the greater of the amount paid or actual damages, punitive damages, costs, and attorney's fees. When she brought suit, LifeRing settled out of court for $15,000.

Why do people choose to use credit cards rather than pay for purchases with cash or checks?

© GETTY IMAGES/PHOTODISC

Under federal law, the cardholder also is liable for unauthorized use of the credit card by any other person, such as a thief or a dishonest finder. This liability is limited to $50 and is imposed only under the following conditions:

1. Cardholder had asked for and received the credit card or had signed or used it.
2. Card issuer had given adequate notice of the possible liability for unauthorized use.
3. Card issuer had provided the cardholder with a description of how to notify the card issuer if the card is lost or stolen.
4. Card issuer had provided positive means for identification on the card, such as space for the holder's signature or photograph.
5. Unauthorized use happened before card-holder notified issuer that card was lost or stolen.

Thus, the loss or theft of a credit card should be reported immediately to the issuer. In *What's Your Verdict?* because of her quick action, Beatrice would not be liable for any of the losses. Even if she had given her notification after the unauthorized charges, her maximum liability would have been $50 per card or a total of $200.

Most credit card agreements require the cardholder to pay the amount charged on the card within a specified number of days after the closing date shown on the billing statement. If the cardholder fails to do so, he or she is contractually obligated to pay interest or finance charges on the unpaid balance.

Some states set limits on the rates that can be charged credit card holders. In other states, however, there are no limits whatsoever except those imposed by competitive forces. Regardless, such charges should be avoided whenever possible by paying the full amount due within the grace period. Fifteen days is common but it may be more or fewer. Finally, recall that the provisions of the Fair Credit Billing Act, discussed in detail in the preceding section, apply in full to credit card transactions.

A QUESTION OF ETHICS

Patricia Blakemore's husband often abused her after coming home drunk late at night. Finally, she reported him to the police.

For a while, with the help of intensive counseling, he had not attempted to harm her. But she could tell he was returning to his old ways. Sooner or later, she knew he would beat her again. She needed to get away. However, he kept the checkbook and money under his control and signature. If she could just take one of the credit cards, she could get enough cash advances to live on until she could get a job. The problem was that she was not a cosigner on the cards. Nonetheless, she knew the personal identification numbers for each card and had used them before at his direction. Of course, this time she would be using the money solely for her own use. Patricia paused. Should she go ahead with what she was contemplating?

What effect do you think credit cards have on the television "home shopping" industry?

© GETTY IMAGES/PHOTODISC

Not only does the consumer pay charges to the credit card company but so does the vendor. The vendor must pay for the credit card company's service in bookkeeping and prompt payment for purchases made. Commonly, this cost to the seller is a charge of between 3 percent and 6 percent of the sales prices. Such amounts paid to the credit card company are passed on to customers, both cash and credit, through higher prices for goods sold.

In addition, credit cards have a great potential for abuse through overuse by owners and misuse by thieves or finders of lost cards. Some consumers fail to plan and save for their purchases. Instead, they often use their credit cards for impulse purchases they do not really need. Sometimes, the payments for these purchases, when added to other living expenses, total more than their income. Debtors who find themselves in this situation may consult debt-counseling services that now operate in many cities. These services assist debtors in budgeting their income and expenses in a disciplined plan to pay off creditors and to avoid being forced into bankruptcy.

CHECKPOINT
What is the liability limit for unauthorized credit card charges?

Xtra! Study Tools
lawxtra.swlearning.com

32-2 Assessment

THINK ABOUT LEGAL CONCEPTS

1. The federal Truth in Lending Act does not limit the percentage amounts that may be charged for interest on consumer loans. **True or False?**

2. The Truth in Lending Act does not apply to first mortgage loans on homes. **True or False?**

3. The federal _?_ extends the protection of the Consumer Credit Protection Act to consumer lessees. (a) Leasehold Security Act (b) Lessor-Lessee Rights Act (c) Consumer Leasing Act (d) none of the above.

4. The federal Fair Credit Billing Act provides that creditors must mail bills at least _?_ days before the due date, must acknowledge billing inquiries within _?_ days, and must settle any complaints within _?_ days. (a) 14, 30, 90 (b) 15, 30, 90 (c) 15, 30, 60 (d) none of the above.

5. Under federal law, a credit card holder may be liable for unauthorized use of the credit card by a thief. **True or False?**

6. Both the consumer and the seller of goods or services in a credit card transaction pay charges to the credit card company in most cases. **True or False?**

THINK CRITICALLY ABOUT EVIDENCE

Study the situation, answer the questions, and then prepare arguments to support your answers.

7. During the warranty period, the Arnaudos returned their home computer for repair to the seller, Computerville Inc. Later, after the express warranty period had expired, the Arnaudos stopped making their regular monthly $100 payments for the computer because the problem continued. Computerville then gave its claim for the $900 balance to Bulldog Services, a collection agency. Bulldog had a clerk telephone the Arnaudos at least once a day and once a night, usually after 1 A.M. Every Sunday, a uniformed Bulldog agent would park the company truck in front of the Arnaudos' house. The truck had these words in large type on both side panels: "Bulldog Services. We Chase Deadbeats." The agent would then try to talk about the claim with any person entering or leaving the house. Was Bulldog Services acting legally? Was Bulldog Services acting ethically?

8. Shortly after graduation from college, Matilda Smith applied for credit at a local department store. The store denied her application, citing the unfavorable credit report it had received from the Alpha-Omega Credit Bureau. Matilda assumed that the negative report stemmed from a prolonged dispute with a major retail chain over goods she had not ordered. Recently the retail store acknowledged its error. What can Matilda do to clear her name?

THE BANKRUPTCY ACT

WHAT'S YOUR VERDICT?

Malcolm Eric, owner of Lake Cleaners, decided he had to face the fact that he was overextended. The new store in the Hollistown Mall had such an expensive monthly payment on its five-year lease that it was about to cause Malcolm to close down the whole chain. This would mean the loss of jobs for his 9 employees as well as his own financial ruin. In fact, he had been unable to make his monthly payments on the company truck and to his suppliers for the last three months. Several suppliers had stopped deliveries to him. He had discussed the situation with his attorney and they were to meet later today to consider filing bankruptcy.

If bankruptcy is Malcolm Eric's only alternative, what form of bankruptcy would you recommend?

Many American colonists came from England at a time when debtors had to go to prison if they could not pay their debts. Therefore, at our country's founding, the ability to avoid such harsh treatment through a process of bankruptcy was considered important enough to be included in the U.S. Constitution. Even today, bankruptcy laws in the United States are more lenient than those in other countries.

By Article I, Section 8, of the U.S. Constitution Congress was given exclusive power to establish "uniform laws on the subject of bankruptcies throughout the United States." The bankruptcy law created as a result and in force in its modern form today has a dual purpose. First of all, **bankruptcy** protects creditors by setting up a framework to give them a fair treatment in their competition for the debtor's assets. Secondly, and most importantly, it protects debtors by giving them an opportunity for a new economic start, free from most creditors' claims.

To accomplish these purposes, the federal Bankruptcy Code in its Chapters 7, 11, 12, and 13 provides a variety of possible ways for debtors to seek relief.

ECONOMIC IMPACT

THE COST OF BANKRUPTCIES

Bankruptcies filed in the twelve-month period ending December 31, 2003, totaled 1,660,245, up 5.2 percent from the 1,577,651 bankruptcies filed in the 12-month period ending December 31, 2002. The resulting increased cost of credit due to these filings is estimated at $400 to $500 per consumer per year. However, as of the writing of this book, the Bankruptcy Reform Act, which has been before Congress and the President at various times, has not yet passed.

THINK CRITICALLY

Research the status of the Bankruptcy Reform Act. If it has not yet passed, research to identify the proposals it will contain when the legislation is reintroduced. If it has passed, read the legislation and speculate on whether it will be effective in curtailing the cost of bankruptcies to society.

CHAPTER 7 LIQUIDATION, OR "STRAIGHT BANKRUPTCY"

Chapter 7 involves the sale for cash of the nonexempt property of the debtor and the distribution of the proceeds to creditors. Nonexempt property includes such assets as bank accounts, stocks, and bonds. Lists of exempt property exist at the state and federal level and will be discussed in the section on bankruptcy procedure. Utilizing Chapter 7 will result in the discharge of most of the debtor's financial obligations.

CHAPTER 11 REORGANIZATION

This option for debtor relief is designed to keep a business organization such as a corporation, partnership, or sole proprietorship in operation with no liquidation. The debtor or a committee of creditors files a plan for reorganization. The bankruptcy court must approve this plan and will do so if it is reasonable and if it was created in good faith. In *What's Your Verdict?* a Chapter 11 plan probably would be optimal.

Under Chapter 11, claims of both secured and unsecured creditors, as well as the interests of the owners of the business, may be "impaired," meaning reduced. The plan to reorganize must be in the best interests of the creditors, and each class of creditors that is affected adversely must accept it. A class of creditors accepts the plan when a majority that represents two-thirds of the amount of that group's total claim votes to approve the plan. Even when only one class (for example, the bondholders) accepts the plan the Bankruptcy Court may approve it under a so-called "cramdown provision." This requires that the creditors or the owners who object are either unaffected by the plan, or are paid in full before any junior (or lower) class of claimant is paid.

CHAPTER 12 DEBT RELIEF FOR FAMILY FARMS

Congress added Chapter 12 relief to the Bankruptcy Code in 1986 for family farm owners. Under this chapter an individual or couple or, sometimes, a corporation or a partnership can be eligible to file a petition for relief. This petition entitles them to a court order protecting them from their creditors. The debtor filing cannot have debts totaling more than $1,500,000 and income of at least 50 percent

Law Brief

Although bankruptcies are rising at an alarming pace, efforts to toughen the eligibility and accuracy requirements in the federal bankruptcy law have been defeated or delayed. The objections of the American Bar Association (ABA) helped to block passage of the Bankruptcy Reform Act. Representing some 400,000 attorneys, the ABA suggested that certain requirements in the proposed act were unduly burdensome to the Bar. These provisions included that lawyers certify the accuracy of factual allegations in the debtor's bankruptcy petition and schedules, under penalty of court sanctions, and that lawyers identify and advertise themselves as "debt relief agencies" subject to a host of new "intrusive regulations." (See coverage of Credit Repair Organizations Act on page 578 in Lesson 39-2.) The ABA has a history of successful lobbying against the content of the proposed reforms. It successfully convinced a House-Senate Conference Committee working on the legislation to delete a provision requiring a bankruptcy court to impose sanctions against attorneys for inaccurate bankruptcy schedules and replace it with a discretionary standard.

of the debtor's income has to be from farm sources. At least 80 percent of all debts must be related to the operation of the farm. This plan is similar in operation to the Chapter 13 proceeding for other debtors.

CHAPTER 13 EXTENDED TIME PAYMENT PLAN

Chapter 13 relief is available only to individuals who have regular income. This plan also avoids liquidation of assets. The debtor must have regular income, unsecured debts of less than $269,250, and/or secured debts of less than $871,550. The debtor must submit a plan for the installment payment of debts within three years with a possible extension to five years.

During this time, the creditors may not file suit for payment of any debts. Both secured and unsecured debts (other than a claim, such as a promissory note and mortgage, secured by the debtor's principal residence) may be reduced in amount or extended in time for payment. The plan must be "in the best interests of the creditors," who might otherwise receive even less in a Chapter 7 liquidation.

A major advantage of the Chapter 13 proceeding is that upon completion of payments called for under the plan, the court grants a discharge for almost all debts. The only exceptions are for certain long-term debts, such as payments for a house and payments of alimony and child support. It is interesting to note, however, that only approximately 35 percent of all debtors filing under Chapter 13 complete the three or five year plan but the report of the filing stays on their credit record for 10 years.

CHECKPOINT

Of the various bankruptcy plans, which one involves total liquidation of the debtor's nonexempt assets?

BANKRUPTCY PROCEDURE UNDER CHAPTER 7

WHAT'S YOUR VERDICT?

Jack Gilbert was talking to his fellow law school student, Chase Adamson, about finances and said, ". . . after I graduate, I'm going to declare bankruptcy and get rid of all these student loans." Chase looked at Jack and said, "Whoa, man. I just finished the course on bankruptcy, and there's something about the law you should know that might change your plan."

What does Chase know about bankruptcy that Jack does not?

LEGAL RESEARCH

Research the connection between bankruptcy and student loans in two situations. First, research the effect on a student loan application where the applicant has previously taken bankruptcy. Secondly, research the availability of bankruptcy to someone wanting to discharge the obligations imposed by student loans he or she has received in the past.

As liquidation under Chapter 7 is at the very heart of the Bankruptcy Act, it is important to look at the procedure followed to carry out its provisions.

THE BANKRUPTCY PETITION

Bankruptcy under Chapter 7 may be either voluntary or involuntary. Once the process is begun by either a voluntary or involuntary filing of a petition under Chapter 7, the procedure is basically the same.

VOLUNTARY BANKRUPTCY With a few exceptions, any person, business, or other association may petition for protection from creditors under Chapter 7. This is the beginning of a **voluntary bankruptcy**. A person does not have to be **insolvent** (unable to pay debts when they are due) to file the petition. Husbands and wives may file jointly.

INVOLUNTARY BANKRUPTCY Any person or business, except farmers and charitable institutions, owing at least $11,625 to their petitioning unsecured creditor(s) and unable to pay debts when they come due may be forced into **involuntary bankruptcy**. However, if a person has more than 12 creditors with unsecured claims totaling at least $11,625, at least three must sign the involuntary bankruptcy petition.

REQUIRED INFORMATIONAL FILING In either voluntary or involuntary bankruptcy proceedings, the debtor, under oath, must file the following information with the court:

■ a list of all creditors and amounts owed to each

- a list of all property owned, including property claimed to be exempt from seizure
- a statement explaining the debtor's financial affairs
- a list of current income and expenses

To conceal or fraudulently transfer assets or to provide false information knowingly is a crime under the bankruptcy laws.

SELECTION OF THE TRUSTEE IN BANKRUPTCY

After the petition is filed, a trustee is then selected. The trustee's duties are to find and to protect the assets of the debtor, liquidate them, and pay the claims against the debtor's estate with the proceeds. Such claims would include court costs, back wages owed to the debtor's employees, taxes, and claims of the general creditors. Secured creditors would seek payment of the secured debts directly against the collateral. Secured debts would be enforced ahead of any other claims.

NON-DISCHARGEABLE DEBTS

There are certain types of claims that cannot be discharged by bankruptcy. These include

- certain taxes
- alimony and child support
- claims against the debtor for property obtained by fraud, embezzlement, or larceny
- judgments against the debtor for willful and malicious injury to the person or property of another (but claims for injuries caused by negligence can be discharged)
- student loans owed to the government or to a nonprofit school of higher learning, unless the loan became due more than seven years before the bankruptcy, or an undue hardship would be imposed on the debtor or on his or her dependents. (In *What's Your Verdict?* this is the information Chase thought Jack should have.)
- judgments against the debtor resulting from driving while intoxicated
- claims not listed by debtor

EXEMPT PROPERTY

Certain assets of the debtor are exempt from liquidation to satisfy creditor's claims. These exemptions are specified in the federal bankruptcy laws which are revised every three years. Individual states have been empowered to disallow the use of these exemptions and substitute their own. The states also can create their own list and let the petitioner choose between state and federal exemptions. Under the federal law, exempt property currently includes

- real property (homestead), including co-op or mobile home, to $18,450; any unused portion of this exemption up to $9,250 may be applied to any property
- life insurance payments for person the debtor depended on for support
- life insurance policy with loan value, in accrued dividends or interest to $9,850
- alimony and child support
- pensions and retirement benefits

What two categories of exempt property do this condo and Mercedes represent?

- $475 per item of household goods up to a total of $9,850
- health aids
- jewelry to $1,225
- motor vehicle to $2,950
- personal injury compensation payments to $18,450
- wrongful death payments
- crime victims' compensation
- public assistance
- social security
- unemployment compensation
- veterans' benefits
- tools of the debtor's trade, books, and equipment to $1,850

- unused portion of homestead exemption
- $925 of any property plus up to $9,250 of any amount of unused homestead exemption

LIQUIDATION AND DISTRIBUTION OF PROCEEDS

Once the assets of the debtor not subject to a security interest are brought under the trustee's control, they are liquidated. The proceeds of the liquidation then are used to pay the creditors. After secured creditors have received either the value of their collateral or the collateral itself, the law provides an order of priority for payment of claims against the bankruptcy estate. The following list contains those recipients of general interest in priority order.

1. Expenses of the administration of the bankruptcy case, including trustee's fees and attorney's fees
2. Claims for wages, salaries, and commissions with a maximum of $4,300 per creditor
3. Claims for contributions to employee benefit plans up to $4,300 per employee
4. Up to $1,950 per claim on unsecured claims for money deposited with the debtor for purchase or lease of property or for services contemplated for the personal, household, or family use of the debtor that were not provided
5. Unsecured claims of governmental units for taxes and penalties
6. Claims of all general unsecured creditors and those with residual unsatisfied claims from the above categories

If any amount is left after all the classes of claimants have been satisfied, it is turned over to the debtor. After the procedure is concluded, all eligible debts of the debtor are considered discharged. The debtor cannot file a petition in bankruptcy again until 6 years have elapsed. Bankruptcy stays on a credit report for 10 years.

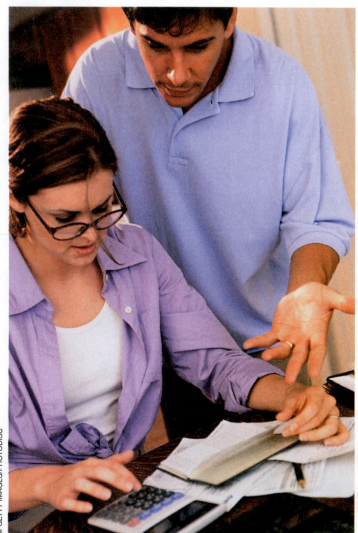
© GETTY IMAGES/PHOTODISC

What is your opinion of using bankruptcy as a tool if you find yourself in trouble financially? What do you see as the pros and cons of filing bankruptcy?

CHECKPOINT

What are the two types of bankruptcy under Chapter 7?

THINK ABOUT LEGAL CONCEPTS

1. "Straight bankruptcy" is obtained under what chapter of the Bankruptcy Act? (a) 7 (b) 11 (c) 12 (d) 13

2. Congress added Chapter 12 relief to the Bankruptcy Code in 1986 for the benefit of (a) railroads (b) savings and loans (c) furniture makers (d) none of the above

3. A major advantage of the Chapter 13 proceeding is that upon completion of payments called for under the plan, the court grants a discharge for almost all debts. **True or False?**

4. Alimony and child support cannot be discharged under either Chapter 7 or 13. **True or False?**

5. Can involuntary petitions be filed under Chapter 7 against farmers? **Yes or No?**

6. Top priority in the distribution of proceeds from a Chapter 7 liquidation belongs to claims for unpaid wages, salaries, and commissions with a maximum of $4,300 per creditor. **True or False?**

7. Lowest priority in the distribution of proceeds from a Chapter 7 liquidation belongs to the claims of all general unsecured creditors and those with residual unsatisfied claims from the categories with higher priorities. **True or False?**

THINK CRITICALLY ABOUT EVIDENCE

Study the situation, answer the questions, and then prepare arguments to support your answers.

8. Mark is greatly upset and wonders if he should report what appears to him to be an obvious abuse of the bankruptcy law. The individual debtor in question has been living for years in a house that is worth at least $100,000 and maybe much more. Recently, the debtor went through a bankruptcy, yet he and his family still live in the house. Is such a result possible without violating the bankruptcy laws? What chapter of the laws might make it possible?

9. Under the state exemptions to the bankruptcy act allowable under the law of a large southwestern state, there is a one-acre exemption for the debtor's home. Two brothers, Robert and Lyle Quest, are forced into involuntary bankruptcy due to some precious metal speculations. Robert lives in a penthouse atop a $62 million office building he owns. Lyle's penthouse is atop a $71 million building that he owns. Each claims the one acre due under the state law. The creditors claim that they should be able to reach all the value in the one acre except for the $15,000 exemption allowed by the federal law. Who wins?

PREVENT LEGAL DIFFICULTIES

Be wise about credit...

1. In applying for credit, always be accurate and honest. Lies about one's credit history are often exposed.

2. If you give property as security for a debt, be sure it is returned or properly released when the debt is paid.

3. Protect your rights as a debtor by learning about them and exercising them when appropriate. The Fair Credit Reporting Act, Fair Credit Billing Act,

Equal Credit Opportunity Act, Fair Debt Collection Practices Act, and related statutes are of limited value without consumer demand for their enforcement.

4. A person who repairs your television, watch, car, or other personal property can exercise an artisan's lien on the property, retaining possession until paid, or eventually selling the goods. Before work is begun get a detailed written estimate of anticipated cost.

Chapter 32 Assessment

CONCEPTS IN BRIEF

32-1 Legal Protection of Creditors

1. It is in the interest of all society that fair and honest loans be collectible with minimum difficulty and expense.

2. Taking a security interest in personal property and fixtures or a mortgage on real property are common ways the law allows creditors to protect themselves.

3. Some secured debt arrangements protect the creditor by allowing the creditor possession of the collateral until the debt is paid.

4. Other means of protection are available to creditors. These means involve third parties and are known as suretyship and guaranty.

32-2 Legal Protection of Debtors and Credit Card Users

5. The law tries to protect debtors from unfair practices and situations by setting maximum interest rates, requiring disclosure of loan terms, chang-ing the terms of unconscionable contracts, correcting specific abuses of the credit system, requiring the creditor to record a public notice when certain debts have been paid and providing a procedure to allow canceling most debts so as to give the debtor's financial life a fresh start.

32-3 Bankruptcy

6. The ability to avoid harsh treatment for unpaid debts through a process of bankruptcy was considered important enough to be included in the U.S. Constitution.

7. Bankruptcy laws in the United States are more lenient and the costs thereof to society far greater than those in other countries.

8. The federal Bankruptcy Code in its Chapters (7 for liquidation, 11 for reorganization, 12 for family farms, and 13 for an extended payment plan) provides a variety of possible ways for debtors to seek relief.

YOUR LEGAL VOCABULARY

Match each statement with the term that it best defines. Some terms may not be used.

1. Repairperson's right to retain possession of the item being repaired until paid or if not paid, to sell the item to pay the repair bill

2. Status of being unable to pay debts when they become due

3. A debt in which the creditor lacks a secured interest in collateral

4. A claim against real property given to a repairperson and others

5. A court-ordered procedure by which a portion of a delinquent debtor's wages are paid to satisfy the debt

6. The total added cost when one pays in installments for goods or services

7. Procedure based on federal law that protects creditors and debtors in cases in which the latter are unable or unwilling to pay their debts

8. The evaluation of a party's ability to pay debts

9. Party who agrees to be primarily liable for debt created in favor of the principal debtor

10. A party who agrees to be secondarily liable to the principal debtor

a. artisan's lien
b. bankruptcy
c. credit rating
d. finance charge
e. garnishment
f. guarantor
g. insolvent
h. involuntary bankruptcy
i. lien
j. mechanic's lien
k. pawn
l. pledgee
m. pledgor
n. principal debtor
o. surety
p. suretyship
q. unsecured debt
r. voluntary bankruptcy

REVIEW LEGAL CONCEPTS

11. What makes the artisan's lien so powerful?

12. What makes the mechanic's lien so powerful?

13. What is the legal difference between a surety and a guarantor?

14. What does a signature on a credit card indicate? If the card is lost or stolen, generally what is the cardholder's liability?

15. Why do usury laws not govern interest charges imposed on credit purchases of goods and services?

WRITE ABOUT LEGAL CONCEPTS

16. Contrast the differences between bankruptcy liquidation and dissolution for the various types of businesses, including sole proprietorship, partnership, and corporation.

17. Compare the bankruptcy options available to a business debtor versus an individual debtor. Compare especially the list of exemptions and the priority of payout of liquidated funds.

18. **HOT DEBATE** Write a persuasive opening statement that emphasizes the legal, ethical, and economic points in Norm's favor. Or, write a persuasive opening statement for the jeweler that encompasses the economic and legal reasons why the loss should fall on Norm.

MAKE ACADEMIC CONNECTIONS

19. **ENGLISH** Read the sections of Little Dorrit, David Copperfield, and the Pickwick Papers by Charles Dickens about debtor's prisons. Each refers to a different debtor's prison in London in the nineteenth century many years after the United States took a stance against them. Realize Dickens' father had been imprisoned in one of them during the son's childhood. Write a paragraph contrasting your feelings about punishment of debtors with those of nineteenth century England. Identify why your feelings coincide with or differ from those of that period.

THINK CRITICALLY ABOUT EVIDENCE

Study the situation, answer the questions, and then prepare arguments to support your answers.

20. You are thinking of buying an automobile and plan to borrow money from a financial institution to help you pay cash for the purchase. Is there a limit on how much interest a lender can charge you? Suppose you decide to rely on dealer financing, paying the dealer or finance company a series of monthly installments. Is there any limit on the annual percentage rate (APR) of the financing charge the seller may add to the price of the car?

21. An acquaintance brags that she will finance her college education with government-insured student loans and then go bankrupt after graduation to avoid paying them. Is this possible? Is this ethical?

22. All five of your credit cards are stolen from your motel room while you are skiing. Fortunately you discover the loss within a few hours and immediately notify the credit card companies by telephone. On the following day, you also notify them by mail. However, within a week, the thief uses your credit cards to charge $1,875 in purchases. Eventually, each credit card company bills you for $50 of the purchases made with its card. By what authority did they do this? Must you pay these bills?

23. Garrotte took his new flat screen TV to Tesla Technology Inc. for repairs. The bill came to more than $500. As Garrotte was short of money, he gave Tesla a 90-day promissory note for the amount due. Tesla then returned the TV to Garrotte. Has Tesla improved his position as a creditor by so doing? Why or why not?

24. When Lola came home from college for spring break, her mother gave her a credit card. "You can sign my name, but don't spend more than $100," she told Lola. Lola went on a buying spree with her friend Joyce and together they bought $575 worth of clothing using the credit card. Now her mother refuses to pay more than $150, stating, "I authorized $100, and $50 is the legal maximum for unauthorized purchases." The credit card company sues for $575. Who wins?

25. Medias and other pawnbrokers objected to an Indianapolis city ordinance that regulated their business. The ordinance required an applicant for a pawnbroker's license to establish good character by the certificate of three landowners. The ordinance also provided that the licensee keep specified records and supply information to the chief of police. Finally, the ordinance specified that the licensee hold all pledged articles for 96 hours, and it required that the licensee take the thumbprints of all persons from whom he or she bought or received goods. Are these regulations arbitrary and unreasonable? (*Medias v. City of Indianapolis*, 216 Ind. 155, 23 N.E.2d 590)

26. Sniadach owed the Family Finance Corporation (FFC) $420 under a written promise to pay. When this debt became overdue, the creditor obtained a court order that summarily garnished her wages. Her employer had $63 in wages earned by her but not yet paid, and it agreed to hold one-half of them subject to the court order. Sniadach sued the FFC and asked the court to reverse the garnishment order, claiming that it violated her right to due process under the Fourteenth Amendment. She had received the summons and complaint on the same day that her employer was notified and froze her wages. Thus, she had no opportunity to be heard and to present her side of the case before the garnishment took effect. The trial court denied her motion, and the Wisconsin Supreme Court affirmed. She now appeals to the U.S. Supreme Court. How should it rule? (*Sniadach v. Family Finance Corporation*, 395 U.S. 337)

27. Todd was one of seven cosureties. When the principal debtor defaulted, Todd paid the debt and sued the other cosureties under his right of contribution. How much can Todd collect from each? (*Todd v. Windsor*, 118 Ga. App. 805, 165 S.E.2d 438)

28. In his divorce decree, Elliot was ordered to pay $102 of his weekly wages of $467.47 from his job at a General Motors plant for child support. Months later, U.S. Life Credit Corporation (USLC) recovered a judgment against Elliot in municipal court. With court approval, USLC then garnished 25 percent of Elliot's $467.47 per week to pay off the judgment amount. The U.S. Secretary of Labor then filed a lawsuit against the municipal court and USLC contending that the payments to USLC and for child support, taken together, vio-

lated the 25 percent of disposable income restriction on garnishments imposed by law. You decide. (*Donovan v. Hamilton County Municipal Court*, 580 F. Supp. 554)

29. When Hardison filed for bankruptcy, one of his main creditors was General Finance Corporation (GFC) to which he owed $2,800. After the GFC debt and others were discharged as a result of the bankruptcy procedure, he received a letter from GFC informing him that his credit was still good with it. By telephone, Hardison then arranged for a $1,200 loan from GFC. However, when he appeared to pick up the money, GFC informed him that it was going to make the loan only if he agreed to pay back not only the $1,200, but also an additional $1,200 from the first loan. Hardison then signed a consumer credit contract agreeing to those terms. Later, Hardison filed a lawsuit claiming that GFC should have included the amount from the previously discharged debt in the "total finance charge" in the truth-in-lending statement shown him at the time of the transaction, rather than as a part of the "total amount financed." Hardison wanted damages available under the Truth in Lending Act. Should he receive them? (*Hardison v. General Finance Corporation*, 738 F.2d 893)

30. When the Richmonds filed for Chapter 7 liquidation under the Bankruptcy Code, their unsecured debts totaled a little more than $19,000. All but $225 of the unsecured debts was owed on credit cards. The trustee in bankruptcy noted that the Richmond's monthly expenses included voluntary payments in support of their grandchildren. The trustee also pointed out to the court that, if these payments were stopped, the Richmonds would have an additional $300 per month with which to pay off the credit cards. In fact, under a three year Chapter 13 plan, the Richmonds could pay off more than 90 percent of the credit card debt in 36 months. As a consequence, the trustee filed a motion to dismiss the Richmond's case, contending that to grant relief to them would be an abuse of Chapter 7. The court noted that in making such a decision, it must decide whether the debtors are seeking an advantage or are truly needy in the sense that their financial situation warrants dismissal of the debts. How should the judge decide this case, and why? (*In Re Richmond*, 144 Bankruptcy Reporter 539)

CASE FOR LEGAL THINKING

IN RE BAKER, U.S. BANKRUPTCY COURT
10 BANKRUPTCY REPORTER 870

FACTS Prior to 1976, a student could attend school on student loans guaranteed by the government and then discharge them immediately upon graduation, before starting employment, under the terms of the Bankruptcy Act. Congress ultimately closed the loophole except for those for whom paying back the loans posed an "undue hardship."

Mary Lou Baker filed for bankruptcy protection under the "undue hardship" provisions to relieve her of the burden of repaying educational loans totalling some $6,635. The loans were from three institutions of higher learning: The University of Tennessee at Chattanooga, Cleveland State Community College, and the Baroness Erlanger School of Nursing.

Mary Lou Baker was a mother of three with a monthly take-home pay of less than $650. Her monthly expenses for herself and the children (her husband had left town) were nearly $1,000. She did not receive any public aid and had no other income according to the record. However, just prior to filing this action, her church had paid her January heating bill to prevent her from being without heat in her home.

Of her three children, one had difficulty reading and another required special and expensive shoes. Baker herself had not been well and her medical bills had gone unpaid prior to the bankruptcy filing. In the bankruptcy petition she filed, Mrs. Baker seeks a discharge of her educational loans based on the hardship provision.

REASONING Ralph Kelley, Bankruptcy Judge, rendered the court's decision:

"In 1976 the Congress passed the Educational Amendments which restricted a discharge in bankruptcy (of student loans). The restriction was designed to remedy an abuse by students who, immediately upon graduation, would file bankruptcy to secure a discharge of educational loans. These students often had no other indebtedness and could easily repay their debts from future wages . . .

In passing the Educational Amendments of 1976 and including these amendments in the Bankruptcy Reform Act of 1978, Congress intended to correct an abuse. It did not intend to deprive those who have truly fallen on hard times of the 'fresh start' policy of the new Bankruptcy Code."

CONCLUSION The court concludes that under the circumstances of this case, requiring the debtor to repay the debts owed to the three defendants of $6,635 plus interest would impose upon her and her dependents an undue hardship.

PRACTICE JUDGING

1. What sort of standard does the court identify here for future debtors when it says petitioner Baker had "truly fallen on hard times"? What sort of standard would you propose?

2. Presume Mrs. Baker did her best at each institution but still ended up either without the sought-after degree or without a job commensurate with the money expended to qualify for it. Does the government, as guarantor of such educational loans, find itself being forced into evaluating how successful each applicant may be before issuing them the money?

© GETTY IMAGES/PHOTODISC

Entrepreneurs and the Law

PROJECT 7 BORROWING MONEY AND PAYING BILLS

FINANCIAL SETBACK

Several years passed. JJ's businesses prospered and grew. At long last, he saw an opportunity to move into even more lucrative fields such as contracts with the Department of Defense and various package shipping companies. Unfortunately, his plan to completely finance the major expansion of his current plant by personally borrowing money from his bank and in-laws hadn't worked. Construction delay after delay had stretched the reservoir of financial resources to the limit. The business was still going strong, but his personal "fortune" was exposed and bankruptcy loomed if he couldn't get more financing to complete the plant. He finally told Amber about the problem. She immediately suggested that he talk it over with a bankruptcy attorney. She also called another attorney who specialized in corporate financing. As usual JJ went ahead with her suggestion for the meeting.

FINANCIAL SOLUTION

JJ looked down in total dismay as he listened to the bankruptcy attorney's report. Not only would he go down in flames, but he probably would take his in-laws with him. Finally, he realized that the bankruptcy attorney had stopped speaking. "That's it then, isn't it?" JJ said. "Not quite, sir," said the attorney. "I'd like to introduce you to an expert in corporate finance, Mr. Whorton. I think he may have some good news for you." JJ looked up. "Haven't had any of that since our daughter was born." JJ pointed to a picture on his desk of his beautiful daughter.

© GETTY IMAGES/PHOTODISC

The attorney smiled and began, "Well, Mr. Adamski, I think you could have saved yourself a lot of grief if you had just come to us in the first place. You have a great deal of unencumbered capital equipment and ground around here. We could go to your current creditors and offer them secured positions in return for their backing off on trying to collect according to their current schedule. However, the best idea would be to set up a financing package that will let you complete your current expansion and even give you capital to buy whatever supplies and equipment you need to make even more money. I've taken the liberty of preparing a plan with several options, including secured and unsecured instruments, equity capitalization and some combinations of the two."

JJ felt unbelievably relieved. If he understood correctly, not only would he be able to save the company but complete the expansion as well. When the attorneys left, JJ emerged from his office with a big smile on his face. For the first time in more than six months, he was going home early to his wife and daughter.

ACTIVITIES

Divide into teams and perform one or more of the following activities as directed by your teacher.

Present

Assume members of your team are the firm's associates accompanying the bankruptcy attorney who explained the bankruptcy issues to JJ. Each team member should consider one of the following issues and prepare a short presentation on it:

1. Which form of bankruptcy might be most helpful to JJ?
2. What will be the effect of bankruptcy on the business?
3. What should be JJ's plan to pay off his in-laws?
4. What could be salvaged for JJ if he does declare bankruptcy?

After each member presents to the team, the team should prepare a presentation covering all the issues for the class.

Brainstorm

As a team, brainstorm a list of financing options for the business—a public stock or bond issue, mortgaging real or personal property, debentures, etc.

Debate

After your list from the brainstorming activity is compiled, debate the pros and cons of each alternative, given JJ's current position. Make a recommendation about which financing option seems best for JJ's company.

COMMUNITY ACTION

Protect Against Identity Theft

Did you know your identity can be stolen? Whenever someone uses your name, address, phone number, credit card, driver's license, or other personal information without your permission to commit fraud or another crime, they are guilty of identity theft. You can help protect yourself and others against identity theft.

Do Your Part

1. Create a multimedia presentation titled Protecting Against Identity Theft. Offer the presentation to your whole school.
2. Use the Internet for information to include in your presentation. Modify your research to be school and age appropriate. For example, include information on safeguarding backpacks and lockers as well as purses and wallets.
3. Make an outline of your presentation before you write the full presentation.
4. Assign different aspects of the presentation to different students. Some students will be writers, some artists, and other students in your group will work with the electronics or stage lighting.
5. Arrange with the administration for a date the auditorium will be available for your presentation and a date for dress rehearsal.
6. Draw up a timeline that details each step that must be taken from beginning of the project to the date of presentation.
7. Write press releases for the school newspaper and radio station.
8. The day before the presentation, and again the morning of, check to make sure all the electronics are available and working properly.

Extemporaneous Speaking

Participants will choose to prepare a speech about "Legal Aspects of Bankruptcy" or "Credit—Good, Bad, Legal Responsibilities."

Each participant will be provided ten (10) minutes to develop a speech for the topic they choose. Notes can be taken on the cards provided by the teacher. No materials or previously prepared notes will be allowed into the preparation or presentation room with the contestant.

The length of the speech will be no less than one (1) minute and no more than three (3) minutes. The contestant will speak before a panel of judges and a timekeeper. No audience will be allowed. One-minute and 30-second warnings will be given during the speech. Points will be awarded per speech, not per judge.

Performance Indicators Evaluated
• Demonstrate effective communication skills.
• Describe the legal requirements and responsibilities for credit.
• Demonstrate effective speech presentation with the introduction, body, and conclusion.
• Utilize nonverbal gestures to effectively explain the legal aspects of credit.
• Define bankruptcy.

For more detailed information about performance indicators, go to the BPA web site.

Think Critically
1. What is bankruptcy?
2. Why have so many people chosen to declare bankruptcy?
3. What are long-term effects of bankruptcy?
4. What responsibilities are attached to the use of credit?

http://www.bpa.org/

CONSTITUTION OF THE UNITED STATES

We the People Of the United States, in Order to form a more perfect Union, establish Justice, insure domestic Tranquility, provide for the common defence, promote the general Welfare, and secure the Blessings of Liberty to ourselves and our Posterity, do ordain and establish this Constitution for the United States of America.

ARTICLE I

Section 1. All legislative Powers herein granted shall be vested in a Congress of the United States, which shall consist of a Senate and House of Representatives.

Section 2. The House of Representatives shall be composed of Members chosen every second Year by the People of the several States, and the Electors in each State shall have the Qualifications requisite for Electors of the most numerous Branch of the State Legislature.

No Person shall be a Representative who shall not have attained to the Age of twenty five Years, and been seven Years a Citizen of the United States, and who shall not, when elected, be an inhabitant of that State in which he shall be chosen.

*Representatives and direct Taxes shall be apportioned among the several States which may be included within this Union, according to their respective. Numbers, which shall be determined by adding to the whole Number of free Persons, including those bound to Service for a Term of Years, and excluding Indians not taxed, three fifths of all other Persons. The actual Enumeration shall be made within three Years after the first Meeting of the Congress of the United States, and within every subsequent Term of ten Years, in such Manner as they shall by Law direct. The number of Representatives shall not exceed one for every thirty Thousand, but each State shall have at Least one Representative; and until such enumeration shall be made, the State of New Hampshire shall be entitled to chuse three, Massachusetts eight, Rhode Island and Providence Plantations one, Connecticut five, New-York six, New Jersey four, Pennsylvania eight, Delaware one, Maryland six, Virginia ten, North Carolina five, South Carolina five, and Georgia three.

When vacancies happen in the Representation from any State, the Executive Authority thereof shall issue Writs of Election to fill such Vacancies.

The House of Representatives shall chuse their Speaker and other Officers; and shall have the sole Power of Impeachment.

Section 3. The Senate of the United States shall be composed of two Senators from each State, chosen by the Legislature thereof, for six Years; and each Senator shall have one Vote.

Immediately after they shall be assembled in Consequence of the first Election, they shall be divided as equally as may be into three Classes. The Seats of the Senators of the first Class shall be vacated at the Expiration of the second Year,

*Sections of the Constitution which are crossed out in this text have been amended and are no longer in effect.

of the second Class at the Expiration of the fourth Year, and of the third Class at the Expiration of the sixth Year, so that one third may be chosen every second Year; ~~and if Vacancies happen by Resignation, or otherwise, during the Recess of the Legislature of any State, the Executive thereof may make temporary Appointments until the next Meeting of the Legislature, which shall then fill such Vacancies.~~

No Person shall be a Senator who shall not have attained to the Age of thirty Years, and been nine Years a Citizen of the United States, and who shall not, when elected, be an Inhabitant of that State for which he shall be chosen.

The Vice-President of the United States shall be President of the Senate, but shall have no Vote, unless they be equally divided.

The Senate shall chuse their other Officers, and also a President pro tempore, in the Absence of the Vice-President, or when he shall exercise the Office of President of the United States.

The Senate shall have the sole Power to try all Impeachments. When sitting for that Purpose, they shall be on Oath or Affirmation. When the President of the United States is tried, the Chief Justice shall preside: And no Person shall be convicted without the Concurrence of two thirds of the Members present.

Judgment in Cases of Impeachment shall not extend further than to removal from Office, and disqualification to hold and enjoy any Office of honor, Trust or Profit under the United States: but the Party convicted shall nevertheless be liable and subject to Indictment, Trial, Judgment and Punishment, according to Law.

Section 4. The Times, Places and Manner of holding Elections for Senators and Representatives, shall be prescribed in each State by the Legislature thereof; but the Congress may at any time by Law make or alter such Regulations, except as to the Places of chusing Senators.

The Congress shall assemble at least once in every Year, ~~and such Meeting shall be on the first Monday in December,~~ unless they shall by Law appoint a different Day.

Section 5. Each House shall be the Judge of the Elections, Returns and Qualifications of its own Members, and a Majority of each shall constitute a Quorum to do Business; but a smaller Number may adjourn from day to day, and may be authorized to compel the Attendance of absent Members, in such Manner, and under such Penalties as each House may provide.

Each House may determine the Rules of its Proceedings, punish its Members for disorderly Behaviour, and, with the Concurrence of two thirds, expel a Member.

Each House shall keep a Journal of its Proceedings, and from time to time publish the same, excepting such Parts as may in their Judgment require Secrecy; and the Yeas and Nays of the Members of either House on any question shall, at the Desire of one fifth of those Present, be entered on the Journal.

Neither House, during the Session of Congress, shall, without the Consent of the other, adjourn for more than three days, nor to any other Place than that in which the two Houses shall be sitting.

Section 6. The Senators and Representatives shall receive a Compensation for their Services, to be ascertained by Law, and paid out of the Treasury of the United States. They shall in all Cases, except Treason, Felony and Breach of the Peace, be privileged from Arrest during their Attendance at the Session off their respective Houses, and in going to and returning from the same; and for any Speech or Debate in either House, they shall not be questioned in any other Place.

No Senator or Representative shall, during the Time for which he was elected, be appointed to any civil Office under the Authority of the United States, which shall have been created, or the Emoluments whereof shall have been encreased during such time; and no Person holding any Office under the United States, shall be a Member of either House during his Continuance in Office.

Section 7. All Bills for raising Revenue shall originate in the House of Representatives; but the Senate may propose or concur with Amendments as on other Bills.

Every Bill which shall have passed the House of Representatives and the Senate, shall, before it becomes a Law, be presented to the President of the United States; If he approve he shall sign it, but if not he shall return it, with his Objections to that House in which it shall have originated, who shall enter the Objections at large on their Journal, and proceed to reconsider it.

If after such Reconsideration two thirds of that House shall agree to pass the Bill, it shall be sent, together with the Objections, to the other House, by which it shall likewise be reconsidered, and if approved by two thirds of that House, it shall become a Law. But in all such Cases the Votes of both Houses shall be determined by yeas and Nays, and the Names of the Persons voting for and against the Bill shall be entered on the Journal of each House respectively. If any Bill shall not be returned by the President within ten Days (Sundays excepted) after it shall have been presented to him, the Same shall be a Law, in like Manner as if he had signed it, unless the Congress by their Adjournment prevent its Return, in which Case it shall not be a Law.

Every Order, Resolution, or Vote to which the Concurrence of the Senate and House of Representatives may be necessary (except on a question of Adjournment) shall be presented to the President of the United States; and before the Same shall take Effect, shall be approved by him, or being disapproved by him, shall be repassed by two thirds of the Senate and House of Representatives, according to the Rules and Limitations prescribed in the Case of a Bill.

Section 8. The Congress shall have Power To lay and collect Taxes, Duties, Imposts and Excises, to pay the Debts and provide for the common Defence and general Welfare of the United States; but all Duties, Imposts and Excises shall be uniform throughout the United States;

To borrow Money on the credit of the United States;

To regulate Commerce with foreign Nations, and among the several States, and with the Indian Tribes;

To establish an uniform Rule of Naturalization, and uniform Laws on the subject of Bankruptcies throughout the United States;

To coin Money, regulate the Value thereof, and of foreign Coin, and fix the Standard of Weights and Measures;

To provide for the Punishment of counterfeiting the Securities and current Coin of the United States;

To establish Post Offices and post Roads;

To promote the Progress of Science and useful Arts, by securing for limited Times to Authors and Inventors the exclusive Right to their respective Writings and Discoveries;

To constitute Tribunals inferior to the supreme Court;

To define and punish Piracies and Felonies committed on the high Seas, and Offenses against the Law of Nations;

To declare War, grant Letters of Marque and Reprisal, and make Rules concerning Captures on Land and Water;

To raise and support Armies, but no Appropriation of Money to that Use shall be for a longer Term than two Years;

To provide and maintain a Navy;

To make Rules for the Government and Regulation of the land and naval Forces;

To provide for calling forth the Militia to execute the Laws of the Union, suppress Insurrections and repel Invasions;

To provide for organizing, arming, and disciplining, the Militia, and for governing such Part of them as may be employed in the Service of the United States, reserving to the States respectively, the Appointment of the Officers, and the Authority of training the Militia according to the discipline prescribed by Congress;

To exercise exclusive Legislation in all Cases whatsoever, over such District (not exceeding ten Miles square) as may, by Cession of particular States, and the Acceptance of Congress, become the Seat of the Government of the United States, and to exercise like Authority over all Places purchased by the Consent of the

Legislature of the State in which the Same shall be, for the Erection of Forts, Magazines, Arsenals, dock-Yards and other needful Buildings; And

To make all Laws which shall be necessary and proper for carrying into Execution the foregoing Powers, and all other Powers vested by this Constitution in the Government of the United States, or in any Department or Officer thereof.

Section 9. The Migration or Importation of such Persons as any of the States now existing shall think proper to admit, shall not be prohibited by the Congress prior to the Year one thousand eight hundred and eight, but a Tax or duty may be imposed on such Importation, not exceeding ten dollars for each Person.

The Privilege of the Writ of Habeas Corpus shall not be suspended, unless when in Cases of Rebellion or Invasion the public Safety may require it.

No Bill of Attainder or ex post facto Law shall be passed.

No Capitation, or other direct, Tax shall be laid, unless in Proportion to the Census or Enumeration herein before directed to be taken.

No Tax or Duty shall be laid on Articles exported from any State.

No Preference shall be given by any Regulation of Commerce or Revenue to the Ports of one State over those of another: nor shall Vessels bound to, or from, one State, be obliged to enter, clear, or pay Duties in another.

No Money shall be drawn from the Treasury, but in Consequence of Appropriations made by Law; and a regular Statement and Account of the Receipts and Expenditures of all public Money shall be published from time to time.

No Title of Nobility shall be granted by the United States: And no Person holding any Office of Profit or Trust under them, shall, without the Consent of the Congress, accept of any present, Emolument, Office, or Title, of any kind whatever, from any King, Prince, or foreign State.

Section 10. No State shall enter into any Treaty, Alliance, or Confederation; grant Letters of Marque and Reprisal; coin Money; emit Bills of Credit; make any Thing but gold and silver Coin a Tender in Payment of Debts; pass any Bill of Attainder, ex post facto Law, or Law impairing the Obligation of Contracts, or grant any Title of Nobility.

No State shall, without the Consent of the Congress, lay any Imposts or Duties on Imports or Exports, except what may be absolutely necessary for executing its inspection Laws: and the net Produce of all Duties and Imposts, laid by any State on Imports or Exports, shall be for the Use of the Treasury of the United States; and all such Laws shall be subject to the Revision and Controul of the Congress.

No State shall, without the Consent of Congress, lay any Duty of Tonnage, keep Troops, or Ships of War in time of Peace, enter into any Agreement or Compact with another State, or with a foreign Power, or engage in War, unless actually invaded, or in such imminent Danger as will not admit of delay.

ARTICLE II

Section 1. The executive Power shall be vested in a President of the United States of America. He shall hold his Office during the Term of four Years, and, together with the Vice-President, chosen for the same Term, be elected, as follows

Each State shall appoint, in such Manner as the Legislature thereof may direct, a Number of Electors, equal to the whole Number of Senators and Representatives to which the State may be entitled in the Congress: but no Senator or Representative, or Person holding an Office of Trust or Profit under the United States, shall be appointed an Elector.

The Electors shall meet in their respective States, and vote by Ballot for two Persons, of whom one at least shall not be an Inhabitant of the same State with themselves. And they shall make a List of all the Persons voted for, and of the Number of Votes for each; which List they shall sign and certify, and transmit sealed to the Seat of the Government of the United States, directed to the President of the Senate. The President of the Senate shall, in the Presence of the Senate and House of Representatives, open

~~all the Certificates, and the Votes shall then be counted. The Person having the greatest Number of Votes shall be the President, if such Number be a Majority, of the whole Number of Electors appointed; and if there be more than one who have such Majority and have an equal Number of Votes, then the House of Representatives shall immediately chuse by Ballot one of them for President, and if no Person have a Majority, then from the five highest on the List the said House shall in like Manner chuse the President. But in chusing the President, the Votes shall be taken by States, the Representation from each State having one Vote; A quorum for this Purpose shall consist of a Member or Members from two thirds of the States, and a Majority of all the States shall be necessary to a Choice. In every Case, after the Choice of the President, the Person having the greatest Number of Votes of the Electors shall be the Vice-President. But if there should remain two or more who have equal Votes, the Senate shall chuse from them by Ballot the Vice President.~~

The Congress may determine the Time of chusing the Electors, and the Day on which they shall give their Votes; which Day shall be the same throughout the United States.

No Person except a natural born Citizen, or a Citizen of the United States, at the time of the Adoption of this Constitution, shall be eligible to the Office of the President; neither shall any person be eligible to that Office who shall not have attained to the Age of thirty five Years, and been fourteen Years a Resident within the United States.

~~In Case of the Removal of the President from Office, or of his Death, Resignation, or Inability to discharge the Powers and Duties of the said Office, the Same shall devolve on the Vice-President, and the Congress may by Law provide for the Case of Removal, Death, Resignation or Inability, both of the President and Vice-President, declaring what Officer shall then act as President, and such Officer shall act accordingly, until the Disability be removed, or a President shall be elected.~~

The President shall, at stated Times, receive for his Services, a Compensation, which shall neither be increased nor diminished during the Period for which he shall have been elected and he shall not receive within that Period any other Emolument from the United States, or any of them.

Before he enter on the Execution of his Office, he shall take the following Oath or Affirmation: "I do solemnly swear (or affirm) that I will faithfully execute the Office of President of the United States, and will to the best of my Ability, preserve, protect and defend the Constitution of the United States."

Section 2. The President shall be Commander in Chief of the Army and Navy of the United States, and of the Militia of the several States, when called into the actual Service of the United States; he may require the Opinion, in writing, of the principal Officer in each of the executive Departments, upon any Subject relating to the Duties of their respective Offices, and he shall have Power to grant Reprieves and Pardons for Offenses against the United States, except in Cases of Impeachment.

He shall have Power, by and with the Advice and Consent of the Senate, to make Treaties, provided two thirds of the Senators present concur; and he shall nominate, and by and with the Advice and Consent of the Senate, shall appoint Ambassadors, other public Ministers and Consuls, judges of the supreme Court, and all other Officers of the United States, whose Appointments are not herein otherwise provided for, and which shall be established by Law: but the Congress may by Law vest the Appointment of such inferior Officers, as they think proper, in the President alone, in the Courts of Law, or in the Heads of Departments. The President shall have Power to fill up all Vacancies that may happen during the Recess of the Senate, by granting Commissions which shall expire at the End of their next Session.

Section 3. He shall from time to time give to the Congress Information of the State of the Union, and recommend to their Consideration such measures as he shall judge necessary and expedient; he may, on extraordinary Occasions, convene both Houses, or either of them, and in

Case of Disagreement between them, with Respect to the Time of Adjournment, he may adjourn them to such Time as he shall think proper; he shall receive Ambassadors and other public Ministers; he shall take Care that the Laws be faithfully executed, and shall Commission all the Officers of the United States.

Section 4. The President, Vice-President and all civil Officers of the United States, shall be removed from Office on Impeachment for, and Conviction of, Treason, Bribery, or other high Crimes and Misdemeanors.

ARTICLE III

Section 1. The judicial Power of the United States, shall he vested in one supreme Court, and in such inferior Courts as the Congress may from time to time ordain and establish. The Judges, both of the supreme and inferior Courts, shall hold their Offices during good Behaviour, and shall, at stated Times, receive for their Services, a Compensation, which shall not be diminished during their Continuance in Office

Section 2. The judicial Power shall extend to all Cases, in Law and Equity, arising, under this Constitution, the Laws of the United States, and Treaties made, or which shall be made, under their Authority; to all Cases affecting Ambassa-dors, other public Ministers and Consuls; to all Cases of admiralty and maritime Jurisdiction; to Controversies to which the United States shall be a Party; to Controversies between two or more States; between a State and Citizens of another State; between Citizens of different States between Citizens of the same State claiming Lands under Grants of different States, and between a State, or the Citizens thereof; and foreign States, Citizens or Subjects.

In all Cases affecting Ambassadors, other public Ministers and Consuls, and those in which a State shall be Party, the supreme Court shall have original Jurisdiction. In all the other Cases before mentioned, the supreme Court shall have appellate Jurisdiction, both as to Law and Fact, with such Exceptions, and under such Regulations as the Congress shall make.

The Trial of all Crimes, except in Cases of Impeachment, shall be by Jury; and such Trial shall be held in the State where the said Crimes shall have been committed; but when not committed within any State, the Trial shall be at such Place or Places as the Congress may by Law have directed.

Section 3. Treason against the United States, shall consist only in levying War against them, or in adhering to their Enemies, giving them Aid and Comfort. No Person shall be convicted of Treason unless on the Testimony of two Witnesses to the same overt Act, or on Confession in open Court.

The Congress shall have Power to declare the Punishment of Treason, but no Attainder of Treason shall work Corruption of Blood, or Forfeiture except during the Life of the Person attained.

ARTICLE IV

Section 1. Full Faith and Credit shall be given in each State to the public Acts, Records, and judicial Proceedings of every other State; And the Congress may by general Laws prescribe the Manner in which such Acts, Records and Proceedings shall be proved, and the Effect thereof.

Section 2. The Citizens of each State shall be entitled to all Privileges and Immunities of Citizens in the several States.

A Person charged in any State with Treason, Felony, or other Crime, who shall flee from Justice, and be found in another State, shall on Demand of the executive Authority of the State from which he fled, be delivered up, to be removed to the State having Jurisdiction of the Crime.

No Person held to Service or Labour in one State, under the Laws thereof, escaping into another, shall, in Consequence of any Law or Regulation therein, be discharged from such Service or Labour, but shall be delivered up on Claim of the Party to whom such Service or Labour may be due.

Section 3. New States may be admitted by the Congress into this Union; but no new State shall be formed or erected within the Jurisdiction of any other State; nor any State be formed by the Junction of two or more States, or Parts of States, without the Consent of the Legislatures of the States concerned as well as of the Congress.

The Congress shall have Power to dispose of and make all needful Rules and Regulations respecting the Territory or other Property belonging to the United States; and nothing in this Constitution shall be so construed as to Prejudice any Claims of the United States, or of any particular State.

Section 4. The United States shall guarantee to every state in this Union a Republican Form of Government, and shall protect each of them against Invasion; and on Application of the Legislature, or of the Executive (when the Legislature cannot be convened) against domestic Violence.

ARTICLE V

The Congress, whenever two thirds of both Houses shall deem it necessary, shall propose Amendments to this Constitution, or, on the Application of the Legislatures of two thirds of the several States, shall call a Convention for proposing Amendments, which, in either Case, shall be valid to all Intents and Purposes, as Part of this Constitution, when ratified by the Legislatures of three fourths of the several States, or by Conventions in three fourths thereof, as the one or the other Mode of Ratification may be proposed by the Congress; Provided that no Amendment which may be made prior to the Year One thousand eight hundred and eight shall in any Manner affect the first and fourth Clauses in the Ninth Section of the first Article; and that no State, without its Consent, shall be deprived of its equal Suffrage in the Senate.

ARTICLE VI

All Debts contracted and Engagements entered into, before the Adoption of this Constitution, shall be as valid against the United States under this Constitution, as under the Confederation.

This Constitution, and the Laws of the United States which shall be made in Pursuance thereof; and all Treaties made, or which shall be made, under the Authority of the United States, shall be the supreme Law of the Land; and the Judges in every State shall be bound thereby, any Thing in the Constitution or Laws of any State to the Contrary notwithstanding.

The Senators and Representatives before mentioned, and the Members of the several State Legislatures, and all executive and judicial Officers, both of the United States and of the several States, shall be bound by Oath or Affirmation, to support this Constitution; but no religious Test shall ever be required as a Qualification to any Office or public Trust under the United States.

ARTICLE VII

The Ratification of the Conventions of nine States, shall be sufficient for the Establishment of this Constitution between the States so ratifying the Same.

Done in Convention by the Unanimous Consent of the States present the Seventeenth Day of September in the Year of our Lord one thousand seven hundred and Eighty seven and of the Independence of the United States of America the Twelfth In Witness whereof We have hereunto subscribed our Names,

G.o Washington Presid.
and deputy from Virginia

AMENDMENT I

Congress shall make no law respecting an establishment of religion, or prohibiting the free exercise thereof; or abridging the freedom of speech, or of the press, or the right of the people peaceably to assemble, and to petition the Government for a redress of grievances.

AMENDMENT II

A well regulated Militia, being necessary to the security of a free State, the right of the people to keep and bear Arms, shall not be infringed.

AMENDMENT III

No Soldier shall, in time of peace be quartered in any house, without the consent of the

Owner, nor in time of war, but in a manner to be prescribed by law.

AMENDMENT IV

The right of the people to be secure in their persons, houses, papers, and effects, against unreasonable searches and seizures, shall not be violated, and no Warrants shall issue, but upon probable cause, supported by Oath or affirmation, and particularly describing the place to be searched, and the persons or things to be seized.

AMENDMENT V

No person shall be held to answer for a capital, or otherwise infamous crime, unless on a presentment or indictment of a Grand Jury, except in cases arising in the land or naval forces, or in the Militia, when in actual service in time of War or public danger; nor shall any person be subject for the same offence to be twice put in jeopardy of life or limb, nor shall be compelled in any criminal case to be a witness against himself, nor be deprived of life, liberty, or property, without due process of law; nor shall private property be taken for public use without just compensation.

AMENDMENT VI

In all criminal prosecutions, the accused shall enjoy the right to a speedy and public trial, by an impartial jury of the State and district wherein the crime shall have been committed; which district shall have been previously ascertained by law, and to be informed of the nature and cause of the accusation; to be confronted with the witnesses against him; to have compulsory process for obtaining witnesses In his favor, and to have the assistance of counsel for his defence.

AMENDMENT VII

In Suits at common law, where the value in controversy shall exceed twenty dollars, the right of trial by jury shall be preserved, and no fact tried by a jury shall be otherwise re-examined in any Court of the United States, than according to the rules of the common law.

AMENDMENT VIII

Excessive bail shall not be required, nor excessive fines imposed, nor cruel and unusual punishments inflicted.

AMENDMENT IX

The enumeration in the Constitution of certain rights shall not be construed to deny or disparage others retained by the people.

AMENDMENT X

The powers not delegated to the United States by the Constitution, nor prohibited by it to the States, are reserved to the States respectively, or to the people.

AMENDMENT XI

The Judicial power of the United States shall not be construed to extend to any suit in law or equity, commenced or prosecuted against one of the United States by Citizens of another State, or by Citizens or Subjects of any Foreign State.

AMENDMENT XII

The Electors shall meet in their respective states, and vote by ballot for President and Vice-President, one of whom, at least, shall not be an inhabitant of the same state with themselves; they shall name in their ballots the person voted for as President, and in distinct ballots the person voted for as Vice-President, and they shall make distinct lists of all persons voted for as President, and of all persons voted for as Vice-President, and of the number of votes for each, which lists they shall sign and certify, and transmit sealed to the seat of the government of the United States, directed to the President of the Senate; The President of the Senate shall, in the presence of the Senate and House of Representatives, open all the certificates and the votes shall then be counted; The person having the greatest number of votes for President shall be the President, if such number be a majority of the whole number of Electors appointed; and if no person have such majority, then from the persons having the highest numbers not exceeding three on the list of those voted for as President, the House of Representatives shall choose immediately, by ballot, the President. But in choosing the President, the votes shall be taken by states, the representation from each state having one vote; a quorum for this purpose shall consist of a member or members from two-thirds of the states, and a majority of all the states shall be necessary to a choice. And if the House of

CONSTITUTION OF THE UNITED STATES

~~Representatives shall not choose a President whenever the right of choice shall devolve upon them, before the fourth day of March next following, then the Vice-President shall act as President, as in the case of the death or other constitutional disability of the President~~ The person having the greatest number of votes as Vice-President, shall be the Vice-President, if such number be a majority of the whole number of Electors appointed, and if no person have a majority, then from the two highest numbers on the list, the Senate shall choose the Vice-President; a quorum for the purpose shall consist of two-thirds of the whole number of Senators, and a majority of the whole number shall be necessary to a choice. But no person constitutionally ineligible to the office of President shall be eligible to that of Vice-President of the United States.

AMENDMENT XIII
Section 1. Neither slavery nor involuntary servitude, except as a punishment for a crime whereof the party shall have been duly convicted, shall exist within the United States, or any place subject to their jurisdiction.

Section 2. Congress shall have power to enforce this article by appropriate legislation.

AMENDMENT XIV
Section 1. All persons born or naturalized in the United States and subject to the jurisdiction thereof, are citizens of the United States and of the State wherein they reside. No State shall make or enforce any law which shall abridge the privileges or immunities of citizens of the United States; nor shall any State deprive any person of life, liberty, or property, without due process of law; nor deny to any person within its jurisdiction the equal protection of the laws.

Section 2. Representatives shall be apportioned among the several States according to their respective numbers, counting the whole number of persons in each State, excluding Indians not taxed. But when the right to vote at any election for the choice of electors for President and Vice-President of the United States, Representatives in Congress, the Executive and Judicial officers of a State, or the members of the Legislature thereof, is denied to any of the male inhabitants of such State, being twenty-one years of age, and citizens of the United States, or in any way abridged, except for participation in rebellion, or other crime, the basis of representation therein shall be reduced in the proportion which the number of such male citizens shall bear to the whole number of male citizens twenty-one years of age in such State.

Section 3. No person shall be a Senator or Representative in Congress, or elector of President and Vice-President, or hold any office, civil or military, under the United States, or under any State, who, having previously taken an oath, as a member of Congress, or as an officer of the United States, or as a member of any State legislature, or as an executive or judicial officer of any State, to support the Constitution of the United States, shall have engaged in insurrection or rebellion against the same, or given aid or comfort to the enemies thereof. But Congress may by a vote of two-thirds of each House, remove such disability.

Section 4. The validity of the public debt of the United States, authorized by law, including debts incurred for payment of pensions and bounties for services in suppressing insurrection or rebellion, shall not be questioned. But neither the United States nor any State shall assume or pay any debt or obligation incurred in aid of insurrection or rebellion against the United States, or any claim for the loss or emancipation of any slave; but all such debts, obligations and claims shall be held illegal and void.

Section 5. The Congress shall have power to enforce, by appropriate legislation, the provisions of this article.

AMENDMENT XV
Section 1. The right of citizens of the United States to vote shall not be denied or abridged by the United States or by any State on account of race, color, or previous condition of servitude.

Section 2. The Congress shall have power to enforce this article by appropriate legislation.

AMENDMENT XVI

The Congress shall have power to lay and collect taxes on incomes, from whatever source derived, without apportionment among the several States, and without regard to any census or enumeration.

AMENDMENT XVII

The Senate of the United States shall be composed of two Senators from each State, elected by the people thereof, for six years; and each Senator shall have one vote. The electors in each State shall have the qualifications requisite for electors of the most numerous branch of the State legislatures.

When vacancies happen in the representation of any State in the Senate, the executive authority of such State shall issue writs of election to fill such vacancies; Provided, That the legislature of any State may empower the executive thereof to make temporary appointments until the people fill the vacancies by election as the legislature may direct.

This amendment shall not be so construed as to affect the election or term of any Senator chosen before it becomes valid as part of the Constitution.

AMENDMENT XVIII

~~**Section 1.** After one year from the ratification of this article the manufacture, sale, or transportation of intoxicating liquors within, the importation thereof into, or the exportation thereof from the United States and all territory subject to the jurisdiction thereof for beverage purposes is hereby prohibited.~~

~~**Section 2.** The Congress and the several States shall have concurrent power to enforce this article by appropriate legislation.~~

~~**Section 3.** This article shall be inoperative unless it shall have been ratified as an amendment to the Constitution by the legislatures of the several States, as provided in the Constitution, within seven years from the date of the submission hereof to the States by the Congress.~~

AMENDMENT XIX

The right of citizens of the United States to vote shall not be denied or abridged by the United States or by any State on account of sex. Congress shall have power to enforce this article by appropriate legislation.

AMENDMENT XX

Section 1. The terms of the President and Vice-President shall end at noon on the 20th day of January, and the terms of Senators and Representatives at noon on the 3rd day of January, of the years in which such terms would have ended if this article had not been ratified; and the terms of their successors shall then begin.

Section 2. The Congress shall assemble at least once a year, and such meeting shall begin at noon on the 3rd day of January, unless they shall by law appoint a different day.

Section 3. If, at the time fixed for the beginning of the term of the President, the President elect shall have died, the Vice-President elect shall become President. If a President shall not have been chosen before the time fixed for the beginning of his term, or if the President elect shall have failed to qualify, then the Vice-President elect shall act as President until a President shall have qualified; and the Congress may by law provide for the case wherein neither a President elect nor a Vice-President elect shall have qualified, declaring who shall then act as President, or the manner in which one who is to act shall be elected, and such person shall act accordingly until a President or Vice-President shall have qualified.

Section 4. The Congress may by law provide for the case of the death of any of the persons from whom the House of Representatives may choose a President whenever the right of choice shall have devolved upon them, and for the case of the death of any of the persons from whom the Senate may choose a Vice-President whenever the right of choice shall have devolved upon them.

CONSTITUTION OF THE UNITED STATES

Section 5. Sections 1 and 2 shall take effect on the 15th day of October following the ratification of this article.

Section 6. This article shall be inoperative unless it shall have been ratified as an amendment to the Constitution by the legislatures of three-fourths of the several States within seven years from the date of its submission.

AMENDMENT XXI

Section 1. The eighteenth article of amendment to the Constitution of the United States is hereby repealed.

Section 2. The transportation or importation into any State, Territory, or possession of the United States for delivery or use therein of intoxicating liquors, in violation of the laws thereof, is hereby prohibited.

Section 3. This article shall be inoperative unless it shall have been ratified as an amendment to the Constitution by conventions in the several States, as Provided in the Constitution, within seven years from the date of the submission hereof to the States by the Congress.

AMENDMENT XXII

Section 1. No person shall be elected to the office of the President more than twice, and no person who has held the office of President, or acted as President, for more than two years of a term to which some other person was elected President shall be elected to the office of the President more than once. But this Article shall not apply to any person holding the office of President when this Article was proposed by the Congress, and shall not prevent any person who may be holding the office of President, or acting as President, during the term within which this Article becomes operative from holding the office of President or acting as President during the remainder of such term.

Section 2. This article shall be inoperative unless it shall have been ratified as an amendment to the Constitution by the legislatures of three-fourths of the several States within seven

years from the date of its submission to the States by the Congress.

AMENDMENT XXIII

Section 1. The District constituting the seat of Government of the United States shall appoint in such manner as the Congress may direct:

A number of electors of President and Vice-President equal to the whole number of Senators and Representatives in Congress to which the District would be entitled if it were a State, but in no event more than the least populous State; they shall be in addition to those appointed by the States, but they shall be considered, for the purposes of the election of President and Vice-President, to be electors appointed by a State; and they shall meet in the District and perform such duties as provided by the twelfth article of amendment.

Section 2. The Congress shall have power to enforce this article by appropriate legislation.

AMENDMENT XXIV

Section 1. The right of citizens of the United States to vote in any primary or other election for President or Vice-President, for electors for President or Vice-President, or for Senator or Representative in Congress, shall not be denied or abridged by the United States or any State by reason of failure to pay any poll tax or other tax.

Section 2. The Congress shall have power to enforce this article by appropriate legislation.

AMENDMENT XXV

Section 1. In case of the removal of the President from office or of his death or resignation, the Vice-President shall become President.

Section 2. Whenever there is a vacancy in the office of the Vice-President, the President shall nominate a Vice-President who shall take office upon confirmation by a majority vote of both Houses of Congress.

Section 3. Whenever the President transmits to the President pro tempore of the Senate and the Speaker of the House of Representatives his written declaration that he is unable to discharge the powers and duties of his office, and until he transmits to them a written declaration to the contrary, such powers and duties shall be discharged by the Vice-President as Acting President.

Section 4. Whenever the Vice-President and a majority of either the principal officers of the executive departments or of such other body as Congress may by law provide, transmit to the President pro tempore of the Senate and the Speaker of the House of Representatives their written declaration that the President is unable to discharge the powers and duties of his office, the Vice-President shall immediately assume the powers and duties of the office as Acting President.

Thereafter, when the President transmits to the President pro tempore of the Senate and the Speaker of the House of Representatives his written declaration that no inability exists, he shall resume the powers and duties of his office unless the Vice-President and a majority of either the principal officers of the executive department or of such other body as Congress may by law provide, transmit within four days to the President pro tempore of the Senate and the Speaker of the House of Representatives

their written declaration that the President is unable to discharge the powers and duties of his office. Thereupon Congress shall decide the issue, assembling within forty-eight hours for that purpose if not in session. If the Congress, within twenty-one days after receipt of the latter written declaration, or, if Congress is not in session, within twenty-one days after Congress is required to assemble, determines by two-thirds vote of both Houses that the President is unable to discharge the powers and duties of his office, the Vice-President shall continue to discharge the same as Acting President; otherwise, the President shall resume the powers and duties of his office.

AMENDMENT XXVI
Section 1. The right of citizens of the United States, who are eighteen years of age or older, to vote shall not be denied or abridged by the United States or by any State on account of age.

Section 2. The Congress shall have power to enforce this article by appropriate legislation.

AMENDMENT XXVII
No law, varying the compensation for the services of the Senators and Representatives, shall take effect, until an election of Representatives shall have intervened.

THE DECLARATION OF INDEPENDENCE

IN CONGRESS, JULY 4, 1776. A DEC-LARATION BY THE REPRESENTATIVES OF THE UNITED STATES OF AMERICA, IN GENERAL CONGRESS ASSEMBLED.

WHEN in the Course of human Events, it becomes necessary for one People to dissolve the Political Bands which have connected them with another, and to assume among the Powers of the Earth, the separate and equal Station to which the Laws of Nature and of Nature's God entitle them, a decent Respect to the Opinions of Mankind requires that they should declare the causes which impel them to the Separation.

WE hold these Truths to be self-evident, that all Men are created equal, that they are endowed by their Creator with certain unalienable Rights, that among these are Life, Liberty, and the Pursuit of Happiness That to secure these Rights, Governments are instituted among Men, deriving their just Powers from the Consent of the Governed, that whenever any Form of Government becomes destructive of these Ends, it is the Right of the People to alter or to abolish it, and to institute new Government, laying its Foundation on such Principles, and organizing its Powers in such Form, as to them shall seem most likely to effect their Safety and Happiness. Prudence, indeed, will dictate that Governments long established should not be changed for light and transient Causes; and accordingly all Experience hath shewn, that Mankind are more disposed to suffer, while Evils are suf-ferable, than to right themselves by abolish-ing the Forms to which they are accustomed. But when a long Train of Abuses and Usurpations, pursuing invariably the same Object, evinces a Design to reduce them under absolute Despotism, it is their Right, it is their Duty, to throw off such Government, and to provide new Guards for their future Security. Such has been the patient Sufferance of these Colonies; and such is now the Necessity which constrains them to alter their former Systems of Government. The History of the present King of Great-Britain is a History of repeated Injuries and Usurpations, all having in direct Object the Establishment of an absolute Tyranny over these States. To prove this, let Facts be submitted to a candid World.

HE has refused his Assent to Laws, the most wholesome and necessary for the public Good.

HE has forbidden his Governors to pass Laws of immediate and pressing Importance, unless suspended in their Operation till his Assent should be obtained; and when so suspended, he has utterly neglected to attend to them.

HE has refused to pass other Laws for the Accommodation of large Districts of People, unless those People would relinquish the Right of Representation in the Legislature, a Right inestimable to them, and formidable to Tyrants only.

HE has called together Legislative Bodies at Places unusual, uncomfortable, and distant from the Depository of their public Records, for the sole Purpose of fatiguing them into Compliance with his Measures.

HE has dissolved Representative Houses repeatedly, for opposing with manly Firmness his Invasions on the Rights of the People.

HE has refused for a long Time, after such Dissolutions, to cause others to be elected; whereby the Legislative Powers, incapable of Annihilation, have returned to the People at large for their exercise; the State remaining in the mean time exposed to all the Dangers of Invasion from without, and Convulsions within.

HE has endeavoured to prevent the Population of these States; for that Purpose obstructing the Laws for Naturalization of Foreigners; refusing to pass others to encourage their Migrations hither, and raising the Conditions of new Appropriations of Lands.

HE has obstructed the Administration of Justice, by refusing his Assent to Laws for establishing Judiciary Powers.

HE has made Judges dependent on his Will alone, for the Tenure of their Offices, and the Amount and Payment of their Salaries.

HE has erected a Multitude of new Offices, and sent hither Swarms of Officers to harrass our People, and eat out their Substance.

HE has kept among us, in Times of Peace, Standing Armies, without the consent of our Legislatures.

HE has affected to render the Military independent of and superior to the Civil Power.

HE has combined with others to subject us to a Jurisdiction foreign to our Constitution, and unacknowledged by our Laws; giving his Assent to their Acts of pretended Legislation:

FOR quartering large Bodies of Armed Troops among us:

FOR protecting them, by a mock Trial, from Punishment for any Murders which they should commit on the Inhabitants of these States:

FOR cutting off our Trade with all Parts of the World:

FOR imposing Taxes on us without our Consent:

FOR depriving us, in many Cases, of the Benefits of Trial by Jury:

FOR transporting us beyond Seas to be tried for pretended Offences:

FOR abolishing the free System of English Laws in a neighbouring Province, establishing therein an arbitrary Government, and enlarging its Boundaries, so as to render it at once an Example and fit Instrument for introducing the same absolute Rule into these Colonies:

FOR taking away our Charters, abolishing our most valuable Laws, and altering fundamentally the Forms of our Governments

FOR suspending our own Legislatures, and declaring themselves invested with Power to legislate for us in all Cases whatsoever.

HE has abdicated Government here, by declaring us out of his Protection and waging War against us.

HE has plundered our Seas, ravaged our Coasts, burnt our Towns, and destroyed the Lives of our People.

HE is, at this Time, transporting large Armies of foreign Mercenaries to compleat the Works of Death, Desolation, and Tyranny, already begun with circumstances of Cruelty and Perfidy, scarcely parallelled in the most barbarous Ages, and totally unworthy the Head of a civilized Nation.

HE has constrained our fellow Citizens taken Captive on the high Seas to bear Arms against their Country, to become the Executioners of their Friends and Brethren, or to fall themselves by their Hands.

HE has excited domestic Insurrections amongst us, and has endeavoured to bring on the Inhabitants of our Frontiers, the merciless Indian Savages, whose known Rule of Warfare, is an undistinguished Destruction, of all Ages, Sexes and Conditions.

IN every stage of these Oppressions we have Petitioned for Redress in the most humble Terms. Our repeated Petitions have been answered only by repeated Injury. A Prince, whose Character is thus marked by every act which may define a Tyrant, is unfit to be the Ruler of a free People.

NOR have we been wanting in Attentions to our British Brethren. We have warned them from Time to Time of Attempts by their Legislature to extend an unwarrantable Jurisdiction over us. We have reminded them of the Circumstances of our Emigration and Settlement here. We have appealed to their native Justice and Magnanimity, and we have conjured them by the Ties of our common Kindred to disavow these Usurpations, which, would inevitably interrupt our Connections and Correspondence. They too have been deaf to the Voice of Justice and of Consanguinity. We must, therefore, acquiesce in the Necessity, which denounces our Separation, and hold them, as we hold the rest of mankind, Enemies in War, in Peace, Friends.

WE, therefore, the Representatives of the UNITED STATES OF AMERICA, in GENERAL CONGRESS, Assembled, appealing to the Supreme Judge of the World for the Rectitude of our Intentions, do, in the Name, and by Authority of the good People of these Colonies, solemnly Publish and Declare, That these United Colonies are, and of Right ought to be, FREE AND INDEPENDENT STATES; that they are absolved from all Allegiance to the British Crown, and that all political Connection between them and the State of Great-Britain, is and ought to be totally dissolved; and that as FREE AND INDEPENDENT STATES, they have full Power to levy War, conclude Peace, contract Alliances, establish Commerce, and to do all other Acts and Things which INDEPENDENT STATES may of right do. And for the support of this Declaration, with a firm Reliance on the Protection of divine Providence, we mutually pledge to each other our Lives, our Fortunes, and our sacred Honor.

Signed by ORDER and in BEHALF of the CONGRESS,
JOHN HANCOCK, President.

ATTEST.
CHARLES THOMSON, SECRETARY.

PHILADELPHIA: PRINTED BY JOHN DUNLAP.

Glossary of Legal Terms

A

Acceleration clause clause making the entire balance of a debt due and payable upon a certain event, typically default

Acceptance in contracts, occurs when a party to whom an offer has been made agrees to the proposal; in commercial paper, drawee's promise to pay the draft when due

Accession right of an owner of property to an increase in that property

Accommodation party party lending his or her credit standing to insure the payment of an instrument

Accord agreement between the parties to a contract to change the obligation required

Accord and satisfaction parties' agreement to change the obligation required by their original contract and the performance of the new obligation

Actual bailment bailee's receipt and acceptance of the goods themselves

Administrative agency governmental body formed to carry out particular laws

Administrator/administratrix court-appointed representative for a decedent (male/female)

Adoption legal process that creates a parent-child relationship

Adverse possession occurs when someone adversely and exclusively possesses, in an open and notorious way, the land of another private person; possession is continuous and for the statutory period

Affirmative action plan court-ordered plan to remedy past discrimination by bringing the percentages of minorities and women in the workforce up to their corresponding percentages in the pool of qualified applicants

Age of majority age at which a person can be legally bound to contracts

Agency legal relationship in which one person is authorized to alter another's legal relationships

Agency shop establishment in which nonunion members are not required to join the union but must pay union dues

Agent one who is authorized to alter the legal relations of another

Alien corporation corporation chartered in another nation

Alteration in contracts, material change in the terms of a contract made intentionally by one party without consent of the other; in commercial paper, party's unauthorized change to or completion of a negotiable instrument intended to change the obligation of a party

Amendment change or alteration

Americans with Disabilities Act of 1990 (ADA) prevents employers from engaging in unjustified discrimination against people based on their disabilities

Annulment court order that cancels a marriage because of a problem that existed from the beginning of the marriage

Antedated dated earlier than the date of issuance

Anticipatory breach notification, before the scheduled time of performance, of refusal to perform contractual terms as agreed

Antitrust laws laws that prohibit competing companies from price fixing or dividing up sales regions

Apparent authority agency authority created when a principal leads the third party to believe that someone has particular agency authority

Appellate brief written argument on the issues of law submitted by opposing attorneys

Appellate court reviews decisions of lower courts to determine if a significant error of law was made during trial

Applicant pool people qualified for a particular job

Arbitrator independent third party who develops a binding and enforceable resolution to a dispute

Arson willful and illegal burning of a building

Articles of Confederation loose form of charter for common government adopted by the thirteen colonies prior to adoption of the Constitution

Articles of incorporation application to a state for a corporate charter

Articles of organization document filed with the state to organize an LLC

Artisan's lien lien for unpaid services assessed against personal property that has been improved

Assault intentional threat to physically or offensively injure another

Assignment transaction by which a party transfers contractual rights to another

Assignment of a lease tenant transfers to a third party his or her interest in a lease

Associate circuit court court that hears minor criminal cases, state traffic offenses, and lawsuits involving amounts of no more than $25,000

Assumption of risk person is aware of a danger on the job but agrees to do it anyway

Attractive nuisance something that attracts children to trespass

Auction public sale to the highest bidder

Authorization card signature on card indicates that a worker wants to be represented by a particular union

Automobile insurance insurance providing liability and other coverages for the operation of a motor vehicle

B

Bailee person having temporary possession and control of another person's goods, holding them in trust for a specified purpose

Bailee's lien right of a bailee to retain possession of the bailed property until payment is made

Bailment transfer of possession of personal property without transfer of ownership

Bailor party who gives up possession of the property

Bait and switch improper business practice involving luring buyers to the store with an understocked, low-priced good and then redirecting them to a more expensive product

Bankruptcy legal proceedings discharging debts and distributing assets

Bargaining unit any group of employees whose employment contract is negotiated together

Barter exchange of goods for goods

Battery harmful or offensive touching

Bearer party in possession of bearer paper

Bearer paper commercial paper legally collectible by the party in possession

Beneficiary party for whose benefit a trust is managed; also, recipient of the amount to be paid under an insurance policy

Bid rigging competitors' agreement that one bidder will have the lowest bid for a particular job

Bilateral contract offeree can accept offer by giving a promise to the offeror instead of performing the contracted-for act

Bill of exchange (also called **draft**) unconditional written order from one person directing another to pay money to a third person

Bill of Rights first ten amendments to the U.S. Constitution

Bill of sale receipt that serves as written evidence of the transfer of ownership of goods

Blank indorsement indorsement consisting only of the indorser's signature

Blue-sky laws laws prohibiting the sale of worthless stocks and bonds

Bona fide occupational qualification (BFOQ) job requirement that compels discrimination against a protected class

Bona fide seniority system system that rewards employees for length of employment rather than merit

Bonds written promises to pay back money borrowed by the corporation

Boycott refusal to buy or use someone's goods or services

Breach of contract failure to provide complete performance of contractual obligations

Bribery offering or giving something of value to improperly effect performance of another party

Bulk transfer transfer, generally by sale, of all or a major part of the goods of a business in one unit at one time

Burglary entering a building without permission when intending to commit a crime

Business ethics ethical principles used in making business decisions

Business judgment rule rule that protects management and other parties involved in a corporation from being held personally liable (criminally or civilly) for honest errors in judgment made in the course of business

Business law group of laws that governs business situations and transactions

Business necessity defense to a disparate treatment employment discrimination case showing that an employer's actions were meant to advance the business rather than to create unjustified discrimination

Bylaws rules and regulations for the internal management of corporate affairs

C

Cancellation ending a contract for sale of goods because of breach, while retaining other remedies; also, any act that shows an intent to end the obligation of payment of commercial paper

Capacity ability to understand

Carrier's lien carrier's right to retain possession of the goods until the charges for transportation and incidental services are paid

Case law made when an appellate court endorses a rule to be used in deciding court cases

Cashier's check check drawn by a bank on itself

Casual seller seller who does not meet the definition of a merchant

Casualty insurance insurance that covers for losses due to accident, chance, or negligence

Casual workers persons who do not work regularly for a certain employer

Causation linking a job requirement with underrepresentation of a protected class in the workforce

Caveat emptor let the buyer beware

Caveat venditor let the seller beware

Cease-and-desist order governmental order requiring that certain improper conduct be stopped

Certificate of deposit (CD) bank's written acknowledgement of the receipt of money with an unconditional promise to repay it at a definite future time

Certification selecting a bargaining representative by a majority secret vote of the workers in the bargaining unit; NLRB then recognizes that union as the exclusive negotiator for employees in the bargaining unit

Certified check check upon which liability has been accepted by the drawee bank

Charitable trust created for the fulfillment of an altruistic purpose

Check draft written on a bank by a depositor

Child custody care and control of a minor

Child support money paid by a parent to provide a child with economic maintenance

CIF "cost, insurance, freight" price

Civil disobedience open, peaceful violation of a law to protest its alleged injustice

Civil law group of laws used to provide remedy for wrongs against individuals

Civil rights personal, human rights recognized and guaranteed by the U.S. Constitution

Class action court procedure allowing a party to bring suit on his or her behalf and for those similarly situated

Closely held corporation private corporation whose stock is held by only one or a small number of shareholders

Closed shop employer agrees that workers must belong to the recognized union before they can be hired

COD collect on delivery

Code laws grouped into an organized form

Codicil formal, written, and witnessed amendment to a will

Coinsurance clause in a fire policy that requires the insured to maintain coverage equal to a certain percentage of the total current value of the insured property

Collateral property subject to the security interest of the creditor

Collateral note note on which personal property is offered for collateral

Collateral promise promise to pay a debt or default of another

Collective bargaining process by which the union and employer negotiate a contract of employment that binds both sides

Collision insurance automobile insurance that protects against upset and direct and accidental damage due to colliding with another object

Commercial paper unconditional written promise or order to pay a sum of money

Commingling mixing the money of the agent and the principal together

Common carrier enterprise that agrees, for a fee, to transport goods that are lawful and fit for shipment for anyone who applies

Common law law based on current standards or customs of the people

Common-law defenses defenses in a negligence suit that include the employee's assumption of risk, the employer's contributory negligence, and co-worker negligence

Common-law marriage marital relationship legalized by the couple holding themselves out as husband and wife and sharing home and property for an extended period

Common stock basic stock in a corporation conveying to its owner the right to vote and to receive dividends

Community property property owned equally by spouses

Compensatory damages amount of money awarded to compensate for a plaintiff's loss

Competency license state requirement for people in certain occupations and businesses to pass exams and receive a license

Composition of creditors agreement by all creditors to accept something less than the total amount of their claims as full payment

Compounding a crime accepting something of value for a promise not to inform on or prosecute a suspected criminal

Comprehensive insurance insurance that covers against all damage to the insured's car except that caused by collision or upset

Condemnation proceeding forcing a property owner to transfer property to a government in exchange for just reasonable compensation

Conditional estate estate where continued ownership is dependent upon some act or event

Consent order voluntary, court-enforceable agreement between the government and an offender requiring the termination of an illegal or questionable practice

Consequences-based reasoning form of ethical reasoning that evaluates the results of an action

Consequential damages money awarded to a party for foreseeable injuries caused by the other party's breach

Consideration what a person demands and generally must receive in order to make his or her promise legally binding

Consignment bailment in which ownership remains with the manufacturer or wholesaler until the goods are sold

Consolidation two or more corporations combine to form a new one

Conspiracy agreement between two or more persons to commit a crime

Constitution document that sets forth the framework of the government and its relationship to the people it governs

Constitutional law law made when the fundamental, supreme law of the land is adopted, amended, or interpreted

Constructive bailment occurs when the bailee receives and accepts a symbol of the personal property rather than the property itself

Constructive delivery having a symbol of a gift substituted in its delivery

Constructive eviction tenant moves out of leased premises because the landlord caused the premises to become unfit for its intended use

Constructive notice legal presumption that everyone has knowledge of facts on public file

Constructive trust created to require a person holding property to transfer it to another because retention would be a wrongful and unjust enrichment of the holder

Consumer individual who acquires goods primarily for personal, family, or household use

Consumer Product Safety Commission (CPSC) agency regulating the safety of various products including toys

Consumer transaction transaction in which a party buys goods or services for personal or household use

Contempt of court action that hinders the administration of justice in court

Contract agreement between two parties that creates an obligation

Contract of adhesion contract in which the more powerful party dictates all the important terms

Contract to sell transaction in which transfer of ownership is to take place in the future

Contractual capacity ability to understand that a contract is being made and its general meaning

Contributory negligence in personal injury law, plaintiff's own negligence is a partial cause of an injury; in employment law, employee does something carelessly to contribute to her or his injury or death

Conversion using property in a manner inconsistent with the owner's rights

Conveyance transfer of an estate from a grantor to a grantee by a deed

Cooling-off period stopping a labor dispute by federal court order for a period of 80 days when a national emergency strike is threatened

Co-ownership ownership existing when two or more persons have the same ownership rights in the same property

Copyright protects the expression of a creative work, such as the work of an artist, author, or composer

Corporate charter certificate of incorporation

Corporation legal entity treated as an artificial person by the law and created by the authority of federal or state law

Corrective advertising advertising to correct improper and false impressions

Counteroffer offeree's response to an offer which modifies it

County court See **Associate circuit court**

Court governmental forum that administers justice under the law

Court of record accurate, detailed report of what went on at trial

Co-worker negligence one worker causes the injury of another

Credit purchase by which whole or partial payment is delayed

Creditor party to whom a debt is owed

Credit rating evaluation of a party's ability to pay debts

Credit sale sale that, by agreement of the parties, calls for payment for the goods at a later date

Crime punishable offense against society

Criminal act specific conduct that violates a criminal statute

Criminal insanity defense based on the accused's inability to know right from wrong

Criminal intent intent to commit an evil act in violation of a statute

Criminal law group of laws that defines and sets punishments for offenses against society

Cumulative preferred stock preferred stock whose dividends remain due and payable beyond one corporate fiscal year

Custody care and present control of another's personal property under the owner's direction

Cyberlaw law that is intended to govern the use of computers in e-commerce and the Internet

D

Damages monetary award to compensate for the loss caused by a tort

Deadlock collective bargaining situation in which the union and employer cannot agree on important issues

Debenture unsecured bond

Debt that which is owed on a purchase on credit

Debtor person or business that owes money, goods, or services to another

Decedent person who dies

Decertification election process by which employees can reject union representation or select a different union

Declaration of Independence document drafted by representatives of the 13 original colonies that asserts the rights desired by the colonists

Dedication transferring real property by donating it to the government, such as to a city for use as a park or roadway

Deed legal document used to transfer ownership of real property

Defamation false statement that injures one's reputation

Default failure to perform a legal duty or failure to perform an agreement

Defendant party complained against in a civil or criminal lawsuit

Defense at criminal law, a legal position that allows the defendant to escape criminal liability

Delegation of duties turning over to another party one's duties under a contract

Delivery subject matter of the contract is placed within the possession or control of the owner

Democracy governmental system in which citizens vote directly to decide issues

Demurrage fee for delay by party shipping goods in loading or by party receiving goods in unloading

Directors individuals elected by the shareholders to be responsible for the overall direction of a corporation

Disability physical or mental condition that substantially limits a major life activity

Disaffirmance both parties to a contract return the consideration

Discharge termination of contractual duties that ordinarily occurs when the parties perform as promised

Discharged for cause employee is discharged due to the violation of an employment obligation

Discharged without cause employee's discharge is not due to his or her conduct

Disclaimer sign, label, or warning reducing a bailee's duty of care; also, notice of exclusion in a warranty

Dishonor bank's refusal to pay a check when due

Disparate impact employer treats members of a protected class less favorably than other employees; has the effect of eliminating members of a protected class

Dissolution change in partnership relationship due to a partner ceasing his association with its ongoing purpose; also, term for divorce or the ending of a marriage in some states

Distributive shares each member's share of profits and losses in an LLC

Dividends distributions of corporate earnings

Divisible contracts contracts for which separate consideration is given for the legal and illegal parts

Divorce court action terminating a marriage

Doctrine of capture grants ownership of fluid minerals to the party who extracts them

Domestic corporation corporation doing business in the state in which it is chartered

Donee person receiving a gift

Donor person giving a gift

Dormant partner partner neither known to the public nor active in management

Double taxation taxation of a corporation as an entity based on its earnings and then of the shareholders on corporate dividends

Draft (also called **bill of exchange**) unconditional written order from one person directing another to pay money to a third person

Drawee party ordered to pay a draft

Drawer party that executes a draft and orders payment to be made

Due process of law constitutional requirement for fundamental fairness in our legal and court system

Duress occurs when one party uses an improper threat or act to obtain an expression of agreement

Duty of accounting requires agent to account to the principal for all money and property of the principal that comes into the agent's possession

Duty of confidentiality requires agent to treat information about the principal very carefully

Duty of loyalty agent may not secretly benefit from the agency transaction

Duty of loyalty and honesty requires employee to look out for the best interests of the employer

Duty of obedience requires employee to follow the reasonable orders and rules of the employer; requires agent to carefully obey the instructions of the principal

Duty of reasonable care and skill requires agent to exercise the degree of care and skill any reasonably prudent person would use in a similar situation

Duty of reasonable performance requires employee to perform assigned duties at the prescribed time and in the prescribed manner

Duty of reasonable skill requires employee to perform job tasks with competence

E

Easement irrevocable right to the limited use of another's land

Economic strike work stoppage in which the dispute is over wages, hours, or conditions of employment

Electronic fund transfer (EFT) debit or credit to an account initiated by the use of a terminal, computer, telephone, or magnetic tape

Emancipation severing the child-parent relationship

Embezzlement taking of another's property or money by a person to whom it has been entrusted

Eminent domain power of the government to take private property for public use in exchange for the fair market price

Employee party who works under the supervision of another for pay

Employer party who engages another to work for pay

Employment contractual relationship in which one party engages another to work for pay under the supervision of the party paying

Employment at will employment relationship whereby employee may be discharged at any time because no agreement was made about length of employment; alternately, employee may quit the job at any time without liability for breach of contract

Employment discrimination treating individuals differently on the basis of race, color, gender, national origin, or religion

Encumbrances claims of third parties against the goods

Endorsements (also called **riders**) modifications made to the standard fire policy to satisfy an insured's needs

Environmental Protection Agency (EPA) agency regulating the creation, marketing, and use of hazardous chemicals, as well as the disposal of toxic waste

Equal Employment Opportunity Commission (EEOC) agency charged with eliminating workplace discrimination based on race, religion, sex, color, national origin, age, or disability

Equity basic fairness

Escheat reversion of property to the state

Estate bundle of ownership rights in, and powers over, realty; also, property of the deceased

Ethics deciding what is right or wrong action in a reasoned, impartial manner

Eviction legal action taken to remove a tenant from possession of all the landlord's real property

Evidence materials presented to prove or disprove alleged facts

Ex parte injunction injunction issued by a judge after hearing only one side of an argument

Exclusions exceptions to insurance coverage

Executed contract contract that has been fully performed

Executor/executrix intestate's personal representative appointed to settle the estate (male/female)

Executory contract contract that has not been fully performed

Existing goods physically existing goods owned by the seller

Express authority agency authority directly communicated by the principal to the agent

Express trust trust in which the terms are explicitly stated by the settlor

Express warranty assurance of quality or performance explicitly made by the seller

Extortion improperly obtaining money or other things of value by use of force, fear, or the power of office

Extraordinary bailment bailment that requires an unusually high standard of care

Extraordinary care duty arising from an extraordinary bailment in which the bailee is liable for all damage, loss, or injury

F

Face value stated maximum amount that could be paid under an insurance policy

Fair use limited use of copyrighted works by critics, researchers, news reporters, and educators

False imprisonment depriving a person of freedom of movement without consent and without privilege

False pretenses obtaining property by lying about a past or existing fact

Featherbedding forcing an employer to pay for services not performed

Federal Communications Commission (FCC) agency regulating all interstate and international channels of communication

Federal Reserve System's Board of Governors agency that regulates interest rates

Federal Trade Commission (FTC) agency that regulates unfair trade practices

Fee simple absolute greatest possible bundle of ownership rights in, and powers over, an estate

Felony crime punishable by more than one year in jail, a fine of more than $1,000, or both

Fidelity bond insurance policy that pays the employer money in the case of employees' theft

Fidelity insurance provides coverage against financial loss caused by dishonesty

Fiduciary duties legal requirement that the agent serve the best interests of the principal; specific fiduciary duties are loyalty and obedience, reasonable care and skill, confidentiality, and accounting

Finance charge total added cost when one pays in installments for goods or services

Financing statement brief, written notice of the existence of a security interest in the identified property

Fire insurance insurance that covers for loss or damage due to fire (and usually smoke as well)

Firm offer binding offer stating in writing how long it is to be held open

Fixture item of personal property that has become permanently attached to realty and is thus transformed from personalty into realty

FOB shipping term meaning "free on board"

Food and Drug Administration (FDA) agency regulating safety of food and drugs on the market

Forbearance refraining from doing what one has a right to do

Foreign corporation corporation doing business in a state other than the one in which it was chartered

Forgery falsely making or materially altering a writing to defraud another

Fraud intentional misrepresentation of an existing, important fact

Fraudulent misrepresentation party to a contract knows that a statement he or she made is untrue

Full warranty express warranty that obligates the seller to repair or replace a defective product without cost to the buyer within a reasonable time

Fungible goods goods of an essentially identical nature

Future goods goods that are not both existing and identified

Future interest nonpossessory estate made up of ownership power retained by the grantor of a conditional estate

G

Garnishment court-ordered procedure by which a portion of a delinquent debtor's wages are paid to satisfy the debt

General duty clause OSHA requirement that employers provide a place of employment free from hazards likely to cause death or serious physical harm

General jurisdiction court that can hear almost any kind of case

General partner assumes full personal liability for debts of the firm

General partnership all partners assume full liability for debts of the firm

Genuine assent agreement to enter into a contract that is evidenced by words or conduct between the parties

Gift voluntary transfer of ownership without consideration

Good faith purchaser innocent third party to a fraudulent transfer of goods who gives value to the goods and acquires rights in them

Goods items of tangible, movable, personal property

Grantee person receiving ownership with a deed

Grantor person giving up ownership with a deed

Gratuitous agency agency relationship where the agent receives no consideration

Gratuitous bailment arises when only one of the parties benefits from the bailment

Guarantor party agreeing to be secondarily liable in case of default by the principal debtor

H

Heir person who, by statute, is entitled to property disposed of by a decedent's will

Holder party in possession of commercial paper payable to his or her order or to bearer

Holder in due course (HDC) party that takes commercial paper in good faith without knowledge of any defect or overdue status and gives value for it

Holder through a holder in due course (HHDC) party that takes commercial paper after an HDC and thereby acquires the same rights

Holographic will will written and signed entirely by the maker

Honor bank agrees to pay a check when due

Hostile environment interference with an employee's ability to work through unwelcome comments, gestures, or touching of a sexual nature

I

Identified goods designated subject matter of a particular sales contract

Immunity freedom from prosecution for a crime

Impartiality idea that the same ethical standards apply to everyone

Impeachment case trying a government official for misconduct in office

Implied authority agency authority that is implied from the grant of express authority or because of an emergency

Implied warranty warranty obligation implicitly imposed by law on all sellers

Incorporators signers of the articles of incorporation

Indemnify to make good a loss

Independent contractor one who contracts to do something for another but is free of the latter's direction and control

Indorsee party to whom commercial paper is indorsed

Indorsement signature on the reverse side of commercial paper

Indorser owner of commercial paper who signs it on the reverse

Infraction minor misdemeanor

Infringement unauthorized copying, sale, display, or performance of a copyrighted work

Injunction court order for a person to do or not do a particular act

Inland marine insurance insurance that covers against loss or damage to personal property where the property is located or while it is being transported by any means other than by sea

Innocent misrepresentation party to a contract does not know that a statement he or she made is untrue

Insolvent status of being unable to pay debts when they become due

Insurable interest potential to sustain loss if the insured property is damaged or destroyed or if the insured person is injured or dies

Insurance agreement under which one party will pay to offset a loss to another

Insured party protected or covered if the loss occurred

Insurer party who will indemnify if loss occurs

Intangible property classification of collateral that represents value in money, goods, or promises to perform specific contracts

Integration clause contract clause stating that both parties agree that the terms written in the contract constitute the entire and final agreement

Integrity doing what is right even under pressure to act otherwise

Intellectual property purely intangible personal property that one cannot touch or move

Intentional tort tort in which the defendant means to commit the injurious act

Inter vivos trust trust created during the lifetime of the settlor

Interference with contractual relations enticing or encouraging a person to break a contract

Interstate commerce trade and other commercial intercourse between or among businesses in different states

Intestate to die without a will

Intoxication mental impairment caused by voluntary use of alcohol, drugs, or inhalants

Intrastate commerce commerce conducted wholly within one state

Invasion of privacy unwelcome and unlawful intrusion into one's private life so as to cause outrage, mental suffering, or humiliation

Involuntary bailment arises without consent of the bailee; raises issue of whether the goods are lost or misplaced

Involuntary bankruptcy occurs when a person or business (except farmers and charities) owe at least $11,625 to petitioning unsecured creditor(s) and are unable to pay debts when they come due

J

Joint tenancy co-ownership of property with equal interests and the right of survivorship

Joint venture partnership formed by two or more persons or firms combining resources and skills for one complex project

Judgment final result of a trial

Jurisdiction power of a court to decide a case

Jury panel of citizens sworn by a court to decide issues of fact in court cases

Justice title of a judge on the state supreme court or federal Supreme Court

Juveniles individuals over 13 and under 18 years of age who have special status under the criminal law

L

Land basic physical element of realty

Landlord (also called **lessor**) one who, through a lease, transfers to another exclusive possession and control of real property

Larceny wrongful taking of another's property with the intent to deny them possession

Laws enforceable rules of conduct in a society

Lease agreement in which one party receives temporary possession of another's real property in exchange for rent

Leasehold estate tenants' ownership interest in real estate

Legal rate of interest rate specified by statute when interest is called for but no percentage is stated in the contract

Legal tender currency or coins

Legal value change in the legal position of a party as a result of a contract

Liability insurance insurance that covers personal injury or property damage claims for which the insured is legally responsible

License in real property, a temporary, revocable right to some limited use of another's land

Licensee person whom the possessor of land has permitted to be on that land

Lien legal right in another's property as security for the performance of an obligation such as the repayment of a loan

Life estate estate that lasts only for the grantee's life

Life insurance insurance that pays to a named beneficiary or the deceased's estate upon the death of the insured

Limited defenses defenses good against all obligees except HDCs and HHDCs

Limited liability corporation (LLC) form of business organization offering limited liability, taxation as a partnership, and few of the restrictions for use encountered in the S corporation or limited partnership

Limited liability partnership (LLP) form of business organization easily converted to a partnership that avoids double taxation and affords partial limited liability protection

Limited partner partner with limited liability in a limited partnership

Limited partnership partnership form authorized by state statute requiring at least one general partner but allowing limited liability for the rest

Limited warranty warranty providing a level of protection less than a full warranty

Liquidated damages damages agreed upon before a possible breach of contract

Liquidated debt debt for which the parties agree that the debt exists and on the amount of the debt

Liquidation process by which a corporation's life is ended

Litigate to resolve disputes in court

Lockout employer shutdown of operations to force a union to agree to the employer's position

Lost property property that the owner unknowingly leaves somewhere or accidentally drops

Lottery game involving the three elements of prize, chance, and consideration

M

Main purpose rule exception to a Statute of Frauds provision making a third party liable for an oral promise to pay another's debt if the main purpose of the promise serves the promisor's own interest

Maker person who executes a promissory note

Marine insurance insurance that covers for loss of or damage to vessels, cargo, and other property exposed to the perils of the sea

Marital consortium mutual obligations of wife and husband undertaken to fulfill the purposes of their union

Marriage legal union of a man and woman as husband and wife

Material facts important facts that influence both parties' decisions about a contract

Mechanic's lien lien against realty available to one who has supplied labor or materials to improve it

Mediation attempt by a neutral third party to achieve a compromise between two parties in a dispute

Mediator independent third party who tries to develop a non-binding solution acceptable to both sides of a dispute

Members owners of an LLC

Mental incapacity condition in which a party to a contract is unable to understand the consequences of the contractual act

Merchant seller who deals regularly in a particular type of goods or who claims special knowledge in a certain type of sales transaction

Merger combination of corporations in which one absorbs another

Mineral rights ownership of the minerals on and beneath a parcel of realty

Minimal care duty arising from a bailment in which the bailee must not ignore, waste, or destroy the property

Minor individual under the age of majority (18 in most states)

Minority minor part of a person's life (typically under the age of 18)

Mirror image rule requires that the terms in the acceptance must exactly match the terms contained in the offer

Misdemeanor crime punishable by up to one year in jail, a fine of less than $1,000, or both

Mislaid property property that is intentionally placed somewhere but then forgotten

Mitigate the damages to act to minimize one's injury

Money official medium of exchange in the United States or any foreign country

Money order draft issued by a post office, bank, express company, or telegraph company for use in transferring funds for the draft's purchaser

Mortgage note note on which real property is used as security for payment

Multinational corporation (MNC) corporation that has a significant investment of assets in foreign countries

Municipal court city court, usually divided into traffic and criminal divisions

Mutual mistake both parties to a contract have an incorrect belief about an important fact

Mutual-benefit bailment consideration is given and received by both bailor and bailee

N

National emergency strike work stoppage that involves national defense or major industries or that would imperil national health or safety

National Labor Relations Board (NLRB) agency regulating collective bargaining

Necessaries things needed to maintain life and lifestyle

Negligence most common tort based on carelessness

Negligence suit suit brought by an employee against an employer that claims the employer's carelessness caused the employee's injury

Negotiable written unconditional promise or order for a sum certain payable on demand or at a definite time

Negotiable instrument another term for commercial paper

Negotiation proper transfer of a negotiable instrument so that the person receiving the instrument has the power to collect on it by overcoming defenses of the person who must pay it off

Neutral on its face label for a workplace policy that does not seem on the surface to discriminate against any protected class

No-fault insurance insurance that requires that the parties to an automobile accident be covered by their own insurance company, regardless of who is at fault

Nominal consideration token amount identified in a written contract when parties either cannot or do not wish to state the amount precisely

Nominal damages token amount awarded when rights have been violated but there is no actual injury

Nominal partner person who is not a partner but who is held out as such

Nonfreehold estate (also called **tenancy**) estate that involves ownership for a limited period of time

Nonprofit corporation business organization for a social, charitable, or educational purpose

Non-trading partnership partnership that provides professional and noncommercial assistance or advice

Novation contractual party's release of the other party from the duty of performance and the acceptance of a substitute party

Nuclear Regulatory Commission (NRC) agency charged with insuring safety of nuclear power plants

Nuncupative will orally made will

Obligor one who owes a duty under a contract

Occupancy acquisition of title by taking possession of personal property that belongs to no one else

Occupational Safety and Health Administration (OSHA) federal agency that administers the Occupational Safety and Health Act of 1970 by enacting safety regulations and inspecting workplaces

Offer proposal by an offeror to do something, provided the offeree does something in return

Offeree party to whom an offer is made

Offeror party who makes an offer to form a contract

Open shop establishment in which nonunion members are not required to join the union or to pay union dues

Operating agreement equivalent of corporate bylaws for an LLC

Option separate contract arising when the offeree gives the offeror something of value in return for a promise to leave an offer open

Order paper commercial paper made payable to the order of a specified payee

Ordinance legislation enacted by a town, city, or county board or commission

Ordinary care duty created by mutual-benefit bailment in which bailee is liable only if negligent in some fashion

Original jurisdiction power to hear the case in full for the first time

Output contract agreement to purchase all of a particular producer's production

Ownership a collection of rights that allow the use and enjoyment of property

Ownership in severalty ownership of all property rights by oneself

Parol evidence spoken words inadmissible in court

Parol evidence rule oral testimony cannot be used to contradict terms in a complete, final, written contract

Participating preferred stock preferred stock whose holder, after the preferred dividends are paid, shares in remaining dividends as a common shareholder

Partnership association of two or more persons, as co-owners, to carry on a business for profit

Partnership agreement explicit statement, orally or in writing, of the terms and conditions agreed to by the partners for running the partnership

Partnership at will partnership in which a partner may withdraw at any time without liability to other partners

Past consideration act that has already been performed cannot be consideration for a promise in the present

Patent government grant of exclusive right to make, use, and sell a product or process which is novel, non-obvious, and useful

Pawn pledge of tangible personal property

Payable at a definite time commercial paper payable on or before an identified calendar date

Payable on demand commercial paper payable on sight or when presented

Payee party to whom commercial paper is made payable

Payment delivery of the agreed-upon price and the concurrent acceptance of it by the seller

Payroll deductions money deducted from an employee's paycheck

Perfected security interest exists when the security interest is superior to all other claims in the collateral

Performance fulfillment of contractual promises as agreed

Periodic tenancy arises when the leasehold is for a renewable period of time with rent due at stated intervals

Perjury crime of lying under oath

Personal property (also called **personalty**) tangible, movable property and intangible property

Picketing members of uncertified unions patrolling near the employer's property with signs, trying to force the employer to bargain with that union

Plaintiff party that initiates a civil lawsuit by filing a complaint

Plea bargaining agreement with prosecutor allowing defendant to plead guilty to a lesser crime than the more serious one he or she likely would be charged with

Pledge secured transaction in which the creditor has possession of the collateral

Pledgee creditor in a pledge who takes possession of property given up by pledgor

Pledgor debtor in a pledge who voluntarily gives up possession of the property

Policy written contract of insurance

Political party private organization of citizens who select and promote candidates for public office

Positive law law based on the dictates of a central political authority

Postdated dated later than the date of issuance

Power of attorney any writing that appoints someone as an agent

Preemptive rights enable shareholders to protect their proportionate voting power and interest in past and future profits

Preferred stock non-voting stock conveying the right to receive a stipulated dividend before any common shareholders receive their dividends

Premium consideration for insurance contract

Prenuptial agreement legal contract resolving property and other claims that might result from a marriage

Price consideration for a contract to sell or sale of goods

Price fixing competitors agree to charge the same amount for a product or service

Primary promise promise to pay another's debt that is not conditioned upon the other person's failure to pay

Principal one who authorizes another to alter his or her legal relations

Principal debtor person who owes the debt or obligation

Private corporation corporation established for a private purpose

Private trust trust created for private reasons

Privity of contract relationship or connection between parties to a legally binding agreement

Probable cause a reasonable ground for belief

Probate court administers wills and estates

Procedural defense defense based on problems with the way evidence is obtained or the way the accused person is arrested, questioned, tried, or punished

Procedural law group of laws that define the methods for enforcing legal rights and duties

Procedural unconscionability element of unconscionability shown by how the contract is created

Product liability the fixing of responsibility to compensate buyers, users, and bystanders for injuries caused by a defective product

Profit-making corporation private corporation organized to produce a profit for its owners

Promisee person to whom the promise or action is given in exchange for the other person's promise or action

Promisor person who gives the promise or action in exchange for the promise or action of another

Promissory estoppel promise is enforced even though no consideration is given for it

Promissory note unconditional written promise to pay money to order or to bearer

Promoters those who sell a business idea and the corporate form for it

Property tangible and intangible things and their corresponding legal rights and interests

Property insurance insurance that covers for losses resulting from perils such as fire, theft, or windstorm

Protected classes groups that employment law protects

Proximate cause legally recognizable cause of harm

Proxy power to vote shares for shareholder

Public corporation corporation established for a governmental purpose

Public service corporation private company that furnishes an essential public service

Puffing greatly exaggerated sales talk

Punishment penalty provided by law and imposed by a court

Punitive damages money a court requires a defendant to pay in order to punish and make an example of the defendant

Purchase money security interest filing is not required to protect a seller's security interest in consumer goods against other creditors of the buyer

Q

Qualified indorsement indorsement limiting or eliminating signature-based liability for the indorser

Quasi-contract obligation that is enforced as if it were a contract in order to prevent unjust enrichment of one party

Quid pro quo one thing exchanged for another; type of sexual harassment case in which a supervisor seeks sexual favors from a subordinate in exchange for continued employment or a favorable term or condition of employment

Quitclaim deed transfers any interest the grantor may have in the real property, but doesn't guarantee that the grantor owns anything or that the grantee receives anything

R

Ratification acting toward the contract as though one intends to be bound by it; principal's assent to unauthorized acts of an agent

Real property (also called **realty**) land, water, and minerals in the earth; airspace above the land; and things permanently attached to the land

Receipt of goods buyer takes physical possession or control of the goods

Receiving stolen property receiving or buying property known to be stolen from another so as to deny the rightful owner of possession

Release party settles a claim at the time the tort occurs, and the liability is unliquidated because the extent of damages is uncertain

Remedy action or procedure followed to enforce a right or to compensate for an injury

Rent consideration given by a tenant in return for temporary possession of a property

Representation election conducted by a union if workers wish to be represented by a union but management will not voluntary recognize it

Republic governmental system in which citizens elect representatives to decide issues

Requirements contract seller agrees to supply all of the needs of a particular buyer

Resale price maintenance manufacturer attempts to influence the retail price of its product

Rescission backing out of the transaction by asking for the return of what you gave and offering to give back what you received

Restitution restoring or making good a loss; repayment of money illegally obtained

Restrictive covenant promise as a part of a contract or deed limiting the owner's use of the realty

Restrictive indorsement directs the use of the proceeds from a negotiable instrument or imposes a condition upon its payment by the indorser

Resulting trust implied trust formed to hold property for its original owner

Revenue license required license imposed by governments on certain occupations for the sole purpose of raising money

Revocation withdrawing an offer before it is accepted

Rider (also called **endorsement**) modification made to the standard fire policy to satisfy an insured's needs

Right of contribution cosurety who pays the full debt is entitled to judgment against the other cosureties for their proportionate share of the debt

Right of partition attribute of co-ownership which allows any co-owner to require the division, usually financial, of the property among the co-owners

Right of repossession right of a secured party to take back collateral to use in satisfaction of the debt

Right of survivorship right of one joint tenant to ownership of property when the other joint tenant dies

Right-to-work laws state laws which prohibit compulsory union membership and ban the union shop, the closed shop, and the agency shop

Riparian rights water ownership system in which those abutting the water own the right to use it

Risk potential loss that is insured against

Robbery wrongful taking of another's property from their person or presence by threat of force of violence

S

Sale contract in which ownership of goods transfers from the seller to a buyer for a price

Sale on approval goods are delivered to the buyer in an "on trial" or "on satisfaction" basis

Sale or return completed sale in which the buyer has the option of returning the goods

Sale of an undivided interest selling a fractional interest in a single good or in a number of goods that are to remain together

Satisfaction performance of the new contractual obligation parties have agreed to substitute for their original obligation

Scofflaw person who does not respect the law

Scope of authority in employment law, range of acts an organization has authorized an employee to do; in agency, range of acts authorized by the principal

S corporation form of business organization governed by subchapter S of the Internal Revenue Code, under which earnings are treated the same as a gain (or loss) from a partnership and only taxed at the individual owner's level

Secret partner partner not known to the public but active as a manager

Secured party person who has a security interest in collateral owned by the debtor-buyer

Secured transaction legal method or device creating a security interest in personal property or fixtures in order to protect creditors

Securities and Exchange Commission (SEC) agency regulating the disclosure of information pertinent to buying and selling stocks as well as the national stock exchanges themselves

Security agreement contract that creates or provides for a security interest

Security interest interest in or claim against specified property of the debtor created for the purpose of assuring payment of the debt

Self-defense use of force that appears reasonably necessary for the self-protection of an intended victim

Separation stage in the divorce process in which the spouses maintain their marital rights and obligations but do not live together

Service mark word, mark, or symbol that identifies a service as opposed to a product

Settlor creator of a trust

Severalty see **Ownership in severalty**

Shareholder (also called **stockholder**) person owning share of stock in a corporation

Shares of stock units of ownership in a corporation

Sight draft draft on which payment is due immediately when presented to the drawee

Silent partner partner known to the public but who takes no active managerial role

Small claims courts state courts that handle disputes in which small amounts, generally $2,500 or less, are involved

Social insurance government-sponsored insurance protecting against financial problems related to retirement, survivorship, disability, and declining health

Sole proprietorship form of business owned by one person who has total unlimited control and liability

Sovereignty freedom from external control

Special indorsement indorsement making the paper payable to the order of a designated party

Special jurisdiction court that hears only one specific type of case

Specific performance remedy for breach of contract that orders the breaching party to do exactly what was required under the contract

Spendthrift trust trust created to protect the beneficiary's interest in a property from the beneficiary's creditors

Spot zoning treatment of a single property in a manner inconsistent with the treatment of similar properties in the area

Standard fire policy fire insurance contract that covers for losses resulting from fire, lightning strike, or removal from premises endangered by fire

Stare decisis doctrine that requires lower courts to follow existing case law in deciding similar cases

Statute law enacted by state or federal legislatures

Statute of Frauds law stating that certain agreements are not enforceable in court unless they are evidenced by a signed writing

Statute of limitations state laws setting time limit for bringing a lawsuit

Stockholder (also called **shareholder**) person who owns a share or shares of stock in a corporation

Stop-payment order instruction by the depositor to a financial institution not to pay a particular instrument drawn on it

Strict liability holding a defendant liable without a showing of negligence

Strike collective work stoppage by employees to pressure the employer to give in to union demands

Subletting tenant transfers to a third party all the property for a period less than the remaining time of the lease or part of the property for part or all of the remaining term of the lease

Subpoena written court order compelling a person to appear and testify

Substantial performance performance of all but a minor contractual duty

Substantive defense defenses that disprove, justify, or otherwise excuse the alleged crime

Substantive law group of laws that define rights and duties

Substantive unconscionability element of unconscionability established by the terms of the agreement

Substitution parties' replacement of their original contract with a new contract

Surety third party agreeing to be primarily liable for debt in case of default by the principal debtor

Suretyship contractual relation in which a third party agrees to be primarily liable for a debt created in favor of the principal debtor

System of checks and balances division and allocation of the powers of government between its various branches

T

Teller's check draft drawn by a bank on its balance with another bank

Tenancy in common form of co-ownership in which the shares may be unequal and there is no right of survivorship

Tenancy by the entireties usual form of co-ownership between husband and wife, carrying equal interest and the right of survivorship

Tenancy in partnership form of co-ownership by which the partners hold partnership property

Tenancy at sufferance tenant remains in possession after a lease has expired

Tenancy at will results if a party possesses land with the owner's permission but without an agreement as to the term of the lease or the amount of the rent

Tenancy for years leasehold that is for a definite period of time, such as six months, one year, or ninety-nine years

Tenant (also called **lessor**) one who, through a lease, is given possession of real property

Tender offer to perform an obligation

Tender of delivery to place the goods at the buyer's disposal or to give notice to the buyer that delivery can be received

Termination following the winding-up process, the ending of the legal existence of the partnership

Termination statement filing by a creditor releasing a security interest in collateral

Testamentary capacity testator must know the kind and extent of property involved, persons who stand to benefit, and that he or she is making an arrangement to dispose of his or her property after death

Testamentary intent clear intention to make a will

Testamentary trust trust created after the death of a settlor in accordance with directions in the person's will

Testate to die with a valid will

Testator/testatrix maker of a will (male/female)

Testimony statements by witnesses under oath

Third party one who deals with an agent who represents the principal

Time draft draft payable on a date set on the instrument or one that is payable after the running of a specified period after the draft's date

Tort private or civil wrong for which the law grants a remedy

Trade secret unpatented formula or process not known to others and which is valuable in business

Trademark unique word, mark, symbol, or device that identifies a product of a particular manufacturer or merchant

Trading partnership partnership that buys and sells goods and services commercially

Transcript verbatim record of what went on at trial

Traveler's check draft drawn by a financial institution on itself and signed by purchaser who must sign again in presence of payee for validation

Trespass (also called **trespass to land**) to be on the land of another without right or permission of the owner

Trial court first court to hear a dispute

Trust legal vehicle used to transfer the immediate control of property to another party

Trust account separate account for the funds of principals

Trustee legal entity having title to the property named in a trust

U

U.S. Constitution document that consists of seven articles that provide a workable framework for our federal government

Unconscionable term or contract that, under the UCC, is grossly unfair and oppressive

Unconscionable contract grossly unfair contract for the sale of goods

Unconstitutional law that conflicts with a constitution and is therefore invalid

Underinsured motorists coverage compensates the insured when the negligent driver does not have sufficient insurance to cover damages

Undisclosed principal principal whose identity is kept secret from the third party by the agent

Undue influence occurs when one party to a contract is in a position of trust and wrongfully dominates the other party

Unemployment compensation government payments to those who recently lost their jobs through no fault of their own

Unequal treatment (also called **disparate treatment**) employer treats members of a protected class less favorably than other employees

Unfair labor practices union or employer actions which violate the rights of employees with respect to union activity

Unfair trade practice dishonest, fraudulent or anti-competitive business method

Uniform Commercial Code widely adopted uniform business law

Unilateral contract offeror promises something in return for the offeree's performance and indicates that this performance is the way acceptance must be made

Unilateral mistake occurs when one party holds an incorrect belief about the facts related to a contract

Uninsured motorists protection allows the insured to collect damages from his or her own insurance company when they are not collectible from the person who caused the harm

Union shop establishment in which all workers must join the union within a stated period

Universal defenses defenses good against all plaintiffs suing on a negotiable instrument

Universalizing mental test to identify irrational, illogical, or demeaning actions

Unqualified indorsement indorsement without wording limiting or eliminating liability for the indorser

Unsecured debt debt in which the creditor lacks a secured interest in collateral

Usury lending money at a rate higher than the state's maximum allowable rate

V

Variance granted by a city or county to allow a landowner to make some use of his or her land that is inconsistent with the general zoning ordinance

Vendee buyer in sales of goods and contracts to sell

Vendor seller in sales of goods and contracts to sell

Verdict jury's decision in a case

Vicarious criminal liability substituted criminal liability

Vicarious liability legal doctrine by which one party is held liable for the torts of another

Vocational rehabilitation retraining an injured worker for a different job

Void without legal effect

Voidable contract contract in which the injured party can withdraw, thus cancelling the contract

Voidable marriage valid marriage that can be terminated by one or both parties due to improper grounds

Void marriage marriage considered invalid from the beginning

Voluntary bankruptcy option that offers a person, business, or other association protection from creditors under Chapter 7

W

Wager bet on the uncertain outcome of an event

Waiver contractual party's intentional and explicit giving up of a contractual right

Warranty statement about the product's qualities or performance that the seller assures the buyer is true

Warranty deed transfers grantor's interest in the property and protects the grantee by providing several enforceable grantor's warranties

Warranty of habitability requires a landlord to provide residential property in a condition fit for human living

Warranty of merchantability warranty requiring that the goods fit the ordinary purposes for which goods are used

Warranty of the principal's capacity assumption of the law that the agent promises the third party that the principal has capacity

Water right ownership of water running over or under a parcel of realty

White-collar crime crime typically committed in the workplace that does not involve violence or force nor does it cause injury to people or physical damage to property

Will legal expression by which a person directs how his or her property is to be distributed after death

Winding-up period period following dissolution in which the ongoing business of the partnership is concluded, its obligations are satisfied, and each partner's share is distributed

Witness individual with personal knowledge of important facts

Work permit document obtained from the state allowing a person under 18 years old to work

Workers' compensation payment employer makes to an insurance fund that compensates employees for injuries that occur on the job

Workers' compensation statutes laws that require most employers to buy insurance to pay benefits to injured employees

Workforce pool persons actually in the workforce

Writ of certiorari order to a lower court to produce the record of a case for the Supreme Court to review

Wrongful discharge firing an employee in retaliation for reporting violations of law by the company

Y

Yellow-dog contract employment contract in which new employees promise not to join a union

Z

Zoning ordinance law adopted by a city or county to regulate the location of residential, business, and industrial districts

Case Index

Index

Financing statement, 560–561
Finding, acquiring ownership by, 275
Fire, types of, 325
Fire insurance, 320, 325–326
Firm offer, 114, 147
Fixtures, 269, 299
    security interest in, 555
Flag burning, 39, 63
Floater, 326
Fluids, ownership of, 300
FOB (free on board), 234
Food
    adulterated, 248
    warranty of merchantability and, 257
Food, Drug, and Cosmetics Act, 78
Food and Drug Administration (FDA), 34, 248
Forbearance, 139
Ford Motor Company, Pinto case, 23
Foreign corporation, 469, 496
Foreign Corrupt Practices Act, 69
Forgery
    as universal defense, 544
France
    criminal procedure in, 71
    Napoleonic Code, 6
Fraud
    buyers in a sale induced by, 229–230
    contract rescission and, 132
    damages and, 132
    defined, 88, 131
    remedies for, 131–132
    voidable marriage and, 202
Fraud in the execution, 543–544
Fraud in the inducement, 543
Fraudulent misrepresentation, 129
Fraudulent Online Identity Sanctions Act, 10
Friendly fire, 325
FTC. See Federal Trade Commission
Full warranty, 255
Fungible goods
    bailments, 286
    transfer of ownership and, 231
    warranty of merchantability and, 257
Future goods, 231
Future interest, 304

G

Gambling Prohibition Act, 91
Gaming, tribal, 169
Gang wars, 5
Garnishment of wages, 574
Gender

denial of right to vote by, 29
    protected class based on, 410
General Electric, 468
General jurisdiction
    defined, 52
    in state court systems, 55
General Motors, Nader case, 101
General partner, 451
General partnership, 451
Genuine assent, 124–137
    as contract requirement, 107
    contractual mistakes and, 128
    defined, 125
    duress and, 125–126
    fraud and, 131–132
    misrepresentation and, 129–130
    undue influence and, 126–127
George II (King of England), 25
Gift
    acquiring ownership by, 273–274
    causa mortis, 274
    defined, 139
    inter vivos, 274
    mutual, 145–156
    of real property, 305
Good faith purchaser, 229
Goods
    bailee's duty to return, 291
    defective, 253
    defined, 215
    existing, 231
    fungible, 231, 286
    future, 231
    identified, 231
    inferior, protection against, 246–249
    mislabeled, 250–251
    receipt of, 216
    sales of, 215–216. See also Sales contracts
Government, federal. See Federal government; U.S. government
Governmental protection
    against inferior services and goods, 246–249
    against unfair trade practices, 249–251
    class actions, 246
    consumer caveats and, 245–246
    licensing, 246–247
    procedure for, 246
    unsafe products, 247–249
Government employees, termination of, 379
Grace period, 332
Grantee, 303
Grantor, 303
Gratuitous agency, 363
Gratuitous bailment, 289
Great Depression

agencies formed during, 34
    labor unions and, 394
Guarantor, 573

H

Habitual drunkard, 543
Hammurabi (King of Babylon), 5
Hard currencies, 526
HDC. See Holder in due course
Health insurance, 321, 334
Henry II (King of England), 7
HHDC. See Holder through a holder in due course
Hilton Hotels Corporation, 78
Hinckley, John, 22
Hispanic Business Woman of the Year, 213
History of the Corporation (Brown), 485
Hit-and-run driving, 73
Holder
    defined, 529
    dishonest, 539
    in electronic data interchange, 548
    limited defenses against, 542
    of negotiable documents of title, 230
Holder in due course (HDC), 540–542
Holder through a holder in due course (HHDC), 541
Holdover tenant, 308
Holographic will, 343
Home solicitation sales, 251
Homicide, 72
    vehicular, 66, 329
Honor (check), 512
Hostile environment, 417–418
Hostile fire, 325
Hot Debate scenarios
    Unit 1, 4, 24, 48, 64, 80
    Unit 2, 106, 124, 138, 154, 168, 188
    Unit 3, 214, 228, 244
    Unit 4, 268, 284, 298, 318, 340
    Unit 5, 360, 376, 392, 408, 424
    Unit 6, 444, 466, 488
    Unit 7, 508, 522, 538, 554, 570
Housing code, 311
HTML. See Hypertext markup language
HTTP. See Hypertext transfer protocol
Hungary, democratic representation in, 33
Hypertext, 37
Hypertext markup language (HTML), 37
Hypertext transfer protocol (HTTP), 37

I

R

Race, protected class based on, 410
Ratification
  of agency authority, 363, 365
  defined, 125, 156, 363
Reagan, Ronald (President), 22, 405
Real property, 298–317
  defined, 269
  as exempt property in bankruptcy, 585
  intangible, 215
  leasing, 307–313
  ownership of. *See* Real property ownership
  quiet enjoyment of, 305
  sale of, disaffirmance and, 162
  Statute of Frauds and contracts to sell, 178
  tenant's duty to take care of, 310
  tenant's right to sublet, 310
  tenant's right to use, 310
Real property ownership
  duties owed to entrants on land, 302–303
  forms of, 303–304
  limitations of, 300–303
  rights of, 299–300
  transfer of, 304
Realty, 269. *See also* Real property
Reasonable care
  partnership duties and, 459
  standard of, 290
Reasonable doubt, 72
Reasonable-person standard, for negligence cases, 90
Reasonable reliance, 130
Receipt of goods, 216
Receiving stolen property, 69
Registered agent, 496
Regulations, administrative, 12
Regulatory agencies, federal, 34
Release, 145
Religion
  freedom of, 28
  protected class based on, 410
Remanded (court decision), 50
Remedy
  bankruptcy as, 197
  conflict of, 196–197
  defined, 194
  duty to mitigate and, 197
  factors affecting choice of, 196–197
  statute of limitations and, 197
  waivers and, 197
Rent
  defined, 307
  tenant's duty to pay, 310
Rental, apartment, disaffirmance and, 162

Repossession, 558
Representation election, 395
Republic, 32
Requirements contract, 143
Resale price maintenance, 171
Rescission
  defined, 125
  discharge of contractual obligation by, 192
  fraud and contract, 132
  as remedy for major breach of contract, 194–195
Restitution, 194–195, 246
Restrictive covenant, 301
Restrictive indorsement, 532
Resulting trust, 350
Retailers Credit association, 578
Retirement insurance, 332–333
Revenue license, 171
Reversed (court decision), 50
Revised Uniform Limited Partnership Act (RULPA), 452, 490–491, 497
Revocation, 112
Riders, 325
Right of contribution, 573
Right of election (to decedent's property), 345
Right of partition, 276
Right of possession, 556
Right of privacy, 30, 87
  Internet and, 41–43
Rights, contract, 189–190
Rights of the accused, 71
Rights of those without capacity, 160–163
Right of survivorship, 277
Right-to-work laws, 396
Riparian, 300
Risk
  assumption of, 90–91, 430
  defined, 319
  of employment, workers' compensation and, 432
Risk of loss
  auction and, 237–238
  breaches after goods are identified, 234
  bulk transfer and, 238
  COD sales and, 236
  goods held by bailee, 234
  goods shipped by carrier and, 233–234
  sale on approval and, 237
  sale or return and, 236–237
  sales on credit and, 236
  sale of an undivided interest and, 237
  transfer of, 233–234
Robbery, 69
  insurance to protect against, 321
Roosevelt, Franklin (President), 394

Roosevelt, Theodore (President), 389
RSDHI, 332
Rule-based ethical reasoning, 17
Rules, administrative, 12
RULPA. *See* Revised Uniform Limited Partnership Act

S

Sale
  bailments for, 287
  bill of, 217
  defined, 215
  of real property, 305
  See also Sales; Sales contracts
Sale on approval, 237
Sale or return, 236–237
Sales
  COD, 236
  tie-in, 258
  transfer of insurable interest in, 235
  transfer of ownership, 229–232
  transfer of rights and risks in specific, 235–236
  transfer of risk of loss in, 233–234
  See also Sale; Sales contract
Sales contract, 214–227
  acceptance of goods and, 218
  bill of sale, 217
  cancellation of, 190
  law of contracts vs., 216
  material alteration, 220
  payment and delivery, 216–218
  proposal for addition, 220
  special rules for merchants, 220–222
  Statute of Frauds and, 221–222
  unconscionable, 218–219
  use of credit and, 217–218
  See also Sale; Sales
Salesperson, scope of authority of, 158
Sarbanes-Oxley Act, 481
Satisfaction, 192
  accord and, 145
Scofflaws, 18
Scope of authority, 158, 362
  agent exceeding, 368
Scope of employment
  committing tort within, 384
  workers' compensation and, 431–432
S corporation
  defined, 492
  eligibility requirements for, 492
  formation of, 492
SEC. *See* Securities and Exchange Commission